Community Residences for Persons with Developmental Disabilities

Community Residences for Persons with Developmental Disabilities

Here to Stay

Edited by

Matthew P. Janicki, Ph.D.
New York State Office of Mental Retardation
and Developmental Disabilities
Albany, New York

Marty Wyngaarden Krauss, Ph.D.
Brandeis University
and Eunice Kennedy Shriver Center
Waltham, Massachusetts

and

Marsha Mailick Seltzer, Ph.D.
Boston University
Boston, Massachusetts
and
Eunice Kennedy Shriver Center
Waltham, Massachusetts

Baltimore · London · Toronto · Sydney

Paul H. Brookes Publishing Co.
Post Office Box 10624
Baltimore, MD 21285-0624

Typeset by The Composing Room, Grand Rapids, Michigan.
Manufactured in the United States of America by
The Maple Press Company, York, Pennsylvania.

Richard I. Krauss, AIA, is gratefully acknowledged for his assistance with the cover design.

Library of Congress Cataloging-in-Publication Data

Community residences for persons with developmental disabilities: Here to stay / edited by Matthew P. Janicki, Marty Wyngaarden Krauss, Marsha Mailick Seltzer.
    p.   cm.
  Bibliography: p.
  Includes index.
  ISBN 0-933716-86-9
    1. Group homes for the developmentally disabled—United States—Management. I. Janicki, Matthew P., 1943.-   . II. Krauss, Marty Wyngaarden. III. Seltzer, Marsha Mailick.
  HV3006.A4C648   1988
  362.1'968—dc19

                                                  87-19864
                                                    CIP

Contents

Contributors

Mary Ann Allard, M.P.A.
Florence Heller School
Brandeis University
Waltham, MA 02254

Michael Apolito, M.A.
Boston College
Chestnut Hill, MA 02167

Bruce L. Baker, Ph.D.
Department of Psychology
University of California
Los Angeles, CA 90024

Jan Blacher, Ph.D.
School of Education
University of California
Riverside, CA 92521

Roger Blunden, B.Sc.
University of Wales
Mental Handicap in Wales
Applied Research Unit
St. David's Hospital
Cardif CF1 9DU, Wales
UNITED KINGDOM

Robert H. Bruininks, Ph.D.
Department of Educational Psychology
University of Minnesota
178 Pillsbury Drive, S.E.
Minneapolis, MN 55455

Sara N. Burchard, Ph.D.
Department of Psychology
John Dewey Hall
University of Vermont
Burlington, VT 05405

Daniel W. Close, Ph.D.
Rehabilitation Research and Training Center in
    Mental Retardation
2nd Floor, Clinical Services Building
University of Oregon
Eugene, OR 97403

Jason R. Dura, M.A.
Departments of Pediatrics and Psychology
Children's Hospital
The Ohio State University
Columbus, OH 43205

Jules Feiman, M.S.W.
Young Adult Institute, Inc.
460 West 34th Street
New York, NY 10001-2382

David Felce, Ph.D.
British Institute of Mental Handicap
Wolverhampton Road
Kidderminster

Worcestershire DY10 3PP
ENGLAND

Donald N. Freedman, J.D.
Concannon, Rosenberg, and Freedman
93 Union Street
Suite 315
Newton Centre, MA 02159

Ruth I. Freedman, Ph.D.
Concannon, Rosenberg, and Freedman
93 Union Street
Suite 315
Newton Centre, MA 02159

Stephen Freeman, M.S.W.
Young Adult Institute, Inc.
460 West 34th Street
New York, NY 10001-2382

Joni Fritz, B.A.
National Association of Private Residential
    Facilities for the Mentally Retarded
6400 Seven Corners
Falls Church, VA 22044-2009

Sheldon R. Gelman, Ph.D.
Department of Sociology
The Pennsylvania State University
University Park, PA 16802

Norman E. Groner, Ph.D.
1607 King Street
Santa Cruz, CA 95060

Andrew S. Halpern, Ph.D.
Rehabilitation Research and Training Center in
    Mental Retardation
217 Clinical Services Building
University of Oregon
Eugene, OR 97403

Barbara A. Hawkins, Re.D.
Indiana University
Institute for the Study of Developmental Disabilities
2853 East 10th Street
Bloomington, IN 47405

Tamar Heller, Ph.D.
Evaluation and Public Policy Program
Institute for the Study of Developmental Disabilities
University of Illinois at Chicago
1640 West Roosevelt Road
Chicago, IL 60608

Bradley K. Hill, M.A.
Center for Residential and Community Services
University of Minnesota
207 Pattee Hall
150 Pillsbury Drive, S.E.
Minneapolis, MN 55455

John W. Jacobson, M.S.
New York State Office of Mental Retardation and
  Developmental Disabilities
44 Holland Avenue
Albany, NY 12229

Matthew P. Janicki, Ph.D.
New York State Office of Mental Retardation and
  Developmental Disabilities
44 Holland Avenue
Albany, NY 12229

Dorothy Butterfield Jenkins, M.L.A.
School of Landscape Architecture
302 Design Building
Louisiana State University
Baton Rouge, LA 70803

Barbara A. Kenefick, Ed.D.
New York State Office of Mental Retardation and
  Developmental Disabilities
44 Holland Avenue
Albany, NY 12229

Marty Wyngaarden Krauss, Ph.D.
Star Center for Mental Retardation
Florence Heller Graduate School
Brandeis University
Waltham, MA 02254
and
Social Science Research Department
Eunice Kennedy Shriver Center
200 Trapelo Road
Waltham, MA 02254

K. Charlie Lakin, Ph.D.
Minnesota University Affiliated Program
University of Minnesota
150 Pillsbury Drive, S.E.
Minneapolis, MN 55455

Sharon Landesman, Ph.D.
Frank Porter Graham Child Development Center
University of North Carolina at Chapel Hill
071 A
Chapel Hill, NC 27514

Joel M. Levy, M.S.W.
Young Adult Institute, Inc.
460 West 34th Street
New York, NY 10001-2382

Philip H. Levy, Ph.D.
Young Adult Institute, Inc.
460 West 34th Street
New York, NY 10001-2382

Dianne Manfredini, Ph.D.
University Affiliated Facility
Robert Wood Johnson Medical School
University of Medicine and Dentistry of New
  Jersey
Piscataway, NJ 08854-5635

James A. Mulick, Ph.D.
Departments of Pediatrics and Psychology
Children's Hospital
The Ohio State University
Columbus, OH 43205

Cal Robert Regula, Ph.D.
New York State Office of Mental Retardation and
  Developmental Disabilities
44 Holland Avenue
Albany, NY 12229-1000

Julia Williams Robinson, AIA
School of Architecture and Landscape Architecture
University of Minnesota
Minneapolis, MN 55455

Louis Rowitz, Ph.D.
School of Public Health
University of Illinois at Chicago
2121 West Taylor Street
Room 113
Chicago, IL 60612

Perry Samowitz, M.A.
Young Adult Institute, Inc.
460 West 34th Street
New York, NY 10001-2382

Gary B. Seltzer, Ph.D.
Boston University
School of Social Work
264 Bay State Road
Boston, MA 02215

Marsha Mailick Seltzer, Ph.D.
Boston University
School of Social Work
264 Bay State Road
Boston, MA 02215
and
Social Science Research Department
Eunice Kennedy Shriver Center
200 Trapelo Road
Waltham, MA 02254

Wayne Smith, Ph.D.
Health Care Financing Administration
6325 Security Boulevard
Baltimore, MD 21207

Jacqueline Thousand, Ph.D.
Department of Special Education, Social Work,
  and Social Services
Center for Developmental Disabilities
University of Vermont
Burlington, VT 05405

H. Rutherford Turnbull, III, LL.B., LL.M.
Bureau of Child Research
Haworth Hall
The University of Kansas
Lawrence, KS 66045

Preface

*C*ommunity Residences for Persons with Developmental Disabilities: Here to Stay *focuses on the cornerstone of the community services system for persons with developmental disabilities—the residential component. Nothing is more critical to the continued viability of community-based services than respecting the trust that thousands of families of handicapped persons place every day in the residential programs that house their family members. This trust must be earned, and it is this challenge that propelled us to assemble the carefully researched and thoughtful essays that comprise this book.*

We began this venture based on the conviction that after more than 20 years of development, the residential system warranted a review of the enduring management, programmatic, and operational issues it poses to administrators, direct care staff, consultants, clinicians, and evaluators. It is clear that the quality of life for tens of thousands of developmentally disabled persons rests in large part on the capacity of the community residential system to demonstrate its ability to support stable and effective management structures that can operate creative and effective programs. Much is asked of a residential program. It must be a home for its residents, a rewarding place of employment for its staff, a competent deliverer of services, and a respectful and respected member of its community. Enormous public and private resources are expended daily in support of these residences. The impressive development of the residential system over the last two decades makes it truly a national resource in which many justifiably take pride. However, if the next 20 years are to witness equally impressive progress, it is necessary to take stock of what has been learned, to distill key findings from the research literature, and to creatively adapt these findings to the diverse environments in which residences operate. It is our hope and intention that this book will form a basis for progress over the coming years.

Our ambitions for this book were matched by the enthusiasm of the authors who were invited to contribute their reasoned perspectives and scholarship to a host of diverse topics that collectively capture the expertise and knowledge required to operate a community residence. The volume's title reflects our profound belief that what has developed in earnest over the last 20 years is here to stay.

Acknowledgments

This text examines critical issues in the management, operation, and evaluation of community residences for persons with developmental disabilities. Each author has brought a wealth of experience, scholarship, and insight into the specific problems and issues addressed in his or her chapter. However, there is a larger pool of contributors to this text whose members deserve special acknowledgment. The development of a community *system* of residential services has depended from its inception on the care, wisdom, and dedication of thousands of direct care staff, clinicians, administrators, family members, and advocates for persons with developmental disabilities. One lasting legacy of this community of concerned citizens is the opportunity for persons with a developmental disability to live in and be a part of the community. We pay public tribute to and graciously acknowledge the critical and pathbreaking work of the people ''in the field.''

We have received support from and have benefited from the dedication of persons who are ''in our field.'' Gladys Rivera and Amy Sheperdson set new standards for conscientious secretarial work. Assistance in editing and checking references was provided by Marjorie Erickson. We are particularly grateful to Melissa Behm, our editor, at Paul H. Brookes Publishing Co., who was supportive and thoughtful throughout the conceptualization and work phases of this project. Finally, our families, to whom this text is dedicated, deserve special acknowledgment for their understanding of the time we needed to devote to this effort.

Dedicated to
Bonnie, Marc, and Davin
Richard, Jake, Rebecca, and David
Gary, Beth, and Rebecca

Section I

HERE TO STAY

How We Got Here

Chapter 1

Context, Models, and Issues for Community Residences

Matthew P. Janicki, Marty Wyngaarden Krauss,
and Marsha Mailick Seltzer

Community residences have become a predominant living arrangement for persons with mental retardation and other developmental disabilities who no longer reside at home or who are in transition from other care settings. This chapter explores some of the antecedents of the community residences model and prevalent typologies of residence programs. The authors consider a range of issues that warrant attention as the community residence "movement" becomes a firmly rooted service delivery system. Finally, the authors provide an overview of the book's chapters and offer a context for the issues addressed by each.

The past 20 years have witnessed considerable growth in the numbers and types of community-based residential programs for developmentally disabled persons in the United States as well as in other industrialized countries. This growth period, which can be termed the first stage of community residential development, was fueled by legal, social, and political reform movements that have established community living as the preferred residential option for all handicapped persons. This major transition in public policy has been well documented in terms of the development of community-based residential options (Baker, Seltzer, & Seltzer, 1977; Bruininks, Hauber, & Kudla, 1980; Hauber, Bruininks, Hill, Lakin, Scheerenberger, & White, 1984; Hill & Lakin, 1986; Janicki, Mayeda, & Epple, 1983; O'Connor, 1976); the range of programmatic supports necessary to operate residences (Cherington & Dybwad, 1974; Lakin & Bruininks, 1985); the fiscal impact on state and federal government (Braddock, 1986; Intagliata, Willer, & Cooley,

1979), and the impact on individual residents (Birenbaum & Re, 1979; Bruininks, Meyers, Sigford, & Lakin, 1981; Conroy, Efthimiou, & Lemanowitz, 1982; Edgerton, Bollinger, & Herr, 1984; Gollay, Freedman, Wyngaarden, & Kurtz, 1978).

Much less attention has been focused on distilling the results of these analyses for use by administrators, clinicians, and other staff who singly and collectively are charged with establishing and maintaining supportive, nurturing, and in many cases, therapeutic environments for developmentally disabled persons. With the passing of the initial phase of community residential development, administrators and program staff must now wrestle with a variety of issues related to maintaining the residential system at as high-quality a level as possible. In this context, an examination of substantive information about "system maintenance" issues is warranted. It is important to consider the range of legal, administrative, programmatic, and physical design concerns that are critical to the

3

day-to-day operation of community residential settings. The purpose of this text is to provide managers, program staff, agency board members, consultants, and other workers involved with community residences with practical and strategic information derived from the research literature and from the direct experience of the contributing authors on the provision of community residential services to developmentally disabled persons.

This chapter begins with a review of selected factors and events that have shaped America's contemporary residential service delivery system. This review is brief because a number of historical reviews of the development of community residential settings for persons with developmental disabilities are already available (Kugel & Shearer, 1976; Scheerenberger, 1987). Next, a description of the most prevalent types of community residential settings is presented. Throughout this text, the term *community residence* is used to refer to what are, in fact, a diverse range of program models; this diversity is highlighted in the discussion that follows. An examination of some persistent issues faced by managers and administrators of all residences, regardless of type, in the management and operation of these environments is then presented. The chapter concludes with an overview of the organization of this text.

A BRIEF HISTORICAL PERSPECTIVE

The roots of today's community residences can be traced to historical phenomena associated with two aspects of transitioning among disabled adults. The first phenomenon was the gradual emergence of foster family care as a transitional setting for persons who moved from the nation's institutions back to community settings. The second phenomenon was the development of residential settings (primarily group homes) for developmentally disabled adults, which enabled them to move from their family homes to more independent settings.

Fernald (1917), writing at the beginning of this century, noted that although publicly supported residential institutions were helpful in providing education and work training for young, more intellectually adept residents, the

development of living situations in the community was the essential next step as these individuals became adults. To this end, many institutions developed "colonies" in both rural and urban areas to provide housing and work for mentally retarded adults who could not yet fully live on their own but who did not need to remain at the institution. These colonies served as an important precursor for today's community residences (Rosen, Clark, & Kivitz, 1976).

While the colony model was abandoned during the depression years, derivatives evolved in many states that, in today's terminology, are called foster family care homes (Janicki, Castellani, & Lubin, 1982; Merges, 1981; Willer & Intagliata, 1984). Foster family care homes were established by families willing to provide board and care to residents from a local institution. In return, the family received a stipend and the services of the adult boarder. In many states, the distribution of foster family care homes for persons with mental retardation shows circular proximity to an institution. Modeled after these original foster family care homes, the first group home residences in the 1960s provided a home-away-from-home (which for these persons was the institution) in the care of "houseparents."

A second influence on the development of community residences emerged from the revolution of an active parent movement following World War II. Many parents, not wanting to institutionalize their developmentally disabled child, fought hard for appropriate educational and other community services (Vitello & Soskin, 1985). As parent groups organized into legal entities (e.g., Associations for Retarded Children—later renamed Associations for Retarded Citizens), many began operating their own programs and services. As their children grew into adulthood, these parent organizations also began to develop group homes. Parent organizations drew from their own experiences and developed community residences modeled on their own homes.

These early community residences were originally transitional programs—half-way houses—designed to bridge the individual's movement from his or her own home to independent living. However, in the early 1970s, widespread legal challenges to the practices and purposes of institutions resulted in judicial decrees to both improve the conditions within institutions and to deinstitutionalize residents to supervised, habilitation-oriented community-based settings (Conroy & Bradley, 1985; Herr, 1983; Rothman & Rothman, 1984). The deinstitutionalization movement soon overwhelmed the capacity of existing community-based residences and their operators. The growth of residences—both in number and types—since the early 1970s has indeed been phenomenal. The influx of previously institutionalized residents into newly developed community residences has altered these programs' character so that they now range from minimally supervised settings to those offering long-term care and structured supervision and staffing.

One of the earliest studies of this new "breed" of community residences was conducted by Baker et al. (1977). Their national survey showed that the range of residences available in the early 1970s consisted of the following types of programs:

1. *Small-group homes,* serving 10 or fewer mentally retarded adults. This was the most prevalent type of community residence.
2. *Medium-group homes,* serving 11 to 20 mentally retarded adults.
3. *Large-group homes,* serving 21 to 40 mentally retarded adults.
4. *Mini-institutions,* serving 41 to 80 mentally retarded adults.
5. *Mixed group homes,* serving mentally retarded adults and adults with other disabilities, including mental illness, physical disabilities, and ex-offenders.
6. *Group homes for older adults,* serving elderly mentally retarded persons and, at times, nonretarded elders.
7. *Foster family care,* serving 5 or fewer mentally retarded adults in a family's own home.
8. *Sheltered villages,* which provide a self-contained community for mentally retarded adults and live-in staff, usually located in a rural setting.

9. *Workshop dormitories,* living units for mentally retarded adults, which are programmatically and physically associated with a vocational training programs.
10. *Semi-independent units,* providing less than 24-hour-a-day supervision of mentally retarded residents.

This typology of residential environments has shown remarkable durability despite the passage of over a decade and the remarkable growth in the number of residential programs available across the country. The continuing need to classify or describe different types of settings has also persisted (Landesman, 1986; Landesman-Dwyer, 1985). What follows is a review of more contemporary classification efforts in order to illustrate the broad array of residential programs that are subsumed under the term *community residence.*

CONTEMPORARY MODELS OF COMMUNITY RESIDENCES

It is widely acknowledged that a range or continuum of residential settings should exist for persons with developmental disabilities (Glenn, 1976; Janicki, Castellani, & Norris, 1983; Madle, 1978; Wolfensberger, 1972). Defining the settings that currently exist has proven, however, to be a complicated and unresolved issue. There is no nationally recognized or utilized classification system under which all types of licensed community residences are identified (Jaffe & Smith, 1986). Indeed, Hill and Lakin (1986) note three critical problems in establishing uniform terminology for community residences: 1) each state uses its own unique licensing/classification system, 2) the variation in basic characteristics within seemingly comparable program models may be as great as between models, and 3) there is little professional consensus regarding the basic dimensions on which a nationally uniform classification system should be developed.

Based on a national survey conducted in 1982 of 15,633 residential facilities, Hill and Lakin (1986) proposed the following definitions of six common residential settings:

1. *Foster home*—a residence owned or rented by a family as their own home, with one or more mentally retarded persons living as family members
2. *Group home*—a residence with staff who provide care, supervision, and training for one or more mentally retarded persons
3. *Semi-independent living program*—a residence consisting of semi-independent units or apartments with staff living in a separate unit in the same building
4. *Board and supervision facility*—a residence with staff who provide sleeping rooms, meals, and supervision, but no formal training or help with dressing, bathing, and so forth
5. *Personal care facility*—a residence with staff who provide help with dressing, bathing or other personal care, but no formal training of residents
6. *Nursing home*—a facility that provides daily nursing care with primary emphasis on residents' health care needs

Others have distinguished among residential settings with respect to whether the setting provides primarily individual versus group care (Vitello & Soskin, 1985). Another schema, proposed by Janicki, Jacobson, and Schwartz (1982), uses the following typology:

1. Family living situations (i.e., living within the context of a surrogate family)
2. Group living situations (i.e., living with a group of nonrelated persons for the benefit of both individual growth and collective welfare)
3. Congregate or therapeutic care situations (i.e., living in an environment in which therapeutic care is provided in structured residential settings)

In the Janicki, Jacobson, and Schwartz (1982) schema, the principal type of family living situation is foster family care. This type of care is based upon a naturally occurring family constellation, emphasizing the individuality, diversity, and intimacy that such settings typically provide. Supervision is provided by family members in their own home to the nonrelated

disabled resident. An important aspect is that care is provided in a nonmedical setting by parental figures who are not professionals. Specific variants of this type of setting range from housing for individuals with minimal supervision needs to housing for individuals who need assistance with personal and other daily living skills.

Group living situations were originally intended for developmentally disabled adults who were mildly or moderately disabled. Increasingly, however, severely and profoundly handicapped persons are living in such settings. Supervision and training is provided by staff specifically employed to work in the residence. Staff are involved in establishing the residents' programs and routines to promote interpersonal relationships, functional skills, social maturation, and physical well-being. These residential programs are typically located in family-sized dwellings in neighborhood settings; in urban areas, these programs are also found in multiunit buildings. Specific variants of this type of setting include the small- and large-group homes and supervised apartment programs.

Therapeutic or congregate care settings, in which the program's emphasis is therapeutic, generally serve more severely impaired persons, who because of substantial intellectual deficits, severe behavior problems, or chronic medical conditions and/or secondary physical handicaps, require a more intensively structured and professionally staffed residential program. Whereas the emphasis in foster care is on "family," and in group living settings on "community participation" and "peer relations," the emphasis in therapeutic care is on "therapeutic habilitation." Typical of the community-based programs within this category are residences certified as intermediate care facilities for the mentally retarded (ICFs/MR) under the federal Medicaid program.

An alternative method of characterizing community residences is to describe programs according to three dimensions of the program's character (Janicki, Jacobson, & Schwartz, 1982). Rather than forming a typology based on unidimensional features, such as size or staffing structure, a multidimensional scheme provides a mechanism for capturing diverse elements of residential programs. The first dimension, *program environment,* is a composite of the factors that define the residential setting. These factors include the setting's physical design and use, the staff who support it, the manner in which the setting provides for its residents, and the overall effects of resident characteristics upon day-to-day events.

The second dimension, *rehabilitative intent,* defines the fundamental purpose of the residence in terms of its goals (i.e., behavior change, social and community-living skills development, etc.) and the processes by which these goals will be obtained. This aspect is critical in distinguishing among residential programs, for without defined rehabilitative intent and appropriate methods for achieving this intent, the residence serves primarily as a domicile.

The third dimension, *management systems,* subsumes two major operational considerations: the administration's understanding of the purpose of the residence and the manner in which it administers. To successfully effect change or growth among a residence's occupants, there must be a coherency between the explicit purpose of the home's program and the role and actions of management. Such coherency is demonstrated by the statements of purpose espoused by management, the programmatic resources provided in support of the home's activities, and the dedication of budget to the program and its staff.

These three dimensions of a residence are important in analyzing the content in which the program operates. They further assist in identifying salient questions that can and should be posed of any program. Does the physical design of the residence support the residents' functional capacities? Are the program staff trained to effectively supervise and assist residents in meeting their individual goals? Does the residence conform to its stated purposes? Does the residence provide services in a manner that promotes the personal growth of its residents? Does the setting support individual change? Do the management structures for the residence facilitate program success? Are these structures

effective in monitoring program activity and detecting areas where improvements are needed?

MANAGEMENT ISSUES IN COMMUNITY RESIDENCES

The ability to achieve desired outcomes within any residential program is partially dependent upon the capacity of the program's management staff to anticipate and respond to operating constraints and opportunities. The range of skills required of contemporary managers is increasingly sophisticated and specialized. As discussed below, these skills are necessary for both proactive and reactive responses to a diverse set of administrative, programmatic, and evaluative issues that face managers of community residences.

Administrative Aspects

As indicated earlier, the past two decades have seen a dramatic increase in the number of community residences for developmentally disabled persons. The variations in program types reflect the diversity in resident characteristics and needs, program philosophies, and rehabilitative intent. Indeed, as noted by Lakin, Hill and Bruininks (this volume), in 1982 there were over 6,500 foster care homes, over 3,500 group homes serving 6 or fewer residents, and over 2,800 group homes serving between 7 and 15 residents in the United States alone. Consequently, the diversity of the types, sizes, and management sophistication of agencies that operate these programs is considerable. For example, in one state with a large community residential system, about half of all agencies licensed to operate community residential programs operate 5 or fewer community residence program sites, and about a third operate only 1 or 2 programs. In contrast, about 25% of these agencies are large multipurpose agencies, each operating a dozen or more program sites (Office of Mental Retardation and Developmental Disabilities [OMRDD], 1984). Further, agencies range from small, single-purpose, not-for-profit agencies, to large, diversified, private, not-for-profit agencies, to public systems managed by state mental retardation/developmental disabilities service agencies, to proprietary corporations (whose residences are but one division of their long-term care or health care operations). In terms of sponsorship, data from one study showed that 68% of the nation's community residences are privately operated by not-for-profit agencies, 19% are publicly operated, and 13% are operated by proprietary agencies (Janicki, Mayeda, & Epple, 1983).

Sponsoring agencies' governance and organizational structures have important implications for the administrative aspects of system maintenance. There are a number of germane issues, including how to:

Effectively underwrite the cost of the program

Structure agencies so that their boards and administrators can effectively manage the programs under their control

Allocate personnel so that the most effective and efficient use is made of their time

Ensure that monies spent for programs are used to the best advantage of the agency's clientele

The complexity of the residential system, with the often conflicting requirements from funding and control agencies, will tax the capacity of any organization. Now that most of the nation's residential provider agencies are beyond the initial stage of agency and program development, the critical aspects are how to live within the agency's resources and not grow beyond the capacity to manage, how to administer effectively, how to coordinate supervision and oversight in a manner that produces a high level of job satisfaction and commitment on the part of employees, how to ensure continued recruitment of workers to a system that is dynamic and constantly growing, and how to provide high-quality habilitative services to residents.

Programmatic Aspects

Given the heterogeneity of the population of developmentally disabled persons, the residential system requires a variety of approaches to program design and implementation. However, the need for program standards is also widely acknowledged. These standards operationalize professional and public mandates for basic guarantees of program quality, safety, and rehabilitation intent.

The variability in rehabilitation philosophies and approaches attests to the fact that there is no one prototypical community residential system. Rather, there is a healthy and functional diversity in clinical practice and program orientation among and within service delivery systems (Hill & Bruininks, 1981; Matson & Mulick, 1983). This diversity, while signifying the system's maturation, is also a focal point for controversy and legitimate debate. For example, a heated debate continues regarding the impact of program size (i.e., number of residents) on the effectiveness of the residential program with respect to management issues (such as efficiency) and to client or resident outcomes (such as developmental growth, social relationships, etc. [Baroff, 1980; Landesman-Dwyer, 1981]).

Although most program administrators and clinicians admit that diverse programmatic perspectives will always exist (for example, behavioral versus humanistic approaches), most also agree that some uniformity in safety and quality of services is warranted. Nearly all developmentally disabled individuals who reside in a community residence are there because they need some level of supervision. This supervision is necessitated by their undeveloped or limited judgment, impaired mobility, or degree of physical infirmity. Consequently, a paramount issue for agencies (in terms of liability) and for residents (in terms of physical well-being and developmental growth) is the safety of the residence. However, balanced against the need to maintain safe conditions is the danger of benevolent overprotection and the need to foster "dignity of risk" (Perske, 1972). Given that fires, injuries, and accidents do occur in community residential programs (as they do in any environment), administrative and programmatic attention to safety is an important consideration.

Quality of services is a critical concern for agencies who have evolved from the development stage to a stage in which program maintenance and evaluation are increasingly important. Agencies are now judged by their outcomes rather than their processes. Important programmatic concerns include how to:

Maintain safe (yet not unduly restrictive) environments

Ensure desired clinical outcomes from resident programs

Encourage the resident's interaction with the community at large

Use architectural design to the greatest effect to support program provision

Define effective program models for different types of residents

Determine the effects of differential staffing patterns upon program quality and on resident development

Effectively use consultants as adjuncts to clinical and direct care staff

Resident movement in and out of programs also raises questions related to the stability of such programs. Should staff skills and intervention technologies by adapted to each successive wave of new residents? What is the role of the residence in preparing for the transition of the residents? Are less-structured living arrangements available so that residents can move on when they want to and/or are ready? A related and strategic question concerns program financing. Many residences are dependent upon stable sources of funds and payment schemes (such as Medicaid funding of ICFs/MR). Others are dependent on funds that shift dramatically with changing political and economic events. To what extent should and does dependency upon one or another source of funding define the character of the program?

Evaluation Aspects

One sign of the maturation of an organization is its willingness to take stock of where it is and consider what improvements or changes may be warranted. This introspective process is heightened by the initiation and application of evaluative, research, and planning activities. Effective evaluation, which is critical to any organization, must be applied at the levels of both the organization and the program. It is important for an organization to implement an

evaluation without overburdening the staff, to develop a strategy for using the results, to determine in advance how adverse findings will be handled, and to effectively weave evaluation into self-renewal.

Research is another critical aspect for management. There is a need and obligation to analyze effective applications of program models, intervention strategies, staff employment and training, dwelling design, and a host of other concerns. However, the costs of research are not easily underwritten, and community residences must often collaborate with outsiders (often academicians) to obtain the funding and to serve as the principal investigators. Notwithstanding these constraints, community residence staff should be encouraged to undertake limited research endeavors that would add to their understanding of agency clientele, clinical approaches, and other aspects of agency work. Development of effective strategies to incorporate these additional responsibilities along with the other demands placed on agency resources and staff time is an obvious concern.

Planning for the continued use and further development of community residential programs is a necessary function. However, many organizations do not have the internal capacity for planning and are primarily reactive to outside direction. Planning concerns can be addressed by a consortia effort in which agencies share information with each other and cooperate with local planning bodies. The determination of need for residential services is not "hard science," and in developing projections for the development or maintenance of community residences, planners have yet to agree upon a single methodology for effectively determining these needs. Some have proposed population-derived (Hogan, 1982) or rate-based (Alpha Center, 1980) planning methodologies. In regard to the latter, one state has proposed that a rate of up to 18/10,000 be used for out-of-home residential care needs (OMRDD, 1984). However, the application of any rate is highly dependent upon local conditions such as degree of in-home supports, demographic characteristics of the population of developmentally disabled persons, financing availability, and political considerations in effecting public policies. Further, planning of residential need requires consideration of both short-term and long-term demands. Although important, planning is not always easy, and established goals can be adversely affected by outside influences such as changes in federal funding systems or in state policies.

Issues of most concern to "system maintenance" include how to:

Mount a successful evaluation effort

Use the outcome of the evaluation to the best interest of the agency, its personnel, and the clientele it serves

Identify the appropriate research strategies to investigate the most salient or pressing program issues

Balance the need to add to the science of service provision in the field of mental handicap, yet protect the integrity of the program and the privacy of its personnel and clientele

Develop a planning capacity

Evaluate short-term and long-range need estimates

Implement planning recommendations

This brief overview of current administrative, programmatic and evaluation issues facing today's community residential system suggests that successful program operators need considerable assistance in making sound decisions that are accountable to both the business and programmatic aspects of human service delivery.

This text provides an insightful, contemporary perspective on issues pertinent to administrators, operators, and staff of community residences as they continue to serve developmentally disabled populations. The intent is to synthesize the most salient findings from the considerable research that is available on most of the areas covered in this text. For those areas in which research findings are either sparse or inconclusive, the chapters on these topics offer reasoned analyses of known problems based on the substantial experience of their authors. The underlying goal of this book, however, is to equip the community residential system, which plays such a pivotal role in the lives of thousands of developmentally disabled individuals,

with new knowledge regarding a broad spectrum of the legal, administrative, programmatic, and physical design issues it faces.

OVERVIEW OF THE TEXT

The chapters in this book are organized to provide a detailed examination both of basic issues facing any agency operating community residences and of specialized concerns that exist given the maturation of the community residential system. Administrative issues are addressed in Sections I, II, and IV, programmatic concerns are examined in Sections III and V, and evaluative issues are woven throughout Sections II, III, and IV.

Section I's chapters provide a broader background for the remainder of the text. Turnbull's provocative chapter reviews some of the major underlying forces that have fueled the development of community residences. His analysis of the legal history that has played such a central and powerful role in laying the foundation for the contemporary residential system illustrates that this system is but a part of the broader civil rights movement for disabled Americans.

Lakin, Hill, and Bruininks's chapter presents a national picture of the expansion of community residential services. Their particular focus on small residential settings offers a valuable perspective on the pressures such settings are likely to experience as the system continues to mature.

The four chapters in Section II examine different aspects of the operating environment for agencies sponsoring community residences. The scope of the chapters attests to the technical sophistication required of agencies to establish and manage both themselves and their programs in the community. The fact that sponsoring agencies assume legal responsibilities and liabilities for the services they provide is reflected in the range of legal concerns to which they must attend (see Freedman and Freedman), in their need to construct and be governed by a legally responsible board of directors (see Gelman), in their need to creatively obtain secure financing for their residences (see Allard), and in their being held accountable for their overall performance (see Jacobson and Regula).

Section III includes eight chapters that examine internal programmatic issues of community residences. While there is considerable debate within the residential care system regarding what constitutes a high-quality program, these chapters suggest administrative and programmatic mechanisms for ensuring that residential services are delivered in a responsible and stimulating way. Landesman, drawing on years of observations of community residences, describes the subtle ways in which program goals can be jeopardized if conscious and sensitive oversight of day-to-day decision making is neglected. The dangers of routinized care are vividly articulated in her chapter. Blunden offers a resident-oriented perspective of some of the key features that contribute to quality environments, identifying a number of ways that service quality can be defined.

One of the hallmarks of the community residential service system for developmentally disabled persons is the use of individualized plans to ensure that residents' needs and goals are concretely identified. A prevalent practice to protect residents from purely custodial care is reflected in the development and implementation of an active treatment plan. This core programmatic process is described in Manfredini and Smith's chapter, which reviews the origin of the concept and presents a detailed explanation of its scope, uses, and effectiveness.

Felce's chapter challenges agencies to view high-quality programming within a larger context that includes the fundamental structure and management style of the sponsoring agency. His analysis, based on studies conducted in Great Britain, indicates the importance of controllable environmental features on the achievement of resident and residence goals.

While no residential system is static, management strategies for ensuring smooth transitions for residents within the system have not been widely disseminated. Heller's chapter focuses on identifying effective strategies and reminds agency and program operators that planned transitions can take advantage of proven methods for reducing the degree of stress that any residential change can engender.

Close and Halpern's chapter describes the semi-independent living program, a type of residential setting that poses unique challenges to management while offering residents an opportunity for greater residential independence. This innovative residential model is likely to appeal to agencies interested in expanding their services to mildly retarded residents.

The relationship between residential service providers and the families of the individuals they serve is the focus of Baker and Blacher's chapter. They offer a review of the literature and a series of recommendations designed to maximize the inherent interest many family members have in maintaining an active supportive role in the lives of their disabled relative. The chapter illustrates that with careful planning, program administrators and staff can utilize a variety of methods to be responsive to family styles and to differing levels of family participation.

Section III concludes with three chapters relevant to a high quality of life for residents: communication, health care and use of leisure time. Kenefick explores the nuances of language and discusses how communicative competence can aid in improving both the climate of a home and the interpersonal competence of its occupants. Rowitz's description of the health care needs of developmentally disabled persons across their life cycle points out both general and unique health issues. Hawkins discusses methods by which program staff can assist residents to derive maximum benefit from their leisure time. She suggests that the role or purpose of leisure time for developmentally disabled individuals is rich in opportunities for continued personal growth when coupled with careful planning by residential staff. These chapters attest to the fact that community residential programs occupy a pivotal position in the lives of disabled persons with respect to fostering and supporting personal well-being as well as habilitative programming.

Section IV includes six chapters on the key ingredient to successful community residences—staff. These chapters are intended to unravel some of the complexities faced by administrators and managers of community residences in ensuring that the program's goals and operations are implemented as planned. Lakin's chapter analyzes the strategies and decisions available to managers to maximize the stability of direct care staff. He highlights the staggering amount of turnover that is experienced in the direct care staff labor market and offers practical suggestions for alleviating the problem through the judicious use of management options. The second chapter in this section, by Levy, Levy, Freeman, Feiman, and Samowitz—all senior managers of a large, private not-for-profit community agency—describes established techniques for recruiting and retaining staff. The authors' emphasis is on career growth paths and the information presented is especially useful for large agencies seeking to groom staff for long-term employment in an environment that can offer staff progressively more responsible and well-paid positions.

Burchard and Thousand's chapter examines ways that agencies can identify the skills and competencies needed by staff to achieve program goals. Their discussion highlights the fact that ongoing staff training and skill development is both within the control of program managers and is a key task in meeting the changing needs and characteristics of residents.

While recruiting, training, and retaining direct care staff are obvious concerns to any residential program administrator, paying staff and protecting their rights as employees are equally complex management issues. Fritz's chapter provides a wealth of technical information on the regulations governing compensation for various direct care staffing patterns. Her chapter also illustrates how the growth of diverse community residential programs with their attendant staffing irregularities has pushed the federal government to devise creative solutions to issues of employee compensation and work conditions.

Few agencies can afford to employ the full range of therapists that may be periodically needed by residents. The use of consultants to supplement direct care staff is an obvious method available to community residences. However, how to derive maximum effectiveness out of consultants presents a serious and potentially costly problem. Seltzer and Apolito's chapter provides a clear description of how programs can obtain specialized knowledge and skills from consultants and incorporate that expertise into their ongoing, daily operation. The chapter focuses on the use of behavioral consultants; however, the techniques described are generalizable to a wide range of other diciplines.

The last chapter in this section explores the ways that microcomputers can facilitate the work of staff and managers in operating community residential programs. Jacobson, Dura, and Mulick describe the key elements of computer systems and illustrate the enormous potential such systems hold for streamlining routine management tasks as well as for aiding resident-oriented, programmatic activities.

Section V's three chapters focus on safety and design issues. The role of the physical environment both as a shaper of behavior and a catalyst for new learning is becoming increasingly appreciated. Community residence managers are often painfully aware of the programmatic constraints imposed by poorly designed facilities. Groner's chapter on fire safety practices describes a variety of approaches—both programmatic and design oriented—that should be considered with respect to resident fire safety. Robinson's chapter examines the ways that interior spaces in a community residence can be designed to promote resident growth without sacrificing the "homey" atmosphere that residences are committed to maintaining. Her chapter contains numerous suggestions for exploiting the architectural properties of residences to ensure resident privacy and individuality as well as to accommodate the realities of group living arrangements. Jenkins's chapter covers similar issues but focuses on exterior spaces. She exposes the possibilities inherent in exterior spaces for both programmatic and recreational use and offers a sensitive approach for recognizing the artful use of landscape materials.

Finally, an epilog by the text's editors summarizes the various themes interwoven throughout the chapters. These closing comments look ahead to the range of management issues likely to be confronted by the community residential system in the coming decades.

REFERENCES

Alpha Center. (1980). *The relationship between health planning and mental retardation/developmental disabilities planning*. Bethesda, MD: Alpha Center for Health Planning.

Baker, B., Seltzer, G., & Seltzer, M. (1977). *As close as possible: Community residences for retarded adults*. Boston: Little/Brown.

Baroff, G. (1980). On size and the quality of residential care: A second look. *Mental Retardation, 18*, 113–117.

Birenbaum, A., & Re, M.A. (1979). Resettling mentally retarded adults in the community—Almost four years later. *American Journal of Mental Deficiency, 83*, 323–329.

Braddock, D. (1986). *Federal policy toward mental retardation and developmental disabilities*. Baltimore: Paul H. Brookes Publishing Co.

Bruininks, R., Hauber, F., & Kudla, M. (1980). National survey of community residential facilities: A profile of facilities and residents in 1977. *American Journal of Mental Deficiency, 84*, 470–478.

Bruininks, R.H., Meyers, C.E., Sigford, B.B., & Lakin, K.C. (Eds.). (1981). *Deinstitutionalization and community adjustment of mentally retarded people*. Washington, DC: Monograph of the American Association on Mental Deficiency.

Cherington, C., & Dybwad, G. (Eds.). (1974). *New neighbors: The retarded citizen in quest of a home*. Washington, DC: President's Committee on Mental Retardation.

Conroy, J.W., & Bradley, V.J. (1985). *The Pennhurst longitudinal study: A report of five years of research and analysis*. Philadelphia: Temple University Developmental Disabilities Center; and Boston: Human Services Research Institute.

Conroy, J., Efthimiou, J., & Lemanowitz, J. (1982). A matched comparison of the developmental growth of institutionalized and deinstitutionalized mentally retarded clients. *American Journal of Mental Deficiency, 86*, 581–587.

Edgerton, R.B., Bollinger, M., & Herr, B. (1984). The cloak of competence: After two decades. *American Journal of Mental Deficiency, 88*, 345–351.

Fernald, W.E. (1917). The growth of provision for the feebleminded in the United States. *Mental Hygiene, 1*, 34–59.

Glenn, L. (1976). The least restrictive alternative in residential care and the principle of normalization. In M. Kindred (Ed.), *The mentally retarded citizen and the law*. New York: Free Press.

Gollay, E., Freedman, R., Wyngaarden, M., & Kurtz, N. (1978). *Coming back: The community experiences of deinstitutionalized mentally retarded people*. Cambridge, MA: Abt.

Hauber, F. A., Bruininks, R.H., Hill, B. K., Lakin, C., Scheerenberger, R.C., & White, C.C. (1984). National census of residential facilities: A 1982 profile of facilities and residents. *American Journal of Mental Deficiency, 89*, 236–245.

Herr, S. S. (1983). *Rights and advocacy for retarded people*. Lexington, MA: Lexington Books.

Hill, B., & Bruininks, R. (1981). *Family, leisure, and social activities of mentally retarded people in residential facilities*. Minneapolis: University of Minnesota, Department of Psychoeducational Studies.

Hill, B.K., & Lakin, K.C. (1986). Classification of residential facilities for individuals with mental retardation. *Mental Retardation, 24*, 107–115.

Hogan, M.F. (1982). Comprehensive community services: How much is enough? *Mental Retardation* (Canada), *32*, 10–19.

Intagliata, J., Willer, B., & Cooley, F. (1979). Cost comparison of institutional and community-based alternatives for mentally retarded persons. *Mental Retardation, 17*, 154–156.

Jaffe, T.P., & Smith, M. (1986). *Siting group homes for developmentally disabled persons*. (Report No. 397.) Chicago: American Planning Association.

Janicki, M.P., Castellani, P.J., & Lubin, R.A. (1982, June). *A perspective on the scope and structure of New York's community residence system*. Paper presented at the 106th Annual Meeting of the American Association on Mental Deficiency, Boston.

Janicki, M.P., Castellani, P.J., & Norris, R.G. (1983). Organization and administration of service delivery systems. In J.L. Matson & J.A. Mulick (Eds.), *Handbook of Mental Retardation* (pp. 3–23). New York: Pergamon Press.

Janicki, M.P., Jacobson, J.W., & Schwartz, A.S. (1982). Residential care settings: Models for rehabilitative intent. *Journal of Practical Approaches to Developmental Handicap, 6*, 10–16.

Janicki, M.P., Mayeda, T., & Epple, W. (1983). Availability of group homes for persons with mental retardation in the United States. *Mental Retardation, 21*, 45–51.

Kugel, R.B., & Shearer, A. (Eds.). (1976). *Changing patterns in residential services for the mentally retarded*. Washington, DC: President's Committee on Mental Retardation.

Lakin, K.C., & Bruininks, R.H. (Eds.). (1985). *Strategies for achieving community integration of developmentally disabled citizens*. Baltimore, MD: Paul H. Brookes Publishing Co.

Landesman-Dwyer, S. (1981). Living in the community. *American Journal of Mental Deficiency, 86*, 223–234.

Landesman-Dwyer, S. (1985). Describing and evaluating residential environments. In R.H. Bruininks & K.C. Lakin (Eds.), *Living and learning in the least restrictive environment* (pp. 85–196). Baltimore: Paul H. Brookes Publishing Co.

Landesman, S. (1986). Toward a taxonomy of home environments. In N.R. Ellis & N.W. Bray (Eds.), *International review of research in mental retardation*. (Vol. 14, pp. 259–289). New York: Academic Press.

Madle, R.A. (1978). Alternative residential placements. In J.T. Neisworth & R.M. Smith (Eds.), *Retardation, issues, assessment, and interventions*. New York: McGraw-Hill.

Matson, J.L., & Mulick, J.A. (Eds.). (1983). *Handbook of mental retardation*. New York: Pergamon Press.

Merges, R. (1981). Checking the cycle: The decline of community-based residential programs in New York State, 1925 to 1950. *Mental Retardation, 29*, 180–182.

O'Connor, G. (1976). *Home is a good place*. Washington, DC: American Association on Mental Deficiency Monograph Series.

Office of Mental Retardation and Developmental Disabilities. (1984). *New York State developmental dis-*

abilities plan—1984–87. Albany, NY: Office of Mental Retardation and Developmental Disabilities.

Perske, R. (1972). The dignity of risk and the mentally retarded. *Mental Retardation, 10,* 24–27.

Rosen, M., Clark, G.R., & Kivitz, M.S. (Eds.). (1976). *The history of mental retardation: collected papers. Vol. 2.* Baltimore: University Park Press.

Rothman, D.J., & Rothman, S.M. (1984). *The Willowbrook wars: A decade of struggle for social justice.* New York: Harper & Row.

Scheerenberger, R.C. (1987). *A history of mental retarda-tion: A quarter century of promise.* Baltimore: Paul H. Brookes Publishing Co.

Vitello, S.J., & Soskin, R.M. (1985). *Mental retardation: Its social and legal context.* Englewood Cliffs, NJ: Prentice-Hall.

Willer, B., & Intagliata, J. (1984). *Promises and realities for mentally retarded citizens: Life in the community.* Baltimore: University Park Press.

Wolfensberger, W. (1972). *The principle of normalization in human services.* Toronto: National Institute on Mental Retardation.

Chapter 2

Ideological, Political, and Legal Principles in the Community-Living Movement

H. Rutherford Turnbull, III

The community-living movement is the result of three powerful principles, each of which fueled the others and collectively created a force greater than the sum of the three. These three principles are normalization (a human service ideology), egalitarianism (a political philosophy), and equal protection (a constitutional doctrine). Together, these principles gave life to three other reforms. They include: 1) a new version of *parens patriae*, a doctrine that holds that paternalism and altruism are best expressed by moving policy away from institutional placements; 2) anti-institutionalism, which goes beyond deinstitutionalization by seeking to abolish institutional placement; and 3) rebalanced power relationships between professionals and parents, on the one hand, and disabled persons, on the other. This chapter defines these six principles, places them in historical context, and suggests what they mean for community-care providers.

The community-living movement would not have been possible without the confluence of three forces—the ideological stream called normalization, the political stream called egalitarianism, and the legal stream called equal protection. Each force, starting independently as a separate stream of activity, flowed into a common mainstream, fueled the others, and collectively created a force that was and is greater than the sum of its parts. These three streams simultaneously gave life to smaller tributaries. These are the reformed *parens patriae* doctrine, with its reshaped notions of social altruism; the anti-institutional reform movement, which consists of more than the traditional efforts at deinstitutionalization; and the acceptance, albeit reluctant at this point, of rebalanced power relationships between professionals and parents, on the one hand, and disabled persons, on the other.

Although these doctrines are explained in detail later in this chapter, it is helpful to briefly define them here. The *parens patriae* doctrine allows a state to intervene in the lives of dependent citizens, such as those with mental retardation, in order to provide them with services that they seem to need because of their special vulnerability. Although the doctrine's impetus is paternalistic and protective, it often results in creating a dual system of law and thereby a second-class citizenship for the persons who are supposed to benefit from it (Turnbull & Barber, 1984; Turnbull & Wheat, 1983). The tripartite policy of deinstitutionalization seeks to improve the conditions of public residential facilities for persons with mental retardation; to prevent the institutionalization of persons into such facilities; and to depopulate public residential facilities by creating community and family-based placements. The drive to rebalance power relationships seeks not only accountability in public services but also greater recognition that persons with mental retardation have situation-specific capacities and the right to chose the degree of independence, dependence, or interdependence they want in life, subject to their own inherent limitations and the restraints on choice experienced by all other members of society (Turnbull & Turnbull, 1985; Turnbull, 1978; Turnbull & Barber, 1985; Turnbull, Biklen, Brooks, Boggs, & Ellis, 1981). Today, many people realize that these efforts simply have not produced the system reforms that seemed desirable several years ago and that, in fact, these efforts actually have legitimized public residential facilities. Accordingly, advocates now seek to divert funding streams away from those facilities and toward community and family-based programs, hoping thereby to create not just new opportunities for liberty, equality, and community for persons with mental retardation but also new forms and norms in society (Turnbull, 1986).

This chapter discusses these streams and tributaries, with the aim of providing ideological, political, and legal contexts for the other chapters in this book.

THREE MAJOR STREAMS

Normalization

In its initial formulation in Scandanavia (Nijre, 1969) and in the United States (Wolfensberger, 1972), normalization called for the accommodation of society to persons with mental retardation and other developmental disabilities so that they could lead lives as nearly normal as practicable. The principle's many contributions include adjusting the fit between society and the person with a disability. No longer does human service ideology allow professionals simply to work with a person, remediating deficits and building on strengths so that the person can meld into the society as well as possible. Instead, it has become imperative for human service ideology, and by extension for human service professionals, to mold society and its environments to fit the person with a disability. Thus, the single-focused professional role has

become a double-focused one. The principle has compelled not just the habilitation of people with disabilities but also the reformation of the society into which they were born and are now seen to have a rightful place as full citizens.

The consequences of this vision are well known to human service professionals and include, among other things, the development of accreditation standards for institutions and community residences that insist on matching the developmental needs of people with disabilities with opportunities and experiences in the normal environment. Whether these standards are those emanating from the Accreditation Council for Services to People with Developmental Disabilities or the Commission for the Accreditation of Rehabilitation Facilities, they reflect, not just in their development and articulation but especially in their implementation, an insistence on the normalization principle.

In recent years there has been a difference of opinion in the literature about the intent and application of the normalization principle. Wolfensberger (1983) has reformulated the principle, claiming that it has been misinterpreted and now should be thought of in terms of "social role valorization." Under this reconstruction, normalization calls on human service professionals to apply habilitation methods whose goal is to enable persons with disabilities to acquire socially valued roles. On the other hand, Nijre's (1985) restatement adheres to the original doctrine and explains why it is still valid. My intent is not to pass judgment on the relative merits of Wolfensberger's or Nijre's views, but only to show how the social-role valorization principle can be useful.

The principle of social role valorization emphasizes not so much the mutual accommodation of society and persons with disabilities as the enhancement of these persons' intrinsic value. One benefit of social role valorization may not be readily apparent. This is its assumption that persons with disabilities have essential worth and that the role of professional intervention is to enhance that value. Some human service professionals may feel that it is unnecessary to make the assumption of intrinsic value more explicit. However, evidence of the withholding of medical care and treatment from newborns with birth disabilities, increased use of amniocentesis and of abortion to avoid the birth of such children, and professional and family willingness to withhold life-sustaining care and treatment of elderly persons provide sufficient reason to impress the worth of such persons upon society.

Another important end of the principle of social role valorization is that of giving impetus to integration efforts. If social role valorization can come to mean that human service professionals and other caregivers (especially parents) strive to enable persons with disabilities to achieve a higher status in their work, education, residence, and social-personal relationships, the "entry-level mentality" that characterizes society's and some human service professionals' perceptions about disabled persons can be replaced by a more potentiating one.

What is an "entry-level mentality" and how is it made manifest? Currently, a vast legion of human service professionals in the United States—especially those in secondary and postsecondary education and in sheltered workshops—believe that persons with disabilities may develop just so far and no further. On the basis of increasingly outmoded data and ideology, these professionals, along with many parents and other family members of disabled children, hold that with sufficient training and societal adaptations, persons with mental retardation may qualify, at a maximum, for simple work, a year or two of special instruction in junior colleges or technical institutes, a group home or perhaps even a semisupervised apartment, and special segregated relationships and friendships. They are convinced, however, that persons with disabilities, no matter how trained or motivated, never will qualify for higher-level work, education, or social relationships (such as marriage and even parenthood). This is the entry-level mentality.

Such a limited vision—one that imposes its own limitations on itself—is the most dangerous type, because (being self-imposed) it lies in the minds and hearts of the most powerful constituency with whom persons with disabilities must deal—professionals and parents. If social role valorization can result in habilitation programs that exceed the entry-level men-

tality and that lead to an increased accommodation of society to such people, it will have done what it may have intended—to continue and to expand, on fronts not previously thought possible, the community-living revolution. The "new institutions" are harbored in our minds and are evident in our communities; they are the "workshop" visions of the past and the workshop settings of the present. (Parenthetically, let us stop calling workshops *sheltered workshops,* a term that suggests and therefore invites segregation, under the aegis of protectionism; it also implies that the workshops do in fact provide shelter, which they may, but of what kind and why?)

Egalitarianism

Beginning with the "legislative years" of the 1950s and continuing through the "executive period" of the 1960s and 1970s (Boggs, 1977; 1978), the currents of American political rivers were distinctly egalitarian. Many human service professionals and parents remember this period fondly—when the federal government was fueled with a dedication to reform not only the inherent characteristics of persons with disabilities by expanded education, habilitation, and medical interventions but also America's communities. The largely white-dominated human service community has yet to fully acknowledge the great debt it owes Thurgood Marshall and the Legal Defense Fund of the National Association for the Advancement of Colored People, and such political activists as Martin Luther King, Jr. In the face of nearly overwhelming odds, they sought to establish equal educational opportunities for blacks—where equal meant integrated, not "separate but equal." Marshall's and King's successes as impassioned, articulate advocates for civil rights laid the foundation for the integration into society of persons with disabilities. This foundation was clear even in the early 1950s. When the U.S. Supreme Court was hearing arguments in the first *Brown v. Board of Education* (1954) case, legal counsel for South Carolina, which was resisting integration-by-race, maintained that such integration would lead to integration by ability/disability. The prophetic vision of that defense would become more and more obvious as time went by and as strict segregation by race, sex, income, and, eventually, disability, increasingly but not fully became the hallmarks of the past.

The climate in which *Brown* and its progeny were argued and then were gradually and ever so painfully implemented was fundamentally accommodating. The nation's political and moral leadership insisted that equal opportunities in education should be matched by equal opportunities in housing and employment. In education, the federal government's initial foray in 1966 with PL 89-750, which amended the Elementary and Secondary Education Act of 1965 and provided federal funds for disabled children's education, tapped a wellspring that became a gusher in 1976 with the passage of the Education for All Handicapped Children Act (PL 94-142). The federal housing initiative at first targeted only poor and minority citizens but, with predictable incrementalism, included some housing opportunities for people with disabilities. Recognizing that housing required ancillary services, federal policy also stressed food-supplement programs, community-based health care, transportation accessibility, architectural accessibility, family-based care, and vocational training. In employment, the federal vocational rehabilitation laws, coupled with an emphasis on vocational education and employment-training partnerships with private industry and/or elimination of employment disincentives in the Social Security Act's provisions for Supplemental Security Income, gave expression to the desire and practicability of bringing people with disabilities into the workforce.

Political egalitarianism called for equal treatment, with emphasis on equal opportunities, for people whose inherent and unalterable personal characteristics (such as race, sex, or disability) historically had rendered them politically, economically, and socially powerless to break out of their present life conditions. Writers analyzing the federal legislation of this period (Boggs, 1977, 1978; Turnbull & Barber, 1985) have demonstrated, among other things, that the egalitarian flavor of the times set the stage for the legal revolution that followed and that truly empowered the human service ideological and programmatic revolution embodied in normalization.

Today, egalitarianism seems but a memory. Vigorous efforts to defederalize human services have put persons with disabilities, and others, on the razor's edge of public selfishness (Turnbull, 1983). Current federal legislative responses to a debt-bloated economy imperil those same citizens, but with different mechanisms—this time, the Gramm-Rudman-Hollings Act and the incipient tax reform (Turnbull, 1986). For the human service professional delivering and trying to protect and even expand community-based services, the question of service delivery now must be cast increasingly in economic terms: cost-benefit, cost-efficacy, and cost-efficiency (Turnbull & Barber, 1985). If this means that professionals learn to do more, with greater proficiency, and with less or the same funding, then people with disabilities—who increasingly are becoming taxpayers—and other citizens will have little to complain about. If, on the other hand, human service professionals do not learn these lessons, they will shortchange not only themselves but their clientele and other taxpayers as well. Egalitarianism created tremendous opportunities, and fortunately was accompanied by the willingness and ability to put money behind policy. But it likewise requires, for the future, fiscally responsible citizenship by caregivers, persons with disabilities, and advocates alike.

Equal Protection

The creative use of legal precedent is the special genius of the lawyer bent upon achieving law reform. Those disability-rights lawyers who followed in Marshall's footsteps used his own fundamental argument, namely that the equal protection doctrine (applicable to the federal government through the Fifth Amendment and the states through the Fourteenth Amendment) forbids a government from discriminating against any member of a large class of people solely on the basis of that person's unalterable or unchosen characteristics, such as a disability.

Without a doubt, the high-water mark of equal protection was made by the first wave, in *Brown v. Board*. No clearer, firmer, or more insistent message that governments may not segretate by race has been given since. *Brown's* progeny—the many cases that have held that education, housing, public facilities, and employment opportunities may not be denied or abridged on the basis of race—were the first members of a new body of law. *Brown's* doctrines came to be applied to people who are indigent, illegitimate, addicted to alcohol or drugs, convicts, or female. And eventually, despite sloppy scholarship overlying wholesome motives, *Brown's* doctrines also reached the education of children with disabilities (Turnbull, 1986) and the accommodation of people with disabilities in other aspects of life as well (Turnbull, 1978).

Even today, when the Supreme Court is (sometimes falsely) accused of civil rights retrenchment, *Brown's* legacy is apparent. Thus, in an attempt to carry out normalization and egalitarianism in community services, advocates for persons with mental retardation sought to persuade the Court in *City of Cleburne v. Cleburne Living Center, Inc.* (1985), that the Fourteenth Amendment, as applied to blacks in school desegregation cases or to other minority groups in other civil rights cases, should be applied as well to people with disabilities. It was argued that the Court must strike down a local zoning ordinance that, as applied, excluded group homes for persons with mental retardation but tolerated other congregate living arrangements (see Freedman & Freedman, Chapter 4, this volume.) Fundamentally, advocates sought to have either the "strict scrutiny" doctrine applied, giving persons with mental retardation the same special protection from governmental discrimination as blacks, or to have a less stringent but nearly as protective doctrine applied, giving people with mental retardation the same special protection from governmental discrimination as women.

Advocates were unsuccessful in both attempts, but they succeeded in their general efforts to purge some zoning discrimination and to establish a legal beachhead in the community. For example, they were able to persuade the Supreme Court to hold unanimously that the zoning ordinance was unconstitutional because it required a group home to obtain a special use permit but did not impose similar requirements

on other congregate facilities such as nursing homes or fraternity houses. Noting that the denial of the permit was based on "irrational prejudice" and that the arguments purporting to express a concern for the safety of the residents of the home and neighborhood were nothing but a smokescreen for prejudice, the Court said that negative attitudes and fears, "unsubstantiated by factors which are properly cognizable in a zoning proceeding," are not "permissible bases" for differential treatment of the group home. "Private biases may be outside the reach of the law, but the law cannot, directly or indirectly, give them effect." Thus, some exclusionary zoning laws and neighbor prejudices are not valid legal objections to community placement. However, state and local governments are still permitted, under *Cleburne,* to exclude group homes from residential zones if they also exclude other congregate facilities on the same basis. State and local legislative reform must outlaw that kind of exclusion to enable the community movement to succeed fully.

Moreover, advocates apparently have persuaded the Supreme Court to create *some* special protection for persons with mental retardation. The Court seems to have created a new class of individuals that will receive some special protection, namely, those who have mental retardation and, arguably, similar disabilities. While rejecting the arguments that persons with mental retardation are entitled to "strict scrutiny" protection (like blacks) or "heightened scrutiny" protection (like women), the Court also made it clear, by its language and approach to the arguments that supported the zoning exclusion, that persons with mental retardation will not be made automatically subject to the progovernment "rational basis" analysis, one that permits *any* governmental action so long as *any* conceivable rationale can be adduced in its favor. The Court underscored that rationalizations of discrimination are not acceptable when the connection between the statute and a legitimate governmental purpose is wholly irrational or simply does not exist. Moreover, it also emphasized that a law that seeks to harm a politically powerless group is not an expression of a legitimate state interest. To a large degree, then, *Cleburne* both retreats from the equal protection doctrine in its potential application to persons with disabilities, and at the same time preserves a special measure of protection for them. The legal beachhead established by *Cleburne* still must be pushed onward, into the depth of residential zones, by state and local legislative reforms. Community-based service providers will have to help finish the legal reform of zoning laws.

THREE RELATED TRIBUTARIES

Normalization, egalitarianism, and equal protection were ideological principles that coexisted in several ways. Not only were they contemporaries of each other, but they also were of the same genre—streams that were so compatible in purpose that they merged easily into a common mainstream of service delivery, politics, and law. Once merged, they quickly overflowed their banks and in turn created new tributaries that generated other forces in the community-living movement. It is to those forces that this writer now turns.

Social Altruism and Parens Patriae

A powerful impetus behind the laws is social altruism (Turnbull & Barber, 1985). The word *altruism* means an unselfish regard for and devotion to the welfare of others. It is exemplified by attitudes and behaviors that regard persons with developmental disabilities as entitled to society's protection and best efforts. Social altruism is a collective effort by members of society, acting through voluntary associations, professional groups, and government, to improve the lives of disabled persons and to rehabilitate them by making them physically and mentally more capable and less disabled. Social altruism acts on the principle that persons with disabilities are essentially and intrinsically important, in other words, a person may have a disability, but he or she is no less worthy (Turnbull, 1976). When social altruism is expressed through law, it rests on the legal principle of *parens patriae*. As indicated earlier, this doctrine enables the government to be responsible for people who are unable to take care of themselves without assistance and to act as a parent would toward children (*parens patriae* literally

means "parents of the country"). Thus, some laws are based on the principal of *parens patriae* and are motivated by *social altruism*.

Unquestionably, the community-placement movement—based on normalization, egalitarianism, and equal protection and usually described accurately in terms of integration, mainstreaming, and least restrictive placement— reflects both individual and social altruism. This is because it represents an effort to "free" individuals with disabilities from the often isolated institutional placements that were common before the reform decades and to afford them the opportunity for a more regular, typical way of life, with environments, associations, opportunities, and rhythms that nondisabled persons take for granted.

Both the now generally out-moded interventions (based on "medical models" that assumed that all persons with mental retardation or other developmental disabilities are "sick" and therefore should be cared for under the supervision of physicians) and generally outmoded placements (in large, publicly supported institutions that end up segregating disabled persons from nondisabled persons and vice versa) often were founded on the purest and most altruistic motives. The mental hygiene reformers of the late 1800s and early 1900s were, in part, people of extreme goodwill, creating what they thought would become wholesome, habilitating, protective environments. No doubt, other misguided hygiene leaders favored segregation to prevent the "contamination" of nondisabled persons by the disabled population.

Whether the motive was to protect the disabled person or the nondisabled person, it often was expressed in terms of altruism and was usually justified by law under the doctrine of *parens patriae*. Given motives that spoke appealingly to the reformers who wanted to habilitate and protect persons with disabilities as well as to others who wanted to shield the nondisabled population from such people (who often were not disabled in any developmental or medical sense but only socially and economically), the institutionalization movement gained momentum easily and had phenomenal success when judged solely by the numbers of people who were institutionalized. Indeed, during the "legislative era" in mental retardation policy and legal reform, and even in the early 1970s, it was commonplace for state governments, assisted financially by the federal government under the authority of the Social Security Act and amendments creating the Medicaid program, to enlarge the institutional system and neglect the development of community-based residential programs. By many, if not most accounts, however, enlargement of the institution did not correlate with, much less assure, the provision of acceptable services.

Yet, it was obvious to many persons that this kind of policy was ultimately destructive not only of the human potential of institutionalized residents but also of opportunities for their equal treatment in and integration into the community. Opponents of institutionalization argued, ultimately with success, that institutionalization was tantamount to victimization; that the residents whose interests were supposedly being protected were the very people whose interests in education, habilitation, health, and even life itself were in the greatest jeopardy. The new reformers essentially maintained that social altruism and the *parens patriae* doctrine had caused a massive and unacceptable reversal of the original intention to assist persons with disabilities.

Anti-Institutionalization

At the start (in the early and middle 1970s), it seemed that the reformers were intent on a policy of deinstitutionalization, entailing three strategies. The first of these was to substantially and immediately change the conditions of life in the institutions. This required the development, first by federal courts and then by Congress, state legislatures, and various accrediting agencies, of at least minimal professional standards of habilitation. The second strategy was to significantly and quickly reduce the number of residents in institutions. This meant the discharge into the community of former residents and the creation of community-based residential options. The third strategy was to reform—so as to discourage new admissions—the procedures by which people, especially minors and persons deemed dangerous to themselves or others, are admitted voluntarily or committed involun-

tarily. This involved the creation by courts and legislatures of new procedures and standards for admission and civil commitment.

Throughout, it seemed clear that improved habilitation standards, reduced institutional populations, and more stringent admission-commitment procedures would have a double-barreled effect. First, they would drive up the cost of doing business in the institutional system. Second, they would compel the creation of community-based alternatives to institutions. Indeed, for many years thereafter, the state and federal investment in institutions continued to rise, largely in response to the judicial and legislative mandates for increasingly rigorous standards of care (Braddock, Hemp, & Fujiura, 1986). Concurrently, the institutionalized population became progressively smaller and the number of community-based placements increased (see Lakin, Hill, & Bruininks, Chapter 3, this volume).

Simultaneously, the federal government began to commit itself in seemingly inconsistent ways to the deinstitutionalization movement. On the one hand, Congress enacted the Developmental Disabilities Assistance and Bill of Rights Act of 1978 (PL 95-602, the "DD Act"). Among other things, this has provided federal funds to assist states to plan, coordinate, and deliver specialized services to persons with developmental disabilities and to do so in a manner consistent with their rights to habilitation in the least restrictive environment. On the other hand, Congress also enacted the amendments to the Social Security Act creating the Medicaid program and authorizing the payment of federal funds to institutions that are certified by the federal government as intermediate care facilities for persons with mental retardation (ICFs/MR). The DD Act and the Medicaid provisions both responded to and sought to improve the conditions in institutions. But interesting and unanticipated developments rendered these laws inconsistent and unacceptable.

In the case of the Developmental Disabilities Act, the Supreme Court held that the act does not bind a state that receives federal funds under its authority to deinstitutionalize by discharging residents to appropriate community placements (*Halderman v. Pennhurst State School and*

Hospital, 1981). The result of that decision was to dilute the enforcement provisions of the DD Act; no longer could advocates rely on them as a tool for state-based legal reform. In the case of the Medicaid ICF/MR program, federal dollars began to increase dramatically while state dollars began to level off and in some states decline to almost an inconsequential, if not zero, level (Braddock et al., 1986). The result was that the hoped-for reduction in the population of institutions simply did not occur at a rate satisfactory to many advocates. Together, these two developments signified that existing federal legislation (in the case of the Developmental Disability Act) was insufficient to reform conditions through depopulation and (in the case of the ICF/MR program) too sufficient to induce depopulation.

To date, Congress's response has been to amend the ICF/MR program to allow federal funds to be "waived" and diverted from institutional use to community-based use. In the future, many advocates hope the ICF/MR program will be amended to require the phaseout of federal support for institutions, the implementation of binding state plans to depopulate institutions, and the diversion of all or a significant portion of federal funds into community-based care programs. If such legislation is enacted, the deinstitutionalization movement will have become a full-fledged anti-institutionalization movement. Currently, deinstitutionalization is an imperfectly realized policy, as a matter of law, funding, and implementation. Fifteen years of experimentation with it have proven too frustrating to too many, and numerous former advocates are now committed, with good cause, to abolishing the institutional model altogether.

In light of these developments, the challenge for the community provider must be to assure not only that the segregative and debilitating conditions of institutional care (at its worst) are not replicated, indeed are not even approached; but to assure as well that improvements in habilitation, integration, interpersonal relationships, and client choice become realities (see Landesman, this volume). This is no easy task. The risk that the community service system will become the institutional model of the future is

apparent to many advocates, however, and can only be avoided by aggressive advocacy by human service professionals and other concerned citizens.

Rebalanced Power Relationships

It is often instructive to analyze the relationships of providers and clients in terms of who has more power within the relationship. Trilling's (1953) paradox (the objects of pity become the objects of concern, study, and, finally, coercion) has become all too real for persons with disabilities, as parents and professionals have compelled them to live apart from the rest of the community, often in injurious conditions. Accordingly, many legal reforms of the past have been predicated on the fact that the provider (including the parent or family as well as the professional) has power, has exercised it unacceptably, and should be required to share power with the individual with a disability.

Self-representation or parent/family participation was intended to be an antidote to the power relationship, a means for rebalancing it and giving the disabled person, or his or her family, a way to protect against the unbridled and often unwelcome authority of professionals (Turnbull, 1986; Turnbull, Turnbull, & Wheat, 1982). Thus, at the federal level the Education for All Handicapped Children Act, the Developmental Disabilities Assistance and Bill of Rights Act, and the Vocational Rehabilitation Act provide opportunities for students, persons with a disability, and their parents, families, or guardians to participate in the development of individualized education or habilitation/rehabilitation plans. These acts also allow such individuals to obtain due process—essentially, an independent administrative or judicial review of professionals' decisions. At the state level, reform of the guardianship laws has been undertaken in many states, with the result that in some states it is no longer necessary for a court to adjudicate a person to be wholly competent or incompetent. Instead, a court may find that the person has limited competence and therefore needs only partial or limited guardianship. (It is fitting, here, to pay tribute to Ralph

Nader, who gave power to consumerism and thereby indirectly affected the self-advocacy and consumer-participation reforms in mental retardation policies.)

Unfortunately, there is a vast difference between law as written and law as implemented. In fact, the law as written—with respect to both the client/family participation components and the limited guardianship component—is not nearly so fully realized in actuality as it might be. The type and amount of student participation in the development of individualized education programs, like the type and amount of adult participation in developmental disabilities and vocational rehabilitation programs, is low, suggesting that the power relationship in favor of the professional is still alive and well. Likewise, limited guardianship is being used far less than might be anticipated. The reason may be that some parties in guardianship hearings wish to preserve the current status of the power relationship, or that courts have no grounds (given the extent of disability of the person) to overcome the power relationship.

Moreover, the self-advocacy movement in mental retardation and developmental disabilities is not nearly so established as it is in the independent-living movement (which consists largely of physically disabled but mentally competent adults). Parents and professionals seem unwilling to train a person with a mental disability to be more competent to make choices; they seem content to teach responses, not reasoning (Turnbull & Turnbull, 1985). Self-advocacy research and curricula are rudimentary and largely not validated. And independence for a disabled person still seems to mean doing what a parent or professional tells the person to do, but doing it with less assistance. It does not yet mean choosing what to do or how much assistance to solicit, consistent with one's capabilities and preferences, as some professionals advocate (Guess, Benson, & Siegel-Causey, 1985; Turnbull & Turnbull, 1985). (This writer dislikes the term *self-advocacy,* believing that it reflects poorly on parents and professionals by seeming to say that self-advocacy is what *we* who are parents and professionals let *them* who have mental disabilities enjoy. This writer prefers the term *di-*

rect advocacy because it emphasizes the direct participation and consent of the person with a disability. As for advocacy by others, this can be termed *representational advocacy,* a term that calls for parents and professionals to represent the interests of the person with a disability. However, some persons with disabilities prefer the term *self-advocacy.* Out of respect for their efforts, it will continue to be used here.)

The challenge to the community-care provider, whether working with children or adults, is to avoid still more mandated rebalanced power relationships and to do so by initiating and assisting the self-advocacy movement, both in its collective form and in its individual expression. The path ahead is difficult. Parents and clients are inculcated with obedience to professionals (Gliedman & Roth, 1980; Zola, 1983). Professional traditions and training, coupled with defensible altruism, make it difficult for professionals to let go. Parental loyalty and concern for minor and adult children with disabilities may make it difficult for them to let go, too, and may impede their support of client-student choice and self-advocacy. Inherent and undeveloped limitations of people with mental retardation and other developmental disabilities stand in the way of client choice in many, but not all, aspects of life. The seductive elements of control of another person's life, sometimes disguising errant paternalism and altruism, are particularly insidious because they are not often explicitly acknowledged and addressed. There is a real danger of negative consequences to the service-delivery system and to professional autonomy if self-advocacy and client choice are taken too far. And, of course, courts are exceedingly deferential to professional judgment.

Yet, healthier client-professional relationships (and effectively redressed power relationships), coupled with more effective service-delivery techniques and systems, may well emerge from the professionals' and parents' actions in, first, training a person to become more competent to exercise choice and, second, in allowing the person to make the choice. For the community-service provider, that can be a challenging and rewarding role, one that moves the client farther toward independence than other types of skill training and that also obviates the necessity for legal reform that changes power relationships by fiat.

CONCLUSION

We all know, at least intellectually, that those who do not study the mistakes of the past are bound to repeat them. Yet we also must be can-

did and admit that we do not often seek to discover our history and its relevance to our actions. This brief chapter has attempted to highlight the most salient events and lessons of the community-living movement, along with its ideological, political, and legal principles so that community providers of today and tomorrow can apply this knowledge to their practice, and be liberated from the dead hand of the past.

REFERENCES

Boggs, E. (1977). Federal legislation, 1966–1971. In I. Wortis (Ed.), *Mental retardation: An annual review* (pp. 162–198). New York: Grune & Stratton.

Boggs, E. (1978). A taxonomy of federal programs affecting developmental disabilities. In J. Wortis (Ed.), *Mental retardation* (pp. 214–241). New York: Brunner-Mazel.

Braddock, D., Hemp, R., & Fujiura, G. (1986). *Public expenditures for mental retardation and developmental disabilities in the United States*. Chicago: University of Illinois at Chicago.

Brown v. Board, 347 U.S. 483 (1954).

City of Cleburne, Texas, et al. v. Cleburne Living Center, Inc., et al., 473 U.S. 432, 87L. Ed. 2d 313, 105 S. Ct. 3249 (1985).

Gliedman, J., & Roth, W. (1980). *The unexpected minority: Handicapped children in America*. New York: Harcourt Brace Jovanovich.

Guess, D., Benson, H., & Siegel-Causey, E. (1985). Concepts and issues related to choice-making and autonomy among persons with severe disabilities. *Journal of the Association for Persons with Severe Handicaps, 10*, 79–86.

Halderman v. Pennhurst State School and Hospital, 451 U.S. 1 (1981).

Nijre, B. (1969). The normalization principle and its human management implications. In R. Kugel & W. Wolfensberger (Eds.), *Changing patterns in residential services for the mentally retarded*. Washington, DC: President's Committee on Mental Retardation.

Nijre, B. (1985). The basis and logic of the normalization principle. *Australia and New Zealand Journal of Developmental Disabilities, 11*, 65–68.

Trilling, L. (1953). *The liberal imagination: Essays on literature and society*. New York: Doubleday.

Turnbull, A.P., & Turnbull, H.R. (1985). Developing independence. *Journal of Adolescent Health Care, 6*, 108–119.

Turnbull, H.R. (1976). Families in crisis. In T. Tjossem (Ed.), *Intervention strategies for high risk infants and young children* (pp. 765–769). Baltimore: University Park Press.

Turnbull, H.R. (Ed.). (1978). *Consent handbook. (Special Publication No. 3.)* Washington DC: American Association on Mental Deficiency.

Turnbull, H.R. (1983). Parents, disabled children, and defederalization: Life on the razor's edge of public selfishness. In S. Pueschell (Eds.), *Parent-professional participation in developmental disabilities services (pp.207–231)*. Cambridge, MA: Ware Press.

Turnbull, H.R. (1986). *Free appropriate public education: Law and interpretation*. Denver: Love Publishing Co.

Turnbull, H.R., & Barber, P. (1984). Future policy issues in mental retardation. In E.L. Meyen (Ed.), *The future of mental retardation*. Reston, VA: Council for Exceptional Children.

Turnbull, H.R., & Barber, P.A. (1985). Federal laws and adults with developmental disabilities. In J.A. Summers (Ed.), *The right to grow up: An introduction to adults with developmental disabilities* (pp. 255–285). Baltimore: Paul H. Brookes Publishing Co.

Turnbull, H.R., Biklen, D., Brooks, P., Boggs, E.M., & Ellis, J. (1981). *The least restrictive alternative—Principles and practices*. Washington, DC: American Association on Mental Deficiency.

Turnbull, H.R. Turnbull, A.P., & Wheat, M.J. (1982). Parent participation: A legislative history. *Exceptional Education Quarterly*, No. 3, 1–8.

Turnbull, H.R., & Wheat, M.J. (1983). Legal responses to classification of people as mentally retarded. In J. Mulick & J. Matson (Eds.), *A handbook of mental retardation* (pp. 157–169). New York: Pergamon.

Wolfensberger, W. (Ed.). (1972). *The principle of normalization in human services*. Toronto: National Institute on Mental Retardation.

Wolfensberger, W. (1983). Social role valorization: A proposed new term for the principle of normalization. *Mental Retardation, 21*, 234–239.

Zola, I. (1983). Toward independent living: Goals and dilemmas. In N.M. Crewe, I.K. Zola, and Associates (Eds.). *Independent living for physically disabled people: Developing, implementing, and evaluating selfhelp rehabilitation programs*. San Francisco: Jossey-Bass.

Chapter 3

Trends and Issues in the Growth of Community Residential Services

K. Charlie Lakin, Bradley K. Hill, and Robert H. Bruininks

This chapter examines the contemporary status, recent changes, and some of the pressing issues in the development of community-based residential programs for persons with developmental disabilities. Between 1977 and 1982, the total number of developmentally disabled persons in both institution and community-based residential facilities licensed, contracted, or operated by state mental retardation/developmental disabilities (MR/DD) agencies was relatively constant (approximately 245,000), but there was a marked shift toward small community-based residences, including specialized foster homes. During that period the number of persons residing in state licensed, contracted, or operated facilities for 15 or fewer residents increased from 16% to 26% of the total population of facilities of all sizes. This chapter describes the characteristics of various community-based residential program models and their residents, and concludes with general comments about the challenges facing residential care systems in the future.

A number of national surveys from the mid-1970s to the mid-1980s documented substantial growth in community-based (generally small and privately operated) residential facilities for persons with developmental disabilities not living in their natural homes (Baker, Seltzer, & Seltzer, 1977; Bruininks, Hauber, & Kudla, 1980; Hill, Lakin, & Bruininks, 1984; Janicki, Mayeda, & Epple, 1983; O'Connor, 1976). These studies provide a counterpoint to other surveys documenting a steady decrease in the number of developmentally disabled persons in state institutions over the same period (Lakin, Krantz, Bruininks, Clumpner, & Hill, 1982; Scheerenberger, 1983). Overall, research on populations of residential programs in the past decade has documented considerable success in realizing the widely acknowledged social goals of deinstitutionalization and placement in less restrictive environments (discussed in Chapter 1 of this volume). Gathering and analyzing these national statistics on utilization patterns of residential services remains important to the formulation, evaluation, and modification of national and state policies affecting residential care for persons with developmental disabilities.

Since 1967 there has been a relatively stable population of approximately 250,000 persons with developmental disabilities living in public and private residential facilities (Lakin, Hill, & Bruininks, in press). However, perceptions about the appropriateness of various types of residential care settings, as well as the distribution of their residents, have been anything but

Research reported in this chapter was funded by grants from the Health Care Financing Administration and the Administration on Developmental Disabilities, both of the U.S. Department of Health and Human Services. Opinions expressed in this chapter do not necessarily represent the official position of these agencies.

stable. There is a growing consensus that institutional care is unnecessary and inappropriate for the vast majority of (if not all) persons with developmental disabilities. Further, smaller community-based alternatives to institutional placement have been demonstrated to be consistently associated with better developmental outcomes (Conroy & Bradley, 1985; Lakin, Bruininks, & Hill, 1986). Thus, it is increasingly expected that the approximately $6 billion in annual public expenditures for extra-familial care for persons with developmental disabilities (see estimates by Braddock [1985] and the Inspector General of the U.S. Department of Health and Human Services [DHHS], [1983]) should purchase services that respond to evolving social and professional standards for such care.

As states have continued to depopulate traditional state institutions and concurrently have attempted to stimulate multiple option, cost-contained private residential service industries, state residential care systems have become much more complex (i.e., greater numbers and diversity of placements) than could have been dreamed possible in the mid-1960s. At that time, it would have seemed almost inconceivable that by the end of 1985, residents of private facilities for persons with developmental disabilities would outnumber those in publicly operated (state, county, and city) programs (Lakin, Hill, & Bruininks, in press). Yet, it is also possible to overestimate the magnitude of the change that has occurred. For example, the shift to small community-based programs has lagged behind the transition to a primarily privately operated state care system. On June 30, 1982 (the most recent date for which national data are available), almost two-thirds (63.3%) of the people in state residential care systems (public and private) were in facilities of 64 or more residents, and over one-half (55.9%) were in facilities of more than 100 residents. Clearly, then, the goal of developing a socially integrated and community-based residential care system for all persons with developmental disabilities is still far from being reached.

This chapter examines the program models, contemporary status, recent changes, and ongoing issues in the development of community-based residential facilities for persons with developmental disabilities. *Residential facilities for persons with developmental disabilities* refers to facilities that states license, contract with, or operate to provide full-time room, board, and supervision (excluding time spent in daytime activities) to persons with developmental disabilities (see Hauber, Bruininks, Hill, Lakin, Scheerenberger, & White, 1984, for a description of the definitions and procedures used to identify and survey these facilities). To examine the status of "community-based" facilities nationally, an arbitrary size standard must be adopted as an operational definition of *community-based*. Readers will recognize that in so doing, size is used as a proxy for qualities that would more precisely determine whether a particular facility is community-based (e.g., located in a residential neighborhood, of the same scale and general appearance as surrounding homes, affording opportunities for interaction with neighbors, and providing opportunities to participate in normal community activities). However, since a standard is needed, the writers have adopted the general convention of defining facilities of 15 or fewer disabled persons living in the same residential unit as community-based. This convention derives primarily from the distinction in the 1967 *Life Safety Code* of the National Fire Protection Association between institutional on the one hand and lodging or rooming house standards on the other, a distinction that in turn has been reflected in other federal and state regulations.

EXPANSION OF COMMUNITY-BASED RESIDENTIAL FACILITIES

Recent years have brought rapid change in the residential care system for persons with developmental disabilities. Most of that change is taking place at the extremes of facility sizes. In 1977 only 16.3% of the approximately 247,800 residents of residential care facilities for persons with developmental disabilities were in facilities containing 15 or fewer residents; 57.7% were in facilities of more than 300 residents. By 1982 26.1% of the approximately 243,700 residents of such facilities were in residences of 15 or fewer residents, while 44.2% remained in

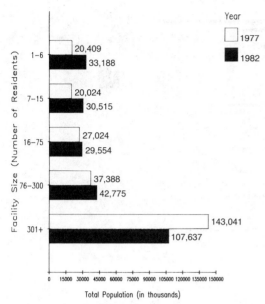

Figure 1. Overall changes in total number of residents with developmental disabilities by facility size from 1977 to 1982.

facilities of more than 300 residents. Figure 1 shows overall shifts in the relative distributions of residents in a number of facility size categories between 1977 and 1982. Four of the five size categories in the figure showed an increase in residents. Only the largest facility size category, of over 300 residents, declined substantially, by approximately 35,000 residents. It should be noted that the apparent growth in facilities with 76–300 residents is actually an artifact of the shift of facilities of more than 300 residents in 1977 into the next lower category of 76–300 residents by 1982 as they reduced their populations. The largest proportional increases occurred in the lowest size categories of 1–6 and 7–15 residents, respectively. These facility categories increased their resident population by over 50% from 1977 to 1982.

INTERSTATE VARIATION IN COMMUNITY-BASED PROGRAM DEVELOPMENT

Information about "the community-based residential care system" has thus far been presented here as though residential services reflected a single national program. Although federal programs contribute substantially to the residential services provided to developmentally disabled individuals, in reality there are 51 residential care systems in the United States, each reflecting the goals and policies of their respective states and the District of Columbia. The variation among these 51 systems with respect to the community orientation of residential services is pronounced. So, too, is the rapidity with which states have been moving to increase availability of community-based programs for residents of the residential care systems. Figure 2 shows the interstate variation in both the overall development of relatively small settings and the speed of that development. Nearly all states showed an increase in residents living in small facilities in proportion to the total numbers of developmentally disabled persons in licensed residential care. In 1977 only 3 states had more than a third of their residential care residents in facilities of 15 or fewer residents; by 1982 this number had grown to 15. By 1982 4 states (Alaska, Hawaii, Montana, Vermont) had predominantly community-based systems.

FACILITY TYPES

This chapter distinguishes between facilities with 15 or fewer residents and those with more than 15 residents. However, within these categories there are a number of different residential care models. A variety of taxonomies have been developed (Baker et al., 1977; Heal, Novak, Sigelman, & Switzky, 1980; Scheerenberger, 1978, 1983). For use in its surveys, the Center for Residential and Community Services (CRCS), University of Minnesota, developed its own taxonomy of residential models (Hill & Lakin, 1986). Table 1 identifies the types and definitions of full-time supervised residential settings used in CRCS research. These types are used to categorize community-based facilities in the data presented later in this chapter. The nature of the services typically provided in these subtypes is described in the paragraphs following, along with two other important residential situations for which national population data are not available (supported living arrangements and living with one's own family).

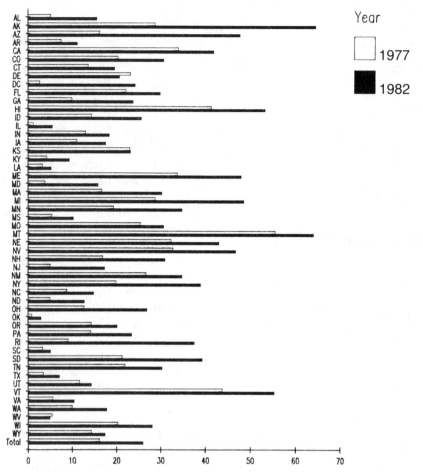

Figure 2.   Percentage of states' total residential care residents living in facilities with 15 or fewer residents, 1977 and 1982.

Specialized Foster Care Homes

The primary characteristic of a foster home placement is that an existing family brings into its home one or more dependent persons who are not family members. There are two types of foster or family care programs in the United States—*generic* and *specialized*. Generic foster homes are operated at a county or other substate level and exist in all states primarily to serve children; often these children have been identified as having handicaps. These homes are not, however, specifically or exclusively licensed to serve developmentally disabled and other handicapped children. In 1980, a U.S. Office for Civil Rights (1981) survey of all counties nationwide found 21,400 mentally retarded children and youth (aged 18 and under) in generic foster care. These children were most likely placed there for reasons other than mental retardation, but were concurrently identified as having mental retardation while in school.

In addition to generic foster care, many states sponsor specialized foster care programs for persons with developmental disabilities. Specialized foster homes differ from generic foster homes in several respects. First, the former are generally specifically licensed, often at the state level, to provide family care services to mentally retarded and other developmentally disabled persons. Second, most specialized foster homes serve adults (63% of the residents are 22 years or older). Third, specialized foster care providers are generally required to receive training specifically related to developmental disabilities. Fourth, while generic foster care is usually temporary (median length of stay is 1.6 years [American Public Welfare Association,

Table 1. Taxonomy of facility models used for community-based care

Model	CRCS definition[a]	Average resident per facility
1. Special foster family care	A residence owned or rented by a family or their own home, with mentally retarded persons living as family members	2.8
2. Small-group residence	A residence of 15 or fewer people with staff who provide care, supervision, and training to mentally retarded clients	6.8
3. Semi-independent living	A residence consisting of semi-independent units of apartments, with staff living in a separate unit in the same building	10.3
4. Board and supervision	A residence with staff that provides sleeping rooms, meals, and supervision, but no formal training or help with dressing, bathing, or other personal care	13.8
5. Personal care	A residence with staff who provide help with dressing, bathing, and/or other personal care, but no formal training of residents	13.6

Note: Although the facility types listed above are primarily small facility models (i.e., 15 or fewer residents), they are not exclusively so. Residential facilities of the types listed had a total population of 67,369 mentally retarded persons in 1982, while 63,703 (95%) were actually in facilities with 15 or fewer residential clients. See Hill and Lakin (1986) for a description of the development and reliability of the taxonomy.

[a]CRCS = Center for Residential and Community Services.

1985]), specialized foster home placements are usually long-term. Fifth, specialized homes have higher reimbursement rates than generic foster care, under the presumption of greater difficulty of care and/or as payment for special services. Despite these higher levels of reimbursement, specialized foster care tends to be the least expensive form of long-term care for persons with developmental disabilities. A major reason for this is the extensive amount of donated capital (e.g., house, furniture, appliances) and time provided by the foster family. In terms of the in-home ratio of caregivers to residents, foster care also tends to offer the highest level of supervision. Furthermore, specialized foster homes are considered an excellent means of providing developmentally disabled persons with normal living experiences, community involvement, and contact with non-handicapped persons (Sherman, Frenkel, & Newman, 1984). New York, Nevada, Michigan, New Jersey, Arizona, California, Delaware, and Missouri are among the states that have strong specialized foster care programs

serving thousands of disabled individuals who need out-of-home care.

Small-Group Residences

Small-group residences consist of dwelling units that are specifically built, owned, or rented for the purpose of providing residential care and active habilitation to 15 or fewer persons with developmental disabilities. They have a paid staff (live-in or shift) that provides 24-hour supervision and in-home training. In general, small-group residences represent the most highly structured and professionalized model of community-based residential services. In many states, these residences are both privately and publicly operated. Of the community-based care models, these facilities (usually called "group homes") come closest to providing the level of care and types of programs offered in large institutions. This may explain why their rate of growth has closely mirrored the depopulation of state institutions. The professionalization of service, the capital investment in the facility and equipment, the intensity of care, and the provision of in-home habitation programming are all factors contributing to the small-group residence being the most expensive model of community-based residential care.

Although there has been a rapid growth in small-group residences nationally, there is also substantial variation among states as to how and what types of programs are developed. For example, Minnesota has been primarily oriented toward developing small group facilities financed through the Medicaid Intermediate Care Facility for the Mentally Retarded (ICF/MR) program (this program is described later); Nebraska, on the other hand, has avoided a "single model for all" approach, and has attempted to develop different levels of care that can be matched to resident characteristics and program needs.

Semi-Independent Living Arrangements

In semi-independent living arrangements, residents have their own living quarters (typically with a roommate). Staff are usually in the same building to provide general supervision, support, and training. To the extent they are able, residents are encouraged to run their own household (e.g., do their own shopping, cooking, and cleaning), while receiving training in skills for daily living in culturally typical residential environments. Such programs assist many residents in developing the skills and confidence to move to even greater levels of independence.

Based on a 1982 survey of residential facilities in the United States (Hill et al., 1984), the average semi-independent living facility (building or contiguous staffed buildings) had 10 handicapped residents with 2 direct care staff on duty in the same building on a typical weekday evening. Semi-independent facilities tend to be somewhat less costly than small-group residences, although costs are often underestimated because residents may receive subsidized rent or pay some of their own expenses from earnings. Also, although relatively few severely retarded persons reside in semi-independent settings (only 150 in 1982), the number is growing steadily as training technologies are improved and the potential of severely impaired persons is

increasingly recognized. The successes of such programs pay dividends not only in the increased proficiency of daily living of their residents but also in the significant financial savings that can result when the individual is enabled to make the transition to less costly residential arrangements (Halpern, Close, & Nelson, 1986).

Board and Supervision Facilities

Board and supervision facilities can be divided into two general types: boarding homes, and board and care facilities. Traditionally, boarding homes provide sleeping rooms and meals, but no or little formal supervision of their residents. Some states specially license or contract with boarding homes to provide care for persons with developmental disabilities. These specially licensed/contracted boarding homes are often obligated to provide formal supervision and sometimes minimal amounts of training. A variation of the boarding home is the board and care facility, which includes some personal services as needed.

Because board and supervision facilities typically provide less intensive supervision than most other facility models, most developmentally disabled residents in boarding homes are adults and have mild to moderate retardation (less than one-third have severe retardation). Most of these facilities are operated by individuals or family proprietors, who provide services at costs that are relatively low in comparison with other models. The states currently utilizing board and supervision placements include Maine, Vermont, and Hawaii. In 1982, only four states—Montana, Vermont, Hawaii, and Arkansas—served greater numbers of developmentally disabled persons in facilities of 15 or fewer beds than in larger facilities (see Figure 2), partially assisted by the vigorous use of boarding and supervision programs.

Personal Care Homes

Small family-run personal care homes frequently resemble foster homes; large personal care homes are often similar to convalescent or rest homes. The characteristic that defines this program model is the provision of supervision and personal care (e.g., help with eating, dressing, bathing, toileting, getting out of bed into a chair, and performing paraprofessional medical/therapeutic services), but without specialized nursing care and with little emphasis on active training. In some states, homes that provide a less intensive level of care (assistance with only one or two personal care skills such as eating and dressing, but not toileting or bathing) are called domiciliary care homes. Generally, personal care homes serve a relatively larger proportion of severely/profoundly retarded persons and older persons (60% of residents in 1982 were 40 years or older) than boarding homes do. Like nursing homes, personal care homes are frequently used for persons who have severe/profound retardation, and are often more oriented toward physical and health services than habilitation. Thus, such homes must be closely monitored to ensure that the services they provide are appropriate and sufficient to promote resident development.

In addition to the models just described, two other important residential categories—supported independent living and natural/adoptive homes—are being selected by increasing numbers of persons with developmental disabilities. These categories have not been the subject of national research to enumerate or estimate the size or characteristics of their populations. However, because of their vital role in a comprehensive system of community-based residential care, they are described here as part of the contemporary array of residential services.

Supported Independent Living Arrangements

The supported independent living model involves arrangements in which residents have their own homes or apartments and are responsible for their own day-to-day activities. Full-time, on-site supervision is not provided, but supporting training and counseling staff visit residents periodically to assist with problem solving, budgeting, crisis intervention, or general independent living skills development. Supported living programs are usually designed as a service with special staff. In areas with a low service population density, such as rural areas, social workers sometimes perform the

support role. As residents become more independent, they receive less support, and some eventually may require little or no support beyond that provided as part of other developmental or entitlement programs in which these individuals participate.

Halpern et al. (1986) conducted a comprehensive study of supported living programs for developmentally disabled persons in four western states. The level of successful adjustment was high for the residents of these programs. Most residents had mild retardation and showed few behavior problems in the community. The study cites some problems encountered by the residents in achieving community integration, in attaining adequate levels of employment, and in receiving needed support services. Overall, the study's findings present an optimistic profile of retarded adults living in these settings, at costs far lower than most residential alternatives, and with limited help and supervision. Several western states and the Association for Retarded Citizens of Maryland have been among the leaders in providing such services.

Natural/Adoptive Homes

The natural/adoptive home is another critically important community-based "placement" and represents by far the most common residential situation for people with developmental disabilities. As indicated earlier, large-scale studies of developmentally disabled persons living in natural or adoptive family settings are scarce. Meyers, Borthwick, and Eyman (1985) studied the demographic characteristics and level of mental retardation of about 59,000 residents in the California service system. Approximately half of the recipients of services lived in the natural home and 14% in family care settings. There is substantial evidence from the California study and those of the CRCS (e.g., Hill, Lakin, & Bruininks, 1984) that this is an increasingly popular "placement." In 1967, public and private residential facilities of all sizes and types had about 130 developmentally disabled residents per 100,000 of the general population; in 1982, this number had dropped to 106 per 100,000. Some of the difference may be accounted for by the use of alternate placement sites such as generic nursing homes, generic foster care homes, or supported living arrangements. For example, there were an estimated 42,000 residents in nursing homes who were indicated as having a primary diagnosis of mental retardation in 1977, according to the CRCS reanalyses of the 1977 National Nursing Home Survey (Lakin, 1986). But, in addition to the decreasing placement rates in residential facilities, important evidence of increased use of natural and adoptive homes as "placements" is seen in the increasing average age at which people with developmental disabilities are first entering residential care. That average increased substantially from the mid-1960s to the late 1970s (from about 12 to 18 years of age). This has resulted in fewer children and youth in out-of-home placements at any one time (Hill et al., 1984; Lakin, Hill, Hauber, & Bruininks, 1982). It is hard to overstate the cost and service implications of the larger natural/adoptive family populations on local, state, and federal costs to supported residential services. Home care not only reduces the demand for expensive and slow-to-develop extrafamilial services, but it actually provides the environment that most community-care settings are attempting to emulate (Boggs, 1979; Bruininks & Lakin, 1985; Moroney, 1979).

ADMINISTRATIVE CHARACTERISTICS OF COMMUNITY-BASED RESIDENTIAL FACILITIES

A major administrative difference between institutions and small community-based facilities is in the operating agency. Individuals residing in small facilities are primarily residents of privately operated programs; individuals residing in large facilities are primarily residents of publicly operated programs. The difference in public versus private operation is directly related to differences in such factors as how the cost of care is established and reimbursed; the nature, costs, and intensity of staffing; and amounts and sources of funding available for capital costs. As shown in Table 2, while community-based residential types are usually privately operated, they exhibit substantial variations in a range of important administrative and demo-

graphic characteristics. Table 2 presents information by residential models on operator characteristics, residents per direct-care staff member, extent of ICF/MR certification, percentage of facilities opening during 1977–1982, and average per diem reimbursement rates.

Residential Models

Most persons with developmental disabilities in community-based residential settings live in facilities designated in the CRCS taxonomy as "group residences" or group homes. These programs provide services for nearly two-thirds (66%) of the small facility residents. The second most commonly used model of community care is the specially licensed foster care home. There were 17,147 persons in these homes as of June 30, 1982. Together, board and supervision and personal care models accounted for 8.4% of community-facility placements, or 5,334 individuals. It is notable that these latter placements tend to be the most "generic" in nature. Only about half their residents were reported in these facilities to have mental retardation, as compared with over 90% of the residents in each of the other care models.

Operator

There are major differences among the community-based residential care models in terms of their patterns of ownership. First, specialized foster care is by its administrative nature a "private proprietary" service, even though "profits" are usually negligible and profitability may not be a primary factor in the decision to provide care. Other primarily private proprietary models are board and supervision and personal care homes. Group homes and semi-independent living programs, on the other hand, are predominantly operated by private, nonprofit agencies. Public (state and county) involvement in operating small facilities remains minimal, with only 6% of residents in publicly operated facilities. In sharp contrast, among large facilities with 16 or more residents, publicly operated facilities house most residents, nearly three-quarters of the residential population (Hill et al., 1984).

Table 2. Administrative and demographic characteristics of different models of community-based residential care—1982

	Residential program models						
	Specialized foster care	Small-group residence			Semi-independent	Board & supervision	Personal care
Characteristics		1–6	7–15	Total			
Total facilities	6,587	3,557	2,857	6,414	306	185	583
Total residents	18,252	15,982	27,606	43,588	3,155	2,559	7,956
Mean residents per facility	2.8	4.5	9.7	6.8	10.3	13.8	13.6
Total mentally retarded residents	17,147	15,701	26,317	42,018	2,870	1,264	4,070
Type of operator							
Private/ proprietary	100.0%	28.6%	25.3%	27.1%	13.4%	94.6%	90.4%
Nonprofit	0.0%	64.0%	63.2%	63.6%	80.4%	4.3%	4.8%
Public	0.0%	7.4%	11.5%	9.2%	6.2%	1.1%	4.8%
Residents per direct care staff at 7:30 P.M. on typical weekday	1.9	2.9	4.9	3.8	5.2	6.2	6.6
Percentage opening between 1/78 and 6/82	46.7%	70.7%	47.2%	60.0%	62.5%	21.4%	27.4%
Percentage of facilities with ICF/MR certification	0.0%	14.1%	24.6%	18.7%	5.9%	0.0%	0.5%
Average reimbursement per resident per day	$16.15	$41.22	$36.60	$38.31	$27.40	$15.97	$17.05

Residents per Direct Care Staff Member

Staffing ratios in different residential facilities can be compared in two general ways. One way is to compute the ratio of all staff full-time equivalents (FTEs), resident contact FTEs, or direct care staff FTEs to residents (i.e., compute an "average" daily staff to resident ratio). A second way is to pick a particular time of day and to compute the ratio from total or direct care staff and total residents actually in the facility at that time. The second method has the advantage of allowing more meaningful comparison across facilities whose staffing arrangements may include foster parents, live-in staff, split shifts, augmented staff complements at critical times, and other efforts to meet staff needs through flexible use of personnel.

Table 2 shows the average resident to staff ratios computed from the reported number of direct care staff (adult household members in the case of foster homes) and the number of residents actually in facilities at 7:30 P.M. on a typical weekday. As can be seen, the resident-to-direct-care staff on-hand ratio is highly related to the size of a facility. Specialized foster care shows by far the best ratio, although one must note that the number of adult caregivers in a foster home at 7:30 P.M. does not necessarily equal the number actually fulfilling a direct care function at that time. Even if one assumes that only half the adults in these homes were performing a direct care function, specialized foster care appears to represent a considerable bargain in the purchase of direct care service, given the relatively low cost of these placements. Although this chapter focuses on small facilities, it is relevant to compare the staffing of community-based placements with that of large institutions. Using the preceding methods of computing ratios, community facilities (an average 3.6 residents per direct care staff member at 7:30 P.M.) compared favorably with large private facilities (7.7 residents per direct care staff member) and large public facilities (7.1 residents per direct care staff member) (Hill et al., 1984).

ICF/MR Certification

Participation in Medicaid's ICF/MR program, in which the federal government currently shares from 50% to 77% of the cost of care depending upon the state's per capita income, is almost exclusively confined to the training-oriented small-group residences and semi-independent living programs. Of these two types of facilities, 19% of the group residences and 6% of the semi-independent living programs were ICF/MR certified as of 1982. This compares with 59% of large private and 87% of large public facilities in 1982 (Lakin, Hill, & Bruininks, 1985). This disparity has led critics (see Taylor et al., 1981) to charge that Medicaid (and specifically the ICF/MR program) has been a major disincentive to the depopulation of state institutions. Indeed, the ICF/MR program was originally developed to assist states in funding improved institutional services. Transposition of its institutional standards to fit small facilities has at times been ambiguous. Nevertheless, the number of small ICF/MR facilities has been growing rapidly. Over two-thirds (68%) of the small ICF/MR facilities operating on June 30, 1982, opened in 1978 or later (as compared with 35% of ICF/MR facilities with 16–75 residents and 10% of those with 76 or more residents). From June 30, 1977, to June 30, 1982, the number of small ICF/MR facilities increased from 188 to 1202. Despite this rapid growth in the number of small ICF/MR facilities, only 6.8% of all ICF/MR facility residents in 1982 were in settings of 15 or fewer residents (Lakin et al., 1985). This statistic suggests why many state mental retardation agency officials responded negatively to proposed federal legislation (i.e., the Community and Family Living Amendments to the Social Se-

curity Act) that would shift Medicaid reimbursement away from support of large institutional settings to smaller community-based settings. Under this legislation, only a tiny minority of present ICF/MR program participants, specifically those in small ICF/MR facilities, would be in residences not targeted for a phasedown of federal Medicaid cost-sharing.

Between July 1982 and July 1985, the number of small ICF/MR programs doubled from 1,202 to 2,453 facilities (according to data gathered by the CRCS National Recurring Data Set Projects), although about a quarter of that growth (nearly 300 facilities) took place in New York alone. New York, California, and Indiana together accounted for 50% of the growth. Concentration of program growth in just a few states does not necessarily suggest a slowing of general program growth; small-sized ICF/MR programs have historically been concentrated in a limited number of states. In mid-1977, 60.1% of all publicly and privately operated small ICF/MR facilities were in Minnesota (which pioneered its use), and three-quarters (74.5%) were in Minnesota and Texas; in mid-1982, 46.4% of small ICF/MR facilities were in Minnesota and New York, and 65.1% were in Minnesota, New York, Michigan, and Texas; by mid-1984, 48.2% of small ICF/MR facilities were in Minnesota and New York, and 62.0% were in Minnesota, New York, Michigan, and Texas. The most notable change in this concentration of small ICF/MR programs in the future probably will be caused by the development of small ICF/MR programs in states that have had relatively small numbers of certified groups until recently (e.g., California) (Lakin et al., 1985).

Percentage of New Facilities

Table 2 also shows the percentage of community-based facilities of the different types operating on June 30, 1982, that opened in 1978 or later. These percentages reflect the particularly rapid growth in small-group residences and semi-independent living programs and the relatively stable or decreasing number of personal care and board and supervision facilities. Specialized foster care settings showed a relatively high rate of new facilities in contrast to the relatively small growth in the number of residents between 1977 and 1982. This probably reflects a combination of the two factors: 1) the more common "movement" of foster homes as foster families, for whom the facility is the primary domicile, move into new homes, and 2) a more rapid real entry and exit of foster care facilities into the system. When foster parents stop providing care the "facility" closes, whereas, in other types of facilities, staff who leave are generally replaced without affecting the survival of the facility itself. Altogether, the 55% rate of new-openings among community (small) placements from January 1978 through June 1982 compares with 16% for public and private facilities of more than 15 residents and 1% for facilities of more than 300 residents (Hill, Bruininks, Lakin, Hauber, & McGuire, 1985).

Cost of Care

Small facility models tend to show considerable variation in cost of care, ranging from foster, board and supervision, and personal care settings with daily reimbursement rates in 1982 in the $16–$17 a day range to small-group homes with an average daily cost of about $38. However, all community models compare favorably with large-group facilities, which average $45 and $84 a day for large private and public facilities, respectively (Greenberg, Lakin, Hill, Bruininks, & Hauber, 1985). Primary factors associated with (but not fully accounting for) the higher costs in large facilities are: 1) the more frequent participation of large facilities in the ICF/MR program, which sets relatively stringent and costly conditions of participation, and 2) the greater numbers of severely impaired populations in large facilities (Greenberg et al., 1985).

CHARACTERISTICS OF RESIDENTS

The continuum of community-based residential living that has evolved in recent years is in direct contrast to the provision of total institutional care as a sole source of residential care to persons of widely ranging abilities that largely existed prior to the mid-1960s. The continuum concept developed to help conceptualize a residential care system that offered a range of services of varying types and intensities, available to people with varying levels of care and training needs, at various times in their life cycle. Earlier conceptualizations of a continuum of residential care often put community-based services toward the least intensive end and institutional care toward the most intensive end. However, such a design can be criticized in that it: 1) implies a justifiable and permanent role for institutions in the residential care system, and 2) assigns those persons with the most intensive level of care needs to institutional placements without specific consideration of whether they would be more beneficially served in community-based settings. Because of diminished acceptability of these propositions, emphasis is being placed on the development of a full continuum of care within a community-based residential care system. Indications that such a system can be viable are reflected in the data on the characteristics of people already in community residences that are summarized in Table 3.

Level of Retardation

Most of the population (60.5%) of public and private residential facilities for persons with developmental disabilities (of all sizes) in 1982 had severe or profound mental retardation. However, only 38% of the persons in facilities of 6 or fewer residents and 30% of the persons in facilities of 7–15 residents had severe/profound retardation (see Table 3). Obviously, community-based programs still fall short of being the primary sources of residential services for severely and profoundly retarded persons. However, between 1977 and 1982, progress was being made within community-based programs in their inclusion. In 1977, only 31% of the population of community-based facilities of 6 or fewer residents and 23% of the population of facilities with 7–15 residents had severe or profound retardation. Although the percentage increases between 1977 and 1982 are in themselves significant, more impressive was the total number of severely/profoundly retarded persons affected. As the community-based care system itself grew, the number of persons with severe or profound retardation in community facilities nearly doubled, from just under 11,000 to about 21,200. Over 6,000 of

Table 3. Characteristics of different models of community-based residential care (1982)

Resident characteristics	Specialized foster care	Small-group residence			Semi-independent	Board & supervision	Personal care
		1–6	7–15	Total			
Level of retardation							
Borderline/mild	25.9%	25.1%	31.8%	29.3%	61.8%	47.1%	31.2%
Moderate	37.7%	37.1%	38.4%	37.9%	32.5%	33.6%	39.8%
Severe	26.0%	25.6%	21.9%	23.2%	5.3%	17.6%	20.6%
Profound	10.4%	12.2%	7.9%	9.5%	.4%	1.7%	8.4%
Functional limitations							
Nonambulatory	9.3%	7.4%	4.1%	5.3%	3.7%	2.7%	5.4%
Cannot talk	24.9%	23.0%	14.1%	17.4%	3.7%	4.8%	16.1%
Not toilet trained	13.1%	9.4%	5.1%	6.7%	.1%	3.9%	6.5%
Age							
<22	37.4%	25.8%	16.4%	19.8%	7.7%	5.9%	10.2%
22–39	32.0%	51.6%	54.4%	53.3%	65.4%	38.3%	31.6%
40–62	23.1%	20.5%	25.7%	23.8%	25.5%	40.5%	41.1%
63+	7.6%	2.2%	3.5%	3.0%	1.5%	15.3%	17.1%

these were profoundly retarded persons, attesting to the belief that a full community-based continuum of residential care can serve virtually all persons with developmental disabilities. As the continuum is currently developing in the community, very small group facilities (6 or fewer residents) and specialized foster homes appear to be the most intensive levels of care. These two types of facilities have the greatest proportion of severely and profoundly retarded residents and also the highest staff-to-resident ratio with which to care for them. In 1982, one-third of the total residents in these facilities had severe/profound retardation, and more than 10% had profound retardation. Group homes of 7–15 residents and personal care homes appear to occupy an intermediate position within the continua, followed by board and supervision and semi-independent living arrangements. Supported living arrangements represent the least restrictive end of the continuum of community-based facilities and typically serve those who have the least severe disabilities (Halpern et al., 1986).

Functional Limitations

Three functional limitations found among developmentally disabled children and adults who live in different residential program models are listed in Table 3. These limitations include lack of independent mobility, lack of speech, and lack of toileting skills. In 1982 the percentage of residents with different functional limitations in the various types of facilities generally paralleled the statistics by type of program model for severe and profound levels of retardation. A substantial percentage of recipients of residential services showed major functional limitations, particularly in speech and language. As with level of mental retardation, specialized foster homes and small-group residences served many persons with substantial functional limitations. The somewhat greater proportion of special foster care residents with significant functional limitations is due in part to the higher proportions of young children in foster care placements and greater proportions of those with severe and profound degrees of mental retardation.

Age

Age distributions of residents in the various types of community residences show a predominantly adult population. In 1982 the popular models of care for children (persons 21 or younger) were foster homes and group homes serving 6 or fewer residents. Overall, between 1977 and 1982 there was a modest increase in the number of children and youth in community-based facilities (from about 13,000 to 15,200). Notably the total population of people below age 22 in the largest institutions (those with more than 300 residents) decreased by 1982 to less than 50% of the 1977 total (from 49,800 to 23,350). However, the proportional distribution of persons under 22 within the different types of facilities in 1982 or the distributional shifts between 1977 and 1982 may be less significant than the overall decrease in the total number of children and youth in the entire residential care system from 1977 to 1982, from about 91,000 to about 60,000. These decreases took place as the existing residential facility populations aged into adulthood without corresponding new admissions of children and youth occurring at anywhere near a full replacement rate. Over one-half of the decrease of about 31,000 in the number of persons under 22 was accounted for by the decrease of about 16,000 in the number of children under 10 (to about 22,200). Such changes and the related rapidly increasing median age at which people are first being admitted to residential care (Lakin, Hill, Hauber, & Bruininks, 1982), must be attributed primarily to increased community-based special education and other developmental programs, parent supports, and other services for persons with developmental disabilities and their families (Lakin et al., 1986).

RESIDENT MOVEMENT/MODEL CHANGE IN POPULATION

Throughout this chapter there have been frequent references to the changing nature of the community-based residential care system. This final section concentrates on elements of that change as reflected in resident movement statistics. *Resident movement* refers to any occurrence that changes an individual's status with respect to his or her residence in a particular facility. Therefore, the components of resident movement are: new admissions (admissions to facilities of persons who had never before lived there); readmissions (admissions to facilities of persons who had lived there earlier); releases (discharges of residents from facilities); deaths (deaths of persons still "on the books" of facilities); and facility closures (facilities closing, moving to another address, or discontinuing service to persons with developmental disabilities). Table 4 presents data on these various movement categories for community-based placement types for the period of July 1, 1981 to June 30, 1982.

Admissions

Rates of admission in 1982 were the highest in semi-independent living programs and in the smallest group homes (6 or fewer residents). The number of admissions to these programs

Table 4. Resident movement in different models of community-based residential care in fiscal year 1982

| Type of movement | Specialized foster care | Small-group residence | | | Semi-independent | Board & supervision | Personal care |
		1–6	7–15	Total			
New admissions	19.0%	29.0%	23.9%	25.7%	31.9%	12.7%	14.7%
Readmissions	.9%	.9%	1.4%	1.2%	1.0%	.9%	2.3%
Releases	7.9%	12.0%	14.2%	13.4%	18.5%	13.0%	8.5%
Deaths	.9%	.6%	.5%	.5%	.3%	.9%	.8%
Estimated movement due to closure[a]	8.8%	7.3%	4.9%	5.8%	9.4%	6.8%	5.7%
Estimated net 12-month change[b]	2.3%	10.0%	5.7%	7.3%	4.9%	−7.1%	2.0%

[a]Estimated movement of residents due to facility closure was computed as 20% of the rate of closure of facilities in each category from June 30, 1977, to June 30, 1982 (see Hill et al., 1985, for a full description of methods and findings).

[b]Estimated net 12-month change is the sum of new admissions (including residents of newly opened facilities) and readmissions less the sum of releases, deaths, and the estimated number of residents in facilities moving or closing.

over the year was equal to 33% and 30%, respectively, of their total June 30, 1982, populations. Board and supervision and personal care homes had the lowest rates of admission (13% and 15%, respectively). Overall in 1982, for community-based facilities (15 or fewer residents), new admissions equaled about 25% of the end-of-the-year population, while readmissions equaled only 1.2%. While the readmissions rate for "small" facilities was not dramatically lower in 1982 than the 1.9% readmission rate of facilities with 16 or more residents, new admission rates were very different. The new admission rate to large facilities in 1982 was only 9%, with progressively larger facilities having lower rates (i.e., 20% for facilities with 16–63 residents, 12% for facilities with 64–299 residents, and 5% for facilities with 300 or more residents) (Hill et al., 1984; Lakin et al., 1986).

Releases

Release rates across community facility types were fairly stable in 1982, with rates falling between 8% in foster care facilities and 18.5% in semi-independent living programs. The high resident turnover in semi-independent living arrangements is consistent with the program's general aim to prepare residents to live in independent or supported living arrangements. The relatively low release rate of specialized foster care settings suggests that the basis of concerns about the stability of placements made into existing households may be somewhat exaggerated, even though caregivers: 1) receive relatively low compensation for service, at least if computed on an hourly rate, 2) have no or low direct capital investment to sustain involvement, and 3) have their entire life-styles affected by their care role. Moreover, such placements tend to serve on average a more severely disabled and less independently mobile population.

Comparison of release rates between small and large facilities is also interesting for what it reveals about how deinstitutionalization is progressing in the different state systems. Deinstitutionalization policy is often considered primarily a process in which people are being moved from large institutions to small facilities, where they then live in relative stability. In reality, the release rates of large facilities are lower than those of small facilities (11% versus 13.5%). If one looks at movement patterns over the past two decades, it becomes apparent that the decreasing populations of state institutions (private institutions have not decreased populations) are primarily attributable to the greatly reduced number of new admissions. For example, in 1967, there were 12,834 new admissions to state institutions for mentally retarded persons and 11,665 discharges (Lakin, 1979); in 1982 there were an estimated 11,076 discharges from state institutions, but only an estimated 3,569 first-time admissions to state institutions (Lakin et al., in press).

Deaths

Death rates in community-based facilities tend to be relatively low and related to the proportion of older residents (see Table 3). The overall small facility death rate of 0.5% is less than half that of larger facilities (1.3%). However, because most state and many private institutions have hospital and nursing units, they have a much higher tendency to retain some acutely and chronically ill residents that smaller facilities would discharge to other health care facilities. They also have a slightly older resident population than smaller community facilities (Hill et al., 1985; Lakin et al., 1986).

Resident Movement by Facility Closure or Movement

A substantial amount of resident movement in community-based residences is caused by the closure or movement of entire facilities. Altogether, the 6.7% estimated resident movement rate caused by facility closure/movement in 1982 was half the rate of actual releases (13.5%). The relatively high closure/movement rates in semi-independent living programs probably reflects the programs' being housed in apartment complexes so that program movement is relatively easier than for programs housed in a purchased facility. Foster homes also showed a relatively high rate of closure/movement (estimated at 8.8% in 1982), but it is unknown how closure (discontinuing care for persons with mental retardation) versus movement (relocation of an intact foster family to a new domicile) contributes to this rate. The 1980 U.S. Census found that 11.8% of households in owner-occupied units moved within 15 months of the census interview (an estimated annual rate of 9.4%), which suggests that considerable movement of intact households (including foster members) may well have occurred (see Hill et al., 1985).

Net Change

Net change in the different models of residential care in 1982 generally parallels the observed change between June 30, 1977, and June 30, 1982. The only type of community-based facility that showed a net decrease in residents in 1982 was the board and supervision category, which decreased about 7%. From 1977 to 1982 the number of residents in the facilities classified as board and supervision decreased about 24%. Part of this decrease is undoubtedly due to increased requirements on residential placements to include training components, which tend to cause board and supervision facilities that meet new licensing standards to be reclassified as small-group residences. Group residences with 6 or fewer residents were the fastest growing type of facility, with a net increase of about 10% in 1982. Although facilities with more than 16 residents lost residents at a −4.4% annual rate in 1982, facilities with 16–63 residents were among the most rapidly growing (at an annual rate of 8%).

SUMMARY OF ISSUES IN COMMUNITY-BASED RESIDENTIAL CARE

In 1968 the first drop occurred in the annual average daily population of public institutions for mentally retarded persons, a drop of about 600 persons from 194,650 to 194,000 (Lakin, 1979). A decade later, there were 148,752 mentally retarded persons in public institutions, a decrease of 23% in 10 years (Lakin, 1979).

Steady annual declines in average populations have occurred every year since, reaching a 1985 average of 105,158 (Lakin, Krantz, et al., 1982; Scheerenberger, 1986).

Matching this extensive decline in public institution placements was the rapid growth of community-based, primarily private proprietary and nonprofit, residential facilities. From 1969 to 1982, the number of residents living in privately managed, generally smaller community-based facilities quadrupled, from 24,000 to approximately 98,000 (Lakin et al., 1985). Paralleling this increase, the mean number of residents per private facility decreased from 47 (34 of whom had mental retardation) in 1969 to 15 (12 of whom had mental retardation) in 1982. Equally important, the focus of residential services changed from a few hundred facilities in the 1960s (mostly large public institutions) to well over 16,000 mostly privately operated programs by the mid-1980s (Lakin et al., 1985).

These national statistics suggest that community-based care programs for persons with developmental disabilities have generally responded to the major challenges that have confronted them in recent years, including: 1) continued expansion to absorb much of the steady rate of institution depopulation that has been maintained since 1968 (about 4% per year); 2) provision of services for increasing numbers of severely and especially profoundly retarded individuals; 3) creation of more numerous and flexible models of supervision and training for persons who are capable of living in settings that permit higher degress of individual autonomy, self-assertiveness, and self-subsistence than typical group home settings; 4) avoidance or delay in the entry of children and youth into residential care, especially institution placements; 5) maintenance of the costs of community residential programs and related habilitation and support services at or below the cost levels of existing institutional programs; and 6) increased association beween dollars spent for service and staff time actually allocated to residents' care, supervision, and training.

At the same time, in examining the nationally aggregated statistics and service trends, it should not be overlooked that there really is no national program of residential services, but, instead, there are 51 state programs (including the District of Columbia), many of which are further subdivided into regional and county programs. Examination of these state programs shows wide diversity. For example, Figure 2 showed substantial differences across states with respect to the distribution of residents by facility size (e.g., four states have more than 50% of their residents in small facilities, and seven states have less than 10%). With respect to the relative size of state residential populations (i.e., the number of people in state residential care systems per 100,000 of their general populations), states again very substantially, with eight having fewer than 70 and eight having more than 140. With respect to funding allocated to the care of residents, eight states averaged less than $50 per day and seven states more than $75 per day (the national average being $62 per day). Clearly, the movement toward small, community-based facilities is a national movement, but it is still at the state, local, and program levels that the major decisions affecting its course are made.

Many important characteristics of residential services changed during the past 25 years. One important change was the dramatic shift from public to private forms of management. This shift radically altered the role of state government agencies in residential services, decreasing the role of direct centralized management and sharply increasing the need for indirect, decentralized management responsibilities (carried out largely through program approval, rate setting, quality assurance, and technical assistance rather than through direct administration). A second change resulted in a phenomenal decentralization of authority and responsibility. Rather than continuing to administer a few large programs that provided nearly all services in one location, states and local government units had to organize highly diverse forms of services in many different agencies and locations. A third dimension was the changing role of government agencies, from being direct managers of programs and policies to being mediators of many conflicting forces

including legislators, parents, providers, employee groups, and the legal system.

Despite such near-revolutionary changes in views and practices, residential and related service programs are organized today at the state and local government levels much as they were 10 to 20 years ago. Policies are carried out by a maze of largely independent and autonomous agencies. Community residential programs, for example, are often administered by a different state office than the one that manages institutional programs. The placement of people from institutions into community settings is further impeded by the autonomy of local government social service agencies, whose financial responsibility is often increased by deinstitutionalization and social integration practices. To complicate matters, state and local services involving education, income maintenance, employment training, health, and other services are all generally controlled by separate, autonomous agencies and boards.

States are rarely actual community care providers, but they play an important role in the size and quality of their community-based care system. Several of the many important challenges facing states and local communities today (albeit to different extents) include:

1. Gaps must be filled in the community-based continua of care, particularly at the most intensive end, so that all persons with developmental disabilities will have the opportunity to live in community settings. Probably the main challenges for small-group residences in the future will be to increase the number of programs that can provide high-quality services to severely/profoundly and multiply handicapped persons, while promoting the movement of current residents not needing highly structured residential care to less structured, less costly, and more appropriate settings.
2. Closer parity in funding must be achieved between community care and institutional care of persons of similar service needs (community care is generally allocated less).

3. Community residences must be adequately supported with critical complementary services (e.g., developmental and work training programs, recreation programs, therapeutic services).

4. Opportunities (i.e., programs) and incentives must be implemented for moving residents toward less structured, more independent residential settings once they have entered community residential services systems. Semi-independent programs tend to serve many of the higher functioning residents in the residential care system, and in this role appear to be important to the future of deinstitutionalization for several reasons. The efforts of states to move severely/profoundly impaired persons into community settings with high levels of supervision can be greatly facilitated by moving mildly/moderately impaired individuals out of such settings, thus increasing the availability of existing community sites for the severely impaired persons still institutionalized or just entering the system.

5. Employees of community facilities must be well-prepared and adequately compensated, and must deliver services that reflect contemporary standards of adequate care and training.

6. Services must be provided to natural and adoptive families of sufficient quality, frequency, and intensity so as to permit and encourage the retention of family members with developmental disabilities within their own homes.

If state and local governments can begin to consistently fulfill these central responsibilities in promoting community-based services for persons with developmental disabilities, continued development of quality community-based residential living systems will be facilitated. To the extent that states differ in their performance of these responsibilities, the state-by-state variations in the availability of community-based living will be maintained or increased and people with developmental disabilities will be differentially provided with minimally adequate services. Continued reform of policies and procedures at all levels of government is necessary to sustain recent national trends toward greater social integration and more appropriate forms of community-based living for developmentally disabled citizens.

REFERENCES

American Public Welfare Association. (1985). *Characteristics of children in substitute and adoptive care.* Washington, DC: Author.

Baker, B.L., Seltzer, G.B., & Seltzer, M.M. (1977). *As close as possible: Community residences for retarded adults.* Boston: Little, Brown.

Boggs, E.M. (1979). Economic factors in family care. In R.H. Bruininks & G.C. Krantz (Eds.), *Family care of developmentally disabled members* (pp. 47–60). Minneapolis: University of Minnesota.

Braddock, D. (1985). *Federal spending in mental retardation and developmental disabilities.* Chicago: University of Illinois at Chicago, Institute for the Study of Developmental Disabilities.

Bruininks, R.H., Hauber, F.A., & Kudla, M.J. (1980). National survey of community residential facilities: A profile of facilities and residents in 1977. *American Journal of Mental Deficiency, 80,* 470–478.

Bruininks, R.H., & Lakin, K.C. (Eds.). (1985). *Living and learning in the least restrictive environment.* Baltimore: Paul H. Brookes Publishing Co.

Conroy, J.W., & Bradley, V.J. (1985). *The Pennhurst longitudinal study: A report of five years of research and analyses.* Philadelphia: Temple University, Developmental Disabilities Center.

Greenberg, J.A., Lakin, K.C., Hill, B.K., Bruininks, R.H., & Hauber, F.A. (1985). Costs of residential care in the United States. In K.C. Lakin, B.K. Hill, & R.H. Bruininks (Eds.), *An analysis of Medicaid's Intermediate Care Facility for the Mentally Retarded (ICF-MR) program* (pp. 7-1-7-82). Minneapolis: University of Minnesota, Department of Educational Psychology.

Halpern, A.S., Close, D.W., & Nelson, D.J. (1986). *On my own: The impact of semi-independent living programs for adults with mental retardation.* Baltimore: Paul H. Brookes Publishing Co.

Hauber, F.A., Bruininks, R.H., Hill, B.K., Lakin, K.C., Scheerenberger, R.C., & White, C.A. (1984). *1982 census of residential facilities for mentally retarded people* (Report No. 19). Minneapolis: University of Minnesota, Department of Educational Psychology.

Heal, L.W., Novak, A.R., Sigelman, C.K., & Switzky, H.N. (1980). Characteristics of community residential facilities. In A.R. Novak & L.W. Heal (Eds.), *Integration of developmentally disabled individuals into the community* (pp. 45–56). Baltimore: Paul H. Brookes Publishing Co.

Hill, B.K., Bruininks, R. H., Lakin, K.C., Hauber, F.A., & McGuire, S.P. (1985). Stability of residential facilities for people who are mentally retarded, 1977–1982. *Mental Retardation, 23,* 108–114.

Hill, B.K., & Lakin, K.C. (1986). Classification of residential facilities for mentally retarded people. *Mental Retardation, 24,* 107–115.

Hill, B.K., Lakin, K.C., & Bruininks, R.H. (1984). Trends in residential services for people who are mentally retarded: 1977–1982. *Journal of The Association for Persons with Severe Handicaps, 9,* 243–250.

Inspector General of Health and Human Services. (1983). *Transition of developmentally disabled young adults from school to adult services.* Washington, DC: U.S. Department of Health and Human Services, Office of the Inspector General.

Janicki, M., Mayeda, T., & Epple, W.A. (1983). Availability of group homes for persons with mental retardation in the United States. *Mental Retardation, 21,* 45–51.

Lakin, K.C. (1979). *Demographic studies of residential facilities for mentally retarded people.* Minneapolis: University of Minnesota, Department of Educational Psychology.

Lakin, K.C. (1986). *Estimated mentally retarded populations in nursing homes according to the National Nursing Home Survey of 1977* (Brief #26). Minneapolis: University of Minnesota, Department of Educational Psychology.

Lakin, K.C., Bruininks, R.H., & Hill, B.K. (1986). Habilitative functions and effects of residential services. *Remedial and Special Education, 7*(6), 54–62.

Lakin, K.C., Hill, B.K., & Bruininks, R.H. (Eds.) (1985). *An analysis of Medicaid's Intermediate Care Facility for the Mentally Retarded (ICF-MR) Program.* Minneapolis: University of Minnesota, Department of Educational Psychology.

Lakin, K.C., Hill, B.K. & Bruininks, R.H. (in press). Basic trends and facts in residential services. In R.B. Kugel (Ed.), *Changing patterns of residential services for persons with mental retardation* (3rd ed.). Washington, DC: President's Committee on Mental Retardation.

Lakin, K.C., Hill, B.K., Hauber, F.A., & Bruininks, R.H. (1982). Changes in age at first admission to residential care of mentally retarded people. *Mental Retardation, 20,* 216–219.

Lakin, K.C., Krantz, G.C., Bruininks, R.H., Clumpner, J.L., & Hill, B.K. (1982). One hundred years of data on public residential facilities for mentally retarded people. *American Journal on Mental Deficiency, 87,* 1–8.

Meyers, C.E., Borthwick, S.A., & Eyman, R.K. (1985). Place of residence by age, ethnicity, and level of retardation of the mentally retarded developmentally disabled population of California. *American Journal of Mental Deficiency, 90,* 266–270.

Moroney, R.M. (1979). Allocation of resources for family care. In R.H. Bruininks & G.C. Krantz (Eds.), *Family care of developmentally disabled members* (pp. 63–76). Minneapolis: University of Minnesota.

O'Connor, G.O. (1976). *Home is a good place: A national perspective of community residential facilities for developmentally disabled persons.* Washington, DC: American Association on Mental Deficiency.

Scheerenberger, R.C. (1978). *Public residential services for the mentally retarded: 1977.* Madison, WI: National Association of Superintendents of Public Residential Facilities for the Mentally Retarded.

Scheerenberger, R.C. (1983). *Public residential services for the mentally retarded: 1982.* Madison, WI: National Association of Superintendents of Public Residential Facilities for the Mentally Retarded.

Scheerenberger, R.C. (1986). *Public residential services for the mentally retarded: 1985.* Madison, WI: National Association of Superintendents of Public Residential Facilities for the Mentally Retarded.

Sherman, S.R., Frenkel, E.R., & Newman, E.S. (1984). Foster family care for older persons who are mentally retarded. *Mental Retardation, 22,* 302–308.

Taylor, S., Brown, K., McCord, W., Giambetti, A., Searl, S., Milnarcik, S., Atkinson, T., & Lichter, S. (1981). *Medicaid institutions and deinstitutionalization: The ICF-MR program.* Syracuse: Syracuse University, Center on Human Policy.

U.S. Office for Civil Rights. (1981). *1980 Children and Youth Referral Survey of Public Welfare and Social Service Agencies.* Washington, DC: U.S. Department of Health and Human Services, Office for Civil Rights.

Section II

OPERATING WITHIN THE REALITIES OF THE COMMUNITY

Chapter 4

Legal Issues
Facing Community Agencies

Donald N. Freedman and Ruth I. Freedman

The legal and human rights of mentally retarded residents need to be protected and incorporated into the day-to-day operations of community residences. This chapter covers a series of legal issues of key importance to agencies planning, developing, or operating community residences.

In the first part of the chapter, legal issues that are often encountered in the preoperational phase of planning community residences are discussed; these include zoning restrictions and building codes. The second part examines legal issues of primary importance in the ongoing operation of community residences, including liability, negligence, battery, and residents' right to privacy. Finally, methods of assuring the protection of residents' human rights are described.

We are largely past arguing about whether mentally retarded persons have, in principle, the rights to treatment and to education, to live in the community, and to a humane and safe living environment. These rights, originating in broadly accepted concepts of human rights, federal and state[1] constitutions, statutes, administrative regulations, and local ordinances, have been affirmed repeatedly by the courts (*O'Connor v. Donaldson*, 1975; *Romeo v. Youngberg*, 1982; *Rouse v. Cameron*, 1966; *Welsch v. Likins*, 1974; *Wyatt v. Stickney*, 1971; cf. *Pennhurst State School and Hospital v. Halderman*, 1981) and by government at all levels, as well as by international organizations. Although, plainly, much remains to be done to enlarge the scope and extent of official confirmation of these rights on all governmental levels, it is also critically important to understand and implement these rights on the day-to-day

level of service provision in the community. At this level, rights are not legally rarified statements of principle, but are often expressed as conflicting interests requiring balance and compromise and procedural safeguards for their effective implementation. The concept of legal rights must be reflected in the day-to-day operation of the agency. While agencies are increasingly sensitive to issues involving the legal rights of mentally retarded persons, they must also acknowledge conflicts with other legal interests, such as local zoning and building standards, as well as fears of liability.

These three areas of legal interest—resident rights, siting/building constraints, and liability—do not have to be altogether "other things" to which the agency must attend, absorbing staff time and diverting services and resources from "direct" services to residents. Rather, legal interests can be reflected in the

---

[1] Habilitation and treatment for mentally retarded persons is mandated by statute in 25 states. See Brakel, Parry, and Weiner (1985, table 6.1, column 1, page 352).

attitude, the procedures, and the services provided by the agency.

By understanding these interests and incorporating them into agency planning, staff training, and resident procedures, the legal and service interests of the agency need not be either conflicting or duplicative, but, rather, aspects of the same overall interest of the mentally retarded persons served.

PREOPERATIONAL CONSIDERATIONS

Zoning

To deal effectively with potential zoning constraints, the agency must be aware of the general policies and principles underlying zoning law, as well as the specific zoning restrictions that are in force in the community or communities in which siting is under consideration. Unless the agency explicitly decides to test, through litigation, a specific ordinance, and is prepared to bear the expense and delay necessarily entailed, final site selection must be made with either prior approval by municipal authorities or with the utmost confidence that the site and intended use complies with local zoning ordinances.

Zoning is a system of legal controls over the use of land in a community. Its valid purposes include the protection of the health, welfare, and safety of citizens, by, for example, separating industrial, commercial, open space, and residential zones (*Village of Belle Terre v. Borass*, 1974). Zoning laws have historically served other interests as well, such as the exclusion of certain groups or socioeconomic classes. Many such zoning ordinances have been ruled invalid on their face. Most of the conflict today in community programming, however, involves the unfair application of zoning restrictions. Communities or neighborhoods opposed to the establishment of community residences may attempt to prevent the opening of these facilities through the enforcement of zoning ordinances that are restrictive by their nature or in their application. Local zoning laws typically separate commercial and industrial districts from residential areas, and distinguish between areas restricted to single-family residences and neighborhoods where multifamily residences are allowed.

While several types of zoning ordinances may exclude community residences, the most frequent difficulty involves the placement of community residences in "single-family residence" zones, typically the most desirable residential areas. Communities may attempt to prevent the establishment of community residences in single-family neighborhoods by arguing that community residences do not fall under the definition of *single family*. *Family* is typically defined in zoning ordinances as a group of persons of any number who are related by blood, marriage, or adoption; or a group of a specific limited number, such as up to two, three, or four, who are unrelated but function as a single housekeeping unit. However, numerous court cases in various states have challenged this use of exclusionary zoning. In most cases, courts have maintained that because a community residence functions like a family, and with residents living in a single unit, participating in housekeeping, cooking, and other activities as a "family" group, such a home fits within the definition of *family* (*Tucker v. Special Children's Foundation*, 1984; *West Monroe v. Quachita ARC*, 1981).

In a 1985 zoning appeal, the U.S. Supreme Court struck down as unconstitutional a Cleburne, Texas, zoning ordinance excluding community residences for mentally retarded persons from "apartment house districts." Although the Court did not find that people with mental retardation were a "quasi-suspect class," entitled to the highest degree of constitutional protection against discrimination, it did invalidate the Cleburne zoning ordinance as based on "irrational prejudice" depriving mentally retarded persons of equal protection under the law (*City of Cleburne v. Cleburne Living Center, Inc.*, 1985).

Another type of zoning ordinance excludes community residences from single-family areas on the grounds that community residences are commercial or business ventures, and thus must be located in business or commercial zones (*Costley v. Caromin House*, 1981; *Harbour v. Normal Life of Louisiana*, 1984). In several recent cases, plantiffs claimed the houses were being used for commercial rather than residential purposes because they were operated by corporations that received money from various state and federal agencies. In these cases, the court rejected the argument, maintaining that the fact that a community residence receives subsidies, pays staff salaries, or even operates on a for-profit basis does not make the home a commercial venture; rather, the family-living style of the home and the emphasis on teaching residents home-living skills were held as the determining factors in classifying community residences as residential in purpose.

Restrictive covenants (private agreements that become part of a contract to buy or sell land) are also a major strategy used to exclude community residences. In some cases, these private covenants have been upheld in court challenges (*Crane Neck Association, Inc. v. New York City of Long Island County Servs. Group*, 1983; *Omega Corporation of Chesterfield v. Malloy*, 1984). In other cases, however, protective state statutes and/or policies have overridden the covenants (*Concord Estate Homeowners Associates Inc. v. Special Children's Foundation, Inc.*, 1984; *Craig v. Bossenberg*, 1984; *Knudtson v. Train*, 1984).

Responding to zoning challenges involves enormous amounts of time, effort, and money on the part of agencies that sponsor community residences. Often agencies simply do not have the time or resources necessary to appeal exclusionary zoning ordinances or practices. As a result, community residences frequently are forced to open or relocate in neighborhoods least likely to enforce restrictive zoning, that is, in multifamily areas, industrial, commercial, or institutional zones. Unfortunately, these areas usually do not afford optimal opportunities for community integration. Moreover, there is often an overconcentration of community residences in neighborhoods with the least resistance. A "ghetto" of community residences can threaten the residential character of a neighborhood and deny disabled persons the opportunity to live in a typical residential area. Some states (either through statute or licensing regulations or both) have limited the number of com-

munity residences within any town or municipality in order to prevent excessive concentration of these facilities.

In an effort to overcome exclusionary tactics, many states have enacted protective state statutes that override or preempt local zoning regulations. According to a 1978 survey of zoning laws (American Bar Association Commission on the Mentally Disabled, 1978), 16 states had enacted statutes limiting local discretion to exclude community homes. In a more recent review (Bogin, 1983), 26 states had legislation limiting exclusionary zoning. These recent state enactments generally specify the types of community homes exempt from local zoning, the types of populations served, the number of residents permitted in community residences, the types of zones in which community residences are permitted, and licensing procedures. For example, Rhode Island's statute designates the residents of community homes (six or fewer residents) as a "family" and waives all local zoning requirements pertaining to them. In Texas, S.B. 940, which went into effect in September 1985, provides that a family home that houses no more than six unrelated persons with disabilities and two supervisory personnel is a "permitted user" in any residential zone or district. The law also prohibits the establishment of a family home within one-half mile of a previously existing family home.

Other states (e.g., Arizona, Minnesota, Ohio, Vermont) treat community residences as "conditionally permitted uses," requiring them to meet certain requirements or standards in order to be located in residential areas and to remain exempt from zoning regulations. Fifteen states limit the types of residents who may live in community homes—for example, persons who have developmental disabilities, mental retardation, mental illness, children who have physical handicaps or persons in need of supervision and care.

In related court cases on governmental immunity from the application of local zoning laws, some courts have held that community residences owned by state or county government or even when operated under contract with state government are immune from the application of local zoning ordinances (*Brownfield v. State of Ohio*, 1978; *Temple Terrace v. Hillsborough Ass'n. for Retarded Citizens,* 1976).

Community residences in Massachusetts have often claimed exemption from local zoning regulations on the basis of a state statute that stipulates that "no ordinances or bylaw shall . . . prohibit, regulate, or restrict the use of land or structures . . . for educational purposes on land owned or leased by the Commonwealth or any of its agencies, subdivisions or bodies politic or by . . . a non-profit educational corporation"(Mass. Gen. Laws C. 40A, § 3). Several recent cases have applied the law supportively to the context of community residences (*South Norfolk County Association for Retarded Citizens Inc. and the Commonwealth of Massachusetts v. Randall Riley and DiSangro,* 1982).

The American Bar Association Commission on the Mentally Disabled (1978) has developed a model statute establishing the right to locate community homes for developmentally disabled persons in residential neighborhoods. The statute includes features that facilitate the location of community residences and at the same time addresses legitimate local concerns about health, fire, and safety regulations. The proposed act: 1) establishes a state licensing program for community homes to ensure safe and appropriate care; 2) gives the state licensing agency authority to prevent overconcentration of homes; 3) provides municipalities with the right to petition the licensing director to deny a license to a particular home; and 4) prohibits the exclusion of community residences by restrictive covenants.[2]

Community residences across the country have faced local zoning challenges. In cases that have been appealed at higher court levels, courts have generally ruled in favor of the community residences. But only a handful of zoning cases are ever brought to appeal because of the enormous amount of time, money, and effort involved.

Building Codes

Zoning law restricts the use of a building according to its site location. Generally, buildings cannot be used for community programming without zoning approval; but zoning approval is not enough. Local and state building codes also contain requirements that must be met for the building to be used, independent of zoning matters.

The public purpose of building codes again relates to the interest of the citizenry in ensuring that buildings are safe and healthful for the persons occupying or using them. Fire safety is a predominant theme. Codes ordinarily include specific requirements for building materials, area and height standards, means of egress, structural and foundation loads and stresses, energy conservation, fire protection systems, and electrical and plumbing systems. Code requirements vary according to proposed building use, such as public assembly, business, industrial, and institutional buildings, with the strictest standards applicable to hazardous uses and uses involving persons who are physically or mentally incapacitated, such as in a hospital or nursing home.

Typically, different standards apply to new construction (where the most stringent standards will apply) and to substantial reconstruction. The codes can also be very strict in situations where a change of use is sought, however. This is particularly true where the proposed new use is considered a higher risk in terms of fire safety, even in the absence of new or substantial construction.

Although building codes relate specifically to the building itself, they may significantly affect programming in several ways. First, the nature of the code requirements for the particular planned use of the building (for example, a group residence) may be so extensive as to make building costs prohibitive. Second, the nature of the renovations required may render the building inappropriate from the viewpoint

---

[2]A copy of the model statute is available through the American Bar Association Commission on the Mentally Disabled, Developmental Disabilities State Legislative Project, 1800 M St., NW, Washington, DC 20036.

of normalization, such as a requirement that all rooms face from a common corridor. Third, the codes may have the effect of limiting the types of persons served by the program. For example, exemption from some of the most problematic requirements, such as a sprinkler fire protection system, may be contingent upon the facility serving only persons who can meet certain requirements pertaining to self-preservation in a fire or other emergency.

Sometimes the argument used by an agency in seeking to resolve its zoning problem may create difficulties regarding application of the building code. For example, in Massachusetts, reliance by group residence providers upon that state's liberal educational use zoning exemption has led several local building inspectors to seek to apply the stringent institutional use building code requirements usually applied to schools, rather than the single-family requirements sought by the provider.

A third source of siting and building restriction often lies in the regulations of the state agency or agencies that pertain to the particular kind of facility. Such regulations often overlap (and occasionally conflict) with zoning law (for example, by barring the siting of facilities within a minimum distance of one another to prevent overconcentration) and building law (by setting special standards for rooms and room dimensions, exterior appearance, means of egress, etc.).

Questions to Ask

Persons and organizations planning to establish a community residence need to address a number of questions when trying to avoid or minimize the likelihood of zoning or building code challenges. These questions include the following:

1. What are the state and local zoning and building laws and agency licensing regulations pertaining to siting and physical plant? What are the applications to the kind of use planned and the specific site location?

2. In what ways is the planned use characterized under zoning, building, and licensing law? For example, is it a single-family use, multifamily use, educational use, health facility use, or institutional use? Within reason, characterization of a group residence or other specialized facility will, to some degree, be within the discretion of the provider. To the extent that the circumstances allow, the facility should be characterized in a way that minimizes legal complications.

3. Is the proposed use exempt altogether from local zoning control under the state zoning statutes?

4. Does the state have legislation that exempts community residences from local zoning or permits them *under certain conditions* (e.g., licensing standards, size regulations, overconcentration standards)? For example, the exemption may apply only to a use in particular kinds of zones; or even though the use is allowed generally, special "land use" approval procedures may apply, such as for parking.

5. Is the intended use permitted in the desired location of the town? The desirability of a location will in any event be determined by evaluating a number of sometimes competing factors. While normalization considerations may create a preference for a single-family zone, access to transportation, business centers, and places of work, as well as the present concentration of other special residential facilities, may weigh in other directions.

Consulting with existing group homes in the area regarding their experiences in establishing the residence is a helpful process. The Supplementary Resources at the end of this chapter list publications that address these issues and offer steps to take in dealing with zoning problems.

OPERATIONAL CONSIDERATIONS

Liability

In our litigious society, legal action of one kind or another is frequently utilized as a means of redressing grievances. Community mental retardation programs are not immune from this trend, which is most directly reflected in the escalation of liability insurance rates. Of equal concern, however, is the danger of overreaction, and the adverse effects of such overreaction not only on the integrity and dynamics of the agency but on the program and mentally retarded persons it serves. With every effort to decrease liability comes the risk of undue restriction of staff flexibility and of resident freedom of choice, factors that are essential to the development and implementation of truly individualized and effective programs.

This section briefly describes basic liability principles and areas of liability, and proposes guidelines for risk management that could mitigate exposure risks at reasonable economic and programmatic cost to the agency and its residents. Chapter 5 in this book also addresses liability issues pertaining to agencies and their governing boards. For another comprehensive resource on liability issues in community residences, see VanBiervliet and Sheldon-Wildgen (1981).

Negligence The most common legal liability to which community programs are vulnerable originates in negligence. The law requires that each of us owes a duty of reasonable care in our dealings with one another. If one of us, by action or inaction, breaches this duty, and injury to another results, there may be the basis of a lawsuit for damages in compensation for the injury.

Negligence may arise in an unlimited number of circumstances such as avoidable accidents arising from unsafe conditions within the home or when transporting residents. These are probably the most common sources of litigation. Other potential sources abound—for example, inappropriate admission, discharge, or transfer; inadequate resident supervision; inadequate planning, implementation, or monitoring of behavior modification programs; failure to provide adequate entry security to the residence; or failure adequately to orient, train, and supervise staff.

It is clear that injury caused, for example, when a resident trips on a long-damaged stair tread may well give rise to a lawsuit against the agency for possible failure to recognize and correct an obvious defect and a safety risk. However, most injuries are far more problematic as to

the potential for assignment of fault. When a resident walks out the front door of a community residence and is hit by a car, agency liability is possible, but will depend on the assessment of a variety of factors. For example, was the agency acting irresponsibly in allowing the resident to leave without supervision? What was the resident's level of skill in handling street risks? Could the driver of the car have avoided the accident?

In general terms, "reasonable care" is defined as what a reasonable and prudent person would do under the circumstances to minimize the risk of injury. In the context of community programming, reasonable care encompasses essentially every aspect of the agency's relationship to the individual. The agency must take reasonable steps to maintain a safe and healthful environment for its residents, and must provide sufficient care, training, and supervision of residents to mitigate the risk of physical and emotional injury.

The standard of reasonable care varies depending on the relationship between the persons involved, with a higher degree of care required for situations involving persons served under contract ("business invitees") and persons in a special trust or dependency ("fiduciary") relationship to the agency. The standard may also be higher where the dependent person is known to have a diminished capacity for self-protection, or poor social judgment, especially as evidenced by past behavior.

Whereas agencies will thus ordinarily be held to a fairly high standard of care in agency actions affecting residents, several critical countervailing factors need to be emphasized. First, the law takes into consideration the intended value of the action in furthering proper social objectives for the agency or individual involved, as, for example, where it is necessary to expose the individual to an element of risk in order to help him or her learn to use public transportation. Second, the agency cannot do more to prevent injury than it is legally capable of doing, given the nature of its relationship with its residents. If a resident is not under guardianship and is participating in a community residence program on a legally voluntary basis, and wishes to travel to a district considered by staff to be unsavory or unsafe, the scope of alternatives available to the agency to try to forestall the trip is, in reality, limited. While the agency can counsel against the trip, keeping the person within the residence would probably itself constitute false imprisonment, and would, in any event, be a practical impossibility for an indefinite time period.

In order for agency action or inaction to constitute negligence, the injury must involve a foreseeable harm preventable through the exercise of reasonable care. That is, the injury must be the *direct result* of the negligence. Thus, an agency would not likely be liable for injuries to a resident in an accident while riding a public bus, even if the resident were on the bus without necessary supervision or training, since the extent of his or her exposure to injury would probably be no greater than that of other passengers. Being better supervised or better trained might not mitigate the fact or extent of injury. In other words the agency's negligence in failing to provide adequately for the resident cannot be shown to have caused the injury. If one cannot say, "but for the agency's action or inaction the resident would not have been injured," the agency will not be liable for negligence.

The bottom line for the agency is that while it bears a high degree of responsibility regarding resident injuries, it does not assume total responsibility. Each individual, including the resident, is primarily responsible for his or her own behavior, and is expected to act in a reasonable manner. If the agency itself acts with reasonableness and prudence in managing the risks to which residents are exposed, it will be doing all that it can to avoid negligence liability.

What does this mean in concrete terms? While it is impossible to project and plan against negligence in every conceivable circumstance, some guidelines are feasible:

1. Know your residents. Be as familiar as possible with their clinical backgrounds and behavior patterns prior to placement. Make observation and evaluation of residents an ongoing part of the agency's standard operating procedures, both to max-

imize protection against injury and assure appropriate services. "We had no idea he would respond that way" is an inadequate defense if the resident has in fact been responding that way for years, but because you never asked, you just did not know it.

2. Plan services carefully, with particular attention to assuring adequate supervision in new situations.

3. Undertake carefully the exposure of residents to new risks, taking into account the frequent unpredictability of resident behavior and responses to new situations.

4. Hire prudent and mature employees, and discipline or dismiss imprudent ones.

5. Train employees in safety, accident prevention, and first aid. Orient them early to the needs of your residents, especially to supervision needs in emergency situations.

Battery Another area of potential liability is that of battery. A battery occurs with the intentional and offensive touching of one person by another. Battery is usually thought of in the context of a physical attack. However, it may also, and more problematically, be based on the well-intentioned but excessive use of force in behavior control. Examples include the inappropriate utilization of physical restraints, certain behavior modification procedures, and physical contact in self-defense or in defense of others.

Various legal factors beyond our scope mitigate against liability under circumstances that otherwise might be an actionable battery, such as explicit or implied consent, necessity, self-defense, and privilege. However, several guidelines concerning the avoidance of liability for battery can be drawn broadly from the legal principles involved.

Particularly in programs involving residents who are known to be assaultive or self-abusive, it is essential that staff be trained from the outset to handle such behaviors. Agency procedures must rely first and primarily on noncontact means of protecting the resident and others. Second, where noncontact means are inadequate, and where the nature of the interest to be protected is substantial, such as the physical well-being of the individual or others, then use of physical force may be legally appropriate. It should, however, be used only to the minimum extent and for the shortest period of time necessary to mitigate the risks of injury. The determination of the nature and extent of physical force to be utilized must ultimately depend on the working judgment of staff on the scene, and will vary with the risk apparently posed by the resident and the vulnerability of the ostensible victim. Events are likely to occur under circumstances not allowing reference to a manual or the individual's service plan. Staff must be given adequte training regarding alternative means of physical restraint in emergency circumstances, and must be made aware of the effectiveness and appropriateness of specified procedures in individual cases.

If physical contact is to be involved in behavior modification programming, such as in certain overcorrection, aversive, or hand-over techniques, agency procedures must minimally: 1) assure compliance with applicable state law and regulations, 2) be based on assessments demonstrating that less intrusive treatment means have been tried and found wanting or clearly would be ineffective, 3) incorporate procedures for individualized planning, implementation, and monitoring of individual programs, 4) incorporate procedures to assure the informed consent of the individual or court-appointed guardian, 5) provide a mechanism for independent review, as by a human rights committee (see discussion later in this chapter), and 6) assure the assignment only of adequately trained and supervised staff to the program.

Right to Privacy   The resident's right to privacy can also constitute an area of liability for an agency. This area of law is still in its early developmental stages, and the definition of the right varies from state to state. However, this much is generally clear: each of us has the right to be protected from intrusions into areas of our lives traditionally viewed by society as private. Areas in which the individual may have a legally protected interest include use of photographs in relation to program publicity, disclosure to third persons of personal resident information, or undue restriction on residents' sexual behavior. Generally, there are greater protections where the question of invasion

arises from the action of a government entity (or probably also from that of a private entity involved, as by contract or under regulation, with a governmental purpose, such as the provision of special residential programming).

What constitutes a reasonable expectation of privacy lies at the heart of litigation in this area, and plainly varies with the individual's circumstances. For example, persons who voluntarily undertake to become public figures are generally considered to have implicitly consented to many kinds of intrusion and disclosure that would otherwise be potentially actionable. Similarly, an individual's voluntary admission to a group residential program can probably be taken as implied consent (even if not explicitly incorporated into a placement agreement) to the enforcement of at least certain kinds of restrictions during his or her stay. Such restrictions, if reasonable, may appropriately arise from the need to reconcile the privacy interest of the individual against the privacy rights of the other residents, as, for example, in establishing clear and enforceable parameters around sexual behavior within the residence. Also, the individual's consent can be taken to extend to reasonable restrictions on privacy in the form of counseling, supervision, and monitoring necessary either to assure the safety of the resident or others, or to accomplish specific training objectives of the placement itself.

To ensure that the rights of residents to privacy are properly protected and to avoid liability in this area, the agency must evaluate all of its existing and proposed procedures and house rules relating to resident behavior and prerogatives of staff persons to enter personal living areas.

HUMAN RIGHTS AND THEIR PROTECTION

Broadly speaking, a *right* may be defined as a capacity residing in one person of controlling, with the assent and assistance of the state, the actions of others. While one may speak generally of human rights, most of the rights of residents are well-defined legal rights, in the sense that they are specifically determined in federal and state constitutions, statutes, court decisions, and agency regulations. Given this broad definition, however, the field of the legal rights of mentally retarded persons is hardly a limited one. It spans all of the rights that nonhandicapped citizens have, from the right to vote, to due process and equal protection, to free speech, to the right to privacy and to protection as consumers, to freedom from discrimination, and to freedom of association. In addition, the special needs of some persons who have mental retardation have given rise to special statutory and regulatory protections to assist in maintaining their health, safety, and welfare, through the provision of residential, educational, and treatment services.

The human service agency has multiple responsibilities regarding the mentally retarded persons it serves. It must refrain from actions that in themselves violate residents' rights, but it must also act affirmatively to provide services in a manner consistent with residents' legally protected expectations. In the context of the agency's responsibility to train, counsel, and supervise the resident in becoming a functioning member of the community to the fullest extent possible, the agency must help protect the rights of the resident in contexts far outside the control of the agency itself. Given the vulnerability of mentally retarded persons, who by reason of their need are deficient in their capacity to advocate for themselves, this means that the agency must undertake the responsibility to know, interpret, and apply the law properly in all areas of its dealings with its residents. Whether the issue is the legal propriety of a behavior modification program involving overcorrection techniques, or the right to privacy and sexual expression in the context of a group residential program, the agency must find, and implement, answers to questions for which there simply are no handbooks or rules clearly applicable to every nuance of every situation.

While it may be easy to accept the broad contention that every resident has a "right to privacy," there is less agreement about acceptance of specific rights. For example, how does an agency go about ensuring the right to privacy in the context of a resident's desire for sexual expression in a group residence? What of the agency's concurrent responsibility to protect the resident from exploitation? to train him or her in appropriate social relations and responsibilities? to protect the privacy and sensitivities of other residents? to maintain an adequately high level of community acceptance of the facility and program?

As a further example, certainly no one would question the resident's "right to be free of physical abuse" by staff, but how is this right to be protected in the context of behavior modification programming for severely self-abusive or self-destructive persons? Even aside from aversive techniques, many behavior modification approaches, such as overcorrection, may involve significant nonconsensual physical contact. Is it the motive behind the contact, or the planning underlying it, that distinguishes proper from improper contact?

In order to protect the rights of residents on an ongoing basis, an agency should undertake certain specific actions and procedures. First among these is staff training, both at the administrative and direct service levels. Unless the nature and scope of the legal rights of residents, within the program and the community, is well understood by the persons charged with their protection, nothing positive can result.

The second step is the development of written agency guidelines to serve as an ongoing reference for staff and residents. These should contain descriptive statements of rights and of their general application to the various aspects of programming and resident life. In addition, there should be written grievance procedures, as well as procedures for the management of situations in which legal rights are particularly vulnerable within the program—such as behavior modification programming, medication, resident labor, research, informed consent, records privacy, or restraint authorization procedures. House rules should also be developed regarding restriction of movement (curfew), visitation and communication policies, and sexual activity. (State agency regulations and guidelines should serve as basic references for such procedures.)

The third necessary component in protecting resident rights is the human rights committee. The existence of human rights committees is seldom mandated by law, although in some states regulations and licensing rules require them. While no single model exists, the essential characteristics of the committee appear to be as follows:

1. The human rights committee must be specifically empowered, by the agency or governmental regulation, or both, to review, monitor, and investigate the activites of the agency in the areas of legal risk previously discussed here. The committee must have independent access not only to the executive and direct care staff of the agency but also to its governing board and to the state agencies responsible ultimately for resident care and agency licensing or regulation. While the committee will ordinarily not have, and probably should not have, direct executive authority within the agency (in order to avoid confict-of-interest problems that would inevitably accompany shared executive authority), independent access to external regulating, licensing, and law enforcement agencies will give the committee the credibility and authority it requires to function properly.

2. The committee's members should represent a diversity of the professional (psychological, social welfare, health, legal, and education) and consumer interests affected by the program and its residents. In many states, a majority of the committee members must be either residents or members of families of residents or other similarly situated consumers.

3. The committee must be composed largely of persons who are not employees of the agency or otherwise financially linked to it, to avoid actual conflict of interest or even the appearance of conflict of interest, which can undercut the committee's effectiveness.

4. The committee must be active, familiar with the agency's residents and programs, and recognized as an authoritative adjunct to agency operation by staff, residents, families, the governing board, and other public and private agencies. In most programs, monthly meetings are essential, particularly in programs where residents are actively involved in behavior modification or behavioral medicine programs.

CONCLUSIONS

Legal issues are of concern both in the planning and operation of community residences. Incorporating legal rights and principles into the day-to-day operation of the residence enhances the quality of the overall program. The protection of human rights of residents underlies all of the legal conflicts and concerns discussed in this chapter. Although there are no hard and fast rules that are specific to each potential human rights problem or conflict, community residence staff must constantly be aware of the need to balance potentially conflicting rights, needs, responsibilities, and concerns of residents, staff, agencies, and families.

REFERENCES

American Bar Association Commission on the Mentally Disabled. (1978). Zoning for community homes serving developmentally disabled persons. *Mental Disability Law Reporter, 2,* 794–810.

Bogin, M. (1983). Group homes for persons with handicaps: Recent developments in the law. *Western New England Law Review, 5,* 423–430.

Brakel, S., Parry, J., & Weiner, B. (1985). *The mentally disabled and the law* (3rd ed.) Washington, D.C.: American Bar Foundation.

Brownfield v. State of Ohio (No. 77-12-2995, Ohio C.P., 1978).

City of Cleburne v. Cleburne Living Center, Inc. 105 S. Ct. 3249 (1985).

Concord Estate Homeowners Associates Inc. v. Special Children's Foundation, Inc., 459 So. 2d 1242 (LA. Ct. App. 1984).

Costley v. Caromin House, 313 N.W. 2d 21 (Minn. 1981).

Craig v. Bossenberg, 351 N.W. 2d 596 (Mich. Ct. App. 1984).

Crane Neck Ass'n, Inc. v. New York City of Long Island County Servs. Group, 460 N.Y.S. 2d 69 (App. Div. 1983), overturning a restrictive covenant earlier upheld by the same court, in Tytell v. Kaen, New York Sup. Ct., Special Term, Bronx County 1979.

Harbour v. Normal Life of Louisiana, 454 So. 2d 1208 (LA. Ct. App. 1984).

Knudtson v. Train, 345 N.W. 2d 4 (Neb. Sup. Ct. 1984).

O'Connor v. Donaldson, 422 U.S. 563 (1975).

Omega Corporation of Chesterfield v. Malloy, 319 S.E. 2d 728 (Va. Sup. Ct. 1984).

Pennhurst State School and Hospital v. Halderman, 451 U.S. 1 (1981) (refusing to recognize constitutional right to treatment).

Romeo v. Youngberg, 457 U.S. 307 (1982).

Rouse v. Cameron, 373 F. 2d 451 (D. C. Cir. 1966).

South Norfolk County Association for Retarded Citizens Inc. and the Commonwealth of Massachusetts v. Randall Riley and DiSangro, C.A.N. 137972 (Superior Court, Norfolk County, Mass. 1982).

Temple Terrace v. Hillsborough Ass'n for Retarded Citizens, 322 So. 2d 610 (Fla. 1976).

Tucker v. Special Children's Foundation, 449 So. 2d 45 (LA. App. 1984).

VanBiervliet, A., & Sheldon-Wildgen, J. (1981). *Liability issues in community-based programs: Legal principles, problems areas, and recommendations.* Baltimore: Paul H. Brookes Publishing Co.

Village of Belle Terre v. Borass, 416 U.S. 1 (1974).

Welsch v. Likins, 373 F. Supp. 487 (D. Minn. 1974).

West Monroe v. Quachita ARC, 402 So. 2d 259 (CA. App. 1981).

Wyatt v. Stickney, 325 F. 2d 781 (M. D. Ala. 1971).

SUPPLEMENTARY RESOURCES

Bates, M.V. (1983). *State zoning legislation: A purview.* Madison, WI: Council on Developmental Disabilities.

Chandler, J., & Ross, S. (1976). Zoning restrictions and the right to live in the community. In M. Kindred, J. Cohen, D. Penrod, & T. Shaeffer (Eds.), *The mentally retarded citizen and the law.* New York: Free Press.

Combatting exclusionary zoning: The right of handicapped people to live in the community. Mental Health Law Project (1220 Nineteenth St., NW, Washington, DC, 20036).

Deinstitutionalization, zoning, and community placement. (1983). *Mental Disability Law Reporter, 7,* 375–377.

Janicki, M. (1983). *Group homes: Property values, zoning, and attitudes: A working bibliography.* Albany: New York State Office of Mental Retardation and Developmental Disabilities.

United States General Accounting Office (1983). *An analysis of zoning and other problems affecting the establishment of group homes for the mentally disabled.* Gaithersburg, MD: GAO Office, Document Handling and Information Services Facility.

Wildgen, J.S. (1976). Exclusionary zoning and its effects on group homes in areas zoned for single-family dwellings. *Kansas Law Review, 24,* 677–699.

Zoning for community homes serving developmentally disabled persons. (1978). *Mental Disability Law Reporter, 2,* 794–810.

Chapter 5

Roles, Responsibilities, and Liabilities of Agency Boards

Sheldon R. Gelman

The role of the board of directors in initiating, designing, and monitoring residential programs serving developmentally disabled persons is explored in this chapter. The discussion addresses board functions and responsibilities, raises critical policy issues faced by the board in organizing an agency, and examines a series of structural issues related to effective agency operation. The responsibilities of board members and potential areas of board negligence and liability are discussed. The chapter examines the importance of board credibility and accountability in an era of increasing litigation and insurance crises in the human service field.

A community service program begins with the coming together of individuals with common interests, needs, or purposes. Community-based residential programs for persons with developmental disabilities may be initiated by parents, existing service agencies, or newly formed corporate entities. Those involved will need to acquire information and commit time and energy to make an idea operational. Goals have to be identified, resources acquired, programs developed, and staff hired. Although the roles played by the initiators will shift as the organization develops (Perlmutter, 1969; Perske, 1974; Wolfensberger, 1973), the usual structure created to oversee the enterprise—the board of directors—is critical to its success.

This chapter explores the role of the board of directors of residential programs serving developmentally disabled persons. It discusses board functions and responsibilities, raises critical policy issues that the board must address in organizing an agency (i.e., relating to for-profit versus nonprofit, incorporation, and client selection), and examines a series of structural issues related to effective agency operation (i.e.,

board composition, size, length of service, board/executive and board/staff relations). The chapter also examines in detail the standard of care required by board members in performing their responsibilities, and identifies potential areas of board negligence and liability. The need for board accountability and oversight in an era of increasing litigation in the human service field is stressed. The intent of this chapter is to facilitate the creation of agencies that are responsive to both clients and the community of interests they serve.

ROLES AND FUNCTIONS OF THE BOARD

The roles, functions, and responsibilities of the board of directors are identified in an agency's bylaws and specified in the charter granted by the state under its corporation statutes (Gelman, 1987; Mitton, 1974). The board in both nonprofit and for-profit agencies is responsible for determining organization philosophy, setting policy, and monitoring the implementation of both philosophy and policies on a regular basis

(Gelman, 1983, 1987; Mitton, 1974; Robins & Blackburn, 1974). The board determines the clientele to be served, sets priorities, and hires administrative staff to carry out its mission.

Board members have a legal duty to assure the achievement of the agency's goals and objectives. Members are legally accountable for both the fiscal and programmatic management of the agency, and share collective responsibility for its overall performance. The board is responsible to funding sources, to the community, to governmental and/or private regulating bodies, to the organization's members, and to the consumers of the agency's services.

The board of directors as a group manages the organization. It may delegate responsibilities where appropriate, but retains ultimate responsibility to its various constituencies (Hanson & Marmaduke, 1972). A board that fails to either determine policy or evaluate achievement in support of those policies is negligent in performing its responsibilities (Gelman, 1983).

Boards function in the following six areas:

Policy development—General direction and control of the agency
Program development—Short- and long-range planning
Personnel—Identification and employment of competent administrative staff
Finance—Identification and facilitation of access to necessary resources
Public relations—Interpretation of the organization to the community at large
Accountability—Evaluation (Gelman, 1987)

A well-structured board establishes appropriate mechanisms to fulfill these functions. Generally, the entire board needs to address the first area; the other five functional areas are more typically handled by working subcommittees of the board, which are responsible for reporting their activities to the full board at regular intervals. Each subcommittee should have a clearly defined charge or span of responsibility and should include board members with specific expertise in the given area. These functions are explored throughout the remainder of this chapter.

CRITICAL POLICY ISSUES

Three policy issues need to be addressed by the board as the organization takes form: the nature of the organization (profit-making or nonprofit), incorporation, and client selection.

Profit versus Nonprofit

Depending on the interests or intention of the organizers, the organization can be formed either as a for-profit or a nonprofit enterprise. A for-profit or proprietary organization provides services with the expectation that those involved as initiators, owners, and/or board members will receive monetary compensation or capital appreciation for their service. Such individuals have a pecuniary interest, unlike those who serve as initiators or board members of nonprofit organizations. Nonprofit organizations are formed for charitable purposes and therefore are treated differently than for-profit organizations under the federal Internal Revenue Service Code and the incorporation statutes of most states.

Incorporation

Incorporation refers to the creation of a legally recognized entity, which has an identity separate from the individuals who created it. The new entity (hereafter referred to as the *agency*), rather than the individuals involved, contracts for and provides various services. The board of directors becomes the vehicle through which the organization functions and becomes the employer of a range of personnel (Dimieri & Weiner, 1981).

Under the traditional doctrine of "respondeat superior," an employer can be held vicariously responsible for harm caused by an employee in the course of his or her employment (Brown, 1977; Chute, 1983; VanBiervliet & Sheldon-Wildgen, 1981). The act of incorporation shields individual board members from personal liability for any harm or damage, real or perceived, that may be attributed to the agency's operations or management. It should be noted, however, that the corporate shield does not protect board members who have committed intentional wrongs that result in harm or injury, nor will it provide protection for individual board members named as codefendants in litigation brought against the organization (Harvey, 1984; Jarvis, 1982).

Client Selection

One of the most important roles of the board is to identify the population to be served by the agency. While the agency charter or the original board may have defined the client population, client priorities should be reviewed periodically. A key aspect in deliberations about client population will be the risk factors associated with particular populations. For example, the complexity of medical needs, level of aggressiveness, age, psychiatric problems, and geography may increase an agency's costs and potential vulnerability. Risk factors will influence both administrative and programmatic issues such as staffing patterns, level of supervision, training, treatment modalities, and the availability and cost of insurance. Agencies that provide services to medically fragile and/or aggressive residents are at risk for litigation when staffing patterns provide less coverage than is necessary to meet the identified and documented needs of residents. Similarly, those agencies providing services to children and/or to those involved in residential care have in recent years become subject to charges of physical and sexual abuse. The more dangerous the situation, or the more vulnerable the population served, the greater the need for board oversight. The board must determine what risks are involved in serving a particular population, how and at what cost those risks can be minimized, and whether the agency will serve particular populations. An agency's mission, community need, or the level of reimbursement available may influence whether certain risks are assumed by an agency.

STRUCTURAL ISSUES

The following structural issues are presented to assist those initiating residential service programs as well as those currently involved in service provision in creating effective and accountable boards.

Board Composition

In constructing the board, it is crucial to select individuals whose personal commitment, energy, and areas of knowledge are related to the agency's mission and to the specific tasks to be performed. It cannot be overemphasized that board members must have the time, interest, and willingness to be of service to the agency. Individuals who are overcommitted or who spend large blocks of time away from the community tend to slow down the board in carrying out its mandated responsibilities. Unavailable or unresponsive board members force other committed individuals to assume more responsibility than they can or should. Irregular attendance at board meetings is one indicator of a board member's failure to meet the required standard of care.

Board members should possess the ability to work cooperatively and tactfully with each other. Interpersonal skills are critical, since board members will be interacting not only with their peers on the board but also with the agency's executive director, staff, community leaders and/or officials, and members of the community at large who may be supporters and/or residents served by the agency. Members of the board should also have legitimacy or standing in the community. Board members should, furthermore, have the expertise to address, monitor, and evaluate the various elements of the agency's operation (Gelman, 1983). Ideally, agency boards should develop into cohesive work groups.

It may be necessary to include in the composition of the board representatives of designated constituencies in order to conform to agency charter (i.e., bankers, politicians, clergy, parents, various professional groups). Again, these individuals should be screened for interest and relevant expertise. Consideration should also be given to appointing prestigious community leaders as honorary board members. This approach prevents the potential lack of time, interest, or commitment of these individuals from diluting or delaying the board in conducting its business. All board members should fully understand the nature of the organization that they serve as well as their individual and collective responsibilities as board members.

The board selects its officers according to the provisions of its bylaws. Customarily, a president, vice-president, and secretary and/or secretary/treasurer is designated. These officers comprise the board's executive committee and are usually empowered to act for the board in certain circumstances. The president and treasurer will usually be required to sign various documents (i.e., grants, contracts, checks, tax forms). These individuals should be bonded, that is, provided with insurance protection against financial loss caused by employee dishonesty and/or acts of omission by those in key positions.

To summarize, in selecting board members, every effort should be made to identify individuals with the following characteristics: 1) interest in the organization and in its mission; 2) ability to work with other individuals; 3) time and willingness to be of service to the board; 4) specific knowledge or expertise in an area or areas of the agency's overall functioning; 5) a community as well as organizational point of view.

Size

It is difficult to specify the optimal size for the board of directors of a nonprofit organization. However, the size should be such that each board member recognizes the importance of his or her role and unique contribution to the overall effectiveness of the agency. Boards that are excessively large tend to lack strong feelings of commitment and obligation, resulting in poor or sporadic participation and attendance at board meetings. Often the size and composition of the board are dictated by agency charter or by the organization's bylaws. Although Weber (1975) suggests that boards be composed of 30 to 36 individuals, a board this size may be too large for effective group interaction.

As a rule of thumb, the board size must be workable—neither too large nor too small (Swanson, 1984). Size and composition should be related to the agency's goals and objectives. Sufficient members must be regularly present and involved to assure an equitable division of labor so that no individual member or small group has to carry responsibility disproportionately. In general, a board of 15 to 18 members is sufficient to monitor the six earlier mentioned areas of board responsibility. Large and complex organizations do not require large boards to accomplish goals. Regardless of the size of the agency board, responsibilities fall into the six areas previously noted. The work of any board can be supplemented through the appointment of committees responsible to it.

Length of Service

The term of board members' service should be limited to 3 years. Reappointment to a second 3-year term should be an option for members who have competently fulfilled their obligations. Service beyond 6 years by any one board member should be broken by a sabbatical before the individual can stand for reappointment or reelection. Those who have been unable to meet the expectations set for board members or who can no longer commit themselves to board service should not be recommended for reelection or reappointment. Individuals who fail to meet their obligations during their term of office should be asked to resign. Board members should serve on a rotating basis, with one-third of the board's positions becoming vacant and replaced each year. Such a format allows for continuity of activities, grooming of new leaders, ongoing monitoring of the organization, and the regular infusion of new blood. The systematic addition of new members, with identified expertise and commitment as well as ongoing training of board members, contributes to the agency becoming self-evaluating and accountable.

Orientation and Training

The orientation of new board members and ongoing training for continuing members is essential. Board members should be fully aware of their roles and responsibilities in terms of time commitments. All members should be provided with written position descriptions detailing expectations and obligations. They should be familiar with the agency, its facilities, programs and/or services, and personnel. Based on their interests, expertise, and the agency's needs, individual board members should be assigned to committees corresponding to the six already-mentioned areas of responsibility. Board members should be aware of the potential for personal liability inherent in accepting a board position. "Directors and officers liability insurance," marketed by various commercial carriers, should be carried by the agency.

Board/Executive Relations

Although some authors suggest that the agency executive must provide leadership to the board in formulating policies (Tripodi, 1976), such an arrangement has the potential of contradicting both the agency's charter and the requirements of law. Unfortunately, many writers dealing with the structuring of board/executive relations treat the subject as if two separable spheres of activity exist—one occupied by the board and the other by the professional executive (Harris, 1977). While the executive may sit as an ex officio board member, allowing the executive to vote on policy matters not only creates a potential conflict but also grants disproportionate power to the executive (Senor, 1965). Granting such power furthermore has no basis in law and permits the executive to function without the traditional constraints placed on other board members by the agency charter.

The board can draw on the expertise and knowledge of the executive, but it cannot allow its legal responsibility to be diluted or coopted by overdependence on the hired executive. A collegial working relationship is essential between board and executive. However, the executive, no matter how long employed, remains an employee of the organization. Although it may be easier or more convenient for a board to delegate all responsibilities, this can result in the board losing control and placing itself and the agency in a vulnerable position.

Board/Staff Relations

Appropriate, effective, and efficient board/staff relations are based on a clear and common understanding by both board members and staff of their respective functions and responsibilities (Trecker, 1981). As already indicated, the board is responsible for developing and establishing policies to guide the organization. The staff is responsible for implementing policies that have been adopted by the board and transmitted to the staff through the executive. While staff may choose among several alternatives to implement and achieve board policy, the board is ultimately responsible and therefore must hold staff, including the executive, accountable for implementing its policies. On the surface, this description may appear one-sided, but ongoing interaction between board and staff is essential for the process to result in a responsible and accountable agency.

It is crucial for staff to have the opportunity to interact regularly with the board and its members in order for staff to share their experience in implementing various policies, solving problems, and identifying unmet needs. Quarterly reports and semiannual meetings of board members and program staff are crucial to the achievement of agency goals. In addition, board members should routinely visit program sites to assure firsthand knowledge of agency operations. In this way the board can adjust or modify its policies based on the experience of its staff members. Staff members should feel comfortable with board members examining various programs. Although the evaluation of staff should rest with the designated administrator or supervisory staff, the collective performance of the staff reflects on the agency's goals or mission and on the board's performance in meeting its responsibilities.

A three-way partnership should exist between board, executive, and staff. Such a partnership is facilitated by clear job descriptions that specify obligations and responsibilities.

STANDARDS OF CARE REQUIRED

Four standards of care (called the charitable immunity standard, gross negligence standard, business judgment rule, and trustee standard) have been used by a court in determining liability of board members:

Immunity This doctrine, usually referred to as charitable immunity, absolves organizations and their directors from any liability for harm that may occur as a result of actions or inaction.

Gross negligence This standard requires that a director's actions must be reckless, extravagant, wrongful, corrupt, or fraudulent to be held liable for harm or damage that may occur.

Business judgment rule According to this rule, a director is expected to act in good faith and with the diligence, care, and skill that an ordinarily reasonable person would exercise under similar circumstances (Purdon's, 1972).

Trustee This standard requires that the highest level of care be exercised by a director, that is, care greater than that expected of an ordinarily prudent (reasonable) person.

Today, the business judgment rule is most often applied (Brown, 1977; Chute, 1983; Dimieri & Weiner, 1981; Harvey, 1984; Pasley, 1966; *Stern v. Lucy Webb Hayes,* 1974). This standard views nonprofit organizations and their directors in the same way as business corporations (Brown, 1977; Chute, 1983; Henn & Boyd, 1981). Board members are expected to approach their responsibilities as they would approach other "business" transactions. Proper concern, oversight, and monitoring are required.

The application of the business judgment rule in nonprofit situations should not discourage civic minded individuals from involving themselves in community affairs. If a board member attends most meetings of the board and any committee on which he or she sits, reads financial statements and other reports, raises questions when inconsistencies or other problems surface, takes appropriate steps to investigate and rectify those problems that come to his or her attention from various sources—in other words, if the member acts in good faith—the business judgment rule will usually afford protection from personal liability (Brown, 1977). While the "good faith" defense has been honored in the past, and in certain instances "good faith" immunity has been provided by state legislatures, its effectiveness today is uncertain (Besharov, 1985). Courts have, in certain instances, expanded the legal concept of "duty" and have come to expect professionals to take affirmative steps in applying their expertise where clients or the public are endangered (i.e., the duty to warn).

It is unfortunate that the model Nonprofit Corporation Act of 1973 (American Law Institute–American Bar Association [ALA–ABA], 1973) does not contain language pertaining to the standard of care expected of board members. This leaves the courts in various jurisdictions free to impose any of the four standards when reviewing the actions of boards and their members. The one thing that is clear in terms of responsibility is that the doctrine of charitable immunity is no longer applicable in most jurisdictions. Charitable (nonprofit) organizations, their governing boards, and employees are liable for harm resulting from negligent actions.

NEGLIGENCE AND POTENTIAL LIABILITY

Legally, board members are bound to exercise due care in the performance of their duties. Their actions should avoid exposing others (i.e., residents, board members, the organization itself) to unreasonable risk of harm. Failure to meet these expectations may leave individual board members personally responsible for harm that occurs.

Following the demise of the doctrine of charitable immunity (Zelman, 1977), most states have included provisions in their nonprofit incorporation statutes for both limited liability and indemnification for board members. However, these provisions are conditioned on actions that are taken in good faith and are reasonable for the circumstances (Henn & Boyd, 1981). Actions involving misconduct or negligence (i.e., failure to act like a reasonable person would in similar circumstances) are not covered by either indemnification or insurance (Chute, 1983). Careless, indifferent, or unreasonable behavior on the part of a board member constitutes negligence. Negligence can occur from acts of omission as well as acts of commission by responsible persons acting in their official capacity as a member of the board of directors.

Negligent actions on the part of board members generally fall into six areas, each of which is discussed in the paragraphs following:

Failure to manage and supervise the activities of the corporation

Neglect or waste of corporation assets

Conflict of interest or self-benefit

Improper delegation of authority

Harm done to third parties through a tort (wrongful action) and/or breach of contract

Offenses against taxing authorities (Harvey, 1984)

Failure to Manage and Supervise

Good management requires knowledge, awareness, and regular, ongoing involvement in the agency on the part of board members. While boards may appropriately delegate many duties and responsibilities, oversight is required. Oversight can be achieved through periodic (at least annual) on-site visitations, program audits, staff evaluations, reports of subcommittees or consultants, feedback from clientele and other community agencies, and accreditation or licensing reviews.

The type and extent of monitoring will vary according to the stage of the agency's development. Similarly, the degree and extent of supervision by the board should be related to the quality and experience of staff, the nature of service provided, the type of clientele served, the type of facility, and the potential risks or exposure faced by the agency. The services and programs offered by an agency must be related to the competence and expertise of its staff. Staff members who are inadequately or inappropriately trained should not be requested or permitted to perform roles beyond their capacity or level of expertise.

Appropriate management includes responsiveness to items or problems brought to the attention of board members by administrative staff, such as defects in the building or physical plant, shortages of resources and personnel, and unmet needs that may endanger employees, residents, or visitors. Such management also involves the development of personnel policies and procedures that provide direction to employees.

Neglect or Waste of Assets

Nonprofit organizations are created for charitable purposes—their activities cannot result in gain, profit, or private advantage to individuals. The organization's resources are acquired for

the purpose of achieving identified goals, and in most instances, board members have a fiduciary responsibility with respect to resources entrusted to the organization. Board members must be aware of and knowledgeable about the disbursement of funds.

Distinctions must be drawn between expenditures that are essential or necessary and those that might be considered extravagant. Prudent accounting procedures must be followed that include adequate documentation and justification for all expenditures. Funds should be maximized through prudent investment practices. Careless, speculative, risky, or extravagant expenditures are to be avoided.

The organization's budget and assets must be reviewed at regular intervals (at least annually) to assure compliance with the organization's purpose. Assets that are being managed for wards of the agency that are accrued when the agency serves as the representative payee must be carefully monitored. Funds received as grants or contracts must be utilized only for the purposes for which they were intended. The responsibility for monitoring assets and their disbursement is a broad responsibility that can be facilitated by a working subcommittee.

Conflict of Interest

Conflicts of interest may arise in numerous situations. For example, agency hiring practices often generate allegations of patronage or nepotism. The purchasing of supplies or services, rental of property or real estate acquisitions, and referral practices for professional services present opportunities where the influence of board members may result directly or indirectly in personal gain or benefit.

Board members serve for a variety of reasons. Some members have purely altruistic motives while others may serve out of self-interest (Klein, 1968; Stein, 1962). Self-interest may include financial gain or power and control. Caution must be exercised to avoid the actual or perceived appearance of such self-serving actions (i.e., when a board member provides professional services or products to the agency or its clientele). Board members may legitimately derive emotional satisfaction from their involvement and/or gain status in the eyes of the community, but they must avoid situations that may result in personal financial gain or benefit. Board members must individually monitor their own activities and collectively those of other board members.

Improper Delegation of Authority

Although the executive director is delegated the authority for the day-to-day operations of the agency as well as for handling the majority of personnel matters, the power and authority to make policy is given by law and charter to the board. In other words, the ultimate responsibility for agency functioning and the performance of the executive and staff resides with the board. Critical to the issue of delegation of authority is the role assumed by staff and the degree of supervision provided by both board and administrative personnel. While it is proper to assign or delegate tasks to line personnel, those tasks should be related to defined job descriptions and related educational or experiential requirements for the position. Inappropriate delegation of authority is a major issue in residential care settings where line staff are hired at minimum wage, are provided little or no training, have minimal supervision, and are expected to be "all things to all people." Given the special needs of many clients served by residential programs—including the need for medication and/or specialized treatment—appropriate supervision becomes a necessity. Staff members should not be put in the position of doing more than they are capable of doing, nor should they have to, by default, do what they are not trained to do. Low wages, lack of supervision, and long working hours not only contribute to staff burnout and staff turnover but leave the agency vulnerable to criticism from staff, clients, and the community. Dissatisfaction from any of these constituencies can lead to court action alleging board negligence in operating the agency.

Harm Done to Third Parties

Harm may occur through acts of omission or commission on the part of anyone associated with an organization. The resulting harm may be either intentional or unintentional—real or perceived. A tort (the legal term used to describe such claims) is any wrong, injury, injustice, or damage except breach of contract inflicted by one party on another for which the aggrieved party can seek remedy and/or compensation. These actions may result in litigation and claims of liability against the organization. As the employer of a range of personnel the board may, and in all likelihood will, be named as a party to the action. The English common law concept of "joint and several" holds that an injured party may recover losses from anyone with some responsibility for the harm or injury that occurs. This concept, like the doctrine of "respondeat superior" discussed earlier, has clear implications for board members of private nonprofit organizations as well as for those involved in the delivery of public services. There are also implications in terms of agency utilization of volunteers and the degree of oversight or supervision provided.

VanBiervliet and Sheldon-Wildgen (1981) discuss 8 potential liability claims that may result in action brought against an agency. Besharov (1985) also identifies 17 liability pitfalls that may be encountered by social services personnel in the course of their involvement with clients. Since such personnel are often the employees (agents) of agencies, the agency itself and its board may be named as parties in litigation. While there are common areas in both authors' lists, they can serve as a base for identifying more than 25 potential areas of vulnerability related to "harm done" in working with handicapped persons living in community residences. These areas can be grouped into the following six categories reflecting program structure and personnel:

Service/Treatment

- False or misleading advertising or claims
- Failure to deliver what is promised—may involve breach of contract
- Inappropriate treatment
- Failure to consult with a resident or failure to refer a resident to a specialist
- Contribution to a resident's suicide
- Failure to be available when needed
- Termination of treatment
- Abandonment

Supervision

- Failure to adopt or to follow policies and regulations
- Inappropriate handling and administration of medication
- Failure to prevent a resident's suicide
- Failure to provide adequate care or supervision for residents
- Inadequate supervision

Safety

- Failure to protect residents from harm
- Failure to inspect, repair, and maintain premises
- Maintaining an attractive nuisance (i.e., unsafe playground, unfenced swimming pool)
- Failure to properly care for resident injuries
- Failure to protect third parties—duty to warn

Privacy

- Invasion of privacy
- Breach of confidentiality
- Defamation (i.e., libel and slander)
- Violation of resident's civil rights (i.e., constitutional violations)
- Assualt and battery
- Sexual involvement with a resident

Custody

- Treatment without consent
- False imprisonment (i.e., failure to discharge)
- Inappropriate release of resident from confinement or inappropriate supervision

Fiscal

- Inappropriate bill or fee collection methods

These actions can be committed by board members or professional/nonprofessional or volunteer staff, all of whom are agents of the organization.

Offense against Taxing Authorities

An organization's status as nonprofit and/or as a 501 (C)(3) (Internal Revenue Code) corpora-

tion for federal tax purposes requires that certain structural and financial procedures be followed. Forms must be filed at regular intervals, and resources withheld for tax purposes (i.e., Social Security; workmen's compensation; unemployment insurance; federal, state, and local income tax; etc.) must be forwarded to the appropriate authorities. When violations of the tax code occur, the nonprofit designation and the privileges associated with it can be revoked and criminal prosecutions initiated.

INSURANCE COVERAGE

Until recently, providers of social services—both governmental and voluntary—were able to purchase reasonably priced insurance to indemnify their organizations in negligence actions brought by injured consumers. In addition to providing personal protection for both staff and board members, insurance coverage minimized the risk to the resources of the organization. However, the current insurance crisis has left various organizations vulnerable (Bayles, 1985a, 1985b; Schrieberg, 1985; Shapiro, 1985; Siegel, 1985; Venezia, 1985), owing to larger and more frequent damage awards, the erosion of charitable and sovereign immunity, and the contingency-fee arrangements that encourage lawyers to file suit. (Fees are a percentage of the settlement award—the plaintiff need not have money to bring suit.) The fear of more costly litigation has caused insurance companies to either raise premiums dramatically or stop writing liability policies altogether. The crisis appears most acute among municipal governments (many of which operate or are responsible for social service delivery), but many nonprofit voluntary providers (particularly those involved in child care and/or residential services) have also experienced dramatic increases in insurance premiums. Revelations of physical and/or sexual abuse as well as concerns about inadequately trained staff and unsafe physical facilities have resulted in an increased demand by consumers for satisfaction and monetary compensation. This trend has serious implications for all who are involved in service provision.

Insurance appropriately tailored to the needs of the organization and with levels of coverage sufficient to satisfy potential adverse judgments should be maintained. Customary coverage for health care, premises, property, and vehicles should also be obtained. In addition, liability coverage for staff, volunteers, and directors/officers should be provided to indemnify them in their official capacities. The level of coverage, which may range from $500,000 to $10,000,000, will be dependent on size of the organization, type of clientele, services provided, and past claim history (Chapman, Lai, & Steinbock, 1984).

It should be noted that an insurance company is delegated the power, within the language of the policy, to reach a settlement on any claim the company deems necessary. This means that even if the agency and/or its board members have done no wrong; the insurance company may settle with the party that filed the action. The determination of when to settle is made on the basis of what is best for the insurance carrier, not on what is in the best interest of the agency or its board members.

LITIGATION

In seeking redress for perceived or actual harm, legal counsel usually suggests a "shotgun" approach in identifying potential defendants. Such an approach not only maximizes the number of defendants but expands the resource pool that may be available for compensating clients. This differs from the more traditional approach to litigation, which sought out the "deeper pocket" of the corporation. Therefore, the likelihood of an individual board or staff member being named as a party in a suit brought on behalf of an agency client is greatly increased (Chute, 1983). The fact that board members and/or professional staff have or are perceived to have insurance coverage contributes to this practice (Harvey, 1984). Those agencies and/or individuals (both paid staff and volunteers) without adequate or appropriate coverage, or those unable to secure coverage, are in a vulnerable position. The cost of extricating oneself as a named party in a lawsuit can run into thousands of dollars. Adequate and appropriate insurance coverage is an absolute necessity, since most standard liability policies contain provisions that cover the costs of legal services incurred in defense of the policyholder as well as coverage in the event of an adverse judgment.

CONCLUSION

This chapter has identified the roles and obligations as well as potential liability of board members of community-based programs. As community services have grown and become more business-like, the roles of boards and their members have changed. The demise of the doctrine of "charitable immunity," the growth in knowledgeable and aggressive consumers, and the increase in litigation as a means of resolving disputes have given board membership new meaning, expectations, and risks.

Although agency charters and bylaws specify the responsibilities of boards, few board members fully understand their potential personal vulnerability for nonperformance. The board is accountable legally and morally for the actions and activities of the agency and its agents. The need to develop an informed and well-functioning board with adequate structures to assure accountability is essential. Altruism and good faith efforts are only part of the challenge faced by board members in today's agencies.

An effective board understands its responsibilities, knows the purposes and goals of its agency, and is involved on an ongoing basis in monitoring goal achievement. Board members should be able to gauge community response to the programs and services provided under their auspices. In addition, board members have a social responsibility to be informed about the social welfare context in which their agency operates. This enables them to anticipate opportunities as well as obstacles to the achievement of agency goals (Stein, 1962; Teltsch, 1985).

The board serves both a public relations and an educational function for the agency, and therefore must be conversant in the agency's operations. While the residents and staff are most visible, it is the board that is responsible for establishing and maintaining the organization's credibility with various sanctioning authorities and the community-at-large. A well-managed nonprofit organization requires sophisticated techniques of accounting; comprehensive program and responsiblity structures; and systematic performance evaluation (Dimieri & Weiner, 1981; Wildavsky, 1972). Put slightly differently, the organization must continuously monitor its own activities so as to determine whether its goals are being achieved. A board that cannot assure the accountability of its enterprise cannot effectively serve the community of interests or needs that led to its creation (Gelman, 1983).

REFERENCES

American Law Institute—American Bar Association (1973). Model Nonprofit Corporation Act. Washington, DC: American Bar Association.

Bayles, F. (1985a, November 18). Liability coverage scarce, costly. Centre Daily Times (PA), p. D-7.

Bayles, F. (1985b, November 20). Insurance loss blamed on litigation. Centre Daily Times (PA), p. B-3.

Besharov, D.J. (1985). The vulnerable social worker. Silver Spring, MD: National Association of Social Workers.

Brown, K.M. (1977). The not-for-profit corporation director: Legal liabilities and protection. Federation of Insurance Counsel Quarterly, 28, 57–87.

Chapman, T.S., Lai, M.L., & Steinbock, E.L. (1984). Am I covered for? A guide to insurance for non-profits. San Jose, CA: Consortium for Human Services.

Chute, C. (1983). Personal liability for directors of nonprofit corporations in Wyoming. Land and Water Review, 18, 273–311.

Dimieri, R., & Weiner, S. (1981). The public interest and governing boards of nonprofit health care institutions. Vanderbilt Law Review, 34, 1029–1066.

Gelman, S.R. (1983). The board of directors and agency accountability. Social Casework, 64, 83–91.

Gelman, S.R. (1987). Boards of directors. In Encyclopedia of social work (18th ed., pp. 206–211). Silver Spring, MD: National Association of Social Workers.

Hanson, P.L., & Marmaduke, C.T. (1972). The board member—decision maker for the non-profit corporation. Sacramento, CA: HAN/MAR Publications.

Harris, J.E. (1977). The internal organization of hospitals. Bell Journal of Economics, 8, 467–482.

Harvey, B.B. (1984). The public-spirited defendant and others: Liability of directors of not-for-profit corporations. John Marshall Law Review, 17, 666–741.

Henn, H.G., & Boyd, J.H. (1981). Statutory trends in the law of nonprofit organizations: California, here we come! Cornell Law Review, 66, 1103–1122.

Jarvis, W.F. (1982). The nonprofit director's fiduciary duty: Toward a new theory of the nonprofit sector. Northwestern University Law Review, 77, 34–47.

Klein, P. (1968). From philanthropy to social welfare. San Francisco: Jossey-Bass.

Mitton, D.G. (1974). Utilizing the board of trustees: A unique structural design. Child Welfare, 53, 345–351.

Pasley, R.S. (1966). Non-profit corporations—accountability of directors and officers. Business Lawyer, 21, 621–642.

Perlmutter, F. (1969). A theoretical model of social agency development. Social Casework, 50, 467–473.

Perske, R. (1974). New role of associations for the mentally retarded. Mental Retardation/Deficience Mentale, 24, 9–11.

Purdon's Annotated Statutes. (1972). Pennsylvania Nonprofit Corporation Law, Title 15, Section 7316 (or see the nonprofit incorporation statutes of any other state).

Robins, A.J., & Blackburn, C. (1974). Governing boards in mental health: Roles and training needs. Administration in Mental Health, 2, 37–45.

Schrieberg, D. (1985, August 22). Child care centers face insurance crisis. Centre Daily Times (PA), p. A-6.

Senor, J.M. (1965). Another look at the executive board relationship. In M.N. Zald (Ed.), Social welfare institutions: A sociological reader (pp. 418–427). New York: John Wiley & Sons.

Shapiro, W. (1985, August 26). The naked cities: Rising insurance rates force officials to pay or pray. Newsweek, pp. 22–23.

Siegel, J. (1985, August 22). Insurance costs too high for some governments in PA. Centre Daily Times (PA), p. B-1.

Stein, H.D. (1962). Board, executive, and staff. In Proceedings of the 89th Annual Conference (pp. 215–230). New York: Columbia University Press.

Stern v. Lucy Webb Hayes National Training School for Deaconesses and Missionaries, 381F. Supp. 1003 (1974).

Swanson, A. (1984). Building a better board: A guide to effective leadership. Washington, DC: Taft Corp.

Teltsch, K. (1985, August 4). Community service society to rethink goals. New York Times, p. 41.

Trecker, H.B. (1981). Boards of human service agencies: Challenges and responsibilities in the 80s. New York: Federation of Protestant Welfare Agencies.

Tripodi, T. (1976). Social workers as community practitioners, social welfare administrators, and social policy developers. In T. Tripodi, P. Fellin, I. Epstein & R. Lind (Eds.), Social Workers At Work (2nd ed.), (pp. 162–169). Itasca, IL: F.E. Peacock Publishers.

VanBiervliet, A., & Sheldon-Wildgen, J. (1981). Liability issues in community-based programs. Baltimore: Paul H. Brookes Publishing Co.

Venezia, J.A. (1985, November 19). City insurance: Costs climb as suits increase. Centre Daily Times (PA), p. A-5.

Weber, J. (1975). Managing the board of directors. New York: Greater New York Fund.

Wildavsky, A. (1972). The self-evaluating organization. Policy Administration Review, 9, 509–520.

Wolfensberger, W. (1973). The third stage in the evolution of voluntary associations for the mentally retarded. Toronto: National Institute on Mental Retardation.

Zelman, W.N. (1977). Liability for social agency boards. Social Work, 22, 270–274.

SUPPLEMENTARY RESOURCES

Anthes, E., Cronin, J., & Jackson, M. (Eds.). (1985). The nonprofit board book: Strategies for organizational success (rev. ed.). West Memphis and Hampton, AK: Independent Community Consultants.

Anthony, R.N., & Herzlinger, R.E. (1975). *Management control in non-profit organizations.* Homewood, IL: Richard D. Irwin.

Attkisson, C.C., Hargreaves, W.A., Horowitz, M.J., & Sorensen, J.E. (1978). *Evaluation of human service programs.* New York: Academic Press.

Austin, M.J., Cox, G., Gottlieb, N., Hawkins, J.D., Kruzich, J.M., & Rauch, R. (1982). *Evaluating your agency's programs.* Beverly Hills: Sage Publications.

Carter, R.K. (1983). *The accountable agency.* Beverly Hills: Sage Publications.

Chase, G. (1979). Implementing a human services program: How hard will it be? *Public Policy, 27,* 385–435.

Davis, P. (1987). *Nonprofit organizations and liability insurance. Problems, options, and prospects.* Los Angeles: The California Community Foundation.

Houle, C.O. (1960). *The effective board.* New York: Association Press.

Newman, H., & VanWijk, A. (1980). *Self-evaluation for human service organizations.* New York: Greater New York Fund/United Way.

Peters, S., Lichtman, S.A., & Windle, C. (1979). *Citizen roles in community mental health center evaluation: A guide for citizens.* Rockville, MD: National Institute of Mental Health.

Ragland, S.L., & Zinn, H.K. (1979). *Orientation manual for citizen boards of federally funded community mental health centers.* Rockville, MD: National Institute of Mental Health.

Slavin, S. (1978). *Social administration: The management of the social services.* New York: Council on Social Work Education.

Volunteer Bureau of Pasadena. (1972). *So . . . you serve on a board.* Pasadena, CA: Volunteer Bureau.

Wiehe, V.R. (1978). Role expectations among agency personnel. *Social Work, 23,* 26–30.

Chapter 6

Public and Private Financing Options for Community Residences

Mary Ann Allard

In the 1970s, a number of community housing programs became available through federal, state, and local governments to assist organizations serving persons with developmental disabilities. In addition to publicly financed housing, private-sector resources including individual family resources and private investments have been used to expand the number and type of community-living arrangements for persons with disabilities. Numerous public and private programs that can be used for specific housing activities are described in this chapter.

Traditionally, community-based residences for persons with developmental disabilities have been funded through specialized, targeted programs. The sources of funding usually include the following: special categorical or grant programs from a state or local mental retardation/developmental disabilities agency, income supports from Supplemental Security Income (SSI) or Social Security Disability Income (SSDI), and the Medicaid Intermediate Care Facility for the Mentally Retarded (ICF/MR) program.

In addition to these funding programs, community residences use client fees, private donations, and other program funds to cover the shelter or housing costs of the program. By the mid- to late 1970s, a number of generic housing programs became available through the U.S. Department of Housing and Urban Development (HUD), such as rental subsidies (Section

8) and direct loans (Section 202). Within the U.S. Department of Agriculture, the Farmers Home Administration (FmHA) formerly included persons with disabilities in housing programs for rural areas. Since that time, many community organizations have used these resources to expand the community residential system for persons with developmental disabilities.

Funding for community residences for persons with disabilities is continually changing. Public housing resources, especially through HUD and FmHA, are declining, and many organizations have turned to private investors for assistance. Moreover, a new emphasis is being placed on individual home ownership. Much of the success of private investment in homes for persons with developmental disabilities has been due to the tax incentives in the federal tax code. Although the tax system is, of course,

Much of the material in this chapter is adapted or quoted directly from Allard, M., Carling, P., Bradley, V., Spence, R., & Randolph, F. (1986). *Providing housing and supports for people with psychiatric disabilities: A technical assistance manual for applicants for the Robert Wood Johnson Foundation and U.S. DHUD program for the chronically mentally ill.* Rockville, MD: U.S. Department of Health and Human Services, National Institute of Mental Health.

subject to modifications, incentives are expected to remain to encourage investors to develop low and moderate income housing.

Despite the ongoing instability in fiscal resources for housing, opportunities in both the public and private sectors can be used to provide funding for community residences. This chapter highlights some of the programs and strategies that agencies can pursue in developing a comprehensive financing approach for community-based housing in the public and private sectors. However, a significant number of technical details accompanies each option, and interested readers will need to make more extensive inquiries regarding the appropriate program under consideration. Information sources for such inquiries are provided in Table 1.

PUBLIC FINANCING PROGRAMS

Table 1 summarizes the federal, state, and local housing options available to persons with developmental disabilities. Eligible housing-related activities, names of programs, and information sources are listed under each major heading.

Federal Programs

Federal Funds to Acquire, Construct, or Rehabilitate Housing. Some of the more popular programs of the Department of Housing and Urban Development that can be used to build, acquire, renovate, or substantially rehabilitate housing include: 1) the Community Development Block Grant (CDBG) program, 2) Rehabilitation, 3) Section 8 Moderate

Table 1. Public financing sources for community housing

Eligible housing activities	Name of program	Information sources Local[a]	State[b]	Federal
Federal:				
1. Acquire, build, rehabilitate	CDBG	City, county, or town community development or planning office HUD field office	—	Assistant Secretary for Community Planning & Development, DHUD, 451 7th St., SW, Washington, DC 20410
2. Rehabilitate (inquire about existing units)	Rental Rehabilitation	(Same as above) HUD field office	—	(Same as above)
3. Rehabilitate (inquire about existing units)	Section 8 Moderate Rehabilitation	City, county, town public housing agency Individual building owners	—	Assistant Secretary for Housing– Federal Housing Commissioner, DHUD, 451 7th St., SW, Washington, DC 20410
4. Acquire, build, or substantially rehabilitate	Section 202 Direct Loans for Elderly/ Handicapped	HUD field office	—	(Same as above)
5. Acquire	Federally owned properties	HUD field office VA office	—	(Same as above)
6. Mortgage insurance	Single Family 1–4 units (Sec. 203 (b))	Local lending establishment (e.g., bank, savings and loan) HUD field office	—	(Same as above)
7. Mortgage insurance	Multi-Family 221 (d)(4)	(Same as above)	—	(Same as above)

(continued)

Table 1. (*continued*)

Eligible housing activities	Name of program	Information sources		
		Local[a]	State[b]	Federal
8. Mortgage insurance	Sec. 234— Condominium Sec. 213— Cooperatives	Local lending establishment (e.g., bank, savings and loan) HUD field office	—	Assistant Secretary for Housing– Federal Housing Commissioner, DHUD, 451 7th St., SW, Washington, DC 20410
9. Sources of rental units	Public Housing	Local public housing agency	—	Assistant Secretary for Public and Indian Housing, DHUD, 451 7th St., SW, Washington, DC 20410
10. Sources of rental units	Insured projects, moderate rehabilitation	Local public housing agency HUD field office	—	Assistant Secretary for Housing– Federal Housing Commissioner, DHUD, 451 7th St., SW, Washington, DC 20410
11. Rental assistance	Section 8 Existing Housing	Local public housing agency	—	(Same as above)
State:				
12. Acquire, build, rehabilitate	Each state is different	—	State housing finance agency/ housing development authority or state community affairs agency	—
Rental assistance, predevelopment loan programs	Each state is different	—	State housing finance agency or state community affairs agency	—
Local:				
13. Acquire	Tax foreclosed properties	Local public housing agency	—	—

[a]City, county, or town community development, planning, and housing agencies are usually listed in the telephone book. A national directory of local housing agencies can be obtained from the National Association of Housing and Redevelopment Officials (NAHRO), 2600 Virginia Ave., Washington, DC, 20037 (not all local housing authorities may be included in this directory). HUD field or area offices should also be listed in the local telephone book; if there is no field office in a specific area, contact the nearest HUD Regional Office.

[b]State housing agencies are usually listed in the telephone book. For a list of all State Housing Finance Agencies, contact Council of State Housing Agencies (CSHA), 444 N. Capitol St., Suite 118, Washington, DC 20001; for Departments of Community Affairs, contact the Council of State Community Affairs Agencies, 444 N. Capitol St., Suite 251, Washington, DC 20001.

Rehabilitation, and 4) Section 202 (Housing for the Elderly and Handicapped). Organizations can also purchase federally owned properties that have been foreclosed. With the exception of the CDBG program, HUD programs cannot be used to support temporary living (less than 1 year) and medical facilities.

The Department of Agriculture's Farmers Home Administration program also administers several rental housing and community facility loan programs (Sections 501 and 504). FmHA programs are not discussed in this chapter; persons interested in developing housing in rural areas should contact their local FmHA representative.

Community Development Block Grant (CDBG) Program Community Development Block Grants enable local governments to fund a variety of housing and housing-related activities that benefit low- and moderate-income persons, reduce or eliminate urban decay, or address other problems that may lead to community deterioration if left untended (HUD, 1984). Specifically, CDBG funds can be used to support the rehabilitation of existing residential structures, site acquisition, special projects to remove architectural barriers, and housing-related costs such as architectural plans, engineering, and public improvements. CDBG funds have also been used as seed money for other federal housing programs, such as HUD 202 projects, and as a way to subsidize loans from a private lender if the housing sponsor is unable to generate adequate revenue to secure a loan at market rates (Levinson, 1985).

While the CDBG program does not permit new construction of housing, in 1985 HUD determined that new construction of homes for persons with special needs, such as mental retardation/developmental disabilities, would be an eligible activity. This type of housing is considered a ''public facility'' rather than a residence. Private nonprofit entities, however, may operate such public facilities.

Since its inception in 1974, organizations representing persons with developmental disabilities have used CDBG funds for a variety of housing-related activities, such as purchasing sites for group homes and removing architectural barriers in existing housing. Although HUD does not collect data on the proportion of CDBG funds allocated to mental retardation/developmental disabilities activities, a 1978 report of the National Association of State Mental Retardation Program Directors (NASMRPD) identified 60 localities that used CDBG funds for such activities, including housing programs. It is likely that the number of localities using CDBG funds to benefit persons with developmental disabilities has grown

since 1978, but some system observers suggest that CDBG remains an underutilized source of funding for housing persons with disabilities (NASMRPD, 1978).

The Community Development Block Grant program is a flexible source of revenue for nonprofit organizations seeking housing alternatives for their clients, and remains available in most cities and counties. Because of the program's appeal, however, competition for CDBG funds is always great, and agencies wishing to receive financing must develop relationships with their local county or city community development office to acquire such funds.

Rental Rehabilitation The Rental Rehabilitation program provides grants to cities and states to renovate residential rental units. Up to $5,000 per rental unit is available and must be matched by other funds, including private financing. Although one-half of the total eligible rehabilitation costs of the project can be covered by rental rehabilitation funds, an average minimum rehabilitation of $600 per unit is required (HUD, 1984). Rental rehabilitation funds also may be accompanied by Section 8 rental subsidies.

Eligible rehabilitation activities are those that are necessary to correct substandard conditions, to make essential improvements, and to repair major systems in danger of failure. Making housing units accessible for persons with disabilities is considered an eligible activity. In general, the Rental Rehabilitation program is targeted to neighborhoods where the median income does not exceed 80% of the area median and where rents are not likely to increase more rapidly than those in the general housing market (DHUD, 1984).

Rental rehabilitation funds can be used in two ways by organizations representing persons with developmental disabilities: 1) an agency currently owns housing units that are in need of renovation, such as for accessibility purposes, and meets other program requirements; and 2) an agency obtains a list of building owners participating in the rental rehabilitation program from its local community development office. Owners can then be contacted to ascertain the availability of rental units for persons with developmental disabilities. A variety of supervised living arrangements could be developed using the Rental Rehabilitation program.

Section 8 Moderate Rehabilitation This program provides rental assistance payments to property owners who lease units to lower-income tenants of buildings rehabilitated either according to HUD Housing Quality Standards or local housing codes. The rental subsidy is based on the difference between the gross rent and the tenant's contribution, which is set at 30% of his or her adjusted household income.

The Section 8 Moderate Rehabilitation program is operated by local public housing agencies (PHAs) who are responsible for selecting property owners to participate in the program. Property owners must secure their own financing for the rehabilitation and must spend at least $1,000 per unit for the rehabilitation. All improvements must be accomplished within the Fair Market Rent structure that governs both the Section 8 Moderate Rehabilitation and Existing Housing programs.

The Moderate Rehabilitation program has several advantages: 1) the rental subsidy remains with the housing unit, unlike Section 8 Existing Housing, thus allowing a community organization greater flexibility in placing eligible persons in vacated units; and 2) it provides assurances to the private lender that the loan for the rehabilitation of the property will be repaid.

Organizations serving persons with developmental disabilities who are interested in rehabilitating rental housing for their clients should contact their local PHA to ascertain the availability of funds for the program. In addition, the PHA can provide to agencies a list of housing owners who have available Section 8 Moderate Rehabilitation units. Individual housing owners can then be approached about their Moderate Rehabilitation units. As already described, a variety of supervised living arrangements can be developed (e.g., supported group living with live-in staff).

Section 202 Direct Loan Program for the Elderly or Handicapped The Section 202 program provides 100% direct loans and Section 8 rental subsidies for multifamily housing for persons who are elderly or who have physical, developmental, or chronic mental disabilities. Since 1978, HUD has funded approx-

imately 7,955 units in 514 group homes and independent living complexes (small apartment buildings) for persons with developmental disabilities. Although roughly 50% of all nonelderly units are targeted to persons with developmental disabilities, nonelderly handicapped projects have comprised only 9% to 10% of all Section 202 new construction over the past few years (NASMRPD, 1985).

Most of the pertinent guidelines and requirements for Section 202 can be found in the HUD Section 202 Handbook (4571.1 Rev.). The program has many components, including size limitations, specification of service packages for clients, cost and design limitations, and others. For example, group homes can serve up to 15 persons per site and independent living complexes up to 40 units (no more than 40 individuals or families per site). HUD staff are encouraged to select projects that include 6 to 8 persons per site. In addition, 202 projects can be linked with Medicaid ICF/MR funding, but HUD staff must be assured that the residence will not be a medical facility.

Section 202 loans are provided at a statutory interest rate of 9.5%. The maximum term of the loan is 40 years, and the accompanying Section 8 rental subsidies are guaranteed for 20 years. The Section 8 rental subsidies pay the mortgage and other housing-related expenses. To be eligible, sponsors must be incorporated nonprofit organizations or consumer cooperatives. They must also be prepared to contribute 0.5% of the loan amount (up to $10,000) and cover all front-end financing costs up to loan closing.

Under the Section 202 program, housing can be built, purchased as is, or rehabilitated. For substantially rehabilitated housing, the cost of rehabilitation must comprise at least 25% of the total loan amount. Residences must meet HUD's minimum property standards (MPS), as well as provide architectural accessibility for persons with physical handicaps. Finally, all tenants in Section 202 housing must be elderly or persons with a handicap. Tenants must also meet a means test that limits incomes to less than 50% of the median income for the locality (exceptions can be made up to 80% of the median income).

As already illustrated, the Section 202 program has been used extensively by organizations representing persons with developmental disabilities to develop group homes and small apartment complexes. Even though it is a highly competitive program, it is one of the few federal sources of capital development funds for financing community residences. The disadvantages of Section 202 financing are numerous, including the length of time involved from loan processing to final construction of the home— an average of 2½ to 3 years. Moreover, many professionals stress that the Section 202 program is best suited for established and sophisticated organizations that have financial backing and a strong history of providing services to persons with developmental disabilities. Indeed, many organizations hire consultants, whose fees can be built into the projected costs, to help them through the morass of paperwork and requirements.

The limitations associated with the Section 202 program, such as the delays in completing the loan process and the layers of review that accompany each application, have led numerous professionals and advocates to suggest various alternatives to the current program structure. In general, the Section 202 program was never intended to support small, community living arrangements, since its antecedents went toward large, congregate housing projects for the elderly. Even though there has been some "tinkering" with program requirements, Section 202 remains cumbersome and costly to implement. As a result, a number of reform efforts have been initiated both administratively and legislatively to address the specific problems associated with housing for persons with disabilities.

Federally Owned Properties Federal agencies, such as HUD and the Veterans Administration (VA), sell properties that they have repossessed through mortgage defaults to the public at fair market prices. Properties may be rental units, single-family homes, or commercial sites. Qualified buyers for single-family housing must have a credit rating, stable employment (or sources of income), and adequate income to cover the mortgage and other costs (i.e., taxes, insurance) (Levinson, 1985).

Obtaining foreclosed property can be very attractive to organizations in the disability field, since such housing tends to be available at reasonable prices. While some of the properties may be run-down, others are in good enough condition so that agencies can purchase and renovate them as supportive living arrangements for persons with disabilities (Levinson, 1985). Agencies interested in this option should work with their local HUD Field Office to determine the kinds of properties available for such housing.

Federal Mortgage Insurance Programs to Assist in Financing Residential Properties A number of mortgage insurance programs are available through the Federal Housing Administration (FHA), an arm of HUD. FHA protects lenders against potential losses by providing insurance for mortgage loans made by private lending institutions. Organizations representing persons with disabilities have often overlooked these programs as a way to enhance the procurement of federal or state funds for housing programs. Since these programs provide only insurance, construction and permanent financing for the residence must be secured elsewhere. FHA insurance may facilitate the process of finding long-term financing from a private lender, and may reduce interest costs (Urban Systems Research and Engineering, 1983).

A few of the major insurance programs that may be used by agencies developing community residences are highlighted in the paragraphs following. Agencies, however, should inquire at their local HUD field office to determine whether more sophisticated FHA insurance programs may be appropriate.

Single-Family Insurance for One- to Four-Unit Properties—Section 203(b) This program may be used to facilitate home ownership and the financing of housing. HUD insures loans made by private financial institutions for up to 97% of the property value and for a term of up to 30 years. The loan may finance homes in both urban and rural areas (except farm homes) (HUD, 1984). The major advantages of this insurance program include very low down payment requirements and a greater willingness on the part of lenders to loan money that is insured.

Agencies could encourage families of persons with developmental disabilities to purchase a home for their relative using Section 203(b) to insure the loan. Although the program is targeted to owner-occupied units, nonowner-occupied units may be insured for up to 85% of the property value. Lending institutions, however, may be reluctant to use the 203(b) program for nonowner-occupied home loans. Interested organizations should contact both their local lending establishment and the HUD/FHA Field Office.

Multifamily Insurance—Section 221 (d)(4) Section 221 (d)(4) provides insurance for new construction or substantial rehabilitation of rental or cooperative multifamily housing for low- and moderate-income households. Mortgages are insured at the FHA ceiling interest rates. Acceptable projects must have a minimum of five units and meet statutorily controlled development cost limits. A number of different housing types from semiattached to elevator structures are eligible (HUD, 1984).

Mortgages may be obtained by public agencies; nonprofit, limited-dividend, cooperative organizations; and profit-motivated sponsors. Under Section 221 (d)(4), only 90% of the mortgage may be insured. Further, tenant occupancy is not restricted by income limits.

Organizations serving persons with developmental disabilities could apply for a mortgage either through a commercial lending establishment or a state housing agency and insure it with 221 (d)(4). Any type of multifamily project (e.g., a five-unit townhouse or a small apartment building) could be insured in this way.

Condominium Unit Insurance—Section 234—and Cooperative Insurance—Section 213 Section 234 provides mortgage insurance to finance ownership of individual units in multifamily housing projects. A project must contain at least four dwelling units. HUD will insure mortgages on individual units in existing condominiums. In addition, sponsors of housing may also obtain FHA insurance to finance the construction or rehabilitation or housing projects that they intend to sell as individual units under Section 234. Any qualified for-profit or nonprofit sponsor may apply for the

latter, while any person with sufficient credit may apply for a mortgage on individual units in a project.

Section 213 provides comparable insurance for cooperative housing projects. At least five or more dwelling units must be occupied by members of the nonprofit cooperative housing corporation. Eligible applicants for cooperative insurance include nonprofit organizations or trusts organized to construct homes for members of the corporation or beneficiaries of the trust; and qualified sponsors who intend to sell the project to a nonprofit corporation or trust (HUD, 1984).

These two insurance programs can be used to encourage individual home ownership. More discussion of these housing options is presented in the second part of this chapter on private financing of community residences.

Potential Sources of Units to Rent for Persons with Developmental Disabilities

Public Housing For many years, HUD provided aid to public housing agencies (PHAs) to develop, own, and operate low-income public housing projects. Although most public housing is associated with large, high-rise projects that are often located in undesirable urban areas, there are many examples of quality, low-density public housing that have been integrated into local neighborhoods. Today, federal funding to help PHAs finance *new* public housing is severely limited. Existing public housing units, however, may be available to persons with disabilities, depending upon the demand for such units and other concerns.

Although persons with developmental disabilities have gained access to public housing, a major problem for organizations serving these persons is that the original public housing legislation specifically prohibits subleasing arrangements (Urban Systems Research and Engineering, 1983). Agencies will frequently lease a block of apartment units or a home on behalf of persons with disabilities. As an alternative to subleasing, HUD will allow organizations to enter into a "management contract" with local public housing authorities (PHAs). This procedure enables the service agency to assume management responsibility for their clients.

This housing option was illustrated, for example, in the cooperation that developed in the late 1970s between the Dallas, Texas, HUD Area Office, several local PHAs, and organizations representing persons with disabilities. Twenty-eight homes and apartments in conventional public housing were established for persons with mental retardation and psychiatric disabilities (Harwell, 1980). As another example, in Albuquerque, New Mexico (formerly part of the Dallas Area Office), the local Association for Retarded Citizens and other private nonprofit organizations were successful in placing 90 residents in existing public housing apartments.

Other Sources of Rental Units (Insured Projects, Moderate Rehabilitation, and Rental Rehabilitation Units) Community agencies should request from their local public housing authority the names of housing owners or buildings where rental units under the Moderate Rehabilitation or Rental Rehabilitation programs may be available. Moreover, HUD field office staff can assist agencies in locating FHA insured projects, such as 221(d)(4) or others, that may have units suitable for persons with developmental disabilities.

As an example, the Dallas HUD Area Office worked with several mental health and mental retardation agencies to secure approximately 15 apartments for 29 persons in FHA insured projects. A variety of supervised living arrangements was available in the rental units.

Rental Assistance for Persons with Disabilities

Section 8 Rental Assistance for Existing Housing The Section 8 Existing Housing Program is one of the more flexible and popular HUD supported programs to benefit persons with disabilities. HUD subsidizes a living unit for income-eligible "households" such that each household is required to contribute no more than 30% of its adjusted monthly income to the cost of the rent. The Section 8 subsidies can be provided for up to 15 years to individuals who remain income eligible and live in suitable housing in their original jurisdiction. HUD pays the landlord the difference between the tenant's contribution and the Fair Market Rent (FMR).

The FMR structure, set by HUD, is based on local housing market surveys.

The Section 8 Existing Housing Program is usually administered by a local Public Housing Agency (PHA); in some cases a state agency administers the program. A public housing agency is defined by HUD as a public body that is authorized to engage or assist in the operation of housing for low-income families. Many different types of agencies may qualify as a PHA, including state or local housing authorities, departments of community affairs, urban renewal agencies, and others. Income-eligible persons apply to the PHA to obtain a "certificate of participation," which allows them to "shop" for an apartment. The major requirements are that the monthly rent cannot exceed FMR limitations, the housing must meet certain minimum standards of quality, and the landlord must be willing to participate in the program. As soon as an acceptable apartment is located, the tenant and the landlord sign a lease, and the PHA and the landlord sign a contract that specifies various agreements and financing arrangements (Urban Systems Research and Engineering, 1983).

In the early 1980s, HUD issued regulations specifying how Section 8 could be used in group living situations called Independent Group Residences (IGRs). Because of the way in which Section 8 subsidies were designated for IGRs, very few organizations took advantage of the program. Most agencies preferred to assist consumers to obtain individual or shared apartment units using the Section 8 subsidy to pay the rental costs. The principal difference between using Section 8 for an IGR and for an individual unit is financial. In the past, agencies found that the Fair Market Rents (FMRs) for IGRs were not adequate to cover rental costs. HUD has recently raised the FMRs for units with three or more bedrooms, which may make IGRs more feasible.

There are several drawbacks to the Section 8 existing program: 1) usually there are long waiting lists for Section 8 certificates of participation; 2) often the housing units that are available exceed FMR levels—however, agencies can lease units with rents above the FMR levels if they can make up the difference between the FMR and the actual rent out of their own reserves or by using available subsidies from state sources; and 3) since Section 8 Existing Housing certificates stay with the individual, a new certificate must be obtained each time an individual moves to a new living arrangement (Urban Systems Research & Engineering, 1983).

Although appropriations for the Section 8 Existing Housing Program have been reduced, PHAs have available certificates because of unit turnover. Approximately 20% of the 800,000 Section 8 Existing Housing certificates currently available turn over each year. To obtain certificates, community providers can ask their PHA to amend its administrative plan in order to provide preference for persons with developmental disabilities.

State Programs

In addition to federal housing programs, a variety of state programs support living arrangements for persons with developmental disabilities. In general, three types of state agencies support housing programs: 1) State Housing Finance Agencies (HFAs), in some states called State Housing Development Authorities, 2) State Community Affairs Agencies or Departments of Community Affairs, and 3) State Mental Retardation/Developmental Disabilities agencies. Some states have both HFAs and Community Affairs Agencies, while others have only one agency that incorporates both entities. Note that these are generic terms to describe housing organizations at the state level and that the name of the relevant agency may differ in each state. (See Table 1 for more information.)

State housing agencies may be involved in numerous housing-related activities: financing, rental assistance, predevelopment loans, and other programs. These activities can also be used to promote housing opportunities for persons with developmental disabilities. The following descriptions, therefore, encompass the range of potential activities that may fall under the purview of these state housing units.

State Housing Finance Agencies Since 1960, 40 states and Puerto Rico have estab-

lished State Housing Finance Agencies. HFAs are created by state enabling legislation and are usually independent or semi-independent entities within state governments. Most state housing finance agencies are required to be self-supporting and are limited in the amount of debt they may incur without additional authorization from the state legislature.

HFAs can engage in a variety of financing programs, but the majority provide either direct or indirect financing for single- and multifamily housing units. The most direct way HFAs finance housing is by selling tax-exempt bonds, which creates proceeds to make interim construction loans and long-term permanent financing (mortgages). By selling tax-exempt bonds, the agency is able to offer these financing arrangements at interest rates lower than those offered by conventional lending institutions. Moreover, prospective housing sponsors can secure HFA financing if they demonstrate that a portion of their property will be occupied by persons of low and moderate income. The attractiveness of tax-exempt bonds to develop housing, however, has been modified by national tax reform measures. Despite the changes in bond financing for low- and moderate-income housing, HFAs will continue to play a strong role in creating affordable housing arrangements.

Although most HFAs lend funds for traditional single-family and multifamily housing, they usually have or can secure the authority to finance alternative projects such as supervised community residences. HFAs can also support housing cooperatives, especially if a majority of persons residing in the units are low or moderate income. Finally, HFAs, and other state housing agencies, can be involved in specialized rent subsidy allocations serving persons with developmental disabilities. As federal Section 8 subsidies for existing housing decline, some states (e.g., Colorado) are considering a comparable state-level rent subsidy program for low-income and disabled persons.

Numerous HFAs have used their resources to finance the construction or rehabilitation of community-based housing for persons with developmental disabilities. Michigan, Minnesota,

Virginia, and Tennessee are among the earliest examples. The Virginia Housing Development Authority (VHDA) began financing group homes for persons with mental retardation in 1976. More recently, the Virginia Department of Mental Health and Mental Retardation submitted a proposal to VHDA to fund a housing subsidy program for persons with disabilities, which would be modeled after the federal Section 8 Existing Housing Program for rental assistance.

State Community Affairs Agencies or Departments of Community Affairs State Departments of Community Affairs (DCAs) perform a variety of community and economic development activities that assist in the dissemination and management of low- and moderate-income housing. DCAs are often involved in the programmatic aspects of housing programs, but in some states they also provide direct financing and rental assistance for housing programs. DCAs can receive allocations of federal Section 8 subsidies for existing housing, but most compete with local housing authorities for such allocations. Several state DCAs (e.g., California, New Jersey, Wisconsin, Utah, Connecticut) have received allocations of Section 8 rental assistance to support persons with developmental disabilities. Finally, DCAs, like other state housing entities, can develop short-term loan programs to help organizations with equity requirements, architectural fees, site control, and other issues.

The Massachusetts Executive Office of Communities and Development (EOCD) is an example of a DCA that has been heavily involved in financing housing for persons with disabilities. EOCD oversees Chapter 689—A Housing Program for People with Special Needs, which provides funds to local housing authorities to develop both single-family and multifamily housing (apartments) for persons with developmental disabilities and other disabling conditions. Public housing authorities are required to affiliate with nonprofit providers to establish and administer the housing programs and services. Although the housing authority maintains ownership of the home, the nonprofit entity can lease the home on a long-term basis. Since 1976, 43 residences housing 370 persons with

mental retardation have been developed throughout Massachusetts, and another 83 residences are in various stages of development.

An example of a DCA rental assistance program benefiting persons with developmental disabilities can be found in New Jersey. The New Jersey Department of Community Affairs began targeting Section 8 Existing Housing subsidies to persons with disabilities in the 1970s. At that time, DCA had only several hundred certificates. Today DCA manages a program that serves approximately 7,000 clients, of whom 11% (770) have disabilities. The DCA determines eligibility and admission to the program through its district offices and works directly with interested organizations in distributing certificates to eligible recipients.

Finally, several states have initiated grant programs to use as down payments for housing programs for persons with disabilities. The California Department of Housing and Community Development (HCD) has a predevelopment loan program available to public and private nonprofit agencies for new construction of subsidized housing. The maximum loan is $100,000 and can be used for site control, preliminary architectural consultations, and other activities. Although these funds are not specifically earmarked for persons with developmental disabilities, they clearly can be used to support community housing for these individuals.

State Mental Retardation/Developmental Disabilities Agencies State Mental Retardation/Developmental Disabilities agencies have traditionally supported community residences through specialized funding programs. As interest grew in the use of generic housing resources, such as Section 8 rental assistance, some state Mental Retardation/ Developmental Disabilities agencies explored the possibility of being designated as "public housing agencies" in order to receive federal rental assistance funds.

Only one state mental disabilities agency has secured this status from HUD—the Colorado Department of Institutions, an umbrella agency that includes the Division of Mental Health, Developmental Disabilities and Youth Services. The Division of Developmental Disabilities is responsible for administering the

Section 8 rental assistance program for persons with developmental disabilities who choose to live independently, in group homes, or in apartment programs. Subsidies are provided to persons through subcontracts with local community boards, who must submit applications to the Division of Developmental Disabilities, describing their intent to develop residential programs for persons with developmental disabilities.

The designation of a state developmental disabilities agency as a public housing agency has not been used extensively, since many states have been able to negotiate successfully for set-asides of Section 8 and new construction programs with their generic state housing agency. Moreover, state developmental disabilities agencies can be designated by state legislatures to oversee the implementation of new housing programs for persons with disabilities. State funding is often broad enough to allow new construction or the purchase/lease of existing housing for group living arrangements, scattered site apartment programs, and others.

Local Programs

Local government agencies, primarily housing authorities, can provide a range of assistance to community organizations seeking appropriate housing for persons with developmental disabilities. Even though local housing authorities may not have the revenues to build/acquire new housing, there are other options that they can offer to interested groups.

Tax-Foreclosed Properties Municipalities foreclosing on properties for nonpayment of taxes will sell their properties through a competitive bid process at public auction, similar to the process that occurs for federally owned properties (Levinson, 1985). Community organizations representing persons with developmental disabilities should develop relationships with the local participating brokers and housing administrators who are knowledgeable about pending property sales that may be suitable for small community residences or independent living settings. Some professionals suggest that organizations purchasing municipal properties may choose to pay the local taxes despite their nonprofit tax-exempt status. In this

way, the agency provides fiscal support to the city and enhances the potential for future cooperative efforts in housing for persons with disabilities (Levinson, 1985).

Contacts for Other Public Programs at the Local Level Housing authorities and community development offices are key information sources regarding housing development, finance, and rental assistance. They may also be aware of other local funding sources such as private development groups and foundations that could be available for community living arrangements for persons with developmental disabilities (see Table 1).

PRIVATE FINANCING OPTIONS

Private Dollars versus Public Dollars

As noted at the beginning of this chapter, public funding of low- and moderate-income housing has diminished in recent years. Attention has turned to the private dollar to fill in the funding gaps and, in some cases, to provide a complete alternative to public resource development.

Private-sector funds for housing are available from a variety of sources—mortgage bankers, thrift institutions, commercial banks, private investors, and private philanthropies. Some of the principal reasons why private-sector dollars should be used to develop housing for persons with developmental disabilities include the following:

- There is *potentially* more money available from the private sector than from the public sector.
- Most government-funded programs, such as those under HUD, do not cover all aspects of housing, and, therefore, other sources of funding must be secured. For example, federal mortgage insurance programs are available only if private financing can be secured.
- Private investment funds are available to agencies serving persons with developmental disabilities through the federal income tax system.
- Community organizations representing persons with developmental disabilities can reduce a private investor's concerns

regarding three major drawbacks to real estate investment: vacancy rates, property management, and maintenance. For example, an agency can establish a long-term agreement with an investor(s) that guarantees as close to 100% occupancy as possible at a fixed rent level. It can also assume responsibility for managing the property—a task most investors would gladly relinquish.

- Community-based housing that is developed using private dollars is usually less expensive, less bureaucratic, and completed in less time than some types of public-sector housing (e.g., HUD's Section 202 program).
- Private investors should be cultivated by local community providers, since they are often tied into influential and powerful local financial and political institutions.

Strategies Using Private Resources

Persons with Developmental Disabilities as Home Owners   A person with a developmental disability can become a home owner either by using his or her own personal resources, or those of family or friends. Even a person on Supplemental Security Income (SSI) is allowed to own a home and still remain income eligible for the program. The variety of possible housing options is endless, including single or multifamily units, housing cooperatives, and condominiums. Consumers can own their own homes through other strategies such as lease/purchase agreements in which the investor relinquishes title to the tenant/lessee after payment of a stated amount of rentals (Laux, 1980).

The number of persons with developmental disabilities who have been able to become home owners both through private and public resources is increasing. Two of the more popular ways to encourage home ownership have been to develop condominium and cooperative housing units. In either case, families and/or a public entity may be involved.

Owning a condominium is like individual home ownership, since each tenant has a "fee simple" interest in his or her own unit. In addition to the unit, the condominium buyer ac-

quires a proportionate individual interest in the common parts of the land and building, with no right of partition (Unger, 1984). Purchasing a condominium can be difficult for individuals or families with low and moderate incomes; however, a blending of private and public resources may enable more persons with disabilities to become home owners than previously envisioned.

Several families in the Boston area, for example, successfully converted a two-family home into condominium units for 10 young adults with mental retardation/developmental disabilities. With the guidance of a social service professional, the families used their resources to assist their family members to purchase individual condominium units. The families created several legal entities in order to purchase the building, finance the individual units, and provide other related services. Family members also contributed their own hard labor, or "sweat equity," to make the project viable.

This approach to housing for persons with developmental disabilities not only highlights an important way of achieving community integration but also is accomplished entirely outside the formal mental retardation/developmental disabilities services system. In the Massachusetts example, the individual condominium owners were involved in selecting staff/friends to help them develop independent living skills. However, there is no formal program within the home. The condominium units are located close to public transportation so that each person can easily commute to work or a day program.

Cooperative housing is another way in which individual home ownership can be promoted. In a housing cooperative, a corporation owns the housing development in which the resident/members live. This type of housing differs from condominium ownership, where individuals own their housing unit and participate in a "simple fee" arrangement. Each resident in a cooperative, however, owns shares in a nonprofit corporation and holds an exclusive right to occupy his or her particular unit. In addition, each resident has an equal vote in selecting the board of directors, who manage the "co-op" and make all policy decisions.

Unlike condominiums, rental assistance programs such as Section 8 or a state subsidy program can be used in cooperatives to help home owners meet monthly costs. If organized and managed successfully, a co-op can provide many benefits to persons with developmental disabilities, including:

A co-op can be organized to limit equity on the resale of the units and, therefore, continues to be affordable over time.
Co-ops are often available at affordable prices.
A co-op owner can deduct interest and taxes paid on his or her unit in a manner similar to the owner of a conventional home (Franklin, 1981).

Cooperatives are usually organized for shareholding by individuals; however, it is possible to substitute the shareholding to nonprofit human service agencies. In this way, nonprofit agencies can have an organizational structure to acquire, rehabilitate, or construct units for individuals in need of services. Agencies could have the shares representing their capital investment but would not have the sole burden of developing housing themselves. By using a nonprofit housing development corporation or forming their own corporation, human services agencies would have the expertise to work collaboratively with the funding agent for the housing project (Schwarzentraub, 1980).

Vignette

An example of a cooperative housing approach combining a human services agency with potential client ownership is underway in Peterborough, New Hampshire. Under this approach, a local housing development team will purchase an eight-unit apartment complex for a housing cooperative. Two of the units will be set aside for persons with developmental disabilities. In the articles of incorporation of the housing cooperative, these units will always be available for clients of the state/local developmental disabilities agency. Possible financing resources include the New Hampshire Housing Finance Authority.

The building will be bought by the housing corporation that will set up the cooperative. Under the rules of the cooperative, each individual will receive stock, like any other corporation. Unlike a condominium arrangement, the stock in the cooperative is issued to the nonprofit organization, which in this case is the local developmental disability agency. The agency will own the two units,

but all the rights and responsibilities of tenancy will be assigned to the individuals with disabilities. SSI and other state subsidies will provide sufficient income to cover the housing costs.

In Canada, housing cooperatives are used extensively to provide opportunities for home ownership to a broad range of people. For example, in Manitoba, the Prairie Housing Cooperative was formed by families, individuals with disabilities, and other interested community members. The cooperative links together small groups of individuals or families who live in duplexes, town houses, or clusters of single-family homes scattered throughout Winnipeg. Each group supports one or more members who have developmental or special needs, or a family with a relative who has a disability.

The Prairie Housing Cooperative is similar to cooperatives in the United States in which members purchase individual shares entitling them to a voice in the cooperative's operations. As the members themselves note, the cooperative is more than just housing. It provides support to encourage members with developmental needs to live with other members of the community. Sources of financial support for the housing come from many individuals and organizations, including the Canada Mortgage and Housing Corporation and the Manitoba Department of Cooperative Development.

Family-Initiated Housing The tasks of encouraging home ownership and of involving families in housing often are intertwined. Some families, for example, can afford to purchase individual housing units like condominiums or cooperatives for their relative with a disability. Other home ownership strategies that families can pursue include creating life estate trusts that allow families to donate their homes to a nonprofit agency to be used for their relative with a disability.

Families have also organized their own nonprofit corporations to develop, operate, and provide affordable housing units over time to their family members. The corporations maintain tax-exempt status and are usually designated as 501 (c)(3) or charitable organizations. Numerous families in the developmental disabilities field have formed corporations and secured federal funds through the HUD Section

202 program or the Community Development Block Grant program to build or renovate single and multifamily housing for their family members. A group of parents in Atlanta, for instance, have built two homes with the Section 202 program and are building two more. Hiring staff and other decisions concerning the residences are the responsibility of the family members. In this example, the family-initiated corporation has received other funding sources to develop residences, including the donation of a home by a local bank. Often families are initially organized by an advocate, professional or a parent who provides the impetus to seek alternatives to the existing service system.

Public-sector and personal resources are not the only funding streams that families have tapped. As described in the following section, family members can link up with private investors to purchase and/or build new housing for persons with developmental disabilities. The extent to which families become involved in developing privately financed housing options for their sons or daughters will depend, in part, on the ability of local lending institutions to respond to the enormous need for such resources. At the same time, families and community agencies serving persons with developmental disabilities must begin to use their resources more creatively: leveraging the funds they have and building equity for future housing projects are important financial strategies that have been overlooked.

Syndications and Limited Partnerships in Housing for Persons with Disabilities Real estate syndications are a complicated way in which to secure capital to develop housing for persons with disabilities. In general, real estate syndications of low- and moderate-income housing projects have been used by big developers to develop large, new construction or renovated housing. Recently, nonprofit organizations and other individuals interested in developing smaller housing projects have successfully used syndication.

A real estate syndication is formed by selling shares of ownership or equity interests in an entity that will build, rehabilitate, or acquire a housing project (Hom, 1984). In most syndications, equity shares are sold through a limited

partnership. A limited partnership usually includes two types of partners: a general partner and a number of limited partners. Limited partners provide the money for the housing development but are not involved in the day-to-day management of the project. Moreover, their liability is limited to the amount of their investment in the project (Hom, 1984).

The incentives to form limited partnerships and syndications are firmly connected to federal tax code provisions. Even though tax reform measures have changed the way in which entities such as limited partnerships may use the tax system, significant efforts were made to preserve incentives for low- and moderate-income housing. For example, tax credits are available instead of depreciation schedules. As a result of these changes, investors will create new mechanisms with which to leverage their funds.

Examples of syndications in housing for persons with disabilities can be found in several states. In San Jose, California, a community provider purchased an eight-unit residential property based on a commitment to use investors to supply the capital needed. The agency prepared an investment prospectus and made a private offering to a large number of friends and associates, including families with disabled members. During the first three months, $115,000 in capital was raised to purchase the complex. Fifty-two percent of the capital came from three individuals who invested more than $10,000 each; the majority of contributors invested approximately $3,000 a piece (Levine, 1984).

Another organizational option that offers latitude and flexibility is that of forming a nonprofit corporation to create and manage the syndications. In the late 1970s, several advocacy and other organizations in Hartford, Connecticut, formed the Corporation for Independent Living (CIL) to develop community-living arrangements for persons with disabilities. Although CIL staff began by competing for Section 202 funds, their focus soon changed to syndication as a way to provide community housing for persons with disabilities. The corporation has developed 70 properties in Connecticut through syndications. CIL acts as the general partner and secures limited partners to invest and purchase various properties.

CIL enters into a contract with local nonprofit agencies to develop housing only if the agencies receive funding for room and board and services. CIL completes all the development work for the home: it identifies and buys the property and ensures that all federal/state requirements are met. The limited partners and CIL own the properties and lease them on a long-term basis, with an option to buy, to community providers or other nonprofit agencies.

In order to develop housing on a large scale, CIL uses a more sophisticated syndication and goes to the "open investment market" to secure investors. With a more extensive investment base, CIL can syndicate 10–15 single-family properties in one limited partnership—these properties are then leased to 8 or 10 nonprofit agencies.

The CIL approach to syndication has many advantages: 1) by using economies of scale, the corporation can develop many more homes than an individual agency; 2) CIL staff have the knowledge and experience to put together investment packages that save the individual nonprofit agency both time and money; and 3) in addition to securing the financing, CIL staff will complete all of the development tasks associated with new housing for persons with disabilities.

Other Financing Strategies Organizations representing persons with developmental disabilities should explore less well-known financing approaches to housing development, such as bargain sales of land or land trusts. These financing options are often based on providing tax benefits to the investor/seller.

Land trusts are governed by nonprofit, tax-exempt corporations that buy land and buildings but hold the land "in trust" and sell the buildings at affordable interest rates to low- and moderate-income families and individuals. Since the land is never bought, up to 25% of the cost of purchasing a home can be eliminated.

Nonprofit agencies may be able to secure permanent housing for persons with disabilities if a land trust is available in their community. If land trusts do not exist, agencies may consider becoming involved with other community organizations to form one.

Housing professionals stress that community agencies must focus on strategies that involve using resources other than their own. The options cited in this section are just a few of the possibilities available to community organizations. Since many financing options involve complicated legal and financial knowledge, especially concerning the federal tax code, housing experts may need to be consulted.

CONCLUSION

This chapter briefly described public and private financing options for housing persons with developmental disabilities. Several themes or guidelines have emerged in the discussion that should be highlighted. First, public housing resources available through HUD and other agencies have decreased significantly, but opportunities still exist to secure resources for community residences. Organizations must develop working relationships with local housing authorities, community development offices, and HUD field office staff in order to secure these scarce resources. Second, private financing can lead to a variety of community-living arrangements for persons with disabilities, but organizations must be alert to the changes and nuances of federal tax reform and should seek expert advice on this strategy. Third, both public and private housing resources should be explored, since neither type alone will sufficiently provide the range of housing alternatives many individuals with disabilities need. Finally, community agencies should consider developing statewide or regional entities as necessary, such as nonprofit housing corporations, that facilitate and greatly expand the financing strategies available to persons with disabilities.

REFERENCES

Allard, M., Carling, P., Bradley, V., Spence, R., & Randolph, F. (1986). *Providing housing and supports for people with psychiatric disabilities: A technical as-* *sistance manual for applicants for the Robert Wood Johnson Foundation and U.S. Department of Housing and Urban Development program for the chronically mentally ill.* Rockville, MD: National Institute of Mental Health.

Franklin, S. (1981). Housing cooperatives: A viable means of home ownership for low income families. *Journal of Housing, 7,* 392–398.

Harwell, J. (1980). A primer on using HUD programs. *Challenge!, XI* (11), Washington, DC: U.S. Department of Housing and Urban Development.

Hom, S. (1984). Does real estate syndication provide a viable financial strategy for low income housing? *Brooklyn Law Review, 50,* 913–938.

Laux, R. (1980). *The use of private investment sources to create residential alternatives.* Falls Church, VA: National Association of Private Residential Facilities for the Mentally Retarded.

Levine, I.S. (1984). *Developing community support service programs: A resource manual for family groups.* Boston: Center for Psychiatric Rehabilitation and Washington, DC: National Alliance for the Mentally Ill.

Levinson, G. (1985). *Residential financing for low income and disabled persons.* East Orange, NJ: Community Health Law Project.

National Association of State Mental Retardation Program Directors. (1978). *Housing for developmentally disabled citizens: An analysis of policy issues.* Washington, DC: U.S. Department of Health and Human Services, Office of Human Development Services.

National Association of State Mental Retardation Program Directors. (1985, April 18). Handicapped housing bill introduced in House. *Intelligence Report,* Bulletin No. 85-28, p. 2.

Schwarzentraub, K. (1980, June 18) *Cooperatives and its implications to individuals who have special needs.* Internal Memorandum. Sacramento, CA: California Department of Housing and Community Development.

Unger, M. (1984). *How to invest in real estate.* New York: McGraw-Hill.

Urban Systems Research and Engineering, Inc. (1983). *Community residences for the chronically mentally ill. A sponsor's guide to development planning.* Washington, DC: U.S. Department of Housing and Urban Development.

U.S. Department of Housing and Urban Development. (1984). *Programs of HUD.* Washington, DC: U.S. Department of Housing and Urban Development.

Chapter 7

Program Evaluation in Community Residential Settings

John W. Jacobson and Cal Robert Regula

This chapter provides an overview of program evaluation processes and issues in community-living situations. Topics covered include a definition of *program evaluation*, identification of evaluation issues and development of an evaluation plan, selection and employment of consultants, and instruments that are useful in conducting community program evaluations.

Program evaluation is the application of scientific research methods to applied settings (for example, industrial, human services, and educational situations) for the purpose of providing information that promotes better managerial decision making. Evaluations serve many purposes, including the measurement of program impact, the assessment of the efficacy of different methods of service delivery, the provision of accountability for continuation of funding, and the identification of program elements associated with different outcomes (Guba & Lincoln, 1981; Hawkins, Fremouw, & Reitz, 1981; Krapfl, 1975; Schalock, 1983). Most program evaluations are conducted within limited time periods and are expected to generate concrete information, enabling managers to make more informed decisions.

Program evaluation activities differ from classical experiments in several ways. First, most evaluations draw data from settings that do not permit random sampling, random assignment, or matching of groups on a variety of relevant parameters. Studies often involve groups that do not remain constant in their treatments over time. Further, many evaluations are conducted in settings where it is impractical or

unethical to maintain control groups. Hence, a variety of quasi-experimental designs have been developed, often entailing the use of multiple measures so that the impact of program features can be demonstrated. These designs are discussed in detail by Campbell and Stanley (1963) and Cook and Campbell (1979).

Monitoring of program activities and processes is only one component of program evaluation. When evaluation procedures are first instituted, it is valuable to monitor and document specific activities and events that occur to establish a baseline of performance. Unless the agency has a reliable, credible data base to begin with, it is usually necessary to build or refine such information. Many initial efforts will be devoted to collection of reliable statistical information on services and costs, upon which more elaborate analytic studies may be structured. Monitoring does not constitute program evaluation, but remains an important aspect of the realm of program evaluation. The crux of program evaluation activities lies in the development of strategies that permit management to make inferences from information and to render more effective decisions. Therefore analyses of intervention design, program implementation, and program benefit are inherent in program evaluation (Rossi & Freeman, 1982).

The decision by management to engage in program evaluation demonstrates management's willingness to examine critically its processes of delivering services. Some programs are contractually required to evaluate their programs, particularly when grant funding is received. In general, it is also good business practice to continually reexamine both programs and internal processes to assure that substantive operational problems are recognized and remediated. Program evaluation is also an activity that both oversight agencies and the general public respect as a way of responding to an unexpected crisis or of uncovering problems.

DEVELOPING AN EVALUATION PLAN FOR THE AGENCY

Management's Blueprint

A good evaluation plan is a blueprint that tells management what specific evaluations will be produced, by whom, at what times, at what costs, and the major decision bodies that will be given information. The plan affords management an understanding of the full staff and monetary costs to the agency. A good evaluation plan includes at least 12 major steps, as follows:

1. Define the goals.
2. Define the objectives.
3. Define the activities.
4. Determine data collection needs.
5. Designate project responsibility.
6. Specify reporting needs.
7. Specify who will write the reports.
8. Specify reporting schedules.
9. Specify the audiences for reports.
10. Estimate resource requirements.
11. Conduct a feasibility assessment.
12. Place issues of concern in order of priority.

Define the Goals The plan must specify the goals to be evaluated. Goals are general statements describing what the agency or program activities are designed to accomplish. Goal statements tend to be abstract descriptions

of changes in people, places, or conditions of the larger society in which the agency is embedded.

Surprisingly, for many managers this is the most difficult task in formulating the plan. Many social programs lack clear or complete specifications of agency goals, therefore making it difficult to see the relationships between the agency's activities and its goals. One method of making both goals and objectives explicit is through a "nominal group process." According to this method, staff, in small groups, write down the major goals and objectives, as they see them, without critiquing them. Next, these goals are examined and placed in order of priority (Bogdan & Biklen, 1982; Delbecq & VandeVen, 1971; Williamson, 1978; Williamson, Braswell, Horn & Lohmeyer, 1978).

Define the Objectives The plan should specify an objective for each goal. Objectives are concrete, specific, and measurable statements detailing what the agency activities are designed to accomplish in relation to a specific goal.

Define the Activities Clear, concrete statements of the activities to be measured, and which are linked to each objective, must be constructed. It is important that measurement or evaluation criteria for each activity be mutually agreed upon by the persons conducting the study and by those planning to use the results. There should be a consensus as to which and how the activities are to be measured, in order to assess whether the objective has, in fact, been accomplished.

For example, one goal of a community-based residential program may be independent resident usage of public transportation. If there are frequent transit strikes, it may be better to measure readiness for independent travel (i.e., knowing where to board the bus or subway, knowing transit schedules or where to get information, counting correct change to purchase tokens, behaving appropriately when awaiting pickup or in transit) rather than documenting who used what modes of transportation at which frequency and at what times. Proficiency in independent transportation usage may be a better measure of program accomplishments than usage per se in times of transit strikes.

Care must be taken in using such surrogate measures, however, as they may mask the failure to provide training that is relevant to the desired skill or behavior.

Determine Data Collection Needs Next, statements of the desired frequency of the measurement of the particular activity are developed. How often the criterion activity is to be measured depends upon management's intended uses of the information. If, for example, a resident satisfaction questionnaire is to be administered prior to resident discharge, management may want to aggregate the information each month for internal monitoring purposes. Other data may be needed on a quarterly, semi-annual, or annual basis. However, by specifying the frequency of measurement in advance, evaluators can efficiently schedule the collection of information, data "bottlenecks" can be avoided, and management's monitoring of the plan is facilitated.

Designate Project Responsibility The importance of designating specific responsibilities for data collection should not be overlooked. Frequently, external evaluators find that when they depend on agency staff to gather information, it is not collected within the specified time period. If agency staff collect the information for external consultants, clearly communicated specification of data collection responsibility can help to avoid misunderstandings and missed deadlines.

Specify Reporting Needs The frequency and types of reports that will be required must be considered. Reports should be issued at a frequency appropriate for their practical use. Therefore, before the evaluation starts, management should decide how the reports will be integrated into the organization's decision-making process. Reports can be issued weekly, monthly, quarterly, semi-annually, or annually. Some reports may be formal documents, while others may be simple memos. Specification of the frequency and types of reports will allow the individuals responsible to plan their workload smoothly and efficiently. It is important to consider the range and form of reports—for instance, reports prepared for board members and administrators should be brief and non-technical, but accurate and specific, in content. Presentations and reports should also demonstrate the potential benefits of the new information for decision making (Windle & Bates, 1974).

Specify Who Will Write the Reports Designation in the evaluation plan of the person responsible for issuing reports is important, because that person may not be the same one collecting the information. This specification minimizes misunderstandings regarding the roles of staff or consultants. In addition, it indicates which individuals must work together to produce evaluation products.

Specify Reporting Schedules Specification of clear deadlines for evaluation reports is necessary to assure accountability and manageability of the evaluation plan.

Specify the Audiences for Reports The specific decision-making groups or committees to whom each report is to be sent for required action must be made clear. This step indicates where in the organizational structure the evaluation results are to be used. Management should take sufficient time to assure that evaluation results will be used in the agency's decision-making processes.

Estimate Resource Requirements Estimation of resources required to complete the evaluation of each objective is critical to proactive evaluation planning. Many evaluations already in progress have been abandoned when management realized the actual costs of evaluation. While evaluations are not necessarily costly, an estimate of costs prior to implementation of the plan should be made. Estimates of staff time involved in gathering and analyzing information, and in writing reports are needed to allow management to decide if the time demands seriously interfere with other duties.

In community residential programs the generalization is often heard that time spent on paperwork is time not available for services to residents. This factor must be kept in mind and weighed in deciding what paperwork is considered essential and the costs and benefits of particular program evaluation strategies.

Conduct a Feasibility Assessment After each element of the plan is developed for each goal and its associated objectives, the plan can be reviewed to determine if the component parts are feasible. To help managers make this feasibility assessment, the following questions can be asked:

1. Is the information needed for a particular aspect of the evaluation obtainable or currently available? (Any agency planning to institute program evaluation activities should develop a list of information and data elements available either at the agency or through other sources [i.e., government programs]. This information inventory can often indicate the availability of information that may preclude the need for new data collection.)

2. Have issues such as confidentiality, reliability of the information, and intrusiveness of the evaluation process been fully discussed between management and the evaluation staff?

3. Are the program objectives sufficiently explicit?

4. Will management authorize the resources necessary to carry the project to completion?

5. Will the results of the evaluation be available at a time appropriate to their use in decision making?

6. Will the results (i.e., reports, memos) be available in a form usable by staff not trained in the special techniques and technologies of the program evaluators?

7. Will agency personnel willingly cooperate with the evaluators to produce the necessary information?

8. Will the information be gathered and displayed in a manner that will allow staff and others to see the evaluation results as credible?

9. Can the evaluation results actually be used to effect changes in agency processes? (Some requirements of funding sources make it difficult to change ways of providing services even if the evaluation results indicated that this might be beneficial. It is appropriate to focus on modifiable program elements).

Consideration of project feasibility is often referred to as evaluability assessment. For further information on useful criteria, see Wholley (1977).

Place Issues of Concern in Order of Priority To place goals and objectives of the evaluation plan in order of priority, the following five areas of inquiry can be addressed:

1. How important is each goal and objective to the agency?

2. Regardless of priority, for which areas is evaluation information needed in order to improve services or accountability?

3. What demands for accountability does the agency face from funding agencies, certification bodies, and citizen or advisory groups that the evaluation can help the agency to address?

4. How much of the agency resources, in terms of budget and personnel time, can realistically be devoted to the evaluation effort?

5. What possible outcomes could result from doing the evaluation?

The first two areas of inquiry imply that the goals being evaluated are important to major policy deliberations. The third area emphasizes that evaluation components should reflect the divergent interests of both internal and external constituencies who are concerned with the agency's performance and policies (Krapfl, 1975; Neufeldt, 1974; Twain, Harlow, & Nerwin, 1970). There must be some payoff for each participant if cooperation is to be assured (Twain et al., 1970). The fourth and fifth focus areas concentrate on the cost, cost-effectiveness, and benefit-cost associated with each evaluation effort. Use of these focus areas should permit management to identify a limited number of projects that will have maximum benefit to the agency. Frequently federal and state certification bodies will demand that a particular program evaluation plan measure the impact or outcome of delivering particular services. The agency with limited resources will want to assure that these concerns are addressed in the plan, while also balancing these areas of focus.

INTERNAL OR EXTERNAL EVALUATION?

Consultants are often called in when management requires technical skills not available within the agency. In the construction of the initial evaluation plan, management may decide to develop its own internal resources, to rely on external resources, or to have a blend of both internal and external program evaluation resources. Building an internal evaluation structure has several long-term advantages. First and foremost is the development of an evaluation staff who over time fully understand the agency's goals, organizational style, structure, strengths, and weaknesses. Once the original investment is made in staff, the products of evaluation can be developed in formats conducive to managerial use, and can be readily altered as these uses change. Finally, an internal technical capacity supports flexibility and responsiveness to crisis situations.

Consultants may have specialized technical knowledge but often do not understand the organizational factors that may affect the agency's receptivity to the evaluation findings. Internal evaluators typically have been found to be as effective as external evaluators (King, 1979). However, in some instances having an outside evaluator has a ceremonial value of greater objectivity. If the outcome to be measured is considered central to management's survival or to a vested interest, then the perceived objectivity of an external evaluator should be seriously weighed as an asset. Likewise, if the project is short-term or requires highly specialized skills, the consultant may be the best or only option.

MANAGEMENT'S USE OF CONSULTANTS

Briefing Prospective Consultants

Rarely does a consultant hired on a short-term basis have full knowledge of an agency's decision-making structure. Therefore, it is management's responsibility to fully explain why a particular study needs to be done, and how the results of the study will be used and/or in-

terpreted both within the agency and by other significant groups (i.e., boards of directors, funding sources, oversight agencies). Consultants must also be apprised of the extent management is willing to allow the evaluation process to intrude upon the normal operations of the agency, the types of resources the agency is willing to provide, and the types of staff resistance that should be expected. Other considerations affecting the consultant's ability to provide acceptable products include the level of reporting dictated by relevant characteristics of internal and external decision-making bodies (i.e., education level, tolerance of lengthy reports) and the importance of adhering to defined timeframes. Management's ability to explicitly communicate these expectations clearly will increase the likelihood of obtaining a useful product from the consultant.

In managing consultation, the two most vital elements are: 1) the consultant's ability to communicate effectively, and 2) the full disclosure and understanding of the resources required to complete the evaluation. Consultants vary in training, skills, preferences for specific theoretical perspectives, and knowledge of developmental disabilities. It is critical that the orientation, abilities, and values of potential consultants be compatible with the program's philosophy and evaluation interests (Budde & Summers, 1983; Neufeldt, 1974).

Budde and Summers (1983) have described evaluation as consisting of four phases: entry, design, service delivery, and feedback. During the entry phase, management presents the general nature of the planned study and obtains initial responses of interest from potential consultants. Management should expect consultants to discuss their knowledge of the program type and its purposes, their philosophical perspective and relevant implications for the nature of services that can be offered, and their degree of familiarity with the technical skills involved in this type of study. The consultant should also be prepared to provide copies of reports from previous studies and to comment on their positive and negative aspects.

This interchange allows the consultant to determine whether she or he can provide the needed services, and enables management to evaluate the consultant's interpersonal style and ability to provide comprehensible reports. Upon selection of a consultant, management can expect to receive a memorandum of agreement or contract for consultative services (Budde & Summers, 1983).

The Final Evaluation Plan

In the second phase of the evaluation design, the consultant will require periodic assistance by management and contact with staff in order to fully assess options for measurement, confirm the adequacy of available documents, and determine the best means by which more information can be gathered. Of special concern in the final evaluation plan are the technical considerations for which the consultant's assistance was sought. Technical aspects may suggest alterations in some, although not necessarily all, of the procedures or objectives selected by management in the construction of its evaluation plan.

The final evaluation plan should be comprehensive in form and should include: 1) a statement of the consultant's abilities, qualifications, and resources, and how these relate to the proposed study, 2) a logical and detailed work plan, 3) a description of the roles and responsibilities of agency staff, the consultant, and consultant staff, 4) costs for the study and the means of cost estimation, 5) the types of analyses to be performed, their limitations, and applicability to the study goals, and 6) assurances that confidentiality of client and program records will be maintained (Budde & Summers, 1983; Morris & Fitz-Gibbons, 1978). Agreement on final content for the evaluation plan is essential to an efficient evaluation process. The following vignette illustrates the importance of the factors discussed in this section.

Vignette

A consultant was asked to develop a new department of program evaluation for a complex mental health/mental retardation residential services agency with federal, state, and county funding sources. When the consultant arrived at the agency, he found that management had previously hired another consultant to "develop evaluation for them." Management knew that they would need an evaluation system because of federal funding requirements. The agency had no previous experience utilizing program evaluation activities and therefore had left it entirely to the original consultant to develop whatever was necessary. A fee had been agreed upon without any plan, specifications of mutual responsibilities, or details of the number or types of reports to be produced. Upon completing his work, the original consultant handed management a report over 300 pages long detailing measurements made to test a theoretical model that was his special expertise. However, the problem areas identified in the report, results, and import had absolutely no impact on any relevant decisions that had to be made by management!

The report was also written in a highly complex, specialized, technical vocabularly that was incomprehensible to anyone not involved with the theoretical system that was studied. Thus, management was already prejudiced against the utility of program evaluation when the second consultant was hired. It was necessary for the second consultant to give management an entirely new perspective on the development of an evaluation blueprint before productive efforts could begin.

Management had not clearly communicated their expectations to the first consultant, who was trained in the theoretical aspects of organizational decision-making but had not worked in the day-to-day environment and was unaware of which decisions were vital to management. The results of this evaluation could not be utilized.

Fortunately, management was flexible and willing to learn; and after a brief period they began to utilize their prerogative to make their needs explicit. The final result was that program evaluation became an integral part of the agency's decision-making structure and was recognized as a valuable tool. Interestingly, when the director of a similar agency asked the director of this agency how useful he found program evaluation to be, the director replied, "It's like air conditioning. Before you had it, you didn't need it. Now you can't understand how you ever did without it."

Management of the Evaluation Process

Management must critically review the final evaluation plan to assure that it is manageable, is within the budget agreed upon, can be used by management in a timely manner, and contains mutually acceptable managerial and consultative responsibilities. Agreement on the final content for the evaluation plan forms the basis for the evaluation contract.

Agency management is responsible for monitoring the evaluation process, assuring staff conformance to their roles, and promoting cooperative activity between staff and the consultant. The third phase of evaluation, service delivery, involves acquiring or developing instruments; training agency or consultant staff in their use; data collection; computerization of data; generation of statistical findings; presentation to management of draft reports; revisions of draft reports; and provision of final reports.

Specific agency staff should be assigned to regularly monitor the evaluation process. Monitoring activities includes attention to unexpected consequences for the organization, adherence to established timeframes, expenditures of resources according to plan, and ensuring that reports are usable (i.e., in terms of length, usage of technical terms, and clarity). Management must also anticipate staff resistance. For instance, staff will often question the motives of management in implementing evaluation. Furthermore, staff assigned to collect information may be uncomfortable with this process, especially if they must monitor the activities of other staff. Evaluation should be presented to staff as a strategy to promote program development and to identify staff development and resource allocation needs, rather than as a vehicle for assigning blame.

PROGRAM ISSUES
AND EVALUATION MEASURES

Beyond the management processes underlying effective evaluation, it is also useful to consider what aspects of programs may be evaluated and related to each other through analysis. Group homes, foster care, and other community living situations are complex settings. While programs may be similar, in that they provide residential care, their specific goals and objectives may vary widely. For example, social integration, enhanced quality of life, improved societal acceptance, and satisfaction with services and setting have been recommended as appropriate goals against which the benefits of community living should be assessed (Emerson, 1985). However, depending on one's perspective, these goals may be considered as part of the process by which other goals (i.e., adaptive, social and vocational development) are pursued. This plausible interplay explains why many evaluation designs include several aspects of programs.

The remainder of this chapter reviews instruments that have been used to measure important features of community-based residential program activity. We have grouped instruments into four broadly defined categories according to whether they assess: 1) developmental progress, 2) environmental adequacy, 3) service adequacy, or 4) organizational performance.

Developmental Progress

Community-based residential programs are generally expected to support the developmental progress of their residents (Conroy, Efthimiou, & Lemanowicz, 1982; Janicki, 1981). There are many ways to evaluate such progress. An evaluation can focus simply on documenting that progress has occurred (providing evidence that, at a minimum, the residence has not had a severe adverse effect). Or evaluations can compare progress obtained among a number of settings, perhaps all operated by a single management team. In the latter instance, one may try to predict the amount of documented progress using other measures (service, climate, staff performance and attitudes, or resident satisfaction) that could reasonably be related to adaptive changes. For example, Seltzer, Sherwood, Seltzer, and Sherwood (1981) have suggested that community adaptation is critical to the evaluation of program performance and is measured most appropriately through assessment of changes in residents' community-living skills, rates and types of behavior problems, and satisfaction with their life-style.

It may be difficult to detect change within a small group of people. Statistical methods for analyzing repeated measures on the same group of people should be chosen. The use of the same assessment tool or instrument at the beginning and end of the evaluation period is especially important. Assessments should be completed independently (i.e., at the second assessment, the rater should not have the results from the first assessment available for reference). Bias, or error of measurement, is an important consideration in repeated measurements. Possible sources of bias include differences in raters, such as tendencies to score items too leniently or too strictly, variation in familiarity with the persons being assessed, and differences in assessment settings (e.g., relating to differences in behavior caused by varying demands of the settings). Rater differences can be controlled in several ways. One is to have two raters independently assess each resident and then have the raters explain and conciliate differences (or average the resulting scores). Other rater biases result when the same persons cannot be made available to perform the second assessment. Even when the same raters are available, their biases may have changed by the time of the second assessment. Detailed training and practice in completing the instrument(s) before both administrations, and exploration of discrepant rating practices, are the most common methods for dealing with staff rater bias. Setting bias is best controlled by using raters who are familiar, and preferably equally familiar, with the resident's behavior in the residential setting. For example, a staff member who has recently begun working in the program should not be used as a rater when more experienced personnel are available.

Adaptive behavior scales are commonly used to address developmental progress (Walls, Werner, Bacon, & Zane, 1977). Because comprehensive adaptive behavior scales are very time-consuming, some brief, potentially useful, measures are shown in Table 1.

Three scales have been used successfully in previous evaluation efforts. These scales are more responsive to adaptive performance than to maladaptation. The short form of the Minnesota Developmental Programming System Behavioral Scales (MDPS–AF—Heiner, 1978; Joiner & Krantz, 1978) and the Behavior Development Survey (BDS—Individual Data Base, 1979) are extracts from longer measures. The MDPS–AF, is an 80-item, 8-domain instrument that provides scores for performance of motoric and instrumental activities of daily living. The BDS is a short research version of the American Association on Mental Deficiency (AAMD) Adaptive Behavior Scale (Nihira, Foster, Shellhaas, & Leland, 1974). It provides information about specific skills and includes five factor scores, which have been widely used

in evaluations of community programs (see Conroy et al., 1982). However, the measurement ceilings on these instruments may be too low for the most able residents. For such persons a more appropriate, albeit a slightly longer, instrument is the Camelot Behavioral Checklist (Foster, 1974).

If maladaptation is an evaluation issue (i.e., one wishes to consider if adaptivity is enhanced and maladaptivity is decreased), useful instruments are the Revised Behavior Problem Checklist (RBPC—Quay & Peterson, 1984), the Devereux Adolescent Behavior Rating Scale (DABRS—Spivack, Haines, & Spotts, 1967), the Revised Behavior Impediments Scale (RBIS—Silverstein, Olvera, Schalock, & Bock, 1984), and the Problem Behavior Scale of the Scales of Independent Behavior (PBS/SIB—Bruininks, Woodcock, Weatherman, & Hill, 1985). Each of these is a relatively brief measure. Comparative data for some of these measures (i.e., the RBPC, the DABRS, and the PBS/SIB) include nondisabled children or adults, as well as developmentally disabled persons and individuals with a psychiatric disability. A wide range of checklists potentially useful in the measurement of problems in interpersonal functioning is reviewed by Achenbach and Edelbrock (1978). Such measures may reflect less overt aspects of maladaptation and may have potential utility in assessment of persons who have developmental disabilities and are comparatively able, but who experience social skill problems.

Checklists of maladaptive behaviors generally show lower reliabilities than do adaptive measures. Although adequate reliabilities have been reported for the more recently developed scales, cautious interpretation of changes in maladaptation ratings is warranted. With either type of checklist, changes in performance are measured by using scale scores, factor scores, or total scores. Over short timeframes, (3-month to 1-year), measurement sensitivity may be enhanced by considering the number of individual items on which improvement is noted, and by analyzing which factors or scales are associated with these items. Over time, there may also be a tendency for persons with extremely high or low scores to approach the

Table 1. Measures of adaptive and maladaptive behavior

Authors	Name of measure	Scales/factors
Heiner (1978); Joiner & Krantz (1978)	Minnesota Developmental Programming System Behavioral Scales–Abbreviated Form (MDPS–AF)	1. Gross motor 2. Eating 3. Toileting 4. Dressing/grooming 5. Communication 6. Reading/writing 7. Quantitative 8. Independent living
Individual Data Base (1979)	Behavior Development Survey (BDS)	1. Personal self-sufficiency 2. Community self-sufficiency 3. Personal-social responsibility 4. Social adaptation 5. Personal adaptation
Foster (1974)	Camelot Behavioral Checklist (CBC)	1. Self-help 2. Physical development 3. Vocational 4. Numerical 5. Communication
Quay & Peterson (1984)	Revised Behavior Problem Checklist (RBPC)	1. Conduct disorder 2. Socialized aggression 3. Attention problems—immaturity 4. Anxiety—withdrawal 5. Psychotic behavior 6. Motor tension excess
Spivack, Haines, & Spotts (1967)	Devereux Adolescent Behavior Rating Scale (DABRS)	1. Defiant—resistive behavior 2. Domineering—sadistic behavior 3. High need for approval 4. Inability to delay gratification 5. Bizarre behavior
Silverstein, Olvera, Schalock, & Bock (1984)	Revised Behavior Impediments Scale (RBIS)	1. Twenty-four behaviors graded by degree of severity and frequency
Bruininks, Woodcock, Weatherman, & Hill (1985)	Scales of Independent Behavior–Problem Behavior Scale (SIB/PBS)	1. General maladaptive behavior 2. Internalized maladaptive behavior 3. Asocial maladaptive behavior 4. Externalized maladaptive behavior

group average. For this reason, unless objective data are collected as part of the evaluation of individual treatment interventions, data are best analyzed on a group basis; claims of change based on information about only the most problematic persons may overstate benefits in improvement of behavior or social competence.

Developmental progress may be reflected not only in changes in the skills displayed (and documented in a scale) but also in the range of community-integrated activities in which residents participate. One means of assessing socially integrative activities is the Rehabilitation Indicators (Brown, Diller, Fordyce, Jacobs, & Gordon, 1980), a measure that contains items descriptive of the extent and type of residents' community experiences. Other methods for measuring community integration have been provided by Crapps, Langone, and Swaim (1985) and Gothelf (1985). Also related to social integrative opportunities is the extent of disabled persons' satisfaction with their living situation and social life (Burchard, Pine, Gordon, & Widrick, 1983). Measures completed in individual interviews have been used to assess satisfaction with the programs and their services (see Heal & Chadsey-Rusch, 1985; Seltzer, 1981). However, interview mesaures must be applied with care; persons with mental retardation tend to answer yes to yes/no interview questions (Sigelman, Budd, Spanhel, & Schoenrock, 1981). Consequently, one interview schedule, the Lifestyle Satisfaction Scale (Heal & Chadsey-Rusch, 1985), includes items to control for inordinate acquiescence.

Environmental Adequacy

The environmental adequacy of a program is a critical concern in many evaluations (Eyman, Silverstein, & Miller, 1977; Intagliata & Willer, 1982; Wandersman & Moos, 1981). *Environment* in this context refers not only to the physical setting but also to the program's climate. *Climate* is usually defined by the typical interaction patterns between staff, residents, neighbors, and friends, including daily rhythms of interaction, as well as by any physical aspects of the program that may affect opportunities for interpersonal behavior. In addition, the extent to which interaction reflects consideration of residents as individuals with varying needs and preferences is thought to be critical to a setting's capability to promote social adaptation. Social interaction may be measured through observation of exchanges between staff and residents (Ittelson, Rivlin, & Proshansky, 1976; Jones, Risley, & Favell, 1983; Landesman-Dwyer, Stein, & Sackett, 1978; Romer & Heller, 1984). However, this approach can be technically difficult to carry

out, data collection can be time-consuming, and data analysis can be costly. Several brief instruments have been developed to describe social climate and are described in Table 2.

Moos and Lemke (1980) developed the Multiphasic Environmental Assessment Procedure (MEAP) to assess sheltered care settings for older persons with regard to physical, programmatic, resource, and social climate features. Consisting of several separate checklists, this instrument provides a comprehensive picture of important environmental sources of support and constraint for residents. As noted by Wandersman and Moos (1981), although the measures were not developed for application in settings for persons with developmental disabilities, there are similarities among community settings and environmental concerns that justify their use. An earlier measure, the Community-Oriented Program Environment Scales (COPES), described by Moos (1972) and Insell and Moos (1974), remains pertinent to the assessment of program climate.

The Group Home Management Schedule (GHMS—Pratt, Luszcz, & Brown, 1980; Zigman & Silverman, 1982) is a brief instrument assessing whether daily routines differ from day to day and among residents, whether residents take part in activities as a group or individually, whether friends of staff or relatives and friends of residents participate in activities in the home, and whether staff act toward residents in ways that emphasize disablement or individuality. The Characteristics of the Treatment Environment (CTE—Jackson, 1969) assessment is a somewhat longer instrument that measures whether staff promote independence in residents' decision making, whether residents have meaningful daily schedules of activity, and whether opportunities for both self-expression and maximal freedom of movement are provided. Either of these instruments can be completed by a group home manager in an hour or less.

The Program Analysis of Service Systems 3 (PASS 3—Wolfensberger & Glenn, 1975) is a more elaborate instrument for assessing: 1) age-appropriateness of activities, physical setting, program rules and services, individualization, and use of generic resources; 2) propriety of

Table 2. Measures of environment and climate

Authors	Name of measure and no. items	Scales/factors
Moos & Lemke (1980)	Multiphasic Environmental Assessment Procedure (MEAP)—35 dimensions	1. Physical and architectural resources 2. Policy and program resources 3. Resident and staff resources 4. Social climate resources
Pratt, Luszcz, & Brown (1980)	Group Home Management Schedule (GHMS)—37 items	1. Rigidity of routine 2. Block treatment 3. Depersonalization 4. Social distance
Jackson (1969)	Characteristics of the Treatment Environment (CTE)—72 items	1. Autonomy 2. Activity
Wolfensberger & Glenn (1975)	Program Analysis of Service Systems 3 (PASS 3)—50 items	1. Normalization—program 2. Normalization—setting 3. Administration 4. Proximity and access

physical and design aspects of the program; 3) management control practices, staff development initiatives, and evaluation practices; and 4) general features of location and accessibility to physical and cultural resources. PASS 3 uses a complex set of ratings; a PASS review may require several days to complete. A short form of PASS is available that may be completed in a single day (Flynn, 1980). Regardless of which version is used, raters require formal training in order to accurately complete a review. Many developmental disabilities professionals have received such training and are likely to be available locally.

Studies linking variation in ongoing interaction patterns to scores on these measurement instruments have not been conducted, although relationships to changes in adaptive behavior over time have been found (Eyman, Demaine, & Lei, 1979). Furthermore, these instruments have not been normed, and they are most useful in comparing two or more living settings, or living units within a larger facility, or, if applied repeatedly in the same setting, to ascertain whether changes in social climate have occurred. These scales, moreover, may not reflect service provision or clinical practices on-site

(Jacobson, Silver, & Schwartz, 1984). Although most evaluative studies measuring program climate have assumed this to be a fairly stable characteristic (and thus have measured climate only at the beginning of an evaluation period), a complete evaluation plan would include a measure of climate at both the beginning and end of the evaluation period. This procedure assures the ability to document possible shifts in climate.

Service Adequacy

The specificity, individuality, and adequacy of the services and interventions developed, provided, or monitored by professionals are critical distinctions between a custodial, a maintaining, and an habilitative setting (Bjannes & Butler, 1974). Inevitably, small residential providers must draw upon other providers in order to acquire the full range of services residents require (see Donnellan, LaVigna, Zambito, & Thvedt, 1985). Unfortunately, it appears that problems with access to such services persist (Close, O'Connor, & Peterson, 1981). Then, too, research on clinical service practices in community living settings has often addressed the behavioral and physical care needs of residents rather than the professional practices associated with these needs (cf, Crawford, Thompson & Aiello, 1981).

Measures of service adequacy should reflect the outcomes of periodic resident reviews and could include: 1) frequency of instances of services received by each resident, by discipline, and the sources of these services with special attention to the types of resources drawn from other agencies; 2) conformance of individualized program plan content with standards for specification of goals (for example, using the Goal Activity Program Analysis—Living Alternatives Research Project, 1982); 3) individualization in goal plan content (for example, using the Tennessee Goal Domain Dictionary—Tennessee Department of Mental Health and Mental Retardation, 1980); and 4) met and unmet needs for resident training, experience, and integration (i.e., determination of clinical consultation and social integration needs).

Few benchmarks and basic principles for clinical practice or organization of service provision have been objectively tested. Thus, there are few verified measures of clinical service quality, notwithstanding the accreditation standards of public agencies and national organizations. However, in general, it is reasonable to assume that a program should seek to both enhance residents' competencies and to ameliorate maladaptations. Because maladaptation is of great concern to most clinicians and managers, evaluations could focus on the extent to which services are disproportionately directed to controlling resident behavior rather than to promoting increased ability. A likely source of information is the content of the individual program plan. Although the accomplishment of goals is one measure of program effectiveness, this strategy requires either use of a uniform goal sequence or some means of scaling goal difficulty (see Cytrynbaum, Ginath, Birdwell, & Brandt, 1979; Schalock, 1984).

Organizational Performance

Organizational Dynamics Little research has been reported on the impact of management's performance upon programmatic attainments in small community program settings. There is, however, some evidence that less bureaucratic organizational structures promote more positive resident outcomes (King, Houghland, Shepard, & Gallagher, 1980). Organizational analyses have focused on bureaucracies in the development and testing of models of structure (see Holland, 1973; Inkson, Pugh, & Hickson, 1970; Perrow, 1967; Pugh et al., 1963) and of effectiveness (Hrebiniak & Alutto, 1973; Pennings, 1975; Steers, 1975).

In any community residential setting, and particularly within a multisite agency, it is appropriate to consider organizational structure and processes. Relevant issues include whether the typical span of control is desirable, whether lines of authority are distinct, whether management personnel are consistently or proportionately dedicated to certain sites, whether communication lines are direct or intact, and whether a middle-management capability exists that can deal with agency expansion. These issues are more appropriately addressed with a management consultant, given the inherent conflict-of-interest for the manager.

Employee-Oriented Measures It is also appropriate to focus on the individual workers in the program, because effectiveness is dependent upon the relatively few staff in the small work-group environment and their competencies (Sulzer-Azaroff, Thaw, & Thomas, 1974). Cherniss (1981) has presented an organizational model that relates workers' roles (job design, role strain), the setting's power structure, job satisfaction, motivation, and attitudes toward residents. A number of instruments have been developed to address these issues (see Table 3), all of which are usable in group homes and similar staffed settings. These instruments can usually be completed in a few minutes by staff. Because of their brevity, it is possible to use all of these measures in a single group home in order to develop a comprehensive picture of the management situation, and to have them completed by all staff who work in a home.

Other facets of organizational activity that can be evaluated are information from exit interviews of staff, reports of burnout by staff or managers, work-oriented stress measures, and patterns of work activity.

Benefit-Cost and Cost-Effectiveness Most human service programs, including resi-

Table 3. Organizational measures

Authors	Name of measure	Scales/factors
Smith, Kendall, & Hulin (1969)	Job Descriptive Index	Job Satisfaction 1. With work 2. With supervision 3. With pay 4. With promotion 5. With coworkers
Bensberg & Barnett (1966); Living Alternatives Research Project (1980)	Attendant Opinion Scale/Personnel Opinion Scale	1. Job dissatisfaction 2. Job insecurity 3. Encourage verbalization 4. Irritability 5. Equality 6. Fostering dependency
Hackman & Oldham (1974)	Job Diagnostic Survey	1. Skill variety 2. Task identity 3. Task significance 4. Autonomy 5. Feedback
Tannenbaum (1968)	Employee Influence Schedule	Decision-making practices 1. Participation 2. Centralization
Halpin & Winer (1957)	Leadership Behavior Description Questionnaire	1. Initiation 2. Consideration
Kerr & Jermier (1978)	Measurement of Substitutes for Leadership	Provisions for management continuity/consistency

dential programs, must attend to benefit-cost and cost-effectiveness issues. These two analytic approaches have been comprehensively described in nontechnical terms by Yates (1985). Benefit-cost addresses the ratio between revenues realized versus costs to acquire these revenues. For such analyses, all aspects of the program's outcomes must be quantified in terms of dollar value. Setting dollar values can be difficult because treatment benefits that do not result in wage-earning by residents are not translated easily into monetary terms. Further, in for-profit settings, one may compare income to costs; in non-profit settings, costs may rise to meet revenues (or may exceed revenues under certain payment methods). These factors make benefit-cost analyses in small community residential settings of potentially less interest than cost-effectiveness analyses.

In cost-effectiveness analysis it is necessary to determine how effectiveness will be measured; multiple quantitative measures (for example, of resident groupings, goals achieved,

integrative activities provided) are usually required. However, these measures are needed for any formal evaluation, and only the issue of cost ascertainment is truly new here. Costs, for example, may be specified with respect to certain outcomes (i.e., costs for staff or consultants to provide care and treatment) or with respect to general costs supporting the capability to provide services. A number of different models for cost classification and tracking have been provided for residential programs. The assumptions made in tracking costs and grouping them can greatly affect the accuracy of the analyses, and even whether the conclusions are acceptable. For these reasons cost-related analyses should not be undertaken without familiarity with previous work on this topic (see Ashbaugh, 1984; Intagliata, Willer, & Cooley, 1979; Murphy & Datel, 1976; Neenan, 1974; Nihira, 1979; Schalock, 1984; Schalock & Thornton, 1984; Templeman, Gage, & Fredericks, 1980; Yates, 1985). In general, the accuracy of cost-effectiveness analysis and findings will mirror the precision of agency accounting procedures.

SUMMARY

Program evaluation is intended to provide management with timely data in a form that can facilitate sound decision making. Program evaluation is a management tool. Utilization of program evaluation results demonstrates management's willingness to examine critically agency practices and exert effort to improve practices.

The core of a strong, sound program evaluation system is a management blueprint or plan that spells out, in detail, the purposes, methods, and results of evaluation activities. The evaluation plan must be assessed for feasibility and need for external assistance. The development of an internal evaluation capability that is responsive to management's needs and promotes flexibility in performance is an organizational asset. When an internal evaluation capability cannot be developed, the selection of an appropriate, knowledgeable consultant will often be a necessity. The consultant's introduction to the agency and to its evaluation needs, his or her cooperative efforts with other staff, and the

development of acceptable products must be actively managed.

Similarly, the quality of continuing program evaluation efforts and staff participation in this process cannot be taken for granted, once set into motion. At each step in evaluation, from initial conception, to assessment of feasibility, propriety, and benefit, to final design and implementation, direction from management constitutes a critical influence contributing to long-term utility.

Program evaluation efforts should be based, at least in part, on measures that have demonstrated value and credibility, and should be integrated into operations in a manner that least disrupts the completion of assigned duties.

Because of increasing emphasis on accountability throughout human services, and because of finite resources accessible to management in most community program settings, expertise in resource allocation constitutes an essential component of effective evaluation management. In turn, improved capability to demonstrate accountability for program benefits and implementation provides an important support to the acceptability of the program to concerned constituencies.

REFERENCES

Achenbach, T.M., & Edelbrock, C.S. (1978). The classification of child psychopathology: A review and analysis of empirical efforts. *Psychological Bulletin, 35,* 1275–1301.

Ashbaugh, J. (1984). *Comparative analysis of the costs of residential, day, and related programs within institutional and community program settings* (Final Report). Boston: Human Services Research Institute.

Bensberg, G.J., & Barnett, C.D. (1966). *Attendant training in southern residential facilities for the mentally retarded: Report of the SREB attendant training project.* Atlanta: Southern Regional Education Board.

Bjannes, A.T., & Butler, E.W. (1974). Environmental variation in community care facilities for mentally retarded persons. *American Journal of Mental Deficiency, 78,* 429–439.

Bogdan, R.C., & Biklen, S.K. (1982). *Qualitative research for education: An introduction to theory and methods.* Newton, MA: Allyn & Bacon.

Brown, M., Diller, L., Fordyce, W., Jacobs, D., & Gordon, W. (1980). Rehabilitation indicators: Their nature and uses for assessment. In B. Bolton & D.W. Cook (Eds.), *Rehabilitation client assessment* (pp. 102–117). Baltimore: University Park Press.

Bruininks, R.H., Woodcock, R.W., Weatherman, R.F., & Hill, B.K. (1985). *Development and standardization of*

the Scales of Independent Behavior, Allen, TX: DLM Teaching Resources.

Budde, J.F., & Summers, J.A. (1983). Consultation and technical assistance. In J.L. Matson & J.A. Mulick (Eds.), *Handbook of mental retardation* (pp. 381–394), New York: Pergamon Press.

Burchard, S., Pine, J., Gordon, L., & Widrick, G. (1983, October). *Manager competence and program quality of community residential programs.* Paper presented at the 13th Annual Conference of Region X, American Association on Mental Deficiency, Portland, ME.

Campbell, D., & Stanley, J. (1963). *Experimental and quasi-experimental designs for research.* Chicago: Rand McNally.

Cherniss, C. (1981). Organizational design and the social environment in group homes for mentally retarded persons. In H.C. Haywood & J.R. Newbrough (Eds.), *Living environments for developmentally retarded persons* (pp. 103–123). Baltimore: University Park Press.

Close, D.W., O'Connor, G.O., & Peterson, S.L. (1981). Utilization of habilitation services by developmentally disabled persons in community residential facilities. In H.C. Haywood & J.R. Newbrough (Eds.), *Living environments for developmentally retarded persons* (pp. 155–167). Baltimore: University Park Press.

Conroy, J., Efthimiou, J., & Lemanowicz, J. (1982). A

matched comparison of the developmental growth of institutionalized and deinstitutionalized mentally retarded clients. *American Journal of Mental Deficiency, 86,* 581–587.

Cook, T., & Campbell, D.T. (1979). *Quasi-experimentation: Design and analysis issues in field settings.* Boston: Houghton Mifflin.

Crapps, J.M., Langone, J., & Swaim, S. (1985). Quantity and quality of participation in community environments by mentally retarded adults. *Education and Training of the Mentally Retarded, 20,* 123–129.

Crawford, J.L., Thompson, D.E., & Aiello, J.R. (1981). Community placement of mentally retarded persons: Clinical and environmental considerations. In H.C. Haywood & J.R. Newbrough (Eds.), *Living environments for developmentally retarded persons* (pp. 169–194). Baltimore: University Park Press.

Crnic, K.A., Friedrich, W.N., & Greenberg, M.T. (1983). Adaptation of families with mentally retarded children: A model of stress, coping, and family ecology. *American Journal of Mental Deficiency, 88,* 125–138.

Cytrynbaum, S., Ginath, Y., Birdwell, J., & Brandt, L. (1979). Goal attainment scaling: A critical review. *Evaluation Quarterly, 3,* 5–40.

Delbecq, A.L., & VandeVen, A.H. (1971). A group process model for problem identification and program planning. *Journal of Applied Behavioral Science, 7,* 466–492.

Donnellan, A.M., LaVigna, G.W., Zambito, J., & Thvedt, J. (1985). A time-limited intensive intervention program model to support community placement for persons with severe behavior problems. *Journal of the Association for Persons with Severe Handicaps, 10,* 123–131.

Emerson, E.B. (1985). Evaluating the impact of deinstitutionalization on the lives of mentally retarded people. *American Journal of Mental Deficiency, 90,* 277–288.

Eyman, R.K., Demaine, G.C., & Lei, T. (1979). Relationship between community environments and resident changes in adaptive behavior. A path model. *American Journal of Mental Deficiency, 83,* 330–338.

Eyman, R.K., Silverstein, A.B., & Miller, C. (1977). Effects of residential settings on development. In P. Mittler & J. deJong (Eds.), *Research to practice in mental retardation: Care and intervention* (pp. 305–314), Baltimore: University Park Press.

Flynn, R.J. (1980). Normalization, PASS, and service quality assessment: How normalizing are current human services? In R.J. Flynn & K.E. Nitsch (Eds.), *Normalization, social integration, and community services* (pp. 323–359). Baltimore: University Park Press.

Foster, R.W. (1974). *Camelot Behavioral Checklist manual,* Lawrence, KS: Camelot Behavior Systems.

Gothelf, C.R. (1985). Variations in resource provision for community residences serving persons with developmental disabilities. *Education and Training of the Mentally Retarded, 20,* 130–138.

Guba, E.G., & Lincoln, Y.S. (1981). *Effective evaluation.* San Francisco: Jossey-Bass.

Hackman, J.R., & Oldham, G.R. (1974). *The Job Diagnostic Survey: An instrument for the diagnosis of jobs and the evaluation of job redesign projects* (Tech. Rept. 4). New Haven: Yale University Department of Administrative Studies.

Halpin, A.W., & Winer, B.J. (1957). A factorial study of the leader behavior descriptions. In R.M. Stodgill & A.E. Coons (Eds.), *Leader behavior: Its description and*

measurement. Columbus, OH: Ohio State University Bureau of Business Research.

Hawkins, R.P., Fremouw, W.J., & Reitz, A.L. (1981). A model for use in designing or describing evaluations of mental health or educational intervention programs. *Behavioral Assessment, 3,* 307–324.

Heal, L.W., & Chadsey-Rusch, J. (1985). The Lifestyle Satisfaction Scale (LSS): Assessing individuals' satisfaction with residence, community setting, and associated services. *Applied Research in Mental Retardation, 6,* 475–490.

Heiner, K. (1978, September). *Item selection and the development of a management information data base.* Paper presented at the 86th Annual Convention of the American Psychological Association, Toronto.

Holland, T.P. (1973). Organizational structure and institutional care. *Journal of Health and Social Behavior, 14,* 241–251.

Hrebiniak, L.G., & Alutto, J.A. (1973). A comparative organizational study of performance and size correlates in inpatient psychiatric departments. *Administrative Science Quarterly, 18,* 365–382.

Individual Data Base. (1979). *Behavior Development Survey user's manual,* Pomona, CA: UCLA Neuropsychiatric Institute Research Group at Lanterman State Hospital.

Inkson, J.H.K., Pugh, D.S., & Hickson, D.J. (1970). Organizational context and structure: An abbreviated replication. *Administrative Science Quarterly, 15,* 318–329.

Insell, P.M., & Moos, R.H. (1974). Psychological environments: Expanding the scope of human ecology. *American Psychologist, 29,* 179–188.

Intagliata, J., & Willer, B. (1982). Reinstitutionalization of mentally retarded persons successfully placed into family-care and group homes. *American Journal of Mental Deficiency, 87,* 34–39.

Intagliata, J., Willer, B., & Cooley, F. (1979). Cost comparison of institutional and community-based alternatives for mentally retarded persons. *Mental Retardation, 17,* 154–156.

Ittelson, W.H., Rivlin, L.G., & Proshansky, H.M. (1976). The use of behavioral maps in environmental psychology. In H.M. Proshansky, W.H. Ittelson, & L.G. Rivlin (Eds.), *Environmental psychology: People and their settings* (pp. 340–351). New York: Holt, Rinehart & Winston.

Jackson, J. (1969). Factors in the treatment environment. *Archives of General Psychiatry, 21,* 39–45.

Jacobson, J.W., & Schwartz, A.A. (1983). The evaluation of community living alternatives for developmentally disabled persons. In J.L. Matson & J.A. Mulick (Eds.), *Handbook of mental retardation* (pp. 39–66). New York: Pergamon Press.

Jacobson, J.W., Silver, E.J., & Schwartz, A.A. (1984). Service provision in New York's group homes. *Mental Retardation, 22,* 231–239.

Janicki, M.P. (1981). Personal growth and community residence environments: A review. In H.C. Haywood & J.R. Newbrough (Eds.), *Living environments for developmentally retarded persons* (pp. 59–101). Baltimore: University Park Press.

Joiner, L.M., & Krantz, G.C. (1978) (Eds.), *Assessment of behavioral competence of developmentally disabled individuals: The MDPS.* Minneapolis: University of Minnesota.

Jones, M.L., Risley, T.R., & Favell, J.E. (1983). Ecological patterns. In J.L. Matson & S.E. Breuning (Eds.), *Assessing the mentally retarded* (pp. 311–334). New York: Grune & Stratton.

Kerr, S., & Jermier, J. (1978). Substitutes for leadership: Their meaning and measurement. *Organizational Behavior and Human Performance, 22,* 375–403.

King, K.P. (1979). Internal versus external evaluation: Consequences and implications. *Ripple, 16,* 6–10.

King, R.D., Houghland, J.G., Shepard, J.M., & Gallagher, E.B. (1980). Organizational effects on mentally retarded adults: A longitudinal analysis. *Evaluation & the Health Professions, 3,* 85–101.

Krapfl, J.E. (1975). Accountability for behavioral engineers. In W.S. Wood (Ed.), *Issues in evaluating behavior modification* (pp. 219–236). Champaign, IL: Research Press.

Landesman-Dwyer, S., Stein, J., & Sackett, G.P. (1978). A behavioral and ecological study of group homes. In G.P. Sackett (Ed.), *Observing behavior (Vol. 1): Theory and applications in mental retardation* (pp. 349–378). Baltimore: University Park Press.

Living Alternatives Research Project. (1980). *The identification and description of environmental conditions affecting growth in personal competence of persons with developmental disabilities: Phase One* (Final Report). Staten Island, NY: NYS Institute for Basic Research in Developmental Disabilities.

Living Alternatives Research Project. (1982). *Goal plans of severely and profoundly disabled persons* (Brief Rept. 82-2). Staten Island, NY: NYS Institute for Basic Research in Developmental Disabilities.

Moos, R. (1972). Assessment of the psychosocial environments of community-oriented psychiatric treatment programs. *Journal of Abnormal Psychology, 79,* 9–18.

Moos, R., & Lemke, S. (1980). Assessing the physical and architectural features of sheltered care settings. *Journal of Gerontology, 35,* 571–583.

Morris, L.L., & Fitz-Gibbons, C.T. (1978). *How to measure program implementation.* Beverly Hills: Sage Publications.

Murphy, J.G., & Datel, W.E. (1976). A cost-benefit analysis of community versus institutional living. *Hospital and Community Psychiatry, 27,* 165–170.

Neenan, W.B. (1974). Benefit-cost analysis and the evaluation of mental retardation programs. In P.O. Davidson, F.W. Clark, & L.A. Hamerlynck (Eds.), *Evaluation of behavioral programs* (pp. 175–200). Champaign, IL: Research Press.

Neufeldt, A.H. (1974). Considerations in the implementation of program evaluation. In P.O. Davidson, F.W. Clark, & L.A. Hamerlynck (Eds.), *Evaluation of behavioral programs* (pp. 65–82). Champaign, IL: Research Press.

Nihira, K., Foster, R., Shellhaas, M., & Leland, H. (1974). *A.A.M.D. Adaptive Behavior Scale, 1974 revision,* Washington, DC: American Association on Mental Deficiency.

Nihira, L. (1979). *Costs for care for matched developmentally disabled clients in three settings* (Report), Pomona, CA: UCLA Neuropsychiatric Institute Research Group at Lanterman State Hospital.

Pennings, J.M. (1975). The relevance of the structural contingency model for organizational effectiveness. *Administrative Science Quarterly, 20,* 393–410.

Perrow, C. (1967). A framework for the comparative analysis of organizations. *American Sociological Review, 32,* 194–208.

Pratt, M.W., Luszcz, M.A., & Brown, M.E. (1980). Measuring dimensions of the quality of care in small community residences. *American Journal of Mental Deficiency, 85,* 188–194.

Pugh, D.S., Hickson, D.J., Hinings, C.R., MacDonald, K.M., Turner, C., & Lupton, T. (1963). A conceptual scheme for organizational analysis. *Administrative Science Quarterly, 8,* 289–315.

Quay, H.C., & Peterson, D.R. (1984). *Revised Problem Behavior Checklist.* Coral Gables, FL: University of Miami.

Romer, D., & Heller, T. (1984). Importance of peer relations in community settings for mentally retarded adults. In J.M. Berg (Ed.), *Perspectives and progress in mental retardation (Vol. 1): Social, psychological, and educational aspects* (pp. 99–107). Baltimore: University Park Press.

Rossi, P.H., & Freeman, H.E. (1982). *Evaluation: A systematic approach.* Beverly Hills: Sage Publications.

Schalock, R.L. (1983). *Services for developmentally disabled adults: Development, implementation, and evaluation.* Baltimore: University Park Press.

Schalock, R.L. (1984, May). *The cost of care and training within facilities for the developmentally disabled.* Paper presented at the 108th Annual Convention of the American Association on Mental Deficiency, Minneapolis.

Schalock, R.L., & Thornton, C.V.D. (1984, May). *Benefit-cost analysis and program evaluation.* Paper presented at the 108th Annual Convention of the American Association on Mental Deficiency, Minneapolis.

Seltzer, G. (1981). Community residential adjustment: The relationship among environment, performance, and satisfaction. *American Journal of Mental Deficiency, 85,* 624–630.

Seltzer, M.M., Sherwood, C.C., Seltzer, G.B., & Sherwood, S. (1981). Community adaptation and the impact of deinstitutionalization. In R.H. Bruininks, C.E. Meyers, B.B. Sigford, & K.C. Lakin (Eds.), *Deinstitutionalization and community adjustment of mentally retarded people* (pp. 82–88). Washington, DC: American Association on Mental Deficiency.

Sigelman, C.K., Budd, E.C., Spanhel, C.L., & Schoenrock, C.J. (1981). When in doubt, say yes: Acquiescence in interviews with mentally retarded persons. *Mental Retardation, 19,* 53–58.

Silverstein, B., Olvera, D., Schalock, R., & Bock, W.B. (1984, May). *Allocating direct care resources for treatment of maladaptive behavior: The Staff Intensity Scale.* Paper presented at the 108th Annual Convention of the American Association on Mental Deficiency, Minneapolis.

Smith, P.C., Kendall, L.M., & Hulin, C.L. (1969). *The measurement of satisfaction in work and retirement.* Chicago: Rand McNally.

Spivack, A., Haines, P.E., & Spotts, J. (1967). *Devereux Adolescent Behavior Rating Scale manual.* Devon, PA: Devereux Foundation.

Steers, R.M. (1975). Problems in the measurement of organizational effectiveness. *Administrative Science Quarterly, 20,* 546–558.

Sulzer-Azaroff, B., Thaw, J., & Thomas, C. (1974). Behavioral competencies for the evaluation of behavior modifiers. In W.S. Wood (Ed.), *Issues in evaluating behavior modification* (pp. 47–98). Champaign, IL: University Park Press.

Tannenbaum, A.S. (1968). *Control in organizations,* New York: McGraw-Hill.

Templeman, D., Gage, M., & Fredericks, H. (1980). Cost effectiveness of the group home. *Journal of the Association for the Severely Handicapped, 6,* 11–16.

Tennessee Department of Mental Health and Mental Retardation. (1980). *Tennessee Goal Domain Dictionary.* Nashville: Author.

Twain, D., Harlow, E., & Nerwin, D. (1970). *Research and human services: A guide to collaboration for program development.* New York: New York Research and Development Center, Jewish Board of Guardians.

Walls, R.T., Werner, T.J., Bacon, A., & Zane, T. (1977). Behavior checklists. In J.D. Cone & R.P. Hawkins (Eds.), *Behavioral assessment: New directions in clinical psychology* (pp. 77–146). New York: Brunner/Mazel.

Wandersman, A., & Moos, R.H. (1981). Assessing and evaluating residential environments: A sheltered living environments model. *Environment and Behavior, 13,* 481–508.

Wholley, J.S. (1977). Evaluability assessment. In L. Rutman (Ed.), *Evaluation research methods: A basic guide* (pp. 41–56). Beverly Hills: Sage Publications.

Williamson, J.W. (1978). Formulating priorities for quality assurance activity: Description of a method and its application. *Journal of the American Medical Association, 239,* 631–637.

Williamson, J.W., Braswell, H.K., Horn, S.D., & Lohmeyer, S. (1978). Priority setting in quality assurance: Reliability of staff judgements in medical institutions. *Medical Care, 16,* 931–940.

Windle, C., & Bates, P. (1974). Evaluating program evaluation. A suggested approach. In P.O. Davidson, F.W. Clark, & L.A. Hamerlynck (Eds.), *Evaluation of behavioral programs* (pp. 395–435). Champaign, IL: Research Press.

Wolfensberger, W., & Glenn, L. (1975). *PASS 3: A method for the quantitative assessment of human services.* Toronto: National Institute on Mental Retardation.

Yates, B.T. (1985). Cost-effectiveness analysis and cost-benefit analysis: An introduction. *Behavioral Assessment, 7,* 207–234.

Zigman, W.B., & Silverman, W.P. (1982). *Socio-environmental characteristics of community residential environments* (Tech. Rept. 82-7), Staten Island, NY: NYS Institute for Basic Research in Developmental Disabilities.

SUPPLEMENTARY RESOURCES

On technical issues that affect the credibility of evaluations:

Campbell, D., & Stanley, J. (1963). *Experimental and quasi-experimental designs for research.* Chicago: Rand McNally.

Cook, T., & Campbell, D.T. (1979). *Quasi-experimentation: Design and analysis issues in field settings.* Boston: Houghton Mifflin.

Hawkins, R.P., Fremouw, W.J., & Reitz, A.L. (1981). A model for use in designing or describing evaluations of mental health or educational intervention programs. *Behavioral Assessment, 3,* 307–324.

Jacobson, J.W., & Schwartz, A.A. (1983). The evaluation of community living alternatives for developmentally disabled persons. In J.L. Matson & J.A. Mulick (Eds.), *Handbook of mental retardation* (pp. 39–66). New York: Pergamon Press.

Schalock, R.L. (1983). *Services for developmentally disabled adults: Development, implementation, and evaluation.* Baltimore: University Park Press.

On information relevant to foster care and family living service models:

Crnic, K.A., Friedrich, W.N., & Greenberg, M.T. (1983). Adaptation of families with mentally retarded children: A model of stress, coping, and family ecology. *American Journal of Medical Deficiency, 88,* 125–138.

Gray, S.W., & Wandersman, L.P. (1980). The methodology of home-based intervention studies: Problems and promising strategies. *Child Development, 51,* 993–1009.

Nihira, K., Meyers, C.E., & Mink, I.T. (1980). Home environment, family adjustment, and the development of mentally retarded children. *Applied Research in Mental Retardation, 1,* 5–24.

Sherman, S.R., Frenkel, E.R., & Newman, E.S. (1984). Foster family care for older persons who are mentally retarded. *Mental Retardation, 22,* 302–308.

Section III

OPERATING A HIGH-QUALITY PROGRAM

Chapter 8

Preventing "Institutionalization" in the Community

Sharon Landesman

The community movement has not been immune from the process by which a setting actively or passively adopts the depersonalized or regimented practices that have been associated with negative consequences in large public residential institutions. This chapter addresses how to prevent "institutionalization" from occurring in the community. Four broad categories of functional features that can influence the nature of a residential setting are examined: administrative organization, social interaction of staff and residents, resource utilization, and relationships with others outside the residence. The chapter then explores three broad issues that become involved when quality of care declines (difficulties in long-term operation of a facility, inadequate self-evaluation, and loss of self-direction), and three ways residences can avoid suboptimal care (self-appraisal, the coupling of functional objectives with structural regulations, and cross-residence staff interaction).

The past 15 years have given this author the opportunity to conduct a series of in-depth field studies of residential facilities that serve individuals with mental retardation. A primary thrust of this research was to compare traditional and new or remodeled institutions to the broad spectrum of community residential facilities, including group homes, general board-and-care facilities, halfway houses, nursing homes, model training programs, intensive behavioral treatment centers, and foster care homes. Many of these studies were conducted collaboratively with Washington State's Department of Social and Health Services, and often were designed to answer specific questions about residents' service needs or the effectiveness of alternative residential programs (e.g., Landesman, 1987; Landesman-Dwyer, 1984a, 1984b; Landesman-Dwyer & G. Butterfield, 1983; Landesman-Dwyer & Mai-Dalton, 1981; Landesman-Dwyer, Schuckit, & Keller, 1976; Landesman-Dwyer, Stein, & Sackett, 1978; Landesman-Dwyer, Sulzbacher, Edgar, Keller, Wise, & Baatz, 1980). The people who live and who work in these residential settings come from almost every walk of life, range in age from old to young and in capabilities from highly capable to severely impaired, and in terms of investment from those filled with optimism, energy, and love to those overwhelmed with pessimism and too demoralized to initiate new activities.

Reporting from the perspective of a social scientist, an objective description of these diverse residential environments was sought and has been reported elsewhere (Landesman, 1986b; Landesman-Dwyer, 1985; Sackett & Landesman-Dwyer, 1977). Of special interest were the new community residences that had been planned by parents and professionals to meet the social and developmental needs of individuals who once were considered too disabled to benefit from living in the community. As the momentum of the community movement accelerated, so did the number of conflicting stories about the success, or the failure, of de-institutionalization. There were many unanswered questions. What factors were the most important in determining whether a person would adjust well or poorly to a new home? Were certain types of residential programs more suited than others were for certain types of people? What types of friendships developed in different community facilities, and was the social life available satisfying for the individuals? The facts about the quality of day-to-day life in community residences were all too few and uncertain. What was needed were firsthand observations of the activities that occurred in these homes, including information about who participated and about the quality of social interactions. Of particular interest was determining whether systematic and quantitative behavioral observations could be useful in evaluating the quality of residential care in the community. Of importance, too, to this author was learning more about the process of human adaptation to changing environments, so that people and places could be better matched.

The findings of this research have been presented to a range of scientific audiences (e.g., Landesman-Dwyer, Berkson, & Romer, 1979; Landesman-Dwyer & E. Butterfield, 1983, 1987; Landesman-Dwyer, Sackett, & Kleinman, 1980; Landesman-Dwyer & Sulzbacher, 1981). The results of these investigations also have been shared with a variety of other groups, including legislators, parent and advocacy organizations, state officials, direct service providers, and reporters. In every instance, the author has tried to restrict statements to ones that could be backed by "hard," scientifically verified facts. The reason is that social scientists have a valuable and unique contribution to make — one that will be best fulfilled by sharing scientific discoveries as accurately as possible. Scientific inquiry relies on the use of systematic techniques that, when properly applied, yield a neutral or unbiased evaluation that cannot be obtained by casual, subjective, or anecdotal methods. Through careful design of a study and application of proper statistical analy-

ses, investigators can reach sound conclusions about many (although not all) of the key issues concerning the effects of alternative forms of service provision. Balanced against this are personal impressions, untested ideas, and a desire to improve things that we see as vital elements in any social reform.

Substandard care has been observed in many institutional settings by this author. In recent years, some community residences have changed (usually gradually, sometimes precipitously) from stimulating, responsive, and warm homes to more routinized, socially neglectful, or impoverished homes. To see such deterioration in residential programs that originally aspired to and often succeeded in providing high quality care is a saddening experience. Fortunately, during this same period, other community homes have achieved continued success, often reflecting the commitment and creativity of staff, residents, administrators, and families who together learned to resolve their problems without resorting to the adoption of rigid rules and regulations.

This chapter examines how to prevent "institutionalization" from occurring in the community. As used here, *institutionalization* differs from the conventional connotation of removing a person from the community and placing that individual in a formal institutional facility. Instead, this term identifies the process by which a setting actively or passively adopts depersonalized and regimented practices that were associated with negative consequences in large public residential institutions.

WHAT DOES *INSTITUTIONALIZATION* MEAN?

Institutionalization captures a multitude of negative impressions and feelings associated with large, segregated, understaffed, and highly regimented public or private institutions. Such institutions prevailed as recently as the 1950s and 1960s and were exposed dramatically, through court cases and investigative reporting, in the 1970s. All too often, these institutions merely housed individuals without providing active habilitation or attempting to meet their social and personal needs. Not all residents, however, were treated inhumanely, and institutions varied widely in the quality of care they provided (Crissey, 1975; Klaber, 1969; Zigler & Balla, 1977). In fact, many institutions developed highly effective training programs, even if these model programs were limited in scope or in continuity. Nonetheless, there were general characteristics of most institutional environments that appeared detrimental to the well-being of residents. In this chapter *institutionalization* refers to some or all of these negative aspects, *regardless of whether they occur in traditional institutional or community settings.*

In reviewing the history of institutions, it is useful to remember that institutions were designed initially to provide special training for children with mental handicaps within a nurturing, safe, and accepting environment. Over the years, these once-exemplary training schools were transformed into larger, less effective custodial care facilities because of increased admissions, decreased discharges, and corresponding reductions in per capita resources. The founding leaders of these institutions often were visionaries who inspired their staff, largely through example, to work patiently and diligently to educate all children. The techniques they developed for each pupil often were highly innovative and effective. As these charismatic leaders retired or moved on to other work, the overall quality of their programs declined (Crissey, 1975). Institutions then entered a long period of routine careproviding (Berkson & Landesman-Dwyer, 1977), showing little or no evidence of the hopes and dreams once held for these training schools. Much has been written about the rise and fall of institutions (e.g., Meyers & Blacher, 1987). What seems most important today is to prevent the neglect and suffering caused by institutionalization from ever happening again.

There are at least two ways to think about institutionalization. One is to focus on structural features; the other is to consider functional features. The *structural features* of a residential facility refer to such characteristics as location, size, ownership (public, proprietary, or nonprofit), and staff-to-client ratio. In contrast, *functional features* indicate the actual way a residence operates. Examples of functional features include the amount and quality of interaction between staff and residents, the types of activities in which residents engage, and the degree to which an individual's personal needs are met. The emphasis in this chapter is on functional features. This does not mean that structural features are not at all important, but rather reflects the perspective that what happens from day to day is what matters the most for residents and careproviders. For example, two group homes may be similar in terms of their structural features, but may differ substantially in how they function. They may have the same number of residents and staff members. In the first home, the staff-to-resident ratio may be perceived as inadequate, perhaps due to the heavy transportation needs of residents and the intensive supervision required by one or two residents. In contrast, staffing in the second home may be sufficient, perhaps because staff members do not need to transport residents as much and there may be local volunteers or relatives who assist in meeting the special needs of a few residents. Even though the structural features of size and staff-to-resident ratio of these two homes are equivalent, the functional consequences for the residents are quite different.

There are many negative functional features that make residential settings institutional in nature. These negative features fall into four broad categories: 1) administrative organization, 2) behavior of direct care staff toward residents, 3) resource utilization, and 4) relationships with others outside the residence. Each of these features has implications for the prevention of institutionalization within community residential programs, as discussed later in this chapter.

Rigid Administrative Organization

Generally, the administrative organization in traditional institutions is cumbersome and complicated. Typically, there is a hierarchical reporting structure, with primary decisions about residential care made at the top and carried out at the bottom. When direct care staff perform their jobs well, they often are promoted — usually into positions that take them away from the residents and the everyday settings where they have excelled (see Levy et al., Chapter 19, this volume). This practice is unfortunate, since it maintains a system in which the least experienced and the least ambitious employees have much of the front-line responsibility for the residents' quality of life. Also, this practice may engender an ineffective management system: a first-rate careprovider will not necessarily be good at supervising others, managing programs, or fitting into a larger bureaucracy.

Another administrative characteristic of traditional institutions is that they have many rules and detailed procedures. These usually are endorsed and expanded upon by administrators, and purport to govern almost every activity that can or does occur. Ironically, despite the many hours that are spent writing and re-writing procedures, most staff members openly admit that many of these procedures and operating policies are not followed. In the majority of large institutions, there is a well defined division of staff into direct care workers *versus* supervisors, professionals, and administrators. Even though institutions encourage teamwork by all staff, this historical division still remains. This split among employees contributes to an adversarial (we versus they) attitude within the institution and provides a ready excuse for programs being less effective than they should be. In some sense, both sides are right. Professionals justly complain that the direct care workers do not consistently carry out programs to achieve specified objectives. The direct care workers complain that many professionals and administrators hold expectations that cannot reasonably be met within the existing setting. In many instances this is true, as the behavioral programs for residents are often too time consuming, too technical, or too tedious for direct care staff to conduct. At other times, professional teams select behavioral goals that appear insensitive, superficial, or excessively ambitious to the direct care staff. Most importantly, because so many aspects of institutional life are highly routinized, and almost every decision about a resident requires the approval and signature of others, the direct care staff and their supervisors rarely engage in active, on-the-spot problem solving in a cooperative fashion.

The administrative organization of most institutions is one in which change occurs very slowly, if at all, because each proposed change must be submitted for careful review within the hierarchical system before translating it into action at the level of the residential unit. By having decisions made at a distance, those responsible for enacting these decisions naturally feel uninformed and remote, and are relatively unmotivated to comply enthusiastically. There is a well-known syndrome in institutions in which ambitious, eager new employees soon "learn the ropes" and become jaded and cynical. They realize all too quickly that there will be few rewards for working energetically. In fact, to win friends among the staff, most new employees quickly adjust their behavior to the norm of their peer group, which in turn helps maintain the status quo within the institution.

One of the most discouraging observations is that the problems associated with the administrative organization of institutions are well recognized by the institutional staff themselves (Raynes, Pratt, & Roses, 1979). Serious efforts to overcome these problems have been and continue to be initiated, but rarely are they sufficient to make a visible difference. Restrictive rules and regulations continue to dominate conduct within institutions, and ultimate authority for all important decisions remains in the distant hands of administrators who have lost touch with the everyday lives of the individual residents. Consequently, the administrative and organizational features that contribute to institutionalization include depersonalization in decision making, rigidity in organizational policies and procedures, diffusion of responsibility, and lack of autonomy among direct care staff. All of these factors have obvious implications for the administrative environment of community residential programs.

Inadequate Social Interaction

The primary fault in the behavior of direct care staff is lack of sufficient social interaction with residents. The vast majority of direct care workers genuinely like the residents and want to help improve the quality of their lives. Just as importantly, most staff believe that their own jobs are important and valued ones. Direct care employees consistently indicate that they would like to spend more time with residents, especially on a one-to-one basis. They further report that they want to learn more about mental retardation and about new techniques for interacting effectively with residents (Landesman-Dwyer & Knowles, 1986). Why then is interaction so minimal?

Despite the special relationships that develop between some staff members and residents, staff generally spend very little of their time directly interacting with residents. Findings from my observational studies indicate that the amount of time direct care staff spend in social interaction with residents (which includes all forms of social exchange) averages only 10%–15% of their total time on the job. The overwhelming majority of direct care staff believe that this low amount of interaction is the result of the staff shortage in institutions. Unfortunately, there is contrary evidence: merely adding more direct care staff will not significantly improve the situation (Baumeister & Zaharia, 1987; Knight, Weitzer, & Zimring, 1978; Landesman-Dwyer, 1981; Landesman-Dwyer, 1984b). This should be called the *myth of understaffing*. It is a myth that is widely believed. In most public institutions, there are as many, or more, staff members as there are residents. Yet even on those days or shifts when there is a surplus of direct care workers (that is, no one is absent and/or extra help is available), the residents do *not* actually receive more attention from the staff. Apparently, it is very difficult for staff to break the well-established habit of interacting only minimally or briefly with residents, even when they have sufficient time to do so. Moores and Grant (1977) describe this as the *avoidance syndrome*. Unlike making beds or giving out medications on time, being highly sociable with residents and attending to their social needs are not staff behaviors that have been highly valued or emphasized in traditional institutions. Very few procedures deal directly with how much positive social interaction should occur between staff and residents.

Another misconception is that the limited social interaction is caused by the unresponsive

resident. This *myth of the unresponsive resident* is used by some to explain why staff do not interact more frequently or for longer periods of time with residents. The premise is that when staff members do not detect a social response from residents, they gradually stop paying attention to the residents. Interestingly, most careproviders *do* perceive the residents as being responsive to them. In fact, some careproviders pay more attention to the less responsive (that is, more passive or less skilled) residents than they do to the more socially active individuals. Just as new parents can truly enjoy playing with their very young infants (who are far less capable and responsive than are older children), so too can careproviders find personal rewards in interacting with residents, regardless of their level of mental retardation or the degree of their sensorimotor impairment. To date, there is no compelling evidence that the cause for social neglect within institutions is attributable primarily to the residents' lack of responsiveness or to the condition of mental retardation per se.

There are several noteworthy characteristics about social interactions in institutions. First, they tend to be very brief and infrequent. Second, they often seem pat and perfunctory. Demonstrations of patience, concern, genuine interest, or pleasure on the part of the staff rarely accompany the staff-resident interactions that take place. Third, almost all direct care workers show evidence of being good *natural teachers*, even though they seldom employ this ability. In a way, this third observation may seem to be at odds with the first two statements. What this author has observed repeatedly, always with some surprise, is that regardless of how distant or abrupt a staff member may seem during routine activities, there are moments when that same individual displays his or her ability to teach, to encourage, or to provide constructive feedback to residents. Remarkably, the situations in which this natural teaching seems to occur most often are those that are unplanned or spontaneous, and that are not associated with any formally assigned staff teaching activities. Outings, holidays, unexpected minor disasters, and the entry of newcomers or visitors usually provide the context for such positive staff-resident interaction. This finding is especially encouraging, because it indicates that the skill level of staff may be more advanced than is recognized, and that correcting the problem may be possible by engineering the environment to be more supportive of staff (Landesman-Dwyer & E. Butterfield, 1983; Landesman-Dwyer & Knowles, 1986). This third observation also helps explain the apparent contradiction between what direct care staff verbally express — namely, that they genuinely care about the residents' well-being — and how they typically behave.

What clearly has been missing in institutional environments is a true appreciation of the significance of informal talking, everyday teaching, the sharing of feelings, or just having fun together (Landesman-Dwyer & Berkson, 1984). As a result, both staff and residents are denied the joys of engaging in unstructured activities, the type of behavior that often is described as "just hanging out together" or "goofing off." In an era when, increasingly, every moment of the day must be accounted for, there is little room in institutional settings for casual encounters. In theory, leisure social time could become an integral and highly valuable component in a person's individualized habilitation plan (see Hawkins, Chapter 17, this volume). In practice, the emphasis in such individual plans has been on the attainment of highly specific behavioral goals and skills via rigidly structured programs in which progress can be monitored carefully and objectively, rather than on the provision of more interactive and responsive social environments for both residents and staff.

Finally, staff in institutions rarely encourage the development of friendships among residents themselves. Because staff turnover and reassignment are so frequent, peer friendships can serve to buffer this social disruption and to provide some social continuity for many residents. In a review of the findings related to friendships and peer interactions among mentally retarded individuals (Landesman-Dwyer & Berkson, 1984), the conclusions were: 1) that peer relationships can be fostered by high-quality environments and 2) that intelligence level is far less important than is environmental support in

maintaining friendships. By orienting staff in community residences toward the value of a socially stimulating environment, there can be more effective facilitation of positive, long-term relationships. Within such socially rewarding settings, there are many natural opportunities for incidental learning and spontaneous teachings.

Insufficient Resource Utilization

Another area in which traditional institutions have done poorly is that of resource utilization. In the past, many of the extremely large rural institutions became self-sufficient communities with their own farms, schools, chapels, hospitals, pharmacies, sewing areas, bakeries, beauty parlors, and even cemeteries. Currently, even the more modern urban institutions duplicate many services available in the general community. The rationale for this duplication is that a centralized facility is more efficient in providing specialized services of some reasonable quality for the residents. This is a questionable assumption since comparisons of the quality of services received within the institution (such as physical and occupational therapy, behavior management programs, and routine medical care) and those provided in the outside community to individuals with comparable needs indicate either: 1) that there is no difference or 2) that the community services are more effective. Often the community service providers complain that they need to invest much time and effort to obtain these higher quality services, but the rewards are great once they do.

What is especially disappointing about resource allocation is that many residents do not receive the services that presumably are available to them. For example, routine medical and dental care, opportunities to use recreational equipment on campus, special therapeutic evaluation (in areas such as communication and motor skills), and needed prosthetic equipment have been woefully inadequate in traditional institutions. This finding is one that parents and legislators are reluctant to accept, since it weakens one of their major reasons for maintaining institutions. The principle to be learned is that the visible presence of services and professional expertise does not ensure that individuals actually receive or benefit from resources.

The concept of resource utilization extends beyond the issues of where services are delivered and who controls them. Resource utilization also may include making the most of the human talent available within a residential facility. Because institutions have compartmentalized daily activities into many distinct areas, with assignment of responsibility to many different staff members, employees hired to fill a specific job rarely are able to participate in activities not included in their job description. Similarly, most institutions have rules that prohibit residents from helping with routine maintenance—rules that originally were intended to protect residents from functioning as unpaid employees, but now actually restrict residents' freedom to engage in certain activities that they might choose voluntarily, or from which they might learn. This creates a living environment that differs markedly from that of most homes. Ideally, members of a group pitch in when needed, providing flexibility to individuals to negotiate minor shifts to accommodate their schedules, preferences, and skills. If the natural interests and abilities of direct care staff were utilized more fully and in a flexible fashion, then the opportunities for staff to become more personally involved and more enthusiastic in initiating positive changes should increase. The idea that the individual personalities of the direct care staff could, and should, contribute to creating a dynamic, unique home environment is foreign to most institutional settings. Instead, most staff members are viewed as interchangeable. This is evidenced by the practice of reassigning staff from their regular living unit to others at the last minute, with little or no orientation to the new environment, whenever absences or vacancies occur. Similarly, staff often leave their home unit and go to a new one to obtain a better work schedule or to be promoted. The functional consequences of treating staff in this depersonalized way certainly are problematic and need to be remedied.

To utilize resources effectively, community residences first need to consider what types of social and physical assistance could be beneficial. Next, the availability of resources within the home and surrounding community should be appraised, recognizing the possibility that there may be some "hidden treasures" that may enrich the lives of residents, staff, and family members. Finally, clear responsibility for resource management is important to establish and to keep current. Most of all, it is important to remember that variety and novelty are desirable elements in a residence, and that the interests and needs of residents should influence the acquisition and use of resources.

Limited Relationships with Others

Institutions have had a varying history of involvement with their local communities and with the families of their residents. One highly successful program that has brought individuals from the community into the institutions is the federally sponsored foster grandparent program. One or two children or adolescents are assigned to a foster grandmother or grandfather, with the goal of establishing close personal relationships between the foster grandparents and children. Parent groups also have been a reliable source of support within traditional institutions, although these have declined in recent years as residents age and fewer young children are admitted. Volunteer programs also have lost vitality, largely because of the lowered status and increased criticism of institutions in general. Thus, institutions continue to remain relatively socially isolated. This is especially apparent when quality of life is evaluated from the perspective of the individual resident (Landesman, 1986a) and when consideration is given to the amount and variety of social contacts that a person has with others outside the institution.

At the agency level, institutions are criticized for their rigidity in dealing cooperatively with other service agencies. In all fairness, this is a two-way complaint, with staff in institutions claiming that community-based professionals and service providers are not sufficiently responsive, knowledgeable, or cooperative with the institution. The emotions associated with such interactions often color the outcome, and in turn reinforce the initial prejudices of each side and prevent forming closer ties.

Finally, many institutions have established formal policy regarding visitation, which serves to further segregation. Like most institutional policies, there were reasons for its creation — to protect residents from having their privacy invaded and to maximize the safety of residents. Without an open door policy, however, residents are limited in their options to form friendships and to invite visitors into their homes whenever they so choose. Family members also report feeling hesitant about visiting too often, sensing that staff do not really welcome them. In practice, few institutions actively foster positive ties between residents and their families. In fact, when family members visit more, they are more likely to notice things that they do not like or that they want to change. This indirect consequence of more active involvement with others outside the institution is not desirable in an environment that generally seeks to maintain the status quo.

To prevent segregation from occurring, community residences can establish a broad network of relationships with individuals and agencies. As much as possible, these contacts should be open, frequent, and mutually beneficial. If administrators insist on knowing about all contacts that staff members and residents have with others, then such social links to the community are likely to be limited or guarded. In contrast, if everyone is encouraged to discover special friendships and support services on his or her own, and if visits and telephone calls can occur spontaneously and with minimal monitoring, then the incentives for having *diverse,* strong relationships with others will be high.

WHY QUALITY OF CARE DECLINES

Defining and measuring quality of life for individuals who live in community homes is extremely difficult (Landesman-Dwyer, 1981, Landesman, 1986a, 1986b). Similarly, providing a thorough description or evaluation of a home is not easy, because there are no clear-cut guidelines or commonly accepted outcomes (Jacobson & Regula, Chapter 7, this volume; Landesman-Dwyer, 1985). What works for some people, for some communities, or at some times may not necessarily succeed under different circumstances.

Why do some of the best community residences eventually become more institutional in character? At least three issues are involved: 1) they are not prepared for the difficulties associated with long-term operation of a residential program; 2) they have no built-in means of self-evaluation; and 3) they lose some of their own sense of internal direction and personal goals, accepting instead the standards and programs of other agencies or advocacy groups.

Concerning the first issue, *difficulties in long-term operation of a facility,* there are many aspects to consider. These include dealing with major changes in staff, residents, community support services, funding sources, and outside criteria used for licensing and evaluation. Invariably, community residences experience the daily hassles and frustrations inherent in any group living arrangement, often exacerbated by the shifting needs of individual residents and new demands generated by the residents, their families, and/or their case managers. The enthusiastic and idealistic staff who help to open community residences are likely to move on to other jobs or to return to school to advance their own education. Salary and opportunities for promotion are limited, although these are not necessarily the primary reasons why talented staff move on. Similarly, the parents who help a community residence in its early phases, by contributing time, money, and ideas, often do so to help create a second home for their own sons and daughters. Over time, some of these parents will withdraw, because their children may move on to live in other places (such as supervised apartments or independent living) or they may experience changes in their own lives, such as retirement, re-marriage, or illness, that alter their ability and motivation to participate actively. And in some cases, parents recognize their own feelings of fatigue, discouragement, or anger associated with constantly battling for better services, reduced red tape, and increased security and amount of funding for community residences. Withdrawal is a solution that some parents and advocates accept only with great reluctance, usually after years of dedicated caring and effective volunteering coupled with chronic problems that stem from insensitive or excessive outside regulation of the programs to which these parents are committed.

Program expansion is another component of long-term operation. Somewhat sadly, once-outstanding community residences may decline in quality after their administrators and advisory boards decide to expand. That is, after succeeding with one residence, these individuals often are encouraged to open a second, then a third, or more new residences. Unfortunately, the managerial skills needed to succeed in operating community residences, especially in a cost-effective and organizationally sensible manner, may be quite different from those that contributed to success in the first "model" program. When talented and charismatic leaders shift their attention away from the original home and the residents there — directing their energy instead into opening new facilities, getting to know new residents, training new staff, and finding ways to make things run more efficiently and with less effort — the first residence may suffer from neglect. Unfortunately, the subsequent community residences in such expansion efforts often seem to be carbon copies *structurally,* but *functionally* they may lack the spontaneous, creative, high levels of activity and caring energy that characterized the first home.

Are the administrators, parents, and professionals of these once-successful homes aware of what may accompany this transition phase? Usually not, although a few admit that they have chosen to open new residences because they miss the challenge and excitement of the planning and early operation period of the other home. Once success was achieved, these individuals wanted to move on, not realizing that equal creativity in problem solving and especially in problem avoiding was vitally needed to maintain a home environment that promoted a *continuous,* but not stagnant, high quality of care for those who lived and worked there. More typically, the leaders show little or no awareness of the decline in the day-to-day quality of life. Since these individuals are very busy with expanding their programs, they are at risk for losing touch with daily activities and the

subtle aspects of social life that are vital to real success.

Whether individuals can fully prepare themselves for the strains that accompany long-term management of a community residence may be uncertain. A danger might be that if service providers fully realize what the future holds, they may never enter into the valuable "honeymoon period" in which they commit themselves wholeheartedly to a program. Alternatively, if those involved are willing to consider openly the experiences of other homes, to build in means to deal with the most likely practical problems (namely, those that have negatively influenced other residences), and to discuss these issues regularly with others who face the same challenges and share the same long-term goals, then they may secure the future of quality community-based care.

The second issue relates to *inadequate self-evaluation.* Because community residences exert much effort in proving to outsiders that they can provide high quality services, they are less motivated to be highly introspective. Self-critique often is feared as a negative process that may demoralize staff, families, or residents. This may reflect the doubts that many staff experience daily about their competence to handle many of the complex, sensitive, and important matters that are central to their jobs. At the same time, effective self-evaluation permits detecting positive program elements as well as negative ones. Just as important, when individuals recognize the strengths and weaknesses of their own programs, they are less likely to feel defensive and more likely to be willing to engage in problem-solving behavior to correct the weaknesses. Because cooperation is vital to success in residential settings, self-evaluation may be a constructive way to prevent programs from becoming stagnant or merely reactive to outside criticism.

A third point that relates to quality decline in residential programs is the *loss of self-direction.* This may be caused by the need to comply with standards established by others. Such outer-directedness may lead to less active engagement of staff, families, and community. It may appear to them that federal, state, and local regulatory agencies are in control. Few normal families could handle the regulations and demands, much less understand them, that even very small group residences or foster homes must. In the past 15 years, all community residences have experienced numerous changes in licensing, funding, and/or routine evaluation procedures for their operation. The shifts in the standards and expectations for ICF/MR facilities, for example, have been major and continue to evolve. This process of evolution is needed and healthy, but the consequences on residents and service providers should be taken into account. In particular, it is important to foster an atmosphere in which ups and downs, mistakes, and changes can be seen as positive, because they provide the context for human experience and learning. For years, psychologists warned about the "Hawthorne effect" — the finding that new things may work simply because they are new and being observed. Variety and trial-and-error are needed, especially when they occur in a caring and committed environment. Excessive structural regulations constrain creative new program efforts, and eventually contribute to a situation in which blame for substandard care can be placed outside the facility—comparable to the unfortunate situation in institutions in which individuals, including staff, administrators, residents, or volunteers, lose their motivation to try to improve things.

Ideally, external standards should become increasingly based on the *functional aspects* of what occurs and how residential programs actually support the development and well-being of residents, as active citizens in their community, rather than the current reliance on structural components. The problems with primary reliance on structural features are that: 1) adherence to these may be used to substitute for (that is, merely comply with stated standards) more individualized adjustment of a home to the varying preferences and needs of those who live there; 2) the minimal costs of meeting these may be so high that homes have virtually no extra funds to initiate programs of their own; and 3) their *own* goals for program development and resident progress are subordinated to external standards. Overall, there is little doubt that formal standards and evaluations are here to

stay. What needs to be considered is how to improve these so that the positive objectives are fulfilled and self-direction enhanced.

There are three ways to help prevent suboptimal or declining care, each of which can be implemented within the present system and with existing resources.

STRATEGIES FOR PREVENTING INSTITUTIONALIZATION

One of the best ways to prevent institutionalization is to encourage service providers and recipients to evaluate things on their own. Self-analysis implies a willingness to reflect on one's activities and motives, and to investigate their consequences. When the incentives for such self-appraisal come from within a home, the process is likely to be more effective.

There have been a number of instruments designed to help evaluate residential programs. These are available, often at no or minimal cost, but rarely will a single instrument that was created for a particular purpose at a particular time meet the current needs of someone else. The dream of having a perfected, multi-purpose tool to measure the success of a residential program is probably not realistic (Windle, 1962), and may not even be desirable for self-analysis. The individuals involved in self-appraisal should be able to shape the process and make changes along the way, for ultimately they will be the ones to decide on and implement changes.

Second, an intensive national effort is needed to remedy existing regulations that are not sound or that lead to program restrictiveness. To succeed, many individuals must speak up about these problems, even if they continue to comply in the interim. One of the most straightforward ways to improve existing regulations would be to provide a *functional objective* for every *structural regulation*. For example, if the staff-resident ratio is mandated (a structural regulation), then the corresponding functional consequences should be stated. Perhaps the functional intent is that residents each receive a certain amount of individual attention from staff on a daily or weekly basis, or that there be sufficient coverage to handle emergencies. Once the functional objectives become as clear as the structural ones, then a substitute or an equivalency formula could be used for homes with exceptional circumstances. This does not mean that they are requesting an exemption from compliance with a policy, but instead are offering to homes flexibility in how to choose to meet an objective. Many homes will continue to adopt the general structural recommendations because these appear reasonable and helpful. Others may prefer more freedom in developing their own proposals. In such a system all homes remain accountable for their own outcomes. This means that compliance with a conventional structural recommendation is not sufficient evidence that the objective is achieved.

Finally, more interaction among staff in community residences should be promoted. Staff need to be in contact with others who also are striving to provide a high quality program for persons with developmental disabilities. By frequent and informal sharing of ideas as well as complaints, staff are likely to feel supported and to develop professionally. This is similar to what happens in natural families in which parents communicate with good friends and other family members over many years about their problems and their accomplishments. Similarly, most other professionals have a peer group to provide social, informational, emotional, and instrumental help. If staff members have the opportunity to visit other residences they will be more likely to observe both positive and negative features they can translate into action in their own programs.

In sum, institutionalization refers to suboptimal, routinized, and depersonalized care. *This can occur anywhere.* The community has passed beyond its turbulent and enthusiastic infancy. Serious efforts to prevent institutionalization must be initiated. This may be achieved by frequent self-evaluation, improvement of existing formal regulations and evaluation activities, and expanded efforts to create a peer network for direct care providers.

REFERENCES

Baumeister, A.A., & Zaharia, E.S. (1987). Withdrawal and commitment of basic care staff in residential programs. In S. Landesman & P. Vietze (Eds.), *Living environments and mental retardation (pp. 229–267).* Washington, DC: American Association on Mental Retardation.

Berkson, G.B., & Landesman-Dwyer, S. (1977). Behavioral research in severe and profound mental retardation (1955–1974). *American Journal of Mental Deficiency, 81,* 428–454.

Crissey, M.S. (1975). Mental retardation: Past, present, and future. *American Psychologist, 30,* 800–808.

Klaber, M.M. (1969). *Retardates in residence: A study of institutions.* West Hartford, CT: University of Hartford Press.

Knight, R.C., Weitzer, W.H., & Zimring, C.M. (Eds.). (1978). *Opportunity for control and the built environment: The ELEMR Project.* Amherst, MA: The Environmental Institute, University of Massachusetts.

Landesman, S. (1986a). Quality of life and personal life satisfaction: Definition and measurement issues (guest editorial). *Mental Retardation, 24,* 141–143.

Landesman, S. (1986b). Toward a taxonomy of home environments. In N.R. Ellis & N.W. Bray (Eds.), *International review of research in mental retardation* (Vol. 14, pp. 259–289). New York: Academic Press.

Landesman, S. (1987). The changing structure and function of institutions: A search for optimal group care environments. In S. Landesman & P. Vietze (Eds.), *Living environments and mental retardation (pp. 79–126).* Washington, DC: American Association on Mental Deficiency.

Landesman, S., & Butterfield, E.C. (1987). Normalization and deinstitutionalization of mentally retarded individuals: Controversy and facts. *American Psychologist, 42,* 809–816.

Landesman-Dwyer, S. (1981). Living in the community. *American Journal of Mental Deficiency, 86,* 223–234.

Landesman-Dwyer, S. (1984a). *Assessing the quality and appropriateness of services for residents of Interlake School.* Olympia, WA: Department of Social and Health Services.

Landesman-Dwyer, S. (1984b). Residential environments and the social behavior of handicapped individuals. In M. Lewis (Ed.), *Beyond the dyad* (pp. 299–322). New York: Plenum Press.

Landesman-Dwyer, S. (1985). Describing and evaluating residential environments. In R.H. Bruininks & K.C. Lakin (Eds.), *Living and learning in the least restrictive environment* (pp. 185–196). Baltimore: Paul H. Brookes Publishing Co.

Landesman-Dwyer, S., & Berkson, G. (1984). Friendships and social behavior. In J. Wortis (Ed.), *Mental retardation and developmental disabilities: An annual review* (Vol. 13, pp. 129–154). New York: Plenum Press.

Landesman-Dwyer, S., Berkson, G.B., & Romer, D. (1979). Affiliation and friendship of mentally retarded residents in group homes. *American Journal of Mental Deficiency, 83,* 571–580.

Landesman-Dwyer, S., & Butterfield, E.C. (1983). Mental retardation: Developmental issues in cognitive and social adaptation. In M. Lewis (Ed.), *Origins of intelligence: Infancy and early childhood* (2nd ed., pp. 479–519). New York: Plenum Press.

Landesman-Dwyer, S., & Butterfield, G. (1983). *Evaluation of specialized group homes for developmentally disabled persons.* Olympia, WA: Department of Social and Health Services.

Landesman-Dwyer, S., & Knowles, M. (1986). Ecological analysis of staff training in residential settings. In J. Hogg & P.J. Mittler (Eds.), *Staff training in mental handicap* (pp. 3–31). London: Croom Helm Press.

Landesman-Dwyer, S., & Mai-Dalton, R. (1981). *A statewide survey of individuals receiving case management services for the Division of Developmental Disabilities.* Olympia, WA: Department of Social and Health Services.

Landesman-Dwyer, S., Sackett, G.P., & Kleinman, J.A. (1980). Small community residences: The relationship of size to resident and staff behavior. *American Journal of Mental Deficiency, 85,* 6–18.

Landesman-Dwyer, S., Schuckit, J.J., & Keller, L.S. (1976). *Survey of developmentally disabled individuals in nursing homes and congregate care facilities.* Olympia, WA: Department of Social and Health Services.

Landesman-Dwyer, S., Stein, J.G., & Sackett, G.P. (1978). A behavioral and ecological study of group homes. In G.P. Sackett (Ed.), *Observing behavior, Vol. I: Theory and application in mental retardation* (pp. 349–377). Baltimore: University Park Press.

Landesman-Dwyer, S., & Sulzbacher, F. MacL. (1981). Residential placement and adaptation of severely and profoundly retarded individuals. In R.H. Bruininks, C.E. Meyers, B.B. Sigford, & K.C. Lakin (Eds.), *Deinstitutionalization and community adjustment of mentally retarded people* (pp. 182–194). Washington, DC: American Association on Mental Deficiency, Monograph 4.

Landesman-Dwyer, S., Sulzbacher, S., Edgar, E., Keller, S., Wise, B., & Baatz, B. (1980). *1979 Rainier School placement study.* Olympia, WA: Department of Social and Health Services.

Meyers, C.E., & Blacher, J. (1987). Historical determinants of residential care. In S. Landesman & P. Vietze (Eds.), *Living environments and mental retardation (pp. 3–16).* Washington, DC: American Association on Mental Retardation.

Moores, B., & Grant, G.W.B. (1977). The "avoidance" syndrome in hospitals for the mentally handicapped. *International Journal of Nursing Studies, 14,* 91–95.

Raynes, N.V., Pratt, M.W., & Roses, S. (1979). *Organisational structure and the care of the mentally retarded.* London: Croom Helm Press.

Sackett, G.P., & Landesman-Dwyer, S. (1977). Toward an ethology of mental retardation: Quantitative behavioral observation in residential settings. In P. Mittler (Ed.), *Research to practice in mental retardation, Vol. II: Education and training* (pp. 27–37). Baltimore: University Park Press.

Windle, C. (1962). Prognosis of mental subnormals: A critical review of research. *American Journal of Mental Deficiency Monograph Supplement, 66,* 1–180.

Zigler, E., & Balla, D. (1977). Impact of institutional experience on the behavior and development of retarded persons. *American Journal of Mental Deficiency, 82,* 1–11.

Chapter 9

Programmatic Features of Quality Services

Roger Blunden

The quality of life of the developmentally disabled persons who live in community residences must feature prominently in any discussion of service quality. Most importantly, the design of community services should lead to a demonstrable improvement in the quality of residents' lives. This chapter examines some dimensions of quality of life and indicates how services for persons with developmental disabilities can influence these in both constructive and adverse ways. In particular, residential services, which assume control over most aspects of residents' lives, can have a major positive or detrimental effect on a person's well-being. Techniques for avoiding negative effects of service design and management are stressed.

With the development in recent years of community services for persons with handicaps, there has been an increasing interest in the quality of the services provided. For example in Great Britain, an early key government policy document (Department of Health and Social Security, 1971) emphasized the provision of *places* within the community. In the last several years, great concern has been expressed about the quality of community services (Independent Development Council, 1982; King's Fund, 1980). And a 1985 House of Commons report stressed the need for government agencies "to take on an inspectorial and evaluative function, both to satisfy Ministers and Parliament that services are of the expected quality and quantity, and to help those locally to judge their own performance" (para. 209).

This chapter contributes to the continuing review of this issue by considering the concept of quality of life and suggesting some dimensions along which quality might be analyzed. It also examines ways in which services influence the quality of lives of their users. It is clear that different types of service can influence different aspects of clients' life-styles, and also that many services have unintended adverse effects on users' lives. Consequently, this chapter considers what can be done in practice to minimize the damaging effects of services and promote positive life-styles. Although there are no easy answers to these complex problems, some programmatic concepts are discussed that may aid

The Mental Handicap in Wales–Applied Research Unit is supported by the Department of Health and Social Security and the Welsh Office. Much of the material in this chapter was first presented at the International Conference on Aging and Disabilities, University of Calgary, July 1986.

in the development of more quality-oriented services for dependent populations.

SOME DIMENSIONS OF QUALITY OF LIFE

Although the term *quality of life* is often used in general conversation, it is an elusive concept to define. We sense that we all know it when we see it, but we find it difficult to agree what "it" is. However, there is some consensus about some of the factors that contribute to quality of life. "Health, wealth, and happiness" are often identified as essential prerequisites of a satisfying life. People's satisfaction with their own lives is often taken as a key indicator. Many of the scandals that have arisen in institutions have highlighted the impoverished social and material environments of their residents, conditions that are indicative of these persons' quality of life.

In general, four key factors may be said to influence quality of life: physical well-being, material well-being, social well-being, and cognitive well-being. These dimensions are not mutually exclusive; aspects of one often influence the other. However, they do help identify a range of issues that might usefully be taken into consideration when evaluating the impact of services.

Physical Well-Being

Physical well-being can be thought of as the ability to use one's body as effectively as possible. Factors contributing to physical well-being include good health, fitness, and the absence of disability. Physical well-being receives a great deal of emphasis in today's society, with much popular concern for exercise and healthy eating. An important part of the intuitive concept of quality of life is freedom from the debilitating effects of illness and disability. When a person has an illness or disability, his or her physical well-being is dependent on the extent to which he or she is able to overcome these limitations, through medical treatment or prosthetic devices.

In community residential services, a number of steps should be taken to ensure that residents enjoy a high standard of physical well-being:

The residents' general health and fitness should be safeguarded; effective medical treatment should be sought promptly where necessary; dental care should be provided; eye glasses and hearing aids should be used by those requiring them; and arrangements should be made for persons with physical disabilities to exercise the maximum independence possible (for example, by the use of walking aids, bath rails, and special eating utensils).

Material Well-Being

Material well-being also features strongly in present-day Western society. Most of us share a firm interest in obtaining an adequate income, and in enjoying the housing, private transportation, and range of possessions that this affords. While conventional wisdom holds that "money isn't really important," most of us nevertheless place a high priority on maintaining or enlarging our personal incomes and in extending the range of our material possessions. Thus, for people living in community residences, material well-being would be in evidence by the amount of disposable income that is available to residents and under their control, by the physical quality of the setting, and by the quantity and quality of residents' personal possessions.

Social Well-Being

Less explicit recognition is given to *social well-being,* although it is a vital element in most people's lives. Human beings are generally social animals and depend heavily on their social networks for both survival and personal satisfaction. An analysis of social well-being that is particularly useful in the context of service provision for dependent populations is provided by O'Brien (1987). O'Brien identifies five components of a valued social life:

1. *Community presence* is the physical location of an individual within a community setting. To have access to other people in a range of community settings, such as shops, leisure facilities, and places of education and employment, is a prerequisite of a satisfactory social life.
2. *Relationships* are a crucial aspect of social well-being. Most people rely heavily on a

range of relationships with friends, family members, colleagues, and peers.

3. *Choice,* another important component of human social existence, includes small, everyday decisions such as what to eat or what to wear, and extends to major life decisions such as where to live or work and with whom. A major part of our social existence involves the exercise of rights—for example, a citizen's right to vote and the right to refuse to engage in particular activities.

4. *Competence,* a fourth aspect of social well-being, requires basic abilities in communication, mobility, self-help, and social and leisure skills in order to participate fully in social relationships.

5. *Respect,* the final element of social well-being, is perhaps dependent on attaining each of the other components. The literature on normalization stresses the importance of valued social roles as an essential requirement for quality of life. It is difficult to think intuitively of a high quality of existence that does not involve a role worthy of the respect of others.

The issue of social well-being may be particularly important in the context of community residential services. Are residents encouraged to have a wide circle of friends and acquaintances outside the residence? Are they helped to form relationships with nonhandicapped persons? Is there an active program to enhance people's competence in basic skills that will enable them to participate more fully in community life? Does the service present its users to the local community as valued citizens, deserving of the respect of others?

Cognitive Well-Being

Cognitive well-being, the individual's own perception of his or her quality of life, is the fourth factor to be discussed here. Much material written on quality of life concentrates on the individual's life satisfaction. One way to interpret life satisfaction is to have a person write a commentary on his or her life or relate orally a "story" about his or her life in which judgments are made about his or her satisfaction with it.

Community residential services may need to pay particular attention to the cognitive well-being of their residents. The way in which staff and others interact with persons with handicaps may significantly influence how they view themselves. Thus a positive, respectful approach may do much to enhance people's cognitive well-being.

IMPLICATIONS FOR THE DESIGN AND MANAGEMENT OF SERVICE SETTINGS

The foregoing discussion has highlighted some important dimensions of quality of life and has suggested how service systems can influence their clients' quality of life. What more can be done to encourage services to promote a positive quality of life among the people they serve?

Interestingly, the issue of quality has also received considerable prominence in the context of commercial organizations. A number of writers in recent years have addressed the problem of how manufacturing and service organizations can effectively meet their customers' needs (e.g., Gilbert, 1978; Hickman & Silva, 1985; Peters & Austin, 1985; Peters & Waterman, 1982). The advice given and lessons drawn from these accounts of successful businesses appear to have relevance for the development of effective services for persons with handicaps.

One major lesson is that successful organizations have a clear value system and devote considerable energy to the active promotion of those key values at all levels in the organization. These values are mainly about *outcome,* rather than *process.* The successful organization has a well-defined notion of what it is trying to achieve. These achievements form the focus of attention. The ways in which people within the organization work to achieve these ends can, to some extent, be of secondary consideration. This approach contrasts strongly with that used in many services for persons with handicaps, where *process* is of prime concern (obtaining funding, organizing staffing schedules, arranging skill teaching, maintaining health and safety standards, financial accounting, etc.) and where outcomes for clients (in terms of improving or maintaining their quality of life) are often left unstated or are assumed to be implicit in the way the service works. This is not to say that the process variables just mentioned are unimportant. However, it may be that explicitly recognizing what a service intends to achieve for its clients' quality of life may be an important step in promoting that quality. Organizations that actively promote core values in terms of client outcomes are then in a position to hold staff accountable for the attainment of these outcomes and to build in mechanisms to review quality and take appropriate action.

Two further important features emerge from the literature on quality in organizations. One is sensitivity to the needs of the consumer. Organizations with a reputation for quality maintain close links with their customers. Everyone, from senior management down, spends time in discussions with customers, ensuring that the organization is receptive and responsive to customer views. This feature is sometimes absent in human service organizations, where senior managers may be far removed from contact with the people served and where the prevailing attitude may be that users should be grateful for any service they are receiving. Thus, the current move to closely involve persons with hand-

icaps, and people speaking on their behalf, in service planning and monitoring may be one important step toward promoting quality.

Another feature of successful organizations is a commitment to action and innovation. Given this commitment, there is the expectation that new ideas will be tested in practice and that some of these may fail. Such a posture allows the organization to be alive and developing, rather than stagnating. Where unmet consumer needs are identified, action is taken to meet the needs. This action orientation is an important part of the "quality circle" approach in industry (Dewar, 1980), in which small groups of workers are encouraged to identify problems, formulate solutions, and put these into practice.

One recent attempt in Britain to make these ideas on quality operational in the field of mental retardation is found in the work of the Independent Development Council (1986). According to their approach—summarized in Figure 1—a Quality Action Group, comprising service users, staff, and other key "stakeholders" is formed with a specific mission to examine aspects of the service system's quality and to take appropriate action. The group first devotes energy to clarifying the values within which a ser-

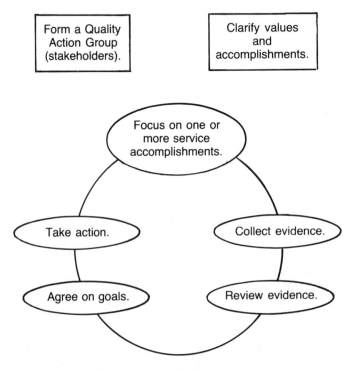

Figure 1. The Quality Action approach.

vice system operates and the important outcomes in terms of clients' life-styles. A review and action process is then started. The group focuses on one or more of the ways in which the service intends to benefit clients' lives. They collect evidence to evaluate how successful the service is in this area. After reviewing the evidence, specific goals are set to improve the service's effectiveness. The process is then repeated by identifying other client outcomes and initiating further reviews and action (Blunden & Beyer, 1987). Some early practical experience in the use of this system has been reported by Beyer (1987).

SUMMARY AND CONCLUSION

This chapter has examined the interaction between services and the quality of life of their users. It has been suggested that the concept of quality of life is complex, but that it may be useful to consider four dimensions—physical well-being, cognitive well-being, material well-being, and social well-being. An effective service may need to address all of these aspects.

Further examination of the interaction between services and quality of life suggests that many services can have a major influence on all aspects of their users' lives. Clearly, service systems must find ways to organize themselves so as to promote high-quality life-styles and to minimize damage.

Literature on the pursuit of quality in commercial organizations is expanding, and much of it may have relevance for the development of high-quality service systems. In particular, three key features of successful organizations have been identified: the identification and promotion of key *values* in terms of client *outcomes;* sensitivity to the needs of clients; and a commitment to action and innovation. One attempt in Britain to apply these lessons to services for persons with mental handicaps has been briefly mentioned.

This chapter was designed more to raise questions than to offer answers. However, it is vital that the community-living movement for persons with handicaps address the issue of quality as well as quantity. There is no guarantee, for example, that simply putting people into small, community-based residences will automatically improve their quality of life. Community living provides major opportunities for people to develop each component of a high-quality life. Whether residents are able to take advantage of these opportunities will depend greatly on the way that services are organized and the attention given to quality of life in the organizational process.

REFERENCES

Beyer, S. (1987). Pursuing quality through a Quality Action Group: Experiences in the CUSS Home Support Service. In L. Ward (Ed.), *Getting better all the time: Issues and strategies for ensuring quality in community services for people with mental handicap.* London: King's Fund Centre.

Blunden, R., & Beyer, S. (1987). Pursuing quality: A practical approach. In L. Ward (Ed.), *Getting better all the time: Issues and strategies for ensuring quality in community services for people with mental handicap.* London: King's Fund Centre.

Department of Health and Social Security. (1971). *Better services for the mentally handicapped (Cmnd. 4683).* London: HMSO.

Dewar, D. (1980). *The quality circle handbook.* Red Bluff, CA: Quality Circle Institute.

Gilbert, T.F. (1978). *Human competence: Engineering worthy performance.* New York: McGraw Hill.

Hickman, C., & Silva, M. (1985). *Creating excellence.* London: George Allen & Unwin.

House of Commons. (1985). *Second report from the Social Services Committee: Community care with special reference to adult mentally ill and mentally handicapped people.* London: HMSO.

Independent Development Council for People with Mental Handicap. (1982). *Elements of a comprehensive local service for people with mental handicap.* (Available from IDC, 126 Albert St., London NW1 7NF, England.)

Independent Development Council for People with Mental Handicap. (1986). *Pursuing quality: How good are your local services for people with mental handicap?* (Available from IDC, 126 Albert St., London NW1 7NF, England.)

King's Fund. (1980). *An ordinary life: Comprehensive locally-based residential services for mentally handicapped people.* (Project Paper No. 24.) London: King's Fund Centre. (Available from King's Fund Centre, 126 Albert St., London NW1 7NF, England.)

O'Brien, J. (1987). A guide to personal futures planning. In G.T. Bellamy & B. Wilcox, *A comprehensive guide to the activities catalog: An alternative curriculum for youth and adults with severe disabilities.* Baltimore: Paul H. Brookes Publishing Co.

Peters, T., & Austin, N. (1985). A passion for excellence: The leadership difference. London: Collins.

Peters, T., & Waterman, R. (1982). *In search of excellence: Lessons from America's best-run companies.* New York: Harper & Row.

Chapter 10

The Concept and Implementation of Active Treatment

Dianne Manfredini and Wayne Smith

Active treatment refers to the consistent, aggressive, continuous, and accountable application of habilitative interventions by caregivers of persons with developmental disabilities. The concept is predicated on the belief that each individual is capable of continued change and can benefit from participation in individually prescribed programs. Interventions are carried out in structured and unstructured settings alike, and are directed toward enhancing each individual's developmental progress throughout the life cycle. Active treatment is accomplished through the development of a comprehensive individualized plan for each individual. This plan is derived from functional assessments. The plan, which contains precise objectives and indices of expected outcomes of the interventions, is translated into a program of daily activities, therapies, experiences, and interactions focusing on the acquisition, reinforcement, generalization, and/or transfer of skills and behaviors within the environments in which the individual functions.

HISTORICAL BACKGROUND OF ACTIVE TREATMENT

The origin of the term *active treatment* can be found in the legislative history surrounding the development of the 1971 legislation authorizing payment of federal Medicaid matching funds to states for reimbursement of the cost of care of eligible Medicaid recipients with mental retardation or related conditions living in public institutions. (Through legal interpretation, private facilities were later permitted to participate.) The statute (Section 1905(d) of the act) specifically states that a facility can claim payment only for the cost of care of individuals who are receiving "active treatment."

This provision was included to ensure that federal Medicaid funds would not be used by states simply to continue the long history of deplorable custodial care that characterized many public facilities at the time.

Burton Blatt's famous pictorial essay *Christmas in Purgatory* (1966) provides a stark reminder of what life in a public institution for persons with mental retardation was like in the mid-1960s. The statutory requirement that facilities had to provide "active" rather than "custodial" care to Medicaid recipients in order to gain Medicaid reimbursement was a dramatic and powerful impetus to institutional improvement, as was the growing power of litigation in the 1970s, which compelled changes in care practices.

The views expressed by Dr. Smith in this chapter do not necessarily reflect the policies and/or position of the U.S. Department of Health and Human Services or the Health Care Financing Administration (HCFA), and no official endorsement of the department or of HCFA should be inferred.

123

Because the U.S. Congress did not define *active treatment*, it was not until the former U.S. Department of Health, Education & Welfare published final rules in January 1974, implementing what became known as the Intermediate Care Facility for the Mentally Retarded (ICF/MR) program, that the term was defined. Interestingly, the definition was placed in the section for definitions under the rules governing Federal Financial Participation (FFP), in Section 42 CFR 435.1009, instead of as a part of the ICF/MR facility requirements, found in Section 42 CFR 442, Subpart G, of the *Code of Federal Regulations*.

According to the original regulations, active treatment consists of:

(a) the individual's regular participation, in accordance with an individual plan of care, in professionally developed and supervised activities, experiences or therapies;
(b) an individual written plan of care that sets forth measurable goals or objectives stated in terms of desirable behavior and that prescribes an integrated program of activities, experiences or therapies necessary for the individual to reach those goals or objectives. The overall purpose of the plan is to help the individual function at the greatest physical, intellectual, social, or vocational level he can presently or potentially achieve;
(c) an interdisciplinary professional evaluation that:
(1) is completed, for a recipient, before admission to the institution but not more than 3 months before and, for an individual applying for Medicaid after admission, before the institution requests payment;
(2) consists of complete medical, social, and psychological diagnosis and evaluations and an evaluation of the individual's need for institutional care; and
(3) is made by a physician, a social worker, and other professionals, at least one of whom is a qualified mental retardation professional as defined in [42CFR] 442.401 of this subchapter.

In 1986, the U.S. Department of Health and Human Services proposed a general revision of the standards for ICFs/MR and included a revised definition of *active treatment*, both as an FFP requirement (42 CFR 435.1009) and as a central requirement stated explicitly in the facility standards to ensure that providers recognize active treatment as a necessary component of an individual's program.

Inherent in both definitions is the requirement that *active treatment* is the provision of services, interactions, and environments that provide individuals with developmental disabilities living in ICFs/MR the best chance possible to progress to more complex levels of skills, to more independent life-styles, and to more active participation in society. In other words, the meaning of *active treatment* holds forth the same expectation for growth and development as that expected from the parenting and educational experiences received in the broader community by other members of society.

In essence, *active treatment* is simply a descriptive characterization used to convey Congress's intention that ICFs/MR provide individuals "something" better than custodial care. Its meaning is no different from earlier concepts of care for persons with developmental disabilities. Falvey (1986, p. 4) cites a 1926 text stating that "the dull and retarded should be taught everything they are capable of learning that will [assist them to] function in life." Further, the concept of *continuum of care* described by the President's Panel on Mental Retardation in 1962 is embodied in contemporary notions of active treatment. Continuum of care was described by the panel as:

the selection, blending, and use, in proper sequence and relationship, of medical, education, and social services required by a retarded person to minimize his disability at every point in his lifespan. Thus, "care" is used in the broadest sense and the word "continuum" underscores the many transitions of liaisons, within and among various service and professions, by which the community attempts to secure for the retarded the kind and variety of help and accommodation he requires. A "continuum of care" permits fluidity of movement of the individual from one type of service to another while maintaining a sharp focus on his unique requirements. The ongoing process of assuring that an individual receives the services he needs when he needs them and in the amount and variety he requires is the essence of planning and coordination. (President's Panel on Mental Retardation, 1962, p. 197)

Public Law 94-142, the Education for All Handicapped Children Act of 1975, and Public Law 95-602, the Developmental Disabilities Assistance Act of 1978, also addressed the issue of individualized planning based on unique and particular needs, and on the provision of services delivered in a manner so as to most benefit the individual. In particular, the Developmental Disabilities Assistance Act speaks to the need for a "combination and sequence of special, interdisciplinary or generic care, treatment, or other services which are of lifelong or extended duration and are individually planned and coordinated" (42USC 3102(7)(E)). More recently Turnbull and Barber (1986) articulated similar goals for the service system:

> Services to persons should be individualized, that is, tailored to fit each individual's diverse needs. All persons with developmental disabilities have capacities to learn, to develop new skills, and to improve their existing skills. They may also need medical care, but they are not inherently "sick," and thus should not be treated under a "medical" model. This concept is based on the developmental model, the precept that the intellectual and physical development of a person (overcoming the effects of a disability) can best be ensured by education, training and habilitation or rehabilitation, not by medical treatment (unless the person is medically ill, of course). (p. 260)

Both the concept and components of active treatment have consistently been incorporated in various perspectives regarding the attributes of effective program planning and service implementation for individuals with varying types of developmental disabilities (Accreditation Council for Services for Mentally Retarded and Other Developmentally Disabled Persons, 1984; Casey, McGee, Stark, & Menolascino, 1985; Paine, Bellamy, & Wilcox, 1984). Indeed, the term *active treatment* may be seen as a rubric under which the commonalities of such particular plans as individualized education plans, individualized habilitation plans, individualized service plans, individualized program plans, and the like are subsumed.

THE ACTIVE TREATMENT PLAN PROCESS

The process for developing an active treatment plan begins when an individual is identified as having a developmental disability, which (by definition) impairs his or her ability to function such that some level of specialized intervention or supportive service (to the family and/or the individual) is required to maintain or achieve the highest degree of functional independence possible. Thus, the first step in the development of an active treatment plan process is assessment.

A series of questions shape the assessment/evaluation process, including:

What is known about the person?
What can the person do?
What additional information is needed?
Who are the most appropriate people to provide this information?
What is the best method(s) to gather this information?

Historically, most assessments were made by professionals from discrete areas of specialization with tests designed for their particular area of interest. Additional information was typically gathered from families and/or other caregivers. In today's care environments, the most productive information is derived from performance-based, criterion-referenced, functional assessments of individual skills across the developmental spectrum. Simply put, a *functional assessment* identifies what the individual actually can do across a range of skills and environments. Effective implementation of an active treatment program plan will depend directly on the effectiveness with which the individual's developmental needs and strengths are identified through functional assessment.

Functional assessments do not eliminate the need for discrete in-depth professional evaluations, especially when sophisticated programs are to be implemented (e.g., a psycholinguistic training program for a nonverbal individual whose functional assessment showed aggressive efforts to communicate). Instead, functional assessments capture most areas of needed intervention. Functional assessments are widely available commercially, but some program managers find that the best assessment devices are developed in-house, tailored specifically to the individuals served in the program. For example, parts of existing assessment instruments can be "patched" together with segments produced by the program staff to make a more tailored instrument. All the caregivers (professionals, paraprofessionals, and nonprofessionals, including parents and family members) can then use their own assessment devices for detailed analyses of pertinent domains.

One value of performance-based, criterion-referenced, functional assessment is that the identification of the individual's current performance level on a specific skill leads directly to an objective for teaching. For example, if an individual's assessment shows that he or she can grasp a spoon, but cannot scoop food, the teaching objective might be to scoop food on a spoon.

At the conclusion of the assessment process, a comprehensive picture of the person has emerged. This serves as the basis for determining skills and abilities that can be built upon, the barriers to continued development, and the available input and output channels for learning and performance.

Each person participating in an active treatment program functions in an environmental context. The environment consists of physical characteristics (buildings, rooms, heat, light, noise, color, etc.), social characteristics (parents, siblings, substitute caregivers, teachers, aides, professionals, other clients, etc.), and affective characteristics (quality of interactions, administrative staff attitudes and behaviors, etc.). All of these characteristics are blended into an "interactional ecology" that directly affects each person's well-being as well as performance and growth.

Thus, in addition to assessing the individual's performance, it is essential to assess the ecological environment in which the individual is expected to function, and those situational elements that facilitate or mitigate against skill application and acquisition. The combined information obtained from the individual functional assessments and the assessment of the individual's environment provides the basis for the development of the individual active treatment program plan.

CONTENT OF AN ACTIVE TREATMENT PLAN

Effective and efficient teaching and learning does not occur in a casual "seat of the pants" atmosphere. Although from the casual observer's viewpoint, effective teaching and learning may appear to be informal, it is more likely to occur when the skills to be taught and the behaviors to be acquired and/or eliminated are carefully manipulated by competent individuals who consistently and correctly apply specified techniques to achieve the objectives set for the individual. Therefore, in order for the information gained from functional assessments to be translated into effective interventions, it is necessary for the individuals responsible for teaching to organize and implement a plan tailored to the needs of the individual, based upon the assessment findings.

The individualized active treatment plan is the foundation of the person's intervention program. It identifies in precise, objective, and measurable terms the instructional focus for the period of time covered by the plan. It also specifies:

How this focus is to be carried out
Who is responsible
Necessary supportive or specialized services
Necessary specialized equipment
Needed alterations to the interactional ecology
The documentation mechanisms most appropriate to that program plan or to a specific objective or service
The general approach to be used in accomplishing the objective

The development of the plan, therefore, transcends particular disciplines, although each discipline's perspective is necessary to ensure coordination, consistency, and maximum benefit from the program. The plan is predicated on the assumption that each individual is capable of change, or development, both horizontally (e.g., applying skills in various environments and situations) and/or vertically (e.g., acquiring new skills or behaviors based on current skills or behaviors).

Typically, the plan is implemented through the development and implementation of an *activity schedule*. This schedule identifies those factors that serve as the prime instructional environments for particular objectives and those that provide opportunities for reinforcement, practice, and refinement. The schedule serves as a "map" of the day, a practical, daily translation of what is specified in the plan. Its purpose is to guide the instructor in directing activities that will benefit the individual participating in the activity.

However, a common pitfall in the implementation of the activity schedule is the mistaken notion that the plan's objectives are taught in discrete settings at particular times, and that the rest of the time is simply "free." While the activity schedule does structure teaching times, which is especially important when establishing new behaviors, refining teaching techniques, testing reinforcement schedules, or establishing behavior-reduction programs, implementation of an active treatment program is better defined in terms of the competency with which all caregivers implement techniques and programs in all settings any time the opportunity is presented. Thus, active treatment is a continuous process of competent interactions, responsive to each opportunity for individually targeted interventions based on the plan and established through the more formal teaching that takes place in the scheduled activities.

From a program standpoint—whether a residential program, a home-based parent training program, or school setting—the individualized program plans and activity schedules assist in identifying types and numbers of needed staff, and the staff competencies necessary to implement the plan effectively. Activity schedules also may be used as a management tool for resource allocation decisions, internal quality assurance systems, and management/supervisory systems. Viewed as a whole, then, the active treatment process establishes a continuous feedback loop in which the documentation of individual performance becomes the basis for subsequent assessment, objectives development, and implementation.

The following example of "Carrie P." illustrates the process and impact of a properly developed and implemented active treatment program plan.

Vignette: Carrie P.

Carrie P., a 52-year-old woman with Down syndrome, had lived in a large state institution for 37 years. She recently moved into a group home with seven other individuals and was enrolled in a local sheltered workshop. According to the records that were given to the group home, she had been diagnosed as being moderately mentally retarded and as having a moderate speech impairment, a mild right-side hearing loss, juvenile onset diabetes with early cataracts, diabetic reti-nopathy, peripheral and diabetic neuropathy, osteoporosis, and fibrocystic breast disease. For the first 3 weeks after she moved to the group home, she refused to participate in any house activities or to attend the sheltered workshop, and averaged seven incidents of inappropriate behavior a day. These took the form of sitting on the floor and refusing to move for periods of 20 to 30 minutes.

In order to develop an active treatment program for Carrie, it was necessary to identify her current performance-based functional status across the social, physical, cognitive, and behavioral domains, and to assess her ability to function in the areas of personal care, mobility, communications, social, leisure/recreational, vocational, and adaptive/community living. The questions to be considered were:

What are the environments in which she currently functions?

How does she function in those environments?

What skills does she currently have?

What skills is she learning?

What are the impacts of her varying diagnoses on her ability to function in those environments or to learn additional skills?

Where is she expected to function?

What are priority areas of instruction for her?

What modifications must be made in the instructional and daily programs, as well as in the environment, because of her disabilities?

Which disabilities can be remediated, and to what extent?

What are the ways, if any, of circumventing nonremedial disabilities?

What specialized equipment does she require?

Of greatest importance in developing an individual's active treatment program is to assemble a team that can acquire all the necessary information from a variety of sources. Although each person providing information does not have to be physically present at a planning session, it is crucial that key individuals meet to process all of the information provided. In Carrie P.'s case, because of her diverse problems, the team consisted of a large number of individuals. For example, a social worker, psychologist, nurse, communications therapist, audiologist, physical therapist, occupational therapist, dietition, pharmacist, direct care staff person, employment specialist, as well as Carrie and her guardian, participated in the development of her active treatment program plan. Not all of these individuals attended the actual team meeting, but the information supplied by them was taken into account.

Each team member's assessment identified either no need for services or provided sufficient detail to enable the core team to develop an appropriate program. Team members not physically present at the planning session were asked to review the final objectives and implementation plans. The plan then evolved into an activity schedule, and outlined the staff competencies necessary to implement the plan in all settings in which Carrie P. lived and worked. For example, one principal objective was to decrease resistance behavior and increase cooperative behavior. The techniques necessary to implement these two complementary objectives had to be known and used by all of the staff and family members who interacted with Carrie P. on a routine basis. Likewise, all aspects of the plan and the information needed to implement it had to be known and used correctly and consistently in all settings.

In summary, the individual's active treatment program plan should reflect the current status and problems experienced by the person, should present a coordinated treatment plan for the particular constellation of problems and disabilities, and should assist that individual to improve or maintain an optimum level of independent functioning. Although the team composition, individual objectives, range of supportive services, documentation mechanisms, and activity schedules will differ from person to person, the process by which the plan is achieved is the same. Thus, active treatment is not context-bound because it focuses on the individual, and not the setting or particular delivery system. Active treatment allows for a variety of ideological approaches and methodologies. Its mandates are client- and content-oriented. The decisions as to "how" remain with each assessor, implementor, and service provider.

The preceding discussion has centered on the technical aspects of developing an active treatment program. However, even if the plan is technically "correct," it is still quite possible that active treatment will not occur. Once functional, an active treatment program can best be thought of as a process rather than as a product or discrete applications of organized therapies. As a process, active treatment assumes that any given interaction between a caregiver and a resident—in formal and informal settings alike—will result in a productive outcome for that resident. The following vignette illustrates this point:

Vignette

It is 7:00 P.M. on a Thursday evening in a group home. There are six residents—three men and three women, and one staff person who lives with them. Dinner is over, the dishes are done, and everyone is watching television. The staff person notices out of the corner of his eye that a resident across the room is beginning to engage in stereotypical head-rocking and hand movements, and that the pattern is rapidly accelerating. The staff person quietly goes over to the resident and takes the resident's hands and gently places them in her lap while stating, "Can we watch TV together?" The resident refocuses on the program and the staff person begins to distance himself from the resident until he finally returns to his own chair.

The staff person *knew* that there was a specific program in place for dealing with this resident's stereotypic behavior, he *knew how* to intervene in the behavior, and did so *correctly and appropriately*. Thus, in the midst of a casual, informal time, the staff person implemented an active treatment intervention because it was needed. This example can be generalized across all interactions, residents, and caregivers. To reiterate, then, active treatment is the *competent* interaction with a resident in service of that person's specific objectives.

ACTIVE TREATMENT VARIABLES

Philosophy and Attitudes

The perspectives from which the service provider and staff view the individual create an atmosphere in which active treatment either flourishes or withers. If the individual is viewed as the core of the program and is seen from a positive, proactive stance as someone capable of change, a solid foundation for the delivery of active treatment exists. If, however, the orientation is toward merely maintaining the status quo of the individual, staff, and/or programs, active treatment will not occur or will occur only in isolated situations dependent upon particular people.

Philosophy and attitudes are translated into behaviors: how individuals are talked to and interacted with, the issues that are given priority when there are changes or problems, how the environment is structured, how decisions are made, how staff are trained and supervised, and how individuals advocate or are advocated for. The presence of written policies and procedures with a positive orientation is not sufficient; translation of these into observable acts offers proof of incorporation and acceptance.

Allocation of Resources

Allocation of resources refers to the manner in which fiscal, physical, and personnel supports are supplied and maintained within a program. Implementation of active treatment requires that each resource be decided relative to the needs of the individuals served. Those resources that are most relevant to a resident's needs and welfare receive first consideration. Allocation of resources should acknowledge that active treatment is a 24-hour-a-day task. The recognition that evening, weekend, holiday, and vacation times require the same commitment to active treatment as do weekdays means that the service provider considers the total program when setting staffing patterns, buying equipment, offering training, or securing service contracts.

The existence of political, financial, or organizational constraints does not absolve the provider from providing active treatment. Rather, such constraints necessitate a proactive posture on the part of the provider; a coordination with other elements in the community; an active advocacy for individual needs; and a willingness to move out of traditional service delivery patterns.

Staff

The quality of the development and implementation of program and services has a direct relationship to staff. Job descriptions, hiring practices, pre-service and in-service training, and staff supervision form a cohesive system designed to develop and promote attitudes and behavioral competencies necessary to deliver an appropriate, consistent, positive program. Since many small programs often have clinical personnel on contract for a limited number of hours, the day-to-day implementation of specialized programs rests with entry level or direct care personnel. The provision of adequate training and monitoring thus assumes critical importance. Staff must understand the bases of each resident's program, must be able to demonstrate the skills and techniques necessary to implement individual programs, must keep adequate data on performance, and must be able to access necessary supports and information. In addition, monitoring and supervision of programs in a variety of settings is required to ensure consistency.

Environment

The combination of physical plant, furnishings, materials, equipment, and general ambience comprises the physical environment. The environment either supports and is conducive to active treatment or represents an obstacle to be overcome or circumvented. An individual's responses or behaviors are often determined or influenced by the environment. A good environment contains things that are not only appropriate to individual needs but that also encourage interaction, response, and positive participation. Such an environment provides the clues individuals may need to develop or manifest certain skills or behaviors. For example, any residence for persons with developmental disabilities should be planned and decorated around the concept of "home," so that the residence does not look like or function as a workplace for staff, and cues appropriate adaptive behavior.

Clearly, the attitudes and values of staff may influence the specific characteristics of an active treatment program. Further, the perceived focus of the program affects how staff react. For example, an individual who does not have a repertoire of appropriate social behaviors may require a program that, for a given time period, subordinates an emphasis on particular skill domains to the shaping and reinforcing of the social behaviors, using the environment and normal rhythms of the day as a context in which certain behaviors are encouraged or discouraged. Staff may find themselves responding to a behavior rather than a person, or to an historic perception of the person. The key factors become the focusing of objectives, resources, staff, and environment on those behaviors; the consistency and continuity of the program; and the ability of the program to change as the resident changes.

Likewise, individuals who present medical problems, are aging, are dependent, or have severe and multiple disabilities would necessitate the development and/or modification of a program to reflect these abilities and needs. The objectives prepared for residents, the staff requirements, patterns and training, and the resources and environment should be tailored to the needs of those individuals. What remains constant, however, across individuals is the emphasis on the development of the individual and the enrichment of his or her life.

Program Type

The size, location, and nature of a program does not change what constitutes active treatment. These factors do, however, influence or affect the ease with which it is achieved. A small-group home in a rural area offering one type of living environment may face problems of coordination, consistency, and staffing, whereas a program that is a part of a large agency may need to grapple with issues related to size, communication, compartmentalization, and bureaucracy. In each instance, the provider is accountable both for the delivery of active treatment in his or her own program or department and for active advocacy to ensure the provision of such a program in all other areas.

SUMMARY

Active treatment requires seven-day-a-week, 24-hour-a-day programs that carefully and consistently seek to maintain and improve the ability of a person with developmental disabilities to function in the most independent manner possible, given that person's skills, preferences, behaviors, and choices. Every element of the program, from dwelling, to the documentation, to the staff, needs to be directed toward that end. While active treatment is typically associated with the ICF/MR program, it has, by legislation, regulation, and best practice standards, become a core criterion by which all program effectiveness is judged. Active treatment, as a concept, focuses services on the needs of the individual, rather than on the service provider.

REFERENCES

Accreditation Council for Services to Mentally Retarded and Other Developmentally Disabled Persons. (1984). *Standards for services for developmentally disabled individuals*. Boston: Accreditation Council for Services to Mentally Retarded and Other Developmentally Disabled Persons.

Blatt, B., & Kaplan, F. (1966). *Christmas in purgatory: A photographic essay on mental retardation*. New York: Allyn & Bacon.

Casey, K., McGee, J., Stark, J., & Menolascino, F. (1985). *A community based system for the mentally retarded: The ENCOR experience*. Lincoln: University of Nebraska Press.

Donnellan, A.M., & Neel, R. (1986). New directions in educating students with autism. In R. Horner, L. Meyer, & H.D. Fredericks (Eds.), *Education of learners with severe handicaps: Exemplary service strategies* (pp. 99–126). Baltimore: Paul H. Brookes Publishing Co.

Elder, J.O., & Magrab, P.B. (Eds.). (1980). *Coordinating services to handicapped children: A handbook for interagency collaboration*. Baltimore: Paul H. Brookes Publishing Co.

Falvey, M. (1986). *Community-based curriculum: Instructional strategies for students with severe handicaps*. Baltimore: Paul H. Brookes Publishing Co.

Gaylord-Ross, R., Stremel-Campbell, K., & Storey, K. (1986). Social skills training in natural contexts. In R. Horner, L.H. Meyer, & H.D. Fredericks (Eds.), *Education of learners with severe handicaps: Exemplary service strategies* (pp. 161–187). Baltimore: Paul H. Brookes Publishing Co.

Guess, D., & Helmstetter, E. (1986). Skill cluster instruction and the individualized curriculum sequencing model. In R. Horner, L.H. Meyer, & H.D. Fredericks (Eds.), *Education of learners with severe handicaps: Exemplary service strategies* (pp. 221–248). Baltimore: Paul H. Brookes Publishing Co.

Horner, R., Meyer, L.H., & Fredericks, H.D. (Eds.). (1986). *Education of learners with severe handicaps: Exemplary service stratgies*. Baltimore: Paul H. Brookes Publishing Co.

Meyer, L.H., & Evans, I.M. (1986). Modification of excess behavior. In R. Horner, L.H. Meyer, & H.D. Fredericks (Eds.), *Education of learners with severe handicaps:*

Exemplary service strategies (pp. 315–350). Baltimore: Paul H. Brookes Publishing Co.

Paine, S.C., Bellamy, G.T., & Wilcox, B. (Eds.). (1984). *Human services that work: From innovation to standard practice.* Baltimore: Paul H. Brookes Publishing Co.

President's Panel on Mental Retardation (1962). Washington, DC: U.S. Government Printing Office.

Public Law 92-223. (1971, December [Effective 1/1/72]). Section 1905(d) of the Social Security Act, *42 Code of federal regulations,* Section 435.1009.

Public Law 94-142. (1975, November 29). *Education for All Handicapped Children Act of 1975,* 20 U.S.C. 1401 et seq.

Public Law 95-602. (1976). *Developmental Disabilities Assistance and Bill of Rights Act of 1978,* 42 U.S.C. 6000 et. seq.

Summers, J.A. (Ed.). (1986). *The right to grow up: An introduction to adults with developmental disabilities.* Baltimore: Paul H. Brookes Publishing Co.

Summers, J.A. (1986). Who are developmentally disabled adults? In J.A. Summers (Ed.), *The right to grow up: An introduction to adults with developmental disabilities* (pp. 3–16). Baltimore: Paul H. Brookes.

Turnbull, H.R., & Barber, P. (1986). Federal laws and adults with developmental disabilities. In J.A. Summers (Ed.), *The right to grow up: An introduction to adults with developmental disabilities* (pp. 255–277). Baltimore: Paul H. Brookes Publishing Co.

Chapter 11

Behavioral and Social Climate in Community Group Residences

David Felce

Orientation, structure, and procedures are three defining features of housing programs for persons with mental retardation. *Orientation* refers to the objectives to which a program aspires. *Structure* includes the relatively permanent features of the residential environment that are decided upon in the initial planning. *Procedures* are the training and operational systems that guide staff performance. This chapter addresses how these characteristics affect the behavioral and social climate of community residences. The findings of past research conducted by the author on these issues are presented and related to a proposed residential model.

The provision of community residences for adult mentally retarded citizens has expanded considerably during the past two decades. This chapter describes the evaluation of such a community residence program in England, a program that has used ordinary housing to comprehensively fulfill the needs of severely retarded adults, including those with disruptive behavior. The program's aim was to test the feasibility of providing a normalized life-style for a group of persons considered by many to be one of the most difficult to care for. In particular, it attempted to approximate as closely as possible a normal adult pattern of activity appropriate to the residents' chronological ages, both inside the home and in the community. Research accompanying the development and evaluation of the program provided insight into the variety of factors that may determine service quality and resident experience.

The literature and popular characterization of residential settings emphasize certain defining features of different residential models. Size, location, and building characteristics are cited frequently as major factors in defining the dichotomy/continuum between "small, community-based, domestic, normalized" and "large, isolated, institutional" settings. However, those familiar with service provision are aware of the myriad decisions concerning other aspects of a residential project that are made from the initial conceptualization and continuing through implementation. Many of these decisions are not discussed in the general debate on successful residential service arrangements, and, yet in practical terms, they exert a crucial influence on how the service operates and the scope of resident experience. This chapter describes in detail the components of a particular residential model and relates these components

The research reported in this chapter was supported by DHSS Grant 0780, and the chapter was prepared under a grant from Portsmouth Health Authority, England.

to empirical findings concerning: a) the behavioral and social ecology within the community homes and b) the extent, quality, and acceptability of community integration. The chapter draws upon experiences from a series of studies conducted by this writer and his colleagues, both to illustrate and amplify the text.

DEFINING THE RESIDENTIAL SETTING

In general, the literature on community residential alternatives to traditional institutions reports that residents in community-based housing demonstrate higher skill development, increased amount and range of activity, and greater community contact (e.g., Close, 1977; Conroy, Efthimiou, & Lemanowicz, 1982; Felce, de Kock, & Repp, 1986; Felce, Kushlick, & Smith, 1983; MacEachron, 1983; O'Neill, Brown, Gordon, Schonhorn, & Greer, 1981; O'Neill, Brown, Gordon, & Schonhorn, 1985; Rawlings, 1985; Schalock, Harper & Carver, 1981). However, there is considerable variation among different forms of community programs, resulting in different outcomes for the individuals served (Bjaanes & Butler, 1974). Some community facilities have been found to restrict resident participation and to lack community involvement or active habilation (Birenbaum & Re, 1979; Butler & Bjaanes, 1978). It is therefore essential to precisely and comprehensively describe programs so that all factors contributing to beneficial outcome are identified. Unfortunately, there is little definitive evidence on the exact combination of factors constituting high-quality care (Landesman-Dwyer, 1981). Explanation remains largely at the level of facility type however categorized; when researchers have looked for powerful effects attached to single-provision variables, such as size, staffing levels, or architectural design, they have often failed to find them. For example, although two separate studies (King, Raynes, & Tizard, 1971; McCormick, Balla, & Zigler, 1975) consistently found that care practices were more resident-oriented in group homes than in large institutions, there were inconsistencies concerning the factors that might contribute to such a result. Empirical findings do not support a precise relationship between size of residence and

outcome (Balla, 1976; King et al, 1971; Landesman-Dwyer, 1981; Landesman-Dwyer, Sackett, & Kleinman, 1980). Provision variables are confounded, and the terms used to characterize settings are often arbitrarily selected from a larger list of differences that may separate them. Sandler and Thurman (1981) have pointed out that, in many studies showing positive behavioral changes in favor of community residences, it is not possible to separate the contributions of the characteristics of the settings (service structure) from those of staff training and quality of programming (staff procedures).

The scope of variation between types of program that could be crudely categorized as similar is recognized. Butler and Bjaanes (1977) have discussed the development of a typology for community settings to distinguish custodial, therapeutic, and maintaining environments. In a similar vein, Janicki (1981) has argued the importance of establishing the rehabilitative intent within the setting as an independent factor, one that cannot be assumed from other setting characteristics. Our work in the United Kingdom on the provision of residential services has led us to a similar view. In the course of an evaluation of staffed community-based alternatives to traditional institutions (Felce, Kushlick, & Smith, 1983), it was clear that even the new community residences generally lacked formal procedures designed to promote individual or group goals. The mere fact of a program being community-based may not imply either an hab-ilititive as opposed to custodial orientation or a well-organized internal regime directed toward explicit objectives.

In seeking to develop a housing model (described in the next section) for severely and profoundly mentally handicapped adults, we focused on three independent dimensions: 1) the *program orientation*, which defines in operational terms the service's therapeutic direction, 2) the *program structure*, which defines the major organizational parameters of the service setting, and 3) the *program procedures*, which define how staff work with residents within the setting.

The definition of service orientation underpins decisions concerning program structure and operational procedures. In designing our project, we sought a service structure that would both facilitate accomplishment and would minimize potential barriers to achieving stated objectives. It was also our intention to develop some systematic guide to staff performance for each explicit objective of the service. We believed that the eventual outcome would be a consequence of the interaction between these structural and procedural factors. The implementation of staff procedures may not be possible without a conducive service structure. Conversely, without attention to staff procedures, the opportunities of a beneficial service structure may go unrealized.

The notion that outcome is generated by the interaction of several factors in combination not only has intuitive appeal but may also help explain inconsistencies apparent in the literature. For example, McCormick et al. (1975) suggested such an interaction effect could be the basis of the difference between their study and that of King et al. (1971) concerning the association between aide-turnover rate and care practices: "It may well be that such human factors as continuity of staffing can only become operative in certain settings" (p. 15). Manipulation of a single factor such as continuity or level of staffing may produce different results depending on other characteristics of the setting. There may be no overridingly powerful independent variables that have predictable effects in isolation, and the nature of the task in establishing high-quality residences is therefore to be meticulous to detail.

DESCRIPTION OF THE RESIDENTIAL MODEL

Table 1 lists the parameters and salient features of the community home model. We were interested in developing a residential environment that gave people living there effective opportunities to participate in a wide range of daily activities and to continue to grow in competence. These objectives were set within a broader context of a continuing relationship with immediate family and an ordinary community life. To these ends, the residences were small, enriched, well-staffed, managerially autonomous,

and served people with local ties. They also had a structured approach to individual plan review, to how staff arranged their responsibilities for resident care and the provision of activity, to how staff supported residents in the conduct of the household routine, and to monitoring resident experience.

The first two homes established were the subjects of our study. They each provide places for eight individuals and are both ordinary detached houses in residential neighbourhoods located a few minutes' walk from the shopping area of the main town in the catchment territory served. Each house is fully equipped with high-quality furnishings that emphasize a comfortably domestic character. Environmental deprivation (e.g., not having carpeting or breakable objects) and overprotection (e.g., vinyl-covered furniture) as resident management strategies were avoided, and there is no wholesale restriction of resident access to areas that may have greater inherent risks, such as the kitchen. These concerns do mean that staff need to be able to cope with difficult behavior, incontinence, and other accidents arising from lack of skill among residents. But these abilities are integral to a high-quality program.

Each house has one person in charge, a deputy, seven other day staff and four half-time night staff. The day staff work from 7.30 A.M. to 3.00 P.M. and from 2.30 P.M. to 10.00 P.M., with two or three staff on duty at a time. The caregiving role is to help residents lead as full an ordinary home life as possible, in which they do their own cooking and other domestic tasks. To support this orientation, the houses have considerable autonomy over budgeting and purchasing, they do not receive externally organized services such as centralized laundry or supply of provisions, and senior staff are responsible for house maintenance and junior staff recruitment.

The program aims to provide each resident the same range of home and community activities that are important to anyone else of similar age. The program takes a structured approach to staff performance and staff:resident interaction. Specific staff procedures promote a goal-setting approach in formulating individualized resident plans, in writing formal

Table 1.   Components of the residential model

Orientation	Structure	Staff procedures
Definition of service function To provide a permanent home	**Size and building design** Eight places in ordinary domestic house **Location** In community residential area close to town center amenities **Clientele** Severely/profoundly retarded adults with local next-of-kin in defined catchment area Heterogeneous grouping within those eligible	**Individual programs** Behavioral goal-setting/program implementation: Global individualized program plan reviews Formal skill-teaching programs Behavior-reduction programs **Organization of the residential day** Weekly household routine Daily planning of staff duties Daily allocation of staff to client groups
Service competencies To provide: Continuing behavioral development Extensive, meaningful age-appropriate occupation Sustained family relationships Community involvement Status-enhancing appearance appropriate to age Alternatives to damaging disruptive behavior	**Material enrichment** As high-quality family home Unrestricted client access throughout home **Staffing level** Nine day staff and two night staff provide 24-hour, 7-day-per-week cover Two to three day staff on duty at a time **Staff roles and job description** All staff assume caregiving role to support clients in living full household life No domestics or catering staff **Management autonomy** Staff in the house have control over: Own catering, laundry, house and grounds maintenance Staff recruitment Purchase of provisions and materials Budget and expenditure	**Staff interaction with clients** Guided by: Specific client programs Routine use of instruct/show/guide antecedent hierarchy Routine deployment of staff attention contingent on client adaptive behavior **Monitoring and review** Daily recording on each client Client participation in household activity Teaching implementation and success Community use Family/friendship contacts Feedback at 3-hour weekly staff meeting

teaching programs, and in preparing daily plans by which staff plan each resident's activities during the day. Staff are taught to use an instruct/show/prompt/guide hierarchy to enable severely retarded residents with little adaptive behavior to participate effectively but as independently as possible. Staff are also taught to motivate resident participation by giving contingent attention. During the course of each day, staff record what household and community activities residents have been involved in, the implementation and success of teaching, and any social contact residents have had with family or friends. The information is summarized to provide a source of feedback and critical review.

THE BEHAVIORAL AND SOCIAL ECOLOGY WITHIN HOUSES

The purpose of our research was to evaluate whether the residential model better achieved the desired objectives than other available services. Community-based residences were compared to two types of settings: 1) traditional institutions, where the majority of the community-based residents previously lived and where a substantial majority of similar residents in Great Britain still live; and 2) larger community-based units that have been recently provided as an alternative to such institutions. The two houses we evaluated served all of the most severely intellectually impaired adults requiring

Table 2. Sex, age, mental age, social impairments, and length of institutionalization of subjects

Subject	1	2	3	4	5	6	7	8	9	10	11	12	13	14
Sex	F	F	M	M	F	F	M	F	M	F	F	F	F	F
Chronological age (years)	50	21	50	27	31	53	66	24	35	40	56	43	40	51
Mental age (months)	8	14	18	21	25	28	30	31	32	33	42	42	45	48
Triad of social impairments[a]	•	•		•	•				•					
Institutionalization (years)[b]	44	FH	1	18	FH	36	1	13	33	34	50	FH	FH	2

[a] *Source:* Wing and Gould (1979).
[b] FH—admitted from family home.
•—has triad.

residential care with next-of-kin in a defined research territory of approximately 60,000 total population. The group included persons characterized as severely behavior disordered with many years of prior institutional experience, some in specially restricted environments. In all, 14 individuals living in the small homes were studied. Their characteristics are summarized in Table 2. Similar residents living in institutions and larger community units served as controls. Studies examining the ecology of the houses have employed measures of staff-resident interaction and resident engagement in activity based on the observational categories listed in Table 3.

Adaptive resident activity found in three studies spanning a 2-year period is categorized in Figure 1. The purpose of Study #1 was to measure the extent of meaningful engagement in the first house and to determine the degree to which household activity could provide a source of age-appropriate activity for considerably intellectually impaired subjects. The results showed that appropriate engagement among the first five permanent residents occupied an average of 46% of the waking day,

Table 3. Measurement categories

Client behaviors:

Appropriate engagement
a. Leisure
b. Personal
c. Domestic
d. Formal program
e. Interacts with client
f. Interacts with staff

Inappropriate engagement
a. Self-stimulation
b. Aggression to self
c. Aggression to others
d. Aggression to property
e. Inappropriate vocalization
f. Other inappropriate

Neutral engagement
a. Passive
b. Aimless ambulation
c. Smoking
d. Watching TV
e. Unpurposeful

Staff behaviors:

Antecedents
a. Instruction
b. Demonstration
c. Physical guidance

Consequences
a. Positive verbal
b. Positive physical
c. Neutral verbal
d. Neutral physical
e. Negative verbal
f. Negative physical

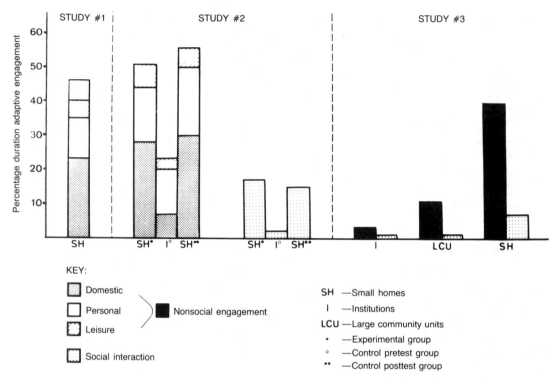

Figure 1. Appropriate client engagement in three studies in small homes, institutions, and large community units.

and that domestic activity generated almost half of it (range, 30%–65%) (Mansell, Jenkins, Felce, & de Kock, 1984).

The results of this initial study were confirmed in the second study, which provides a within-subject and a between-subject comparison of the resident experience in the small homes with that in traditional institutions (Felce et al., 1986). The experimental group (n = 6) lived in the first small home, the control pretest group (n = 6) lived in institutional settings, and a control posttest was achieved by observing the same individuals after transfer to a small home. The experimental and control groups were demographic samples matched on mental age, language age, chronological age, and adaptive functioning. Resident engagement in activity, both nonsocial and social, was considerably higher in the small homes (experimental and control posttest) than in the institutions, where little was done to support resident activity. This picture of low levels of activity and interaction

with staff in institutions and considerably higher levels in the small homes was further confirmed in Study #3 (see Figure 1), which also considered larger (25-place) community environments (Thomas, Felce, de Kock, Saxby & Repp, 1986). Appropriate engagement in the larger community units was slightly greater than in the institutions, but still substantially lower than in the small homes.

In addition, data on staff interaction with residents were simultaneously collected. Staff interaction whether in the form of antecedent support, encouragement, or discouragement to residents was extremely low in both the institutions and large community units. In comparison, small-home residents received instruction for an average of 20% and 11% of the time and physical guidance for an average of 5% and 3% of the time in the two houses, respectively (Felce et al., 1986). Moreover, the duration of antecedent interaction was appropriately related to degree of retardation, with those individuals with lower mental ages receiving more help, thereby enabling them to approximate the levels of meaningful occupation of the more able. Further, a Spearman rank correlation coefficient of 0.97 was found within subjects between the levels of staff antecedent support and nonsocial engagement.

In another study, the relationship of activity to the physical environment was examined (Felce, Thomas, de Kock, Saxby, & Repp, 1985). Residents in the small homes had a greater variety and extent of activity than in institutions. Much activity was found to be dependent on materials and equipment present in the functional areas of the homes such as in the kitchen and utility room, areas to which institutionalized residents typically are not given access.

To further examine differences in the ecologies of the residential environments, data on resident engagement and staff:resident interaction were collected for nine matched groups of 10 severely and profoundly mentally handicapped adults living in four institutional settings, three large community units, and two sets of small homes (Felce et al., 1987). In this study, the size of the staff:resident group of which the subject being observed was a part was continuously recorded, and staff and resident functioning were related to the absolute group composition and to the staff:resident ratio. Where a relationship existed between the staff:resident ratio and the extent of staff interaction or appropriate resident engagement, two findings applied to all three types of settings. First, resident improvement accompanied an increase in the staff:resident ratio only as a result of a reduction in the number of residents being looked after by one and sometimes two staff. Little improvement was found by increasing the numbers of staff present. Second, when the resident group was 5–9 or 10 or more in the institutions and large community units, staff interactions and resident engagement were low irrespective of whether there were one, two, three, or four staff members present.

Table 4 summarizes the social ecologies of the three types of settings. The data reveal important differences that support the earlier

Table 4. Percentage occurrence of each staff : resident ratio condition for various numbers of staff

# of Staff	Setting	Percentage occurrence of each ratio[a]							
		# of residents				# of residents			
		1–4	5–9	10+	Total[c]	1	2	3–4	Total[c]
Zero	Institutions	26	16	2	44				
	Large community units	37	9	2	48				
	Small homes					16	6	—	22
One	Institutions	5	8	4	17				
	Large community units	15	7	4	27				
	Small homes					13	14	15	42
Two	Institutions	2	11	6	19				
	Large community units	4	5	2	11				
	Small homes					6	12	11	29
Three	Institutions	—	6	6	12				
	Large community units	3	3	2	7				
	Small homes					—	2	5	7
Four	Institutions	—	2	5	7				
	Large community units	—	—	—	—				
	Small homes					—	—	—	—
Total[b,c]	Institutions	8	27	20					
	Large community units	22	15	8					
	Small homes								77

[a]Data for institutions and large community units are listed separately from those for small homes because there were no small homes with resident groups larger than 4.

[b]A single total for 1–3 staff and 1–4 residents is given for small homes. Totals for institutions and large community centers are for 1–4 staff according to three categories of resident group size; the total for small homes compares to the smallest (1–4) of these.

[c]Totals may not sum precisely because of rounding errors.

findings of greater staff and resident activity in the small homes: a) residents were unsupervised far more in the institutions (44% of the time) and in large community units (48%) than in the small homes (22%); b) residents were with staff alone or in small groups of two to four more often in the small homes (77% of the time) than in the institutions (8%) or the large community units (22%); c) staff worked alone with groups of residents far more in the small homes (42% of the time) than in the institutions (17%) or the large community units (27%); and d) institutional and large community unit staff were with residents when the resident group size exceeded five for 47% and 23% of the time, respectively.

Another aspect of the social ecology of the residential environment is the responsiveness of staff to resident behavior. In an associated study (Felce, Saxby, de Kock, Repp, Ager, & Blunden, 1987), the relationship between appropriate, inappropriate, or neutral resident behavior and staff contact was investigated (Table 5). The density of staff encouragement of appropriate resident behavior was three times greater in the small homes than in the institutions and large community units. A discrimination index, calculated by deriving the ratio of staff contacts given to appropriate behavior over all staff contacts, shows that staff in the large community units and small homes gave the majority of their attention contingent on appropriate engagement (2:1 and 3:1, respectively), but that the distribution of staff attention in the institutions was noncontingent.

COMMUNITY INTEGRATION

In addition to the belief that a better home environment will be established with the change in service provision from institution to community, the community-living movement has also derived momentum from the assumption that mentally handicapped persons will be able to participate more in the mainstream of community life. Our studies addressed the community integration issue by measuring the *frequency of social contact* that residents have with family and friends (henceforth referred to as *family contact*), the *frequency of use of community amenities* such as shops, bars, cafés, and leisure facilities (henceforth referred to as *community contact*), and the *resident participation in activity* when using community amenities. The views of amenity proprietors and staff concerning the level of integration experienced were also obtained. Two comparisons of the rate of family and community contact in the small homes were conducted: with the subjects' prior institutional experience and with that of control subjects in larger community units (de Kock, Felce, Saxby, & Thomas, 1985). Figure 2 combines the results by giving comparative average annual rates. Small-home residents received an average of 70 family contacts per year, half in the form of visits to the houses and the remainder split evenly between trips out during the day or overnight stays. This level compared to only 11 contacts per year in the previous residential institutions and 48 contacts per year in the larger community environments. In the latter, which also had local residents, frequencies of trips out during the day and overnight stays were similar to those in the small homes. Almost 250 community contacts were experienced per person in the small homes. This compared to only 7 events per year in the previous institutions and 72 in the large community units. Shopping accounted for 54% of small-

Table 5. Percentage staff response to appropriate client behavior and percentage of total contacts to appropriate client-behavior (staff discrimination) in institutions, large community units, and small homes

Setting	Staff response			Staff discrimination
	No response	Encouraging	Other	
Institutions	67.4	15.9	16.7	50.8
Large community units	66.5	16.5	17.0	69.3
Small homes	42.3	42.6	15.1	76.8

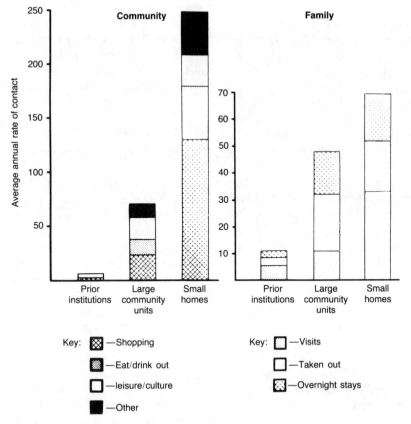

Figure 2. Average annual rates of community and family contacts in prior institutions, large community units, and small homes.

home events; eating or drinking out in a bar, café or restaurant a further 19%; and cultural or leisure events 11%.

The most frequent community contacts were shopping and visits to bars, cafés, and restaurants. A direct observational study of activity while using these amenities was conducted to gain information on resident experience (Saxby, Thomas, Felce, & de Kock, 1986). Specifically, we were interested in whether the residents participated in the substantive activity that the amenities occasioned and interacted with community citizens or whether their role was one of passively accompanying staff and remaining uninvolved and isolated from contact with the public. Nonsocial participation while shopping or in bars and cafés occupied 29% and 36% of the time, respectively. These figures are somewhat lower than engagement levels within

the homes, but the level of social interaction between staff and residents was similar. However, interactions with the general public were short, occupying an average duration of 2% (range across subjects was 0% to 6%). Finally, inappropriate behavior occurred for an average of 6.4% of the time in shops and 11.3% of the time in bars/cafés. This was limited mainly to four individuals and in particular to one who spent 53% of her time in self-stimulation in bars/cafés and 21% of her time similarly engaged in shops.

In order to assess the acceptability of this level of community involvement from the viewpoint of the businesses, proprietors, managers, and other staff from the six large shops, six small shops, two bars, and two cafés used most frequently were interviewed. All respondents found the frequency of use of their amenity—

which varied from daily to about once a week—acceptable, and found one or two hand-icapped customers at a time the preferable group size. In response to whether they thought the residents stood out from other customers, 10.8% said they did to a considerable degree, 21.6% said a moderate degree, 45.9% little, and 21.6% not at all. Noisiness was singled out most frequently as an intrusive characteristic. One respondent felt that resident behavior needed improvement, and one expressed "a lit-tle concern." Caregivers were rated as dealing well with problematic behavior. The substantial majority of community respondents (92.1%) considered the residents' appearance to be as presentable or more presentable than the average customer. Residents were also seen as being involved in the community; only 5.6% of re-spondents said they were rarely involved in ac-tivities and only 11.1% said they were rarely involved in interactions with them. A similarly high proportion of respondents (97.4%) felt the individuals benefited from community involve-ment, 63.2% felt their business benefited, 21.1% felt they benefited personally, and 42.2% felt other customers benefited.

FACTORS INFLUENCING THE BEHAVIORAL AND SOCIAL CLIMATE

The data show that in many areas of adaptive functioning, range of environmental oppor-tunity, and appropriateness of staff interaction, the small-home model was superior to the other types of settings evaluated. However, as in nu-merous other research studies, we can only ex-plain the differences in resident and staff behav-ior on a global level by reference to facility type. Many factors are implicated in the dif-ferences between the residential settings ana-lyzed, and the research design does not allow the influence of these differences to be sepa-rated. The key question is: Why are the small homes better environments? It is not possible to prove empirically the relationship between components of the model and resident outcome. However, it is useful to return to the factors itemized in Table 1 and to discuss their possible contribution. In so doing, the distinction be-tween necessary and sufficient conditions is helpful. The evaluation shows that the small-home model had conditions sufficient to pro-duce markedly more beneficial outcomes. Of interest is which of the factors constituting the model are necessary for which outcomes.

Staff Performance

Staff performance within the houses has been demonstrated to be related to resident function-ing. Staff were taught to employ a simple hier-archy of antecedent conditions from instruction to extended physical guidance, and to reinforce engaged adaptive behavior differentially. It seems likely that this routine interactional style was also strengthened by the monitoring of resi-dent experience, the feedback generated, and the demonstration of skills required to formu-late specific programs (setting educational ob-jectives in behavioral terms, task analysis, and explicit attention to reinforcement and correc-tion). Given that the character of staff perfor-mance was not typical of that reported in the research literature (e.g., Burg, Reid, & Lat-timore, 1979; Moores & Grant, 1976; Repp & Barton, 1980), and given the lack of effect of major structural variables on staff performance (e.g., Landesman-Dwyer et al., 1980), the con-gruence between the aims of the staff training and procedural systems implemented and the observed staff behavior suggests that the train-ing and systems were important determinants in the quality of care established.

However, to attribute outcome solely to suc-cessful training and programming would over-look the contribution of the inherent structure of the residences. Data on the social ecologies of the three types of residential environments and their associated patterns of staff and resi-dent activity suggest that deployment of staff so that each works with small numbers of residents is important. Other research has also shown be-havioral gains arising from defined staff alloca-tion (e.g., Harris, Viet, Allen, & Chinsky, 1974; Mansell, Felce, de Kock, & Jenkins, 1982; Porterfield, Blunden, & Blewitt, 1980). The size and the physical design of ordinary housing may facilitate the establishment of such desirable conditions. An initially small resident group, a limited number of staff on duty at a time, and a variety of domestic-scale activity areas that are each of different function may naturally occasion staff:resident groupings conducive to interaction. However, again it is important to recognize the interdependency of structure and procedure. Staff:resident groupings were not left to chance in the small homes; a system of daily planning operated in which staff determined their allocation to residents and their particular responsibility for the conduct of the household routine (Felce & de Kock, 1983).

The material enrichment of the homes is also a factor that, although arguably not sufficient for high resident activity, is a necessary precondition for it, particularly for residents who largely lack language and for whom much adaptive engagement and social interaction is therefore materials-based. Moreover, the extent of use of materials by residents (as opposed to by staff on their behalf) is also dependent on the orientation and structure of the service. There were no restrictions placed on resident access to particular activity areas such as the kitchen or utility room in the small homes, even though the use of these may have associated risks. In contrast, access to these areas in the larger settings was generally not permitted. Moreover, unlike many residential settings in Britain run by statutory agencies, domestic and catering staff were not employed in the small homes. As a result, the full range of household tasks was available for residents to engage in with staff. Again, this was not the case in the institutions and large community units studied. However, the assumptions, first, that the residents were people who could conduct their household life for themselves and, second, that the staff role was to support them stem ultimately from the definition of the service itself. The houses were defined as the residents' permanent homes where they would be involved in all spheres of adult domestic life; they were not "halfway" houses (implying a through-put model with a specific educational or habilitative emphasis) or "caring" environments (implying a "custodial" or "maintaining" model where staff are active on behalf of but act independently of residents). Household life was regarded as sequences of separate, often simple, motor and

cognitive responses, each of which if necessary could be instructed, prompted, or guided by staff to help a substantially retarded person do them successfully. No self-care, domestic, food preparation, shopping, or household maintenance task was viewed as the independent province of staff; all required activity was seen as being accomplished through the hands of the persons living in the home. This orientation was the central theme of the staff training, and is reflected in the procedures for monitoring the extent of opportunity for household and community engagement afforded to residents.

The structure of the homes supported these emphases in other ways. Caring environments in Britain tend to be organized by statutory agencies, which have many features of large bureauracies, including hierarchical management and organizational methods that exploit economies of scale. Often the result is that control is located in essential areas of day-to-day operation (e.g., in decisions concerning budgeting, staff recruitment, and acquisition of materials) at some distance from the residential staff. In particular, centralized arrangements are made for the supply of provisions, other materials, house and grounds maintenance, laundry, and even catering. In line with the orientation of the houses and the decisions not to appoint specialist domestic and catering staff, these structures were also avoided. The budget was fully devolved, senior staff were responsible for the recruitment of junior staff, and centralized means of supply were not used. These alternative conditions not only set the occasion for resident involvement in ordinary pursuits such as shopping but also gave staff the necessary means to respond to what was required of them. As outlined, the model is clearly dependent on an intensive, if well-deployed and well-trained, level of staffing.

To this point the discussion has concentrated on the determinants of the quality of the internal household life; however, many of the same factors contribute to the picture of community integration found. In the same way that material enrichment may be considered a precondition of adaptive engagement, community location and proximity to community amenitites may be considered preconditions of community utilization. Again, in itself physical location may not be considered a sufficient condition for high community use (e.g., Birenbaum & Re, 1979). Certain other structural variables promote community integration: for example, the absence of centralized supply necessitates shopping, and budget devolution gives staff flexibility to make many normal household decisions involving the use of community resources, such as to eat out after shopping rather than to return for lunch. Although the larger community units studied were equally advantageously placed in terms of proximity to amenities, community use was less in these. One possible reason was that there was less need to use community resources in the larger units, and staff also had less flexibility to do so because of a greater input of independently organized supply and catering services. Expenditure of revenues was not under the control of caregivers.

The level of resident participation in community amenities shows evidence that staff generalized the approach taken to resident involvement in the home to the outside world. For instance, the purpose of shopping was not seen simply as a means of obtaining provisions but also as a way to promote residents' skills and experience. In addition, the level of integration was found to be highly acceptable. It is possible to characterize the good opinion of shopkeepers and bar staff as resting on an unstated bargain between the service and community. Groupings were normative: one or two residents with a staff member while shopping, and sometimes slightly larger parties for a social gathering at a bar. Considerable effort had been given, particularly in the initial resident program review, to ensure that residents' clothing and personal appearance was appropriate to their chronological age. Staff were diligent in their responsibility for resident behavior, although it is perhaps important to note that aggressive behavior to members of the public was not observed, and community response might well be different if such behaviors occurred frequently. The residents were also clearly identifiable as financial contributors to the local economy. The earlier mentioned decision not to use centralized supply arrangements resulted in residents shopping regularly (with staff) for a relatively large

household. Full budget devolution has meant that, despite most residents being personally poor, they have been able to act as ordinary consumers. Most businesses said they benefited from having the residents as customers, for two major reasons: first, the extra business the residents brought them; and second, a good public image was created by their being open to handicapped members of the community.

Community acceptance may also have been promoted by the fact that residents of the smaller homes were local. Each house had a defined catchment area, and eligibility for residence was established by address of next-of-kin. This factor permitted two features of the service. First, the decision as to who would reside in the community houses was not the result of an arbitrary policy on the part of the service agency; when the properties were originally acquired, a strong argument for the rights of particular individuals to live in the locality could be made. Second, after the initial return of people from distant institutions was achieved, other residents came directly from their family homes and were generally known within the community. This policy may arguably establish the most favorable conditions possible for a community to accept and assimilate its handicapped members as it establishes an equitable distribution of services in relation to total population. Moreover, long-standing familiarity can make programming gains recognizable to the public. One such example was of an overweight young woman who on admission to one of the small homes wore a one-piece rear-fastening jump suit to combat obsessive stripping and who in the eyes of the community was nonambulant. She could only walk short distances because of her excessive weight, and her parents had always taken her to town in a wheelchair. Hardly more than 6 months after moving in, she was of normal weight for her height, was wearing ordinary fashionable clothes, and was fully ambulant. On several occasions staff were stopped by community citizens to talk about the "marvelous work" that they were doing.

The local nature of the service is also an important aspect in determining family contact rates. Distance between family home and residential services has been a factor consistently implicated in this area (Anderson, Schlottman, & Weiner, 1975; Balla & Zigler, 1971; Ballinger, 1970; Burrows, Pasewark, & Gillette, 1968; Campbell, 1968; Felce, Lunt, & Kushlick, 1980; McKeown, Cross, & Keating, 1971). Distance can be viewed as representing a cluster of obstacles to contact. Once removed, the frequency of family contact may be influenced by many other variables associated with the quality of the setting: from the many factors already discussed that may promote activity and progress, to simple structural factors such as the availability of individual rooms to host visitors in reasonable comfort and privacy and access to those household resources required to offer normal hospitality.

IMPLICATIONS FOR SERVICE PROVISION, DEVELOPMENT, AND RESEARCH

Given that the residents in our homes were severely mentally retarded, the quality indices presented demonstrate a successful service program. This chapter has described a residential model in terms of a number of central characteristics and the more complex array of factors that interact to influence outcomes. The discussion, although speculative, is intended to shed light on a wider range of issues that may vitally contribute to ultimate success. In residential settings, such a broad range of issues is determined by the planning process, either positively by commission or haphazardly by omission. Given the considerable momentum for large-scale service redesign, it is important that service providers attend to the consequences to residents of the decisions they make. Models that are coherent in orientation, structure, and procedures must be formulated and replicated with precision.

Two directions for future research are apparent from this analysis. First, there is a need for greater understanding of how resident behavior is affected within different residential systems. This can be achieved by drawing more extensively on experimental as well as comparative methodologies and on direct observational research. Second, a more detailed description of residential systems must be encouraged by the

research community. Settings descriptors in comparative research are analogous to the description of the intervention procedure within experimental research; that is, they constitute the independent variables to which the results are considered to relate. If no effort is made to determine a full listing of independent variables, there is a danger that the correlation of exogenous factors will remain undetected and will bias interpretation.

Whereas the task of research may be to isolate the contribution to outcome of single factors within residential models, the task of service providers is different. Service providers must arrange as many factors as possible within their power to promote resident welfare. It is false to assume that high-quality outcomes will be assured by correctly determining a few key variables in the service structure. We believe that the full range of factors discussed here contributes to resident experience. Service planners, accordingly, must be equally comprehensive in their approach to identifying the numerous working arrangements that constitute a residential environment. In so doing, they must assure coherency between the orientation, structure, and procedures of the service. If planning decisions are to be based on assumptions concerning consequences for residents, a prerequisite is an unambiguous statement of program orientation: what the service seeks to accomplish for the user. This statement guides program structure and procedures. In determining structure, the task is to: a) avoid creating obstacles to the achievement of resident objectives, b) provide the conditions necessary for such achievement (i.e. opportunities), and c) create the conditions that allow staff to perform in the manner desired. Thorough attention to procedures designed to promote desired staff performance can realize the opportunities available in the service structure.

Finally, key questions concerning the structure of residences have been viewed as crucial. The attempt to define optimum residence size and staff:resident ratio recognizes the central relationship of these factors to program costs and to establishing the essential conditions for successful program activity. It has been argued here that the complexity of factors makes conclusions concerning the optimum level of single variables difficult. However, because of the need to plan on the best available information, some conclusion is required. The evidence from this research project suggests that residences that serve four or five people, with two staff on duty giving an effective staff:resident ratio of about 1:2.5 throughout the day, are optimal. These conditions promote staff:resident groupings of the size found to be associated with high staff:resident interaction and adaptive resident activity (providing there is a way of ensuring the staff work separately much of the time). Having two staff on duty enables residents to use the community with staff support either individually or with one other person. The second member of the staff can then work with residents remaining at home. Overall, the ratio of residents to staff must allow for a span of control manageable enough to permit senior staff to properly plan the resident program and supervise staff.

REFERENCES

Anderson, W.H., Schlottmann, R.S., & Weiner, B.J. (1975). Predictors of parent involvement with institutionalized retarded children. *American Journal of Mental Deficiency, 79,* 705–710.

Balla, D. (1976). Relationship of institution size to quality of care: A review of the literature. *American Journal of Mental Deficiency, 81,* 117–124.

Balla, D., & Zigler, E. (1971). The therapeutic role of visits and vacations for institutionalized retarded children. *Mental Retardation, 9,* 7–9.

Ballinger, B.R. (1970). Community contacts of institutionalized mental defectives. *British Journal of Mental Subnormality, 16,* 17–23.

Birenbaum, A., & Re, M.A. (1979). Resettling mentally retarded adults in the community—almost 4 years later. *American Journal of Mental Deficiency, 83,* 323–329.

Bjaanes, A.T., & Butler, E.W. (1974). Environmental variation in community care facilities for mentally retarded persons. *American Journal of Mental Deficiency, 78,* 429–439.

Burg, M.M., Reid, D.H., & Lattimore, J. (1979). Use of a self-recording and supervision program to change institutional staff behavior. *Journal of Applied Behavior Analysis, 12,* 363–375.

Burrows, R.E., Pasewark, R.A., & Gillette, L. (1968). Visitation and vacation rates of the institutionally retarded. *Training School Bulletin, 65,* 106–111.

Butler, E.W., & Bjaanes, A.T. (1977). A typology of community care facilities and differential normalization outcomes. In P. Mittler (Ed.), *Research to practice in mental retardation. Vol. 1, Care and Intervention* (pp. 337–347). Baltimore: University Park Press.

Butler, E.W., & Bjaanes, A.T. (1978). Activities and the use of time by retarded persons in community care facilities. In G.P. Sackett (Ed.), *Observing behavior. Vol. 1: Theory and application in mental retardation* (pp. 379–399). Baltimore: University Park Press.

Campbell, A.C. (1968). Comparison of family and community contacts of mentally subnormal adults in hospital and local authority hostels. *British Journal of Preventative Social Medicine, 22,* 165–169.

Close, D.W. (1977). Community living for severely and profoundly retarded adults: A group home study. *Education and Training of the Mentally Retarded, 12,* 256–262.

Conroy, J., Efthimiou, J., & Lemanowicz, J. (1982). A matched comparison of the developmental growth of institutionalized and deinstitutionalized mentally retarded clients. *American Journal of Mental Deficiency, 86,* 581–587.

de Kock, U., Felce, D., Saxby, H., & Thomas, M. (1985). *Community and family contact: An evaluation of small community homes for severely and profoundly mentally handicapped adults.* Highfield, Southampton, England: Department of Psychology, University of Southampton.

Felce, D., & de Kock, U. (1983). *Planning client activity: A handbook.* Highfield, Southampton, England: Department of Psychology, University of Southampton.

Felce, D., de Kock, U., & Repp, A.C. (1986). An eco-behavioral analysis of small community-based houses and traditional large hospitals for severely and profoundly mentally handicapped adults. *Applied Research in Mental Retardation, 7,* 393–408.

Felce, D., Kushlick, A., & Smith, J. (1983). The planning and evaluation of a programme of community based residences for severely mentally handicapped people. In S.E. Breuning, J.L. Matson, & R.P. Barrett (Eds.), *Advances in mental retardation and developmental disabilities* (pp. 237–271). Greenwich, CT: JAI Press.

Felce, D., Lunt, B., & Kushlick, A. (1980). Evaluation of alternative residential facilities for the severely mentally handicapped in Wessex: Family contact. *Advances in Behaviour Research and Therapy, 3,* 19–23.

Felce, D., Repp, A.C., de Kock, U., Thomas, M., Ager, A., & Blunden, R. (in press). Staff: client ratios and their effects on staff interactions and client behaviour in twelve facilities for severely and profoundly mentally handicapped adults. *Research in Developmental Disabilities.*

Felce, D., Saxby, H., de Kock, U., Repp, A., Ager, A., & Blunden, R. (1987). To what behaviours do attending adults respond?: A replication. *American Journal of Mental Deficiency, 91*(5), 496–504.

Felce, D., Thomas, M., de Kock, U., Saxby, H., & Repp, A.C. (1985). An ecological comparison of small home and institutional settings: II. Physical setting and the use of opportunities. *Behaviour Research and Therapy, 23,* 337–348.

Harris, J.M., Veit, S.W., Allen, G.J., & Chinsky, J.M. (1974). Aide-resident ratio and ward population density as mediators of social interaction. *American Journal of Mental Deficiency, 79,* 320–326.

Janicki, M.P. (1981). Personal growth and community residence environments: A review. In H.C. Haywood & J.R. Newbrough (Eds.), *Living environments for developmen-*

tally retarded persons (pp. 59–101). Baltimore: University Park Press.

King, R., Raynes, N., & Tizard, J. (1971). *Patterns of residential care*. London: Routledge & Kegan-Paul.

Landesman-Dwyer, S. (1981). Living in the community. *American Journal of Mental Deficiency, 86,* 233–234.

Landesman-Dwyer, S., Sackett, G.P., & Kleinman, J.S. (1980). Relationship of size to resident and staff behaviour in small community residences. *American Journal of Mental Deficiency, 85,* 6–17.

MacEachron, A.E. (1983). Institutional reform and adaptive functioning of mentally retarded persons: A field experiment. *American Journal of Mental Deficiency, 88,* 2–12.

Mansell, J., Felce, D., de Kock, U., & Jenkins, J. (1982). Increasing purposeful activity of severely and profoundly mentally handicapped adults. *Behaviour Research and Therapy, 20,* 593–604.

Mansell, J., Jenkins, J., Felce, D., & de Kock, U. (1984). Measuring the activity of severely and profoundly mentally handicapped adults in ordinary housing. *Behaviour Research and Therapy, 22,* 23–29.

McCormick, M., Balla, D., & Zigler, E. (1975). Resident-care practices in institutions for retarded persons: A cross-institutional, cross-cultural study. *American Journal of Mental Deficiency, 80,* 1–17.

McKeown, T., Cross, K.W., & Keating, D.M. (1971, November 13). Influence of hospital siting on patient visiting. *Lancet,* 1082–1086.

Moores, B., & Grant, G.W.B. (1976). On the nature and incidence of staff-patient interactions in hospitals for the mentally handicapped. *International Journal of Nursing Studies, 13,* 69–81.

O'Neill, J., Brown, M., Gordon, W., & Schonhorn, R. (1985). The impact of deinstitutionalization on activities and skills of severely/profoundly mentally retarded multiply-handicapped adults. *Applied Research in Mental Retardation, 6,* 361–371.

O'Neill, J., Brown, M., Gordon, W., Schonhorn, R., & Greer, E. (1981). Activity patterns of mentally retarded adults in institutions and communities: A longitudinal study. *Applied Research in Mental Retardation, 2,* 367–379.

Porterfield, J., Blunden, R., & Blewitt, E. (1980). Improving environments for profoundly handicapped adults: Using prompts and social attention to maintain high group engagement. *Behaviour Modification, 4,* 225–241.

Rawlings, S.A. (1985). Behaviour and skills of severely retarded adults in hospitals and small residential homes. *British Journal of Psychiatry, 146,* 358–366.

Repp, A.C., & Barton, L.E. (1980). Naturalistic observations of institutionalized retarded persons: A comparison of licensure decisions and behavioral observations. *Journal of Applied Behavior Analysis, 13,* 333–341.

Sandler, A., & Thurman, S.K. (1981). Status of community placement research: Effects on retarded citizens. *Education and Training of the Mentally Retarded, 16,* 245–251.

Saxby, H., Thomas, M., Felce, D., & de Kock, U. (1986). The use of shops, cafes, and public houses by severely and profoundly mentally handicapped adults. *British Journal of Mental Subnormality, 32,* 67–81.

Schalock, R.L., Harper, R.S., & Carver, G. (1981). Independent living placement: Five years later. *American Journal of Mental Deficiency, 86,* 170–177.

Thomas, M., Felce, D., de Kock, U., Saxby, H., & Repp, A.C. (1986). The activity of staff and of severely and profoundly mentally handicapped adults in residential settings of different sizes. *British Journal of Mental Subnormality, 32,* 82–92.

Wing, L., & Gould, J. (1979). Severe impairments of social interaction and associated abnormalities in children: Epidemiology and classification. *Journal of Autism and Developmental Disorders, 9,* 11–29.

Chapter 12

Transitions

Coming In and Going Out
of Community Residences

Tamar Heller

This chapter examines the impact of residential transitions into and out of community residences upon the lives of adults with developmental disabilities, and proposes guidelines for promoting successful community integration. Whether the individual moves from a family home, an institution, or another community residence, major readjustments are required as the newcomer faces changes in the physical setting, in programming, in social relationships, and in behavioral demands. While the literature indicates that residential transfers frequently result in behavioral and physical stress reactions, these effects are often mitigated by improvements in the resident's environment and by proper clinical management of the relocation. Effective management of the transition process is discussed in this chapter along the following guidelines: 1) minimizing social and programmatic disruption; 2) conducting a preparatory program; 3) involving residents in decision making; 4) developing a constructive family/staff partnership; and 5) fostering community integration.

I wanted to move away from home because I wanted to be more independent. I didn't know what to expect in a group home. My parents took me to visit several places and I spent an overnight at two places. The first one was terrible. Everybody was so retarded. I'm not retarded. I called my parents to pick me up as fast as they could. Finally, I visited Maple House which I liked. It took time to get in, but moving day finally came. I was very scared at first. At home Mom and Dad did everything for me, like drive me everywhere. I didn't know how to take a bus or do laundry or use money. I did not like my first roommate. We had lots of fights and then I got a new roommate.

When I first moved into this house I was sad; I wasn't used to it, now I am.

I was happy to move here because my boyfriend was here.

At first it was terrible; I had seizures and fainting spells; the staff made me mad.

These comments depict the varied range of emotional reactions experienced by adults with developmental disabilities upon moving into a community residence. Whether the move is from a family home, an institution, or another community residence, it requires major readjustments for the new resident. This chapter examines the impact of moving into a community residence upon the lives of developmentally disabled adults and proposes guidelines for mitigating stressful reactions and promoting successful community adjustment.

Most of the studies of residential transitions among the developmentally disabled population have focused on transfers from a family home into an institution, from one institution to another, or from an institution to a community-based residence (reviewed in Heller, 1984). As the population in state institutions for developmentally disabled persons has dropped from about 200,000 in 1967 to 125,000 in 1981 (Braddock, 1981), residential relocation to community-based residences has become a likely prospect for this population. At the same time, there is a growing population of adults with developmental disabilities who are living at home and also seeking residential placement in community-based settings. For this group, transitions to community residences frequently occur either as they "age out" of the public school system or as their parent caregivers are no longer able to adequately care for them. Unfortunately, few studies depict the transition into a community residence from a family home.

DEMANDS AND EXPECTATIONS

Relocation to a new residence frequently entails widespread changes not only in physical surroundings but also in social relationships, basic daily patterns, leisure activities, and vocational and educational programming. The behavioral demands placed on residents will also differ in the new settings. For those moving from an insitution, the new setting may entail less restrictiveness and greater privacy, less tolerance of deviancy, and greater utilization of community resources. For example, bizarre behavior may be tolerated on the institution grounds, whereas not in a neighborhood park. To function adequately in a community residence, formerly institutionalized residents need to learn how to do housekeeping, laundry, and cooking, as well as how to interact with the neighborhood environment surrounding the home. Having spent the majority of their lives in the institution, most of these residents have developed well-established routines that are difficult to change.

For individuals moving from a family home, the community residence experience may represent their first opportunity for group living, and for independence from their family. Such transitions are often accompanied by a painful realization of these residents' disabilities. As they move into a home with other disabled persons

and are required to interact more independently with people outside the community home, they become more acutely aware of their disability. For instance, when children with developmental disabilities are reared at home, they tend to be sheltered most of their lives, often lacking many skills needed for independent living (Kauppi & Jones, 1985). Developmentally disabled children might be indulged or permitted to engage in behavior not allowed other children (Skrtic, Summers, Brotherson, & Turnbull, 1984).

Family ambivalence regarding residential transfers of their disabled offspring can influence the residents' experiences during these transitions. Many families have strongly resisted residential transfer out of institutions to community placements, fearing that the residents would suffer "transfer trauma," a severe stress reaction involving physical, mental, or behavioral deterioration. Their opposition to transfers largely centers around perceptions that the large institutions provide better care, more experienced staff, and greater stability for their relatives than would other smaller or community-based facilities (Heller, Bond, & Braddock, 1984; Payne, 1976).

Families' fears about their disabled offspring moving out of the family home and into a community residence frequently translate into separation anxiety and concerns about their offsprings' safety and security. Unfortunately, the decision to find a group residence for their offspring is often not made until there is a crisis in the family (e.g., death or illness) or as parents age and can no longer adequately care for their disabled son or daughter. The literature suggests that families with disabled members tend to avoid disruptions and future planning for their relatives (Birenbaum, 1971). Turnbull, Brotherson, and Summers (1985, p. 136) cite the comments of a father of a 19-year-old disabled son: "I haven't really thought about my son's future in the last 6 months. I have a new job and I'm bushed when I get home. We've never spent much time discussing the future. We didn't think we had options."

Hence, case managers spend much of their time trying to find emergency residential placements following a death or illness of a parent who failed to make plans for his or her disabled offspring (Janicki, Otis, Puccio, Rettig, & Jacobson, 1985). What the families face in such circumstances are long waiting lists and too few satisfactory options. Without sufficient planning, a disabled adult may be quickly placed in an inappropriate setting and indeed face "transfer trauma," as there is no time for psychological preparation and for learning basic skills needed for living in a community residence.

EFFECTS OF RESIDENTIAL TRANSITIONS

An examination of the literature pertaining to residential relocation of elderly and disabled populations in general can shed light on the transition process and its impact on the residents themselves, whether from a family home, another residence, or an institution. Institutionalization studies are excluded from this review, since moves to institutions from family homes often result from deterioration in either the resident's or the caregiver's physical or mental health. On the other hand, transfers to a community residence usually represent a step toward equal or greater independence.

Researchers in mental retardation and gerontology have sought to determine the degree of stress faced by residents transferring from one residential facility to another. The most dramatic effects reported have been increases in mortality rates for elderly nursing home residents (reviewed in Heller, 1984; Kasl, 1972; Marlowe, 1973) and for residents with profound mental retardation (Miller, 1975). However, across relocation studies, the mortality results are mixed. Most recent studies of transfers from institutions have found either no increase or even a decrease in mortality among individuals who are elderly (reviewed in Borup, Gallego, & Heffernan, 1979) or mentally retarded (Cohen, Conroy, Frazer, Snelbecker, & Spreat, 1977; Heller & Braddock, 1985). Hence, while changes in mortality rates following relocation could be serious problems, increased mortality rates following transfers have not been well documented.

Adverse physical health effects reported following transfers have included higher rates of hospitalization and health failure for elderly residents (Miller & Lieberman, 1965) and a higher number of sick days for children with mental retardation who are moved from one community residence to another (Heller, 1982). However, increased health problems are most likely to be limited to those who are already physically fragile.

The most common reactions to residential transitions are in emotional, behavioral, and mental health changes. These effects have included pessimism and decreased social activity (Bourestom & Tars, 1974), depressed mental health, self-care, and social capacities (Marlowe, 1973), and increased confusion, memory deficits, and bizarre behavior (Miller & Lieberman, 1965) among elderly persons. Other effects reported include sleep disturbances, toileting problems (Heller & Braddock, 1985), and a decrement in constructive, social behaviors of residents with severe and profound mental retardation (Carsrud, Carsrud, Henderson, Alisch, & Fowler, 1979; Heller, 1982; Heller & Braddock, 1985). These behavior effects, however, tend to be short-term, often returning to pretransfer levels within several months. Behavioral disturbances may also manifest themselves before the transfer, as residents anticipate moving and staff behaviors toward them change (Carsrud et al., 1979).

SUITABILITY OF ENVIRONMENT

While the literature indicates that residential transfers frequently result in stress reactions, these effects are often mitigated by improvement in the resident's environment and by the proper clinical management of the relocation. The key issue affecting adaptation is the suitability of the receiving facility environment for the new residents. Relocation to a new environment may have positive effects by facilitating changes in individual social and intellectual functioning and the eventual integration into the community. Moving from a family home or institution to a community residence can provide an impetus for learning new skills, developing greater autonomy, and making new friends. Other possible benefits of a transfer are opportunities for better programming and better staff, better housing, or more pleasant physical surroundings.

Studies of placements from institutional to community-based facilities have generally reported long-term resident progress in self-help, socialization, and communication (e.g., Aanes & Moen, 1976; Close, 1977; Conroy, Efthimiou, & Lemanowicz, 1982). Several studies comparing transferees' pre- and postmove residential environments have shown a relationship between changes in resident behavior and changes in either resident-staff interactions or in degree of structured activity (Carsrud et al., 1979; Heller, 1982; Heller & Braddock, 1985; Hemming, Lavender, & Pill, 1981).

Physical features of residences such as facility location and proximity of services, comfort and appearance, and openness and blending with neighborhood have been related to resident progress (Eyman, Demaine, & Lei, 1979). A therapeutic staff orientation emphasizing habilitative programming, community involvement, and staff-resident interaction has resulted in greater client utilization of community services (Butler & Bjaanes, 1977; Felce, Chapter 11, this volume). The habilitative programs and services offered at residential facilities will also contribute significantly to client growth and development (Bjaanes, Butler & Kelly, 1981; Manfredini & Smith, Chapter 10, this volume).

TRANSITION PROCESS

Preparatory Programs

The immediate impact of relocation on residents largely depends on the manner in which the relocation is handled, how it is perceived by the resident, and the amount of social support provided.

An event will be stressful to an individual if it is perceived as highly unfamiliar, ambiguous, and unanticipated (Lazarus, 1966). Anticipatory coping strategies that increase predictability of the residential transfer can alleviate stressful reactions to it. Preparatory programs that foster anticipatory coping have been used successfully with both mentally retarded (Weinstock, Wulkan, Colon, Coleman, & Goncalves, 1979) and elderly persons (Bourestom, Tars, & Pastalan, 1973; Jasnau, 1967; Novick, 1967; Zweig & Csank, 1975) facing residential transfers. These programs provided supportive services, preparatory counseling, site visits, and realistic information about the new settings prior to the move.

Allowing residents greater choice and decision-making powers during the transfer process may also result in greater predictability, optimistic expectations, and better adjustment. Comparisons of voluntary and involuntary relocations of elderly people have indicated that voluntary moves were more likely to result in positive changes in resident well-being and satisfaction (Schulz & Brenner, 1977).

In one study of residents with mental retardation that used a transfer preparatory program (Weinstock et al., 1979), no adverse adaptive behavior or mortality effects were found. In that study, the transfer was voluntary; residents' families were involved in the transfer decision; and those residents who could discriminate the two environments were given voluntary choice with a visit to the new facility. Preparation for the move included notifying the residents of the transfer date, giving them physical checkups, new clothes, explanations of the future transfer, information about their belongings, and opportunities to meet the new staff.

Social Disruption

In addition to preparatory programs, new residents will benefit from continuity of social networks and support from staff, family, and friends. Cassel (1974) and Cobb (1976) have noted that persons undergoing stressful life events are cushioned from harmful psychological and physiological effects when such events are experienced in the presence of social support. During residential transitions there is considerable disruption of ongoing social relationships as new resident groupings, new staff, and changes in family involvement occur. Residents with developmental disabilities typically exhibit short-term decreases in social interaction with other residents and staff after residential transfer (Carsrud et al., 1979; Heller, 1982;

Heller & Braddock, 1985). A study of sheltered workshop participants showed that degree of sociability was related to time they had spent in the workshop. When clients first entered the new setting they tended to be socially isolated, but after 8 weeks their rate of sociability increased significantly (Heller, Berkson, & Romer, 1981).

Disruptions in social networks reduce the predictability and familiarity of new settings, resulting in higher stress for newcomers. Minimizing social disruption can ease the adjustment demands during the transition period. Bourestom and Tars (1974) compared elderly residents who moved to a new physical environment entailing new staff, programs, and patient populations, to those who also experienced a move, but without any accompanying changes in staff, patients, or programs. Following the move, the residents experiencing greater changes had higher mortality, more pessimism about their health, and a greater increase in inappropriate behavior. Greater social disruption was also associated with increased abnormal behavior in a study of children with mental retardation who were moved from one community residence to another (Heller, 1982).

Social support from day and residential facility staff, families, and friends can help to smooth the resident's transition into new settings. During transfers out of institutions entailing large phasedowns, staff are likely to withdraw from their previous attachment to the residents as they anticipate the transfer. At the receiving community residences, staff may be inexperienced (Hemming et al., 1981) and unaccustomed to working with the more severely disabled or behaviorally disturbed population coming from the institution. Residents moving from family homes experience a transition from daily supervision by one set of caregivers (typically parents) to that of another (residential program staff). Sometimes differences in values and philosophy of care result in conflicts between the two groups as each attempts to assert control over the decision making related to the resident. The following vignette of a case noted by Bloomfield, Nielsen, and Kaplan (1984, p. 143) provides a good example of how such conflicts arise and the effects they have on the resident.

Vignette: Donna P.

Donna P. is a 22-year-old woman with mild mental retardation who has been living in a supervised apartment for about a year. Her parents, both in their mid-60s, had arranged with a local agency for Donna's admission to the apartment program because they were concerned that they did not "know how long we have left" and wanted Donna to be settled before they got any older.

The staff at the residence strongly identify with the principles of normalization and are deeply committed to promoting independence among the residents at the program. Recently, staff associated with the residence have reported that Donna has been behaving in a progressively violent manner and exhibiting "psychotic symptoms." They also noted that she would call out her father's name at peculiar times.

Agency policy discourages parental visits to the residence for the first 6 months after the individuals have moved into the program. However, the parents have visited the apartment unannounced. They have also sought out a weekend relief staff member at her regular place of employment to persuade her to spend more time with Donna.

During a meeting set up between the staff and Donna's parents to discuss these difficulties, the staff told the parents that they thought that the parents were overinvolved with Donna and were interfering with the treatment program. The parents expressed feelings of guilt over what they regarded as an abandonment of Donna. They felt that they had been able to care for her for the past 21 years, but now because they themselves were getting old, they had to secure another living arrangement.

Later, in speaking with a consultant to the agency about the meeting, they expressed a distrust of the staff at the residence. The father also expressed puzzlement: he did not understand the staff's attitude. When asked about their visits to the weekend staff person, the parents acknowledged the visits, but explained that the residential staff "were too young to really understand Donna" and that they thought that the relief worker, who was an older woman, could relate better to their daughter. The parents also raised concerns about the medications that Donna was receiving, noting that they thought them to be unnecessary.

In this vignette, the staff's own attitudes or, perhaps, lack of experience, as well as their programmatic emphasis on the resident developing greater independence was in conflict with the parents' values and desires to continue to be actively involved with their daughter and her program. It may be unreasonable to expect families to abruptly relinquish control after caring for their offspring for so many years. In this instance, staff, although well intended, were not sensitive to the separation anxieties that the parents were experiencing and had not developed sufficient rapport to engage the parents in appropriate supports for the program they had developed. Further, staff apparently failed to involve the parents in planning the resident's program, which resulted in the parents' distrust of the staff and their questioning of the program regimen (e.g., the medication issue).

However, asking parents to reduce their involvement with their offspring once their son or daughter enters the community residence may be therapeutically sound and best for the new resident. Landesman-Dwyer, Stein, and Sackett (1978) found that group home residents who maintained active contacts with their parents were at risk for being socially isolated in their group home setting. In a study of young adults with mental retardation living independently, the least well adjusted were those who were enmeshed in conflict-ridden relationships with parents (Zeitlin & Turner, 1985).

On the other hand, families can also provide essential support, by initially visiting the facilities, getting involved in resident habilitation plans, advocating for the resident's rights, and actually helping with the physical move. Family involvement and approval of community placement have been shown to be critical elements in successful community integration (Gollay, Freedman, Wyngaarden, & Kurtz, 1978; Schalock, Harper, & Genung, 1981). Although one might expect an increase in family visits after residents transfer to facilities closer to their families, the findings are inconsistent. Some studies noted increased visits (e.g., Heller & Braddock, 1985), while others did not (e.g., Conroy & Latib, 1982).

Peer social networks play a critical role in the successful adjustment and quality of life of mentally retarded adults in community settings. Low levels of social support have been associated with depression in this population (Reiss & Benson, 1985). There is also evidence that residents with greater degrees of peer contact are more likely to: a) remain in the community (Gollay et al., 1978), b) transfer to less re-

strictive settings, c) demonstrate independence in self-care skills (Heller & Berkson, 1982), d) earn more money, and e) transfer out of vocational workshops for positive reasons (Melstrom, 1982).

Gollay et al.'s (1978) interview study of 440 deinstitutionalized persons indicated that three-quarters of the individuals had friends while they were living in the community. Of those who were successfully maintained in the community (nonreturnees), two-thirds still visited or kept in touch with some of their institutionalized friends. The nonreturnees were more likely to have at least one friend than were the returnees to the institutions. The most severe problems in adapting to the community identified by both families and residents were the absence of satisfying interpersonal relationships and loneliness.

Heller and Berkson (1982) studied a residential relocation in which administrators were sensitive to the potential disruption of friendship networks following a facility closure. In order to maintain peer relationships, residents were interviewed about their friendship choices, and many were moved with their chosen friends. The relocations offered an opportunity to study the effects of friendship stability on posttransfer adjustment. The findings were that stable friendships were associated with higher post-transfer adjustment, greater self-help skills, more sociability, and with later transfers to more independent settings.

IMPLICATIONS FOR MANAGING RESIDENTIAL TRANSITIONS

Minimizing Social and Programmatic Disruptions

As adults with developmental disabilities move into new settings as a result of either deinstitutionalization, changes in their level of competence, or changes in their family situations, the program focus has been primarily on providing them with the least restrictive alternative. Little attention has been paid to maintaining social networks. During relocation we typically move disabled adults away from settings where their friends work and live, in spite of the fact that we know that friendships are important to them (Romer & Heller, 1983). Because a person with developmental disabilities has less access (financially and physically) to transportation and communication services, a move across town or to another part of the state may strongly limit contacts with previous friends. Moving residents with chosen friends or as intact groups, rather than individually, will help preserve a sense of continuity.

In such moves residents are more likely to feel that they are "all in the same boat." If a facility is undergoing a major phasedown, maintaining as much stability as possible for residents will facilitate a smoother adjustment. This involves minimizing internal client and staff transfers during phasedown, keeping resident groupings as intact as possible, allowing residents to keep familiar possessions, and transferring at least some previous staff with residents. During such phasedowns the residential facilities lose staff through layoffs, transfers, and attrition; at the same time resident groupings change as residents are sent to many different facilities at varying time schedules. This results in considerable turmoil for residents, who are suddenly faced with both new staff and new roommates. Disruption for the residents would be lessened significantly if one cottage/home/unit were closed at a time.

Another way to minimize social disruption is to maintain continuity in vocational and day programming. In Heller et al.'s (1981) study of initial social adjustment to workshop placement, affiliations were more likely among individuals who knew each other while undergoing work evaluation than with other workshop participants; as individuals became integrated into the workshop program over a period of 8 weeks, this tendency decreased. Involvement in vocational settings can also provide increased opportunities for learning how to cope with problematic aspects of everyday life. Levine (1985) found that in situations of potentially high stress that involve problem-solving demands and unfamiliar tasks, mildly mentally retarded adults who were employed (competitively or in a workshop setting) were less likely to respond with anxiety than were those adults who were not employed.

The move may also be less traumatic if previous staff and/or family members actually participate in the physical move itself. This entails helping residents pack, organizing their belongings, and introducing them to their new surroundings.

Although the natural inclination is for staff to quickly change the new residents' programming (e.g., switching vocational workshops or instituting new behavioral programs), a gradual approach is preferable. (In the instance of Donna P., presented earlier, a gradual weaning from parental involvement, rather than a precipitous separation, may have best served the new resident; her "acting out" was symptomatic of a lack of effective weaning from people she had known and depended upon all her life.) The demands of the new setting itself may also initially require major readjustments for the newcomers, without the added demands of intensified programming. Also, the staff need time to become acquainted with new residents so that they can properly assess their skills and problem areas.

Conducting a Preparatory Program

The period prior to the actual move is likely to be most stressful as the transferees experience fear of the unknown. Anticipatory coping can be initiated during this period. This could entail site visits to the group homes, counseling sessions dealing with residents' emotional reactions, and informational meetings regarding exact date of entry and specific procedures. Many community residences have a policy that serious applicants spend a night at the facility prior to their acceptance into the residence. This provides the staff and the prospective resident a chance to assess how well he or she fits in. It can also allay the disabled person's anxieties about what life will be like in the new residence.

Involving Residents in Decision Making

Throughout the transition period, the residents, if capable, will benefit from exercising choice and from participating in the movement process and in the habilitation planning.

Certainly if the move is voluntary, the resident will be more satisfied and will adapt better. Some adults with developmental disabilities who have lived all their life in an institution or with their families will strongly resist a move. Gollay et al. (1978) found that among deinstitutionalized residents, over half of the returnees to the institution said they preferred the institution to the community, while none of the non-returnees expressed that sentiment.

In planning residential transitions, it is important to listen carefully to the potential transferee's desires regarding placement and to adhere to them, if possible. During a facility phasedown, priority for transfers can be given to those residents who want to leave and who seek greater independence. Higher-functioning residents may also have preferences regarding the type of residence (group home versus independent apartment), type of furnishings, colors of decor, geographic location, mix of resident population, and specific roommates. Given the earlier discussion of friendships, a suitable roommate can be critical to a happy adjustment for newcomers.

Early in the process, potential transferees can begin planning and making decisions about their move in cooperation with their families, case managers, and residential facility staff. After moving in, the residents will need to be consulted regarding their programming desires, particularly in regard to leisure activities. A mistake often made by staff is to enforce social activities—for example, to coerce newcomers into participating in bowling outings, parties, or YMCA programs. Some residents will prefer more solitary activities. As the newcomers adapt to their new settings and establish rapport with staff, encouragement of greater sociability and community integration will be more effective.

Developing a Constructive Family/Staff Partnership

As noted, families often resist the idea of placing their disabled relative in a community residence. Deinstitutionalization studies have shown that family attitudes change dramatically after transfers, with the majority reporting positive feelings about the placement outcome

for their relatives (Conroy & Latib, 1982; Landesman-Dwyer, 1981; Vitello & Atthowe, 1982). Staff from the sending and receiving facilities and case managers can be instrumental in both preventing early stressful reactions and in changing initial attitudes of families. Providing families with early, clear-cut information regarding the transfer and involving them in the planning to the greatest extent possible, will reduce their fearfulness and opposition. Staff can encourage families to physically help the residents move, to visit the receiving facilities, and to make supportive contacts with other parents.

Sometimes, it is beneficial to invite parents whose relatives have successfully undergone similar transfers to participate in meetings with concerned families. The purpose is to help reduce family anxieties and build support for the positive opportunities that well-planned community placements can bring.

For families whose relatives live at home, it is imperative that case managers or program staff encourage or aid them in planning for their relative's future residential transition. Turnbull et al. (1985) suggest that when it is in the interest of the disabled person, professionals should serve as catalysts for change, as "outside energizers that can penetrate family routine to the point that change can occur" (p. 137).

In developing a working partnership with families, group home staff need to be sensitive to the families' concerns about their relative and their personal and cultural values. Families often complain of staff insensitivity toward their feelings, of patronizing attitudes, and of inadequate communication (as happened with Donna P.'s parents). On the other hand, residential staff need to let families know that within the facility they enforce the rules, whereas during home visits the families are in charge. When conflicts do arise, a third party, such as a case manager, can serve as a mediator of the decision-making process.

Fostering Community Integration

There is evidence that many residents of group homes develop one-way dependency relationships with care providers. Bercovici (1981) pointed out that "in addition to not preparing its charges for or encouraging them to experience the world outside the facility, caretakers tend to discourage, even prohibit, residents from maintaining contact with friends or acquaintances or inviting them to visit the family. This is especially true with the smaller facilities" (p. 135). Such policies not only serve to intensify the loneliness often felt during residential transfers but also inhibit residents' growth in adaptive behavior and independence.

Community integration training programs instituted both prior to and after transfers that focus on basic self-care, home management, independent mobility, and use of community resources will increase the residents' successful adaptation. Such training should be tailored to the specific demands of the new facility and its community. Schalock and Harper (1978) described a program that trained candidates for residential placements in the skills demanded by the new settings. Success within those environments was predictable according to the degree the clients met the specific behavioral requirements of their settings.

SUMMARY

Moving into a group home may cause high stress and disruption to a resident and to his or her family. However, short-term reactions can be far outweighed by the long-term benefits of a successful adaptation to an environment that better meets the resident's current and future needs. Administrators and caseworkers of residential facilities can smooth the transition in or out of community residences by minimizing social and programmatic disruptions, conducting preparatory programs, involving residents in decision-making, developing a constructive family/staff partnership, and fostering the residents' community integration.

REFERENCES

Aanes, D., & Moen, M. (1976). Adaptive behavior changes of group home residents. *Mental Retardation, 14,* 36–40.

Bercovici, S. (1981). Qualitative methods and cultural perspectives in the study of deinstitutionalization. In R.H. Bruininks, C.E. Meyers, B.B. Sigford, & K.C. Lakin (Eds.), *Deinstitutionalization and adjustment of mentally retarded people* (pp. 133–144). Washington, DC: American Association of Mental Deficiency.

Birenbaum, A. (1971). The mentally retarded child in the home and the family cycle. *Journal of Health and Social Behavior, 12,* 55–65.

Bjaanes, A.T., Butler, E.W., & Kelly, B.R. (1981). Placement type and client functioning level as factors in provision of services aimed at increasing adjustment. In R.H. Bruininks, C.E. Meyers, B.B. Sigford, & K.C. Lakin (Eds.), *Deinstitutionalization and community adjustment of mentally retarded people* (pp. 337–350). Washington, DC: American Association on Mental Deficiency.

Bloomfield, S., Nielsen, S., & Kaplan, L. (1984). Retarded adults, their families, and larger systems: A new role for the family therapist. In J.C. Hansen (Ed.), *Families with handicapped members* (pp. 138–149). Rockville, MD: Aspen Publishers.

Borup, J.H., Gallego, D.T., & Heffernan, P.G. (1979). Relocation and its effect on mortality. *Gerontologist, 19,* 135–140.

Bourestom, N.C., & Tars, S. (1974). Alterations in life patterns following nursing home relocation. *Gerontologist, 14,* 506–510.

Bourestom, N.C., Tars, S., & Pastalan, L. (1973). *Alteration in life patterns following nursing home relocation.* Paper presented at the meeting of the Gerontological Society of America, Miami.

Braddock, D. (1981). Deinstitutionalization of the retarded: Trends in public policy. *Hospital and Community Psychiatry, 32,* 607–615.

Butler, E.W., & Bjaanes, A.T. (1977). A typology of community care facilities and differential normalization outcomes. In P. Mittler (Ed.), *Research to practice in mental retardation: Care and intervention* (pp. 337–347). Baltimore: University Park Press.

Carsrud, A.L., Carsrud, K.B., Henderson, C.J., Alisch, C.J., & Fowler, A.V. (1979). Effects of social and environmental change on institutionalized mentally retarded persons: The relocation syndrome reconsidered. *American Journal of Mental Deficiency, 84,* 266–272.

Cassel, J. (1974). Psychosocial processes and "stress": Theoretical formulations. *International Journal of Health Service, 4,* 471–482.

Close, D. (1977). Community living for severely and profoundly retarded adults: A group home study. *Education and Training of the Mentally Retarded, 12,* 256–262.

Cobb, S. (1976). Social support as a moderator of life stress. *Psychosomatic Medicine, 38,* 300–310.

Cohen, H., Conroy, J.Q., Fraser, D.W., Snelbecker, G.E., & Spreat, S. (1977). Behavioral effects of interinstitutional relocation of mentally retarded residents. *American Journal of Mental Deficiency, 82,* 12–18.

Conroy, J., Efthimiou, J., & Lemanowicz, J. (1982). A matched comparison of the developmental growth of institutionalized and deinstitutionalized mentally retarded clients. *American Journal of Mental Deficiency, 86,* 581–587.

Conroy, J.W., & Latib, A. (1982). *Family impacts: Pre-post attitudes of 65 families of clients deinstitutionalized.* Philadelphia: Temple University Developmental Disabilities Center.

Eyman, R., Demaine, G., & Lei, T. (1979). Relationship between community environments and resident changes in adaptive behavior: A path model. *American Journal of Mental Deficiency, 83,* 330–337.

Gollay, E., Freedman, R., Wyngaarden, M., & Kurtz, N.R. (1978). *Coming back: The community experiences of deinstitutionalized mentally retarded people.* Cambridge, MA: Abt.

Heller, T. (1982). Social disruption and residential relocation of mentally retarded children. *American Journal of Mental Deficiency, 87,* 48–55.

Heller, T. (1984). Issues in adjustment of mentally retarded individuals to residential relocation. In N. Ellis & N.W. Bray (Eds.), *International review of research in mental retardation* (Vol. 12, pp. 123–147). New York: Academic Press.

Heller, T., & Berkson, G. (1982, April). *Friendship and residential relocation.* Paper presented at the Gatlinburg Conference on Research in Mental Retardation, Gatlinburg, TN.

Heller, T., Berkson, G., & Romer, D. (1981). Social ecology of supervised communal facilities for mentally disabled adults: VI. Initial social adaptation. *American Journal of Mental Deficiency, 86,* 43–49.

Heller, T., Bond, M.A., & Braddock, D. (1984, August). *Families of the developmentally disabled: Year 2 adaptation to residential facility closure.* Paper presented at the 92nd annual meeting of the American Psychological Association, Toronto.

Heller, T., & Braddock, D. (1985). Institutional closure: A study of resident impact. *Mental Retardation Systems, 2,* 30–44.

Hemming, H., Lavender, T., & Pill, R. (1981). "Quality of life" of mentally retarded adults transferred from large institutions to new small units. *American Journal of Mental Deficiency, 86,* 157–169.

Janicki, M.P., Otis, M.P., Puccio, P.S., Rettig, J.H., & Jacobson, J.W. (1985). Service needs among older developmentally disabled persons. In M.P. Janicki & H.M. Wisniewski (Eds.), *Aging and developmental disabilities: Issues and approaches* (pp. 289–304). Baltimore: Paul H. Brookes Publishing Co.

Jasnau, K.F. (1967). Individualized vs. mass transfer of nonpsychotic geriatric patients from mental hospitals to nursing homes with special reference to the death rate. *Journal of the American Geriatrics Society, 15,* 280–284.

Kasl, S. (1972). Physical and mental health effects of involuntary relocation and institutionalization on the elderly: A review. *American Journal of Public Health, 62,* 377–383.

Kauppi, D.R., & Jones, K.C. (1985). The role of the community agency in serving elderly mentally retarded persons. In M.P. Janicki & H.M. Wisniewski (Eds.), *Aging and developmental disabilities: Issues and approaches* (pp. 403–406). Baltimore: Paul H. Brookes Publishing Co.

Landesman-Dwyer, S. (1981). Living in the community. *American Journal of Mental Deficiency, 86,* 223–234.

Landesman-Dwyer, S., Stein, J.G., & Sackett, G.P. (1978). A behavioral and ecological study of group homes. In G.P. Sackett (Ed.), *Observing behavior, Volume 1: Theory and applications in mental retardation* (pp. 349–377). Baltimore: University Park Press.

Lazarus, R.S. (1966). *Psychological stress and the coping process.* New York: McGraw-Hill.

Levine, H.G. (1985). Situational anxiety and everyday life experiences of mildly mentally retarded adults. *American Journal of Mental Deficiency, 90,* 27–33.

Marlowe, R.A. (1973). *Effects of environment on elderly state hospital relocatees.* Paper presented at the meeting of the Pacific Sociological Association, Scottsdale, AZ.

Melstrom, M. (1982). Social ecology of supervised communal facilities for mentally disabled adults: VII. Productivity and turnover rate in sheltered workshops. *American Journal of Mental Deficiency, 87,* 40–47.

Miller, C. (1975). *Deinstitutionalizational and mortality trends in profoundly mentally retarded.* Paper presented at the Western Research Conference on Mental Retardation, Carmel, CA.

Miller, D., & Lieberman, M.A. (1965). The relationship of affect state and adaptive capacity to reactions to stress. *Journal of Gerontology, 20,* 492–497.

Novick, L.J. (1967). Easing the stress of moving day. *Hospital, 41,* 6–10.

Payne, J.E. (1976). The deinstitutionalization backlash. *Mental Retardation, 3,* 43–45.

Reiss, S., & Benson, B. (1985). Psychosocial correlates of depression in mentally retarded adults: I. Minimal social support and stigmitization. *American Journal of Mental Deficiency, 89,* 331–337.

Romer, D., & Heller, T. (1983). Social adaptation of mentally retarded adults in community settings: A social-ecological approach. *Applied Research in Mental Retardation, 4,* 303–314.

Schalock, R.L., & Harper, R.S. (1978). Placement from community-based mental retardation programs: How well do clients do? *American Journal of Mental Deficiency, 83,* 240–247.

Schalock, R.L., Harper, R.S., & Genung, T. (1981). Community integration of mentally retarded adults: Community placement and program success. *American Journal of Mental Deficiency, 85,* 478–488.

Schulz, R., & Brenner, G. (1977). Relocation of the aged: A review and theoretical analysis. *Journal of Gerontology, 32,* 323–333.

Skrtic, T.M., Summers, J.A., Brotherson, M.J., & Turnbull, A.P. (1984). Severely handicapped children and their brothers and sisters. In J. Blacher (Ed.), *Severely handicapped young children and their families* (pp. 215–246). Orlando, FL: Academic Press.

Turnbull, A.P., Brotherson, M.J., & Summers, J.A. (1985). The impact of deinstitutionalization on families: A family systems approach. In R.H. Bruininks & K.C. Lakin (Eds.), *Living and learning in the least restrictive environment* (pp. 115–140). Baltimore: Paul H. Brookes Publishing Co.

Vitello, S.J., & Atthowe, J.M. (1982, April). *Deinstitutionalization, family reaction, and involvement.* Paper presented at the Gatlinburg Conference on Research in Mental Retardation, Gatlinburg, TN.

Weinstock, A., Wulkan, P., Colon, C.J., Coleman, J., & Goncalves, S. (1979). Stress inoculation and interinstitutional transfer of mentally retarded individuals. *American Journal of Mental Deficiency, 83,* 385–390.

Zeitlin, A.G., & Turner, J.L. (1985). Transition from adolescence to adulthood: Perspectives of mentally retarded individuals and their families. *American Journal of Mental Deficiency, 89,* 570–579.

Zweig, J.P., & Csank, J.Z. (1975). Effects of relocation on chronically ill geriatric patients of a medical unit: Mortality rates. *Journal of the American Geriatrics Society, 23,* 132–136.

Chapter 13

Transitions to Supported Living

Daniel W. Close and Andrew S. Halpern

Supported living refers to the provision of ongoing support services to developmentally disabled persons who live in semi-independent settings. Such settings allow for maximum exposure to family, neighbors, friends, work, community services, and social/recreational resources. This chapter explores the supported living option and examines the following issues: financial and employment supports, the role of the semi-independent living program staff, the role of the family in the semi-independent living program, and the transition from fully supervised living to semi-independent living. Some policy and research concerns for the future are also addressed.

Nearly 20 years ago Edgerton (1967) described the postinstitutional adjustment of a group of adults with mild and borderline mental retardation. This landmark documented the scarcity of community resources and lack of assistance provided by the social service. The subjects in Edgerton's study succeeded in large measure, owing to their ability to obtain and maintain a person who served as a "benefactor" during the initial phase of their adjustment to the community. These benefactors were typically members of the person's social support network and included landlords, employers, neighbors, friends, and family. The assistance they provided took many forms, but typically included help with residential chores, financial dealings, lots of advice, and emotional support. Rarely, if ever, was a benefactor a paid employee of the service delivery system. However, as the community residential facility movement gained momentum during the 1970s, the wisdom contained in Edgerton's research regarding the importance of benefactors had only a limited impact on service design. Further, little attention was paid to the role of families, friends, and other informal supports in the delivery and coordination of services.

Another problem during the early years of the community residential movement was that inadequate attention was paid to the development of quality community-based services (Close, O'Connor, & Peterson, 1981). To meet the needs of this rapidly growing service option, a class of professional staff emerged to provide both training and supervision to clients of residential programs (O'Connor, 1976). Institutional facilities often provided important assistance during these early years in the administration of community-based services.

As program models matured and evolved, the role of quality staff and informal supports received greater emphasis than before, in part because of findings from an emerging body of research (Seltzer & Seltzer, 1978). Many investigators noted that quality programs of habilitation and training were related to positive resident adjustment and satisfaction (Eyman & Call, 1977; Janicki, 1981; Seltzer, 1981). Various research efforts also emphasized the critical role played by friends and family (Gollay, Freedman, Wyngaarden, & Kurtz, 1978; Romer & Berkson, 1980) in the successful community adjustment of persons with developmental disabilities. In sum, research clearly demonstrated that a variety of services and supports was needed to maintain successful community adjustment for persons with disabilities.

The foregoing research focused primarily on facilities and programs providing 24-hour-per-day supervision to persons with mental retardation. During the past 10 years, a new program model has gained impetus that provides training and support within the context of less than 24-hour-per-day supervision. This model is typically identified as a semi-independent living program (SILP). Early mention of such program models appeared in the literature on deinstitutionalization of persons with retardation (Baker, Seltzer, & Seltzer, 1977; Gollay et al., 1978; Seltzer & Seltzer, 1978). In addition, information in the form of anecdotal findings (e.g., Crnic & Pym, 1979; Sitkei, 1980) or local program descriptions (e.g., Close, Taylor, & Pickett, 1981) have also described such service options.

More recently, a longitudinal study conducted in the western United States provided information on the three primary elements of community adjustment in semi-independent living settings: 1) residential environment, including quality of both homes and neighborhoods; 2) occupational and financial security; and 3) social and interpersonal networks of residents, including their family and friends (Halpern, Close, & Nelson, 1986). SILPs are typically viewed as minimally restrictive options in the array of community residential programs for persons with developmental disabilities. A unique feature of the program model is that training and support are provided by non-live-in staff to the resident in his or her home or apartment setting. In this sense, services are provided either as a prelude for transition to a less restrictive setting, or as an ongoing support.

This chapter discusses the concepts and issues related to semi-independent living for persons with developmental disabilities. First, a vignette is presented that describes the utilization of an SILP for assisting in the community adjustment process. The concept of "supported living," which refers to ongoing support in unsupervised (i.e., no live-in staff) settings, is then introduced. Next, a series of strategies for promoting the transition from supervised group care living to unsupervised semi-independent living is provided. Finally, policy and research recommendations are offered.

Vignette: Maury and Judy

Maury was born over 50 years ago in a midwestern state. Abandoned by his parents at a young age, he was raised by an uncle. Maury spent a couple of years in school but was then excluded due to mild mental retardation. He and his uncle barely eked out an existence by farming and selling cut wood.

Upon the death of his uncle, Maury moved to the West Coast to live with a brother. After a series of conflicts with his sister-in-law, Maury was placed in an adult foster home. Maury's roommates were three other adults with varying levels of retardation. The foster caregiver cooked Maury's meals, washed and folded his clothes, and provided limited transportation. Maury traveled by bus to a local work activity center. His wages of approximately $60 per month and his Supplemental Security Income (SSI) subsidy were also managed by the care provider. Maury received approximately $5 per week for miscellaneous expenses.

After several years in the foster home Maury was placed in a semi-independent living program. He and a male roommate lived in a two-bedroom apartment that was attached to another home. In the SILP Maury received training in the use of public transportation, banking facilities, stores, laundromats, and fast food restaurants. In addition, he learned to cook, shop for groceries, and manage his finances. The public transportation system allowed Maury to visit friends, eat at restaurants, and take advantage of other community resources.

Money management was quite difficult for Maury to learn, owing to his lack of basic reading and computation skills. He would frequently state, "I can't read or write." A picture-based curriculum was used to teach him a range of skills, including basic survival skills in reading.

Maury met Judy, who was 43 years old at the time, at the local sheltered workshop where they were both employed. Judy was diagnosed as mentally retarded as a young child and had never attended formal school. She could not read or write, but was able to identify coins and their value. Judy spent most of her time in her family's home, performing simple domestic chores, until a social worker enrolled her in a sheltered workshop at age 30. Her job in the sheltered workshop was to sort used clothing for cleaning and repair.

Maury and Judy usually met during break at work and ate lunch together in a downtown restaurant on Saturdays. Their two-year courtship culminated in marriage, at which time Judy moved into Maury's apartment. This move was Judy's first attempt at living outside the family home.

Maury and Judy developed an interesting relationhip. Maury did all the grocery shopping, cooking, and laundry. They both shared the housekeeping chores. Household bills were paid with the assistance of the SILP staff. Weekends were often spent visiting family and attending church functions.

Maury and Judy now live in a small house adjacent to Maury's in-laws. They maintain their own household, and assume responsibility for their own finances. No assistance is provided by SILP staff. Maury and Judy are essentially living on their own, with occasional support from both families. They both look forward to the time they can retire and spend more time "puttering around the house."

Maury and Judy's transition to supported living was facilitated by a variety of resources. The federal income subsidies of SSI and U.S. Department of Agriculture Food Stamps allowed them a measure of financial security. Their network of family and friends was a primary source of social interaction and leisure. Their employment at the sheltered workshop provided a combination of financial remuneration, directed activity, and social interaction. The services provided by the SILP taught them some needed skills. In addition, the opportunity for real-life experiences in their apartment and occasional support from SILP staff assisted them in their transition from total dependence on government and family to their current state of relative independence.

SUPPORTED LIVING

Much research has focused on the problem of defining successful community living for persons with mental retardation. Many theorists have concluded that simplistic definitions such as tenure in a community setting following a period of institutionalization fail to capture the richness and diversity of adult life (Emerson, 1985; Heal, Sigelman, & Switzky, 1978; Lakin, Bruininks, & Sigford, 1981). Recently Halpern (1985) has proposed a model of community adjustment that attempts to incorporate the complexity of life in the community. His model comprises the outcome dimensions of: employment and finances, quality of life in the residence, and the social and interpersonal networks employed by persons with developmental disabilities. In addition, he utilizes the notion of short-term and ongoing supports intro-

duced by Will (1984) in defining the supported work model. The combination of outcome and varied type and durations of support to maintain community-based living provides the basis for a definition of *supported living.*

Implicit in the concept of supported living is the opportunity to live in a community residential setting with access to ongoing support services that may be needed to maintain an acceptable quality of life. A basic aspect of this definition is the chance to live in typical residential settings that allow maximum exposure to family, neighbors, friends, work, community services, and social/recreational resources. The varied types and levels of support needed to provide these outcomes will require coordinated efforts by citizens with mental retardation, their families, and government and private agencies.

The concept of supported living implies that all persons receive some support in life from others. At present, the lines separating private support from public support are often blurred, with the frequent result being an absence of needed services or poor service coordination. Supported living argues for a partnership between families, private resources, and government agencies. This support may take many forms, including, for example, advice or social contact from parents, support from a landlord to maintain an apartment, or assistance from a friend to utilize leisure resources. A key feature of this support is that it is tied to the goal of semi-independent living for individual residents. Each plan of support will differ, based on the skills and motivation of the resident and the formal and informal services available in the environment. In the end, the level and type of support are evaluated in terms of the role support plays in both maintaining and enhancing the individual's quality of life.

FINANCIAL AND EMPLOYMENT SUPPORT

A full range of financial, medical, nutritional, and public welfare resources are available to persons with disabilities and/or low income. These resources include financial subsidies such as Supplemental Security Income, Social Security Disability Insurance, Housing Subsidies, Food Stamps, and Medical Assistance. Often a person's ability to participate in an SILP is contingent on the availability of such financial resources. The importance of these financial resources should not be underestimated. Halpern et al. (1986) found that governmental assistance represented 75% of the income for disabled persons with low incomes. These persons utilize federal Housing Subsidies, Food Stamps, and other forms of financial assistance at levels significantly above the national average. This high level of use, however, is often accompanied by several highly negative consequences.

Individuals with disabilities are eligible for federal Supplemental Security Income only if their inability to maintain remunerative employment can be documented. Once a specified level of wages has been reached, the person loses both the income support for SSI and the health protection benefits from Medicaid. Furthermore, during the past 5 years, eligibility procedures of SSI have either been tightened or loosened based on changing political policies (Weaver, 1985). As a consequence, long-term financial planning is often not possible, due to the potential for loss of subsidy as regulations are altered.

The impact of this policy creates both a disincentive to employment and an interference with job behaviors. The disincentive stems from the fact that many people with disabilities work in subsidized employment settings at salaries below the minimum wage. Their potential for increased wages is hindered owing to salary and resource limitations specified in state and federal financial subsidy guidelines. For example, Maury's SSI payments were frequently in jeopardy because of his ability to save more money than regulations allowed. He often went on unplanned and inefficient ''spending sprees'' just to get his bank account below the $1,500 resource limit. An interference problem emerges when the work situation conflicts with the necessity of spending numerous hours at state and federal offices in order to maintain financial subsidies. Maury and Judy often received form letters from the Social Security Administration requesting that they appear at the local Social Security office for an interview. In addition, it was always during work hours when applications for Food Stamps assistance had to be made, and when free cheese and butter were distributed. Periodic absence from work both jeopardized Maury's and Judy's progress in vocational training and decreased their wages.

The support required to maintain community adjustment typically involves a variety of resources. The assistance needed to arrange and maintain financial, medical, and nutritional subsidies, in the face of problems such as those just cited, is an example of the ongoing support needed for community adjustment. Another element critical to the success of community adjustment efforts is the coordinated planning and implementation of specific activities to promote increased independence. It is in this regard that SILPs play a critical role.

ROLE OF SEMI-INDEPENDENT LIVING PROGRAM STAFF

SILPs deliver services via direct contact with residents in their homes or in a variety of community settings (e.g., banks, stores, public assistance office, etc.). This direct contact occurs in the form of three primary functions: 1) skill training, 2) support and supervision, and 3) crisis intervention. The actual mix of functions varies from resident to resident and over time for each person. In addition, the frequency and duration of contact varies according to individual need.

Skill Training

Training refers to instruction designed to produce proficiency on a skill or set of skills. One type, *preplanned individual instruction,* typically occurs when a trainer teaches a specific skill or set of skills with the aid of organized curriculum materials. For example, Maury received individualized instruction in budgeting and bill paying while enrolled in an SILP. This instruction followed a carefully sequenced curriculum that taught Maury his sources of income and expenses, how to make purchases and fill out money orders, and when and where to send payment for his bills. All instruction took place between Maury and a skills trainer associated with the SILP. A second form of training consists of *preplanned group instruction*. For Maury, group instruction occurred in grocery shopping, meal planning, and cooking. Small-group instruction included work on the different food groups, identification of sale items in the grocery store, and group meal preparation. The setting for group instruction occurred in a different resident's home each week. A final form of training is *spontaneous* instruction, often in response to a problem encountered. For example, the SILP trainer may teach a resident how to replace a blown fuse or unclog a drain, or how to call a landlord to fix the problem. This incidental, spontaneous form of instruction typically occurs without organized teaching materials.

Support and Supervision

Support and supervision refers to personal or telephone contact by the trainer when the resident is not receiving direct training. The forms of support and supervision include: 1) observation of the resident to identify service needs or to monitor progress; 2) guidance and counseling to provide encouragement or to allow the resident to express his or her feelings; and 3) advice and problem-solving assistance, such as helping the resident with an interpersonal problem or assisting him or her to set up a medical or dental appointment. For example, Maury and Judy often needed support in managing their interpersonal conflicts and setting up medical appointments. These incidental contacts are differentiated from crisis management in that the problems that arise are typical and minor in nature.

Crisis Intervention

Crisis intervention refers to trainer activities on behalf of the resident when *major* problems arise. Often major crises are such that without prompt and effective action, the resident's status in the community is jeopardized. For example, Maury was denied Supplemental Security Income during a routine review of his eligibility status. Staff of the SILP contacted the local Social Security office, the local member of the U.S. House of Representatives, and finally the Legal Aid Society. After months of testifying before Administrative Law judges and much

wrangling and discussion, Maury was determined to be eligible for SSI. Without this crisis intervention, Maury's income support might have been terminated. Other forms of crisis intervention include: taking a resident to the hospital for emergency medical care, assisting him or her in a legal matter, or intervening with a landlord in a dispute.

The amount of training, support, supervision, and crisis intervention allocated to a given resident varies greatly, depending on his or her needs, staffing patterns, and resources. Halpern et al. (1986) reported that residents received substantially varying amounts of training and support from staff. On an average residents received between 6 and 10 hours of training per week, and between 4 and 7 hours of support and supervision per week. Further, they noted that 1 crisis per month was typical, and that the primary reason for crisis intervention involved money matters or health problems.

ROLE OF FAMILY IN SILP PROGRAMMING

While professional staff will continue to perform a major role in the lives of persons with retardation, it is clear that additional resources must be organized to assist in semi-independent living. Naturally occurring sources of support, such as family, are needed to maximize success.

The advent of professional staff in community residential programs has produced a conflict between the service system and families. Professional staff frequently complain of "parental overprotection" and/or of attempts to sabotage or undermine program efforts. Parents, in turn, are concerned about the minimal level of training and the high level of staff turnover.

Although many families do not provide continuity and support for their adult children with disabilities, when one compares the relative instability of paid staff with the stability of many families, one can conclude that a vast, motivated resource is potentially available. A key point is to not attempt to gain support from all families, but primarily from families who care to assist. The Oregon study (Halpern et al., 1986) noted that 80% of the clients studied received some form of assistance from their families. Of those families providing assistance, over 50% provided "just enough" as judged by the resident being served. Further, in the view of service providers, only 20% of the families exerted a negative influence. Hence, it is clear that a substantial group of families do actively participate in the support and nurturance of their adult relative with a disability.

The challenge for service delivery personnel is to attempt to influence the nature and frequency of positive family interactions. This influence can be accomplished in several ways. Initially, the parents should be interviewed during the referral and assessment process. This interview could include ideas for targeting areas for skill training and suggestions for additional support services. As staff prepare the individualized living plan (ILP), the document that guides the delivery of services and provides timelines for evaluation of program effectiveness, family perspectives should be meaningfully incorporated. This effort could reinforce the collaborative nature of service delivery and formalize the partnership between the family and the service agency. Further, family members should be encouraged to attend resident staffings at which the ILP is discussed and program effectiveness is evaluated.

An important point to remember is that many of the activities targeted for training and support involve living skills that are part of daily patterns and cycles. For example, family members can assist their relatives and the SILP by accompanying their relatives on shopping trips, and on visits to the bank and various governmental agencies. In addition, joint participation in leisure activities and family celebrations reinforces family ties and provides opportunities for social interaction.

Involvement of siblings has many potential advantages, including their similar age and interest in activities that are valued by the person with a disability. For example, shared interest in music, sports, and entertainment is often possible between peers. Likewise, parents of young adults will have had years of experience in the individualized education plan (IEP) process in public education. As a bottom line, we must remember that service providers and pro-

grams will come and go, whereas supportive families will remain involved in the ongoing process of life-span growth and development and lifelong adjustment.

FACILITATING THE TRANSITION FROM FULLY SUPERVISED LIVING TO SEMI-INDEPENDENT LIVING

The basic premise underlying programming for transition to semi-independent living is that individuals with mental retardation can learn to function effectively in adult roles with minimal assistance from society. This view, while shared in general, has not clearly been articulated into program policy on a widespread basis. The efforts of parents, persons with retardation, program administrators, and policy developers are not necessarily motivated by the same goals (Emerson, 1985). Parents are often concerned with issues of safety, security, and quality of life for their children. Persons with retardation desire to live on their own in the same manner as their similarly aged peers. Program administrators and policy developers often focus on serving the maximum number of persons with the highest quality at minimal expense. Given these seemingly discrepant views of programming for semi-independent living, program policies and practices must be adopted that maximize the probability of quality life in an efficient, supportive environment.

Traditional models of preparation for increasingly independent living are based on the viability of a systematic continuum of residential options. The typical residential continuum provides a range of options from institutional care, through various levels of 24-hour-a-day community-based supervised living, to semi-independent living. Implicit in the design of such a system is the notion that skills and behaviors learned in one setting will transfer or generalize to subsequent settings.

Recent evidence indicates that the skills and behaviors required in settings with no live-in staff are quite different from those required in environments with residential staff (Close, Irvin, Taylor, & Agosta, 1981; Crnic & Pym, 1979). For example, regulating one's daily schedule, arriving at work and appointments on time, preparing meals, preparing and maintaining a personal budget, saying no to telephone solicitations for money, requesting help when needed, etc., are all performed with limited and occasional help within an SILP. Further, the independent initiation of social contacts for the typical SILP resident, who lives alone or with a single roommate, differs from the social network available in many supervised settings.

A related problem is the difficulty many persons with mental retardation experience when attempting to transfer skills learned in one training setting to a subsequent setting. When generalized performance does occur, the crucial element appears to be the similarity between the materials, tasks, and procedures utilized in the training setting and subsequent requirements in the criterion setting (Stokes & Baer, 1977).

Recent evidence indicates that persons with mild and moderate retardation comprise 40% of the residents in community residential facilities that provide round-the-clock supervision (Hauber et al., 1984). Given the increased pressures to place persons with severe and profound retardation into this type of residential facility, it is desirable to plan for an orderly transition of the many persons with mild and moderate retardation into the less supervised SILPs. The challenge for staff and administrators will be to articulate and implement policies and practices that result in successful semi-independent living for as many persons with mental retardation as possible.

Teaching Functional Skills

The supported living approach to program design stresses functional skills needed for competent performance in a community setting. In this social validation model (Kazdin, 1977), the important tasks in current and future environments are the focus of programming. It bears emphasizing that instruction in functional skills should closely approximate the *actual* skills needed for competent and satisfactory living. In addition, priority is given to the development of skills that afford maximum participation in community living, with support provided only when needed.

Close, Sowers, Halpern, and Bourbeau

(1985) described a system for teaching functional skills in community residential settings. In this system, curriculum content is determined by assessment of future needs, current skill levels, and available support systems. Residents are taught to identify and respond to the regular cues that are available in unsupervised settings. For example, while bills should be paid when they arrive in the mail, residents need to learn not to respond to every request for money received in the mail. A key factor in this process is a well-designed and sequenced set of instructional materials.

The importance of teaching skills that generalize to unsupervised settings cannot be overstated. Program staff must be trained in the use of direct instructional strategies that efficiently teach functional skills. Close et al. (1985) described two techniques as being most useful: 1) direct teaching of functional skills in simulated settings and 2) training via general case programming.

Teaching in Simulated Settings In teaching in simulated settings, the training environment is designed systematically to approximate the characteristics of an unsupervised apartment or home setting. The resident receives training in the group home, not as part of the daily routine, but in ways that specifically aid in the transition process. For example, staff in the group home could teach money management in the following manner. Costs for rent, utilities, phone, and so forth, would be determined for the resident. Resident income in the form of salary and government subsidy would be deposited in the resident's bank account. The resident would pay the program separately for rent and utilities. Adherence to community standards for banking procedures, timelines for bill paying, and allocation of money for personal expenses would be strict. Other useful examples of simulation training include having the resident utilize the public transportation system and using public laundromats for cleaning of clothes.

Another feature of simulation training is the use of charts, picture cues, and other visual displays in instruction. The primary purpose of this type of instruction is to make relevant stimuli in the teaching situation more salient. For example, Bourbeau, Sowers, and Close (in press) utilized enlargements of bank deposit and withdrawal slips to teach banking operations to students with mild and moderate retardation in a simulated setting. Likewise, Close, Taylor, and Pickett (1981) utilized money management charts to remind residents to budget and bank their money and pay their bills. It is important to note that generalization is greatly affected by the degree of similarity between the stimulus features and response requirements of the simulated (group home) setting and the subsequent unsupervised setting. For example, instruction using the actual forms of the resident's bank would help in strengthening learning.

General Case Programming   In the natural environment of an adult, the tasks that must be performed vary considerably over time. Examples such as grocery shopping, cooking, and interacting socially with others readily come to mind. Given the inherent complexity of these tasks or demands, and the relatively short time period allowed for teaching, it is difficult to teach all the skills needed for successful community living. An instructional system must therefore be developed that teaches a small set of skills or behaviors that generate a larger set of applications (Becker & Carnine, 1980).

For program staff, the process of utilizing principles of general case instruction requires a fundamental change in how tasks are selected for instruction. Traditional task-oriented programs seek to teach all of the skills that are noted to be deficient. The general case approach, when implemented properly, allows a restricted range of tasks to be taught and generalized to an expanded set of tasks. For example, it would be difficult to teach all of the cooking operations desired to prepare a range of economical, nutritious, and good tasting meals. Rather than teach a different meal each day, the staff may want to select a set of meals that sample the range of similar tasks such as "boiling" (e.g., boiling noodles, rice, eggs, hot cereal, hog dogs, potatoes, or vegetables). Each of these foods requires a standard set of boiling operations (e.g., pouring water in a pan, adding food to the pan, placing the pan on the stove, setting a timer, heating the water and food, turning off the stove, etc.). Preparation of these foods also requires variation in the following:

amount of water in the pan, degree of heat to use on the stove, whether to place the food in water to boil or to place the food in water once boiling, time allowed for cooking, and period of waiting before eating. By carefully selecting examples for teaching, staff should be able to sample a range of meals with varying characteristics that would teach a wider variety of cooking skills.

Consider also the importance of residents learning the skill of saying no to persons who solicit money over the telephone or at the front door. Teaching a selected number of instances that necessitate a negative response will facilitate generalized responding when similar situations occur in the unsupervised setting. Most skills that are important can and should be taught within this framework of general case programming.

Developing Resident Transition Plans (RTPs)

Another important need is the development of planning and documentation procedures to facilitate the transition from supervised living to semi-independent living. This process results in a resident transition plan (RTP) for each resident. This plan can be implemented as part of a high school student's individualized education plan or a resident's individualized living plan (referred to by some states as an individualized habilitation plan, individualized program plan, individualized treatment plan, etc.). In the case of postschool-age individuals living with their parents or in a foster home, the RTP would be the sole blueprint to guide the transition to semi-independent living.

Developing such a formal plan for transition into a minimally supervised setting is important for several reasons. First, focusing on the resident's needs for the future forces program accountability. Program goals and objectives are stated in terms that facilitate objective evaluation. Second, the RTP incorporates agreements for cooperation among a variety of social service agencies that will impinge on the resident's life after placement in a SILP. These agencies will have clear input into the RTP and will share responsibility for the outcome of placement. Third, parents and significant others are informed, educated, and involved in the selection of options that are available for their family member being placed. The roles that parents, other relatives, and friends must play to support the development of community independence of the resident are clearly specified and delineated. Finally, the RTP provides a clear set of goals and objectives for the resident. Instead of some nebulous concept such as, "I want to live on my own" or "I want to live in an apartment," the resident knows her or his rights and responsibilities in the transition process (i.e., what he or she can expect and will be expected to do to be able to live independently).

The elements of the RTP should address the specific areas that are needed for supported living in an unsupervised setting. Abramowitz (1985) specified eight elements in an ideal transition plan. These include:

1. Vocational and/or occupational placement
2. Income support
3. Continuing education
4. Social, recreational, and leisure options
5. Transportation
6. Residential options (including amount and nature of support required)
7. Social support and advocacy
8. Medical and insurance needs

Abramowitz (1985) further emphasized the need for a broad range of input from various sources to the plan. At a minimum, the resident, parents, program staff, and social service agencies should share responsibility for the development, implementation, and monitoring of the RTP. Someone must be identified as a coordinator of the planning process, and careful attention must be given to specifying the person or agency responsible for each objective of the plan. Tentative timelines indicating important landmarks toward implementation also need to be specified and then reviewed regularly.

POLICY AND RESEARCH DIRECTIONS FOR THE FUTURE

The following section on recommendations for policy and research draws heavily upon the data base and conceptual model provided by Halpern et al. (1986). Three major issues are analyzed here in regard to the concept of semi-inde-

pendent living: 1) eligibility criteria for determining who is to be served; 2) design and implementation of program structure to support persons in criterion settings; and 3) development of methodology for measuring the outcomes of semi-independent living.

Eligibility for Semi-independent Living Programs

Persons with certain types of disabilities are generally excluded from participation in SILPs. These include people with severe disabilities and/or behavior problems, as well as middle aged or elderly persons. In order to reduce these biases over time, we will need to understand and remediate the underlying causes.

Severe Disabilities Eligibility criteria for many semi-independent living programs are based on the assumption that an individual should be able to live without supervision for a given amount of time. Often the question is asked, "Can the client live without supervision for at least 48 hours?" This criterion is plausible given the lack of immediate and direct 24-hour-per-day supervision in all semi-independent living programs. On the other hand, this criterion is unduly restrictive if it automatically excludes people with severe disabilities from gaining access to SILPs. As evidence for the existence of such a bias, Halpern et al. (1986) found that over 80% of the population in SILPs were diagnosed as mildly handicapped.

Expectations concerning the competence of persons with severe disabilities have increased in the past two decades. Gold's (1972) charge that it "takes very little intelligence to live in the community" rings true today. Ten years ago, few persons with severe disabilities lived outside the family home or institutions (O'Connor, 1976). Currently, persons with severe disabilities comprise 60% of the population of community residential facilities (Hauber et al., 1984) and 17% of the SILP population. The critical feature in serving persons with severe disabilities is matching services to the needs of the individual. An example of such a modification is provided by the Seattle Community Home Health Care Model (Carlson, 1985). In this program, six persons with severe disabilities live in adjacent apartments in a typical apartment complex. A staff member responsible for providing supervision and training also lives in an apartment within the complex. During the first 24 months of operation, emergency contacts rarely occurred, and supervision was provided only when needed.

Behavior Problems Another population often screened out of SILPs includes individuals with behavior problems. In the Halpern et al. (1986) study, persons known to destroy property or to be harmful to others were almost totally excluded from SILPs.

Persons with behavior problems also constitute one of the few population groups currently showing an increased rate of institutionalization (Best-Sigford, Bruininks, Lakin, Hill, & Heal, 1982). While institutional facilities typically provide extensive supervision and control, few therapeutic resources in mental health counseling or psychotherapy are utilized in such settings to ameliorate problem behaviors. Training programs often require the resident to conform to strict rules and regulations relevant only to the institutional environment. In contrast, SILP personnel working in conjunction with mental health professionals can design residential services to address the crisis needs of such individuals in the context of realistic adult demands. Many such models exist in the mental health literature (e.g., Anthony, Cohen, & Cohen, 1984); these could serve as a guide for service delivery for persons with mental retardation who exhibit behavior problems. Adaptation of such models will be required if we are to increase the accessibility of SILPs for this population. However, given the risks involved in placing individuals with behavior problems in SILPs, agencies need to carefully evaluate and monitor such placements and to provide more supervision to such residents.

Middle-Aged and Aging Persons Another population that is underrepresented in SILPs comprises persons 40 years of age or older. Halpern et al. (1986) found that less than 10% of the persons they studied were above the age of 40. Given that the over-40 population is the fastest growing segment of the overall population, careful attention needs to be directed toward the development of program structures to *include* this group. Collaborative programs with housing agencies or providers serving older nondisabled persons should be developed.

A common rationale for the exclusion of persons over 40 is that they are "settled" in their current supervised setting. When these residents are given the choice of staying with friends and familiar surroundings of the group home, or to move out "on their own," they often report a desire to stay in the present setting. Unfortunately, commonly the resident has made this decision without the experience of living without 24-hour per day supervision.

In an attempt to provide the option of semi-independent living to older persons with established social networks, adjustments should be made in the service options that are available from SILPs. One such adjustment would be to create small living units of friends within the SILP. Groups of two to five individuals could be organized, based on friendship and desire to live together. Training and support services would be directed to the group as well as to individuals.

A person's medical and health care needs pose another potential impediment to serving persons with disabilities, particularly those over the age of 60. Many of these individuals take medications daily and have frequent appointments with health care providers. A major cause of recidivism from SILPs to more supervised settings is failure to assume responsibility for taking one's own medication. In supervised facilities, staff often view their job primarily as providing care in the daily living and health areas. In such situations, program elements such as specific dietary requirements and medication administration are regular features. This level of supervision, however, is not always required. In fact, all but the most sophisticated medical or dietary needs can be provided by SILP program staff in coordination with existing health care providers. Medications can be administered, monitored, and evaluated on a regular basis with the resident performing a key role in the process.

Program Design and Implementation Issues

Providing training and support to persons with developmental disabilities in *unsupervised* settings represents an important shift from the traditional "flow-through" model of services. In the flow-through model, residents must obtain skills prior to placement in unsupervised settings. Residents often remain in supervised settings because program exit criteria dictate the independent performance of *all* skills needed for independent living. In contrast, the concept of the SILP program model suggests that residents be provided the opportunity for independent living in combination with ongoing support services. The primary challenge in this regard is to design services that clearly match each resident's needs.

This chapter has highlighted the person-specific nature of service design and implementation. The message to be gained from this orientation is that the person's own capacities and skills should determine the quality and quantity of services delivered. Halpern et al. (1986) state: "Low or inappropriate client performance should be matched with high levels of training and supervision, while high or appropriate client performance should be matched by low levels of training or supervision" (p. 172). Clearly, the SILP is in a unique position to implement such a program. For example, an individual may have few skills in money management and bill paying but enjoys a rich social life with an extensive social support network. This resident's individualized living plan may call for weekly classes in budgeting and bill paying, with additional support provided by staff on payday and bill paying days. In addition, staff may want to capitalize on the client's extensive social support network by structuring budget plans to save extra money each week for socializing with friends.

The concept of matching the skill level of the person to service design and implementation implies that program rules be flexible enough to accommodate changes in skill level. It has been noted that many SILPs adopt restrictive program rules on an "across the board" basis. In many cases, uniform program rules and restrictions (e.g., "no alcohol allowed in home" or "no overnight guests of the opposite sex"), independent of a resident's rights, needs, or behavior, was a major source of client dissatisfaction (Halpern et al., 1986).

Measurement of Outcomes

The nature of supported living implies multiple dimensions of outcome and the use of a variety of evaluation methodologies. The Halpern et al. (1986) model of community adjustment includes skills in four major areas of outcome: 1) *occupation and finances,* including employment and financial security; 2) characteristics of the *residential environment,* including quality of home, cost of housing, neighborhood attractiveness, neighborhood safety, and access to community resources; 3) *social network,* including family support, friendship, access to a benefactor, intimate relationships and sexuality, leisure activities, and community integration; and 4) *client satisfaction.* This model is consistent with past research that has identified the complex demands of adult adjustment (Heal et al., 1978).

Given the diverse nature of the residents served, it will be necessary to adopt flexible guidelines for measuring the outcomes of semi-independent living. Multiple sources of information are desirable in order to obtain several perspectives on each of the relevant outcomes. Possible information sources include: direct service staff, parents, and most important, the residents themselves. In addition, multiple types of information could be collected, ranging from quantitative data such as wages, numbers of social contacts, or number of bills paid on time to qualitative data such as client, family, or staff anecdotal information. This mix of quantitative and qualitative data should provide a rich account of the outcomes of service delivery.

SUMMARY

The concept of supported living offers a framework to design, implement, and evaluate residential programs in the least restrictive environment. This concept presents persons with developmental disabilities the opportunity to live a relatively normal life-style. For Maury and Judy, the individuals highlighted in this chapter, the process of living on their own has entailed a mix of exciting challenges and new opportunities, accompanied from time to time by frustration and disappointment. Their goals are achievable through support from a variety of friends, family, SILP staff, and government agencies.

The support required to maintain a quality life is achieved through a coordinated effort of all parties concerned. Parents, residents, agency personnel, staff from supervised group living settings, and staff from SILPs must work together to prevent the development of confusing and contradictory systems.

Finally, the goals and aspirations of persons with developmental disabilities must be incorporated into the design, implementation, and evaluation of supported living. The consumers of services will determine whether this residential option is truly less restrictive or just another modification of more rigid and impersonal programs. The ultimate criterion of success must be client satisfaction with the outcomes that are achieved.

REFERENCES

Abramowitz, D. (1985). *Transition planning for youth with mild handicaps.* Unpublished master's thesis, University of Oregon, Eugene.

Anthony, W.A., Cohen, M.R., & Cohen, B.F. (1984). Psychiatric rehabilitation. In J. Talbott (Ed.), *The chronically mentally ill: Five years later* (pp. 67–79). New York: Grune & Stratton.

Baker, B.L., Seltzer, G.B., & Seltzer, M.M. (1977). *As close as possible: Community residences for retarded adults.* Boston: Little, Brown.

Becker, W.C., & Carnine, D.W. (1980). Direct instruction: An effective approach to educational intervention with disadvantaged and low performers. In B.B. Lakey & A.E. Kazdin (Eds.), *Advances in Clinical Child Psychology: Vol. 3* (pp. 429–473). New York: Plenum.

Berkson, G., & Romer, D. (1981). A letter to a service provider. In H.C. Haywood & J.R. Newbrough (Eds.), *Living environments for developmentally retarded persons* (pp. 167–181). Baltimore: University Park Press.

Best-Sigford, B., Bruininks, R.H., Lakin, K.C., Hill, B.K., and Heal, L.W. (1982). Resident release patterns in a national sample of public residential facilities. *American Journal on Mental Deficiency, 87,* 130–140.

Bourbeau, P.E., Sowers, J., & Close, D.W. (in press). An experimental analysis of generalization of banking skills from simulated to untrained settings in the community. *Education and Training of the Mentally Retarded.*

Carlson, C. (1985). *Intensive tenant support programs for persons with severe retardation.* Paper presented to the 3rd Annual Residential Conference for Persons with Developmental Disabilities, Ellensburg, WA.

Close, D.W., Irvin, L.K., Taylor, V.E., & Agosta, J.M. (1981). Community living skills instruction for mildly retarded persons. *Exceptional Education Quarterly, 2,* 75–85.

Close, D.W., O'Connor, G., & Peterson, S. (1981). Utilization of community services by retarded persons living in residential facilities. In H.C. Haywood (Ed.), *Lifestyles of retarded persons* (pp. 75–85). Baltimore: University Park Press.

Close, D.W., Sowers, J., Halpern, A.S., & Bourbeau, P.E. (1985). Programming for transition to independent living for mildly retarded persons. In K.C. Lakin & R.H. Bruininks (Eds.), *Strategies for achieving community integration of developmentally disabled citizens* (pp. 161–176). Baltimore: Paul H. Brookes Publishing Co.

Close, D.W., Taylor, V.E., & Pickett, M. (1981). Training and support for independent living. *Community Services Forum, 2,* 2–3.

Crnic, K., & Pym, H. (1979). Training mentally retarded adults in independent living skills. *Mental Retardation, 17,* 13–16.

Edgerton, R.B. (1967). *The cloak of competence: Stigma in the lives of the mentally retarded.* Berkeley: University of California Press.

Emerson, E.B. (1985). Evaluating the impact of deinstitutionalization on the lives of mentally retarded people. *American Journal on Mental Deficiency, 90,* 227–288.

Eyman, R.K., & Call, T. (1977). Maladaptive behavior and community placement of mentally retarded persons. *American Journal of Mental Deficiency, 82,* 137–144.

Gold, M. (1972, May). Skill training for the mentally retarded. Paper presented to the Annual Convention of the American Association on Mental Deficiency, Atlanta.

Gollay, E., Freedman, R., Wyngaarden, M., & Kurtz, N.R. (1978). *Coming back.* Cambridge, MA: Abt.

Halpern, A. (1985). Transition: A look at the foundations. *Exceptional Children, 51,* 479–486.

Halpern, A.S., Close, D.W., & Nelson, D.J. (1986). *On my own: The impact of semi-independent living programs for adults with mental retardation.* Baltimore: Paul H. Brookes Publishing Co.

Hauber, F.A., Bruininks, R.H., Hill, B.K., Lakin, K.C., Scheerenberger, R.C. & White, C.C. (1984). National census of residential facilities: A 1982 profile of facilities and residents. *American Journal on Mental Deficiency, 89,* 236–245.

Heal, L.W., Sigelman, C.K., & Switzky, H.N. (1978). Research on community residential alternatives for the mentally retarded. In N.R. Ellis (Ed.), *International review of research in mental retardation* (Vol. 9, pp. 209–247). New York: Academic Press.

Janicki, M.P. (1981). Personal growth and community residence environments. In H.C. Haywood & J.R. Newbrough (Eds.), *Living environments for developmentally retarded persons* (pp. 59–101). Baltimore: Univeristy Park Press.

Kazdin, A.E. (1977). Assessing the clinical or applied importance of behavior change through social validation. *Behavior Modification, 1,* 427–457.

Lakin, C.K., Bruininks, R.H., & Sigford, B.B. (1981). Deinstitutionalization and community-based residential adjustment: A summary of research and issues. In R.H. Bruininks, C.E. Meyers, B.B. Sigford, & K.C. Lakin (Eds.), *Deinstitutionalization and community adjustment of mentally retarded people* (pp. 382–412). Washington, DC: American Association on Mental Deficiency.

O'Connor, G. (1976). *Home is a good place: A national perspective of community residential facilities for developmentally disabled persons* (Monograph No. 2). Washington, DC: American Association on Mental Deficiency.

Romer, D. & Berkson, G. (1980). Social ecology of supervised communal facilities for mentally disabled adults: II.

Predictors of affiliation. *American Journal of Mental Deficiency, 85,* 229–242.

Seltzer, G. (1981). Community residential adjustment: The relationship among environment, performance, and satisfaction. *American Journal of Mental Deficiency, 85,* 624–630.

Seltzer, M.M., & Seltzer, G.B. (1978). *Context for competence: A study of retarded adults living and working in the community.* Cambridge, MA: Educational Projects.

Sitkei, G. (1980). After group home living—what alternatives? *Mental Retardation, 18,* 9–13.

Stokes, T.F., & Baer, D.M. (1977). An implicit technology of generalization. *Journal of Applied Behavior Analysis, 10,* 349–367.

Weaver, C.L. (1985). *Thinking about Social Security disability policy in the 1980s and beyond.* Paper presented at the Conference on Economics and Disability, Washington, DC.

Will, M. (1984). *OSERS programming for the transition of youth with disabilities: Bridges from school to working life.* Washington, DC: Office of Special Education and Rehabilitative Services.

Chapter 14

Family Involvement with Community Residential Programs

Bruce L. Baker and Jan Blacher

This chapter examines family involvement in community residences. Families and service providers alike are often uncertain about how much and what types of family involvement are desirable. Researchers and policy makers have not paid much attention to the family's continuing role in the life of a member placed out of the home. Yet few would deny that the family is a tremendous resource for social support, guidance, and advocacy. Most past research has focused on parental attitudes toward placement in institutions or community residences, and has found that parents generally like the present setting best, whatever it is. Some authors have examined family involvement, although they have been more inclined to count visits than to assess the content and contribution of these visits. Others have considered the parents' role in decision making, examining involvement such as participation in writing individualized program and transition plans or monitoring residential programs and procedures. This chapter reviews these studies and offers additional insight into effective means for family involvement.

I'm under my mother's care still, and I don't like it. I want to be completely on my own, but I can't. Because I have checking accounts and I don't know how to make my own checks . . . but I can make a money order. My mom does my bookkeeping all the time . . . I'll be in her care until the day I die—I mean—the day she dies.
—On My Own

In *On My Own*, an account of semi-independent living programs, Halpern, Close, and Nelson (1986) follow the preceding quotation with this observation: "There is both good news and bad news to be found in the literature on family involvement in the life of adults with mental retardation" (p. 93). The good news is that family involvement can make a positive difference in the lives of retarded adults, providing them with the social support, guidance, and financial assistance that facilitate community integration (Edgerton, 1967). The bad news is that this same family involvement can foster lifelong dependency (Hunt, Browning, & Nave, 1982).

Most striking to us, though, is just how little news there is, how neglected the topic of family involvement has been. In particular, we find few studies of family attitudes toward and involvement in community residential settings. Once families elect to place a son or daughter in a residential setting, their role changes dramatically, it would seem, from that of primary caregiver. Conroy and Feinstein (1985), writing

Order of authorship was determined by a coin toss.

about the lack of systematic attention given to families in relation to policymaking in the developmental disabilities field, noted that "in a formal sense, our service structures generally relegate families to the role of permission-giver. Service programs do not regularly contact families unless some form of consent is needed, e.g., for medical treatment. Conversely, the family rarely makes contact with program officials (other than direct care staff seen during visits) unless they perceive a problem" (p. 3).

We argue here that families and professionals alike, albeit sometimes for different reasons, have resisted closer family involvement in out-of-home placements. Yet we feel that there would be more good news for mentally retarded residents if meaningful family involvement could be enhanced.

RATIONALE FOR
FAMILY INVOLVEMENT

There is a strong rationale for encouraging family involvement in community residences. In general, parental practices, relationships, and expectations affect how positively mentally retarded adults view themselves (Zetlin & Turner, 1984). In two follow-up studies of residents placed from institutions into community facilities, the most significant predictors of successful placement have been family acceptance of the concept of community placement and their involvement in the client's individualized program plan (Schalock, Harper, & Genung, 1981; Schalock & Lilley, 1986). Most parents of handicapped children living at home today are actually quite involved in their son's or daughter's life until the time of placement. They have served as consistent advocates, have provided social support and encouragement, and have assumed much financial responsibility. They have usually been engaged in decision making regarding their child's education or habilitation; for example, they have probably attended annual individualized education plan (IEP) meetings during the school years, and perhaps have helped to write a transition plan if their child has finished high school. And they have struggled long with the decision about if

and when and where to place. Placement should not, then, mean a severing of ties. Reading the literature on community residences might lead one to believe that parents' involvement ends once they have chosen a placement. There is therefore a corollary and compelling rationale for encouraging more research on family roles throughout the retarded offspring's life cycle.

DIMENSIONS AFFECTING
FAMILY INVOLVEMENT

When a new resident walks through the door of a community placement, how will his or her family likely be involved in the ensuing weeks and years? Numerous characteristics of that resident, the family, the resident's service history, and the residential environment are bound to affect the family's attitudes and involvement. Four dimensions are emphasized in this chapter. First is the resident's *status as child or adult*. For instance, one might expect children in out-of-home placements to have greater and different family involvement than adults. Second is the *level of handicap*. This is likely to be important, as it may influence the specific type of family involvement that does occur. A parent of a profoundly retarded daughter, for example, may not choose to call her weekly, but may be very involved in the writing and monitoring of her program plan.

Third is the *placement history*. Is the resident moving from an institution, another community placement, or the natural home? Parental attitudes and potential involvement should be very much affected by whether they have had previous experiences with out-of-home placements, which types, and for how long. Fourth is the *perceived permanence* of the placement. This refers to the mind-set of parents when they actually initiate the placement. Placements that are perceived as short-term and transitional may attract and encourage more active family participation than those that are seen as a permanent new home.

This chapter reviews existing studies of parental attitudes toward community residences, as well as studies of actual parental involvement. We note that parents raising young handicapped children at home today are a "new breed''; they are experiencing an era marked by enhanced rights and services. It is also an era that espouses normalization and ''in-home'' placement of handicapped children. We argue that this has left service providers and parents alike ambivalent about what their relationship might be. Finally, after considering political, social, and research trends, we conclude the chapter with suggestions for family involvement that community residence staff may want to consider.

FAMILY ATTITUDES TOWARD COMMUNITY PLACEMENT

Community residences, like any new kid on the block, have been met with a mixture of anticipation, curiosity, suspicion, and, variously, acceptance or rejection. Many facilities encounter scattered or organized opposition, especially from neighbors (Seltzer, 1985). But professionals and some parent advocacy groups, enlightened by a philosophy of normalization, have pressed ahead, and neighbors have generally ''come around'' with time. Oddly, however, as stated earlier, we still know little about how most families of mentally retarded persons feel about community living alternatives for their own children.

Ferrara (1979), in noting that the community residence movement has been supported by organizations identified as parent/advocate groups, hypothesized that parents might be less enthusiastic about community placement if speaking about their own son or daughter. The general population, for example, is more in favor of community living for handicapped persons in the abstract than of facilities for such purposes located in their own neighborhood (Kastner, Reppucci, & Pezzoli, 1979). Ferrara (1979) surveyed members of organized parent groups in Philadelphia, randomly distributing two forms of a questionnaire about normalization and related ideas. One form had a general referent (mentally retarded children). The other form had a child-specific referent (my mentally retarded child) for the same questions. As predicted, attitudes toward normalization activities were less positive when the referent was specific to the parent's own child.

Most of what we know about parents' attitudes toward community placement is derived from surveys of families with offspring residing in institutions. And what we know is that these families do not like the idea very much.

Families Who Have Placed

"Their praise lavished on institutions was so extravagant as to suggest severe distortions in reality in this area" (Klaber, 1969, p. 180, commenting on his survey of parents of institutional residents.)

Satisfaction with the Institution Studies have consistently reported high satisfaction with institutions among families who have placed relatives there. Payne (1976) surveyed parents of residents in Texas institutions and found that while they were not opposed in principle to the option of small-group homes, especially for higher-functioning residents, they still preferred the institution.

Meyer (1980) surveyed parents of 273 residents in Western Center, an institution near Pittsburgh. Specifically, Meyer contrasted parental attitudes toward continued institutional placement versus placement in a community residence for their son or daughter. Of these families, 79% were satisfied with the programming and care being provided by the institution. When the questionnaire described a small-group home and supervised apartments, the families who felt that the resident would be best served in these alternatives were 13.5% and 0%, respectively for the two types; 83% thought remaining in the institution would be best. When the question was phrased, ''Assuming that the resident reaches his or her highest potential at Western, where do you think he or she would be best served in the future?'' 77% still selected remaining at the institution.

Pressures for deinstitutionalization have had a diverse effect on parents. Advocacy organizations, like the Association for Retarded Citizens–U.S., have pressed for community placements. Yet some parents of institutionalized residents, expressing satisfaction with the institution and negative attitudes toward community placements, have united to produce a counter force for parents' rights to choose placements and for improved institutional care. All, of course, are motivated by what they perceive to be the best interests of the mentally retarded individual. As one parent in Nebraska noted: "It's funny—we all want the same thing but we see it so differently. It's like churches—we all want to go to heaven but believe there are different ways to get there" (Frohboese & Sales, 1980, p. 45).

This divisiveness was particularly noteworthy in Pennsylvania, where the highly emotionally charged climate surrounding the decision to transfer residents of Pennhurst Center to community living arrangements found parent groups opposing each other in court. Fortunately, family attitudes about Pennhurst and community alternatives have been extensively studied.

Attitudes and Attitude Change: The Pennhurst Longitudinal Study Family surveys were part of an ambitious 5-year longitudinal study of the deinstitutionalization of Pennhurst. The study, conducted by James Conroy and his colleagues, offers the best evidence available about parent attitudes prior to deinstitutionalization. Mail surveys were obtained from 472 families with relatives residing in Pennhurst (Conroy, 1985; Conroy & Bradley, 1985; Latib, Conroy, & Hess, 1984; these references apply to all the findings in this subsection). Moreover, this is the only study that reexamined attitudes following community placement. Families of 119 residents were surveyed again by phone 6 months after their relative had moved to a community-living arrangement. We only consider here the 119 families assessed before and after the move, although it should be noted that their initial attitudes were generally similar to those of the overall population of 472.

Before the transition, these 119 families were very satisfied with the institution and opposed any change in placement. At pretest 85% reported being very or somewhat satisfied with the services received in the institution. A key question asked before transition was: "If your relative were to be selected for movement from Pennhurst to the community, how likely would you be to agree with this decision?" Only 27% expressed some degree of agreement, while 52% said they would disagree strongly.

Remarkably, 6 months after relocation these families demonstrated an enormous change in attitude. Whereas the great majority had formerly been satisfied with the institution, at posttest 83% were very or somewhat satisfied with the community placement. Families were asked: "Overall since your relative was selected for movement from Pennhurst to the community, how do you feel about that move?" Now fully 81% expressed some degree of agreement, and only 4% strongly disagreed. At pretest, families were also asked what changes in family life they expected as a result of their relative's community placement (e.g., effects on your general happiness, family recreation activities, your mentally retarded relative's relationships with other people). At post, they were asked what changes they had actually perceived. Twelve of the 14 items showed statistically significant changes, and for each of these the actual post situation was perceived as better than expected. The largest change was in the retarded relative's general happiness. Originally, 42% of families had expected "much worse," but at post none chose this category. For 70% of families, their relative's happiness was greater than they had expected, and for 28%, happiness was the same as they had expected (Latib et al., 1984).

Attitudes and Child Characteristics As already suggested, a child's age and level of retardation may affect parents' attitudes about placement. Conroy (1985) reported that compared with parents of adult residents, parents of children (under 22 years old) were somewhat less likely to report satisfaction with the institution and were much less opposed to deinstitutionalization and related ideas. Other surveys have not been consistent; Ferrara (1979) found that child age related to parent attitudes in general but not when questions concerned their own child, and Meyer (1980) found no relationship between attitudes and child age. Level of retardation did not show much variance in the Pennhurst survey, with 86% of residents classified as severely or profoundly disabled (Conroy & Bradley, 1985). In surveys where roughly half of the residents were so classified, parents' attitudes about their child's placement did not relate to level of functioning (Ferrara, 1979; Meyer, 1980).

Worries about Community Placement

When parents speak about the community-based service system, *permanence* often emerges as the central issue. They are clearly not confident that community residences will assure the degree of permanence that they associate with institutions (Conroy & Bradley, 1985; Frohboese & Sales, 1980; Payne, 1976; Spreat, Telles, Conroy, Feinstein, & Colombatto, 1984). Parents recognize that institutions have a century's history of state and now federal funding, consistent staffing in which the overall operation is not disrupted if a few key persons leave, and a physical plant that will not vanish according to whims of social policy (Bradley, 1985). By contrast, the majority of families in the Pennhurst survey believed that community funding is not secure.

These worries are not unfounded. One survey of community facilities found that the average houseparents remained for less than 2 years, and that smaller programs in particular often changed dramatically with staff changes (Baker, Seltzer, & Seltzer, 1977). Moreover, a recent national study of the stability of 6,340 residential facilities reported that over a 5-year period, 38% closed, moved, or stopped serving clients who have mental retardation (Hill, Bruininks, Lakin, Hauber, & McGuire, 1985). The normalization movement has lobbied for smaller facilities. Yet among foster homes of three to four residents and group residences of six or fewer residents, the closure figures were even higher, at 47% and 41%, respectively (Hill et al., 1985). Clearly, community placements are unwelcome to parents who had expected that the institution would assure a lifelong place for their offspring.

Related worries focus on the *comprehensiveness and quality of care*. Parents are concerned that funding limitations will mean that the wide range of services they perceive as being available in an institution are not continuously available in the community. They are worried, too, about the overall quality of life and, especially, about safety. Many parents see the community as a dangerous place for their sons and daughters to live.

Parents also express concern about the process of deinstitutionalization and, in particular, about their exclusion from it. Conroy and Fein-

stein (1985) found that *control* (whether the parent will have a major say in what happens to his or her relative) and *monitoring* (the ability of the state and region to monitor the quality of the settings and take action against bad programs) were the two primary concerns of parents in institutional and community settings alike. Interestingly, though, concerns were lower for these and other variables (e.g., staff turnover, medical care) for parents with a child already in a community facility. It is true that the increasing involvement of the courts in institutional life has diminished parental control, but it still seems that parents should and could be involved more in the decision-making process.

In contrast to realistic concerns about permanence and safety are those reflecting shifting *ideologies*. Community residences are grounded in a philosophy of normalization, with its concomitant developmental model. Yet families such as those in the Pennhurst study do not generally agree with the principles of normalization and of least restrictive alternative (Conroy & Bradley, 1985). Seventy-five percent of the families believed the resident had no potential for further development. Also, one of the strongest predictors of opposition to community placement was families' perception that their relatives needed considerable medical care—much more, in fact, than was perceived by the institutional staff who worked with the resident (Conroy, 1985).

Conroy (1985) has drawn on cognitive dissonance theory (Festinger, 1957) to help understand the extreme satisfaction families express with the institution and their related beliefs about their relative's potential and needs. Most families experienced severe stress around the decision to place, which was initially allayed somewhat by societal and professional pressure for institutionalization. Yet there certainly would be high dissonance between the decision to place the child in a public institution and the recognition that the institution is unpleasant or detrimental to the child's growth and development. "During the years following institutionalization, families may attempt to reduce dissonance by coming to believe that learning and development are not feasible and/or important goals, by selectively perceiving information supportive of the institution's quality, by rejecting new ideas or options, by emphasizing the medical aspects of the relative's needs, and by generally coming to a position that the institution is what the relative needs" (Conroy, 1985, p. 145).

Given this background, it would seem clearly stressful for such families to confront the idea that the resident could live in a small homelike setting in the community. This challenges the original placement, reraises the guilt and uncertainties surrounding it, and exacerbates these by arguing that someone else ("caregivers," "houseparents") can provide the care and training that the family felt they could not provide. With emotional reasons for favoring the institution and realistic worries about the permanence and safety of the community placement, it is small wonder that parents have resisted movement.

The Present Placement Is Best

There is, moreover, the considerable appeal of the status quo for parents with a handicapped child. As already noted, the Pennhurst survey showed parents of institutional residents clinging to institutional placement, but after movement to the community, equally enamored with community residences (Conroy & Bradley, 1985). In a Connecticut survey of families with offspring in central institutions, regional residential placements, and community residences, the vast majority from each setting expressed satisfaction (Conroy & Feinstein, 1985). In a large study of foster care for mentally retarded children, the natural parents indicated a general satisfaction with their child's placement, and nearly 90% indicated that they had no plans to take their child back home (Lei, Nihira, Sheehy, & Meyers, 1981). Rudie and Riefl (1984) found that parents were happy with whatever placement their child had, whether in an institution or in the community, so long, apparently, as it was not in the natural home. This may in part reflect realistic concerns about the family's abilities to successfully live and cope with the retarded child.

Our society's lack of service alternatives has resulted in a parental search for services that is invariably fraught with difficulties. Consequently, there is often a willingness for parents

to stick with what they have found, even if it means overlooking some shortcomings. Special education teachers, for instance, are often revered by parents as "angels." In our personal experience we know of many decidedly poor educational settings that, when threatened with closing, found their strongest advocates in the parents of their charges. To begin the search all over again is sometimes just too much.

Methodological Shortcomings of Family Attitude Surveys

Although the surveys we have reviewed have been fairly consistent in their findings, we should nonetheless express some methodological caveats. First, as with any survey, respondents may not have been representative of all parents of institutionalized persons. Response rates ranged from 30% to 75% of surveys distributed. The Pennhurst study (Conroy & Bradley, 1985) had the best response rate and, in addition, contacted a random sample of nonresponders, with the encouraging finding that their attitudes did not differ from those of responders. Second, some studies are not reported in sufficient detail. Payne (1976) offered general conclusions but did not report numerical results; Ferrara (1979) did not report whether her respondents had children living in institutions or at home; and only one survey (Conroy & Feinstein, 1985) went beyond the general terms "*parents*" or "*families*" to indicate who respondents were. Third, the methodology of some studies may have a press for pro-institution results. Meyer's (1980) survey was mailed with a supporting letter from the institution superintendent; Frohboese and Sales (1980) talked only with parents who were opposed to deinstitutionalization. Fourth, other studies may press toward a more favorable response to community placements. Conroy and Bradley's (1985) study changed survey methods midstream, from a mailed prequestionnaire to the more personal telephone postinterview. Fifth, much of the work of these studies was conducted in the absence of a theoretical framework. And even recent attempts to propose such a framework regarding child placement and family adaptation (Cole, 1986) have negative overtones, suggesting that placement occurs only when a family can no longer cope with their situation. Finally, an overall shortcoming in this literature is that the much larger population of families with retarded children living at home has not been questioned about their attitudes toward community placements. This issue is discussed next.

Parents with Retarded Children Living at Home

In planning for family involvement in community residences of the future, we must pay attention to families with young retarded children who are currently living at home. The childrearing experiences today of these families are certainly different from those of families represented by the surveys just reviewed. Raising a retarded child in the post-PL 94-142 (The Education for All Handicapped Children Act) era is likely to affect attitudes about the child's potential and about desirable services. We conjecture that families' attitudes toward, and involvement with, community-living alternatives will be more positive in this new generation, although many of their worries will be the same as those of families with institutionalized relatives.

Today's families with a young handicapped child at home are influenced by normalization ideology, favored by many professionals who strongly advocate keeping the child at home. National professional and advocacy groups, such as the Association for Persons with Severe Handicaps (TASH), speak vehemently against out-of-home placement for children. The mood is definitely one of "placement is bad" and "home rearing of handicapped children is good." Institutional placement is usually not even a viable option, given this rhetoric and the reality of increasingly tight admission policies. Conversely, when the child has become a young adult, out-of-home placement into the least restrictive community setting is encouraged.

Today's families with handicapped children also find themselves playing a significant role in their child's education. They are actively involved in the educational process, as advocates, planners, and even teachers of their child. Public Law 94-142 affords their child the right to a free and appropriate education and affords the parents key rights and responsibilities in planning and decision making. A majority of par-

ents are involved in annual educational planning sessions with the school (Meyers & Blacher, 1987), and many maintain ongoing involvement with the school. Moreover, many parents participate in training programs to learn how they can become better teachers of their child at home (Baker, 1984).

Today's family also has greater experience with short-term respite care than families did previously. A number of communities have initiated programs whereby a respite worker comes to the home for several hours or in which the child can be temporarily placed for a few days to a month or more when a family has a special need for respite or the child has a special need for intensive training (Salisbury & Intagliata, 1986). The following comments from parents are illustrative (both cited in Upshur, 1983, p. 13):

> I used to get very depressed never having any time to myself and having the constant care of our severely retarded boy. . . . Now we look forward to respite care and can spend time with our teenage daughter. . . . We parents who choose to bring up our retarded children need desperately to get regular respite care services.
>
> I have been very grateful for respite care. I am a single parent due to the death of my husband. Last summer I was able to go away on vacation, the first time in 23 years I had ever left my retarded son.

There is evidence that respite care can prevent or delay institutionalization (Townsend & Flanagan, 1976), as may be the case in the first of the preceding quotes. Paradoxically, however, some parents report that it reduces their guilt in separating from their child (Joyce, Singer, & Isralowitz, 1983) and can ultimately ease the transition to a community placement (Blacher, 1986a).

These experiences relating to ideologies, legal rights, service involvements, and respite care are very likely to affect parents' attitudes toward eventual community residential placement for their child. While we are aware of no direct research on this issue, a longitudinal study in California illustrates these experiences.

Jan Blacher and C. Edward Meyers have followed 100 families with a severely handicapped child between the ages of 3 and 9 in their Project for the Severely Impaired and Their Families. As part of an extensive assessment battery about their experiences, parents were interviewed regarding their experiences with and perceptions of schooling, respite care, and placement.

Schooling results, coded reliably from audiotapes of the interviews, revealed that 81% of parents were satisfied or extremely satisfied (Meyers & Blacher, 1987). Parents also identified a number of perceived benefits of schooling in addition to the child's education. Among these, schooling was seen as helping to create more positive attitudes toward their child and toward his or her potential capabilities and as teaching the parents new skills and behavior management techniques, thus helping them "cope" better with their child. Parents reported that they were highly involved in all aspects of their child's schooling, from assessment and writing individualized education plans (IEPs), to participating in parent groups. Most remained in regular communication with the teacher, and almost half (47%) did so daily. Only 3% of the parents reported no communication with the school.

It is noteworthy that 89% of parents mentioned that schooling had some respite benefit for them (Blacher & Prado, 1986). In response to the hypothetical question of what action parents would take if school were no longer available, only four parents said they would definitely place the child; 27% said they did not know, or they did not want to think about it, or they preferred to "take each day at a time." The remainder would try to find an equivalent program, a private school, some daycare service, or any alternative so long as the child remained in some kind of educational placement. Once having sampled the freedom, the respite care, and the training provided by public schooling, these parents were no longer willing to even consider the possibility of no day placement.

Out-of-home placement is a separate but not unrelated issue. It usually has been studied retrospectively, by asking parents questions like, "Why did you place your handicapped child?" Attitudes toward changes in placement, as we have seen here, have also been the focus of many researchers. The longitudinal sample currently under study (Blacher, 1986b) affords a

unique opportunity to study the placement process prospectively. Admittedly, the parents in this sample are predisposed toward home placement, as they were initially selected in 1982 because their child still resided at home. We find that this generation of parents makes a clear distinction between eventual placement in an institution versus a community-based facility. Nearly all vowed to keep their child "out of the institution," although many of them considered the possibility of alternative placements (i.e., community residences).

Blacher (1986a) has reported data on these parents' thoughts on placement at three different time points, each about a year apart. The study uses a scale ranging from 1 ("No, I have never thought about placement") to 6 ("The child is placed"), to emphasize that parents experience placement decision making as a process or tendency, not as a sudden decision made on Monday morning after a weekend of bad behavior from their child. While 55% of parents reported a score of 1 and stayed at a 1 over the 3 years, other parents who took the first step did in fact continue to move up the scale. The prediction of ultimate placement (score of 6) from a score of 4 ("We have thought about placement and have inquired about it; we have talked with Regional Center and looked at placements, but have done nothing about it yet") was high.

These data reveal that placement is a process to which parents devote considerable thought over a period of several years. During this time parents remain highly involved with their child and their child's schooling. While one might argue that some form of "detachment" takes place as soon as parents move from a 1 to a 2 ("Occasionally we have given placement a thought") on the scale, complete detachment from their child does not exist until long after the actual out-of-home placement occurs, if ever (Blacher, 1986b). For these parents at least, continued involvement in their child's community residential placement is critical to ensure both a smooth transition for the child and a positive adjustment period for themselves.

FAMILY INVOLVEMENT IN COMMUNITY RESIDENCES

In the months and years following placement in a community residence, family involvement at best remains steady. However, it is more likely to diminish. What, then, do we know about the extent and nature of continuing family involvement in community residences? We consider here two broad types of family involvement: *visitation,* which includes all forms of personal contact for social support, guidance, and the like, and *participation in decision-making.* Although the two types tend to be related, some families choose one type of involvement but not the other.

Involvement through Visitation

The most comprehensive information on family contacts and visitation was obtained in a study by Hill, Rotegard, and Bruininks (1984). They surveyed 2,271 residents of facilities for mentally retarded persons; of these, 965 were randomly selected residents from 161 community residential facilities. Information about family contacts was gathered through interviews with direct care staff. For every 5 residents, staff reported that about 1 had no personal contact with family members although in some cases there were gifts or letters, 3 were visited from one to three times a year, and only 1 was visited more frequently. Sixty percent were visited 1–3 times a year. "Visits," as the term was used here, included both visits at the residential facility and at home. It embraced all possible family members, although 75% of residents' contacts with relatives were with parents.

The impression these statistics convey is essentially one of isolation from families. This becomes more troubling in the context of broader social relationships. Only 15.8% of the residents had social contact once a month or more with a nonhandicapped peer, and only half (50.4%) had a friend (defined as someone whom the residents liked and with whom they did things on their own time). Friends outside of the residence or its organized volunteer programs were rare.

Although all of these social relationships for residents in community facilities surpassed those for residents of public institutions, they nonetheless underscore the social isolation of many residents. Caregivers also reported that lack of someone to accompany residents was a major impediment to their engaging in more leisure time activities. Hill and his colleagues

(Hill et al., 1984) conclude that efforts to increase friendships and family involvement should be more of a priority for program administrators, as these correlates of successful community adjustment are more readily changed than factors such as resident IQ or staff ratios.

It is often assumed that parents will visit community residences more than larger institutions. However, Conroy and Feinstein (1985) found a slightly higher visitation rate to regional institutions than to smaller community facilities. And Latib et al. (1984) did not find that visits to or from families became more frequent following relocation from Pennhurst to community residences. While 44% of families reported visiting their mentally retarded relative at least once a month prior to deinstitutionalization, this figure only increased to 53% after. Similarly, before relocation, 13% reported that their relative came home at least once a month, a figure that climbed only to 16% after. It is important to note, however, that parents did report that after resident relocation, visiting was easier, less "scary" than visiting at the large institution, and more conducive to bringing along younger siblings.

What child, family, and program attributes relate to visitation? Anderson, Schlottmann, and Weiner (1975) studied parent involvement with 200 institutionalized retarded children, selected so that about half were visited often (once a month or more) and half seldom or never (three times a year or less). Of these parents, about three-quarters attended the annual planning conference.

Families with high involvement (both visitation plus decision making) were contrasted with those with low involvement (neither visitation nor decision making) on a number of demographic variables. High-involvement families consistently scored more advantageously. Their children had higher IQs and a lower incidence of physical anomalies, a finding corroborated by Klaber (1968). Their marriages were more likely intact. Their family income was higher, and hence a greater proportion of these families was required to make maintenance payments. Fathers' education and occupational levels as well as mothers' education were higher. Also, parents lived closer to the institution. (Distance as a predictor of visitation has been found by several other investigators [Ballinger, 1970; Schultz & Buckman, 1965], though not by all [Klaber, 1968].)

More recently, it has been suggested that the types of demographic variables that Anderson et al. (1975) found related to visitation may now influence parents' selection of placement setting. Hodapp and Zigler (1985) note that "more capable and involved parents are more likely to insist on a local and more innovative environment when institutionalizing their child" (p. 128). Meyers and Blacher (1987) also found that higher scores on home quality and adjustment variables related to the amount and type of involvement of parents in their severely handicapped child's public school program.

Suggestions to Increase Family Involvement in Visitation

The major limitation to these studies on visitation is that we still know little about the level and extent of families' involvement during

those visits. We also have scanty information about how satisfied residents or their relatives are with that involvement. This would be a useful focus for future research, especially since many parents in the 1980s and '90s will already be accustomed to a high level of involvement with their child's school program. The paragraphs following offer suggestions for increasing visitation by parents and for improving the content of those visits. These and other considerations for family involvement are summarized in Table 1.

First, it is important to give parents or family members a reason to want to visit. The visit itself should be pleasant; parents should not be made to feel guilty or to feel that they are intruding. The residents—whether children or adults—should look "good"—clean, and well groomed. Specially sponsored activities by staff, or opportunities for parents to participate in ongoing activities, also help to encourage visitation. Some parents are eager to have their nonhandicapped children involved as well, so

Table 1. Enhancing family involvement: A self-assessment for service providers

I. PREPARATION FOR MOVEMENT INTO A COMMUNITY RESIDENCE
  1. Does your program encourage forms of "outreach" to parents, informing them of your program (e.g., goals, philosophy, and characteristics) before an applicant is placed there?
  2. Is the resident moving into the community residence (CR) from his or her natural home, or from another placement?
    If from the natural home:
    a. Have the parents expressed any interest in continued involvement with their son or daughter?
    b. If so, what specific types of involvement do they prefer or expect?
    If from another placement:
    a. Have parents (or other family members) been involved in this previous placement?
    b. If so, how or to what extent?
    c. Did they view this placement as inviting involvement?
    d. Is there any indication that they would like more involvement in your placement?
  3. Have you conducted any "parent needs assessment" as part of the preparation for entrance into your CR?
  4. Have you given parents a chance to voice their attitudes toward this particular community placement versus other placement options (e.g., remaining at the institution)?
  5. Have your staff members been prepared for working with parents of new residents?
    a. What exactly did this preparation consist of?
    b. Do staff members demonstrate understanding of the parents' perspective, thoughts, or feelings about placement?
    c. Do staff members hold negative attitudes toward parents?

II. ENTERING THE RESIDENCE
  1. Are staff oriented toward meeting residents' needs as they enter the residence?
    a. Do staff routinely consider the resident's previous social relationships or friendships?
    b. Is the resident encouraged or helped to be integrated into existing social groups at the residence?
  2. Are families included in your transition process?
  3. Do you have separate entrance procedures and requirements for residents who enter directly from their natural home and for residents who have been living out of the home?

(continued)

Table 1. *(continued)*

III. VISITATION

    1. Do you have a visitation policy for parents at your residence?
        a. How does it work; is it fixed, or flexible?
        b. Does it apply to friends and other relatives of the resident as well?
    2. Do you provide any transportation to parents who may have difficulty visiting, or any accommodations upon visiting?
    3. How do families arrange to take their relative out with them for an outing, overnight, or extended vacation?
        a. Is this encouraged by staff?
        b. Are such efforts coordinated with staff (e.g., is there an attempt to continue any programming during this "leave" time)?
        c. Is there any opportunity for families to learn methods to use in programming for their relative when he or she is visiting at home?
    4. When family members visit, are they involved in ongoing residence activities?
        a. Is there programming in progress that families may observe?
        b. Are special activities initiated for the actual visitation?
    5. Is there any support group for parents/families that meets regularly?

IV. DECISION MAKING

    1. Are parents routinely involved in decision making concerning their son or daughter, such as:
        a. Developing education or habilitation plan?
        b. Setting social skills goals?
        c. Planning subsequent transitions (e.g., transition from one vocational placement to another)?
        d. Financial planning?
    2. Are parents involved in decision making concerning the operation of your community residence, such as:
        a. Setting parent involvement policies?
        b. Setting policies for staff-related issues, such as hiring, maintenance, job responsibilities?
        c. Setting policies for appropriate client behaviors, relationships, responsibilities, restrictions?
    3. Do the parents of your residents make decisions about funding their son or daughter (i.e., determine and provide financial support)?
    4. Are parents involved in advocacy, monitoring, or evaluation activities at your residence?

V. TRANSITIONS—MOVING ON

    1. Are parents of your residents consulted before changes in residential placement are made (e.g., movement from one residence to another)?
    2. What methods are used to keep parents posted on resident behavior (social, emotional, adaptive) during the transition process?
    3. Does your program have different family involvement expectations depending upon the next residential setting being planned for?
    4. Have you developed and implemented a formal resident transition plan (RTP) that parents or other family members share in?
        a. If so, are the roles of family members in the writing and implementation of the plan clearly defined?
        b. Are family members educated and informed about the purpose of the RTP?
    5. Does your program maintain contact with residents and their families after residents have moved to another program?

special activities for them are usually well received.

Second, visits can be used to promote positive staff-parent interaction; staff should be available to respond to parents' inquiries rather than retreating from sight. By working as partners with parents, staff may earn their respect and appreciation, and perhaps be less likely to receive criticism. The burden of promoting this outreach to parents should be on the residence staff, as parents may feel anxious, embarrassed, and at a loss as to how to approach them. One is reminded of scenes in the award-winning documentary film, *Best Boy,* where Pearl (the mother of the retarded adult newly placed into a group home for the first time) desperately wants reassurance that her son Philly will be all right.

Third, individualizing parent visits is also a good idea. Some parents will be placing their son or daughter for the first time and still be very attached. They will need to "detach" slowly, engaging in a more frequent visitation pattern at first, with a gradual decrease in contact. However, other parents will undoubtedly choose *not* to be so involved, and to make few visits. Parents should be able to exercise this option as well, without being made to feel guilty by the staff.

Finally, parental visits to any community residence would probably increase if at least one respite care bed were made available. This would enable other families to participate in the residence in at least a limited way. It would create a gradual form of family involvement and would serve as a transition aid for families considering out-of-home placement for their son or daughter.

Decision Making

The other general type of family involvement with a relative in a community-living arrangement is to share in making important decisions that affect his or her life. Three areas are considered here in which family members' involvement can be beneficial: planning activities, transitions, and monitoring activities.

Planning Activities As reported by Close and Halpern (Chapter 13, this volume) families have an important role to play in annual or more frequent meetings to develop long- and short-term goals for the resident's program (e.g., individualized education plans, resident transition plan). This decision-making role is a more comfortable one for many families than is their more personal involvement in visiting and teaching. The Anderson et al. (1975) study revealed that more families were involved in these planning sessions than in regular visitation. Families with children living at home—who will be the future residents of community facilities—are going to want a greater decision-making role than has been the case with families of current residents. As noted earlier, the new generation of parents is accustomed to being involved in planning, and many parents have acquired good programming skills. These parents can be a threat or an asset, depending upon the perspective the staff chooses to take.

Transitions Critical times for professional/parent collaboration involve residential

transitions (e.g., from home to out-of-home placement, from institution to community residence, from one community program to another, from a program back to the home). There is less emphasis at present on permanent placement, with transitions seen as a normal experience. The following vignette illustrates one community residence that pays considerable attention to transitions.

Vignette: Eric

Eric is 11 years old, a thin boy with blue eyes and curly hair. He lives now with five other children on Cape Cod in Massachusetts. The large Cape house with split rail fence and rosebushes blends into its seaside neighborhood. Yet it is a transitional group home operated by the May Institute, a residential program for autistic children. Married houseparents live with their toddler daughter in a separate apartment on the second floor, and the three full-time associate therapists each periodically sleep in the house. The house bustles with teaching and recreational activity.

Before Eric was admitted to the May Institute at age 8, the transitional services staff met at length with his parents to discuss the transitional nature of the program and to agree on the future site that they would program toward. As with most other residents, Eric would return home when specified behavioral goals were met, probably in three or four years. His parents' attitudes toward this community placement was quite positive. As his mother noted: "It's not like putting him away. He'll have a school experience for a while that we can all share in."

After 2 years, Eric was about ready to return home, but his parents had reservations about whether his improved sleeping and self-care behaviors would generalize back home, and the local school wondered about his classroom behavior in a less controlled environment. Eric was moved to the group home and to a special education class in the local community.

Eric's family figures prominently in his program, even though they live 80 miles away in Boston. They completed the May Institute's group parent training program in Boston and carry out teaching with Eric when he is at home. To enable them to have a role in decision making, they are required to observe his program for 2 days each year, split between the group home and the classroom. They also attend the annual individualized educational plan meeting. In addition, there are several social events at the group home each year, which Eric's 9-year-old sister especially enjoys.

Eric returns home for five vacation periods (45 days) each year, and during some of these the houseparents and transitional staff spend extended time at Eric's house. He also returns home every other week, from Friday afternoon through Sunday. The houseparents drive a van that drops off the children near their homes, and then the houseparents spend the weekend at the May Institute's Boston apartment. Every other trip they visit Eric's home for 2 hours or so, to discuss progress and problems with Eric's parents, to demonstrate teaching methods, and to supervise the parents' teaching. Since Eric is almost ready to return home, his new individualized transitional plan involves extended weekends at home, with participation in a local school on Fridays and Mondays.

Eric, then, is living in a community residence with ongoing parent involvement that takes a variety of forms: planning, programming, social support, and just plain parenting. Awareness of the future site, Eric's natural home, guides the program in this transitional facility. (Compiled in part from information provided by Drs. Walter Christian, Stephen Luce, and Stephen Anderson, and by Yvonne Ryan, all of the May Institute).

Monitoring Activities As already noted, parents commonly worry about the quality of care in community facilities. Although parents visiting a community residence may notice ways in which the program quality could be improved, they are unlikely to actively monitor the program or make suggestions to staff about possible changes. Indeed, most community residences have no mechanism by which staff can receive and act upon suggestions. Hence, most parents keep their thoughts to themselves. This reticence may change with the next generation of consumers, who, rather than simply being thankful for any placement, will recognize their rights and the increasing range of program options. Although state agencies have monitoring procedures for certain professional activities, community residences would do well to establish better ways to involve parents as monitors.

One exemplary approach to monitoring is a collaborative program between an Association for Retarded Citizens, staff of group homes, and the Macomb-Oakland Regional Center in Michigan (Provencal & Taylor, 1983). A Parent Monitoring Committee, composed of over 30 volunteer parents and guardians, monitors group and foster homes for over 300 residents. Two-person teams visit each group home every 2 months; they do not visit homes where their own relatives or wards reside.

The monitors' primary responsibility is to evaluate the "feel" of each home; specific areas given attention include home appearance, meals, security, laundry, general environment, staff, support services, and resident rights. Monitors have a list of questions they might ask themselves (e.g., Is there sufficient space for an individual to pursue a quiet activity in the home?"). The Regional Center reimburses mileage and provides program monitors with identification cards, an office, and supplies. In the first 4 years, this program made over 1,500 group home visits and filed as many reports, which recommended an average of five improvements for each home per year. Monitors reported that a large number of these recommendations were acted upon. This inexpensive and seemingly effective program has been well received by parents and, after initial skepticism, by group home providers. An additional benefit has been increased trust and respect between parents and community residence staff.

Suggestions to Increase Family Involvement in Decision Making As we have seen, control, or at least consultation, is an important issue for parents and the one that seems to have generated the most annoyance in the deinstitutionalization process. Parents feel that they have not beeen consulted in a meaningful way about decisions. The community residence staff should ask for families' input about important decisions that arise, and especially should involve them in decision making from the start, as part of the "transitioning in" process.

The community residence might also formalize some decision-making processes, such as establishing an advocacy board or a parent advisory committee on social norms and activities so that parents can find it easier to participate. The staff could also schedule individual semi-annual conferences with each family to discuss the community residence's program and their relative's progress. It is important, of course, to keep a balance between formal and informal activities, giving a consistent message of always being willing to listen to parents. Finally, community residences may want to involve other family members, especially siblings. Since siblings are most likely to be involved in advocacy and financial planning over the long run, community-residence-sponsored half-day informational programs on topics such as estate planning are a good way to involve them meaningfully.

Staff Ambivalence

Parents' decisions about involvement are not made in a vacuum. We find little attention paid in the literature to staff attitudes, although these certainly have an impact on how parents relate to the community residence. When staff see family involvement as integral to the program and are open to it—indeed, invite or even require it—the family's involvement is likely to be greater and more productive (cf., the instance of Eric). Many staff, however, are ambivalent about parents, an attitude that we feel reflects some negative cognitions, role conflicts, and perceived program deficiencies.

Staff ambivalence can arise from negative cognitions about parents who have formerly placed their handicapped son or daughter in an institution. Staff members who did not experience the past professional ideology that pressured parents to place the child may blame parents for this decision ("They gave him up. What right do they have now?"). Moreover, some staff caught up in normalization rhetoric may have overly rejecting cognitions about parent involvement with their adult offspring ("Parents should let go. They are fostering dependency."). Cognitions (or "self-statements") like these can enormously influence staff receptivity to parent involvement. Like many cognitions that influence our behavior, however, these may not be entirely conscious. Community residence staff might usefully meet to discuss their thoughts about parents, to try to get negative cognitions "on the table" so that more positive angles can be explored.

Staff ambivalence can also arise from their unique caregiving role. Especially in settings perceived as permanent, staff may derive much of their gratification from seeing their charges as "my kids" or "my residents." There is some reluctance to share decision making, affection from the resident, or credit for his or her progress with others; indeed, communication is less than would be desirable, not only with par-

ents but also with teachers and job supervisors. When the role is defined in this way (house-*parents,* foster *parents*) some resistance to intrusion with staff parenting is likely. An analogy may be the foster parents who resent and resist intrusion by natural parents. A more helpful model from family configurations may be one of the shared parenting in some divorced families. In community residence staffing models where staff work shifts rather than live in and invest their whole life in the program, a more balanced role definition may be easier to achieve (Baker et al., 1977). Again, it is advisable for community residence staff to meet to discuss how they view their roles and to seek definitions that leave room for parents and others to make important contributions.

Staff ambivalence can also arise from a progam that they perceive as inadequate. The more that staff believe their facility to be appropriate, of high quality, and a caring program, the more likely they are to want to show it off and share it with others. Resistance to parent involvement can arise when there is nothing much to report to parents or ask of them—in short, nothing much happening. We have seen that parents are more likely to visit and to enjoy the visit in well-run programs, and we suspect that this is in part because the staff are more receptive to such visits. Any staff consideration of ways to "make the program better," then, may have spin-off effects on their receptiviity to parent involvement.

CONCLUSION

Families with handicapped relatives are wary of services that move their children back into the neighborhood, and community residence staff are ambivalent about families moving onto their turf. Yet there is good reason to promote opportunities for families to be involved in the life of their relative and in his or her new home. We advocate types of involvement that are individualized according to the placement setting, resident needs, and needs of other family members. All indications from current political and philosophical arenas are that the number of community residences for mentally retarded individuals will increase. The availability of these options allows families to more naturally consider and realistically plan for eventual placement.

For families experiencing the process of placement, programs that promote their involvement will allow them to make this transition at their own pace. As a mother of a severely/profoundly mentally retarded teenage daughter said after placing her child: "You don't just leave them in one chunk." By providing opportunities for meaningful family involvement, community residence staff can make this difficult transition and the years that follow more pleasant for the family, the resident, and themselves.

REFERENCES

Anderson, V.H., Schlottmann, R.S., & Weiner, B.J. (1975). Predictors of parent involvement with institutionalized retarded children. *American Journal of Mental Deficiency, 79,* 705–710.

Baker, B.L. (1984). Intervention with families with young, severely handicapped children. In J. Blacher (Ed.), *Severely handicapped young children and their families: Research in review* (pp. 319–375). Orlando, FL: Academic Press.

Baker, B.L., Seltzer, G.B., & Seltzer, M.M. (1977). *As close as possible: Community residences for retarded adults.* Boston: Little, Brown.

Ballinger, B.R. (1970). Community contacts of institutionalized mental defectives. *British Journal of Mental Subnormality, 16,* 17–23.

Blacher, J. (1986a, March). *Assessing placement tendency in families with severely handicapped children.* Paper presented at Annual Gatlinburg Conference on Research and Theory in Mental Retardation/Developmental Disabilities, Gatlinburg, TN.

Blacher, J. (1986b). *Placement of severely handicapped children: Correlates and consequences.* NICHD Grant # RO1 HD21324. Riverside, CA: University of California, Riverside.

Blacher, J., & Prado, P. (1986). The school as respite for parents of children with severe handicaps. In C.L. Salisbury & J. Intagliata (Eds.), *Respite care: Support for persons with developmental disabilities and their families* (pp. 217–234). Baltimore: Paul H. Brookes Publishing Co.

Bradley, V.J. (1985). Implementation of court and consent decrees: Some current lessons. In R.H. Bruininks & K.C. Lakin (Eds.), *Living and learning in the least restrictive environment* (pp. 81–96). Baltimore: Paul H. Brookes Publishing Co.

Cole, D.A. (1986). Out-of-home child placement and family adaptation: A theoretical framework. *American Journal of Mental Deficiency, 91,* 226–236.

Conroy, J.W. (1985). Medical needs of institutionalized mentally retarded persons: Perceptions of families and staff members. *American Journal of Mental Deficiency, 89,* 510–514.

Conroy, J.W., & Bradley, V.J. (1985). *The Pennhurst longitudinal study: A report of five years of research and analysis.* Philadelphia: Temple University Developmental Disabilities Center. Boston: Human Services Research Institute.

Conroy, J.W., & Feinstein, C.S. (1985, November). *Attitudes of the families of CARC v. Thorne Classmembers.* Interim Report Number 2. Connecticut Applied Research Project. Philadelphia, PA: Conroy & Feinstein Associates.

Edgerton, R.B. (1967). *The cloak of competence.* Berkeley: University of California Press.

Ferrara, D.M. (1979). Attitudes of parents of mentally retarded children toward normalization activities. *American Journal of Mental Deficiency, 84,* 145–51.

Frohboese, R., & Sales, B.D. (1980). Parental opposition to deinstitutionalization. *Law and Human Behavior, 4,* 1–87.

Halpern, A.S., Close, D.W., & Nelson, D.J. (1986). *On my own: The impact of semi-independent living programs for adults with mental retardation.* Baltimore: Paul H. Brookes Publishing Co.

Hill, B.K., Bruininks, R.H., Lakin, K.C., Hauber, F.A., & McGuire, S.P. (1985). Stability of residential facilities for people who are mentally retarded, 1977–1982. *Mental Retardation, 23,* 108–114.

Hill, B.K., Rotegard, L.L., & Bruininks, R.H. (1984). The quality of life of mentally retarded people in residential care. *Social Work, 29,* 275–280.

Hodapp, R.M., & Zigler, E. (1985). Placement decisions and their effects on the development of individuals with severe mental retardation. *Mental Retardation, 23,* 125–130.

Hunt, E., Browning, P., & Nave, G. (1982). A behavioral exploration of dependent and independent mentally retarded adolescents and their mothers. *Journal of Applied Research in Mental Retardation, 3,* 141–150.

Joyce, K., Singer, M., & Isralowitz, R. (1983). Impact of respite care on parents' perceptions of quality of life. *Mental Retardation, 21,* 153–156.

Kastner, L.S., Reppucci, N.D., & Pezzoli, J.J. (1979). Assessing community attitudes toward mentally retarded persons. *American Journal of Mental Deficiency, 84,* 137–144.

Klaber, M.M. (1968). Parental visits to institutionalized children. *Mental Retardation, 6,* 39–41.

Klaber, M.M. (1969). The retarded and institutions for the retarded—a preliminary research report. In S.B. Sarason and J. Doris (Eds.), *Psychological problems of mental deficiency,* New York: Harper & Row.

Latib, A., Conroy, J., & Hess, C.M. (1984). Family attitudes toward deinstitutionalization. *International Review of Research in Mental Retardation, 12,* 67–93.

Lei, T., Nihira, L., Sheehy, N., & Meyers, C.E. (1981). A study of small family care for mentally retarded people. In R.H. Bruininks, C.E. Meyers, B.B. Sigford, & K.C. Lakin (Eds.), *Deinstitutionalization and community adjustment of mentally retarded people.* Monograph No. 4. Washington, DC: American Association on Mental Deficiency.

Meyer, R.J. (1980). Attitudes of parents of institutionalized mentally retarded individuals toward deinstitutionalization. *American Journal of Mental Deficiency, 85,* 184–187.

Meyers, C.E., & Blacher, J. (1987). Parents' perceptions of schooling for their severely handicapped child: Home and school variables. *Exceptional Children, 53,* 441–449.

Payne, J.E. (1976). The deinstitutional backlash. *Mental Retardation, 14,* 43–45.

Provencal, G., & Taylor, R. (1983). Security for parents: Monitoring of group homes by consumers. *Exceptional Parent, 13,* 39–44.

Rudie, F., & Riefl, G. (1984). Attitudes of parents/guardians of mentally retarded former state hospital residents toward current community placement. *American Journal of Mental Deficiency, 89,* 295–297.

Salisbury, C.L., & Intagliata, J. (1986). *Respite care: Support for persons with developmental disabilities and their families.* Baltimore: Paul H. Brookes Publishing Co.

Schalock, R.L., Harper, R.S. & Genung, T. (1981). Community integration of mentally retarded adults: Community placement and program success. *American Journal of Mental Deficiency, 85,* 478–488.

Schalock, R.L., & Lilley, M.A. (1986). Placement from community-based mental retardation programs: How well do clients do after 8 to 10 years? *American Journal of Mental Deficiency, 90,* 669–676.

Schultz, H.F., & Buckman, S.T. (1965). A study of visiting patterns of relatives. *Welfare Reporter, 16,* 72–75.

Seltzer, M.M. (1985). Public attitudes toward community residential facilities for mentally retarded persons. In R.H. Bruininks & K.C. Lakin (Eds.), *Living and learning in the least restrictive environment.* Baltimore: Paul H. Brookes Publishing Co.

Spreat, S., Telles, J.L., Conroy, J.W., Feinstein, C.S., & Colombatto, J.J. (1984). *Attitudes toward deinstitutionalization: A national survey of the families of institutionalized mentally retarded persons.* Philadelphia: Temple University Woodhaven Center and Developmental Disabilities Center/UAF.

Townsend, P.W., & Flanagan, J.J. (1976). Experimental pre-admission program to encourage home care for severely and profoundly retarded children. *American Journal of Mental Deficiency, 80,* 562–569.

Upshur, C.C. (1983). Developing respite care: A support service for families with disabled members. *Family Relations, 32,* 13–20.

Zetlin, A.G., & Turner, J.L. (1984). Self-perspectives on being handicapped: Stigma and adjustment. In R.B. Edgerton (Ed.), *Lives in progress: Mildly retarded adults in a large city* (pp. 93–120). Washington, DC: American Association on Mental Deficiency.

Chapter 15

Communicative Competence

Barbara A. Kenefick

Communication acts as a powerful means of gaining mastery over one's world. In many respects, individuals with mental retardation have difficulty in both expressing themselves competently and in processing information that is directed toward them. This chapter examines some of the basic principles of communication and explores various means that can be employed to teach residents of community residences to be more effective in communicating. It also discusses how the communication patterns of staff can influence the behavior of those around them. Suggestions are offered as aids for habilitative programming.

This chapter explores how interventions directed toward communication skill development can foster growth and effect change for persons with mental retardation living in community residential settings. It is also designed to offer a foundation in the basic principles of communication functions and the habilitative strategies that can be effective in building communicative competence. In this chapter, *communication* is defined as the exchange of messages between two or more individuals in direct relationship through the use of oral language symbols, signs, and behavior, when the meaning of these symbols is understood by all participants in this exchange. Such communication is not limited to verbal acts, but also comprises visual and kinesthetic processes (including telephoning and writing). Consequently, communication skill development includes all of those activities that are directed toward improving an individual's communicative competence (e.g., effective and adaptive use of communication).

Communication acts as a powerful tool in shaping our world. It enables us to probe the dimensions of time and space, while sustaining contact with the people whose lives affect us. Communication connects us with time by providing the opportunity to reconsider the past and plan for the future. Through communicative exchange we are able to share the present as we describe and comment on current experience. Communication orients us to space, as we identify the components of our environment and order them for comfort, convenience, and effective use. Further, communication supports our social being as we express feelings and values, while responding to those of others. Thus, communication functions as an instrument of growth and change.

The chapter begins by examining the notion of communication as an habilitative tool for individuals with mental retardation, for their caregivers, and for members of the community at large with whom they interact. Components of communicative competence are described with particular relevance to the uses of language. Recent research and program designs pertaining to communicative competence are then reviewed as a basis for the formation of practical recommendations for community residential programs and suggestions for further study.

COMMUNICATIVE COMPETENCE

Approaches and Assumptions

To effectively assess changes in the expressive and receptive language abilities that constitute oral communication, it is helpful to define basic terms. First, it is important to understand the distinction between *expressive* and *receptive* language. *Receptive language* comprises the ability to understand the spoken word or other means of communication, such as signing. It is based on auditory memory, as well as the comprehension of the structure, meaning, and functions of speech. *Expressive language* is the ability to prepare oral or signed messages that are meaningful and appropriate to one's listeners. It includes the capacity to organize one's thoughts in concord with the capabilities of other speaker/listeners.

As a concept, communicative competence in relation to conversation comprises three aspects of language: its *structure* or *syntax,* its *meaning* or *semantics,* and its *functions* or *pragmatics.* Thus, *communicative competence* is the ability of a speaker to encode messages that in form, content, and use are congruent with the speaker's intent, are appropriate to the situation, and are understood by the receivers of these messages.

Language can be viewed from a number of perspectives. First, communicative competence can define language on a continuum, with a conceptual approach at one extreme and empirical considerations at the other. It can provide the basis for developing individual intervention programs to build communication skills by elaborating the capabilities that should result from a given series of interventions. Further, communicative competence may comprise the framework for detailing the skills an individual needs to accurately deliver a message that is readily understood by others.

Second, communicative competence can be related to a perspective that views language developmentally from either a longitudinal or cross-sectional point of view. One can either examine changes in communicative abilities that develop over a long period of time or examine changes in communication abilities from various points of time over the course of a short time span.

Third, communicative competence can provide a standard of comparison for the three aspects of language (structure, meaning, and function) mentioned earlier. Workers assessing the capabilities of a resident to effectively communicate can relate their findings in one aspect to capabilities or skill levels in another aspect.

Fourth, communicative competence enables various professionals to share their findings about an individual being assessed. It offers a channel of commonality in discussions of matters of interdisciplinary importance among clinicians from diverse backgrounds.

Communicative competence can also form the basis for drawing assumptions about situational problems among individuals with mental retardation who reside in community residential settings. For example, researchers have reported that both gains and losses have been observed in the language abilities of mentally retarded persons who have moved from institutional to small-group living settings (Heinberg & Galligan, 1983; Hemming, 1986). One possible reason for these discrepant research findings is that changes in language abilities have been described solely in terms of alterations of scores on standardized tests or observational instruments and have not been related to interpersonal situations. The concept of communicative competence can offer a basis for consideration of language changes through analyses of the components of a communicative or speech act (Searle, 1975).

Aspects of Communicative Competence

At least four factors of any situation can influence communicative competence: the characteristics of the speaker, the characteristics of other speaker-listeners who are present, the aspects of the environment, and the nature of the communicative task.

The characteristics of the speaker and other speaker-listeners fall into three general groups: 1) enduring demographic and social characteristics such as age, sex, and educational background; 2) transient personal characteristics (such as cognitive, emotional, and motivational qualities); and 3) the speaker's intent and attention characteristics, including purposes for which one speaks, intended listeners, and whether the speaker is focusing on what is being said or to whom it is being said. In general, enduring characteristics are perceived by the speaker and other speaker-listeners, personal characteristics are behaviorally expressed by the speaker, and intentional/attentional characteristics of the speaking act are known only to the speaker and are assumed by other speaker-listeners.

Several dimensions of the environment require consideration for their relationship to communicative competence: the strange-familiar, person-object, and temporal-spatial. First, a language sample of an individal during her or his first day at the community residence is likely to be quite different than one taken 6 months later. This is because the *strangeness* of the setting affects the immediate demonstration of communication skills. Second, a living room with a formal arrangement will produce speech that differs from that heard in a recreation room, because communication is affected by how people relate to the immediate *objects* around them. Third, *spatial* arrangements found in a theater, gymnasium, park, or store can also shape speech in distinctive ways because people react to how their general environment is structured. The language of a resident should be assessed in a variety of settings because the characteristics of the individual are often confounded by the characteristics of the setting. It is important to remember that often environmental references cannot be separated from speaker-listener effects.

In considering the communicative task (i.e., what is the purpose of the communication), four factors have a bearing on communicative competence. First, there is the specific purpose of the task, which may be *substantive, relational,* or *expressive*. For example, giving directions, teaching a new skill, and most formal training exchanges have a substantive purpose in that these speaking situations depend on data that have a truth value. Deciding on a course of action, developing rules for cooperative living

in a community residence, and planning social or recreational events are relational in that they affect social processes and are judged by standards of appropriateness. Giving opinions, stating preferences, and showing feelings are expressive tasks.

The second factor that influences communicative competence consists of the interpersonal aspects of the task, such as whether it will affect the speaker-listener engaged in its performance, other persons, or both. In this respect, it is important to know how participant and spectator roles are distributed, and whether a common frame of reference is shared by all speaker-listeners. Other pertinent issues include the *code* (language, dialect, etc.) of the communicative act, the *channel* (telephone, conversation), *genre* (sales pitch, prayer, etc.), *topic,* and the *tone or manner* in which the act is performed (Hymes, 1972).

The third factor is the temporal dimension. This dimension determines whether the task can be accomplished in one session or requires several meetings or an extended period of time. Finally, there is the spatial element, which specifies if the task is dependent on a particular setting, a selection of settings, or is "setting-free."

FUNCTIONS OF COMMUNICATON

A Taxonomy and Its Use

The functions of communication comprise the uses governing the exchanges of messages. This field of study, formally known as pragmatics, has been described as the "study of the use of language in context, by real speaker-listeners in real situations" (Bates, 1974).

Workers in the field have constructed several language usage classification systems; however, most classification systems include the functions presented in Table 1. These categories characterize the uses to which language is shaped in conversational interchange and can be helpful in designing interventions to enhance communication skills with residents of community residences. The classification includes *directive, declarative, emotive, volitive, ritualization,* and *creative/metalanguage* functions.

Table 1. Taxonomy of communicative functions

Functions	Definition	Tasks	Forms	Examples
Directive	A use of language that moves listener toward the speaker's goals	Places constraints on the actions of listeners by prescribing or restricting activity	Command Request Advice Questions Activates	"Sit down." "Please give me the package." "I would go if I were you." "Isn't it hot in here?" (or more directly) "Would you open the window?" "Let's go to the game."
Declarative	A use of language to describe the speaker's phenomenological world and interactions with it	Provides information to listeners and/or accompanies action of speaker. This function demonstrates that speaker and listener share the same model of the universe	Regulates speaker's behavior Describe/report Structures relationships, situations States relationships Informs Narrative	"I'll finish the dishes before I read the paper." "She had short brown hair and wore a blue dress." "To complete this agenda it has been suggested we consider the program for the year." "That belongs to her." "There are 320 similar cases." "Once upon a time a fox went hunting."

		Explanation and exposition	
			"From this hypothesis the following conditions are predicted."
Emotive	A use of language that represents the feelings of the speaker and/or elicits the feelings of listeners	Expresses emotional response to persons, objects, and situations	Statement of affect Indication of affect for others Obtaining affective response from listeners	"I'm afraid of lightning." "I am glad you care." "Does this music make you sad?"
Volitive	A use of language that expresses the preferences, wishes, likes, and dislikes of the speaker	Indicates thoughts and behaviors directed toward action and change	Choice Decision Praise Criticism Striving	"I'll take this one." "I have made up my mind to go back to school." "You did that well." "You did not get that right." "I want to learn to ski."
Ritualization	A use of language that identifies an individual as a member of a particular language group	Reflects convention and idiomatic usage that enables members of a given community to recognize one another	Demonstration of membership in a particular language group Performance of ceremonial acts	Cheer for a particular sports team; class or club song "I take thee as my lawful, wedded wife."
Creative	A use of language for literary purposes	Expresses thought by form and content	Figures of speech (e.g., metaphor)	"Evening of life" "Truth is beauty."
Metalanguage	A use of language to communicate about language	Depicts language through use of language	Statement about language	"Every statement has a structure, function, and meaning."

Directive communication occurs when an individual uses language to move others toward his or her goals. Giving orders, advice, or recommendations constitutes direction, as does placing constraints on the behavior of another individual. This communication may be direct, as in issuing a command, or indirect, as in utilizing questions to achieve a specific purpose (e.g., asking "Is it cold in here?" when one wishes someone present to close a window). In certain circumstances one expects direction, as in consulting with a physician or supervisor. In other situations, with friends or family, direction may be less welcome. For example, Kenefick (1986) found that if more than 30% of an interaction between two people constitutes direction by one of them, an argument is likely to take place.

Declarative language gives information about the speaker or the speaker's environment and serves to regulate the speaker's own behavior and/or depict aspects of his or her identity. Emotives comprise expression of affect and include both representation of the speaker's feelings and elicitation of the feelings of others. Volitive communication manifests preferences, likes, and dislikes. On occasion it can be difficult to distinguish between willing and feeling (e.g., "I like being happy.").

Ritualization constitutes a function that identifies an individual as a member of a particular language group. Ritual language reflects conventions and idiomatic usages that enable members of a given community to recognize one another. The jargon used by workers in a particular discipline or field is an example of this. Finally, creative/metalanguage refers to communicative functions of two broad types. First, there is artistic usage, such as that found in poetry, and second, there is the use of language to communicate about language, as occurs in this chapter.

Two vignettes from observation of residential programs indicate how changes in language function of staff alter resident behavior:

Vignette: Mr. E.

Mr. E., a talkative man in his early 60s, participated eagerly in ongoing activities within the house. He enjoyed cooking, cleaning, and working on other household tasks. However, even when he volunteered for an assignment, he often left the tasks undone. For example, when fixing a meal, he frequently forgot to clean up the stove and counter space. When a staff member criticized him or pointed out what he had not done, Mr. E. responded, "I'll kill myself," and started hitting his head with his fist.

After repeated experiences with this type of behavior, the residence staff changed their message from "directives" to perform the omitted task to a "soft directive" embedded in praise: "Mr. E., you did such a good job fixing your sandwich . . . but did you forget something after you made your lunch?" "I'm sure that you can tell me what you forgot and do it now."

Mr. E. has begun to respond by identifying what he had not done and performing the appropriate clean-up activity without the usual accompanying self-abusive behavior.

Vignette: Mr. K.

Mr. K., who is in his mid-30s, was nonverbal and confined to a wheelchair. He had daily periods of prolonged self-abusive behavior when he would hit himself on the head and face. Finally staff had to apply elbow splints to prevent him from seriously injuring himself.

A new staff member in the residence had observed Mr. K.'s behavior for a few weeks. He then decided to take him out for a walk while constantly talking to him about what he could see, hear, and feel. His speech was primarily composed of declaratives. His conversational pattern was similar to one that would be used with anyone else; he spoke and then paused and waited for Mr. K. to respond. Since Mr. K. could not respond, the staff member would act as if he had and would speak for him. This pattern of interchanges continued. It was also associated with a decrease in self-abusive behavior on the part of Mr. K.

WHAT RESEARCH TELLS US ABOUT COMMUNICATIVE CHANGE

It is important to understand some of the directions that have been taken in studying language development and acquisition among persons with mental retardation. However, one limitation of this research literature is that practically all the work on the language development of persons with mental retardation has been done with children. Consequently, the generalization of these findings to the development of interventions for adults must be considered with caution. What follows is a synthesis of the main points of language development research relevant to this discussion.

Although research has been conducted on the development of communicative competence among nonhandicapped children (e.g., Bloom, Lightbown, & Hood, 1975), studies of children with a developmental disability have focused primarily on language use in social situations, rather than on the acquisition of specific patterns and skills per se. As a result, there appears to be no resolution to the issue of whether the acquisition of communicative skills and language use by persons with a developmental disability follows similar but delayed sequences as it does for noncognitively impaired individuals, or whether the stages of development are intrinsically different. Debates over this question have given rise to the "delay/difference controversy" (Leifer & Lewis, 1984; Zigler & Balla, 1982). In general, findings of investigations of the delay/difference controversy depend upon the perspective of the researchers and the experimental methodology employed. For a detailed review of this issue, see Zigler and Balla (1982).

Characteristics of Speaker-Listeners

Of the four components of communicative competence (i.e., characteristics of the speaker, characteristics of other speaker-listeners, communicative environment, and communicative task), the characteristics of other speaker-listeners has received the most attention. The major foci for these efforts have been parents (especially mothers of young children with developmental delay), teachers and fellow students in school settings, and caregivers in group and congregate care settings. The most frequent goals of research and program efforts in this area have been to increase social exchanges between persons with demonstrated deficits in interaction and others with whom they interact or to teach handicapped persons specific communicative skills. Although speaker characteristics (such as age, mental age, sex, and type of disability) are described in detail, the primary aim in these studies has not been to explore these characteristics, but, rather, to change the communicative behaviors of one person through modifications of language by another person.

Communicating with Parents Studies of maternal speech to prelinguistic children with Down syndrome (Cardosa-Martins & Mervis, 1985; Jones, 1980) have shown the maternal-child interaction to be mother-directed in contrast to the child-dependent style used by mothers of normally developing age peers. Levy-Shiff (1986), for example, found that there was less frequent communicative interaction directed by retarded children toward their parents and by mothers toward their impaired offspring. In contrast, fathers of retarded children resemble fathers of nondisabled children in their interactions. Further, communication between parents of retarded children about their youngsters was more frequent than between parents of normally developing children.

Based upon a study of normally developing and mentally retarded children under age 5, Porter (1978) reported that normally developing children stayed in closer proximity and engaged each other more often in social interactions in comparison to mentally retarded age peers who demonstrated no consistent preferences for other retarded or nonretarded peers. Also, although nonretarded children were observed to vocalize more frequently in the presence of peers than did mentally retarded children, this could possibly reflect a greater verbal capacity on the part of nonretarded children.

MacDonald (1981) proposed an intervention model to be used with children with delayed or impaired communication skill development that has application to mentally retarded adults. He suggests that engaging the individual in conversation with significant others in his or her life can serve as a major influence on the development of communicative competence. MacDonald suggested the use of five intervention strategies that have application to adults living in a community residential setting as aids in the development of communicative abilities. The first technique incorporates the use of "minimally discrepant modeling," in which the significant other models for the disabled individual slightly more advanced or complex language usage than is typical of the individual's current level of performance of a given language skill. MacDonald noted that it is important to use a language skill level that stimulates the individual.

The language development path that is to be followed should not be so close to the individual's current repertoire as to bore the individual, nor should it be so advanced that he or she cannot easily attain it.

The second technique makes use of old content in new linguistic form; that is, a staff person working with a resident could shape familiar vocabulary into unfamiliar linguistic structure that requires only a small communicative step forward. For example, a resident's vocabulary could be increased by teaching new words that are based on roots of words already mastered. In the third technique, significant others can treat the individual's idiosyncratic communication as a first language and conventional communication as the second. For example, if a resident points to an object, the staff person can provide a verbal label in order to associate a word with the individual's message. The fourth technique is what could be termed "up the ante." This process involves providing the individual with consistent modeling of higher communicative levels, together with the expectation that the individual will demonstrate them. The fifth technique involves a gradual shift in the balance of communicative power. While the significant other initially leads communication by displaying and modeling patterns of interaction, that person also yields to the individual so he or she can experience success in the social exchange. Thus, communicative turntaking gradually becomes more flexible, with the resident increasing the number of turns he or she initiates.

Communicating with Teacher and Students Communication styles and interventions can play a crucial role in influencing language skill development. For example, the impact of teachers' verbal interventions in enhancing interaction between pairs of severely mentally retarded and nonretarded elementary school students was explored by Cole, McQuarter, Meyer, and Vandercook (1986). Although teacher interventions initially increased communicative exchanges, continuing interventions consisting of instructional prompts and verbal reinforcements were associated with decreased contacts. In this situation, it would appear that although teacher guidance could initially improve socialized play between handi-

capped and nonhandicapped peers, developing interdependence among the children would be a more effective device in sustaining relationships.

In the same vein, Brinker and Thorpe (1986) found that the interactive behavior of nonretarded students had a significant impact on the "social bids" (or approaches) made to them by the retarded students. The authors noted that direct intervention with nonretarded peers is the best means of ensuring school integration. Cosson and Wilton (1985), following an examination of teacher-student interactions, reported that the students who made the largest gains in expressive oral language spent less time in structured/teacher-directed language activities. Following a period of observing supervisors of educational programs, Cherniss (1986) concluded that the supervisors tended to spend more time making directed statements to staff and students than they listened, sought feedback from staff, or participated in goal-setting for the students.

These studies point to the importance of identifying intervention strategies and techniques for use in the learning situation that are associated with improved oral language skill acquisition.

Communicating with Caregivers and Peers Based on the work of Strain (1977), who used a trained peer confederate to elicit social actions from withdrawn children, Dy, Strain, Fullerton, and Stowitschek (1981) used a similar protocol with institutionalized elderly mentally retarded women who were socially isolated. Initially, the confederate's actions and the anticipated response of the woman to whom she would be relating were role-played by the two staff members. Then the confederate practiced her part with one staff member continuing to role-play her communicative target while the other provided coaching and reinforcement to the confederate trainee. Role-play continued when the confederate began her assignment with the withdrawn resident(s) and was gradually decreased over successive sessions. The authors noted that to be successful in this approach, continuing supervision of the confederates was imperative.

Based upon the analysis of taped conversations of developmentally disabled persons and their caregivers in group home settings, Kenefick (1986) identified stable patterns of interaction within and among groups. When staff spoke informally to colleagues at break and mealtimes, approximately two-thirds of their comments were comprised of declaratives (e.g., exchanges of information and discussions of personal happenings). The balance was distributed among volitives, expressing individual preferences and praise and/or disapproval of the actions of others, and other functional categories, with considerable variation by speaker. In contrast, when talking with residents, about 70% of the speech acts were directives, with the balance consisting of volitives (e.g., giving praise to residents for compliance or expressing disapproval for not conforming to staff orders or requests).

When residents spoke to one another, about two-thirds of their verbalizations employed directives, with the remainder divided largely between declaratives and volitives. Most of the residents' remarks to staff consisted of declaratives that were usually partial sentences responding to the constraints of orders, requests, and questions by house staff. The study also revealed that the communicative content of the speech used by the residents was in large part maladaptive (that is, their speech was difficult to understand or uninteresting to the other speaker-listeners). The residents often employed incomplete deixis (e.g., "Bring me this."), which was incomprehensible to the others present, or they reported physical symptoms, complained about behaviors of others, or made comments that bore no apparent relationship to the topic under discussion (e.g., first person: "I went shopping yesterday."; second person: "Once I saw a deer.").

Based on these observations, Kenefick (1986) implemented a training program to sensitize direct care staff to the discrepancies between their speech with peers and with residents, to reduce directives, and to increase declaratives in work assignments. The reported effectiveness of the training program in changing the predominant communication styles of the staff would indicate that staff of community residences should consider the communication styles used in the residence and whether a greater sensitization to the effects those styles have on resident behavior is warranted.

Environmental Effects

Reports on communicative change in individuals who move from large institutional to small community group home settings have indicated an improvement in language skills immediately after deinstitutionalization, but a subsequent decline in skills some time afterwards (Heinberg & Galligan, 1983; Hemming, 1986). In these studies, changes in language use were assessed through the use of standardized tests, such as the Adaptive Behavior Scales' Language Development subscale and the Illinois Test of Psycholinguistic Abilities. Hemming (1986) suggests that the initial increase and subsequent decline in scores could be associated with the frequency and quality of resident-staff interactions. Immediately after moving from an institution, residents often spend prolonged periods of time in their new residences with plenty of opportunity for socialization with caregivers. Later, residents get more involved in their day program activities, and socialization opportunities in the residence become more limited.

Hemming (1986) offers an hypothesis to explain these declines in language use skills: communicative skills may be forgotten without the opportunity for practice. The observations reported by Kenefick (1986) on the variance of staff-resident language patterns may provide another explanation for the failure of some deinstitutionalized group home residents to show continued language usage growth. If staff communications directed to residents do not elicit a higher order of language usage among residents, then initially learned speech patterns may fall into disuse and higher order communicative styles may never evolve. Kenefick's demonstration that staff training in communicative patterns is useful in affecting speech skill loss among residents is indicative that such losses may be reversed.

An integrated environment (e.g., involving both mentally retarded and nonretarded speakers) may be hospitable to expanding communicative skills. In one study, Brinker (1984) observed a number of students in both integrated and segregated settings. Most of the disabled students lacked verbal communication skills and were dependent on others for assistance in self-care. He noted that in the integrated settings, a significant number of social bids were directed by the impaired individuals to their peers and vice versa. Most of the social bids, however, were from nonretarded to retarded individuals. Further, approaches from retarded individuals were more frequently responded to by nonretarded individuals than by other retarded individuals. Brinker noted that integrated social environments promote more communicative exchange than do segregated surroundings.

FUTURE DIRECTIONS

Communication for Behavior Change

This chapter has so far dealt with communicative competence through an exploration of the pragmatics of language and an examination of some applications for program design. The remaining pages of the chapter address the development of intervention programs within community residences.

The first step in designing a language development program in a community residence is to become aware of the importance of language and its role in personal growth and behavior change. The use of language affects those who live in and work within a residence. Consequently, workers should consider the effects of the four distinct factors already cited: the communicators, others who listen and/or take turns communicating, the environment, and the nature and context of the communicative intent.

Research has demonstrated the importance of considering the effects on communication of both enduring attributes of the communicators (such as age, sex, and nature of disability), as well as more temporary characteristics (such as emotional and motivational states). Depending on which of these attributes/characteristics serve as the basis for describing the communicative dysfunction, the language of the handicapped speaker may seem delayed, different from, or similar to that of a nonhandicapped peer.

In considering relationships to other speaker-listeners, two major concerns emerge from the literature. First, as reported by Brinker and Thorpe (1986), Cole et al. (1986), Hendrickson, Gable, Hester, and Strain (1985), and Porter (1978), the interaction of developmentally disabled persons with nonhandicapped peers favorably affects social interaction. However, adult guidance, which may initially support exchange between handicapped and nonhandicapped peers, appears to limit and constrain communicative encounters over a longer period of time (Cole et al., 1986).

Experience has shown that caregivers and significant others can be trained to act as coaches for enhanced communicative skills. In many instances, simple techniques, such as those proposed by MacDonald (1981), can be used by staff and others to elicit more sophisticated speech in residents. Special attention should be paid to the interactions among staff and between staff and residents and note taken of which staff person appears to have the most positive influence over a given resident. Such observations often may reveal the means to shape, influence, or modify communication patterns by using a significant other as role model. Further, staff should be taught about the effective use of reinforcers to reward higher order communication; the use of these paired with the coach model can prove to be a very effective means of developing communication skills. An illustration of varied communicative strategies that resulted in resident change follows:

Vignette: Miss D.

Miss D., a new resident of a community home operated by a small agency in the midwest, had lived in the residence for several weeks without speaking. All attempts to involve her in conversation failed. However, when she was at the state developmental center, she was reported to have good expressive skills and good receptive ability (which she had demonstrated by correctly performing a complicated series of instructions). One day, a musically oriented staff member brought a kazoo (a small wind instrument) to work with her, played it, and then put it in Miss D.'s hand. After a few minutes, Miss D. began to play the instrument, for which she received much praise from the staff and other residents. The staff member then led the group in a song as Miss D. played.

In the days that followed, the staff member sang parts of the songs. At first, Miss D. only played her instrument, but then began to sing along with her. Later, the staff member spoke to her in a singsong manner using rhyming speech. Soon Miss D. began to imitate her. Gradually, the staff member inserted normal talk between song intervals and Miss D. followed her example. Shortly thereafter, Miss D. was talking with the staff and other residents.

Some concern exists relative to the influence of the environment on gains in communicative competence. As previously noted (Heinberg & Galligan, 1983; Hemming, 1986), some formerly institutionalized residents, following an initial improvement in communication skills, appear to lose skills after a period of time following entry to a community residence. Remedies for this problem require special consideration; however, possible solutions may include a training program for caregivers (Kenefick, 1986) and increased contact with nonhandicapped individuals in integrated settings (Brinker, 1984; Cole et al., 1986). Other means should include careful assessment of how variations in the environment affect an individual's speech. For example, is the individual more or less communicative in day program settings, on home visits, or in other settings where there are not other disabled persons?

It is also important to understand what communication patterns are prevalent among supervisors, staff, and the home's residents. Table 1 provides a useful guide to the various communication styles. Some obviously will be more effective than others, depending upon the level of improvement of the individuals residing in the home. Attention should be paid to maladaptive styles or patterns that may be a potential cause of tensions or misunderstandings in the home.

The Unknowns: A Challenge for Action

There is a need for more information about the effects of various communication characteristics on the functions of communication. This will require both longitudinal and cross-sectional clinical studies of language functions for disabled and nondisabled persons. Although there is a relatively large body of knowledge about language acquisition among children, this information does not exist for other age groups. Workers are just beginning to identify differences in language use correlated with age for the nonhandicapped population. Whether these differences also apply to developmentally disabled or other language impaired persons warrants further study. For example, in small-group discussions without an adult present, children often show an affiliative pattern that enables each member of the group to have a chance to speak. In contrast, older adults often demonstrate a higher use of volitive usage and a simultaneous decrease in directives, apparently becoming more inner-oriented, rather than outer-oriented, in communication (Kenefick, 1986). Whether developmentally disabled persons in these age groups show similar shifts in patterns of communicative function has not been established.

Another unstudied area relates to nonspoken languages, such as signing. Topics to be examined include whether stages of language acquisition and functions that are manually represented relate to similar processes that use spoken language. Work is needed that will examine whether language varies with the presence of family members, friends, colleagues, or persons with a specific relationship to the speaker (e.g., physician, supervisor, clergy).

Only limited information is available about the impact of environmental change on communicative function. Further study is needed to describe changes in language patterns that occur when people move from their home environment to a group setting. Such information would be helpful to caregivers in guiding the assimilation process. Familiar and rewarding communicative patterns might be utilized to link those in new surroundings with their unfamiliar housemates and/or caregivers.

Uncertainty exists in describing communicative intent for individuals with language difficulty. An individual with unimpeded communication skills can usually relate the communicative intent to his or her exchange and whether the goal has been achieved. This same information is not generally available from someone with a developmental disability. If the intent of the communicative act is unknown, the listener cannot estimate the appropriateness of the function and the correctness of the time and setting in which it occurs.

The preceding discussion underscores the importance of observation of communication as a prerequisite to installation of communication skill programs within community residential programs. The key to such study is to compare individuals and groups with normally developing/developed communication with those who demonstrate specific deficits.

CONCLUSIONS

Even with the paucity of current knowledge about communicative competence and pragmatics, guidelines and caveats exist for developing a residential milieu that fosters communicative growth. Practical experience has shown that the most essential component for fostering communicative competence for an individual with mental retardation is exposure to others in the unimpaired world. Therefore, access of the persons living in the residence to nonhandicapped peers is a crucial clinical and programmatic goal. This goal can be met both through integration within the residence and by frequent contact with nonhandicapped people in the community by the creation of situations for residents to interact with nonhandicapped peers.

Both research and practical experience have shown that staff, in their own conversations and communications, need to serve as role models and present communication styles that are appropriate and meaningful. Residence staff should be careful listeners and observers to ensure that they model communicative patterns that reflect the language community of which they are a part. They should offer choice rather than constraint to residents, and sharing of experiences rather than isolation.

Frequent in-service training should be available to staff members to acquaint them with relevant research on communicative change and to assist them in maintaining a responsive ear to the messages they receive from residents, as well as in recognizing how common situations can be used as training environments for increasing communication competence.

Shaping speech skills is not a difficult task. Role-modeling, rewarding good language usage, and encouraging communication are all effective devices. However, it is vital for speech and communication skill development to be included in the resident's individualized program plan. Using general common-practice teaching techniques to build vocabulary, appropriate speech and language usage, and communication can prove to be rewarding to staff and an important step toward greater independence for residents of a community home. In this manner communication can function as an instrument of growth and change.

REFERENCES

Bates, E. (1974). Acquisition of pragmatic competence. *Journal of Child Language, 1,* 277.

Bloom, L. Lightbown, P., & Hood, L. (1975). Structure and variation in child language. *Monographs of the Society for Research in Child Development, 40*(2).

Brinker, R. (1984). Interacting between severely mentally retarded students and other students in integrated and segregated school settings. *American Journal of Mental Deficiency, 89,* 587–594.

Brinker, R.P., & Thorpe, M.E. (1986). Features of integrated educational ecologies that predict social behavior among severely mentally retarded and nonretarded students. *American Journal of Mental Deficiency, 91,* 150–159.

Cardosa-Martins, C., & Mervis, C.B. (1985). Maternal speech to prelinguistic children with Down syndrome. *American Journal of Mental Deficiency, 89,* 451–458.

Cherniss, C. (1986). Instrument for observing supervision behavior in educational programs for mentally retarded children. *American Journal of Mental Deficiency, 91,* 18–21.

Cole, D.A., McQuarter, R.J., Meyer, L.H., & Vandercook, T. (1986). Interactions between peers with and without severe handicaps: Dynamics of teacher intervention. *American Journal of Mental Deficiency, 91,* 160–169.

Cosson, L., & Wilton, K. (1985). Teacher-pupil interaction and oral language development of mildly retarded children. *Australia and New Zealand Journal of Developmental Disabilities, 11,* 97–105.

Dy, E.B., Strain, P.S., Fullerton, A., & Stowitschek, J. (1981). Training institutionalized elderly mentally retarded persons as intervention agents for socially isolated peers. *Analysis and Intervention in Developmental Disabilities, 1,* 199–215.

Heinberg, J., & Galligan, B. (1983). Effects of deinstitutionalization on adaptive behavior of mentally retarded adults. *American Journal of Mental Deficiency, 88,* 21–27.

Hemming, H. (1986). Follow-up of adults with mental retardation transferred from large institutions to new small units. *Mental Retardation, 24,* 229–235.

Hendrickson, J., Gable, R., Hester, P., & Strain, P.S. (1985). Teaching social reciprocity: Social exchanges between young severely handicapped and non-handicapped children. *Pointer, 29*(4), 17–21.

Hymes, D. (1972). Introduction to functions of language in the classroom. In C.B. Cazden (Ed.), *Functions of lan-*

guage in the classroom (pp. 3–7). New York: Teachers College Press.

Jones, C.H.M. (1980). Prelinguistic communication skills in Down syndrome and normal infants. In T.M. Field (Ed.), *High-risk infants and children, adult, and peer interactions.* New York: Academic Press.

Kenefick, B. (1986). Studies of language interacting with developmentally disabled persons and care providers. Albany, NY: NYS OMRDD. Unpublished manuscript.

Kogan, K., Wimberger, H., & Bobb, H.R. (1969). Analysis of mother-child interaction in young mentally retarded children. *Child Development, 40,* 799–812.

Leifer, J.S., & Lewis, M. (1984). Acquisitions of conversational response skills by young Down syndrome and non-retarded young children. *American Journal of Mental Deficiency, 88,* 610–618.

Levy-Shiff, R. (1986). Mother-father-child interactions in families with a mentally retarded young child. *American Journal of Mental Deficiency, 91,* 141–149.

MacDonald, J. (1981). *Language through conversation.* Columbus, OH: Parent-Child Communication Project. Nisonger Center, Ohio State University.

Porter, R.H. (1978). Sound interactions in heterogeneous groups of retarded and normally developing children: An observational study in observing behavior. In G.P. Sackett (Ed.), *Theory and applications in mental retardation.* Baltimore: University Park Press.

Searle, J.R. (1975). A taxonomy of illocutionary acts. In G.K. Anderson (Ed.), *Language and knowledge.* Minneapolis: University of Minnesota Press.

Smith, L., & Von Tetzchner, S. (1986). Communicative, sensori-motor, and language skills of young children with Down syndrome. *American Journal of Mental Deficiency, 91,* 57–66.

Strain, P.S. (1977). An experimental analysis of peer social initiations on the behavior of withdrawn pre-school children: Some training and generalization effects. *Journal of Abnormal Child Psychology, 5,* 445–455.

Straus, P.S., Shores, R., & Timm, M. (1977). Effects of peer social initiations on the behavior of withdrawn pre-school children. *Journal of Applied Behavior Analysis, 10,* 288–298.

Zigler, E., & Balla, D. (1982). *Mental retardation: The developmental-difference controversy.* Hillsdale, NJ: Lawrence Erlbaum Associates.

Chapter 16

Health Care Issues
in Community Residential Settings

Louis Rowitz

This chapter discusses the use of health services by developmentally disabled persons. Health services are viewed from the perspective of the total service delivery system. The importance of viewing this system within the continuum of care cycle is stressed. Since coping with illness and the amelioration of health problems is a lifelong task, the problem of providing health services to developmentally disabled persons is discussed in the context of life stages from infancy and childhood to old age. Recommendations are included for improving our understanding of the health care system as it affects developmentally disabled persons who live in community residences.

This chapter addresses health care provision to developmentally disabled persons living in community residences. Since community residences serve people of all ages, the discussion focuses on differences in health care needs across the life cycle. Consideration is given to types of health care problems faced by developmentally disabled persons, in addition to issues of health care access. The chapter is primarily concerned with medical, dental, and other health-related services, as well as federal and state policy pertinent to health care coverage.

It should be noted at the outset that information on the strategies used by operators of community residences to ensure comprehensive health care services for their residents is extremely difficult to obtain. While a number of studies highlight the critical role that the health status of a developmentally disabled child or adult assumes in his or her residential placement (Seltzer & Krauss, 1984), detailed analyses of the variety of health care service options that presumably exist are not currently available.

For most persons, different health-related problems occur at various stages of the life cycle. For example, the greatest use of health care services is typically experienced at the beginning and end of the life cycle. Young children, in particular, are subject to various diseases or illnesses and need routine and frequent monitoring of immunizations, growth development, and adaptive skills acquisition. As people age, problems become more chronic (although they can begin at any age). Older persons become more frequent users of health care services as their body systems begin to show the effects of decades of use. Before discussing specific health care problems experienced at each stage of the life cycle, some general issues are examined.

HEALTH PROBLEMS OF DEVELOPMENTALLY DISABLED PERSONS: AN OVERVIEW

Persons with developmental disabilities face both normal health-related problems associated

203

with different stages in the life cycle as well as difficulties that are exacerbated or associated with their developmental disability. A common health care issue for these persons is the need to recognize general health care needs (i.e., immunizations, routine physical exams, preventive dental care), which exist independent of the developmental disability. Too often, health service providers may concentrate on the specific disability and attribute common health problems (i.e., colds, respiratory infections, balance problems) to the disability rather than to normal and expected health needs. It is also possible to overlook routine health care services in the wake of the often extensive medical interventions needed by persons with more severe disabilities.

Moreover, specific types of residential settings have been implicated with some health problems. For example, studies have documented the increased prevalence of hepatitis B infections in institutionalized mentally retarded persons (Lohiya, Lohiya, & Caires, 1986). The prevalence of hepatitis B surface antigens and hepatitis B virus markers is considerably higher among institutionalized persons than in the U.S. population, and is equal to or higher than that observed in intravenous drug users, homosexual men, hemodialysis patients, and Asian immigrants. A number of studies have reported that institutionalized persons with Down syndrome have a higher risk of developing chronic hepatitis B surface antigenemia after hepatitis B infection than individuals with mental retardation owing to other etiologic causes (Aldershvile et al., 1980; Gust, Dimitrakakis, & Sharma, 1978; Madden et al., 1976; Williamson, Lehaman, Dimitrakakis, & Sharma, 1982).

There has been a growing concern that hepatitis B transmission may be a problem when children from an institutional residential program attend a community school. However, a recent study (Williams, Weber, Culler, & Kane, 1983) found a low rate of transmission of hepatitis B among susceptible students with mental retardation who were placed in daytime educational programs and mentally retarded peers who were carriers. Over the 14 months of the study, no susceptible staff acquired hepatitis B serologic markers.

The issue of whether communicable disease is more prevalent in handicapped populations than among nonhandicapped persons is controversial. Zonia and Goff (1986) examined this issue among retarded and nonretarded populations in three Michigan counties. The authors studied 15 categories of communicable diseases that were reported on a weekly basis between 1980 and 1983 to the Michigan Department of Public Health. The illnesses included shigellosis, chicken pox, scarlet fever, gonorrhea, syphilis, influenza-like diseases, tuberculosis, measles, rubella, pertussis, mumps, hepatitis A, hepatitis B, hepatitis unknown, and salmonellosis. It was found that retarded persons had a significantly higher prevalence rate in 6 of the 15 communicable diseases (measles, chicken pox, tuberculosis, scarlet fever, hepatitis B, hepatitis unknown) than the population at large. Although it is not possible to generalize from the data on these three counties, the study does demonstrate a method for determining specific health problems, which can be useful in local communities' health planning efforts. Epidemiological methods are important tools for monitoring health problems and health care needs of local and state populations (Rowitz, 1974a, 1974b).

MANAGEMENT OF HEALTH CARE SERVICES

The movement of mentally retarded individuals from institutions into the community raises important questions about the subsequent health care management of these persons within community settings. Minihan (1986) investigated these issues in a study in southeastern Massachusetts. She found that a high percentage of previously institutionalized mentally retarded clients were not able to be served within the community. Some physicians refused to serve them. Geographic proximity of specialized services was also a problem. For Minihan's sample, the most frequently required specialties were neurology, orthopaedics, and ophthalmology. These specialty services as well as psychiatric services were not readily available to community residents.

A 25-year follow-up study of families with a severely handicapped person was conducted by Rowitz and Farber (1986). They asked parents about the medical services utilized by their handicapped son or daughter (now aged 31–55) over their life span. Preliminary analyses revealed that a wide variety of medical and dental contacts were made over the years. The most prevalent sources of health care were general practitioners, pediatricians, dentists, and neurologists. The professionals that were seen the least frequently were orthodontists, oral surgeons, plastic surgeons, cardiologists, chiropractors, and gynecologists.

Two major factors affect the delivery of health care services to developmentally disabled persons. First, the fragmentation of the health care system, which results in uneven access for the general population (Cohen, 1979), presents a special dilemma for those with developmental disabilities. Second, health care providers are often poorly prepared to offer appropriate and effective services to persons with cognitive and functional limitations (Garrard, 1982). Thomas (1986), for example, notes that most physicians have neither the education nor the experience to treat adults with developmental disabilities. She cites the following challenges faced by physicians:

1. Development of broader doctor-patient communication skills
2. Development of the ability to distinguish between disability and disease
3. Acquiring knowledge of a disability's long-term complications
4. Management of often intricate medication regimens
5. Acquiring knowledge of the latest medical advances

Thus, the issues of health care provision to developmentally disabled persons include varying health needs over the life cycle, inadequate and poorly coordinated health care systems in which to seek care, and frequently ill-prepared health care providers. Developmentally disabled persons living in community residences typically rely on the operators of the residence to establish and maintain access to health care providers on their behalf. The responsibilities

of direct care staff to detect health problems as they emerge, to alert responsible persons to the need for health care visits, and to assist the resident in managing health care problems represent major activities for which most direct care staff are poorly trained. For these reasons, the necessity of properly managing the health care needs of developmentally disabled persons living in community residences is gaining increasing recognition. Responsible administrators are keenly aware of the need both to develop internal staff capabilities to meet these needs and to keep abreast of major changes in federal and state policies regarding health insurance and service delivery options.

HEALTH CARE ISSUES ACROSS THE LIFE CYCLE

Services for Developmentally Disabled Children

A critical factor in the delivery of services to handicapped children living with their families has been found to be related to the professional who first diagnoses the handicapping condition (Rowitz, 1980). If the original identifier of the problem is a physician or other health provider, the individual with mental retardation will receive much of his or her service within a health or mental health service system. If, on the other hand, the orginal identifier is a social or educational provider (such as a school or social service agency), the individual will receive services in a nonmedical system. Thus, service delivery is greatly affected by where the individual enters the service delivery system and by who first sees the individual (Rowitz, 1981b).

The passage of PL 94-142 (The Education for All Handicapped Children Act of 1975) has had important ramifications for the delivery of services to families with a developmentally disabled or otherwise handicapped child (Rowitz, 1981c; Walker, 1984). Walker (1984) pointed out that the law made the schools responsible for the care of chronically ill children and for children with disabilities; the school, consequently, became a health care provider. Some of the school services needed by these children include support therapies (e.g., speech, occupational, and physical therapy), schedule modifications, adaptive physical education programs, special transportation, special toileting facilities, ramps and other devices to expedite accessibility, counseling services, and school health services (e.g., in administration of medications, implementation of medical procedures, emergency preparations, and case coordinations). All of these health-related services were needed in addition to special educational requirements.

Contacts with the health care system can sometimes be problematic. In an early study, Schwartz (1970) studied 21 mothers with a moderately or severely retarded child. She found that the first contacts with the health care system were usually with a pediatrician or general practitioner, and that these medical personnel did not typically give a clear message to the families regarding the nature or extent of the child's problem. She also found that phsyicians often treated the child's illnesses without consideration of the impact of mental retardation on the occurrence or outcome of the illness. Physicians were also found to be poor sources of information on the community health care system and on the appropriate specialists needed to treat the child. When parents did contact other health care professionals, often they reported being treated harshly.

A recent series of studies examined a random sample of 1,726 special education students in five large metropolitan areas (Charlotte, NC, Houston, TX, Milwaukee, WI, Rochester, NY, and Santa Clara, CA). These studies offer important information on issues related to health problems and service use by these children (Walker, Butler, Singer, & Palfrey, 1984).

For example, among students in special education classes, 44.3% were classified as having a mental impairment (Palfrey, Singer, Walker & Butler, 1986). About 48% of the special education students had at least one health problem, and almost 30% had more than one health problem. The students with two or more health problems had greater than four times the hospitalization rate of those children with no health problems. Children with cerebral palsy, other forms of paralysis, epilepsy, or kidney disease needed the most health services.

In general, parents reported that they had a regular source of health care for their children. Students without a regular source of care varied from 2.1% to 15.4% across the five study sites. Those students receiving health care tended to come either from high socioeconomic status families or from working-class families who were eligible for Aid to Families with Dependent Children (AFDC), or for Medicaid, or who had access to urban health centers or clinics. Palfrey et al. (1986) also reported that physicians rarely attended school conferences related to the development of the child's individualized education plan. One reason was that there were few financial incentives for physicians to become involved in educational planning.

It has also been reported that black and Hispanic children in special education classes are two to three times as likely as white children not to have a regular source of medical care (Singer, Butler, & Palfrey, 1986). Children with medical or categorical conditions (i.e., mental retardation, cerebral palsy, deafness, etc.) were more likely to have a regular source of care than children with behavioral or functional problems (i.e., speech disorder, learning disorder, hyperactivity, emotional disorders, etc.). In addition, it was also found that children who were white, who were from higher socioeconomic status families, and who had mothers with more education were more likely to get services from private practitioners than were children who were black or Hispanic, who came from lower socioeconomic status families, and who had mothers who were less educated. In terms of health insurance, 56% of the children were covered by a private health plan, 32% by a public plan, and 12% had no health insurance coverage. Twenty-six percent of the Hispanic children were uninsured; in contrast, only 8% and 12% of the white and black children, respectively, were uninsured.

Butler, Singer, Palfrey, and Walker (1987) found that among children without insurance, only 42% had been seen by a physician within the preceding year. In contrast, 65% of the children with insurance had seen at least one physician during that time period. If the family had no health insurance, the health care visits were paid for by the parents. The authors also found that whether or not parents received a subsidy influenced their seeking care for their child.

Children with a disability need frequent services. Early intervention and medical monitoring of health problems are important in identifying and lessening problems that handicapped children may face as they get older. Parents must not be alienated by the health care system, since this may lead to their ignoring critical health problems or avoiding the health care system altogether. Both schools and the health care system need to reach out to parents and help them through difficult problems that could adversely affect the entire family.

The growth of early intervention programs for and services to children with biological, established, or environmental risks to normal development has provided new opportunities for parents to receive therapeutic and support services during their child's preschool years (Chinn, Drew, & Logan, 1979). One goal of these programs and services is to support parental efforts in gaining access to needed services and in collaborating with health care providers in treating their children and preventing potential health problems (Demb & Diamond, 1980).

Regardless of whether developmentally disabled children live with their families or in a community residential program, proper pediatric care is needed. Attention to immunizations, monitoring of physical growth and nutritional needs, and consultation on social and behavioral skills are areas in which professional oversight is needed. With various preventive and needed health care intervention strategies at early ages, many potential health care problems in adulthood may be prevented. This does not mean that *all* later onset disorders will be prevented, but rather that the number of these disorders might be significantly diminished. Without appropriate lifetime care, the number of potential health care problems may become major for operators of community residences relative to developmentally disabled adults.

Services for Developmentally Disabled Adolescents

Little is known about the health care needs of adolescents with developmental disabilities. Although adolescence is usually a period of substantial physical and emotional growth, the special medical care problems of developmentally disabled adolescents have often not been adequately addressed. Hammer and Barnard (1966) studied the nutritional, dental, and physical health needs of a group of adolescents with mental retardation who lived in a rural area. The authors found that the diet of these children was high in carbohydrates, since parents tended to give their children candy or desserts for good behavior. Consequently, there was a high degree of dental problems. Demb and Diamond (1980) noted that a major reason that handicapped children did not receive adequate dental care was because their parents concentrated on acquiring medical and educational services and that dental care was considered a low priority.

Poor dental care occurs not only because developmentally disabled persons may not be taken to a dentist but also because of the lack of dentists willing to accept these individuals. While dentists have become increasingly sophisticated in allaying the anxieties of nervous patients, most dentists are not properly trained to treat patients with potentially severe behavioral responses. It is usually suggested that a developmentally disabled person be accompanied to the doctor's office by someone with whom the patient has a strong, trusting relationship.

Chinn et al. (1979) found that adolescence is an emotionally traumatic period for developmentally disabled children. When puberty occurs, these adolescents do not understand what is happening, and parents or other care providers often have trouble communicating with them. Parents also have great difficulty with the frequent inappropriate sexual acting out of their handicapped adolescents. For some families, sex education is still controversial, and many handicapped adolescents are often sexually naive because of lack of information.

Schor, Smalky, and Neff (1981) studied a group of previously institutionalized retarded children and young adolescents (5–17 years of age). A community residential program had been developed to provide 2 to 4 years of protected community living, which would enable the youngsters to eventually move into less restrictive programs. The provision of health care to these residents, most of whom were covered by Medicaid, was initially viewed as a problem. However, the program found a health maintenance organization (HMO) to provide health care services to them. During the first year of the project, residents averaged approximately one primary care encounter with the HMO per month. During the second year, the visits decreased by 50%. Most health problems were related to upper respiratory infections and self-limited febrile illnesses. The most frequently needed specialty clinics were ophthalmology, otolaryngology, podiatry, orthopaedics, and urology. Emergency room visits rather than hospital admissions were the most frequent means of providing acute care services. Further, a significant reduction in medication use occurred while the children were covered by the HMO. The study illustrates that the use of a prepaid system of care can provide comprehensive coverage for persons with mental retardation or other disabilities.

In summary, more attention to the special health care needs of adolescents with developmental disabilities is required. The need for adequate information about human sexuality and emotional and behavioral changes, as well as assistance in identifying personal health care needs, are important areas for both parents and community residence operators to address. Adolescence is also a period in which transitions to adult life with its attendant responsibilities are often contemplated. Mental health counselors can be enlisted along with other relevant service providers to assist personal and family planning for these transitions.

Services for Developmentally Disabled Adults

Obtaining health services for adults with developmental disabilities is a complex challenge. Hill, Bruininks, and Lakin (1983) studied 2,271 people with developmental disabilities who resided in either community residential programs or institutional settings. They found that there was no statistically significant difference in the prevalence rates of chronic health problems in the two types of facilities. For example, circulatory disorders and respiratory or digestive disorders occurred with the same frequency among both groups. However, community residents were found to have fewer seizure disorders and physical handicaps. Also, it was observed that residents of public institutions were more likely to have seen a doctor for a chronic health disorder than community residents.

In a companion study, Hill, Balow, & Bruininks (1985) found that residents of community residential programs and public institutions regularly received at least one type of prescribed medication. In addition, during a one-year study period, 25.9% of community residents and 37.9% of institutionalized residents received psychotropic drugs. The authors expressed surprise at the high rate of psychotropic drug use in the community; however, they felt that the prescription of medication for physical health problems (e.g., epilepsy) was less alarming. This study raises concerns about the overprescription of certain types of drugs. The monitoring of drugs and prevention of overmedication of developmentally disabled residents in community settings is a significant health concern.

O'Connor (1976), in an extensive national survey of community residences, found that 90% of the homes reportedly made medical and dental services accessible to their residents on a regular basis. In addition, it was reported that the community services were generally adequate to meet needs. All the surveyed residential programs had emergency services available to them at a nearby hospital, and some programs had a private physician on call. Practically all homes required potential residents to have a medical examination prior to placement in the home. Usually one physician was responsible for the medical care of all residents in a home. Medical examinations typically took place in the physician's office. Forty percent of the facilities reported that at least one of their residents had seen a medical specialist in the 6 months prior to the study. The specialists included surgeons, ophthalmologists, orthopaedists, and neurologists. Only 15% of the community residences reported no routine medical or dental care available.

A study conducted by the Rehabilitation Institute of Chicago examined the community medical and allied health services system for handicapped developmentally disabled adults (Hamilton et al., 1977). About 3,800 developmentally disabled adults were studied, and over 1,300 specific problems were identified, of which 70% were physiologic in origin and 30% were socioenvironmental. It was argued that many of the problems of these adults would be treatable by today's medical standards, whereas they were not treatable when the population was younger. Medical needs were generally found to be met, while psychological services, recreation, and dental care needs were not.

In a more recent study, Jacobson, Silver, and Schwartz (1984) reported on issues concerning service provision to residents in one state's community residences. A questionnaire, mailed to over 400 community residences, received responses from 368 homes serving 3,249 residents. It was found that the amount of clinical services that were provided on site to occupants of homes varied as a function of type of home, type of operators, and, somewhat, the size of the home. Those who were residents of ICFs/MR (intermediate care facilities for the mentally retarded) and state-operated programs received a greater number of services and greater total hours of health care in comparison to other types of community residences. Smaller homes provided more hours of service per occupant and more hours of each clinical service, excepting service from psychologists, psychiatrists, and rehabilitation counselors. With respect to medical services specifically, the group homes that served the smallest number of occupants with self-direction deficits gave more hours of service than did homes with less disabled residents.

The Jacobson et al. (1984) findings raise an important question regarding the locus of health care service provision. Many community residences are consciously established to provide a homey rather than therapeutic environment for their residents. Providing therapeutic and/or clinical services within the residence, as opposed to receiving such services in the more traditional location of the provider's office, is an important programmatic decision for operators of such community residences. Obviously, this decision is affected by the needs of the residents served, by the physical design of the residence, by transportation considerations, and by the programmatic and service goals of the sponsoring agency.

McDonald (1985) has pointed out that one result of the deinstitutionalization movement is that persons who remain in institutions are now more handicapped than those who moved to community programs. It has been estimated that about 80% of the residents in state-operated residential institutions are severely or profoundly retarded (Garrard & Crocker, 1979; Scheerenberger, 1982). McDonald (1985) studied the medical needs and health care service utilization of 27 severely developmentally disabled persons residing in a small number of ICFs/MR. She found an average of 1.15 health problems per resident. Seven of the 27 residents had seizure disorders that were controlled by medication. In addition, the group had a high prevalence of orthopaedic problems: 70% had scoliosis, 96% had multiple fixed contractures, and 56% had dislocated hips or occlusion. Other problems that she observed included blindness and other eye problems, esophagitis, asthma, dermatitis, heart murmur, megacolon, and fibroepitheliomata.

With regard to services, McDonald (1985) noted that the major source of health care was primary physician contacts (200 visits for the study group in the first year). Most of the service was related to annual physicals and periodic visits made to the physician's office or to the residence. There were also a number of acute care (mostly related to infections) visits and inpatient visits. The residents also utilized a variety of specialist service visits.

The importance of the McDonald (1985) study is that it reveals that severely and profoundly handicapped persons can receive health care services in community settings. McDonald noted that her sample had a low incidence of acute illnesses and emergencies. Consequently, although the residents had medical needs, the level of service was not extraordinarily high. One possible explanation is that because a nurse is a required member of the core staff in ICFs/MR, the sample members received more continuous health care than is possible in residences without nursing staff.

In summary, health care provision for adults with developmental disabilities is an area about which more information is urgently needed. For example, it is notable that there is little information in the literature on provision of gynecological services for adult females. Operators of community residences need to ensure that residents receive routine medical examinations, appropriate dental care, and the specialized services that may be required for residents with specific types of problems. While some types of community residences have the capacity to provide health care monitoring and services within the residence (i.e., ICFs/MR), most residences seek these services from community providers. Locating health care professionals with the appropriate training and willingness to serve developmentally disabled persons remains a major challenge in the expansion of community-based residences.

Services for Developmentally Disabled Elderly Persons

As people age, there is typically an increased need for medical and dental care (Tobis, 1982). Stone and Newcomer (1985) point out that current health care policies have ignored the issue of increased longevity among physical and mentally disabled individuals, and that the health care system has yet to adequately respond to the needs of a larger population of community residence occupants who are elderly. Appropriate and readily accessible health care services need to be in place in order to prevent unnecessary institutionalization or reinstitutionalization of older residents. Changes in health care needs are often the result of a community residence's occupant "aging in place," thus causing a greater demand upon nursing services, medication usage, and physician visits. In other instances homes may be begun with an older population in mind, yet once functioning, the anticipated health services and supports do not materialize.

Janicki and Jacobson (1986) examined population characteristics and service need and utilization patterns of some 10,500 older and elderly developmentally disabled persons living in a variety of residential settings in New York. About a third were residing in either community residences or foster care homes. Among this group, they noted that men outnumbered women until about the sixth decade; then women begin to outnumber men. It is known that life expectancy among women is greater in general and that women are more prone to bone diseases with advancing age. Men, however, are more frequently afflicted with heart disease and other systemic conditions. Janicki and Jacobson observed this as well. They also found differences between older men and women in types of physical disease conditions with advancing age, particularly in cardiovascular, genitourinary, and endocrine system diseases. When these authors examined health service utilization patterns, they found that older residents in group homes saw a physician more frequently than either foster care home residents or those older individuals residing at home. It was also noted that older group home residents appeared to be receiving medical and dental services with sufficient frequency, although from clinics rather than from primary care physicians.

A recent national survey of community residential and day programs serving elderly mentally retarded persons found that one type of residential setting that was used to house older persons was a group home with a nursing component (Krauss & Seltzer, 1986; Seltzer & Krauss, 1986). These homes were similar to other group homes except that they had a nurse as part of the core residential staff. This staffing modification suggests an important adaptation of the residential program to the medical and health care needs of older developmentally disabled persons.

Although the information about the health care needs of elderly mentally retarded persons is limited, studies that are available indicate that staff and administrators of community residences need to be aware that differences in health care needs exist and that these are dependent upon the age and physical state of each individual. People living in community residences are like other people—they get sick, have accidents, develop chronic conditions, have their emotional ups and downs, and need both routine and emergency health care. In some instances, residents will pose a special problem in terms of their health or medical needs. Careful consideration of a range of wellness, nursing, and medical services for each resident is important. Probably the greatest hurdle faced by staff is that of ensuring that linkages to the health care system are adequate and appropriate, and that when medical attention is needed it can be obtained.

Summary

This section of the chapter has examined the health care needs of developmentally disabled persons across the life cycle. While there are specific, age-related concerns that are important to recognize, it is also notable that the developmentally disabled population is very heterogeneous. It is thus not possible to identify a homogeneous pattern of service delivery. Numerous factors affect the delivery of service, from basic demographic factors (e.g., sex, age, race, and socioeconomic level) to the type and characteristics of the residential setting. As pointed out earlier, the type of residential setting in which a developmentally disabled person lives in a community may affect both access to service as well as the funding mechanism or options for these services. Geographic differences in the availability and quality of health care are also commonly recognized factors. Further, the type and severity of the developmental disability is a critical factor in the health care needs of the individual.

While this discussion has concentrated on medical care needs, it should be emphasized that mental health services for developmentally disabled persons are also an important service need (Rowitz, 1981a). Mental health services have developed separately from and parallel to the mental retardation services system. These services are often provided in facilities distinct from the general medical health care system as

well. The dispersion of various types of health and social services for developmentally disabled persons among different administrative and organizational sectors in society poses a considerable challenge to those responsible for ensuring comprehensive care to this population.

FINANCIAL ISSUES IN HEALTH CARE

Payment for health care services is an extremely complex issue. Publicly sponsored health care coverage is difficult to characterize given the maze of federal, state, and local variations in coverage and payment mechanisms. About 90% of group home residents are eligible for Medicaid coverage (V. Bradley, personal communication, 1986). Medicaid is a federal and state financed program that operates as a third-party insurance program and covers a variety of medical and health services. In general, eligibility for Medicaid coverage is automatically met for persons receiving Supplemental Security Income (SSI).

Medicare eligibility for developmentally disabled persons is more complicated. While there is no precise count available of the number of developmentally disabled persons covered by Medicare, some estimates are that 300,000 persons are recipients. If the parents of a developmentally disabled person are eligible for Social Security either because of age or disability, the handicapped child may be covered under both Social Security and Medicare. If the handicapped person becomes eligible for Social Security, eligibility for Medicare is met after 2 years.

Another source of payment for health services emanates from ICFs/MR, which are residential facilities certified to receive Medicaid reimbursement. States that decide to participate in the ICF/MR program receive between a 50% and an 83% match from the federal government for the cost of care (Fernald, 1986). Although the ICF/MR program is the largest source of federal funds for persons with mental retardation, the program benefits only a small percentage (6%) of this population.

Table 1. Medicaid recipients and Medicaid vendor payments for ICF/MR by state, 1984–1985

State	1984 Number of recipients	1984 Amount of medical vendor payments	1985 Number of recipients	1985 Amount of medical vendor payments
Alabama	1,461	48,630,596	1,468	49,319,263
Alaska	118	8,818,038	125	10,147,278
Arizona	0	0	0	0
Arkansas	1,468	40,053,737	1,452	42,381,035
California	10,160	257,004,464	9,740	277,575,882
Colorado	1,696	37,802,851	1,574	49,117,047
Connecticut	1,378	50,897,515	1,309	59,373,051
Delaware	482	10,324,858	442	9,833,868
District of Columbia	521	16,093,014	561	21,487,810
Florida	2,948	98,925,088	3,221	116,325,502
Georgia	1,767	51,545,474	1,750	61,749,501
Hawaii	402	9,447,344	263	8,824,401
Idaho	515	15,096,349	509	15,983,568
Illinois	8,602	188,952,559	8,546	215,970,087
Indiana	2,113	34,450,067	2,195	40,787,772
Iowa	1,726	56,235,124	1,856	60,953,643
Kansas	2,255	47,452,844	2,280	49,483,654
Kentucky	1,464	38,729,488	1,264	39,717,321
Louisiana	5,412	135,221,716	5,710	136,985,194
Maine	730	24,421,150	709	24,884,408
Maryland	0	0	0	0
Massachusetts	3,562	219,491,633	3,533	228,845,654
Michigan	3,591	143,128,505	3,670	157,208,370
Minnesota	7,773	205,705,855	7,808	202,213,106
Mississippi	1,655	23,610,881	1,648	23,210,257
Missouri	2,667	57,263,317	4,698	52,325,352
Montana	268	6,083,131	284	8,087,688
Nebraska	896	23,205,591	894	24,089,931
Nevada	210	7,344,823	205	8,769,109
New Hampshire	380	9,880,877	374	14,880,470
New Jersey	4,246	163,200,365	4,027	166,248,451
New Mexico	594	17,130,824	624	17,294,130
New York	16,128	771,661,702	17,254	974,026,344
North Carolina	2,882	96,700,254	3,083	111,953,929
North Dakota	564	9,820,222	649	18,318,261
Ohio	7,522	176,226,856	7,442	186,708,927
Oklahoma	1,648	39,421,756	2,456	53,675,015
Oregon	1,979	49,212,220	1,856	51,992,014
Pennsylvania	8,546	359,772,985	8,317	344,664,666
Rhode Island	1,094	44,194,215	1,081	47,468,136
South Carolina	2,481	45,977,302	2,487	53,057,144
South Dakota	718	15,612,601	748	15,874,926
Tennessee	2,481	63,325,415	2,762	63,438,297
Texas	13,115	268,855,647	12,807	265,693,713
Utah	1,335	23,101,921	1,386	23,978,567
Vermont	292	12,405,224	282	12,800,197
Virginia	3,285	70,591,768	3,220	94,968,072
Washington	2,844	88,362,351	2,841	101,514,926
West Virginia	235	2,369,905	258	2,606,106
Wisconsin	2,873	72,619,687	2,384	68,139,071
Wyoming	0	0	0	0

Note: 0 = no ICF/MR program or no data available.

Table 1 presents data on the number of Medicaid recipients and amount of vendor payments for the ICF/MR program by state for the years 1984 and 1985. It is notable that the highest number of Medicaid recipients were in New York, Texas, California, and Illinois. A recent analysis of the ICF/MR program indicates that between 1977 and 1982, the proportion of occupied beds in the residential system for developmentally disabled persons that were ICF/MR certified grew from 43% to 58% of the total number of residential beds (Lakin, Hill & Bruininks, 1985). It was also noted that the number of children in ICF/MR facilities has decreased substantially, while the percentage of severely impaired persons served in these facilities has increased.

A major change in the structure of the Medicaid program occurred in 1981. Section 2176 of PL 95-35 (The Omnibus Budget Reconciliation Act) permitted the U.S. Department of Health and Human Services to waive specified statutory requirements in the Medicaid program to allow states to use Medicaid funds to finance community-based services for persons who would otherwise require care in an ICF/MR. A survey of state mental retardation/developmental disabilities agencies conducted by Gardner (1986) in 1983 found that about 15,000 people received services under the waiver. Gardner pointed out that most states intended to integrate the services covered under the waiver program into their existing pattern of service delivery, but were experiencing difficulties in implementing the waiver program.

The development of unique and innovative service delivery systems in health care is necessary as funding for public and private programs is curtailed. The emphasis on cost-effective programs creates additional incentives for the establishment of alternative systems of care (Califano, 1986). Two demonstration projects in this area offer interesting examples of alternative systems.

J. Pulcini (personal communication, 1986) has studied a community-based health care service owned and operated by a group of nurse practitioners. The nurse practitioners have an independent practice that provides health care to developmentally disabled and nondisabled persons in the Laconia, NH, area. Health-related services are provided in various community settings and financed through the state area community agency for mental retardation using Medicaid and Blue Cross reimbursement. When medical intervention is needed, two physicians who serve as consultants to the private nurse practitioner practice are utilized. In areas where the density of service is low, a nurse practitioner model may be particularly effective.

Harrington and Newcomer (1985) have studied the feasibility of a social/health maintenance organization (S/HMO) to serve disabled persons. This model is organized to provide long-term care to people on a prepaid basis and to provide a full range of health care and supportive services. The model uses case management, home care, and social services. It is also designed to give services for acute, primary, and preventive health across the life cycle and could be funded through Medicaid. It is expected that the total cost of care would be less expensive than providing services to people in ICFs/MR and other long-term care programs. In addition, other types of community residences could contract with the S/HMO to provide necessary care.

One important factor that needs to be addressed relative to HMO and S/HMO service is that these prepayment forms of health care services have a financial incentive to screen out Medicare clients (and possibly Medicaid beneficiaries if applicable) whose care will be more costly than usual (Schlesinger, 1986). Thus HMOs and S/HMOs would try to limit services to chronically ill or disabled persons because of cost. This may be a critical problem for group homes trying to get health coverage for their disabled residents.

Summary

This section has discussed some of the problems related to financing medical and dental care for developmentally disabled persons living in community group homes. Two innovative service models were presented as possibilities to provide these services within the given constraints. Other innovative service models need to be developed.

CONCLUSIONS AND
RECOMMENDATIONS

The American health care system is characterized by fragmentation and an unequal geographic distribution. The reimbursement of health services, particularly for developmentally disabled persons, is extremely complex. Obtaining appropriate health care services and paying for it are major issues facing developmentally disabled persons and those charged with their day-to-day care. The readiness of operators and staff in community residences to meet the health care needs of their residents requires deliberate and comprehensive planning. To this end, the following recommendations are offered to increase the level of preparedness of those responsible for this central area of service:

1. Develop training programs for residents and staff on health promotion and disease prevention methods (e.g., nutrition, exercise).
2. Provide in-service training for staff of community residences on the location and capacities of various health services in the community.
3. Expand the case manager model to expedite the utilization of community services and to monitor the process.
4. Assign a staff person the responsibility of being a liaison between the community residence and the health care providing community.
5. Expand the training of health professionals regarding the special health care needs of developmentally disabled persons.
6. Assist state and local health departments in monitoring the health care needs and problems of disabled populations.
7. Undertake a needs assessment for health care services of developmentally disabled persons living in community residences.
8. Encourage the expansion of HMO, S/HMO, and other prepaid plans to serve persons with developmental disabilities.
9. Develop a legal advocacy group to help families obtain insurance coverage and financial security for their handicapped relative.
10. Monitor changing health care needs of disabled persons throughout the life cycle.

REFERENCES

Aldershvile, J., Skinhj, P., Frosner, G.G., Black, F., Deinhardt, F., & Neilsen, J.O. (1980). The expression pattern of hepatitis B antigen and antibody in different ethnic and clinical groups of hepatitis B surface antigen carriers. *Journal of Infectious Diseases, 142,* 18–22.

Butler, J.A., Singer, J.D., Palfrey, J.S., & Walker, D.K. (1987). Health insurance coverage and physician use among children with disabilities: Findings from probability samples in five metropolitan areas. *Pediatrics, 79,* 89–98.

Califano, J.A. (1986). *America's health care revolution.* New York: Random House.

Chinn, P.C., Drew, C.J., & Logan, D.R. (1979). *Mental Retardation: A life cycle approach.* St. Louis: C.V. Mosby.

Cohen, H.J. (1979). Community health planning. In P.R. Magrab & J.O. Elder (Eds.), *Planning for services to handicapped persons: Community, education, health* (pp. 91–120). Baltimore: Paul H. Brooks Publishing Co.

Demb, H., & Diamond, D. (1980). Problems in providing medical services to the developmentally disabled. In H.J. Cohen & D. Kligler (Eds.), *Urban community care for developmentally disabled.* Springfield, IL: Charles C Thomas.

Fernald, C.D. (1986). Changing Medicaid and intermediate care facilities for the mentally retarded (ICF/MR): Evaluation of alternatives. *Mental Retardation, 24,* 36–42.

Gardner, J.F. (1986). Implementation of the home and community-based waiver. *Mental Retardation, 24,* 18–26.

Garrard, S.D. (1982). Health services for mentally retarded people in community residences: Problems and concerns. *American Journal of Public Health, 72,* 1226–1228.

Garrard, S.D., & Crocker, A.C. (1979). *The status of health care for ''deinstitutionalized'' mentally retarded people in Boston, Massachusetts: Present and future directions.* Department of Family and Community Medicine, University of Massachusetts Medical Center and Developmental Evaluations Clinic, Children's Hospital and Medical Center.

Gust, L.D., Dimitrakakis, M., & Sharma, D.L. (1978). The prevalence of HBeAG and anti-HBe in an institution for the mentally retarded. *Australia and New Zealand Journal of Medicine, 8,* 471–473.

Hamilton, B.B., Betts, H.D., Rath, G.J., Gilette, H.E., Greene, A.M., Garrity, S.D., & Libman, A.S. (1977). *A study of the medical and allied health services delivery system for substantially handicapped disabled adults.* Chicago: Northwestern University, Rehabilitation Institute of Chicago.

Hammer, S.L., & Barnard, K.E. (1966). The mentally retarded adolescent. *Pediatrics, 38,* 845–857.

Harrington, C., & Newcomer, R. (1985). Social/health maintenance organizations: New policy options for the aged, blind, and disabled. *Journal of Public Health Policy, 6,* 204–222.

Hill, B.K., Balow, E.A., & Bruininks, R.H. (1985). A national study of prescribed drugs in institutions and community residential facilities for mentally retarded people. *Psychopharmacology Bulletin, 24,* 279–284.

Hill, B.K., Bruininks, R.H., & Lakin, K.C. (1983). Characteristics of mentally retarded people in residential facilities. *Health and Social Work, 8,* 85–96.

Jacobson, J.W., Silver, E.J., & Schwartz, A.A. (1984). Service provision in New York's group homes. *Mental Retardation, 22,* 231–239.

Janicki, M.P., & Jacobson, J.W. (1986, May). *What do the data tell us about the aging and aged mentally retarded population?* Paper presented at the 110th Annual Meeting of the American Association on Mental Deficiency, Denver.

Krauss, M.W., & Seltzer, M.M. (1986, May). *The national survey of programs serving elderly mentally retarded persons: Community based residential program typology.* Paper presented at the 110th Annual Meeting of the American Association on Mental Deficiency, Denver.

Lakin, K.C., Hill, B., & Bruininks, R. (Eds.). (1985). *An analysis of Medicaid's intermediate care facility for the mentally retarded (ICF-MR) program.* Minneapolis: University of Minnesota, Department of Education Psychology.

Lohiya, S., Lohiya, G., & Caires, S. (1986). Epidemiology of hepatitis B infection in institutionalized mentally retarded clients. *American Journal of Public Health, 76,* 799–802.

Madden, D.L., Dietzman, D.E., Matthew, E.B., Sever, J.L., Lander, J.J., Purcell, R.H., Rostafinski, M., & Mata, A. (1976). Epidemiology of hepatitis B virus in an institution for mentally retarded persons. *American Journal of Mental Deficiency, 80,* 369–375.

McDonald, E.P. (1985). Medical needs of severely developmentally disabled persons residing in the community. *American Journal of Mental Deficiency, 90,* 171–176.

Minihan, P.M. (1986). Planning for community physicians services prior to deinstitutionalization of mentally retarded persons. *American Journal of Public Health, 76,* 1202–1206.

O'Connor, G. (1976). *Home is a good place.* Washington, DC: American Association on Mental Deficiency Monograph Services.

Palfrey, J.S., Singer, J.D., Walker, D., & Butler, J.A. (1986). Health and special education: A study of new developments for handicapped children in five metropolitan communities. *Public Health Reports, 101,* 379–388.

Rowitz, L. (1974a). Changing perspectives in social epidemiological research. *Mental Retardation, 12,* 21–23.

Rowitz, L. (1974b). Social factors in mental retardation. *Social Science and Medicine, 8,* 405–412.

Rowitz, L. (1980). Original identifiers of mental retardation in a clinic population. *American Journal of Mental Retardation, 85,* 82–86.

Rowitz, L. (1981a). Mental health services for the mentally retarded individual. In W.H. Silverman (Ed.), *Community Mental Health.* New York: Praeger.

Rowitz, L. (1981b). Service paths prior to clinic use by mentally retarded people: A retrospective study. In R.H.

Bruininks, C.E. Meyers, B.B. Sigford, & K.C. Lakin (Eds.), *Deinstitutionalization and community adjustment by mentally retarded people* (pp. 360–374). Washington, DC: American Association on Mental Deficiency Monograph Services.

Rowitz, L. (1981c). A sociological perspective on labeling in mental retardation. *Mental Retardation, 19,* 47–51.

Rowitz, L., & Farber, B. (1986, October). *Families with a mentally retarded member, 1959–1986.* Paper presented at the 114th annual meeting of American Public Health Association, Las Vegas.

Scheerenberger, R.C. (1982). Public residential services 1981: Status and trends. *Mental Retardation, 20,* 210–215.

Schlesinger, Mark (1966). On the limits of expanding health care reform: Chronic care in prepaid settings. *Milbank Quarterly, 64,* 189–215.

Schor, E.L., Smalky, K.A., & Neff, J.M. (1981). Primary care of previously institutionalized retarded children. *Pediatrics, 67,* 536–540.

Schwartz, C.G. (1970). Strategies and tactics of mothers of mentally retarded children for dealing with the medical care system. In N.R. Bernstein (Ed.), *Diminished people.* Boston: Little, Brown.

Seltzer, M.M., & Krauss, M.W. (1984). Family, community residence, and institutional placements of a sample of mentally retarded children. *American Journal of Mental Deficiency, 89,* 257–266.

Seltzer, M.M., & Krauss, M.W. (1986, May). *The national survey programs serving elderly mentally retarded persons: Community based day program typology.* Paper presented at the 110th Annual Meeting of the American Association on Mental Deficiency, Denver.

Singer, J., Butler, J.A., & Palfrey, J. (1986). Health care access and use among handicapped students in five public school systems. *Medical Care, 24,* 1–13.

Stone, R. & Newcomer, R. (1985). Health and social services policy and the disabled who have become old. In M. Janicki & H. Wisniewski (Eds.), *Aging and developmental disabilities: Issues and approaches* (pp. 27–39). Baltimore: Paul H. Brookes Publishing Co.

Thomas, P. (1986, February). Special adults: New challenge to primary care MDs. *Medical World,* 68–81.

Tobis, J.S. (1982). The hospitalized elderly. *Journal of the American Medical Association, 248,* 874.

Walker, D.K. (1984). Care of chronically ill children in schools. *Pediatric Clinics of North America, 31,* 221–233.

Walker, D.K., Butler, J.A., Singer, J.D., & Palfrey, J.S. (1984, November). *Special education services and parent satisfaction in five urban school districts.* Paper presented at the 112th annual meeting of the American Public Health Association, Anaheim, CA.

Williams, C., Weber, F.T., Culler, J., & Kane, M. (1983). Hepatitis B transmission in school contacts of retarded HBs AG carrier students. *Journal of Pediatrics, 103,* 192–196.

Williamson, H.G., Lehaman, N.I., Dimitrakakis, M., & Sharma, D.L. (1982). A longitudinal study of hepatitis infection in an institution for the mentally retarded. *Australia and New Zealand Journal of Medicine, 12,* 30–34.

Zonia, S.C., & Goff, G.A. (1986). Communicable illnesses in the mentally retarded and nonretarded populations of three Michigan counties. *American Journal of Mental Deficiency, 90,* 453–456.

Chapter 17

Leisure and Recreational Programming

Barbara A. Hawkins

This chapter explores the role of leisure in community residential life. A conceptual foundation for understanding leisure needs is outlined, and practical approaches to program development for persons with developmental disabilities living in community residences are offered. Leisure needs are examined from the perspectives of health/wellness promotion and leisure ability. Program development strategies are discussed, including resident assessment, program planning, implementation, and evaluation. The chapter concludes with a discussion of professional practice and staff responsibilities for providing leisure programming in community residences.

Most community residences seek to create a home environment that provides for a full range of experiences that contribute to personal growth. Thus, a person with a developmental disability living in such a setting should be able to learn basic care skills, make friends, develop recreation interests and leisure-time use skills, and adopt a life-style that integrates responsibility and play. It is in the successful combination of work and leisure that most individuals find meaning to life and experience their fullest potential. Living in a community residence can enhance the quality of life of an individual with a disability through providing an atmosphere where leisure activities are used to promote health/wellness, life satisfaction, and rewarding personal relationships.

This chapter outlines a framework for understanding the role of leisure and offers practical approaches for developing recreational programs for individuals living in a community residence. The role of leisure is examined from the perspective of the promotion of health/wellness and of leisure ability. Recreation program development suggestions include resident as-

sessment and program planning, implementation, and evaluation. The chapter also discusses professional practice and staff responsibilities for providing recreation programming.

THE ROLE OF LEISURE-TIME USE

The notions of health and wellness promotion and of leisure ability provide a framework for understanding why leisure is an integral component in developing a healthy life-style. Further, these notions are essential to the technical aspects of leisure skills assessment and recreational program development. *Health promotion* and *wellness* can be defined as encompassing those activities that are intended to enhance self-fulfillment, personal well-being, and the realization of one's fullest potential (Teague, 1986). These activities are directly influenced by both life-style factors and features of the environment (McDowell, 1983). Ardell (1986), in describing a health/wellness model, notes that wellness is life-style focused and based upon the integration of five dimensions: physical fitness, nutrition, stress management, en-

vironmental sensitivity, and self-responsibility.
Ardell proposes that these dimensions are dynamic, changing throughout one's life according to age and life stage. According to Ardell's
model, health is a direct result of a life-style
that is shaped by each of these wellness dimensions. Health is viewed as freedom from physical, mental, and emotional illness or pain.
Both the health and wellness components of the
model are critical to an individual's ability to
reach his or her potential and experience ful-
fillment.

Leisure traditionally has been viewed as a
diversionary activity of minimal therapeutic
value in the design of habilitation programs.
This view, however, is changing. The incorporation of leisure-time use into formal recreational plan activities is becoming more accepted
as its value is recognized as a significant factor
in improving overall quality of life (see
Blunden, Chapter 9, this volume). Consequently, the residence staff's concern with enhancing health and wellness through a more effective use of leisure time can be a means of
meeting the avocational and personal development needs of the residents.

The rationale for the development of leisure
ability, in conjunction with the notion of health
and wellness promotion, provides the basis for
why recreational activities play such an important role in any person's life. The purpose of
providing recreation services is the development of leisure ability (i.e., the capability to
effectively and successfully use leisure time).
Consequently, recreation services can include
the following three aspects: treatment, leisure
education, and recreation participation (Peterson & Gunn, 1984). Overall, recreation services are directed toward the goals of promoting
independent leisure-time use, health, wellness,
and an enhanced quality of life. The development of the ability to productively use leisure
time, including the promotion of self-responsibility for understanding productive free-time
use, identifying one's leisure interests and preferences through and expansion of experience,
and the promotion of choice-making skills, is
enhanced through leisure-time use education
(Pollingue & Cobb, 1986). The natural consequence of ongoing recreation participation is

the development of fitness, appropriate stress
management strategies, a zest for life, and a
generally enhanced quality of life.

LEISURE PROGRAM DEVELOPMENT

Training for productive leisure-time use is accomplished by implementing activities drawn
from a recreation services plan. A four-step
process is frequently used in developing an individual recreation services plan (Austin, 1982;
Peterson & Gunn, 1984). These steps include
assessment, planning, implementation, and
evaluation.

Assessment

The first step in the development of a recreation
services plan is to conduct a systematic, objective assessment of the individual's health/well-
ness status and current leisure-time use skills by
identifying the problem, stipulating means to
measure growth and progress, and gaining an
understanding of the individual's strengths, interests, and expectations (Austin, 1982; Howe,
1984; Navar, 1980; Peterson & Gunn, 1984;
Wehman & Schleien, 1981).

Although the recreation program plan can be
developed by direct care staff in a community
residence, it is usually based upon assessment
information provided by an interdisciplinary
team. As such, all assessment information obtained by team members is important to the development of the recreation services component
of a resident's individualized program plan (see
Manfredini & Smith, Chapter 10, this volume).
For example, perceptual motor skill and performance information from an occupational or
physical therapist will be helpful in identifying
habilitation recreation activities or the need for
activity adaptation. Also, information on receptive and expressive language skills may be
useful in designing recreation activities that
teach recognition of free time, enhance appropriate social interaction behaviors, develop activity preferences, and encourage choice-making skills. In addition, information provided by
a physician can aid in determining the range of
possible physical activities appropriate for the
individual. In some instances, the recreation
needs or leisure-time use assessment process

can become more elaborate and require coordination by recreation professionals, as in the process described in the next section.

Health/Wellness Status Assessment
Health and wellness promotion is beginning to replace the more traditional approach to health care or treatment for illness and disease (McDowell, 1986). The role of recreation professionals, and specifically that of the therapeutic recreation specialist, in health promotion is rapidly expanding as these service providers focus their attention on leisure, wellness, and life-style (McDowell, 1986; Teague, 1986). The function of a health/wellness status assessment is to identify the individual's strengths and weaknesses as applied to possible applications of recreation services.

The basic components of a comprehensive health/wellness assessment include a general health status evaluation, physical fitness appraisal, nutritional analysis, and stress or emotional adjustment appraisal (O'Donnell & Ainsworth, 1984; Teague, 1986). The general health status evaluation, done by or under the direction of a physician, involves screening the individual for basic health and personal information. A screening instrument commonly used is the General Health Hazard Appraisal (Centers for Disease Control, n.d.); it includes such information as the individual's age, race, sex, life-style practices, and a projected life expectancy. Following the screening, the individual should undergo multiphasic testing of physiometric measurements to identify any possible chronic conditions in an asymptomatic phase (Teague, 1986). The General Health Hazard Appraisal assures that any applications of habilitative programming do not entail undue risk for aggravating existing disability or disease conditions.

The physical fitness appraisal includes the following components: a) exercise history survey, b) body composition, c) flexibility, d) muscle strength and endurance, e) balance and equilibrium, f) cardiopulmonary capacity, and g) exercise contraindication survey (Teague, 1986). Techniques that can be used to assess an individual with a developmental disability are described in American Alliance for Health, Physical Education, Recreation and Dance (1976), Ford (1985), Katch and McArdle (1983), and O'Donnell and Ainsworth (1984). A qualified therapeutic recreation specialist, in conjunction with an exercise physiologist, generally conducts a physical fitness appraisal.

The nutritional analysis, generally performed by a dietician, serves to identify potential risk factors that should be considered in the recreation program plan. Essential information comprising a comprehensive nutritional analysis includes: a) health history, b) food intake and eating patterns, c) amount of exercise and level of physical fitness, d) personal and family situations, e) home and work environments, and f) stress coping mechanisms (Teague, 1986).

Stress or emotional adjustment appraisal, as applied to recreational programming, should entail, at a minimum, an understanding of events that produce stress in the individual's life and how he or she responds to such events. Understanding the resident's response behaviors and the precipitating events are important for effective home management irrespective of their applications to recreation; however, in many instances recreational activities can become a useful management tool in times of stress. Other strategies to employ when an individual is experiencing stress can include relaxation techniques, nutritional and dietary modifications, counseling, and activity schedule modifications.

Leisure-Time Use Skill Assessment
The description and evaluation of resident leisure-time use skills are essential steps in developing an appropriate recreation program. Leisure-time use skills assessment optimally will involve a variety of measures (Wehman & Schleien, 1981). In addition to the use of assessment information from other members of the habilitation team, both recreation and community residence staff should collect information on the resident's repertoire of activities, interests, preferences, expectations, and independence capacity skills (such as use of public transportation, shopping skills, eating in public, and capacity for self-protection). Such information may be collected by using naturalistic techniques and/or standardized instruments (Ferguson, 1983; Parker, Ellison, Kirby, & Short,

1975; Stumbo, 1983). For example, the leisure-time use preferences and leisure-play skill levels of young children are more easily assessed through systematic observation during natural play sessions. In contrast, task analytic testing procedures may be more appropriate when as-sessing leisure or independence capacity skills of adolescents or adults.

Important factors in assessing a resident's leisure-time use skills include understanding what is functional and age-appropriate, and how the environment can be adapted to elicit a mean-

Table 1. Leisure assessment tools

Instruments	Target population	Reliability	Validity[a]	Ease of administration[b]	Response mode
Avocational Activities Inventory (Overs, O'Connor, & Demarco, 1974)	EMR	good	good	quickly	staff
I Can (Wessel, 1976)	TMR-children	good	good	quickly	direct
Joswiak's Leisure Counseling Assessment Instruments (Joswiak, 1975)	DD	N/A	good	time consuming	examinee: direct
Linear Model for Individual Treatment in Recreation (LMIT) (Compton & Price, 1985)	DD	N/A	N/A	time consuming	examinee: direct
Leisure Skills Curriculum Assessment Inventory (LSCDD) (Wehman & Schleien, 1979)	DD	N/A	N/A	time consuming	direct: staff
Minimum Objective System (MOS) (Williams & Fox, 1977)	severely handicapped	N/A	good	quickly	direct: staff
Recreation Therapy Assessment (Cousins & Brown, 1979)	nonambulatory adult	N/A	N/A	time consuming	direct
Sonoma County Organization for the Retarded Assessment System (SCOR) (Westaway & Apolloni, 1977)	DD	N/A	good	time consuming	examinee: staff
State of Ohio Curriculum Guide for Moderately Mentally Retarded Learners (Ohio Department of Mental Health, 1977)	TMR	N/A	N/A	time consuming	direct: staff
Toward Competency: A Guide for Individualized Instruction (Oregon State Department of Education, 1974)	all special populations	N/A	good	time consuming	examinee: staff

Adapted with permission from Wehman & Schleien (1980), pp. 14–15.

[a]The original table by Wehman & Schlein (1980) reported validity for some instruments; however, it did not provide companion reliability information. N/A = not available.

[b]"Quickly" implies 30 minutes or less, and "time consuming" means longer than 30 minutes.

ingful display of the skill (Horst, Wehman, Hill, & Bailey, 1981). Further, it is important to assess leisure-time use skills in terms of health, wellness, habilitation, leisure education, and leisure participation. It is also important to consider the age-appropriateness of the individual's leisure-time use skills, as well as whether the skills are a function of the limits posed by the individual's disability or a lack of sufficient experience. In addition, when needed, the environment should be modified to support the resident's abilities as well as to minimize the limits presented by the disability.

A number of leisure-time use skill assessment instruments are available that can be used with individuals living in a community residence. Table 1 lists 10 such instruments and evaluates them according to their target population applicability; reliability, validity, ease of administration information; and response mode (examinee, direct observation, staff/parent). All of the instruments noted on Table 1 are at a minimum criterion referenced and applicable to individual assessment applications. The *I Can* instrument (Wessel, 1976) is applicable to group assessments as well.

In addition to using a standardized assessment instrument, specially adapted or developed documentation procedures can be used that provide ongoing assessment information regarding an individual's responses to participation, including observed or expressed interests, preferences, particular skills, adaptations, and other special needs. The development of a standard record sheet will enhance interpretation in terms of progress, problem solving, and the identification of environmental adaptation strategies.

Program Planning, Implementation, and Evaluation

Recreation program planning can occur at two levels: 1) the resident's individualized program plan, and 2) the overall recreation program for the community residence.

Individualized Program Planning As noted by Manfredini and Smith (Chapter 10, this volume), the individualized program plan is a written document that translates assessment in-

formation into stated goals and behavioral objectives to provide direction to and accountability for all programming with application to recreation. The leisure-time skill development goals selected should be placed in priority-order and cross-referenced with goals formulated for other discipline areas (e.g., speech communication, physical therapy, vocational training). To help in effecting behavior change that reflects the interrelatedness of all of life's major spheres (work, education, home, community, leisure), a fewer number of cross-referenced goals is preferred to a greater number of unrelated goals (Smith, 1983). This means that recreational objectives should be interrelated with other broader teaching objectives when applicable (e.g., use of board games to teach cooperation, number skills, sight vocabulary, and sequencing; or participation in a ball game to improve eye-hand coordination, teach competition and rules, and instill social affiliation).

In spite of the seeming informality of recreation activities, specific functions can be defined that teach new behaviors. Consequently, with application to formal recreation programs, behavioral objectives should be written to include a description of the performance desired, designation of the specific conditions of that performance, and the criterion that will be applied to demonstrate adequate performance (Wehman & Schleien, 1981). For example, if an overall goal for an individual is to increase skills in using public transportation, then an appropriate recreation-related goal would be: "John will increase his use of the bus transport system so that he can participate in community recreation programs." A specific objective linked to this goal could be: "John will take the Number 8 city bus to and from the YMCA with some assistance." The criterion for measuring the success of this objective could be: "John meets this objective when he responds prior to receiving three or fewer naturally occurring cues, such as the driver calling out the location of his stop." Resources such as Austin (1982), Peterson and Gunn (1984), and Wehman and Schleien (1981) may be consulted for developing and writing recreation-related behavior objectives.

The basic elements common to all individual recreation service plans are:

1. The resident's needs are stated in terms of assessment outcomes.
2. Goals are specified as an outcome of the interdisciplinary team assessment and planning process and with priorities assigned.
3. Specific behavior objectives developed are based on a task or activity analysis process and are modified based on the functional status of the resident.
4. A plan of activities and/or programs is developed that enhances goal/objectives attainment.
5. Strategies and approaches are utilized by staff and other service providers involved with the resident.
6. Information is provided on environment selection, modification, and/or adaptation.
7. A description is provided of the evaluation methods and procedures to be used by staff to document resident performance and progress (Austin, 1982; Peterson & Gunn, 1984).

Residence Program Planning Staff should consider a number of factors prior to designing an overall recreation program plan for the residence. First, there should be agreement upon a philosophy and accompanying goal statements, which form the foundation for the recreation program (Peterson & Gunn, 1984). An example of a philosophy statement is:

> Beach Home, a group home for older adults with a developmental disability, is committed to providing a quality of life and life-style for its residents that is characterized by the promotion of health/wellness, a familylike social environment, activities designed to enhance independent living skills, and opportunities to experience personal life satisfaction.

Goal statements that complement the philosophical foundation should reflect the special needs of residents either by factors of age or disability; the nature and resources of the community residence setting; the nature and resources of the local community; and staff perspectives as reflected in their attitudes and values. Peterson and Gunn (1984) have recommended that goal statements encompass the three functions of recreation: treatment, leisure education, and leisure participation. Sample *treatment* goal statements that could accompany

the foregoing philosophy statement might include:

1. To maintain optimal physical functioning
2. To maintain physical health, including promoting good nutrition and minimizing stressful experiences, thus reducing the potential for illness
3. To maintain or increase social and interactional skills
4. To facilitate the maintenance of independence and choice-making skills

Sample *leisure education* goal statements that could accompany the preceding philosophy statement might include:

1. To facilitate social integration into existing senior citizen programs
2. To provide opportunities to participate in new leisure experiences
3. To stimulate self-directed leisure behavior
4. To expand the personal repertoire of leisure-time use skills

Sample *leisure/recreation participation* statements that could accompany the previous philosophy statement might include:

1. To provide opportunities for experiencing enjoyment
2. To provide an environment that enhances the social integration of residents into the mainstream of community leisure activities
3. To facilitate participation in experiences in which residents show skills and preferences

The scheduling of recreational activities is an important consideration in the residence's overall recreation plan. Coordination of scheduling is important because it integrates the individualized recreation plans of residence occupants into the normal patterns of daily living activities at the residence. Such normal patterns are characterized by personal maintenance times; periods of independent time; opportunities for socialization, school, vocational, or day activity; times for passive or active leisure pursuits; and rest/recuperation time. Also, points of transitions between the major spheres of daily life (such as work/school/day activity,

Table 2. Leisure activities sampler

Life stages	Leisure activity categories						
	Sports and physical activity	Creative experience	Living skills	Social/cultural activities	Outdoor activities	Amusements
Infancy (birth–24 mos.)	rolling, early walking, crawling	peek-a-boo	eating skills family dining	parades	lying on grass	mobiles
Toddler (2–3 years)	climbing, running	story hours	cooperation parallel play	holiday events	outdoor exploration	children's zoo
Early childhood (4–5 years)	kickball, circle games	finger paints	safety and rules games	circus	nature print mold making	carnivals
Middle childhood (6–12 years)	dodgeball, volleyball	puppet shows	reading	playground, music festivals	nature clubs	children's museums
Adolescence (13–19 years)	team sports, billiards	concerts, musicals	using community services transportation	teen dances	nature collections	theme park
Young adulthood (20–40 years)	dancing, tennis, skating	music groups	money management shopping	dining out	camping	movies
Middle adulthood (41–60 years)	basketball, bicycling, bowling	ceramics, wood working, theater	independence restaurants	libraries	picnics	theatrical productions, county fairs
Older adulthood (61 + years)	horseshoes, swimming, walking	wood working, social dancing	social/physical independence senior centers	art museums	gardening	travel

home, leisure) are important to consider in program planning.

At the end of a day of work, or of educational or day activity programming, it is helpful for a resident to be able to choose a leisure activity in which to participate or simply to do nothing. This rest time, permitting recuperation and rejuvenation, can be appropriately spent passively or actively, individually or in groups, inside or out-of-doors doing something of one's own choosing. The critical aspect is choice; having available a range of opportunities will enhance each resident's expression of personal leisure-time use choices and promote relaxation. Such opportunities might include restful activities like lying down; a passive movement like swinging or rocking; diversionary activities such as television viewing, socializing, or individual hobbies; or active pursuits such as gardening, walking, jogging, or other fitness-promoting activities. The attractiveness of the activities made available at the residence can serve as vital incentives in encouraging residents to engage in leisure-time use behavior designed to bridge the pressing nature of daily routines with the more personal and self-expressive characteristics of evening leisure time.

In developing an evening and weekend recreation program, activities that are age-appropriate and meet the needs of the individual, as well as fit into the group's needs, should be used to guide program design. Residence staff should try to balance individual and group experiences and active and passive pursuits in the activities that take place in the home and in the community. In addition, sampling from a range of leisure-time use opportunities should help to increase the breadth of experiences and enhance the development of an individual's ability to make meaningful choices. At a minimum, activities from the following broad categories should be available to residents: sports and physical activities, creative experiences, living skills, social and cultural activities, outdoor pursuits, and amusements. A sampler of activities for these categories across different life stages is presented in Table 2. Technical resources that may be helpful in choosing other leisure activites for each of these areas include Baker, Brightman, & Blacher (1983); Wehman

(1977); Wehman (1979); Witt (1979); and Wuerch & Voeltz (1982).

A further consideration in program planning and implementation is resource assessment (Certo, Stuart, & Hunter, 1983). Identifying the resources that exist in the home helps in planning and implementing the range of activities to be made available to the residents. For example, if the residence is located in the midst of a city where there is little or no outdoor yard space, home gardening and yard use are not likely to be potential recreational activities. On the other hand, if the house is situated in a quiet suburban neighborhood, bicycle riding and walking might be excellent activities to promote fitness as well as stress reduction. Further, the potential of both the house and neighborhood should be considered. A house with an available recreation room could offer a range of indoor sport activities (such as table tennis or pool), while a house located in an area with shops and recreation outlets (such as an ice cream parlor, movie house, or bowling alley) can offer many alternatives for an evening's entertainment.

It is important also to take into account the nature and capabilities of the community resources that are in proximity to the home, many of which can be used for planning and implementing the recreation program (Benest, Foley, & Welton, 1984). Most communities have at least a public park or playing field. Many have recreation and parks departments, which can be called upon for help in setting up recreation activities. Assessing the range of public and private agencies and organizations—which also can be called upon to participate in providing program opportunities (or providing volunteers)—will ultimately contribute to a rich and varied leisure program. Most frequently, the task is one of matching existing outside programs with resident needs or interests, and then preparing the administrators, staff, and participants of those programs to understand and accept the resident.

PROFESSIONAL PRACTICE

Resident assessment, as well as program planning, implementation, and evaluation for leisure-time use in community residences, can involve a variety of professionals and direct care staff from the interdisciplinary team. As suggested earlier, the comprehensive health evaluation component can involve a physician, nutritionist, therapeutic recreation specialist, and a range of other consultants such as an exercise physiologist, all working in conjunction with the residence's staff. In some instances, leisure skills assessment and individualized plan development will be the responsibility of a qualified recreation specialist, who can serve as a consultant to the agency's direct care staff. The implementation of individual resident recreation programs can be carried out by a broad range of persons, including direct care staff, community recreation service providers, and the therapeutic recreation staff. Based upon the number and variety of staff who will be involved with recreation programming in the residence, it is helpful to have a basic understanding of the roles, responsibilites, and credentials of therapeutic recreation specialists.

The National Therapeutic Recreation Society (NTRS), a branch of the National Recreation and Park Association (NRPA), is a professional leadership organization in the area of therapeutic recreation services and standards of practice (NRPA, 1980a, 1980b, 1982, 1986). The NTRS has adopted a statement of philosophy that recognizes three areas of professional services: treatment, leisure education, and leisure/recreation participation. The NTRS (NRPA, 1982) philosophy states:

> The purpose of therapeutic recreation is to facilitate the development, maintenance, and expression of an appropriate leisure lifestyle for individuals with physical, mental, emotional, or social limitations. Accordingly, this purpose is accomplished through the provision of professional programs and services which assist the client in eliminating barriers to leisure, developing leisure skills and attitudes, and optimizing leisure involvement. Therapeutic recreation professionals use these principles to enhance clients' leisure ability in recognition of the importance and value of leisure in the human experience.

The NTRS has developed *Guidelines for Administration of Therapeutic Recreation Services in Clinical and Residential Facilities* (NRPA, 1980a). The guidelines specify the respon-

sibilities of therapeutic recreation staff. If possible, community residence staff should arrange a consultation with a qualified therapeutic recreation professional to assist in assessment and individualized program planning. When applicable, a therapeutic recreation specialist will be a participating member of an interdisciplinary treatment team, and as such will contribute to the development of the overall program plan, as well as develop the recreation services component. A therapeutic recreation specialist can also be helpful in establishing linkages with community recreation services. All of these services, accompanied by consultation and training to direct care staff, will increase the likelihood for quality leisure-time use programming in community residences.

CONCLUSION

Recently, Landesman (1986) made a plea for operationally defining quality of life and personal satisfaction. This chapter introduced a notion of leisure and life-style that should lead to an enhanced quality of life in community residential settings. Factors that contribute directly to enhancing the quality of life include health/wellness and ability to effectively use leisure time. Areas that are basic to leisure-time use ability and health/wellness include self-responsibility, fitness, nutritional balance, stress, environment, and leisure behavior. Each of these areas can be addressed through three functions of leisure/recreation services: treatment, leisure education, and leisure/recreation participation.

Community residences have great potential to provide the context and environment necessary to enrich the lives of persons with developmental disabilities through leisure programming aimed at quality of life and providing a well-balanced life-style. Perhaps it is in leisure that disability can be blurred, fading into the background as the primary deterrent to social integration and acceptance. As persons with disabilities living in community residences increasingly become involved in community leisure activities, opportunities for all segments of society to better appreciate and accommodate their abilities will expand.

REFERENCES

American Alliance for Health, Physical Education, Recreation and Dance. (1976). *Special fitness test manual for mildly mentally retarded persons* (rev. ed.). Reston, VA: Author.

Ardell, Donald B. (1986). *High level wellness, an alternative to doctors, drugs, and disease.* Berkeley, CA: Ten Speed Press.

Austin, D.R. (1982). *Therapeutic recreation process and techniques.* New York: John Wiley & Sons.

Baker, B.L., Brightman, A.J., & Blacher, J.B. (1983). *Play skills.* Champaign, IL: Research Press.

Benest, F., Foley, J., & Welton, G. (1984). *Organizing leisure and human services.* Dubuque, IA: Kendall/Hunt Publishing Co.

Centers for Disease Control. (n.d.). *General health hazard appraisal.* Atlanta: Author (Bureau of Health Education, 1600 Clifton Rd., NE, Atlanta, GA 30333).

Certo, N., Stuart, J., & Hunter, D. (1983). An ecological assessment inventory to facilitate community recreation participation by severely disabled individuals. *Therapeutic Recreation Journal, 17,* 29–38.

Compton, D., & Price, D. (1975). Individualizing your treatment program. A case study using LMIT. *Therapeutic Recreation Journal, 9,* 127.

Cousins, B., & Brown, E. (1979). *Recreation therapy assessment.* Jacksonville, FL: Amelia Island ICF/MR.

Ferguson, D. (1983). Assessment interviewing techniques: A useful tool in developing individual program plans. *Therapeutic Recreation Journal, 17,* 16–22.

Ford, R. (1985). *Health assessment handbook.* Springhouse, PA: Springhouse Corp.

Horst, G., Wehman, P., Hill, J., & Bailey, C. (1981, September). Developing age-appropriate leisure skills in severely handicapped adolescents. *Teaching Exceptional Children,* 11–15.

Howe, C. (1984). Leisure assessment instrumentation in therapeutic recreation. *Therapeutic Recreation Journal, 18,* 14–24.

Joswiak, K.F. (1975). *Leisure counseling program materials for the developmentally disabled.* Washington, DC: Hawkins & Associates.

Katch, F.I., & McArdle, W.D. (1983). *Nutrition, weight control, and exercise.* Philadelphia: Lea & Febiger.

Landesman, S. (1986). Quality of life and personal life satisfaction: Definition and measurement issues. *Mental Retardation, 24,* 141–152.

McDowell, C.F. (1983). *Leisure wellness: Concepts and helping strategies.* Eugene, OR: Sun Moon Press.

McDowell, C.F. (1986). Wellness and therapeutic recreation: Challenges for service. *Therapeutic Recreation Journal, 20,* 27–38.

National Recreation and Park Association. (1980a). *Guidelines for administration of therapeutic recreation service in clinical and residential facilities.* Alexandria, VA: National Therapeutic Recreation Society.

National Recreation and Park Association. (1980b). *Standards of practice for therapeutic recreation service.* Alexandria, VA: National Therapeutic Recreation Society.

National Recreation and Park Association. (1982). *Philosophical position of the National Therapeutic Recreation Society.* Alexandria, VA: National Recreation Society.

National Recreation and Park Association. (1986). *Standards for field placement in therapeutic recreation.* Alexandria, VA: National Therapeutic Recreation Society.

Navar, N. (1980). A rationale for leisure skill assessment with handicapped adults. *Therapeutic Recreation Journal, 14,* 21–28.

O'Donnell, M.P., & Ainsworth, T.H. (1984). *Health promotion in the workplace.* NY: John Wiley & Sons.

Ohio Department of Mental Health/Mental Retardation. (1977). *State of Ohio curriculum guide for moderately mentally retarded learners.* Columbus, OH: Author.

Oregon State Department of Education. (1974). *Toward competency: A guide for individualized instruction.* Salem, OR: Special Education Section.

Overs, R., O'Connor, E., & Demarco, B. (1974). *Avocational activities for the handicapped.* Springfield, IL: Charles C Thomas.

Parker, R.A., Ellison, C.H., Kirby, T.F., & Short, M.J. (1975). Comprehensive evaluation in recreation therapy scale: A tool for patient evaluation. *Therapeutic Recreation Journal, 9,* 143–153.

Peterson, C.A., & Gunn, S.L. (1984). *Therapeutic recreation program design: Principles and procedures* (2nd ed.). Englewood Cliffs, NJ: Prentice-Hall.

Pollingue, A.B., & Cobb, H.B. (1986). Leisure education: A model facilitating community integration for moderately/severely mentally retarded adults. *Therapeutic Recreation Journal, 20,* 54–62.

Smith, W. (1983, April). *Active treatment for the developmentally disabled.* Paper presented at a workshop for the North Dakota State Department of Health, Bismark, ND.

Stumbo, N.J. (1983). Systematic observation as a research tool for assessing client behavior. *Therapeutic Recreation Journal, 17,* 53–63.

Teague, M.L. (1986). Comprehensive health assessment: An algorithmic model. *Therapeutic Recreation Journal, 20,* 39–50.

Wehman, P. (1977). *Helping the mentally retarded acquire play skills.* Springfield, IL: Charles C Thomas.

Wehman, P. (1979). *Recreation programming for developmentally disabled persons.* Baltimore: University Park Press.

Wehman, P., & Schleien, S. (1979). *Leisure skills curriculum for developmentally disabled persons.* Richmond: School of Education, Virginia Commonwealth University.

Wehman, P., & Schleien, S. (1980). Relevant assessment in leisure skill training programs. *Therapeutic Recreation Journal, 14,* 9–20.

Wehman, P., & Schleien, S. (1981). *Leisure programs for handicapped persons, adaptations, techniques, and curriculum.* Baltimore: University Park Press.

Wessel, J. (1976). *I can physical education program,* Northbrook, IL: Hubbard Scientific Co.

Westaway, A., & Apolloni, T. (1977). *SCOR curriculum: Volume 1. Independent living skills assessment system.* Sonoma, CA: Sonoma County Organization for the Retarded and Department of Education, Sonoma State College.

Williams, W., & Fox, T. (1977). *Minimum objective system.* Burlington, VT: University of Vermont, Center on Developmental Disabilities.

Witt, P.A. (1979). *Community leisure services and disabled individuals.* Washington, DC: Hawkins & Associates.

Wuerch, B.B., & Voeltz, L.M. (1982). *Longitudinal leisure skills for severely handicapped learners: The Ho'onanea curriculum component.* Baltimore: Paul H. Brookes Publishing Co.

SUPPLEMENTARY RESOURCES

Audiovisuals

Cast No Shadow (16 mm film, color, 27 min.)
Activities for severely mentally retarded, physically handicapped, multihandicapped, and emotionally disturbed children.

Academic Support Center, Film Library Scheduling, 505. E. Stewart Rd., Columbia, MS 65211.

Count Me In (16 mm film, color, 20 min.)
Process of mainstreaming. Shows disabled individuals in work, recreation, and independent living situations.

Stanfield House Film/Media, 12381 Wilshire Blvd., Suite 203, Los Angeles, CA 80025.

Focus on Ability (16 mm film, color, 22 min.)
Techniques and understanding in swimming instruction for individuals with orthopaedic, mental, emotional, and sensory disabilities.

Academic Support Center, Film Library Scheduling, 505 E., Stewart Rd., Columbia, MS 65211.

Like Other People (16 mm film, color, 37 min.)
Controversial British film about the pleasures and problems encountered by a young couple with cerebral palsy.

Academic Support Center, Film Library Scheduling, 505 E. Stewart Rd., Columbia, MS 65211.

Little Marty (16 mm film, color, 5 min.)
Shows Marty (National Foundation–March of Dimes poster boy), who has artificial arms and built-up shoes, feeding himself, painting, typing, playing soccer and softball.

National Foundation–March of Dimes, 800 Second Ave., New York, NY 10017.

Not Just a Spectator (16 mm film, color, 26 min.)
Forty to 50 challenging and satisfying recreation activities for individuals with various handicapping conditions. Includes activities such as mountain climbing, basketball, angling, sailing, kayaking, caving, wheelchair dancing, and more.

International Rehabilitation Film Library, 20 W. 40th St., New York, NY 10018.

Out of Left Field (16 mm film, color, 7 min.)
Shows techniques for integrating blind and visually impaired youths with sighted peers.

American Foundation for the Blind, 15 W. 16th St., New York, NY 10011.

Out of the Shadow (16 mm film, color, 25 min.)
Shows individuals with different handicapping conditions in recreation activities.

Recreation Center for the Handicapped, 207 Skyline Blvd., San Francisco, CA 94132.

To Serve a Purpose (16 mm film, color, 15 min.)
Shows the scope of therapeutic recreation services and populations served.

Academic Support Center, Film Library Scheduling, 505 E. Stewart Rd., Columbia, MS 65211.

Section IV

STAFFING AND OPERATIONAL SUPPORTS

Chapter 18

Strategies for Promoting the Stability of Direct Care Staff

K. Charlie Lakin

This chapter examines the effects of staff turnover on the operation and programs of community-based residential facilities. It describes the magnitude of the problem of staff turnover and discusses the fiscal, management, and treatment consequences of turnover. The chapter also reviews the factors related to instability for direct care workers and suggests mechanisms and strategies that are available to community residence operators for maximizing the desired tenure of workers in such programs.

Residential care for persons with mental retardation in the United States is a large, complex, and costly social enterprise. Total annual costs of institutional and community-based residential facilities for persons with mental retardation was estimated in 1982 at nearly $5.5 billion (Lakin, Hill, & Bruininks, 1985). Of these total costs, payroll costs (i.e., wages, payroll taxes, and fringe benefits) account for about two-thirds of total operating expenditures (Wieck & Bruininks, 1981). In other words, institutional and community-based residential facilities for persons with mental retardation spent over $3 billion in 1982 to provide residential care personnel for approximately 244,000 mentally retarded persons in all types of residential facilities. Persons providing direct care constitute most of the total personnel in these facilities, numbering nearly 135,000 full-time equivalent positions (Lakin & Bruininks, 1981b). On a typical weekday evening in 1982, nearly 40,000 persons were providing direct care to persons with mental retardation (Hill & Lakin, 1986). Presumably, that number would be greater today.

The majority of persons with mental retardation in residential settings now live outside state mental retardation and mental health institutions. While approximately 112,000 persons lived in such facilities at the end of fiscal year 1985, an estimated 130,000 persons lived in other private and/or community-based facilities (Lakin, Hill, Street, & Bruininks, 1986). Correspondingly, of the direct care personnel working in residential settings on a typical weekday evening in June 1985, only an estimated 42% were working in state-operated institutions; the majority were employed in private, "community" facilities (Hill, Lakin, & Bruininks, 1984; Lakin et al., 1986).

Because this text focuses on community-based residential programs, it is useful to focus on factors specifically affecting employee stability in such settings. However, it soon becomes clear that conditions affecting employee stability in community-based residential facilities are not substantially different from those affecting employee stability in public residential facilities, nor for that matter from those operating in other employment settings. Therefore, this chapter focuses on general principles related to direct care staff stability and, then, on how these principles might be applied to community-based residential settings.

EFFECTS OF DIRECT
CARE STAFF INSTABILITY

An analysis of the salary components of the costs of residential care shows clearly that this is a labor intensive industry. Most of the funds allocated to residential services are paid directly to the people who provide it. These individuals convert their own energy, abilities, attitudes, and information into the residential experiences of facility residents. A visit to two facilities operated under the same management will enable a visitor to note clearly how it is the individual direct care staff members who determine what is experienced and accomplished in this industry.

In residential programs, the raw materials, the processes, and even the products are people. The goals and purposes for each residential program, the needs and characteristics of the residents, and the qualities of staff members are all inextricably interrelated. The nature of the "industry" is such that any concern for the welfare of residents cannot be manifested without simultaneous concern for the welfare of the caregivers. Unfortunately, we have not been very successful at meeting the needs of staff members of residential facilities for persons with mental retardation. Because of our difficulties in this area, recruiting, selecting, training, managing, and retaining direct caregivers has become the most consistently stated problem facing residential programs (Bruininks, Kudla, Wieck, & Hauber, 1980; O'Connor, 1976; Office of the Inspector General, 1981).

In recent years there has been growing acknowledgment that these general personnel problems should be a central focus of research. Major studies of rates of turnover of direct care personnel of residential care facilities have documented a generally high average rate of turnover. These have ranged from unacceptably high rates (from 26% to 33% annually) in public institutions (Bensberg & Barnett, 1966; Lakin, Bruininks, Hill, & Hauber, 1982; Scheerenberger, 1978; Zaharia & Baumeister, 1979) to even substantially higher rates in community-based facilities. The most comprehensive analyses of turnover of direct care employees of community-based facilities for

persons with mental retardation have documented rates of 55% to 73% annually (George, 1980; Lakin et al., 1982). These extremely high turnover rates have been particularly discouraging, as privately operated programs have become the predominant model of care and are continuing to grow steadily in number of residents and employees (by an annual estimate of 4,000 and 2,200 respectively).

Program providers, advocates, and researchers have noted several negative effects of direct care staff turnover on the quality and cost-effectiveness of residential care (see Baker, Seltzer, & Seltzer, 1977; George & Baumeister, 1981; Lakin & Bruininks, 1981a; Levy et al., Chapter 19, this volume; Zaharia & Baumeister, 1978, for summaries). These effects include:

1. *Discontinuity of treatment and care.* While rates of employee turnover such as those just noted would be extremely deleterious to the effectiveness of any organization (Katz & Kahn, 1978), they are particularly magnified in settings where dependent persons experience a steady withdrawal of the individuals upon whom they depend for nurturing, consistency, understanding, and individually appropriate habilitation programs. Such qualities of the residential experience are substantially affected by the stability of the relationships between the resident and direct caregiver. What is more, in a time of increasing emphasis on normalized living patterns for developmentally disabled persons, greater concern is naturally being expressed at the abnormality inherent in the high transience of key nurturing figures in the lives of long-term care residents. Since less than 10% of a representative sample of about 2,000 persons with mental retardation in residential facilities see family members once a week or more often (unpublished 1979 data of the Center for Residential and Community Services, University of Minnesota), the importance of these primary relationships should not be underestimated.

2. *Chronic low productivity and staff shortages.* Not only is there a reduction of

care between the time one employee resigns and another is hired and trained, but as new employees fill vacant positions, experienced staff are required to devote some of their normal direct care time to helping to train these new employees. In residential facilities with high staff turnover there is a wide discrepancy between the financed amounts of contact between residents and staff and what actually occurs.

3. *Administrative intensity of personnel replacement process.* A direct relationship has been found (Lakin et al., 1982) between the rates of turnover in residential facilities for persons with mental retardation and the relative size of the administrative staff. As the proportion of total personnel being replaced annually increases, the relative proportion of the organization's staff devoted to that process also tends to increase; conversely, the relative proportion of the organization's staff devoted to direct service necessarily decreases. Like so many of the findings within residential services, this tendency has also been noted in a wide range of industries (Price, 1977).

4. *Direct cost of personnel replacement.* The direct costs of replacing direct care staff of residential facilities are enormous. Zaharia and Baumeister (1978) estimated a direct care staff replacement cost of $1,600 per position in a sample of public residential facilities in 1977. This would equal approximately $2,800 in 1985 dollars. George (1980) estimated that the average cost of replacing staff members in community-based facilities in Tennessee in 1978 was over $500 per position replaced ($800–$850 per position in 1985 dollars). One might further conclude that the difference in estimated cost of replacing public and community facilities employees is a difference borne by residents, as relatively untrained staff more quickly assume full direct-care responsibilities in community-based settings. Available statistics on the number of direct care personnel, their rates of turnover, and the costs of replacement indicate a nationwide annual public cost of

direct care staff turnover of approximately $70–$90 million dollars. Clearly, few problems within the residential services system more seriously impede the effectiveness and efficiency of residential care and treatment for persons with mental retardation than the difficulties associated with recruiting and retaining a stable force of direct care personnel.

Another reason to be concerned about the extremely high turnover rates that plague residential services is that we are simply failing to meet the human needs of a large share of the persons hired in direct care positions. Given the often pronounced dictum that direct care staff comprise the key ingredient in the quality of residential services, it makes sense to focus carefully on ways to simultaneously meet both organizational needs and the human needs of direct care employees.

In so doing, two central questions arise: 1) What types of employees most frequently have their work needs met in direct care roles as currently structured, and 2) What types of structural changes in direct care delivery systems would increase the numbers or types of workers who would find direct care work adequately satisfying?

FACTORS RELATED TO DIRECT CARE STAFF STABILITY

In the late 1970s and early 1980s there was increased interest in direct care staff turnover in residential facilities as its deleterious effects became better understood (Coleman, 1979; Ganju, 1979; George & Baumeister, 1981). The benefits of this research were not limited solely to identifying a problem area deserving serious attention, but also included the identification of factors that could be manipulated in efforts to ameliorate personnel stability problems. For example, research at the Center for Residential and Community Services, University of Minnesota (Lakin & Bruininks, 1981a; Lakin, Hill, Bruininks, & Krantz, 1983) outlined a number of employee characteristics that were highly predictive of staff turnover in a 1-year follow-up of the occupational status of 1,035 direct care staff of the public and community-based residential facilities. Among factors predicting turnover were: 1) age (older employees were more stable); 2) education (the less formal their education, the more stable employees tended to be); 3) length of service (employees with longer lengths of service tended to be more stable); 4) age at initial employment (the older the employees at initial hiring, the more stable they tended to be over the follow-up period); 5) geographic stability (controlling for chronological age; the longer employees had lived in the vicinity of the residential facility, the more stable they tended to be); 6) prior specialized training (at all education levels, employees who were initially hired with no prior training for the position tended to be more stable); 7) reason for initially accepting position (employees who initially accepted the position because of its economic benefits, simple availability, convenience, etc., or because of past rewarding experiences, general interest, or personal satisfaction in working with handicapped adults or children tended to be more stable); 8) job satisfaction (staff members expressing more general satisfaction with their jobs tend to be more stable); and 9) owning/operating one's own facility (owner/operators are more stable than paid employees).

No matter which variables are analyzed with respect to staff turnover, three are consistently found to be the best predictors of staff turnover: 1) *compensation*—actual pay, pay relative to cost of living, satisfaction with pay, appropriateness of pay to education, fringe benefits; 2) *advancement*—either actual or perceived opportunities to advance in an organization; and 3) *opportunities for other employment*—personal employability or general alternative employment opportunities in the area.

In fact, it can be argued that most institutional and demographic factors predicting turnover are directly or indirectly related to these three major variables. For example, if one wants to explain why institutional employees in this sample tended to be more stable than those in community-based facilities, one might start by noting that the public institutions studied paid starting wages averaging 15% or well over $1,000 more per year than community-based

facilities, and that these institutions' fringe benefit packages averaged over twice the value of those provided to community-based staff members. One might further note that there are generally better opportunities for advancement in institutional settings, and that the institutions were much more frequently located in rural areas where other employment opportunities were relatively scarce. Add to this the fact that the public institution programs tended to be much older and therefore had greater proportions of their staffs made up of people with relatively long tenure, and one begins to understand why community-based facilities generally had considerably higher rates of employee turnover. Moreover, if one wished to analyze the many specific and personal variables associated with these causes of staff turnover, each could be found to bear some relationship to the level of compensation, chances for advancement, and/or chances for other employment opportunities. Each of these crucial factors is reviewed next, in reverse order.

Other Employment Opportunities

It is clear from research on direct care staff stability that the general unemployment in an area is strongly associated with staff turnover (Bensberg & Barnett, 1966; Lakin et al., 1982). Low paying or otherwise undesirable jobs tend to be particularly susceptible to such relationships regardless of the industry. In areas where there are greater numbers of job openings, greater numbers of direct care staff will leave their positions to take these other jobs.

In addition to the general level of opportunity in the local economy, the relative opportunities available to individual or potential employee pools are also critical to analyses of staff turnover. For example, the finding that direct care staff with 11 or fewer years of education are about three times less likely to leave positions over a 1-year period than direct care staff with 16 or more years of education (i.e., 11% versus 39% turnover, respectively, Lakin et al., 1983) is related, at least in part, to the relative opportunities that the two groups have for other forms of employment. Similarly, for employees with on-the-job versus formal training, on-the-job training is less readily translatable into economic opportunity in other settings.

Finally, many persons' employment opportunities are limited by their need or desire for nontraditional work patterns. Some people require hours that correspond to specific life patterns or desires, including part-time work or flexible or atypical work schedules. Agencies that can provide employment to people who because of background or need have relatively restricted employment options will, all other things being equal, be able to develop a more stable body of employees.

Chances for Advancement

Opportunity for advancement in one's organization has long been recognized as an extremely important aspect of one's attitude toward a job. Evidence is strong that when workers perceive a chance for advancement in an organization they are more likely to stay with it (Lakin et al., 1983; Lawler, 1971; Porter & Steers, 1973). Human service agencies, particularly smaller private ones, have generally had difficulty offering such opportunities. Two trends in residential services are helping to overcome this problem. The first is the increase in multiple facility organizations, which are able to provide at least limited opportunities to move on a career ladder. These organizations will continue to evolve in meeting the increasing need for expertise in the development and administration of community-based facilities. Second is the expansion in the number of owner-operated facilities. While not directly offering intraorganizational advancement opportunities, such "facilities" often provide an important difference over traditional direct care employment. The impressive stability among caregivers that has been noted in owner-operated residences is probably due to the fact that these residences permit caregivers to: utilize their skills and commitment independent of formal supervision; develop their own programs; realize some capital formation; obtain greater total profit than is typical of direct care pay (although often less per hour); and develop and supplement as needed their chosen work schedule with family members or other employees.

Compensation

For most people, work serves primarily to provide the means for sustenance, and the amount of pay received determines both life-style and social status. Pay for direct care staff positions tends to be very low, and it is probably unreasonable to expect major improvements in stability in this work role unless the extent of compensation is improved or unless there are significant decreases in the salary expectations of persons providing direct care. The fact that the median per hour pay rate for community facility personnel in 1979 was equal to little more than minimum wage represents an enormous problem for the field. Total funds available for employee compensation in community-based facilities must be examined carefully. This process must begin by recognizing that direct care personnel are in effect subsidizing the residential care system with the difference between the salaries they currently receive and what their qualifications would bring on the open employment market. Most who leave this work do so because they simply cannot afford the size of the contribution they are required to make. As greater proportions of the total residential care system consist of community-based facilities, the significance of this discrepancy for residential care in general will continue to grow.

Unfortunately, human service providers cannot dictate what resources will be allocated to the provision of residential care. Therefore, responses are never optimal, but they can be effective. Administrators can be particularly effective in five areas. Briefly, these are:

1. *Maximizing the use of people who promise stability.* Personal factors predicting stability have been discussed previously. To use these effectively in staff selection, we must overcome many current biases within the services system. Young, well-educated specialized professionals may be "ideal" employees in some respects, but certainly not in regard to the degree of interpersonal and social stability they tend to bring to the lives of persons in residential care (by virtue of their being upwardly mobile). It is important to weigh the immediate advan-

tages of hiring certain types of people for direct care roles against the longer-term probability of retaining them.

2. *Maximizing the new and potential employee's knowledge of and ability to perform the job role.* The fact that nearly one-half of the people leaving direct care positions do so in the first 6 months of employment (Lakin et al., 1982) suggests a great need for better job orientation and initial training. Written and experiential orientation to the organization, to the scope of work, and to the potential employee's own feelings about the job seem extremely important given the dramatic rates of turnover immediately following hiring. This has been clearly pointed out by research showing that when former direct care employees return to the job, they are more stable than new ones (Schiers, Giffort, & Furtkamp, 1980). It also suggests the value of seriously considering institution staff members as a potential employment pool for community-based facilities (Scheerenberger, 1981). In addition, all new employees must be guaranteed the training necessary to be successful and to feel successful in the particular tasks given to them.

3. *Communicating that direct care staff members are valuable and valued.* Direct care personnel must sense that the mission of the facility is the same for everyone: that the role of supervisors is to facilitate effective programs, not to supervise employees. Program administrators must demonstrate true concern for employee interests, providing a sense that staff members are the organization and not merely working for it. Stimulating positive relationships between employees, encouraging staff involvement in developing programs and policies, showing recognition of the staff member as an individual (e.g., through recognition of birthdays, children's birthdays, accomplishments away from work), and providing positive feedback for work efforts are all important in making staff feel that they are indeed the cornerstone of residential programs.

4. *Maximizing potentially attractive aspects of the direct care role.* Particular concern for the human needs of workers is crucial to promoting staff stability. Flexibility is especially important. Since this work is not highly technical, it is possible to maintain low divisions of labor. The encouragement of a sense of sharing in the total program is important to both morale and performance (Raynes, Pratt, & Roses, 1977). Flexibility in dividing work hours is important too. This type of work offers exciting possibilities for two- and three-day workweeks for staff at no additional cost to management. It is also highly conducive to allowing staff to create their own work schedules.

5. *Ensuring that positions are well-designed and adequately supplemented.* Generally speaking, a direct-care position is well-designed if it: a) is well-defined in terms of role and function, b) maximizes the individual's decision-making opportunities and control in relation to his or her potential, c) provides opportunities for each caregiver to enjoy a full sense of what is being accomplished (e.g., opportunities to see residents in other settings like school or work, to read reports from other agencies, to meet with residents' family), and d) incorporates objective ways of measuring resident growth (e.g., a list of a few goals or objectives for the resident that each direct-care staff helps to monitor). Positions are adequately supplemented when periods of understaffing are avoided and when other staff members are available to assist at special activities and to serve as replacements in times of illness, personal business needs, and for periods of respite. Staff supplementation is an area in which much creative work needs to be done.

6. *Maximizing the compensation to employees.* Somewhat simplistically, one can say that Direct Care Wages + Direct Care Fringe Benefits = Per Diem Reimbursement − Per Diem Administration and Program Operation Costs × Residents. Application of such a formula helps identify the limited ways available to improve employee compensation. These include:

a. Raise per diem rates and allocate the increase to employee compensation.

b. Lower administrative/program costs and transfer savings to employee compensation (e.g., savings on indirect administration costs; savings on food, medical costs, home maintenance, use of volunteers; efficient use of more costly professionals—for example, using them to train paraprofessional staff rather than to deliver direct services).

c. Identify and provide desired mixes of direct wages and fringe benefits at no increased cost, including allowing employees to select from a menu of possible fringes.

d. Raise productivity (i.e., increase the ratio of resident to paid direct care staff hours). Among ways to increase productivity are:

Increase effort on the part of staff (e.g., fewer staff persons work with the same number of residents).

Modify scheduling of personnel around level of demand for staff time.

Increase use of resources outside the facility to substitute for facility programs or to reduce demands for staff.

Decrease division of labor to increase efficiency of total staff complement.

Increase resident participation in program/facility administration and maintenance activities that would otherwise consume resources.

Staff members themselves should be encouraged to suggest ways to decrease program costs and increase productivity. It is also important to note that compensation is often not strictly wages and benefits. Good organizations take care of their employees in other ways.

SUMMARY

Direct care staff turnover is one of the major problems in the residential services system today. Present rates of employee compensation and opportunities for advancement are the factors most directly related to this problem, and, unfortunately, the near future appears to hold little promise for substantially improved resources. Clearly in the current context it is not easy to respond to the need to increase the employment longevity of the key persons in the lives of persons with mental retardation in residential settings. Responding effectively to the needs of direct care staff members requires considerable sensitivity, creativity, and flexibility. Failure to meet this challenge will continue to undermine the effectiveness and the efficiency of community-based residential care.

REFERENCES

Baker, B.L., Seltzer, G.B., & Seltzer, M.M. (1977). *As close as possible: Community residences for retarded adults.* Boston: Little, Brown.

Bensberg, G.J., & Barnett, C.D. (1966). *Attendant training in southern residential facilities for the mentally retarded.* Atlanta: Southern Regional Education Board.

Bruininks, R.H., Kudla, M., Wieck, C.A., & Hauber, F.A. (1980). Management problems in community residential facilities. *Mental Retardation, 18,* 123–130.

Coleman, T.E. (1979). *An investigation of staff turnover at five Massachusetts mental retardation facilities.* Boston: Massachusetts Department of Mental Health, Division of Mental Retardation.

Ganju, V. (1979). *Turnover trends among MHMR series employees in Texas state schools.* Austin: Texas Department of Mental Health and Mental Retardation.

George, M.J. (1980). *A statewide study of employee turnover in community residential facilities for developmentally disabled persons.* Unpublished doctoral dissertation, George Peabody College for Teachers, Vanderbilt University, Nashville, TN.

George, M.J., & Baumeister, A.A. (1981). Employee withdrawal and job satisfaction in community residential facilities for mentally retarded persons. *American Journal of Mental Deficiency, 85,* 639–647.

Hill, B.K., & Lakin, K.C. (1986). Classification of residential facilities for mentally retarded people. *Mental Retardation, 24,* 107–115.

Hill, B.K., Lakin, K.C., & Bruininks, R.H. (1984). Trends in residential services for people who are mentally retarded: 1977–1982. *Journal of the Association for Persons with Severe Handicaps, 9,* 243–250.

Katz, D., & Kahn, R.L. (1978). *Social psychology of organizations* (2nd ed.). New York: John Wiley & Sons.

Lakin, K.C., & Bruininks, R.H. (1981a). *Occupational stability of direct-care staff of residential facilities for mentally retarded people.* Minneapolis: University of Minnesota, Department of Educational Psychology.

Lakin, K.C., & Bruininks, R.H. (1981b). Personnel management and the quality of residential services for developmentally disabled people. In T.C. Muzzio, J.J. Koshel, & V. Bradley (Eds.), *Alternative community liv-*

ing arrangements and non-vocational social services for developmentally disabled people (pp. 125–170). Washington, DC: Urban Institute.

Lakin, K.C., Bruininks, R.H., Hill, B.K., & Hauber, F.A. (1982). Turnover of direct-care staff in a national sample of residential facilities for mentally retarded people. *American Journal of Mental Deficiency, 87,* 64–72.

Lakin, K.C., Hill, B.K., & Bruininks, R.H. (Eds.). (1985). *An analysis of Medicaid's Intermediate Care Facilities for the Mentally Retarded (ICF-MR) program.* Minneapolis: University of Minnesota, Department of Educational Psychology.

Lakin, K.C., Hill, B.K., Bruininks, R.H., & Krantz, G.C. (1983). Factors related to job stability of direct-care staff of residential facilities for mentally retarded people. *Journal of Community Psychology, 11,* 228–235.

Lakin, K.C., Hill, B.K., Street, H., & Bruininks, R.H. (1986). *Persons with mental retardation in state-operated residential facilities: Years ending June 30, 1984 and 1985 with longitudinal trends.* Minneapolis: University of Minnesota, Department of Educational Psychology.

Lawler, E.E. (1971). *Pay and organizational effectiveness.* New York: McGraw-Hill.

O'Connor, G.O. (1976). *Home is a good place: A national perspective of community residential facilities for developmentally disabled persons.* Washington, DC: American Association on Mental Deficiency.

Office of the Inspector General. (1981). *Placement and care of the mentally retarded: A service delivery assessment.* Washington, DC: U.S. Department of Health and Human Services.

Porter, L.W., & Steers, R.M. (1973). Organizational, work, and personal factors in employee turnover and absenteeism. *Psychological Bulletin, 80,* 151–176.

Price, J.L. (1977). *The study of turnover.* Ames: Iowa State University Press.

Raynes, N., Pratt, M., & Roses, S. (1977). Aides' involvement in decision-making and the quality of care in institutional settings. *American Journal of Mental Deficiency, 81,* 570–577.

Scheerenberger, R.C. (1978). *Public residential services for the mentally retarded: 1977.* Madison, WI: National Association of Superintendents of Public Residential Facilities for the Mentally Retarded.

Scheerenberger, R.C. (1981). Human service person power for developmentally disabled persons. In T.C. Muzzio, J.J. Koshel, & V. Bradley (Eds.), *Alternative community living arrangements and non-vocational social services for developmentally disabled people* (pp. 172–204). Washington, DC: Urban Institute.

Schiers, W., Giffort, D., & Furtkamp, E. (1980). Recruitment source and job survival for direct-care staff. *Mental Retardation, 18,* 285–287.

Wieck, C.A., & Bruininks, R.H. (1981). *The cost of public and community residential care for mentally retarded people in the United States.* Minneapolis: University of Minnesota, Department of Educational Psychology.

Zaharia, E.S., & Baumeister, A.A. (1978). Technician turnover and absenteeism in public residential facilities. *American Journal of Mental Deficiency, 82,* 580–593.

Zaharia, E.S., & Baumeister, A.A. (1979). Technician losses in public residential facilities. *American Journal of Mental Deficiency, 84,* 36–39.

Chapter 19

Training and Managing Community Residence Staff

Philip H. Levy, Joel M. Levy,
Stephen Freeman, Jules Feiman, and Perry Samowitz

The massive growth of the nation's community residence program has caused many agencies sponsoring community residences to reconsider their approaches to recruiting, training, and managing their personnel. This chapter examines how organizational characteristics and management approaches can help an agency cope with a growing personnel component and extrinsic demands of the labor market. The chapter also addresses the training of community residence staff and managers through an examination of organizational philosophy, supervision practices, recruitment of staff, and job enrichment approaches.

The community residence development movement, initially fueled by a generation of "baby boomers" who were often motivated by a desire to help others, has resulted in an expanded community human service industry. This pool of workers, many college educated, facilitated the dramatic expansion of community residences. However, numerous young adults who entered the human services workforce during the 1970s have now moved on to other careers. The consequence has been that well-meaning and humanistically motivated individuals have needed to be supplemented by highly skilled and often business-oriented professionals. A "good heart" is no longer the sole or major criterion for working in the developmental disabilities field. This employment sector is now competing with other social or health-related organizations, as well as commercial, profit-making industries, for talented, dedicated, and skilled employees.

There is also a growing emphasis on the part of lawmakers, government officials, and the general public on the need for efficient and ef-fective human services. The federal deficits and restricted economies of the early 1980s have led legislators to demand more accountability for public dollars spent (Romanatha & Hegsted, 1980). While in the past voluntary providers of services to persons with developmental disabilities were evaluated primarily on the basis of their commitment to "goodness," evaluative criteria have shifted to viewing human services as an industry that must also be cost-effective. Voluntary, not-for-profit organizations are now pressured to improve their efficiency and are closely monitored in the use of public funds.

The human service industry has been slow to develop training and educational programs for their staff (Tropman, 1984). Voluntary human service agencies face a unique obstacle to effec-tive management. They do not have the "push for profit" as a measure of performance. As a result, it is more difficult to measure perfor-mance objectively, and there is a greater poten-tial for the retention of stale and redundant ideas. These problems are compounded by the fact that these organizations exist in an unstable and dependent environment—where their financial supports are less secure and changes are more frequent (Tropman, 1984).

The day-to-day management of such agencies is further complicated by internal pressures, particularly those placed on middle-level management. At this level, program administrators and supervisors are typically overworked and periodically overwhelmed by daily problems demanding their protracted attention. Because of the preoccupation with detailed human problems, the exigencies of daily routines often preclude attention to short- and long-range program planning and management skill building (Tropman, 1984). Further, it is often the case that staff are promoted to management positions because of clinical or programmatic expertise, but with little formal managerial training or experience.

This chapter addresses the training and management of community residence staff and managers, through an examination of organizational philosophy, supervision practices, recruitment of staff, and job enrichment.

ORGANIZATIONAL PHILOSOPHY AND MANAGEMENT STRUCTURES

Most human service agencies have an explicit (or implicit) organizational philosophy that is made operational through its goals and objectives. Some organizations also adapt a management approach whereby managers, consistent with the organizational philosophy, are trained on the job, have a degree of professional autonomy, and have early access to the decision-making process. In the operation of community residences, such a philosophy offers a framework for the provision of services to residents, and also exemplifies the organization's view of and treatment of its staff.

A statement of philosophy should reflect the agency's mission. If management is to achieve the agency's stated mission, then clear goals and objectives should be delineated. Furthermore, a framework of values and ethics should be formulated. Ideally, these values should speak to the rights of residents and staff.

Agencies providing community residential services to persons with developmental disabilities must have a system for controlling and

monitoring the implementation of their goals and objectives. In organizations with relatively few administrative levels, decision making often rests in the hands of a few. This frequently occurs in small agencies that operate a small number of group homes. Such agencies should be viewed differently than large multi-program organizations. In small agencies, the direct communication from house manager to agency director may enable a more consistent decision-making process, whereas in larger organizations, where top management is less capable of making all decisions, decision-making is generally spread within various levels of the organization (Romanatha & Hegsted, 1980). Therefore, the larger the organization and the more layers of management, the greater the need for structured management controls. Romanatha and Hegsted (1980) have noted that ideally the decisions made by operating managers are the same as would have been made by senior management, if they had actually acted.

In addition to its goals and objectives, an organization can often be characterized from the perspective of its planning process. McConkey (1983) notes the importance of planning and the potential roles of various administrative levels in the planning process (see Table 1). For example, different levels of management involve themselves in different aspects of planning. While strategic planning is most often conducted by senior management, short-term planning is frequently done by immediate program managers. Distribution of planning responsibility is usually allocated as shown in Table 1.

Employee participation is an important factor in effective organizations. Japanese researchers, for example, have noted that employee involvement in problem-solving, planning, and decision-making promotes productivity and success (Ouchi, 1981). The ability of an employee to use initiative and imagination in solving work problems is critical to his or her success. The employee is motivated by a feeling of involvement, and ultimately ownership, which can only come from being treated with respect and having one's views valued.

Participatory management processes can be applied to the operation of community residential facilities. Most services to persons with de-

Table 1. Management involvement and planning

Level of management	Short-term planning	Long-term planning	Strategic planning
Top management	Low to medium	Heavy	Heavy
Middle management	Heavy	Medium to heavy	Low to medium
Lower-level management	Medium	Low	None

Source: Adapted from McConkey (1983).

velopmental disabilities are based on the notion that individuals can make decisions by providing them with the necessary tools and resources to make those decisions. The same philosophy and approach can be logically applied to the treatment of staff, such as house managers or residence supervisors. These middle-level managers are the link between agencywide operations and specific program sites. The methods used by various managers may have a profound impact on staff motivation, on productivity, on the likelihood of stress and burnout; on programming; and on the quality of life of residents.

SUPERVISION

In many large organizations, the house manager or supervisor may be the only agency "higher up" that entry-level or direct care staff meet. The supervisor, therefore, represents power and authority, and has the ability to influence a program in many ways (Frost, Wakeley, & Ruh, 1974). Many human service agencies have a supervisory system that facilitates growth in agency employees and, at the same time, elicits their participation in agency operations. This process of supervision is the main structure by which communication among all levels of administration flows (Amacher, 1981; Burns, 1958). Supervision can be defined as a method of transmitting knowledge of skills from the trained to the untrained, from the experienced to the inexperienced, as well as the administrative process for getting work done and maintaining organizational accountability.

The supervision process has three distinct components: educative, supportive, and administrative (Kadushin, 1976). *Educative supervision* is characterized by a process whereby direct care workers are engaged by an individual,

usually the residence supervisor, to discuss issues related to their knowledge of the field, clientele and program. Also, educative supervision provides house staff with feedback about their performance and a chance to plan upcoming steps in program implementation. The supervisor must be knowledgeable in these areas in order to assist the staff and to have them continue to seek assistance. The supervisor must also be resourceful in order to understand the availability of educational resources outside the program or agency. Encouraging participation in a range of educational experiences provided by the agency (e.g., in-service training, seminars, and workshops) can play an integral role in this educational process.

Educative supervision also calls for an awareness that individuals learn best when they are highly motivated to learn. Therefore, the supervisor must explain the usefulness of the content area being taught. Motivation increases as usefulness and content become clear. Making the learning relevant, in terms of the individual's needs and aspirations, is also important.

The atmosphere in which learning takes place may be as crucial as the content and the individual's motivation. Most of us learn best when we can devote our energies to the learning situation. Regularly scheduled supervisory sessions, free of other work demands, help to enable the staff person to focus on the task to be learned. An accepting, supportive learning atmosphere is critical in these sessions. Supervisors should also use a progressive learning approach tailored to the particular needs of each individual, and should positively reward accomplishments as learning takes place.

Supportive supervision has long been overlooked by the profit-making sector, but in many human service agencies it has been used extensively. Since most supervisors in these agencies tend not to be managers by career design or entry, but rather have become so by promotions from clinical or direct service positions, these individuals tend to understand the need and application of support. The roles of a supervisor as cheerleader, coach, confidante, advisor, and friend are now readily accepted for the manager (Peters & Branch, 1972). According to Bloom and Herman (1958), one of the major functions of the supervisor is to provide certain emotional supports for the worker. The supervisor must encourage, strengthen, stimulate, and even comfort and pacify. The supervisor who attempts to alleviate anxiety and guilt and relieve dissatisfaction often replenishes the worker's energies, offers a supportive environment to try new and innovative approaches, and helps to establish an atmosphere where employees are more likely to feel fulfilled. Supportive supervision is therefore concerned with tension management on the job. Tension may stem from perceived "client hopelessness," short-staffed situations, challenges of the supervisory relationship, or family or community opposition. The numerous forms of tension for the direct care worker in a community residence may contribute to a stress-laden work situation.

Administrative supervision is the third component. It has been described as a process of defining and attaining the objectives of an organization through a system of coordinated and cooperative effort (Kadushin, 1976). The supervisor is a key link in this process, holding individuals accountable for their performance and viewing their performance in the context of the agency's ultimate mission and goals. This is often seen as the most important element in any product-oriented organization. Accountability is the "bottom line" of administrative supervision. However, the process leading to this accountability is somewhat complex. Specific tasks need to be delineated clearly and concisely so that the supervisor and supervisee have mutual understanding and expectations. Work assignments need to be specified in such a fashion that they are appropriate to the function of the individual and to the division of labor as defined by the organizational structure. For example, the number of residents assigned to a particular worker in a residential program can be based on a variety of factors: staff member's background and experience, the resident's needs, or the number of staff available to serve the residents. These work assignments should carefully consider many components, and should be a functional part of administrative supervision.

The supervisor serves as a sounding board and liaison between a specific program and the organization as a whole. This is the most critical connection in the management chain.

RECRUITMENT OF STAFF

With the development of increased numbers of community residences, day programs, and innovative community-based support programs for persons with developmental disabilities, a major issue confronting sponsoring service agencies is the recruitment of qualified, motivated staff. The magnitude of the problem has been underscored by Jacobson and Janicki (1984), who noted the near doubling (from 368 to 762) of the number of community residences in one northeastern state within a 4-year period. This tremendous growth in the number of residences has created an intense competition in recruiting capable and qualified staff to work in both new and existing residences.

The problems of recruitment are compounded by misconceptions among prospective employees and the general population about what it means for an individual to have mental retardation or a developmental disability. Aside from special curricula at some 2- and 4-year colleges and universities, there is no formal skill development training program to lay the foundation for serving as a worker in a community residence for mentally retarded/developmentally disabled individuals. Recruitment programs therefore face the challenge of attracting people to a field that is not as readily known as, for example, hospital work, community center work, or foster care. The public education component is clearly a vital aspect of recruitment.

In addition, ongoing assessment must be made of the best use of time and resources in pursuing a particular phase of a recruitment program. For example, a recruitment program may be divided into short-term, medium-term, and long-term efforts. Short-term efforts, such as the placement of help-wanted advertisements, can draw a large number of applicants. However, many of those responding may not be qualified for the positions offered. Careful screening using a structured interview process will allow suitable applicants to be identified and referred to programs in a timely manner.

Medium-term recruitment efforts such as extensive mailings of job listings, as well as flyers to career offices of universities, colleges, and both commercial and public-operated personnel agencies can be successful in referring qualified applicants, but on a less regular basis than advertisements. These efforts may yield valuable returns over time as career and personnel offices become familiar with characteristics that an agency looks for in employees. In this manner, the employment agency may serve as a screening agent. Relationships with career offices and agencies must be cultivated by recruiters in order to provide continuous reinforcement and familiarity regarding the quality of applicants the agency is seeking and knowledge of who would work well in direct care, supervisory, or clinical positions (Heneman, Schwab, Fossum, & Dyer, 1980).

Long-term recruitment efforts consist of networking with areawide high school guidance counselors, university department chairpersons, and specific professors to recruit the best students possible through word of mouth. This approach assures that the agency is able to target a specific population of individuals who could provide referrals, and also enables more extensive education and recruitment activities by providing information on mental retardation/developmental disabilities.

JOB ENRICHMENT

A vacant position in a community residence can have an adverse impact on residents, staff members, and the program supervisor. It can raise tension levels in both staff and residents, and may also create unnecessary pressures on staff because of the assumption of additional responsibilities. Preventing long-term vacancies is one function of management. Therefore, in filling a

vacant position, supervisory staff need to carefully consider the characteristics of the position and the qualities of the person required to fill it. This information should be utilized in conjunction with a detailed reanalysis of the job, as well as in reviewing the background on why the position is open.

Job analysis is a multistep process in which the supervisor evaluates each task/component of the job (Gael, 1983) as well as qualities possessed by individuals who successfully carried out the responsibilities of the position. Prior analyses should be reviewed to look for commonalities that indicate which factors can have the highest likelihood of matching an applicant with the position. Exit interviews should be reviewed to ascertain what in the past caused individuals to leave the position. Although this information may not always be valid because employees may not give their real reasons for leaving, broad trends may be ascertained (Alexander, 1982, p. 14). Supervisors should be asked to consider the past history of their particular program or unit as well as to assess the relative strengths of employees currently under their supervision.

By analyzing the functional requirements of the job and matching these with an applicant's ability and motivation, one would expect an increased likelihood that the employee will be satisfied in the job and confident that he or she has been placed in the right position. The objective is that better services will be provided through a high-quality job performance that could translate into a commitment to the program and to the overall goals of the agency. This, one hopes, will manifest itself through good attendance and an increased length of service (Henemen et al., 1980).

The process just outlined can assist supervisors in knowing that they are not powerless in influencing an employee's decision to leave the agency. Discussions with staff, as part of the individual supervisory meeting, regarding their short- and long-term career plans can lead to the early identification of the possibility that an employee may wish to leave the agency or move on to another position within the organization. Formal discussions relative to the employee's career plans prior to or during a formal performance evaluation can enhance employee retention.

Often, employees can be retained by job enrichment (Howarth, 1984). Most individuals view a career ladder solely in terms of upward mobility. Therefore, self-perceived position and development is indicated by the receipt of a promotion. When a promotion does not occur, many staff may feel frustrated and may prematurely leave an organization. One way of ensuring upward mobility by competent employees is to increase the responsibilities of staff members within their current position (i.e., job enrichment), and to consciously groom staff to assume positions of greater responsibilities 6 to 12 months hence (i.e., future pacing).

For example, if a staff person indicates a desire to be promoted, the supervisor and the employee can develop a plan to enhance the employee's supervisory and administrative skills. A structured program including supervisory responsibilities over volunteers or interns and education about budget management and compliance could be instituted.

The dual process of analyzing the functional characteristics of a position and of examining why the position is open, coupled with the process of "early intervention" to assure that qualified staff are involved in job enrichment programs, can be quite successful. Success can be measured by: 1) the number of individuals promoted to positions of greater responsibility; 2) a feeling on the part of employees involved in job enrichment that the agency is responsive to their career goals and objectives; 3) staff being convinced that avenues exist along which they can pace themselves to assume greater responsibility and that there is a value in remaining with the agency (Howarth, 1984); and 4) reduced turnover and vacancy time.

The recruitment process is an important first step in increasing staff service longevity. The retention of good employees is an essential index of efficiency and quality of service provision. To this end, creative strategies reflecting short-, medium-, and long-term recruitment and retention efforts must be developed and employed. They must also be accompanied by efforts to educate the general public, which

would serve to enhance the image of working with disabled persons, thus attracting more well-qualified employees.

However, vacancies will occur no matter how effective an agency's efforts at retention. Vacancies present an opportunity to examine staff working conditions, training and supervisory practices, and recruitment procedures. Recruitment can be a means of testing labor receptivity of the agency and its policies. The acceptance or rejection of job offers can be a means of assessing wages and benefits and of evaluating worker response to agency goals. Further, as new employees begin work, early intervention using job enrichment and future pacing can set the stage for a potentially long and productive relationship. In order to make staff retention and continuity a reality, proper training must be available to prepare workers for the job, and subsequently, progressive training must be provided to encourage each employee to grow within the organization.

TRAINING STAFF

A number of problems have emerged that have taxed the capabilities of administrators of community residences. In many localities, some staff who work directly with the residents are undereducated (i.e. have little or no formal education and have limited experience in the field of developmental disabilities [Schalock, 1985; Slater & Bunyard, 1983]). In addition, in some instances, an extremely high percentage of staff leave within a year (George & Baumeister, 1981; Lakin, Bruininks, Hill, & Harber, 1982). Hence, management is often faced with poorly trained staff who are not professionally committed to the field as a lifelong career. Yet, these staff members desperately need training to facilitate resident growth.

Management must not simply react to the needs of labor intensive industries, but, rather, must take a proactive course to ensure that its goals are being met (Roberts & Wolf, 1983). When planning any strategy for training, a managerial team must determine if money spent is adequate to meet the perceived gain, which itself must be attainable and measurable. In corporations that are profit oriented, the measurement of a successful venture is the bottom line of a balance sheet. In a nonprofit company, the bottom line is outcome and quality. Thus, a costly process such as staff training needs to be justified.

Specifically, there are three basic goals of training programs: 1) to improve employee productivity; 2) to reduce turnover rate; and 3) to enhance opportunities for employees to be promoted (Fallon, 1983).

Productivity in a service industry often translates into meeting the needs of the service users. For community-based residences, productivity may be assessed in terms of the extent to which the residents attain goals through the efforts of staff. Training programs must be designed to improve the staff's job skills and to have direct application on the job. Well-trained staff are essential for achieving the resident's goals; poorly trained staff impede this progress.

Career path training for staff is intended to reduce turnover among employees. Employee development programs, which are future-oriented, as well as employee training programs, which are present-oriented, are important elements for maintaining and enhancing the quality of staff life. Training programs should follow the following basic principles: 1) learners should understand why the training is important; 2) the training should teach a concrete skill or convey knowledge that is directly applicable to the job; 3) learners should be given an adequate opportunity to practice the skills learned; 4) learners should receive constructive feedback on their performance; and 5) learners should be reinforced for completing the training process (Bittel, 1978).

Pre-service training programs are typically designed to establish and translate the agency's philosophies, principles, and rules into the everyday routines of its workers. For example, at Disney World, new employees are taken through a carefully scripted pre-service program to ensure that Disney World's purpose of entertainment is carried out (Peters & Waterman, 1981). Consequently, pre-service training can begin with a statement of the philosophy and goals of the agency. Because new staff may see themselves as caretakers rather than professionals, an agency should communicate to its residence staff that their main purpose is to provide a warm caring home, teach functional skills, and facilitate peer group interaction. Each staff member acts as a catalyst/facilitator, assisting the developmentally disabled person to achieve a level of functioning better suited to community living and more fulfilling to himself or herself.

Staff also need to know how the system is structured so that they can understand that their ideas are valued and can influence changes in agency practices and policies. This is akin to the concept of quality circles where the workforce is encouraged to be creative, hence improving worker morale and managerial abilities (Blass, 1983).

Pre-service training is important because it enables staff to understand various facets of their job before they actually begin work. A number of aspects of work within a residential program agency need to be covered within a pre-service training program. These include an orientation to the agency's clientele, the basic philosophy of providing services, health and safety issues, sexuality, and service provision practices.

It is important that new staff understand the types of individuals with whom they will be working and what is expected of them in regard to working with the agency's clientele. Staff may have little, if any, experience with a disabled person and may need to both confront their own attitudes and values related to disablement, as well as understand the capabilities and potentials of disabled persons. This is very important, as it sets a constructive tone for staff attitudes and expectations. However, it is also vital to address residents' limitations so as not to engender staff frustration when residents who are more severely impaired do not display rapid progress in acquiring new skills.

The foundation for the agency's practices—its philosophy of care—should be grounded in a belief system that holds all persons in high esteem, no matter how severe their disabilities, and promotes experiences and activities that are typical of the community. Human management belief systems such as those espoused within the tenets of the normalization principle (Wolfensberger, 1973) are used by many residential

program agencies to orient staff in the philosophy of care. A fundamental understanding of
the principles of normalization will serve as a
good foundation for staff practices within the
community residence.

Issues of Health and Safety

Health and safety issues are also important, and
should be covered with staff as soon as possible
after beginning their employment. All staff
should be required to take first-aid and cardiopulmonary resuscitation (CPR) training;
they should also be taught how to deal with
serious injuries and seizures. Frequently, because residents of a residential program may
often have difficulty exercising independent
judgment, staff also need to be trained in decision making and in exercising good judgment in
situations where residents may be endangered
and need protection. Residents in a typical community are exposed to certain dangers in everyday situations such as crossing streets, riding
buses, cooking and cleaning, and using electric
or power equipment. Staff in a community-
based home must be aware of the inherent dangers of community living, while also helping
residents to take advantage of as many opportunities in the community as possible. Staff
should be trained to lessen the risks as much as
possible while allowing for "dignity of risk."

Sexuality

The issue of human sexuality is often laden with
profound emotional overtones. Many agencies
debate whether to even bring up the issue of sex
education because of the fear of negative reaction from family members of the residents.
However, sexuality is an integral part of any
individual's life and requires an open discussion
to result in accurate knowledge and sound judgment. Many agencies want to be clear that
while they neither encourage nor discourage
sexual activity, they seek to facilitate a resident's understanding of sexuality. Staff are told
that the resident should receive counseling and
teaching regarding the privacy and appropriateness of various behaviors. Staff also come to
the job with their own values, attitudes, and
prejudices concerning sexuality. It is constructive to have them contend with both their own

feelings about sexuality and the sexuality of the
residents. Consequently, including the topic of
sexuality within the pre-service training program can prevent misunderstandings and problems once the staffperson is on the job.

To reiterate, a pre-service training program
should include, at a minimum, the philosophy
of a given agency, an understanding of who the
residents are and of how the agency's philosophy affects the treatment and care of the residents, and basic health and safety topics. If pre-
service training is conducted at a site other than
the community residence, the manager of the
home should review this information with the
new employee, including any aspects specific
to the residence, before the employee begins
work.

Many residential program agencies operate a
number of homes, each of which has a different
mix of residents, depending on the residents'
age, sex, level of intellectual impairment, or
physical handicap. Since, in many instances,
the major differences that staff must adapt to are
those attributed to variations in intellectual impairment, some agencies conduct separate training programs for staff who work with severely
and profoundly impaired residents and for those
who work with mildly and moderately impaired
residents.

Training to Work with Severely
and Profoundly Retarded Persons

When training staff to work with severely and
profoundly retarded residents, agencies need to
first stress that these residents can learn and
achieve. Gold (1975), in his *Try Another Way*
techniques, clearly demonstrated that severely
handicapped individuals can perform complex
tasks through proper training. Similarly, it has
been shown that persons with severe handicaps
can perform in competitive job settings, given
the proper conditions (Brown et al., 1983).
Also, any training must concentrate on those
skills that are critical for residents to learn in
order to better negotiate their environment
(Adams & Sternberg, 1982).

In addition, staff who work with severely and
profoundly retarded persons require a different
level of skills than those who work with mildly

retarded persons, because of the severity of the disabilities (Foxx, 1982). In working with severely and profoundly retarded individuals, staff need intensive training in behavioral techniques, as well as in the use of feedback or reinforcement procedures and in prompting and fading techniques to strengthen positive behaviors (Foxx, 1982; Van Houten, 1980).

To ensure that staff comprehend the approach and perform the skill properly, role-playing and videotapes can be utilized in the training sessions. Simulations can be set up in which staff role-play working with a resident and demonstrate the skills they have learned (Cooper, 1974).

Training to Work with Moderately and Mildly Retarded Persons

When training staff to work with residents who have moderate or mild retardation, staff should be adept at enhancing behavioral, affective, and cognitive abilities. Consequently, staff should be trained to motivate the residents by utilizing proper behavioral feedback techniques, and should also understand the emotional needs of residents.

Mildly handicapped residents need to learn how to better solve problems by developing new adaptive skills. Valuable techniques are those that teach residents strategies to think through problems, not merely to perform the task at hand (Feuerstein, 1980). For example, to teach a resident to vacuum a room, staff first have to train the resident to understand that a problem exists by utilizing all their senses to interact with the environment. They then teach the resident to label the various parts of the room and to plan a strategy for vacuuming, and finally to be precise in checking his or her work.

New staff need to understand that mildly impaired residents may often need more emotional support, because they have a greater understanding of who they are and what their handicap is than does a severely profoundly handicapped person. Because mildly impaired residents sometimes are more aware of the negative attitudes of nonhandicapped people, staff also need training in providing sensitive counseling to help them cope with this problem.

The combination of staff working at three training levels leads to a definable outcome, as reflected in evaluation. If a number of staff do not exhibit a given skill, then the system needs to be reevaluated in terms of how the skill was taught and whether staff practice time was sufficient.

While basic skills are fairly generic when beginning to teach staff to work with residents, unique needs do arise in each residence. A training system should address the ongoing needs of staff in the particular program. Many agencies in the mental retardation field do have continuing in-service training programs. Nevertheless, in our experience numerous complaints are heard from staff that the in-service training is irrelevant and that it contains too much lecturing. Staff training should be applicable to the day-to-day realities of the job, and should teach concrete skills to help staff work more effectively with residents (Bittel, 1978). Two vignettes illustrate some examples of creative training sessions that can be useful in teaching job skills.

Vignette #1

At a suburban community residence serving impaired adults with mild mental retardation, some staff felt pressured by what they perceived as demands placed upon them by family members of residents. These demands resulted in strained relations between staff and families, with staff feeling unappreciated for the good work they felt they were doing. After assessing the problem, the agency operating the community residence requested its training department to devise a training session on how to relate effectively to family members. The trainers prepared a videotape illustrating recommended and not-recommended ways of relating to different personality types among family members (e.g., authoritarian, passive, indulgent, etc.). After the staff had observed the training tapes, they participated in practice exercises involving role-playing. As they learned to use these newly acquired skills, their morale improved and good relations between staff and residents' families were achieved.

Vignette #2

At a small urban residence with seven severely impaired adolescents, staff were constantly over-prompting their residents. The training department created a video-game exercise that not only taught staff the appropriate prompt levels but made learning more enjoyable. On the tape the staff saw a house counselor helping a resident clean up after dinner. Staff were challenged to figure out which prompt was needed to get a resident to perform each given task. This exercise was complex, because within approximately 30 seconds, nine different tasks were performed. The staff next reviewed the tape to find out how many prompt levels they had correctly identified. Each staff person was then given an opportunity to practice the skill while being videotaped, and then to critique his or her own work with the aid of a facilitator. This "game" made training more enjoyable, and reinforced learning. The skill level of the staff was greatly improved after the training.

Training Managers

Another concern is the training offered managers of community residences. When an employee shows the capacity for promotion to management, he or she should be encouraged to pursue this career path. Employees who are given career path training have shown positive improvement in attitude and performance (Bittel, 1978). While some agencies in the mental retardation field promote the best house counselor, the skills of counseling and management do not always correspond. Training is needed to ensure that the prospective manager can truly perform the varied tasks of the new job. It is recommended that a career path system be set up whereby managerial candidates are first promoted to an assistant level before moving to a full management position. In developing a plan, objectives must be clearly delineated, defining the skills needed to manage staff. The training should allow the participant to practice and receive feedback on the skills learned. Although managers should be exposed to a wide range of topical areas, many agencies include the following topics in their training programs for new managers or assistant managers:

1. Managing and communicating with people. (Managers require good listening skills when supervising their staff [McGraw-Hill, 1983].)
2. Personnel practices. (Managers need to know the parameters of their authority and responsibility and the policies and procedures of their agency.)
3. Interviewing techniques. (In many community residences, the managers are responsible for interviewing new staff.)

4. Leadership and motivational skills. (Setting an example for work is an important management asset.)
5. How to run meetings. (Meetings are a way of life for most organizations [McConkey, 1983].)
6. The management process. (Most literature on management breaks it down into a step-by-step process of planning, organizing, directing, and controlling [Bittel, 1978; McConkey, 1983; Terry, 1977].)
7. Disciplinary action. (Managers need to know the disciplinary process to follow if staff do not fulfill the requirements of the job.)
8. Evaluation. (Evaluation measures job performance against job requirements [Terry, 1977].)

SUMMARY

This chapter has focused on the problems and means of training and managing staff to work within a residential program agency at the staff and middle-management level. An agency must first have an organizational philosophy to guide its work with its clientele and employees. Second, an agency must have staff supervision, recruitment, and retention practices that enhance its ability to attract and retain capable staff.

A sound organizational philosophy allows senior management to influence decisions at all levels and provides a framework both for the development of concrete objectives and for a corporate personality. An effective management style is one that involves all levels of the organization to the greatest degree possible. The crucial link in this organizational structure is the program supervisor, who bridges the gap between administration and program.

The most significant problem in the management of community residences is the recruitment and retention of staff. To address this problem, agencies must have policies and procedures that reinforce staff through job enrichment, future pacing, and career path training. Obviously, problems and practices will vary from agency to agency and will be greatly influenced by geography, labor availability, and the size of the agency. The material presented here is a context for agency practices in management and training, adaptable to a range of conditions and situations.

REFERENCES

Adams, G., & Sternberg, L. (1982). *Educating severely and profoundly handicapped students.* Rockville, MD: Aspen Systems.

Alexander, G.G. (1982). *Human resources management planning.* New York: American Management Association.

Amacher, K. (1971). *Explorations into the dynamics of learning in field work.* Doctoral dissertation, Smith College School of Social Work, New York.

Bittel, L.R. (1978). *Encyclopedia of professional management.* New York: McGraw Hill.

Blanchard, M., & Tager, M. (1985). *Working well: Managing for health and high performance.* New York: Simon & Schuster.

Blass, W.P. (1983). Worker morale. In K. J. Albert (Ed.), *Strategic management handbook.* New York: McGraw-Hill.

Bloom, L. & Herman, C. (1958). A problem of relationship in supervision. *Journal of Social Casework, 39,* 402–406.

Brown, L., Ford, A., Nisbet, J., Van Deventer, P., Sweet, M., York, J., & Loomis, R. (Eds.). (1983). Teaching severely handicapped students to perform meaningful work in non-sheltered vocational environments. In *Educational programs for severely handicapped students: Vol. 13* (pp. 1–100). Madison, WI: Madison Metropolitan School District.

Burns, M. E. (1958). *The historical development of the process of casework supervision as seen in the professional literature of social work.* Doctoral dissertation, School of Social Service Administration, University of Chicago.

Cooper, R. (1974, November). Simulated supermarket. *Training,* 37–40.

Fallon, W.K. (Ed.). (1983). *AMA management handbook.* New York: AMACOM.

Feuerstein, R., in collaboration with Rand, Y., Hoffman, M., & Miller, R. (1980). *Instrumental enrichment.* Baltimore: University Park Press.

Foxx, R. (1982). *Decreasing behaviors of severely retarded and autistic persons.* Champaign, IL: Research Press.

Frost, C., Wakeley, J., & Ruh, R. (1974). *The Scanlon Plan for organization development: Identity, participation, and equity.* East Lansing: Michigan State University Press.

Gael, S. (1983). *Job analysis: A guide to assessing work activities.* San Francisco: Jossey-Bass.

George, M.J., & Baumeister, A.A. (1981). Employee withdrawal and job satisfaction in community residential facilities for mentally retarded persons. *American Journal of Mental Deficiency, 85*(6), 639–647.

Gold, M. (1975). *Try another way* [film training series]. Indianapolis, IN: Film Products of Indianapolis.

Heneman, G., Schwab, P., Fossum, A., & Dyer, D.

(1980). *Personnel/human resource management.* Homewood, IL: Richard D. Irwin.

Howarth, C. (1984). *The way people work: Job satisfaction and the challenge of change.* Oxford, England: Oxford University Press.

Jacobson, J.W., & Janicki, M.P. (1984, August). Trends in staff in a large community residence system 1980–1983. Paper presented at the 92nd annual meeting of the American Psychological Association, Toronto.

Kadushin, A. (1976). *Supervision in social work* (pp. 39–198). New York: Columbia University Press.

Lakin, K.C., Bruininks, R.H., Hill, B.K., & Harber, S.A. (1982). Turnover of direct care staff a national sample of residential facilities for mentally retarded people. *American Journal of Mental Deficiency, 87,* 64–72.

McConkey, D.D. (1983). *How to manage by results.* New York: AMACOM.

McGraw-Hill. (1983). Managing people, communicating with people. *McGraw-Hill supervision workbooks.* New York: McGraw-Hill.

Ouchi, W.G. (1981). *Theory 2.* New York: Bard, Camelot, Discus, and Flare.

Peters, T., & Branch, C. (1972). *Blowing the whistle: Dissent in the public interest.* New York: Praeger.

Peters, T., & Waterman, R. (1981). *In search of excellence.* New York: Warner Communications.

Roberts, R.G., & Wolf, M.G. (1983). Training. In K.J. Albert (Ed.), *Strategic management handbook.* New York: McGraw-Hill.

Robinson, H., & Robinson, N. (1975). *The mentally retarded child.* New York: McGraw-Hill.

Romanatha, K.V., & Hegsted, L.P. (1980). *Readings in management control of non-profit organizations.* New York: John Wiley & Sons.

Schalock, R.L. (1983). *Staff development: In-services for developmentally disabled adults.* Baltimore: University Park Press.

Schalock, R.L. (1985). Comprehensive community services: A plea for interagency collaboration. In R.H. Bruininks & K.C. Lakin (Eds.), *Living and learning in the least restrictive environment* (pp. 37–64). Baltimore: Paul H. Brookes Publishing Co.

Slater, M.A., & Bunyard, P.D. (1983). Survey of residential staff roles, responsibilities, and perception of resident needs. *Mental Retardation, 21*(2), 52–58.

Terry, R. (1977). *Principles of management.* Homewood, IL: Richard D. Irwin.

Tropman, J.H. (1984). *Policy management and human services.* New York: University Press.

Van Houton, R. (1980). *How to motivate others through feedback.* New York: H & H Enterprises.

Wolfensberger, W. (1973). *Orientation manual on mental retardation.* Toronto: National Institute on Mental Retardation.

Chapter 20

Staff and Manager Competencies

Sara N. Burchard and Jacqueline Thousand

Research indicates that the attitudes and competence of direct care staff are of utmost importance in advancing program goals, achieving increased independence, enhancing community integration, and improving adjustment of mentally retarded persons living in community settings. This chapter examines the literature to identify those relevant characteristics and competencies of staff and managers of small community residences that are linked to job satisfaction, job tenure, competent performance, and desired resident and program goals. Methods are explored for addressing staffing needs, such as staff training, organizational supports, and utilization of competency-based staff selection and training. Procedures for developing and validating staff competencies are also presented.

Since the inception of community residential service systems for persons with developmental disabilities, the recruitment, training, and retention of high-quality staff have been identified as among the most important problems facing administrators and professionals (Bruininks, Kudla, Wieck, & Hauber, 1980; Lakin, Bruininks, Hill, & Hauber, 1982; McCord, 1981; Morreau, 1985; O'Connor, 1976; Schalock, 1983, 1985). Further, direct care staff are critical to the provision of quality programming (Baker, Seltzer, & Seltzer, 1977; McCord, 1981; O'Connor, 1976). Such staff provide training, social integration opportunities, supervision, and direct care to residents. Despite this critical role, the majority of community residence staff are paraprofessionals and are often the least educated, trained, or experienced in providing developmental services to

persons with retarded development (Schalock, 1985; Slater & Bunyard, 1983). Moreover, annual turnover rates of between 50% to 85% (George & Baumeister, 1981; Lakin, Bruininks, & Hill, 1982) are costly both administratively and programmatically (Lakin, Bruininks, & Hill, 1982; McCord, 1981; O'Connor, 1976).

For these reasons, hiring, training, and retaining qualified staff have been priority concerns of administrators and professionals involved in the provision of community residential programs (Schalock, 1983). A significant prerequisite to the resolution of these concerns, however, is the delineation of specific skills and qualities that constitute quality staff performance.

This chapter examines the literature on the characteristics and competencies of primary

We wish to acknowledge the contribution of the Vermont Department of Mental Health, service providers, consumers throughout the state of Vermont, and particularly Ronald Melzer, Ph.D., director of Community Mental Retardation Programs, the office that supported the research on which much of this chapter is based.

care providers that are associated with program quality in small community residences. Staff retention, burnout, and associated factors are analyzed; and the personal and occupational factors associated with staff competencies are considered within the framework of a number of studies that the writers conducted in this area. Included also are suggestions for what to consider when selecting staff. The writers also examine some of the assumptions made about desirable staffing practices and comment on the most pressing needs for further research and directions for program development.

Our focus is on group community residences serving no more than 8 to 10 individuals in settings whose rehabilitation intent is to assist residents to achieve greater personal independence and community integration through the provision of training and habilitation within a typical home living environment (Janicki, Jacobson, & Schwartz, 1982). Small-group residences are the fastest growing segment of community residential services; by 1982 they accounted for over a quarter of all community living alternatives (Hill, Lakin, & Bruininks, 1984). In these residences, both managers and staff are in direct contact with residents and may serve as primary caregivers. These group living settings include residences identified in the literature as group homes, staffed apartments, and other community living alternatives.

CARE PROVIDERS AND RESIDENT ADJUSTMENT

Research investigating community integration and adjustment of mentally retarded persons has shown that environmental factors affect the acquisition of adaptive living skills, autonomy, community use, social interactions, social support, and normalized life-styles of these individuals (Bjaanes & Butler, 1974; Burchard et al., 1987; Eyman, Demaine, & Lei, 1979; Hull & Thompson, 1981; Seltzer, 1981; Willer & Intagliata, 1981). Among the many factors examined, caregiver characteristics have been identified as being especially important to resident adjustment and integration (Burchard et al., 1987; Intagliata & Willer, 1982; Intagliata, Willer, & Wicks, 1981; Sutter, Mayeda, Yee, & Yanagi, 1981).

Care Providers and Community "Success"

Success or failure to remain in a community-living arrangement is a measure of resident adjustment and appears to be highly affected by primary care providers. For example, Sutter et al. (1981) found that when there was a good match between the careproviders' level of tolerance for maladaptive behaviors and the maladaptive behaviors of the resident, the resident was more likely to remain there; whereas when there was a mismatch, residents tended to leave. Also, more experienced providers tended to retain residents as compared to less-experienced providers, even though both groups had residents who exhibited similar levels and types of maladaptive behaviors (Sutter, 1980; Sutter, Mayeda, Call, Yanagi, & Yee, 1980; Sutter et al., 1981).

Willer, Intagliata, and their colleagues (Intagliata & Willer, 1982; Intagliata et al., 1981; Willer & Intagliata, 1981) found that less competent foster careproviders had residents with more behavior problems 2 to 4 years after placement, and that group home staff tolerated more interpersonal maladaptive behavior than did foster care providers. Schalock, Harper, and Genung (1981) also reported that resident "success" (i.e., no reinstitutionalization) for persons manifesting similar behaviors was related to staff tolerance and attitudes.

Studies such as these validate the importance of caregivers' attitudes, experience, and tolerance with regard to managing individuals with behavior problems in community settings and preventing reinstitutionalization. Since the manifestation of behavior problems has consistently been shown to be a major impediment to community integration, matching care provider characteristics, attitudes, and skills to resident characteristics is an important administrative step (Hill & Bruininks, 1984; Morreau, 1985; Sutter et al., 1981).

Care Providers and Adaptive Living Skills

Care provider characteristics have also been shown to be related to the *performance* of skills of daily and community living. Caregiver expectations and promotion of independence have been found to be associated with resident independent functioning in studies across community residential types (Burchard, Hasazi, Gordon, Rosen, & Dietzel, 1986; Butler & Bjaanes, 1977; Hull & Thompson, 1980; Seltzer, 1981). Care provider characteristics have also been shown to be related to *acquisition* of community skills. Flexible, resident-oriented, normalization practices have been linked to skill acquisition (Eyman et al., 1979), while rigid rules and protective attitudes have been linked to lack of progress (Willer & Intagliata, 1981). Caregivers who encouraged independence and new behaviors had residents who increased their levels of community-living skills (Intagliata et al., 1981). In two studies of group homes, those managers and manager candidates who were assessed as having greater behavioral competence were those who, after employment, had instituted more data-based training plans for teaching residents skills (Burchard, Pine, Widrick, & Creedon, 1985; Burchard et al., 1987).

Care Providers and Community Integration

Areas of resident success that have been consistently associated with care provider characteristics include promotion of resident activities and degree of community use. These are usually more a function of care provider interests, expectations, attitudes, and supports than of type of residence or number of residents (Bjaanes & Butler, 1974; Butler & Bjaanes, 1977, 1978). In studies of foster homes, care providers play a key role in facilitating community integration of residents (Intagliata et al., 1981; Sherman, Frenkel, & Newman, 1984). Caregivers who were rated as more competent as well as being younger, and who had higher levels of psychological well-being, promoted more community integration opportunities for residents, especially for those who were more disabled (Willer & Intagliata, 1981). In studies of group homes and small intermediate care facilities for persons with mental retardation (ICFs/MR), involvement in community activities by residents was also found to be highly related to living in homes whose managers were competent in normalization implementation (Burchard, Pine, & Gordon, 1984; Burchard et al., 1987). Essentially, degree of community

use was not related to the severity of the resident's handicapping condition nor to residence type (whether the program was an ICF/MR or a regular group home).

Care Providers and Social Adjustment

Although staff characteristics have been viewed as critical to the social support and adjustment of residents (Baker et al., 1977; Landesman-Dwyer, 1981; McCord, 1981; O'Connor, 1983), studies demonstrating this are relatively rare. In a study of 57 moderately and mildly retarded persons living in group homes, personal satisfaction was high in homes with more competent managers, with good interpersonal relations, and more community integration opportunities (Burchard et al., 1984). Seltzer (1981) found greater resident satisfaction in homes with supportive staff. In foster care and group homes, social support from family visits was related to care provider efforts (Willer & Intagliata, 1981). These few studies provide some empirical evidence that care provider characteristics are important factors in the social support and personal satisfaction of group home and foster home residents.

The critical relationship of care provider characteristics, attitudes, preferences, and competencies to resident adjustment and community integration in small community residences is suggested by the studies noted here. Caregiver qualities have been related to resident tenure in the community, degree of community integration, performance and acquisition of adaptive daily and community-living skills, social supports, and resident satisfaction.

STAFF RETENTION AND PROGRAM QUALITY

Organizational and personal characteristics are associated with staff staying or leaving jobs in the human services field. In an effort to suggest solutions to the problems of staffing community programs, factors related to staff turnover, staff satisfaction, and staff burnout are considered next.

Staff Satisfaction and Job Tenure

When job satisfaction within community residences is examined, staff report a greater degree of satisfaction with coworkers, supervision, and the nature of the work than with pay or advancement opportunities (George & Baumeister, 1981; Zigman, Schwartz, & Janicki, 1984), and greater satisfaction with resident-related activities than with other aspects of their job (Bersani & Heifetz, 1985). In one study, only a third of the personnel leaving cited job dissatisfaction as the primary reason. Quality of interactions with residents was the main reason cited for staying (George & Baumeister, 1981). However, the group home programs that were examined were only a few years old at the time of the studies, and it is known that both job retention and satisfaction are frequently low in the first years of programs (George & Baumeister, 1981; Lakin, Bruininks, & Hill, 1982).

In an investigation of job stability and job satisfaction in a national sample of some 1,200 direct care residential staff drawn from a cross-section of all types of community and institutional residential settings, staff demographics rather than job satisfaction was more predictive of remaining on the job for at least 1 year (Lakin, Bruininks, & Hill, 1982). Satisfaction with extrinsic work factors was also related to staying. In a group home study, Bersani and Heifetz (1985) also found that measures of caregiver work-related satisfaction (but not resident-related satisfaction) were positively associated with care providers' length of job tenure.

In a University of Minnesota national survey, community residences with 15 or fewer residents had a higher rate of staff satisfaction, were more highly rated as homelike environments, and had greater resident autonomy and activity. These homes, however, had residents who were less disabled than larger residences (Rotegard, Hill, & Bruininks, 1983). When resident ability, residence size, and other factors were statistically controlled, staff job satisfaction was a predictor of resident autonomy and, to a lesser degree, of resident activities. In a controlled study of staff training in group homes, less *decline* in satisfaction after staff training was also associated with increases in positive attitudes toward residents and more frequent and appropriate social interactions with

them (Schinke & Landesman-Dwyer, 1981; Schinke & Wong, 1977).

These studies provide an indication of a relationship between staff satisfaction and certain characteristics of the treatment environment such as more autonomy, greater involvement in activities, and increased interactions for residents. The studies also suggest that some aspects of job satisfaction, particularly aspects related to extrinsic work factors, may be related to job tenure. The relationship of job tenure to quality staffing is examined next.

Staff Characteristics and Tenure

It is commonly assumed that programs and residents will benefit from having staff remain in their position over a long period of time. Many authors point to the role of staff or care providers in providing a stable environment for training, for long-term interpersonal relationships, and for nurturing and understanding (Bruininks et al., 1980; George & Baumeister, 1981; Lakin, Bruininks, & Hill, 1982; Rotegard et al., 1983). Sanderson and Crawley (1982) examined the vocational preferences, attitudes, and interests of 55 family caregivers, comparing those who remained in the service system with a group that had terminated. Care providers who left the field were young and "enterprising" (as characterized by Holland's [1973] vocational interest/personality category). Those who remained were older, less educated, and were characterized as "conventional" or "realistic" in terms of Holland's categories. The age and vocational interest findings were similar to those of other studies of staff turnover where younger, more highly educated, career-oriented persons left employment in institutional (Zaharia & Baumeister, 1978) and community settings (Lakin, Bruininks, & Hill, 1982; Lakin, Bruininks, Hill, & Hauber, 1982). Stability, then, appears to be at the expense of staff who are better educated, better trained, and motivated by "professional" reasons. Stable staff are older, often hired at an older age, less educated, and motivated by other than career interests (Bersani & Heifetz, 1985; Lakin, Bruininks, Hill, & Hauber, 1982; Zaharia & Baumeister, 1978).

In the national sample of residential settings, Lakin, Bruininks, and Hill (1982) found that job termination was not related to quality of job performance; exceptional employees were as apt to leave as poor ones. This was true of public as well as nonpublic residential settings. This study also showed that although small community residences (i.e., those with six or less residents) had the highest separation rate (87% annually), most staff stayed for 1 year and then left. In larger residences and institutions, a considerable proportion of those who left, did so within the first 3 months of their employment (Lakin, Bruininks, & Hill, 1982; Zaharia & Baumeister, 1978, 1979). Since leaving is not correlated with quality of job performance, it is important to examine the characteristics of that group of "stayers" who are also *quality* caregivers as based upon some acceptable criteria of competent performance or resident benefit.

Several recent studies that surveyed employees in small community residences in New York and Vermont reported staff who were educated (2 or more years of college), experienced in the field (5 years with an average of 3 years on the job), fairly young (median age late 20s and early 30s), and predominately female (two out of three) (Bersani & Heifetz, 1985; Burchard et al., 1987; Janicki, Jacobson, Zigman, & Gordon, 1984). These findings suggest that some states can claim a cadre of experienced and educated caregivers working in small residences.

Burnout and Program Quality

Human services is a field with high interpersonal stress frequently leading to burnout. Burnout is a phenomenon of emotional distancing and detachment from clients that occurs in some service providers as a coping mechanism for dealing with intense pressures (Freudenberger, 1975; Maslach, 1976). Burnout does not necessarily lead to staff turnover, but to objectification and dehumanization of persons served. Among the strategies employed to reduce burnout are frequent support groups and meetings at which problems are discussed; opportunities to leave work behind; opportunities

for time-out from direct contact with clients when needed; increased variety in work tasks with increased length of employment; lower client/staff ratios; and training in interpersonal skills (Maslach, 1976). However, in small community residences, opportunities are limited for staff development, support groups (Ebert, 1979; Fiorelli, 1982; Slater & Bunyard, 1983) and training that emphasizes the development of interpersonal skills and value-based attitudes (Schalock, 1985; Schinke & Wong, 1977; Thousand, Burchard, & Hasazi, 1986).

Research examining the issues of stress and burnout in small community residences is limited. One such study found that stress and burnout were present at moderate levels for group home staff (Fimian, 1984). Staff characteristics (unspecified) were the most predictive aspect of stress and burnout. Another such study reported that resident characteristics created more job stress than work-related characteristics for staff of 19 small-group homes (Bersani & Heifetz, 1985). However, stress was *not* related to job satisfaction nor to any staff characteristics including length of employment.

Research regarding caregiver retention and program quality in small community residences suggests that the most competent care providers are not necessarily those who remain on the job for an extended period of time. Research from related service fields suggests that long-term employment without a job change may be *undesirable* in that it can lead to a decrease in quality of interaction and service to clients. The assumption that staff job tenure necessarily promotes quality programs has been questioned (Janicki et al., 1984). However, as already noted, there is evidence that a cadre of experienced, educated, fairly young persons are remaining in the community residential workforce for several years. As suggested earlier, the characteristics of the competent providers among them need to be studied. Strategies used to reduce burnout in related fields, including training in interpersonal skills, staff development opportunities, and job changes within the service system, also need to be employed and evaluated with respect to their effectiveness in maintaining quality staff for community residences. The next section addresses staff competency.

PROVIDING COMPETENT CAREPROVIDERS FOR COMMUNITY RESIDENCES

Identifying Manager and Staff Competencies

Competencies are those skills, knowledge, and behaviors that enable employees to do their job, that is, to assist residents in attaining their habilitation goals. Competencies are the staff activities that mediate those goals or resident outcomes. In the identification of competencies the following steps should be taken: 1) define clearly desired resident outcomes; 2) determine staff activities or performances that enable or mediate those outcomes; and 3) demonstrate empirically that the performance competencies do lead to or are related to the desired outcomes.

Identifying Program Goals Desired resident outcomes should directly reflect the stated goals of the residential program. Staff competencies may be quite different from one community residential program to the next, depending upon the program's stated goals and associated outcome measures. For example, if the overall goal of a program is to increase independence of residents in home and community settings, the role of staff becomes that of mentor or facilitator of independence. Staff competencies should operationalize this teacher/facilitator role. If the stated program goal is to provide residents with an enduring emotionally and socially supportive living environment, the role of staff becomes that of friend or giver of ongoing social and emotional support. Staff competencies should then facilitate this supportive friendship role. Major program goals need to be explicit before useful competencies can be identified.

Methods of Competency Identification Staff performances should lead to the explicit program goal outcomes. A number of methods have been employed to generate competency statements for human service jobs; these include expert opinion, job function analysis, and critical incident analysis. Expert opin-

ion is the most widely used method (Pottinger & Goldsmith, 1979) and has been applied to identify competency among staff of community residential facilities (Bernstein & Ziarnik, 1982; Kane, 1982; RCA Services Company, 1979) as well as among practitioners of applied behavior analysis techniques (Sulzer-Azaroff, Thaw, & Thomas, 1975). In most cases, the "experts" have consisted of notable authors, employers, and supervisors of practitioners, in addition to university-based trainers who have translated coursework into skills to be acquired (Burke & Cohen, 1977; Horner, 1977; Wilcox, 1979; York et al., 1979). Competencies for applied behavior analysis practitioners were developed from a comprehensive survey of nationally known behavioral experts. Competencies were identified in the following areas: 1) the behavior modification model; 2) assessment, goal formation, and setting of priorities; 3) ethics; 4) behavioral observation; 5) measurement; 6) program design; 7) behavioral procedures; 8) communication; 9) consultation and training; 10) administration; and 11) research (Sulzer-Azaroff et al., 1975). These behavior analysis competencies have become the cornerstone of programs preparing educators and caregivers of individuals with severe handicaps (Fiorelli, 1979; Hogan, 1974).

In spite of its popularity, the expert opinion approach has been characterized by Pottinger and Goldsmith (1979) as the least valid method of competency identification. Experts may be more involved in administration or training than in the actual practice of the profession, and tend to emphasize abilities that, in practice, are relatively unimportant (Kane, 1982). Social validation of competencies generated by actual practitioners can strengthen the expert opinion approach, but this has happened only rarely (National Institute on Mental Retardation [NIMR], 1972).

Job function analysis and critical incident analysis are two useful alternatives to expert opinion in generating competency statements. Job function analysis identifies what a worker does or is supposed to do on the job. The observed and implied components of a worker's performance are translated into training objectives and criteria for hiring, licensing, and performance evaluations (Mager, 1972). A limitation of this approach is that knowing what activities a professional performs on the job does not indicate the importance of the activities in delivering quality services (Kane, 1982). For example, a job function analysis of group home staff showed that housekeeping jobs constituted a major portion of their work. Staff, however, rated these activities as relatively unimportant with respect to resident habilation (Thousand et al., 1986). By addressing only readily observable behaviors, job function analysis may also fail to identify the complex behaviors that comprise the affective, attitudinal, interpersonal, and environmental variables that influence human behavior and may characterize the competent job performer (Pottinger & Goldsmith, 1979). The job function analysis approach has been used to generate competencies for employees of community residential facilities (Fiorelli, 1979) and, as might be expected, has yielded knowledge and skill competencies almost exclusively associated with performance of job functions. Complex behaviors such as interpersonal skills, personal characteristics, and attitudes were not identified as competencies through this procedure.

The third approach, critical incident analysis, focuses upon the less observable characteristics of the competent job performer (Flanagan, 1954, 1962). This method examines situations within a job context in which a person has felt particularly effective or ineffective (Mager, 1972; Pottinger & Goldsmith, 1979). Descriptions of situations are elicited through structured interviews from which both overt and covert behaviors may be reconstructed (Goleman, 1981; McClelland & Dailey, 1973). Responses are recorded and analyzed in terms of underlying concepts and unobservable covert behaviors that may precede or lead to competent professional behaviors (Klemp, 1977).

Applications of Methods of Competency Identification In a study of group home workers, Thousand et al. (1986) employed multiple methods for identifying job competencies in an attempt to: 1) ensure a non-biased determination of competency statements; 2) validate identified competencies by demonstrating correspondence of competency state-

ments across methods; and 3) provide social validation by including incumbent practitioners in generating, selecting, and ordering by priority the set of competencies. To supplement the judgment of experts, job function analyses, critical incident analyses, and personally conducted open-ended structured interviews were conducted to tap the knowledge, performance, and opinions of incumbent practitioners.

Thousand et al.'s (1986) study was designed to identify staff and manager competencies in community residences that serve no more than six persons with mental retardation. The residences all shared a common program philosophy and set of program goals, that is, the provision of training to promote the community integration and independent functioning of residents within a typical, age-appropriate and homelike living environment.

The four methodologies employed in this study—expert opinion, job function analysis, critical incident analyses, and personal interviews—yielded a core of 21 competencies essential to effective job performance for managers and staff of small-group residences, regardless of the level of disability of the resident. These 21 competencies are listed in Table 1. A majority (19) of the competencies related to implementation of normalization philosophy; interpersonal skills and characteristics important to working with parents, residents, and colleagues; sensitivity to resident needs; and personal valuation of persons with mental retardation as individuals. Furthermore, most (17) of the core competencies were generated using the open-ended methods (i.e., critical incident analysis and personal interview) rather than expert opinion and job performance analysis.

Social validation for the final competencies selected was provided by the observed similarity between these core competencies and characteristics that have been identified (Klemp, 1977; Rogers, 1962) and validated therapeutically (Carkhuff, 1983; Carkhuff & Truax, 1966; Truax et al., 1966) as critical to a successful helping relationship or successful job performance across a variety of professions. The fact that interpersonal skills and characteristics were assigned such importance by all

Table 1. Core competencies identified as essential prerequisites for staff and managers of small community residences for individuals with mild, moderate, severe, or multihandicapping conditions

Normalization Competencies

Creates a homelike atmosphere in residence
Provides age-appropriate activities, expectations, interactions
Provides appropriate role model for clients and community:
    Represents norms in values, dress, behavior
Assists residents in being interpreted as valuable persons:
    Encourages age-appropriate activities, attractive appearance
    Assists residents with displaying appropriate social behavior
Recognizes importance of household tasks for resident training and maintaining an acceptable residence

Value-Based Interpersonal Skills

Shows investment in resident growth and development:
    Commitment to the developmental model
    Commitment to individualized treatment
    Commitment to most appropriate programs and quality services
    Commitment to individualized resident achievement
Shows positive attitude toward persons with retarded development
    Views residents as interesting and valuable persons
    Is comfortable with residents in home and public settings
    Is tolerant, patient with residents
    Displays good disposition around residents
    Gives of personal time to residents
Shows respect for individual residents:
    Gives positive and corrective feedback
    Shows interest in interacting with residents on verbal, social, physical levels
    Enjoys residents as individuals
    Enjoys participating in leisure activities with residents
    Shows ability to communicate and relate to residents
Shows empathy for residents:
    Identifies what resident has to deal with in everyday life
    Identifies resident needs, interests, desires
Shows concern for residents' social and emotional well being
    Demonstrates general counseling skills with residents:
        Listens to resident concerns, problems
        Assists resident to identify and express feelings
        Assists resident in resolving interpersonal conflicts
        Assists resident in identifying appropriate behavior for social situations

Interpersonal Work Skills

Works as a team member
Takes direction from supervisor
    Cooperates with supervisor
Shows sincere interest in job:
    Shows interest to stay at least 1 year
Shows commitment and ability to work cooperatively with others:
    Staff, professions, service providers, parents
Shows professional manner with public:
    Displays social amenities
    Speaks positively of residence, residents, own job
    Responds to messages and requests
Works independently without supervision:
    Initiates activity with or for benefit of residents
    Carries out routine without prompts
Tolerates heavy workload, long hours
Shows respect for parents:
    Talks with parents in lay terms
    Communicates personal interest in parents
    Listens to parents' concerns and point of view
    Is sensitive to parents' needs

Developmental Programming & Teaching Competencies

Shows concern for training-based resident progress:
    Demonstrates pride in program, service delivery
    Demonstrates interest in data collection and monitoring
    Demonstrates interest in providing the most appropriate programs possible for residents
    Demonstrates concern for consistent and regular implementation of resident programs
Shows concern for using the most positive, least intrusive interventions
Is consistent and positive in consequating residents' behavior

employees questioned is consistent with Klemp's (1977) work on competency identification. Klemp found the personality or covert behavioral characteristics of interpersonal skills, motivation, and cognitive processing to be most highly related to competence.

Other researchers have alluded to the importance of personality characteristics as prerequisites for providing direct care in community settings (Baker et al., 1977; O'Connor, 1976). McCord (1981) noted the importance of basic human awareness and sensitivity, enjoyment in being with persons with mental retardation, and affective human qualities as essential factors in providing an enhanced quality of life to group home residents. Schalock (1983) cited respectful attitudes toward residents and promotion of their independence as necessary and basic staff competencies. Despite the identified importance of these characteristics, however, there has been no systematic use of them in recruiting, hiring, or staff training.

Staff Competencies and Resident Adjustment

The competencies identified as critical for staff of community residences depend, in part, upon both the methodology employed and the group of individuals who prepare the competency statements. Empirical validation of the competencies is needed with respect to their direct relationship to desired resident outcomes (Bernstein & Ziarnik, 1982; Burchard et al., 1987; Ziarnik, Rudrud, & Bernstein, 1981).

Several studies examined care provider competence in relation to identified residential program goals. In a study of foster care in New York, nurses and social workers rated care providers on nine qualities, including, among others, promoting independence, knowledge of resident needs, providing warmth and caring, and implementing treatment plans. Care providers rated highly were those who facilitated more community integration and more social support from families for residents than did providers with lower ratings. Residents in high-quality homes, however, were also younger and had more day programs available (Intagliata et al., 1981).

In Vermont, staff competencies were identified and validated by service providers for staff working in that state's community residences (Thousand et al., 1986). In a series of studies, the authors analyzed the relationship between care provider competence and resident habilitation outcomes. Care provider competence was measured using supervisors' ratings of staff performance of specific functions and by a written test that included the development of an individualized service plan.

The competencies identified in the Thousand et al. (1986) study fell into two general clusters: 1) value-based interpersonal relationship skills, including respectful orientation to residents and implementation of normalization principles; and 2) technical skills related to behavior management and developing and implementing of resident training programs. These competencies are shown in Table 2. Experienced managers with greater-assessed competence in interpersonal skills, resident regard, and implementation of normalization principles worked in homes whose residents experienced a higher degree of individualized community integration regardless of severity of their handicapping condition (Burchard et al., 1987) and who expressed greater personal satisfaction with their living environment, activities, and the interpersonal relations in their homes (Burchard et al., 1984). Managers with greater-assessed competence in technical skills had more complete individualized program plans with data-based training plans and received higher ratings from state program reviewers. Competence was not related to any manager demographic variable such as age, sex, length of employment, education, or experience (Burchard et al., 1987).

Subsequently, competency assessment procedures developed by Burchard and colleagues were used in hiring staff and managers of small community residences. These procedures included competency ratings based upon structured interviews, telephone references, written test performance, and observations (Burchard, Thousand, & Widrick, 1981). Assessment of competence in value-based interpersonal skills including normalization implementation, and in technical skills of teaching and behavior management, was predictive of performance ratings and test performance in those two areas 6 to 10 months after hiring. Competency assessments were also predictive of postemployment pro-

Table 2. Competencies for managers and staff of small community residences for individuals with mild, moderate, severe, and multihandicapping conditions: used as a basis for hiring and for performance evaluations

CLUSTER 1

Normalization Competencies

Has working knowledge of normalization principles
Evaluates programs and services with regard to normalization principles
Interacts with residents in a manner that is socially appropriate to their age
Provides appropriate role model for residents and community by representing local norms in dress, appearance, behavior, values
Recognizes importance of appearance in assisting residents to be valued members of the community
Creates a homelike atmosphere in the residence
Encourages age-appropriate activities and helps residents to display appropriate social behavior
Uses household tasks as part of resident training, maintaining residence in acceptable manner

Value-Based Interpersonal Skills

Appears comfortable with residents
Shows interest in interacting with residents on a social, verbal, and physical level
Shows ability to communicate and relate positively and respectfully to persons with retarded development
Shows interest in residents and views them as valuable persons
Has empathy for residents and ability to identify their needs and interests
Shows commitment to resident growth & development through the provision of services and training
Listens to residents' concerns, assists them to identify and express their feelings, helps them resolve conflicts
Advocates for appropriate goals and improved services for residents in day programs, work, school, etc.
Identifies social and recreational resources and opportunities for residents in the community

Interpersonal Work Skills

Demonstrates physical and emotional resources to meet heavy job-related demands
Presents a professional, competent demeanor: pleasant, confident, knowledgeable, in control of the situation
Shows sincere interest in job
Works as a team member
Takes direction from and cooperates with supervision
Solicits staff input on resident programs (supervisory position)
Shows respect and concern for other employees
Is effective in dealing with supervisory agencies
Works independently without supervision
Schedules and coordinates programs and activities for residents
Works well with professionals, staff members, and parents

CLUSTER 2

Technical Competencies

Demonstrates investment in resident progress through training and data collection
Is confident and able to provide instructional programming for residents
Shows knowledge and understanding of basic behavioral principles
Demonstrates concern for using the least intrusive, most positive interventions
Is effective in implementing the individualized program plans
Is effective in dealing with inappropriate behavior and emotional outbursts of residents
Effectively uses behavioral techniques such as contingent reinforcement and specific behavioral strategies for managing behavior
Effectively uses instructional strategies such as physical guidance, modeling, shaping, prompting, and fading
Is positive and consistent with residents
Implements resident training programs consistently and regularly or sees that consistent, regular implementation takes place
Instructs or assists other staff to develop, modify, or implement individual programs for residents
Is flexible and creative in making needed program changes
Is effective in developing and maintaining an organized and useful record system
Keeps data current and accurate
Uses data to evaluate programs
Writes appropriate instructional programs for resident goals

gram evaluations completed near the end of the first year for participating residences. Technical competence was reflected in more data-based resident training plans and better state program review ratings. Interpersonal skill, client re-

gard, and normalization competencies were predictive of degree of community use and integration (Burchard et al., 1985). Total assessed competence was predictive of later performance evaluations and of program measures of normalization, resident integration, quality of individualized program plans, and program quality by state reviewers. Previous experience and educational preparation were the only demographic variables related to assessed staff and manager competence at hiring and again after 8 months of employment. Based on the results of these studies, the writers feel that competencies related to client outcomes and program goals can be identified and used as a basis for hiring and staff training.

Staff Training and Program Quality

Staff training is regarded as a mechanism for offering quality services for residents. Expanded pre-service and in-service training, the establishment of career ladders, and the "professionalization" of direct care staff are frequently cited as means to promote quality programs (Ebert, 1979; Fiorelli, 1982; Schalock, 1985; Singer, Close, Irvin, Gersten, & Sailor, 1984). Community residence staff training needs have been identified as substantial (George & Baumeister, 1981; Slater & Bunyard, 1983). In institutional settings, training effectiveness has been examined primarily in terms of staff changes in subjective feelings, cognitive information, and turnover, rather than in terms of changes in staff behavior or resident outcomes (Ziarnik & Bernstein, 1982). The results of this research show at best small changes in staff performance immediately after training, with no evidence of persistent effects.

There has been little research on effects of training on staff performance in community residences. In one study, Schinke and Wong (1977) demonstrated that behavioral staff training resulted in increased knowledge, improved attitudes, decreased client maladaptive behaviors, increased staff/client appropriate interactions, and smaller increases in job dissatisfaction immediately posttraining and at a 3-week follow-up among group home staff. The duration of these effects beyond 3 weeks was not assessed.

It is difficult to generalize from existing staff training research. Program goals and staff roles may differ considerably across programs, indicating that different skills may be needed in different programs (Ziarnik et al., 1981). Training curricula are often determined by experts or by needs assessments rather than by empirically and socially validated competencies that are directly related to skills needed to produce desired resident outcomes (Schalock, 1983; Thousand et al., 1986; Ziarnik et al., 1981). While training programs for community staff exist, few are competency based and even fewer examine competency acquisition by assessing staff performance or client benefits after training (Schalock, 1985). Further research is needed to demonstrate the effectiveness of staff training in improving community staff performance, which is then reflected in better resident services and resident benefits (Reid & Whitman, 1983; Schalock, 1985).

Organizational Factors and Program Quality

Staff performance is contingent on more than knowledge, skills, and attitudes. Staff, as well as residents, may be affected by environmental conditions including the residence's management practices. A number of studies have examined management practices based upon behavior management principles, to determine if these can be used to increase staff performance with respect to organizational and/or resident goals. Specifically, researchers have examined the effect of the following strategies on staff performance: 1) clearly stated goals and performance feedback; 2) use of antecedents, prompts, cues, modeling; 3) use of rewards, attention, consequences; and 4) self-management procedures (Lattimore, Stephens, Favell, & Risley, 1984; Reid & Whitman, 1983; Repp & Deitz, 1979; Sajwaj, Schnelle, McNees, & McConnell, 1983; Ziarnik & Bernstein, 1982). These studies have shown that clear goals and performance feedback are effective means of maintaining staff performance. Unfortunately, however, the studies were conducted in institutional settings, and almost no data are available on generalization, on whether these practices are viewed as positive by staff, or on whether the practices are related to important changes in resident behaviors (Reid & Whitman, 1983). The use of behaviorally based staff management practices in community settings to enhance staff performance, satisfaction, or job tenure has not been investigated.

Other researchers have examined organizational characteristics of the work setting that are related to staff satisfaction or to improved resident services. Greater participation in decision making, more comprehensive job responsibilities, more autonomy, and collaborative management have been identified as means to enhance staff functioning and satisfaction. Raynes and her colleagues found that more individualized care and more social interactions were provided residents by staff who were more involved in decision making (i.e., meetings, fewer rules, more independence) (Raynes, Pratt, & Roses, 1979). In a controlled, reversal design study of staff roles, Byrd, Sawyer, and Locke (1983) found that assignment of more comprehensive responsibilities for individual residents resulted in two to five times more resident training and social interaction with residents. These studies, however, were done within institutional, not community, settings.

Tjosvold and Tjosvold (1983) examined the social psychological literature with respect to the differential effects of collaborative versus control management structures on staff performance, satisfaction, and resident skill acquisition. Applying their findings to *both* staff and residents, Tjosvold and Tjosvold suggest that including residents and staff in the collaborative management of the residence will result in higher staff morale, increased resident social skills, greater social competence, improved self-esteem, and decreased dependency by increasing residents' feelings of control over their lives. They point out that collaborative management characterized by shared decision making, expression of opinions, confrontation of differences, and working together, is associated in many environments with higher-quality decision making and higher performance. Collaborative management leads to commitment to implement goals, increased social competence, and increased morale. Tjosvold and Tjosvold suggest using collaborative decision making in group homes to develop peer cooperation as well.

Utilization of collaborative management styles and cooperative learning structures in community residence settings may add an additional set of competencies or skills and practices for residential staff to learn or master. The long-term benefit for residents, though, is that such management styles and learning structures could also lead directly to increased independence and the development of more stable social peer relationships. The development of stable social relationships among peers and persons other than staff who are not permanent residents is a highly desirable and more realistic alternative for providing enduring relationships than relying on staff to do so.

SUMMARY AND FUTURE DIRECTIONS

A number of issues related to the staffing of community residences for individuals with developmental disabilities remain to be resolved. One issue in need of immediate attention concerns the selection of appropriate goals and desired outcomes for community residential programs. All programs must periodically take a hard look at their stated and actual program goals, select those goals that are consistent with their philosophy relative to residents' habilitation, and clearly articulate these goals to all staff and supervisory personnel. The establishment of a program philosophy and program goals is a prerequisite to the identifying staff characteristics or competencies needed to carry out a program.

Once the program philosophy, goals, and objectives have been agreed upon, a variety of staffing concerns can be addressed. First, staff characteristics and competencies consistent with the achievement of stated program goals can be identified. Next, hiring and selection procedures to identify individuals who possess those basic competencies can be implemented. Training content and procedures consistent with the identified competencies, including interests, attitudes, and behaviors, can then be developed and validated by posttraining performance evaluation. Finally, managerial practices that support desired staff behavior and resident outcomes can be instituted.

This chapter has described characteristics and competencies of direct care staff and managers or primary care providers in small community residences that have a demonstrated relationship to resident functioning and adjustment in a broad range of areas related to habilitation goals and community integration. Care provider differences are related to tolerance for and, possibly, remediation of behavioral problems, to implementing plans that should increase skill acquisition and independent functioning, to degree of community use and integration, to the personal satisfaction of the residents, to residents' activities and opportunities, and to degree of social support from families and others.

This chapter also described procedures by which staff competencies can be identified and validated. A set of basic competencies for staff and managers of small group homes was presented. These were used to develop staff hiring and selection procedures that were validated with respect to identified program goals and resident outcomes. A number of value-based, interpersonal skills and attitudes were also identified as essential prerequisites for both managers and staff.

Most research regarding residential environments of individuals with mental retardation has been conducted in institutional rather than community settings (McCord, 1981), making the generalizability of this research to community residences questionable. We know little about the staffing, turnover, or personnel practices and issues among small nonowner-operated residences (Lakin, Bruininks, & Hill, 1982). What research has been published on community staffing issues investigates these factors in a variety of quite different types of residences. Dramatic differences can exist among residences in terms of program goals, staff roles, and organizational climate (Janicki et al., 1982). Clearly, institutions vary from community residences along these and other dimensions. Similarly, smaller community residences likely differ in a number of ways from larger community residences. Live-in residential staff may have very dissimilar relationships or roles with residents than staff who work on 8-hour rotational shifts. These differences are undoubtedly reflected in varying experiences for residents as well as for staff (Burchard et al., 1987; Hemming, Lavender, & Pill, 1981; MacEachron, 1983; MacEachron, Zober, & Fein, 1985; Pine, 1983).

Further research is needed to examine these issues separately for each type of residence of interest. Prospective and longitudinal studies also would be extremely useful in answering critical issues related to staffing community residences and providing quality programs.

Despite these limitations, the literature does suggest answers to some of the questions regarding staff satisfaction, job tenure, and tenure and program quality. Job satisfaction with extrinsic work-related factors such as pay and job security is related to job tenure but not to job performance. Job satisfaction derived from working with residents is higher than satisfaction with extrinsic factors, but is unrelated to job tenure. While there is evidence that the more educated, professionally motivated employee does not remain in a particular staff position, evidence is also accumulating that there is a growing cadre of experienced, educated personnel who continue in the community service programs.

The writers suggest that agencies can affect the capabilities and competencies of their staff by considering the following:

Utilizing cooperative, collaborative management practices to further resident and staff satisfaction as well as facilitate acquisition of needed skills.

Hiring staff who exhibit greater competencies even if they are younger, more career oriented, and therefore less likely to stay in a staff position for more than a few years. Seeking more competent staff who are willing to remain on a time-limited basis rather than staff who will remain on a semipermanent basis may yield programs of greater vitality and quality.

Promoting stable interpersonal relationships for residents by means other than attempting to provide permanent staff. Assisting residents to develop and maintain their own friendship and kin networks independent of staff may be a more realistic way of establishing enduring, stable relationships for residents.

Incorporating value-based interpersonal skills in selection and training processes to enhance efforts to provide quality staff and contribute to improved resident services.

Provide staff with training, other development opportunities, and job changes to mitigate burnout, increase staff satisfaction and competence, and thereby improve the quality of service to residents.

REFERENCES

Baker, B.L., Seltzer, G.B., & Seltzer, M.M. (1977). *As close as possible: Community residences for retarded adults.* Boston: Little, Brown.

Bernstein, G.S., & Ziarnik, J.P. (1982). Proactive identification of staff development needs: A model and methodology. *Journal of the Association for the Severely Handicapped, 7,* 97–104.

Bersani, H.A., & Heifetz, L.J. (1985). Perceived stress and satisfaction of direct-care staff members in community residences for mentally retarded adults. *American Journal of Mental Deficiency, 90,* 289–295.

Bjaanes, A.T., & Butler, E.W. (1974). Environmental variations in community care facilities for mentally retarded persons. *American Journal of Mental Deficiency, 78,* 429–439.

Bruininks, R.H., Kudla, M.J., Wieck, C.A., & Hauber, F.A. (1980). Management problems in community residential facilities. *Mental Retardation, 18,* 125–130.

Burchard, S.N., Hasazi, J.E., Gordon, L.R., Rosen, J.W., & Dietzel, L. (1986, May). *Careprovider competence and attitudes, integrating activities, and the lifestyle and personal satisfaction of adults with retarded development.* Paper presented at the annual conference of the American Association of Mental Deficiency, Denver.

Burchard, S.N., Pine, J., & Gordon, L.R. (1984, August). *Relationship of manager competence and program normalization to client satisfaction in group homes.* Paper presented at the 92nd Annual Meeting of the American Psychological Association, Toronto.

Burchard, S.N., Pine, J., Gordon, L.R., Joffe, J.M., Widrick, G.C., & Goy, E. (1987). The relationship of manager competence to residential program quality in small community residences. In J.A. Mulick & R. Antonak (Eds.), *Transitions in mental retardation: Vol. II.* Norwood, NJ: Ablex Press.

Burchard, S.N., Pine, J., Widrick, G.C., & Creedon, S. (1985, December). *The relationship of entry-level competencies to job performance and program quality in small community residences.* Paper presented at the 11th Annual Conference of the Association for Persons with Severe Handicaps, Boston.

Burchard, S.N., Thousand, J.S., & Widrick, C.G. (1981). *Managers competencies assessment package.* Burlington, VT: University of Vermont, Residential Managers Training Project, Psychology Department.

Burke, P.J., & Cohen, M. (1977). A quest for competence in serving the severely/profoundly handicapped: A critical analysis of personnel preparation programs. In E. Sontag, J. Smith, & N. Certo (Eds.), *Educational programming for the severely and profoundly handicapped* (pp. 445–468). Reston, VA: Council for Exceptional Children.

Butler, E.W., & Bjaanes, A.T. (1977). A typology of community care facilities and differential normalization outcomes. In P. Mitter (Ed.), *Research to practice in mental retardation* (Vol. 1, pp. 337–347). Baltimore: University Park Press.

Butler, E.W., & Bjaanes, A.T. (1978). Activities and the use of time by retarded persons in community care facilities. In G.P. Sackett (Ed.), *Observing behavior: Vol. 1* (pp. 379–399). Baltimore: University Park Press.

Byrd, G.R., Sawyer, B.P., & Locke, B.J. (1983). Improving direct care via minimal changes in conventional resources: An empirical analysis. *Mental Retardation, 21,* 164–168.

Carkhuff, R.R. (1983). *Sources of human productivity.* Amherst, MA: Human Resources Development Press.

Carkhuff, R.R., & Truax, C.B. (1966, March). Toward explaining success and failure in interpersonal learning experiences. *Personnel and Guidance Journal,* 723–728.

Ebert, R.S. (1979). A training program for community residence staff. *Mental Retardation, 17,* 257–259.

Eyman, R.K., Demaine, C.G., & Lei, T. (1979). Relationship between community environments and resident changes in adaptive behavior: A path model. *American Journal of Mental Deficiency, 38,* 330–338.

Fimian, M.J. (1984). Organizational variables related to stress and burnout in community-based programs. *Education and Training of the Mentally Retarded, 19,* 201–209.

Fiorelli, J.S. (1979). *A curriculum model for preservice training of alternative living arrangement direct service personnel.* Philadelphia: Developmental Disabilities Center, Temple University.

Fiorelli, J.S. (1982). Community residential services during the 1980s: Challenges and future trends. *Journal of The Association for the Severely Handicapped, 7,* 14–18.

Flanagan, J.C. (1954). The critical incident technique. *Psychological Bulletin, 51,* 327–357.

Flanagan, J.C. (1962). *Measuring human performance.* Pittsburgh: American Institutes for Research.

Freudenberger, H.J. (1975). The staff burn-out syndrome in alternative institutions. *Psychotherapy: Theory, Research and Practice, 12,* 73–82.

George, M.J., & Baumeister, A.A. (1981). Employee withdrawal and job satisfaction in community residential facilities for mentally retarded persons. *American Journal of Mental Deficiency, 85,* 639–647.

Goleman, D. (1981, January). The new competency tests: Matching the right people to the right jobs. *Psychology Today,* 35–46.

Hemming, H., Lavender, T., & Pill, R. (1981). Quality of life of mentally retarded adults transferred from large institutions to new small units. *American Journal of Mental Deficiency, 86,* 157–169.

Hill, B.K., Bruininks, R.H. (1984). Maladaptive behavior of mentally retarded individuals in residential facilities. *American Journal of Mental Deficiency, 88,* 380–387.

Hill, B.K., Lakin, C., & Bruininks, R.H. (1984). Trends in residential services for people who are mentally retarded: 1977–1982. *Journal of The Association for the Severely Handicapped, 9,* 243–250.

Hogan, E. (1974). *ENCORE direct service personnel competency packet.* Unpublished manuscript, Eastern Nebraska Community Office of Mental Retardation, Developmental and Vocational Services Division, Omaha.

Holland, J.L. (1973). *Making vocational choices: A theory of careers.* Englewood Cliffs, NJ: Prentice Hall.

Horner, R.D. (1977). A competency-based approach to preparing teachers of the severely and profoundly handicapped: Perspective II. In E. Sontag, J. Smith, & N. Certo (Eds.), *Educational programming for the severely and profoundly handicapped* (pp. 436–444). Reston, VA: Council for Exceptional Children.

Hull, J.T., & Thompson, J.C. (1980). Predicting adaptive functioning of mentally retarded persons in community settings. *American Journal of Mental Deficiency, 85,* 253–261.

Hull, J.T., & Thompson, J.C. (1981). Factors contributing to normalization in residential facilities for mentally retarded persons. *Mental Retardation, 19,* 69–73.

Intagliata, J., & Willer, B. (1982). Reinstitutionalization of mentally retarded persons successfully placed into family care and group homes. *American Journal of Mental Deficiency, 87,* 34–39.

Intagliata, J., Willer, B., & Wicks, N. (1981). Factors related to the quality of community adjustment in family care homes. In R.H. Bruininks, C.E. Myers, B.B. Sigford, & D.C. Lakin (Eds.), *Deinstitutionalization and community adjustment of mentally retarded people* (pp. 217–320). Washington, DC: American Association on Mental Deficiency.

Janicki, M.P., Jacobson, J.W., & Schwartz, A.A. (1982). Residential care settings: Models for rehabilitative intent. *Journal of Practical Approaches to Developmental Handicaps, 6,* 10–16.

Janicki, M.P., Jacobson, J.W., Zigman, W.B., & Gordon, N.H. (1984). Characteristics of employees of community residences for retarded persons. *Education and Training of the Mentally Retarded, 19,* 35–48.

Kane, M.T. (1982). The validity of licensure examinations. *American Psychologist, 37,* 911–918.

Klemp, G.O. (1977, March). *Three factors of success in the world of work: Implications for curriculum in higher education.* Paper presented at the Annual Convention of the American Associates of Higher Education, Chicago.

Lakin, K.C., Bruininks, R.H., & Hill, B.K. (1982). *Factors related to job stability of direct-care facilities for mentally retarded people.* Minneapolis: University of Minnesota, Department of Psychoeducational Studies.

Lakin, K.C., Bruininks, R.H., Hill, B.K., & Hauber, F.A. (1982). Turnover of direct-care staff in a national sample of residential facilities for mentally retarded people. *American Journal of Mental Deficiency, 87,* 64–72.

Landesman-Dwyer, S. (1981). Living in the community. *American Journal of Mental Deficiency, 86,* 223–234.

Lattimore, J., Stephens, T.E., Favell, J.E., & Risley, T.R. (1984). Increasing direct care staff compliance to individualized physical therapy body positioning prescriptions: Prescriptive checklists. *Mental Retardation, 22,* 79–84.

MacEachron, A.E. (1983). Institutional reform and adaptive functioning of mentally retarded persons: A field experiment. *American Journal of Mental Deficiency, 88,* 2–12.

MacEachron, A.E., Zober, M.A., & Fein, J. (1985). Institutional reform, adaptive functioning of mentally retarded persons, and staff quality of work life. *American Journal of Mental Deficiency, 89,* 379–388.

Mager, R.F. (1972). *Goal analysis.* Belmont, CA: Fearon Publishers/Lear Siegler.

Maslach, C. (1976, September). Burned-out. *Human Behavior, 5,* 16–22.

McClelland, D.C., & Dailey, C. (1973). *Evaluating new methods of measuring the qualities needed in superior foreign service officers.* Boston: McBer.

McCord, W.T. (1981). Community residences: The staffing. In J. Wortis (Ed.), *Mental retardation and developmental disabilities* (Vol. XII, pp. 111–128). New York: Brunner/Mazel.

Morreau, L.E. (1985). Assessing and managing problem behaviors. In K.C. Lakin & R.H. Bruininks (Eds.), *Strategies for achieving community integration of developmentally disabled citizens* (pp. 105–128). Baltimore: Paul H. Brookes Publishing Co.

National Institute on Mental Retardation. (1972). *A national mental retardation manpower model: A comprehensive planning and organization program for training personnel in the mental retardation and allied developmental handicap fields. Progress report on Project 563-9-6.* Toronto: National Institute on Mental Retardation.

O'Connor, G. (1976). *Home is a good place: A national perspective of community residential services for the mentally retarded.* (Monograph No. 2). Washington, DC: American Journal of Mental Deficiency.

O'Connor, G. (1983). Presidential address, 1983. Social support of mentally retarded persons. *Mental Retardation, 21,* 187–196.

Pine, J. (1983). *Activity as a measure of quality of life in group homes.* Unpublished doctoral dissertation, University of Vermont, Burlington.

Pottinger, P.S., & Goldsmith, N. (1979). *Defining and measuring competence: New directions for experimental learning, No. 3.* San Francisco: Jossey-Bass.

Raynes, N., Pratt, M., & Roses, S. (1979). *Organizational structure and care of the mentally retarded.* New York: Praeger Publishers.

RCA Services Company. (1979). *Section III: Task list development and review submitted to NY State Office of Mental Retardation and Developmental Disabilities.* Cherry Hill, NJ: RCA Services Company, Department of Educational Development.

Reid, D.H., & Whitman, T.L. (1983). Behavioral staff management in institutions: A critical review of effectiveness and acceptability. *Analysis and Intervention in Developmental Disabilities, 3,* 131–149.

Repp, A.C., & Deitz, D.E.D. (1979). Improving administrative-related staff behaviors at a state institution. *Mental Retardation, 17,* 185–191.

Rogers, C.R. (1962). The interpersonal relationship: The care of guidance. *Harvard Review, 39,* 416–429.

Rotegard, L.L., Hill, B.K., & Bruininks, R.H. (1983). Environmental characteristics of residential facilities for mentally retarded persons in the United States. *American Journal of Mental Deficiency, 88,* 49–56.

Sajwaj, T., Schnelle, J.F., McNees, M.P., & McConnell, S. (1983). Organizational behavior management in a community mental health center: The development of a staff performance assessment system. *Behavioral Assessment, 5,* 245–261.

Sanderson, H.W., & Crawley, M. (1982). Characteristics of successful family-care parents. *American Journal of Mental Deficiency, 86,* 519–525.

Schalock, R.L. (1983). Staff development. In *Services for developmentally disabled adults* (pp. 133–156). Baltimore: University Park Press.

Schalock, R.L. (1985). Comprehensive community services: A plea for interagency collaboration. In R.H. Bruininks & K.C. Lakin (Eds.), *Living and learning in the least restrictive environment* (pp. 37–64). Baltimore: Paul H. Brookes Publishing Co.

Schalock, R.L., Harper, R.S., & Genung, T. (1981). Community integration of mentally retarded adults: Community placement and program success. *American Journal of Mental Deficiency, 85,* 478–488.

Schinke, S.P., & Landesman-Dwyer, S. (1981). Training staff in group homes serving mentally retarded persons. *Frontiers of Knowledge in Mental Retardation, 1,* 427–433.

Schinke, S.P., & Wong, S.E. (1977). Evaluation of staff training in group homes for retarded persons. *American Journal of Mental Deficiency, 82,* 130–136.

Seltzer, G. (1981). Community residential adjustment: The relationship among environment, performance, and satisfaction. *American Journal of Mental Deficiency, 85,* 624–630.

Sherman, S.R., Frenkel, E.R., & Newman, E.S. (1984). Foster family care for older persons who are mentally retarded. *Mental Retardation, 22,* 302–308.

Singer, G.H.S., Close, D.W., Irvin, L.K., Gersten, R., & Sailor, W. (1984). An alternative to the institution for young people with severely handicapping conditions in a rural community. *Journal of The Association for the Severely Handicapped, 9,* 251–261.

Slater, M.A., & Bunyard, P.D. (1983). Survey of residential staff roles, responsibilities, and perception of resident needs. *Mental Retardation, 21,* 52–58.

Sulzer-Azaroff, B., Thaw, J., & Thomas, C. (1975). Behavioral competencies for the evaluation of behavior modifiers. In S.W. Wood (Ed.), *Issues in evaluating behavior modification.* Champaign, IL: Research Press.

Sutter, P. (1980). Environmental variables related to placement failure in mentally retarded adults. *Mental Retardation, 18,* 189–191.

Sutter, P., Mayeda, T., Call, T., Yanagi, G., & Yee, S. (1980). Comparison of successful and unsuccessful community-placed mentally retarded persons. *American Journal of Mental Deficiency, 85,* 262–267.

Sutter, P., Mayeda, T., Yee, S., & Yanagi, G. (1981).

Community placement success based on client behavior preferences of careproviders. *Mental Retardation, 19,* 117–120.

Thousand, J., Burchard, S., & Hasazi, J. (1986). Field-based determination of manager and staff competencies in small community residences. *Applied Research in Mental Retardation, 7,* 263–283.

Tjosvold, D., & Tjosvold, M.M. (1983). Social psychological analysis of residences for mentally retarded persons. *American Journal of Mental Deficiency, 88,* 28–40.

Truax, C.B., Fisher, G.H., Leslie, G.R., Smith, S.W., Mitchell, K.M., Shapiro, J.G., & McCormick, A.G. (1966). Empathy, warmth, genuineness. *Rehabilitation Record, 7,* 10–11.

Wilcox, B. (1979). A competency-based approach to preparing teachers of the severely and profoundly handicapped: Perspective I. In E. Sontag, J. Smith, & N. Certo (Eds.), *Educational programming for the severely and profoundly handicapped* (pp. 418–429). Reston, VA: Council for Exceptional Children.

Willer, B., & Intagliata, J. (1981). Social-environmental factors as predictors of adjustment of deinstitutionalized mentally retarded adults. *American Journal of Mental Deficiency, 3,* 252–259.

York, R.T., Burdett, C., Fox, T., Hoffman, R., Sousie, S., & Williams, W.W. (1979). *Intensive special education program: Preparing personnel to teach individuals with severe and multiple handicaps.* Burlington, VT: Center for Developmental Disabilities, University of Vermont.

Zaharia, E.S., & Baumeister, A.A. (1978). Technician turnover and absenteeism in public residential facilities. *American Journal of Mental Deficiency, 82,* 580–593.

Zaharia, E.S., & Baumeister, A.A. (1979). Technician losses in public residential facilities. *American Journal of Mental Deficiency, 84,* 36–39.

Ziarnik, J.P., & Bernstein, G.S. (1982). A critical examination of the effect of inservice training on staff performance. *Mental Retardation, 20,* 109–114.

Ziarnik, J.P., Rudrud, E.H., & Bernstein, G.S. (1981). Data vs. reflections: A reply to Moxley and Ebert. *Mental Retardation, 19,* 252.

Zigman, W.B., Schwartz, A.A., & Janicki, M.P. (1984). Group home employee job attitudes and satisfactions. In J.M. Berg (Ed.), *Perspectives and Progress in Mental Retardation,* (Vol. 1, pp. 401–411). Baltimore: University Park Press.

Chapter 21

Wage and Hour Considerations in Compensating Employees of Community Residences

Joni Fritz

Federal minimum wage and overtime rules governing the ways in which staff who work in residential programs must be compensated are considered in this chapter. Rules originally designed for industrial or commercial applications create staffing and record-keeping problems when used in the human services field. However, such rules still serve to provide workers with protections by requiring payment of minimum hourly wages and overtime for time actually worked. Problems associated with federal wage and hour law as it is applied to community residence settings are identified, as are provisions developed by the U.S. Department of Labor to apply the Fair Labor Standards Act to community residential settings to avoid unnecessary payment of wages for hours not actually worked. Applications of exemptions from minimum wage and overtime rules are also reviewed. The disability field is attempting to have federal rules modified to permit more flexibility in staffing community residences to reduce both staff turnover and burdensome record-keeping requirements, yet keep intact protection of workers. Recommendations for these modifications are discussed as well.

One of the most important, though least understood, issues in staffing community residential programs in the United States is compliance with the Fair Labor Standards Act of 1938 (FLSA), as amended. This act, passed at the end of the depression when many workers had to work long hours and throughout the week, was designed to improve "labor conditions detrimental to the maintenance of the minimum standard of living necessary for health, efficiency, and general well-being of workers . . ." (Sec. 2[a], 29 U.S.C. 201, et seq.), and to assure that as many Americans as possible were employed. To improve the standard of living of workers, the U.S. Congress initiated a minimum wage of 25 cents per hour. To encourage the employment of as many people as possible, the FSLA required that when em-

ployees worked more than 40 hours per week, they had to be paid at a rate of one and one-half times their usual hourly rate of pay for any additional hours worked. This provision served as an incentive for employers to hire more people to avoid having to pay costly overtime wages. Thus, an employer who previously had one employee working 70 hours a week found it less costly to reduce that employee's workweek to 40 hours and to hire an additional employee to work the other 30 hours. As a vehicle for protecting and enlarging the labor force, the FLSA was, and still is, an instrument with greatest applicability to industrial and retail settings.

In 1966, under the administration of President Lyndon B. Johnson, the FLSA was amended by Public Law 89-601 to extend its coverage to many types of employees not previously protected by its provisions. Section 3(r)(1) was added, which specifically applies the FLSA to "any person . . . engaged in the operation of a hospital, an institution primarily engaged in the care of the sick, the aged, the mentally ill or defective who reside on the premises of such institution, a school for mentally or physically handicapped or gifted children, elementary or secondary school, or an institution of higher education (regardless of whether or not such hospital, institution, or school is public or private or operated for profit or not for profit) . . ." In the early 1970s, this section of the FLSA was further amended to extend its coverage to employees of preschools as well.

Despite these amendments, the U.S. Department of Labor (DOL) had an unofficial policy of not enforcing certain provisions of the FLSA in state institutions or private residential programs serving persons with disabilities (except in response to specific complaints). This unofficial policy continued until the 1973 court decision in *Souder v. Brennan*. This decision mandated enforcement of the FLSA as it pertains to persons who reside in such institutions (referred to by the court as "patient workers"). However, when DOL field agents began inspecting residential programs to evaluate compliance for patient workers, they investigated the compensation provided to other institutional employees as well. This eventually resulted in the extension of compliance requirements to community residential programs.

Although small-group living arrangements were increasing in the late 1960s and early 1970s, most providers or sponsoring agencies had little awareness of federal wage and hour rules. It was common, for example, for residences to be staffed by a couple who lived at the home 365 days a year. These people were relieved from duty on weekends, vacation periods, and when personal emergencies occurred. They sometimes did not have every weekend off and often did not leave the home even when relief staff were on duty. They were usually paid a set salary, and little attention was given to hours actually worked. However, as group home and apartment programs proliferated and as persons with more severe disabilities began living in community programs, problems result-

ing from staff turnover and staff scheduling preferences led to the development of more varied staffing patterns to reduce the burden on employees and to enhance the stability of residential programs (see Lakin, Chapter 18, this volume).

At the same time, providers of residential services began to become informed about FLSA requirements. In 1973, the National Association of Private Residential Facilities for the Mentally Retarded (NAPRFMR) contacted the Department of Labor and began to examine how DOL rules applied to residential programs. Because it was clear that most providers were unaware of the need to comply with labor law and implementing regulations, NAPRFMR began disseminating appropriate information to agencies that administered residential programs; NAPRFMR also began seeking interpretations of the rules that would permit the use of more flexible staffing patterns.

There are still agencies and providers who are unaware that they must comply with provisions of the FLSA. There are also some federal compliance officers who are unfamiliar with the ways in which rules may be applied to staff of residential programs. The problems of application are compounded by the variety of administrative practices in staffing community residential facilities. The following discussion focuses on the various aspects of federal wage and hour legislation and regulations that affect the staffing of residential programs in the United States.

MINIMUM WAGE AND OVERTIME PROVISIONS OF FLSA

The staffing pattern generally in use in industry, retail establishments, large state institutions, and traditional nursing homes is a work shift of 8 hours a day (40 hours a week). For this type of pattern, provisions of the FLSA are straightforward. Section 7 of the Act requires that individuals who are not specifically exempt from minimum wage and overtime requirements of the law be paid at least the minimum wage for the first 40 hours worked in a workweek, and one and one-half times the "regular rate of pay" for any hours over 40 worked in the workweek. An employee cannot waive his or her statutory right either to be paid the required minimum wage or to receive overtime compensation for hours worked in excess of the applicable statutory standard. Currently, the minimum wage in the United States is $3.35 per hour and has been so since January 1, 1981, despite periodic efforts by some members of Congress to increase it.

Section 778.105 of Department of Labor regulations defines the workweek as a "fixed and regularly recurring period of 168 hours—seven consecutive 24 hour periods." The rule also states that a workweek need not coincide with a calendar week but may begin on any day and at any hour of the day. Different workweeks may be established for different employees or groups of employees, but once established, the week must remain fixed for each individual or group. The beginning of an employee's workweek may be changed if the change is intended to be permanent and is not designed to avoid the overtime requirements of the FLSA.

Overtime must be based on one and one-half times the "regular rate" of pay. Some erroneously believe that overtime wages may be paid at one and one-half times the minimum wage. This is incorrect unless the employee is paid at the minimum wage. The regular rate of pay has been defined by the U.S. Supreme Court as the "rate actually paid the employee for the normal, non-overtime workweek for which he is employed" (*Walling v. Youngerman–Reynolds Harwood Co.*, 325 U.S. 419).

Section 7(e) of the FLSA requires that the regular rate include "all remuneration for employment paid to, or on behalf of, the employee, [except payments specifically excluded elsewhere in the Act]." This rate must, therefore, include the value of room and board furnished for the benefit of the employee and all promised or routine bonuses. It does not include gifts, discretionary bonuses, or holiday, vacation, and sick pay provided to the employee (see Sections 708.208–708.215 of DOL regulations).

Special Provision for 80-Hour, 14-Day Work Periods

The FLSA contains a special provision for 80-hour, 14-day work periods, which can be applied in most states to employees who work in community living arrangements. This provision, contained in Section 7(j), is applicable to employees of hospitals or facilities engaged primarily in the care of persons who are sick, aged, mentally ill, or mentally retarded and who reside on the premises. Employees of such facilities may agree, in advance of employment, to be compensated over a work period of 14 consecutive days for purposes of overtime compensation. However, if such employees work more than 8 hours on any given day, the law requires that they be paid at one and one-half times their regular rate of pay for the excess hours, even if they do not exceed 80 hours within that 14-day work period.

The advantage of the 80-hour, 14-day work period is realized only when work schedules are arranged so that employees will be working more than 5 days in a row but for no more than 8 hours on any single day. This work period is generally utilized by agencies that schedule staff for 10 days on and 4 days off, or for 7 days on and 7 days off, during the 14-day work period, and whose work can be limited to 8 or fewer hours a day. Shift staff, for example, could work under this provision from 7:00 A.M. to 3:00 P.M. Monday of the first week through Wednesday of the second week, with the second Thursday through Sunday off; or work Monday through Sunday of the first week and be off the second week. In another example, staff could work a split shift either Monday of the first week through the following Wednesday, or Monday through Sunday of the first week, from 7:00 A.M. to 10:00 A.M., be off from 10:00 A.M. to 3:00 P.M., and resume work from 3:00 P.M. to 8:00 P.M.

Any time employees hired under this provision work more than 8 hours on any single day, they have to be paid overtime for the extra hours worked that day. Therefore, in the second example just presented, if a resident, for instance, failed to leave the home for the day program by 10:00 A.M. (when the staff member was supposed to be relieved of duty) and the staff person had to remain in the home until 11:00 A.M., he or she would have to be paid one hour of overtime.

Some state labor laws prohibit use of a 14-day workweek. It is always advisable to obtain information about state and federal laws when arranging staffing patterns. States may always add more stringent requirements, but they may never permit waivers of federal law.

Defining Live-in and 24-Hour Employment

The December 7, 1973, decision in *Souder v. Brennan* arrived on the heels of the national deinstitutionalization movement, and the DOL was confronted with a variety of living alternatives that used a myriad of staffing patterns. Fortunately, the rules that implement the FLSA have some provisions pertaining to other types of employment that are not too different from conditions of work found in group living arrangements. Switchboard operators, for example, and others in similar jobs are sometimes required to remain on duty for 24 hours or more and are permitted to sleep for a portion of that time. The courts have found that in instances where employees are required to be on duty for less than 24 hours, they cannot realistically be expected to sleep and should be paid for all of the hours on duty even when permitted to sleep while at the place of employment. When employees work for periods of 24 hours or more or when they reside on the employer's premises, the courts have decided that it is reasonable to expect them to be able to sleep during regularly scheduled sleeping periods of 8 hours or less. In such circumstances, with prior agreement of the employee, it is not necessary to pay for sleep time.

Sections 785.20–785.23 of the DOL regulations define the criteria that must be met for an employer to avoid compensating staff for bona fide sleep time spent while at the place of work. Because of complications that arose as department investigators examined the conditions of work in community living arrangements, further criteria have been developed that are now applied specifically to employees of group homes and other small living alternatives. These criteria, not codified, appear in letters of interpretation sent to NAPRFMR and others. They are also used as guidelines for DOL staff who enforce the FLSA through routine, random investigations or as a result of complaints filed by employees or other private citizens. Copies of the letters are in the appendix to this chapter.

As noted, during the early development of community living arrangements, the "houseparent" staffing model, in which staff frequently lived in a group home on a rather permanent basis, was the norm. Often the couple that was hired made the group residence their legal address. The couple was usually on duty for at least 5 days a week, sometimes more. Such workers clearly fell under that section of the DOL regulations that applies to employees who "reside on the employer's premises." Employees who live on the premises are not considered to be working all of the time they are there. When agreed to in advance of employment, they need not be paid for up to 8 hours of bona fide sleep time at night, or for time in the middle of the day when they are free to come and go as they please. They are, however, subject to minimum wage and overtime rules for all hours they are actually on duty. In these instances, many live-in staff work more than 40 hours a week, particularly if they are on duty more than 5 days a week, which can require the payment of a considerable amount of overtime compensation.

A number of factors, including a growing awareness of minimum wage and overtime rules and the necessity of developing staffing patterns that minimize the use of overtime pay in addition to trying to cope with staff scheduling preferences and burnout, with resulting problems of staff turnover, have influenced agencies administering group homes to move away from the live-in houseparent staff model. These agencies have found that the demands on an employee's time and energy when living in a group home can be debilitating. For example, unless live-in staff leave the premises when relief staff take over, residents still tend to seek out the live-in staff to ask for help. Thus, live-in staff never seem to be relieved of all responsibilities.

In the mid-1970s, staffing therefore gradually shifted to a reliance on a "house counselor" or "house manager." Direct care staff were less frequently seen in the role of parent and more often were being perceived as peers and role models for adults with developmental disabilities. Administering agencies also began to encourage live-in employees in group homes to have a second residence where they could live on their days off. This eventually necessitated the development by the DOL of a more specific definition of *live-in staff*. A DOL letter of interpretation sent to both NAPRFMR (dated February 3, 1981; see Appendix for the full text) and the National Association of State Mental Retardation Program Directors (NASMRPD), outlined conditions under which employees would be considered "living on the employer's premises. . . for an extended period of time" or "working for periods of duty of 24 hours or more."

The DOL's position in the February 3, 1981, letter (see Appendix) applies when "house-parents" are given private quarters that are separate from the group home residents, and are provided with other amenities that establish a homelike environment. If they spend 5 days or nights at the group residence, they are considered to be "residing on the premises. . . for an extended period of time." If the days are consecutive, staff need not spend 120 hours a week at the living arrangement to be considered live-in employees. The DOL letter provides examples of staffing patterns that meet the criteria for "live-in employees":

> If employees are on duty from 9 A.M. Monday until 9 A.M. Saturday, they will have been on duty for 120 hours (ignoring off-duty time that may be allowed for a few hours each day). Such employees are considered to reside on their employer's premises. The same is true of employees who are on duty from 9 A.M. Monday until 9 A.M. Wednesday and from 9 A.M. Thursday until 9 A.M. Sunday, since they will have been on duty for 120 hours in the week (again ignoring short periods of off-duty time). In each case, the employees reside on the premises for five days and five nights.
> Employees who are on duty from 9 A.M. Monday until 5 P.M. Friday would also be considered to reside on the employer's premises. Even though on duty for less than 120 hours, they are on duty for five consecutive days (Monday through Friday). The fact that they sleep over only four nights does not matter. Similarly, employees who are on duty from 9 P.M. Monday until 9 A.M. Saturday would also be considered to reside on their employer's premises since they are on duty for five consecutive nights (Monday night through Friday night).

DOL also clarified the criteria for staff who are on duty for periods of 24 hours or more in their letter of February 3, 1981, and provided additional clarification in a letter to NAPRFMR in April 1983. In the 1983 letter, DOL stated (see Appendix for the full text):

> Employees who do not reside on the employer's premises on a permanent basis or for an extended period of time but who may remain at the employer's establishment for at least 24 hours (and as long as two or three days), even though they may have off-duty time during the day with complete freedom from all responsibilities, thereby enabling them to use the time effectively for their own purposes, may still have sleep time deducted from their hours worked.

In 1987, DOL officials wrote to NAPRFMR to address a difference of understanding regarding the 1981 and 1983 letters of interpretation as applied to employees who are on duty for 24 hours or more. In the June 29, 1987, letter (see Appendix) they stated that only "relief" employees who perform essentially the same duties as a full-time employee (who in turn meets criteria outlined in the 1981 letter for employees who reside on the employer's premises on a permanent basis or for extended periods of time) may have a mutually agreed-upon amount of off-duty time excluded from compensable hours of work if they are not paid for sleep time. Thus, employees who: 1) have a certain amount of uncompensated "free" time during the workday, 2) do *not* reside on the premises of the group home where they work, and 3) do *not* relieve a full-time employee who resides on the premises *must* be compensated for time spent sleeping.

The alternative method of compensating 24-hour employees who do not "relieve" live-in staff is to pay them for 16 hours of work (exclusive of bona fide meal periods) if they are not compensated for sleep time.

DOL officials have stated that the FLSA will have to be amended by Congress before they can alter this requirement. NAPRFMR and other national associations that represent the disability field are currently exploring ways to overturn this recent letter of interpretation.

Consideration of Special Situations

Employees in group living arrangements are often confronted with atypical work demands. Certain job-related requirements are imposed on employees for the benefit of the group home residents. These may include sleeping on the premises to be available for supervision or to assist in the event of an emergency; eating with residents as part of habilitative activities and to serve as role models; and being on-call in the event of a re-call to work or to deal with a special situation. These special considerations pose difficulties in compensating workers for hours worked. The following discussion examines how the FLSA and implementing DOL regulations address these special work situations.

Treatment of Sleep Time The DOL has determined that live-in and 24-hour employees who work in group living arrangements need not be paid for sleep time, "provided that the employer and employee agree in advance to do so, and that no more than 8 hours per night (or actual, uninterrupted sleep time, if that is less than 8 hours) is deducted" (see Sections 785.22 and 785.23 of the DOL regulations). As noted in the DOL letters appended here, such employees may also have off-duty time during the day with complete freedom from all responsibilities, which need not be compensated.

The decision to permit the inclusion of uncompensated free time in the middle of the day for residential employees working a 24-hour shift of duty was made after a lengthy period of negotiation with NAPRFMR, NASMRPD, and other disability advocacy organizations. As a result, the DOL determined that "because of the home-like environment, an exception can be made where employees do in fact get a reasonable night's sleep." However, unless the employee works 5 or more days in a row, only one sleep period (of up to 8 hours) may be deducted for each 24-hour work period. For example, if a relief employee works from 3 P.M. Monday to 10 A.M. Wednesday, sleep time may be deducted only for the first day of work, but not for the second, since the second day of work comprises a period of less than 24 hours. However, if the employee's tour of duty ends at 3 P.M. Wednesday, two 8-hour sleep periods may be deducted, so long as the employee is actually free to sleep. Unfortunately, it may not always be convenient for the employee to return to duty for an hour or so at the end of the last 24-hour

period, but this inconvenience is required to avoid paying for sleep time.

The DOL requires that no more than 8 hours of sleeptime be set aside each night for both live-in and 24-hour relief employees, and that when sleeptime is interrupted by a call to duty, the time of interruption must be compensated. Furthermore, if an employee is unable to get at least 5 hours of sleep during the 8-hour sleep period, all of the time must be compensated (Section 785.22 of the rules). DOL also has indicated that a period of work may not begin with a sleep period. It is, after all, unreasonable to expect an employee to go to sleep immediately after reporting to duty.

The regulatory definition of duty of 24 hours or more duration includes the requirement that an employee be provided with "adequate sleeping facilities" and that he or she "can usually enjoy an uninterrupted night's sleep" (Section 785.22). In permitting agencies to avoid paying staff for sleeptime (even if they have free time in the middle of the day), DOL has considered the settings in which residential services are being provided, and has determined that "because of the home-like environment afforded to these employees in community residences, with private quarters and other amenities . . . there are ample facilities to enable them to get a full night's sleep." Therefore, it is important that an employee's sleep not be interrupted on a regular basis and that a private room be available with either a bed or a couch that can be made into a bed. It is not necessary for the employee to have a suite of rooms, but he or she must be given privacy and a bed on which to sleep. A couch in the living room or a bed in a room shared by a client is not considered adequate, and staff who sleep under such conditions must be paid for sleep time if they have free time during the 24-hour period of duty.

Treatment of Meal Periods Meal periods, like sleep periods, may be excluded from compensation only if the employee is completely relieved from duty except for rare emergency calls. The rules (Section 785.19) indicate that if a meal is interrupted by a call to duty, the employee must be compensated for actual time spent responding to the emergency. Coffee breaks or time for snacks are not defined as bona fide meal periods and are subject to compensation. Periods of 30 minutes or longer are considered appropriate for uncompensated meal breaks.

In most community-based living arrangements, staff are expected to supervise the meal and at the same time to serve as a role model by eating with the residents. Under these circumstances, employees must be compensated for meal time, as the time spent eating is considered work time.

On-Call Time There are special considerations in compensating "on-call" time. According to the DOL rules (Section 785.17), employees who are not required to remain on the premises, but who leave word where they may be reached or who carry a monitor or beeper that can be used to contact them in times of emergency, are not considered to be working during their free time, and this time is not subject to compensation. These employees must, however, be compensated for the periods of time spent responding to calls.

If calls become so frequent or conditions so restrictive that the employee is not actually free to pursue personal activity, the employee may be considered to be "engaged to wait" and must then be compensated for his or her time. For example, if, in order to respond to a possible emergency, live-in or 24-hour employees are expected to remain in the group living arrangement during the middle of the day while residents are at their day program, this significantly restricts their freedom. In this case, the DOL considers them to be "engaged to wait," requiring payment for the time they are waiting for a call to duty.

Employee Payment for Room and Board The DOL rules permit deduction of the "fair value" or "reasonable cost" of room and board from an employee's wages if room and board are furnished for the benefit of the employee (Section 531, Subpart B). Circumstances surrounding the provision of a room are generally a consideration in determining whether or not the room is provided for the benefit of the employer or the employee. Thus far DOL has provided considerable flexibility to employers, so that the provision of either a room or meals may be treated either way. If

room and/or board are considered part of an employee's compensation, the actual value or "reasonable cost" of the room(s) and food provided must be used in these computations, rather than the fair market value of such facilities and services. It is advisable to check with DOL officials regarding current guidelines for establishing fair value or reasonable cost.

When room and/or board are considered part of an employee's compensation and are deducted from wages, their value is used by the department in computations to determine the "regular rate of pay" used in computing overtime. Further, the value of *free* meals and lodging may be excluded from Social Security, unemployment insurance payments, and withholding taxes. If counted as part of an employee's wages, however, the applicable taxes and insurance payments must be made as with other forms of compensation. It is advisable to check with the Internal Revenue Service to be certain how the value of room and board should be treated for tax purposes.

Establishing a Salary for Hourly Employees

Some employers and employees prefer to establish a regular salary under a prearranged agreement for employees who reside on the employer's premises, and to arrange extra compensation for the infrequent periods that actual sleep, meal, or free time is interrupted, rather than attempt to include all potential interruptions in the regularly scheduled worktime and salary. The DOL calls such an arrangement a "reasonable agreement." Rules for paying an employee on a "salary basis" appear in Section 541.118 of the regulations.

A "reasonable agreement" must take into consideration all of the factors involved and assure that the employee is being paid an amount at least equal to the minimum wage plus overtime for hours scheduled for work each workweek.

Some employers find that computing salaries under these rules at the minimum wage results in an annual salary below that which the employer wishes to pay. In such cases, the hourly rate of pay is increased commensurate with the desired rate of compensation. If, for example,

Table 1. Information to be maintained on each employee

The U.S. Department of Labor (DOL) requires that the following information be maintained on each employee:
1. Employee's full name, as used for Social Security purposes, and any identifying number or symbol used in place of the name on time, work, or payroll records
2. Address, including zip code
3. Date of birth, if under age 19
4. Sex and occupation in which employed (related to equal pay provisions of FLSA)
5. Time of day and day of week on which employee's workweek begins
6. Regular hourly rate of pay for any week when overtime is worked, and basis on which wages are paid (such as "$4 an hour" or "$150 a week")
7. Hours worked each day and total hours worked each workweek
8. Total daily or weekly straight-time earnings, exclusive of overtime
9. Total premium pay for overtime hours (excluding straight-time earnings)
10. Total additions to or deductions from wages paid each pay period, plus nature of items that constitute the additions and deductions
11. Total wages paid each pay period
12. Date of payment and pay period covered by payment
13. Social Security number (a requirement of the Internal Revenue Service rather than the Department of Labor)

Rules governing recordkeeping requirements were published by DOL on July 1, 1987.

an employer wished to pay an employee about $10,000 per year and the employee works 42 hours per week (40 hours of regular time and 2 hours of overtime), at the minimum wage of $3.35 per hour, the employee's weekly wage would be 40 hours at $3.35 ($134) plus 2 hours at $5.03 ($10.06), or $144.06 per week. This would result in an annual salary of just $7,492 per year, about $2,500 less than the employer wishes to pay. If the rate of pay is raised to $4.48 per hour, the weekly wage would be 40 hours at $4.48 ($179.20) plus 2 hours at $6.72 ($13.44), resulting in $192.64 per week, or an annual salary of $10,018.

Overtime hours worked in excess of those accounted for within the agreement still must be compensated at the overtime rate of pay. Therefore, if the employee in the previous example works 44 hours in a given workweek, he or she must receive 2 hours at $6.72 (the overtime rate of pay), or $13.44, in addition to the usual salary paid for 42 hours of work.

If an employee's normal routine changes, the hours worked must be recomputed and a new agreement developed. Thus, if the employee in the example used here were to begin to work 44 hours per week on a regular basis, the hourly rate of pay would have to be recalculated. (There is nothing in the FLSA that prohibits an employer from lowering the hourly rate of pay, so long as it does not drop below the minimum wage.)

Although the DOL does not require agreements to be kept in writing, it is strongly ad-

vised that employers do so to avoid misunderstandings and to provide documentation should a DOL audit occur. The DOL does require that all employers obtain and maintain certain basic information on each person employed (See Table 1). Items numbered 6 and 9 in the table need not be kept for employees who are exempt from minimum wage and overtime rules when they meet the special criteria for exemption as executive, administrative, or professional employees; as houseparents in orphanages; or as outside salespersons (as discussed next).

Special Exemptions from Minimum Wage and Overtime Rules There are a few specific circumstances under which employees of residential programs may be exempted from minimum wage and overtime provisions of the Fair Labor Standards Act. The exemptions apply in instances where: 1) houseparents work in orphanages whose residents also attend a school established by the employer; 2) professional employees meet five clearly defined tests, including a salary of at least $170 per week and work activities that are predominantly "intellectual and varied"; 3) executive employees are paid at least $155 per week and direct the work of two full-time employees; 4) administrative employees are paid at least $155 per week and primarily do work related to the administration of a business or school; and 5) individuals work as outside salespersons. Although most staff of community residences generally do not fit into any of these categories, the exemptions are described to enable those agencies that employ people who qualify for the exemptions to investigate further.

Special Houseparent Exemption A 1974 amendment to the FLSA provides a special exemption for houseparents working in orphanages. To be eligible for this exemption, employees must meet very specific statutory criteria. Section 13(b)(24) of the FLSA requires that a couple be employed who receive a combined salary of at least $10,000 per year, exclusive of room, board, and other facilities. They must live at and be employed by a nonprofit educational institution. In addition, the children they serve must be enrolled in the educational program provided by the institution, and at least one parent of each child must be deceased.

This exemption clearly does not apply to individuals employed in residential programs that serve adults or those serving children whose parents are both living, nor does it apply to group living arrangements not affiliated with an educational program.

Exemption for a Professional Employee The conditions that must be met for employees to be exempt from minimum wage and overtime requirements as "professionals" are outlined in Section 541.3 of the DOL regulations. To so qualify an employee must meet five criteria. He or she must:

1. Be paid on a salary or fee basis at a rate of not less than $170 per week, exclusive of board, lodging, or other facilities.
2. Do work that is "predominantly intellectual and varied," as distinguished from "routine" or "mechanical" duties.
3. Not spend more than 20% of his or her time in the workweek on activities not "essentially a part of and necessarily incident to" professional duties.
4. Consistently exercise discretion and judgment.
5. Finally, and perhaps most important, primary work of the employee must either: a) require advanced knowledge in a scientific or other field, customarily involving a prolonged course of specialized instruction or study; or b) call for originality and creativity in a recognized field of artistic endeavor; or c) involve teaching in the school system or educational institution by which he or she is employed.

Staff members of residential facilities generally are not considered by the DOL to meet this five-category test for exemption as professional employees. Although some agencies whose house counselors spend considerable time instructing residents argue that their staff meet the exemption as teachers, DOL officials maintain that they have not yet seen an example of live-in employees in a residential program serving persons with developmental disabilities who adequately meet the foregoing conditions of employment. It should be noted that it is not necessary for an employee to have a teacher's certificate to be exempt as a teacher. The obverse is also true; people who have bona fide teachers' certificates do not necessarily meet DOL critiera for exemption as teachers.

NAPRFMR, NASMRPD, and several other national organizations based in Washington, DC, have been seeking recognition of "human service professionals" as a category of exempt professionals under the DOL rules. The definition of *human service professional* is equivalent to the one used for *qualified mental retardation professional* (*QMRP*) as defined in proposed federal regulations for intermediate care facilities for the mentally retarded.

The term *QMRP* has existed in federal rules since January 1974. The current definition (in 42 CFR Part 442.401) includes a list of professionals who would meet existing DOL criteria for professionals (e.g., physicians, nurses, educators, occupational therapists). To be acknowledged as QMRPs, these individuals must also have at least 1 year of experience "in treating or working with the mentally retarded." Proposed rule changes published in 1986 would expand the definition to include a human service professional who must have "at least a bachelor's degree in a human service field . . . (such as sociology, special education, rehabilitation counseling)."

Under current federal rules a QMRP is responsible for: a) supervising the delivery of each resident's individualized plan of care,

b) supervising the delivery of training and habilitation services, c) integrating the various aspects of the [home's] program, d) recording each resident's progress, and e) initiating a periodic review of each individualized plan of care.

Duties such as those described are comparable to those required of other professionals in DOL rules. Individuals with a bachelor's degree in a disability-related field, and at least 1 year of experience working with people who have disabilities—who are performing duties comparable to those in the preceding list—should qualify under this exempt category.

Exemption for an Executive The following criteria apply to employees who are exempt from minimum wage and overtime rules as executives (Section 541.1 of the DOL rules):

Payment must be on a salary basis at a rate of not less than $155 per week, exclusive of board, lodging, or other facilities.
The employee's primary duty must consist of management of the enterprise or of a customarily recognized department or subdivision thereof.
The employee must direct the work of two or more other full-time employees or their equivalent.
The employee must have the authority to hire or fire other employees or have great weight in hiring, firing, and promotion decisions.
The employee must regularly exercise discretionary powers.
The employee may not devote more than 40% of the hours of work in the workweek to activities not directly and closely related to the performance of activities just described.

A subcategory under this exemption, called the "sole-charge exception," pertains to employees who are "in sole charge of an independent establishment or a physically separated branch establishment" of a business. The rules specifically require that the establishment be geographically separate from other business/agency property. Only one person in any establishment can qualify as an executive under this exemption, and then only if he or she is the senior person in charge at that location, supervises the work of two or more full-time employees, and ordinarily oversees all agency activities at that site.

The sole-charge exception has been successfully applied to some house managers. It exempts such employees only from the requirement that at least 60% of the workweek be devoted to activities related to the work of an executive in managing the business. Such individuals must still direct the work of at least two full-time employees or their equivalent, which few house managers do. Those who do may be paid on a salary basis, regardless of the number of hours worked each week, if the salary is at least $155 per week, exclusive of board, lodging, and other facilities.

In response to a November 1985 DOL advance notice of proposed rulemaking, NAPRFMR, NASMRPD, and nine other national organizations encouraged the DOL to revise the rules to expand the sole-charge exception to exclude the requirement that such employees supervise the work of at least two other full-time employees. The disability advocacy groups believe that employees who assume management responsibility for a single home or apartment are clearly in charge of activities at a "geographically separated branch establishment" as required by federal rules. Further, those who do not supervise the work of two employees have responsibility for residents, and this generally requires a higher level of oversight and responsibility than may be required in the supervision of other employees. The work is thus comparable to that performed by other persons who are exempt as executives. Readers are advised to check with the DOL regarding the applications of this exemption.

Exemption for an Administrative Employee For an employee to be considered to be in a bona fide administrative capacity, he or she must meet each of the following requirements of Section 541.2 of the DOL's rules:

Payment must be on a salary or fee basis at a rate of not less than $155 per week, exclusive of board, lodging, or other facilities.
No more than 40% of the time spent at work may involve nonexempt duties (work not directly and closely related to administration of a business).
The employee's primary duty must be either a) responsible office or nonmanual work directly related to the management policies or

general business operations of the employer or the employer's customers, or b) responsible work directly related to academic instruction or training carried on in the administration of a school system or educational establishment.

The employee must customarily and regularly exercise discretion and independent judgment.

The employee must; a) regularly assist a proprietor or a bona fide executive or administrative employee; or b) perform work under only general supervision along specialized or technical lines requiring special training, experience, or knowledge; and c) execute special assignments under only general supervision.

The DOL has generally ruled that house counselors who serve persons with disabilities do not meet requirements for exemption as administrators. The tasks required to operate a group living arrangement are not considered to relate closely enough to "administrative" duties, but are seen as more routine in nature. Employees who are paid at least $250 per week need not meet quite such rigorous tests. Some agencies that employ house managers of small-group living arrangements who are paid $250 or more per week believe that their employees meet this exemption, and have used it without being challenged by DOL compliance officers. Others have been ordered to pay back wages to these employees, and overtime wages have been calculated on the basis of a "regular rate" of pay of $6.25 per hour ($250 divided by 40 hours).

The NAPRFMR and other groups have urged DOL to take a closer look at this exemption category as well. Rather than performing non-manual work that is directly related to management policies and general business operations of the employer's *customers* (as required under current rules), employees in residential programs perform management functions related to the employer's *clients*. These functions include exercising discretion and independent judgment very similar to that required of an executive who is exempt under the provision for sole-charge exception, but in this case it may be a shared responsibility more similar to that for adminstrative employees. The work performed regularly and directly assists the executive director or administrator of the human service agency in providing residential services. Again, it is argued, the level of responsibility required to serve an employer's clients is comparable to that required by bona fide administrative employees in an industrial or retail setting who are responsible for serving customers.

General Guidance Unless the staff person is paid the salary necessary for one of the exemptions *and* meets each of the criteria necessary to qualify as either a professional, executive, or administrative employee, compensation must be computed on an hourly basis and at least at the statutory minimum wage of $3.35 per hour.

Few house counselors have been found to meet the categorical tests. If it is felt that some employees legitimately meet all of the tests for an exemption, it is advisable to get a formal determination of such exemption from the local office of the U.S. Department of Labor.

Compensatory Time

With the exception of the special provision for 80-hour, 14-day work periods, and for exempt employees, wages are generally computed on the basis of a workweek of 7 consecutive days. Time may not be averaged over 2 or more weeks when computing wages due. Therefore, if time off can be given later in a week in which overtime hours have been worked, thereby keeping the total number of hours constant, there will be no change in pay for the workweek.

Under certain circumstances, time off may be given in lieu of immediate overtime pay following the week in which overtime is worked. This is often referred to as "compensatory time," or "comp time," and it can be used to avoid extra bookkeeping. *This is permissible only within the same pay period for employees who work in the private sector.* For such employees, if time off is not given within the workweek, but can be provided later within the same pay period, the amount of actual compensation need not be altered if 1½ hours of "comp time" is given for each hour of overtime worked. In no case may "comp time" be taken beyond the pay period by employees in the private sector.

As a result of legislation passed in 1985 (Public Law 99-150), employees of state and local governments who work under a collective bargaining agreement or who agree in advance are permitted to collect overtime hours and take the time off at a future date. Comp-time hours, accumulated over a period of several days or even months, may be taken a day or more at a time, or used to extend a vacation period. Public employees must also be given one and one-half hours off for each hour of overtime worked and public safety employees may accumulate up to 480 hours of comp time.

Volunteer Time

Individuals may volunteer their services to public- or private-sector organizations and receive no compensation. Such persons are excluded from the definition of *employee* and are thus not covered by FLSA. They may be reimbursed for any expenses they incur on behalf of an organization without violating this volunteer status.

A person who is employed by an organization may not volunteer services to his or her own agency that are of the same type the employee is paid to perform. For example, a bookkeeper may not keep the books for his or her agency's special fundraising event without compensation, nor may a direct care staff person accompany a resident to an agency picnic or some other special event as a "volunteer."

DOL has provided some further guidance about conditions under which an employee may have contact with residents outside of the regular work day, which need not be compensated. It is not unusual for staff to invite residents to their home for a weekend or for a special family celebration. In a letter dated March 20, 1980, DOL stated, "If the activity is a form of hospitality, such as any family might occasionally offer to friends or relatives, and entirely voluntary with no coercion by the employer, no promise of advancement or no penalty for not volunteering, then we would be inclined not to consider time spent engaging in such activity as compensable 'work.' " DOL cautions, however, that "if the 'home visiting' represents a continuation of the same services that are provided for the [residents] while on the premises of the [home], and if the visits represent a substantial expenditure of time by the employees on a regular or recurrent basis, then we would consider such time spent as compensable under the Act" (H.J. Cohen, personal communication, March 18, 1980).

FURTHER DISCUSSION OF THE ISSUES

Employees who work with persons requiring support in their residential environment play a critical role in these persons' lives. Those often referred to as "direct care staff" spend more time with residents than any other employees, yet often receive the lowest rate of compensation, the fewest benefits, and the least amount of training. Human service providers decry the low rates of reimbursement that prohibit paying direct care staff the wages they should receive. Sometimes federal wage and hour rules provide the leverage needed to obtain an increase in per diem rates so that staff can at least be paid the minimum wage and overtime for hours actually worked. In this way the Fair Labor Standards Act is performing its function of helping to assure that American workers maintain the "minimum standard of living necessary for health, efficiency and general well-being."

In advocating for higher wages and exemptions from minimum wage and overtime rules, advocacy organizations such as the NAPRFMR are confronted with conflicting interests. The irregular hours frequently worked and the additional bookkeeping that results when staff must keep track of all hours worked can mean added expenses for bookkeeping. These monies spent on administrative costs could better be used for direct client services. The extension of wage and hour exemptions to more staff of community residences would relieve the administrative paperwork burden for many agencies and permit the use of more flexible staffing patterns preferred by most staff. Complicating that desire, however, is the awareness that staff who are not well paid tend to be dissatisfied with their jobs, and dissatisfaction can result in poor client services. It is clearly in the best interests of every human service agency to advocate for higher staff wages and benefits. Exemptions must therefore be crafted in such a way that employees are not disadvantaged. Higher salary tests for exempt employees now being considered by DOL would provide one means of increasing staff protection. The current salary test for administrative and executive employees represents a salary that is equal to the minimum wage plus less than 5 hours of overtime pay per week. The human services field must be certain that efforts to increase flexibility in staffing residential programs is not used to reduce costs at the expense of fair compensation for employee work. Further, wages must be high enough to attract quality personnel to staff group residences.

Programmatic considerations are not the only reasons for complying with requirements of the Fair Labor Standards Act. There are financial incentives as well. If an audit is conducted and wage and hour rules are found to have been violated, the agency will be required to pay employees back wages for the prior 2 years. Since the hours that must be compensated are generally overtime hours, the amount owed adds up quickly, and usually results in tens of thousands of dollars due. In addition, if it is discovered that an employer has deliberately avoided complying with the law, DOL may require payment of back wages due over the past 3 years, rather than for 2 years.

Despite what may sound like perfect conditions for an adversarial relationship between service providers and DOL officials, quite the opposite is generally true. The job of a compliance officer is to assure that provisions of the law are being observed. It is not his or her role to serve as an advocate either for workers or employers. Field agents are generally friendly and cooperative and will go to great lengths to determine the circumstances specific to the work being investigated. They will interview employees and staff to gain an understanding of the conditions of employment. This is particu-

larly helpful if an employee is mistaken about the agreement reached prior to employment. Such interviews enable the field officer to reach an objective conclusion.

The telephone numbers for local Department of Labor offices can be found in the telephone directory under the listings for U.S. Government. DOL officials often answer questions posed anonymously. They are also willing to examine staffing schedules and to recommend ways to comply with statutory and regulatory requirements. If they find an employer out of compliance as the result of such consultations, it will not automatically trigger an audit. However, it is *not* advisable to invite compliance officers to your agency. Once on-site, they are required not just to help you comply in the future, but to compensate for past errors by paying employees wages that should have been paid out over the prior 2-year period.

The information presented here on federal wage and hour rules is not intended to be the sole source of guidance in establishing staffing patterns and wages. Those interested in establishing community residences should contact their federal and state departments of labor for further guidance. It is also advisable to consult an attorney who specializes in labor law to review the specifics of each home's employment relationships.

Operating a residential setting serving persons with disabilities is a task with many complexities. Compliance with federal wage and hour rules is an area that demands the need for skill and a sound knowledge of business practice. A good business management system that can respond to all applicable regulatory requirements is essential. Such appropriate and competent responses to the task of compensating employees within the confines of federal law and regulation will promote program stability and a sound work environment.

REFERENCES

Code of Federal Regulations, 42 Health and Human Services, Parts 435 and 442, *Federal Register,* March 4, 1986.

Code of Federal Regulations, 29 Labor, Parts 500 to 1899, Revised as of July 1, 1979.

Fair Labor Standards Act Amendments of 1985, Report 99-357, November 1, 1985.

Fair Labor Standards Act, as Amended (29 U.S.C. 201, et seq.), WH Publication 1318, U.S. Department of Labor, Revised 1978.

Souder v. Brennan (Civil Action No. 482-73, United States District Court for District of Columbia, December 7, 1973).

APPENDIX

February 3, 1981

Ms. Joni Fritz
Executive Director
National Association of Private
  Residential Facilities for the
  Mentally Retarded
6269 Leesburg Pike, Suite B-5
Falls Church, Virginia 22044

Mr. Robert M. Gettings
Executive Director
National Association of State Mental
  Retardation Program Directors, Inc.
2001 Jefferson Davis Highway
Arlington, Virginia 22204

Dear Ms. Fritz and Mr. Gettings:

This is in response to your request for clarification of our letters of May 27 and March 13, 1980, dealing with the circumstances under which an employer can deduct from hours worked the time spent by houseparents sleeping at privately-operated community residences for the mentally retarded.

The facilities in question are owned or leased by private non-profit corporations. The corporations employ houseparents, and relief staff in many cases, to provide custodial care for mentally retarded individuals who reside in the facilities. The houseparents sleep overnight, sometimes as many as five or six days in a row, after which they get a day or two off. In addition, the houseparents may also have several hours off each afternoon, when they are free to do whatever they choose, including leaving the premises to shop, visit friends, or engage in similar activities.

Many of the houseparents maintain permanent residences elsewhere in the community, but others have as their only residence the facility for the mentally retarded. The relief staff may stay overnight at the facility one or two nights a week, and they maintain permanent residences elsewhere.

The houseparents and relief staff sleep in private quarters separate from the mentally retarded residents of the group home. The actual facts differ somewhat from facility to facility, but the above description sets forth the typical situation as it has been explained to us.

The Department's policy concerning sleep time is generally explained in its Interpretative Bulletin on Hours Worked, 29 CFR Part 785 (copy enclosed). As a general rule, sleep time is compensable unless it falls within either of two exceptions. First, subject to specified conditions, sleep time of up to eight hours need not be considered as working time if the employee is "on duty for 24 hours or more" (§785.22). (If the employee is on duty for less than 24 hours, no sleep time may be deducted from the employee's hours of work (§785.21.)

Second, where an employee "resides on his employer's premises on a permanent basis or for extended periods of time," any reasonable agreement of the parties as to the amount of hours worked will be accepted, if it takes all of the pertinent facts into consideration (§785.23).

Your first question is whether a community home employee who maintains a separate residence is prevented, by that fact alone, from qualifying as an employee "who resides on his employer's premises . . . for extended periods of time" within the meaning of 29 CFR 785.23. The maintenance of a separate residence would not, in itself, disqualify the employee from meeting this test. *In general, we take the position that employees who reside on their employer's premises five days a week are considered to reside there "for extended periods of time."* Where the facilities offered by the employer provide a homelike environment with private quarters separate from the residents of the group home, we would regard such employees as residing there, even though they may have another residence which they may regard as their principal residence. In light of the amount of time they spend at the group home, it is in effect a second residence.

Your second question seeks clarification of the Department's five-day rule described above. In our May 27 letter, we stated that where less than 120 hours in a week are spent residing on the employer's premises, five consecutive days or nights would also qualify as residing on the premises for extended periods of time. Your specific question is whether, under this standard, employees who are required to be on duty for less than 120 hours per week can still be considered as residing on the employer's premises.

The answer to this question is yes. Specifically, *where employees are on duty for less than 120 hours in a week, they can be considered as residing on the employer's premises, provided that they spend five consecutive days or five consecutive nights on the premises.* This rule can best be illustrated by concrete examples. If employees are on duty from 9 A.M. Monday until 9 A.M. Saturday, they will have been on duty for 120 hours (ignoring off-duty time that may be allowed for a few hours each day). Such employees are considered to reside on their employer's premises. The same is true of employees who are on duty from 9 A.M. Monday until 9 A.M. Wednesday and from 9 A.M. Thursday until 9 A.M. Sunday, since they will have been on duty for 120 hours in the week (again ignoring short periods of off-duty time). In each case, the employees reside on the premises for five days and five nights.

Employees who are on duty from 9 A.M. Monday until 5 P.M. Friday would also be considered to reside on the employer's premises. Even though on duty for less than 120 hours, they are on duty for five consecutive days (Monday through Friday). The fact that they sleep over only four nights does not matter. Similarly, employees who are on duty from 9 P.M. Monday until 9 A.M. Saturday would also be considered to reside on their employer's premises, since they are on duty for five consecutive nights (Monday night through Friday night).

Your third and final question related to *employees who do not reside at the community residences but who,* as relief employees, *remain there for at least 24 hours, and often as long as two or three days.* You have informed us that these relief employees, *during a 24-hour period, have off-duty time during the day with complete freedom from all responsibilities,* thereby enabling them to use the time effectively for their own purposes. Such employees, as you have pointed out, *are arguably on duty for less than 24 hours.* Your specific question is whether the sleep time of such employees can be deducted from working time.

Under the particular circumstances you have described, we believe that such sleep time can be deducted from hours worked, provided that the employer and employees agree in advance to do so, and that no more than 8 hours per night (or actual, uninterrupted sleeptime, if that is less than 8 hours) is deducted. We have reached this conclusion, which represents a departure from the general rule under 29 CFR 785.21, because of the home-like environment afforded to these employees in community residences, with private quarters and other amenities. Even where employees sleep over for only one or two nights, there are ample facilities to enable them to get a full night's sleep.

In situations falling within the general rule which forbids the deduction of any sleep time, the demands of the job have seriously interfered with the employee's ability to sleep, or the sleeping facilities have been minimal. Here, however, because of the home-like environment, an exception can be made where employees do in fact get a reasonable night's sleep. In other words, under the particular circumstances described above, we would apply the sleep time rule set forth in §785.22.

We trust that this letter is responsive to your questions.

Sincerely,

Henry T. White, Jr.
Deputy Administrator

Enclosure

April, 1983

Ms. Joni Fritz
Executive Director
National Association of Private
   Residential Facilities for the Mentally
   Retarded
6269 Leesburg Pike, Suite B-5
Falls Church, Virginia 22044

Dear Ms. Fritz:

This is in reply to your letter of February 25, 1983, concerning sleep time. You wish to know how many hours may be counted as sleep time in a situation where an employee works from 3 P.M. Monday to 10 A.M. Wednesday. In this period of time, the employee sleeps from 11 P.M. Monday to 7 A.M. Tuesday, has free time from 10 A.M. to 3 P.M. Tuesday, and then sleeps from 11 P.M. Tuesday to 7 A.M. Wednesday. The employee leaves work at 10 A.M. on Wednesday. In a telephone conversation with a member of my staff, you added that these employees do not reside on the employer's premises on a permanent basis or for a period longer than the work period described in your letter.

As you know, sleep time of up to eight hours need not be considered as working time if the employee is "on duty for 24 hours or more" (see Section 785.22 of 29 CFR Part 785) or if the employee resides on the employer's premises on a permanent basis or for an extended period of time (see section 785.23). If the employee is on duty for less than 24 hours, no sleep time may be deducted from the employee's hours of work (see section 785.21).

Employees who do not reside on the employer's premises on a permanent basis or for an extended period of time but who may remain at the employer's establishment for at least 24 hours (and as long as two or three days), even though they may have off-duty time during the day with complete freedom from all responsibilities, thereby enabling them to use the time effectively for their own purposes, may still have sleep time deducted from their hours worked. We wish to emphasize again that this departure from the general rules is permitted only if the personnel are provided private quarters and other amenities which provide a home-like environment. Further, the employer and the employee must agree in advance that sleep time will be deducted from hours worked and that no more than 8 hours (or actual, uninterrupted sleep time if that is less than 8 hours) is deducted.

Assuming the employees you describe in your example meet the qualifications described above for employees on duty for 24 hours or more, the employer may deduct 8 hours of sleep time in the work period. Only one sleeping period of up to 8 hours may be deducted for each 24-hour period an employee is scheduled to work. In your example, the employee works from 3 P.M. Monday to 3 P.M. Tuesday (a 24-hour period) and works from 3 P.M. Tuesday to 10 A.M. Wednesday (a 19-hour period). Sleep time may be deducted for the first day of work but may not be deducted for the second day of work since the second day is a period of less than 24 hours.

We hope the above has been responsive to your inquiry.

Sincerely,

William M. Otter   James L. Valin
Administrator   Assistant Administrator
                          Wage and Hour Division

June 29, 1987

Ms. Joni Fritz
Executive Director
National Association of Private
  Residential Facilities for the
  Mentally Retarded
6400H Seven Corners Place
Falls Church, Virginia 22044

Dear Ms. Fritz:

This is in further reply to your letter, addressed to former Assistant Administrator James L. Valin, concerning the application of the Fair Labor Standards Act (FLSA) to employees of community residences for the mentally retarded. We regret the delay in responding to your inquiry.

You wish to know if, under certain conditions which you describe, time spent sleeping may be excluded from the compensable hours of work by these employees. The conditions are that the employees in question:

(1) have a certain amount of uncompensated "free" time during the workday,

(2) do *not* reside on the premises of the group home where they work, and

(3) do *not* relieve a full-time employee who resides on the premises.

Employees' time spent sleeping is compensable as hours worked under FLSA unless this time falls within either of two exceptions which are set forth in Interpretative Bulletin, 29 CFR Part 785, a copy of which is enclosed for your information. First, subject to specified conditions, sleeping time of up to 8 hours need not be considered as working time if the employee is "on duty for 24 hours or more" (section 785.22). Second, where an employee "resides on his employer's premises on a permanent basis or for extended periods of time," any reasonable agreement of the parties as to the amount of hours worked will be accepted, if it takes all of the pertinent facts into consideration (section 785.23).

In our letter to you of August 20, 1985 (copy enclosed), we clarified the position of the Wage and Hour Division regarding the exclusion of time spent sleeping from employees' compensable hours of work under FLSA. In that letter, we advised you that "in situations where a community residence employs one or more full-time employees *who reside on the employer's premises on a permanent basis or for extended periods of time* (emphasis added), the employer and a relief employee who performs essentially the same duties as such full-time employees may agree, in advance of the performance of any work, that sleeping time of up to eight hours can be excluded from compensable hours of work, regardless of the length of the tour of duty involved. Also, a mutually agreed-upon amount of off-duty time, during which the employee is completely free from all responsibilities, can be excluded from compensable hours of work."

You refer to certain changes which have evolved in the care of people with mental retardation. You indicate that the continuing movement of patients from institutions to community living arrangements has made it necessary for group homes to implement more innovative staffing patterns. The subject of your opinion request is an example of one of these changes in staffing patterns. Specifically, this is the practice of having the group home completely staffed by two or more employees who work on rotating shifts. However, none of these individuals qualifies as a full-time employee who "resides on the premises" within the meaning of that term or as a "relief employee" as defined in our previous letter to you on this subject. Therefore, it is our opinion that time spent sleeping by the employees who are referred to in your inquiry may not be excluded from their compensable hours of work under FLSA.

We trust that the above is responsive to your inquiry.

Sincerely,

Paula V. Smith
Administrator

Enclosures

Chapter 22

Behavioral Consultation in Community Residences

Gary B. Seltzer and Michael Apolito

This chapter discusses behavioral consultation in community residences for developmentally disabled persons. Following a review of the literature, the consultation process is described in detail, starting with how to select a consultant and covering topics such as the structure of the consultation process, developing programs for residents, and data-keeping strategies. Suggestions are provided for additional reading and staff training materials.

I t is the norm for public institutions for mentally retarded persons to employ specialized staff (e.g., physical therapists, psychologists, etc.) for the development and the coordination of residents' programs. In contrast, community-based residential programs rarely directly employ specialized staff (Hill, Lakin, Sigford, Hauber, & Bruininks, 1982). Instead, it is usually the responsibility of direct care staff in community residences to assess the need for specialized services and to broker such services on behalf of residents. In addition, staff of community residences are expected to teach personal care and housekeeping skills to residents, promote community participation, help residents to improve their social skills, and reduce behavioral excesses that interfere with the ability to learn new skills and live cooperatively with peers. This hefty agenda demands the utilization of a vast amount of technical knowledge and sophisticated clinical skills by direct care staff, who generally are nonprofessionals.

Some sponsoring agencies of community residences hire consultants in order to enable direct

care staff to more effectively promote residents' health, develop their functional abilities, and reduce behavior problems. In any given residence, the type of consultant hired is a function of the programmatic needs of the residents and the skills of the direct care staff. Community residences can utilize consultants from as diverse a set of fields as physical therapy, recreation, nutrition, medicine, social work, and psychology. Each of these types of consultants can contribute to the flow of specialized knowledge into community residences, can help to establish linkages to other community resources, and can develop interventions that teach residents new skills and reduce maladaptive behaviors. The consultation process provides a vehicle by which direct care staff can develop clinical expertise. Hence, consultants have two functions: 1) program development for residents and 2) staff development.

There are many common elements of the consultation process irrespective of the specific discipline of the consultant. In all instances, an outside expert is hired to provide technical in-

The authors wish to gratefully acknowledge the contributions to the model presented in this chapter by the Behavioral Development Center, Providence, RI, with which both authors were formerly affiliated.

formation to staff in order to improve the skills and quality of life of residents and to make the organization function more effectively. Further, although consultants have only a time-limited relationship with an agency, they are expected to make a lasting contribution to its operation.

The most common type of consultation is provided by behavioral specialists, oftentimes psychologists, social workers, or educators, who are hired to assist staff in the development of clinical interventions aimed at improving residents' skills and functional abilities. This chapter focuses on behaviorally oriented consultation to community residences for persons with mental retardation and other developmental disabilities.

In this chapter the use of a behavioral approach to consultation refers to the application of practice principles and theory that often fall under the rubric of behavior modification or behavior therapy. We are not drawing a distinction between *behavior modification* and *behavior therapy*. There are numerous definitions of *behavior modification,* ranging from the application of the principles of operant conditioning (e.g., Skinner, 1953, 1963) or classical conditioning (Wolpe, 1982) to the more generally applied principles of social learning theory (Ullman & Krasner, 1975). More recently there has developed an expanded repertoire of clinical approaches that incorporate the works of such theorists as Bandura (1977) and innovative practitioners such as Lazarus (1976). Although there is no single theoretical underpinning for behavior modification, there is agreement among practitioners to utilize an empirical approach to practice and to experimentally analyze and treat the functional relationships among problem behaviors. There is an ever-changing empirical literature on the study of behavior and its modification, the use of which is expected to be an integral part of the consultant-consultee relationship.

We have elected to focus on a behavioral model of consultation for a number of specific reasons. First, research has clearly indicated that behavioral procedures can be used effectively to teach self-help and community living skills to mentally retarded persons (Reid, Wilson, & Faw, 1983). The range and complexity of behaviors being taught has grown considerably in the last 20 years (Matson & McCartney, 1981). Schibak (1983) noted that there are over 400 studies in the literature demonstrating the efficacy of behavioral procedures with mentally retarded individuals.

Second, staff can be taught to implement behavioral procedures effectively. Professionals, paraprofessionals, and parents have been successfully taught to use behavioral techniques in order to improve the adaptive behaviors of mentally retarded persons (Whitman, Schibak, & Reid, 1982; Yule & Carr, 1980). Furthermore, behaviorally oriented training materials have been developed that can be used by nonprofessionals with a minimum of professional support (Baker, Heifetz, & Murphy, 1980).

Third, state regulatory agencies often require community residences to maintain records on resident goals, programs, and progress in the form of individualized service plans (ISPs). Since ISPs tend to measure progress according to achievement of behavioral objectives, behavioral consultants can help staff to develop data-keeping systems that provide the documentation required by state and federal regulatory agencies.

Although hiring a behavioral consultant is advantageous for all of these reasons, a consultant's long-range effectiveness is dependent upon the development of behavioral expertise among the full-time staff. This chapter describes a model of behavioral consultation in which a full-time staff member is designated to be trained by and to serve as the liaison with the behavioral consultant. The designated staff member functions as an on-site behavioral programmer who eventually assumes responsibility for training other members of the direct care staff.

This model of consultation is intended for use in community residences that serve mentally retarded persons who have substantial impairments in functional skills, who have serious maladaptive behaviors, are multiply handicapped, or have other needs that require the development of clinical treatment interventions. This chapter does not explain how to develop behavioral programs per se, but, rather, how to structure a consultation relationship that fosters the development of behavioral programs for residents. (See Manfredini & Smith, this volume, for a discussion of program development for active treatment in community residences.)

Following a description of the consultation model, behavioral assessment forms and procedures are presented that can enhance the working relationship between a behavioral consultant and community residence staff. Finally, a vignette illustrating the use of behavioral consultation is presented.

BACKGROUND: BEHAVIORAL TREATMENT

In the late 1950s, operant procedures such as reinforcement and extinction, initially developed in laboratory animal studies, were applied in working with mentally retarded children (Bijou, 1963). Using subjects from schools and public institutions, the effectiveness of behavior modification techniques was demonstrated. Researchers noted impressive improvements in skill acquisition and reduction of serious behavior problems previously not believed amenable to change (Lovaas & Simmons, 1969; Watson, 1967). These documented treatment successes helped fuel the deinstitutionalization movement of the 1970s.

Although numerous behavioral studies have been conducted in institutional settings and public schools (Kratochwill, 1985), only a limited amount of research has been conducted in community-based residential settings. Stacy, Doleys, and Malcolm (1979) conducted a study of social skills training in community residences. A behavioral approach was used to improve the social behavior of mentally retarded adults with extended histories of institutionalization. Subjects given the training showed significant reductions in maladaptive behaviors characteristic of institutionalized persons (e.g., overcompliance and helplessness). Schalock, Foley, Toulouse, and Stark (1985) examined the use of medication and behavioral interventions in order to modify compliance and stereotypic behaviors. Again, their findings support the use of behavioral interventions in community residences. Other examples of the use of behavioral treatment methods in commu-

nity residences include studies by Matson on depression (1982) and on preventing home accidents (1980), and by Handen, Apolito, and Seltzer (1984) on modifying verbal behavior.

Handen et al. (1984) noted the difficulty of implementing treatment outcome studies in community residences for persons with a developmental disability. Staffing inconsistencies associated with staff turnover, illness, and vacation schedules were cited as some of the common impediments to behavioral consultation and programming. Further, community residences tend to have limited consultation budgets, which has deterred the utilization of consultants in such settings. The model presented here was designed so that a community residence can efficiently use a small consultation budget to develop a consulting relationship that is flexible enough to succeed even in the context of direct care staff instability.

THE CONSULTATION MODEL

In developing a consultation relationship, it is necessary to decide which type of arrangement best fits the needs of the community residence. The type of possible arrangements are defined by the anticipated length of the relationship, the primary recipient of consultation, the identified target for change, and the type of consultative expertise required. Kadushin (1977) delineated different consultative arrangements based upon the recipient of consultation and the targets for change. In some consultative relationships, the primary target for change is the agency, whereas in others it is the residents. Sometimes the consultant concentrates on improving the skills of the consultee and secondarily on the target of change or vice versa.

Although these foci are not mutually exclusive, these writers are of the opinion that the consultation model that best fits the needs of community residences is one in which a full-time staff member is selected as the consultee. The initial focus of the long-term relationship is on building the skills of the consultee, who in turn is expected to train other direct care staff to implement residents' programs. Kadushin (1977) called this approach ''consultee-centered case consultation'' and noted that the emphasis is on modifying the consultee's behavior so that he or she can more effectively help the residents. He also noted that this type of consultation requires a substantial period of contact between consultant and consultee.

In order to implement this consultation model, it is critically important to have a community residence staff member on site with strong behavioral skills. While community residences are characterized by frequent direct care staff turnover, the process of training, monitoring, and evaluating effectiveness can be made more efficient by having a "resident" expert on staff, usually in the position of house director.

The design of our consultation model borrows from the works of Bernstein (1982) and Tharp and Wetzel (1969). Tharp and Wetzel (1969) proposed a triadic model of consultation that they considered to be consistent with a behavioral approach. In their model, behavioral program development flowed from the consultant to the target (resident) via a mediator (key staff person). They defined the *consultant* as anyone with behavioral expertise, the *mediator* as someone who reinforces the target, and the

target as someone whose behavior the consultant agrees to modify.

Bernstein (1982) noted that the complexity of behavioral interventions has increased considerably since Tharp and Wetzel developed their model in the late 1960s. In order to adapt to this level of complexity, Bernstein proposed that the function of the mediator be differentiated into two functions: behavioral engineer and behavioral manager. She explained that "in this model the client is anyone whose behavior the behavioral engineer agrees to modify; the behavioral manager is anyone who implements change procedures; the behavioral engineer is anyone who designs and adjusts change procedures; and the consultant is a troubleshooter and resource provider who assists the behavioral engineer with program design and revision or the behavioral manager with program implementation" (p. 3).

Figure 1 depicts the elements in the consultative system and the anticipated patterns of information flow. The model is interactive because it assumes that changes in any one element (such as changes in residents' behavior)

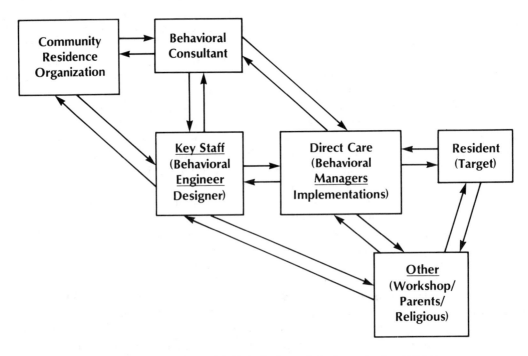

Figure 1. An interactive model of behavioral consultation for community residences.

influence some other element. This interactive, or systems, approach to consultation is consonant with a behavior analytic approach, as most behavioral models specify that in order to change one person's behavior, one has to modify the behaviors of others in that same environment. As noted earlier, the initial focus of consultation is between the behavioral consultant and the key staff person. Over time, the consultant and consultee can shift their focus to other issues. These may include the quality and consistency of programming between community residence and day programs, developing more meaningful ties to community resources, and enhancing residents' familial relationships.

IMPLEMENTING THE CONSULTATION MODEL

To implement this consultation model, four tasks must be accomplished:

1. Selecting the consultant
2. Selecting the on-site key staff member
3. Structuring the relationship between the consultant and the key staff member
4. Developing programs for residents

Selecting the Consultant

There are five important attributes to watch for in selecting a behavioral consultant for a community residence. First, it is essential for a consultant to be knowledgeable about community residential services for developmentally disabled persons. Community residences serve at least two functions: first, providing a home for developmentally disabled persons; and second, creating a habilitative environment that fosters the development of new skills in residents and as independent a life-style for them as possible. Familiarity with this dual purpose of community residences is necessary in order for the consultant to facilitate the development of skill-building programs while recognizing the constraints of operating in a home environment rather than a classroom or clinic. Further, familiarity with community residences enables the consultant to be sensitive to potential problems such as staff turnover, budgetary limitations, community opposition, linkages with day

programs, and other issues that affect the success of programming efforts.

Second, the consultant must have expertise in behavioral programming with developmentally disabled persons. Not only is thorough knowledge of general behavior modification techniques necessary, but it is strongly advised that previous experience in the utilization of these techniques with developmentally disabled persons be a prerequisite of the position.

Third, the consultant needs to be knowledgeable about organizations. Our consultation model is a systems model in which the consultant is building the expertise and capabilities of the organization. Familiarity with how decisions are made and implemented by boards of directors and executive staff immeasurably facilitates this consultation process.

Fourth, it is essential for the consultant to have good social skills, to be willing to work with a wide variety of types of staff, to be flexible in scheduling, and to be a good listener and a good observer.

Fifth, and related to the previous point, the consultant must be willing to nurture the expertise and credibility of the key staff person. Recall that the goal is to transfer expertise from the consultant to the key staff person. Thus, the consultant must be willing to let the key staff person receive much of the credit for the programming that they do together in order to develop the key staff person's credibility and expertise.

Hiring any professional involves making judgments about intangible qualities. While the preceding five attributes may be difficult to assess objectively, they should be kept in mind during the selection process.

A number of strategies have been used successfully by community residences to identify a potential behavioral consultant. Consultants come from many disciplines including social work, psychology, education, and other helping professions. They may be engaged in their own private clinical practice and enjoy the opportunity to participate in a consultation relationship as a contrast from their direct treatment practice role. Universities may be another good source of consultants. Often, academic departments and their faculty seek to establish partnerships with service agencies in order to contribute to the community image of the university and to provide a site for research or field placement for students. Many graduate students are quite skilled in behavioral treatment techniques and are in need of the type of flexibility that consultation work affords. Lastly, national organizations such as the Association for Advancement of Behavior Therapy (AABT) and similar local organizations committed to behavioral treatment publish membership directories, which may serve as a resource for locating behavioral consultants.

Selecting the Key Staff Member

This consultation model is built on the assumption that an on-site staff member can be trained to eventually assume an in-house consultation role. Optimally, this person should have a long-term commitment to the sponsoring agency so that he or she will likely still be affiliated with the agency after the consultation/training process has been completed. The key staff person should also be in a supervisory role or in some other position of authority with respect to the direct care staff members. This person may be the residence director or may have some supervisory or programmatic responsibility for several residences sponsored by a single agency.

In addition, the process of training the key staff member will be easier if he or she already has some familiarity with behaviorally oriented programming methods. While it is possible for the consultant to "start from scratch" in training the key staff person, this will slow the process considerably and delay the development of programs for residents.

Structuring the Relationship between the Consultant and the Key Staff Member

Three phases characterize the relationship between the consultant and the key staff member. In the first phase, the consultant assumes primary responsibility for developing programs for residents. In addition, he or she provides training in program development to the key staff member. In the second phase, the key staff member assumes responsibility for the development of residents' programs, while receiving some supervision from the consultant. Finally, in the third phase, the key staff member trains the direct care staff to develop programs and acts as a consultant to them. In this third phase, the consultant gradually reduces involvement in the community residence or can shift his or her focus to other programming needs within the sponsoring agency (e.g., day programs, family work).

During phase one, the consultant uses the decision tree categories delineated in Figures 2 and 3 as a guide to the specific content that the key staff member needs to learn. The consultant may select one or a group of residents on whom skill and behavior problem assessments are conducted, working with the key staff person. The skill area to be worked on should be selected on the basis of its likelihood to change with a minimum of both environmental modification and use of staff resources. The selection of readily modifiable skill deficits is one way to put into practice the behavioral principle of taking small, gradual steps when learning new skills in order to maximize successful outcomes. Successful outcomes are reinforcing and are likely to result in an increased investment in utilizing the consultant's expertise to advance the skills of the key staff member. Once the consultant and key staff member have collaborated on the development of approximately 15 skill and behavior problem programs by running through the series of steps listed in Figures 2 and 3, the consultant should begin to implement a fading-out procedure. Fading out of assistance is a common behavioral technique (involving a gradual withdrawal of some stimulus) that is used to increase independent performance, which is the goal of phase one.

During phase two, the key staff member assumes more responsibility for programming and for making decisions on how and when to implement the steps in Figures 2 and 3. The consultant must be sure to emphasize independent program initiation and completion as much as if not more than the specifics of program development. The consultant should also be aware of himself or herself as a teaching model to be used by the key staff member during phase two.

In practice, the third phase begins earlier than its consecutive order implies. During phase

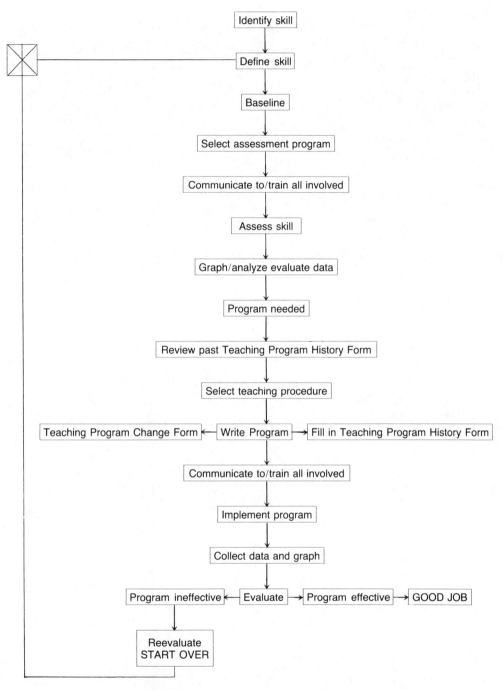

Figure 2. Decision tree for skill teaching programs.

two, the direct care staff have already begun to implement the programs first designed by the consultant and then by the key staff member. Direct care staff will thus have been trained in the collection of assessment, baseline, and treatment data. Once the key staff member establishes the record-keeping system and data book (described later in the chapter), he or she and the consultant can provide training to the direct care staff.

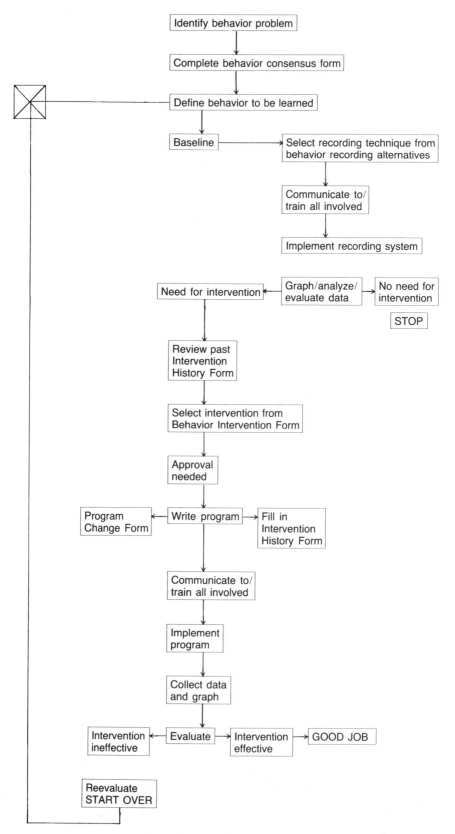

Figure 3. Decision tree for behavior problem programs.

The training format should include assigned readings, group discussions of the readings, quizzes, role-playing, and direct feedback. Again, a structured system of questions and answers for each procedure, role-playing scripts, and rating forms, are helpful exercises. Evaluations of these training exercises can be conducted through direct observation of the staff's implementation of behavioral procedures. Materials that may be useful in the training process are listed in the Supplementary Resources at the end of this chapter.

The process of training the key staff member typically spans a 1- or 2-year time period. During the early months, the expense to the agency is the highest because the consultant's involvement is most intense. Weekly meetings between the consultant and the key staff member generally are needed. In addition, it is advisable for the consultant to attend staff meetings and to help the key staff member put in place the data collection procedures (described later) that are needed to develop and implement behavioral programs for residents. Over time, the consultant can reduce his or her contact with the direct care staff, while continuing to meet with the key staff member. Finally, the frequency of these meetings should be reduced, as the key staff member assumes primary responsibility for programming.

Developing Programs for Residents

The consultation model conceives of consultation as a problem-solving process consisting of four stages: 1) problem identification, 2) problem analysis, 3) plan implementation, and 4) problem evaluation. These four stages are described in considerable detail by Bergan (1977). Together these stages offer an empirically grounded approach to consultation. Starting with the identification of the problem and the collection of baseline data, the model requires the delineation of treatment interventions and the evaluation of treatment effectiveness based upon observable, quantitative changes in the residents' behavior. The decision trees in Figures 2 and 3 were developed in order to specify a series of steps in the process of developing, implementing, and evaluating skill teaching and behavior problem programs con-

sistent with the four stages. The programming direction begins at the point of problem identification and concludes with program success or reevaluation.

In a study of consultation effectiveness, Bergan and Tombari (1976) found that those consultants who failed the first of the four stages, that of problem identification, never reached the stages of problem analysis, plan implementation, or evaluation. In contrast, consultants successful in identifying the problem were almost invariably able to effectively develop and evaluate programs. The Bergan behavioral model of problem solving and the Bergan and Tombari (1976) findings suggest that a strong emphasis should be placed on behavioral assessment as a part of the consultation process. The remainder of this chapter analyzes behavioral assessment in consultation.

BEHAVIORAL ASSESSMENT IN CONSULTATION

The process of behavioral assessment begins with the collection of reliable information about a resident. Many community residential programs have poor data collection and record-keeping systems. The consultant and designated key staff member should evaluate the community residence's data-keeping systems. Early collaboration on effective data-keeping systems is critical. The more comprehensive and reliable the record-keeping systems, the greater the chance that consultation will be successful. A variety of assessment forms and data collection procedures is offered throughout the remainder of this section.

Data Books

A separate program data book should be developed for each resident. The data book contains a compilation of the resident's initial skill assessments, a listing of skills that have been taught, periodic reassessments, detailed teaching plans and associated data, behavior problem interventions and data, correspondence with the resident's day program, and medical information. The data book should be sectioned into each of the areas just mentioned, with a cover sheet describing what information/forms are to be kept in each section. A single direct care staff member is assigned responsibility for the content and maintenance of a resident's data book. In this way, the designated direct care person functions as a case manager for his or her assigned resident, following a case management model.

The key staff member should review the data books weekly in order to provide supervision and feedback to staff and to monitor the pro-

gress made by residents. In addition, these data books provide a compendium of information that is readily available for review by the consultant. The key staff member and consultant can use the data books for program planning and as a way to evaluate how well direct care staff can observe and collect data. Reliability checks on specific programs in the data book enhance the evaluation of the direct care staff's competence. In addition, during weekly staff

---

Behavior Consensus Form

This form is to be used to ascertain the scope of a resident's behavior problem. The form should be sent to the resident's respective day or residential settings.

This section is to be filled out by practitioners in the setting where the behavior problem was first observed.

Resident: _____   Setting: _____   Date: _____

Behavior/description: _____

_____

_____

_____

_____

_____

_____

_____

Staff signature: _____

This section is to be filled out by the recipient of this form.

Setting: _____   Date: _____

    The described behavior has been observed in this setting: Yes/No
                                                  (Circle one)

    The described behavior is a problem in this setting: Yes/No
                                                  (Circle one)

    Scheduled program meeting: Date: _____   Time: _____

Behavior/description. (This section should be filled in if the behavior observed differs in any manner from the above description.)

_____

_____

_____

_____

_____

Staff signature: _____

Figure 4. Behavior Consensus Form.

meetings, a direct care staff person may be responsible for presenting an overall review of one of his or her resident's programs. The key staff member can provide feedback to the direct care staff about the quality of the programs developed and help to redesign programs that may not be effective.

Data-Keeping Forms

An important element of the data book is a list of the skills to be taught within each of a series of areas (e.g., hygiene and grooming; community living skills, etc.). Each skill to be taught should be broken down into component steps (i.e., task analyzed). Records should be kept of the date training began and the mastery date. The resident should be assessed in all of the program's curriculum areas as an aid in identifying target skill deficits.

Separate series of forms should be developed for use by the day program and community residence. Most residents attend day programs separate from the residential program. If a resident has serious skill deficits or problem behaviors,

it is important to assess whether these are manifested differently in the residential and day program settings. The Behavior Consensus Form was developed for this purpose (see Figure 4). This form should be sent to the resident's day program. A description of the behavior of concern should be recorded on the form by staff in both settings, and then a planning meeting should be arranged to discuss appropriate assessment strategies. Once the behavior problem or skill deficit has been identified and adequately described, recording procedures can be selected and documented. The operational definition and data recording procedure should be documented jointly by the key staff member and consultant in order to identify target behaviors and implement programming strategies. Regular graphing of data from this form allows for synthesis of information. Visual inspection of these graphs tends to enhance communication across settings.

Figure 5 is an example of a Behavior Problem Form, which includes the name of the person writing the plan, the date, goals, objectives,

---

Behavior Program Form

1. Resident: _____ Staff/title: _____ Date: _____

2. Goal: _____

3. Objective: _____
   (Whenever the goal is to decrease/extinguish a behavior, provide an alternative behavior and a program to initiate and increase it.)

4. Target behavior definition: _____

5. Baseline data: _____

6. Data-recording procedures (how, where): _____

7. Treatment procedures (who, what, where, when, how): _____

8. Procedures for maintenance: _____

9. Procedures for generalization: _____

10. Bonus: _____

11. Penalty: _____

12. Signed—resident: _____ Clinical director: _____

    Guardian advocate: _____ Service coordinator: _____

    Human rights committee: _____

    Other: _____

13. Review date(s)—fill in date of each review:

    ____ ____ ____ ____ ____ ____ ____ ____ ____ ____

    ____ ____ ____ ____ ____ ____ ____ ____ ____ ____

    ____ ____ ____ ____ ____ ____ ____ ____ ____ ____

Figure 5. Behavior Program Form.

Level I.   Procedures requiring supervisor approval; formal approval of the clinical director not needed
    A. Contingent positive reinforcement
       1. Social
       2. Activity
       3. Edible
       4. Token
    B. Differential Reinforcement of
       1. Other behavior (DRO)
       2. Incompatible behavior (DRI)
       3. Low rates of behavior (DRL)
    C. Modeling
    D. Contingency contracting (not including procedures in Levels II or III)
    E. Environmental changes
    F. Extinction

Level II.   Procedures requiring approval of clinical director, guardian/client, and human rights committee; and service coordinator's signature.
    A. Response cost (loss of points, tokens, nonessentials such as tea, coffee, or dessert)
    B. Restitution (making amends), which is not physically enforced
    C. Positive practice (practicing the correct behavior in massed trials)
    D. Nonexclusionally/observational timeout
       1. Client removed from activity while remaining in full view (maximum 5 minutes)
       2. Activity removed from the client (maximum 5 minutes)

Level III. Procedures requiring approval of clinical director, guardian/client, human rights committee, and DMH area human rights committee; and service coordinator's signature
    A. Overcorrection (correcting the environmental consequences of the behavior and then practicing an alternative incompatible behavior) in which physical guidance is used.
    B. Exclusionary timeout
       1. Removal to an area out of view (maximum 10 minutes)
       2. Removal to a lighted, ventilated room, door open (maximum 10 minutes)
       3. Removal to a lighted, ventilated room, door closed (unlocked, maximum 10 minutes)
    C. Response cost (less of an activity, or less of an activity recommended in the individualized service plan)

Figure 6. Intervention alternatives.

baseline data, data recording procedures to be used, and a detailed outline of the treatment strategy. Procedures for generalization, maintenance, review dates, and approval signatures should also be recorded. The use of a detailed form such as this helps structure the writing of programs and aids in ensuring that all program components are adequately addressed.

When developing programs to change maladaptive behaviors, it may be helpful for the consultant and staff to prepare a set of intervention procedures listed in order from the least intrusive to the most intrusive (see Figure 6). Further. the listing should specify the level of approval (i.e., key staff approval, resident director approval, resident/guardian approval, and human rights committee approval) needed to use each level in the intrusiveness hierarchy. This procedure not only assists in the selection

of the least intrusive intervention but also in protecting the resident's rights.

An example of how behavioral consultation can be used is shown in the following example of Mark (see vignette). This complicated behavioral program was successfully implemented at Mark's community residence (see Handen et al., 1984, for a full description of the program and its effects). Over time, the consultant and key staff member had developed the necessary data-keeping systems and had trained the direct care staff in carrying out the reinforcement program. After conferring with the consultant, the key staff person wrote Mark's program on a Behavior Problem Form and placed it in Mark's data book. Also, the key staff person trained Mark's direct care staff in the specific assessment and intervention strategies required for his program. The program was reviewed weekly with the consultant and during weekly staff meetings. Any program changes were documented, and the staff were informed of the changes by the key staff person.

Vignette: Mark

Mark is a 16-year-old adolescent with a diagnosis of autism and mental retardation. He had lived at home with his parents until the age of 14, when he moved into a community residence. At the residence, he lived with five other male residents of his approximate age and with similar diagnoses. The staff-to-client ratio was 1:2. Mark attended a year-round day treatment and educational program.

Mark had a 5-year history of extremely repetitive speech, the pattern of which involved repeating statements or asking the same questions literally hundreds of times each day. In his school program, he had been treated using a variety of behavioral techniques, as well as timeout, but with little or no success. Mark's repetitive speech was highly distracting and caused residents and staff to avoid interacting with him whenever possible.

The consultant and the key staff person worked together to develop an intervention strategy. First, they operationally defined the target for change— Mark's repetitive speech. Repeating was defined as saying any word, phrase or sentence two or more times in a row, or making a verbal response that was similar in content to what was previously said. Audiotapes were used in the process of defining repetitive behavior and later as a means of assessing the reliability with which staff identified and recorded repeats.

Mark was encouraged to avoid repeating by rewarding him when he made fewer than a criterion level of repeats within a predetermined time interval. The criterion was gradually made more and more stringent. At the end of an interval, if Mark had met the criterion he received a token. He could then exchange the token for a reinforcer or save it and exchange the token at a later time.

Mark continued on the program for approximately 18 months. During baseline data collection, Mark was averaging 4.7 repeats per minute. At posttest, he averaged one repeat every 3 to 4 minutes. Now that his repeats were reduced to a level that did not interfere with his learning ability, Mark was taught more appropriate ways to get attention from staff and other residents. Over time, Mark became well accepted by the other residents, who previously had avoided interacting with him.

CONCLUSIONS

This chapter presented a consultation model that brings behavioral expertise into the daily routine of community residences. The model requires a structured long-term relationship of at least a year's duration between the consultant and designated key staff person from the community residence. This relationship is pivotal to the consultation objectives. Over time, the consultant and key staff person collaborate to: 1) establish a compendium of behavioral assessments and data collection forms; 2) develop an individual behavioral program for each of the residents; and 3) develop an ongoing training program for direct care staff. An ongoing training program is critical because of the high turnover rate among direct care staff. The third of these objectives assumes that the residents served warrant intensive programming. In community residences that serve developmentally disabled persons whose skill deficits and maladaptive behaviors are not severe, a less intensive consultation model would be more appropriate.

As noted earlier, a commonly used behavioral programming strategy is to fade out reinforcement and other programming implements in order for the skill to be performed independently and perhaps to generalize beyond the specific environmental contingencies. The intent of the consultation relationship is also to reduce the dependence of the key staff person on the consultant and for the behavioral expertise to become an integral part of the setting. Furthermore, as residents' skills improve, it may be possible to move from the highly structured mode of operation as described in this chapter to a less structured one.

The writers strongly suggest that the quality of the consultation model be assessed on the basis of achieved residents' goals. The purpose of the model is to facilitate the use of behavioral techniques in order to enhance the quality of life for residents. The model's success rests on the degree to which residents are gaining independence in their lives and feel satisfied and happy about the quality of their lives.

REFERENCES

Baker, B.L., Heifetz, L., & Murphy, D. (1980). Behavioral training for parents of mentally retarded children: One year follow-up. *American Journal of Mental Deficiency, 85,* 31–38.

Bandura, A. (1977). Self-efficacy: Toward a unifying theory of behavioral change. *Psychological Review, 84,* 191–215.

Bergan, J.R. (1977). *Behavioral consultation.* Columbus, OH: Charles E. Merrill.

Bergan, J.R., & Tombari, M.L. (1976). Consultant skill and efficiency and the implementation and outcomes in consultation. *Journal of School Psychology, 14,* 3–14.

Bernstein, G. (1982). Training behavior change agents: A conceptual review. *Behavior Therapy, 13,* 1–23.

Bijou, S.W. (1963). Theory and research in mental (developmental) retardation. *Psychological Record, 13,* 95–110.

Handen, B.L., Apolito, P.M., & Seltzer, G.B. (1984). Use of differential reinforcement of low rates of behavior to decrease repetitive speech in an autistic adolescent. *Journal of Behavior Therapy and Experimental Psychiatry, 15,* 359–364.

Hill, B.K., Lakin, K.C., Sigford, B.B., Hauber, F.H., & Bruininks, R.H. (1982). *Programs and services for mentally retarded people in residential facilities.* Minneapolis: University of Minnesota, Department of Psychoeducational Studies.

Kadushin, A. (1977). *Consultation in social work.* New York: Columbia University Press.

Kratochwill, T.R. (1985). Selection of target behaviors in behavioral consultation. *Behavioral Assessment, 7,* 49–61.

Lazarus, A.A. (1976). *Multimodal behavior therapy: Vol. 1.* New York: Springer.

Lovaas, O.I., & Simmons, J.O. (1969). Manipulation of self-destruction in three retarded children. *Journal of Applied Behavioral Analysis, 2,* 143–157.

Matson, J.L. (1980). Preventing home accidents: A training program for the retarded. *Behavior Modification, 4,* 397–410.

Matson, J.L. (1982). The treatment of behavioral characteristics of depression in the mentally retarded. *Behavior Therapy, 13,* 219–218.

Matson, J.L., & McCartney, J.R. (Eds.) (1981). *Handbook of behavior modification with the mentally retarded.* New York: Plenum.

Reid, D.H., Wilson, P.G., & Faw, G.D. (1983). Teaching self-help skills. In J.S. Matson & J.A. Mulick (Eds.), *Handbook of mental retardation* (pp. 429–442). New York: Pergamon.

Schalock, R.L., Foley, J.W., Toulouse, A., & Stark, J.A. (1985). Medication and programming in controlling the behavior of mentally retarded individuals in community settings. *American Journal of Mental Deficiency, 89,* 503–509.

Schibak, J.W. (1983). Behavioral treatment. In J.L. Matson & J.A. Mulick (Eds.) *Handbook of mental retardation* (pp. 339–350). New York: Pergamon.

Skinner, B.F. (1953). *Science and human behavior.* New York: MacMillan.

Skinner, B.F. (1963). Behaviorism at fifty. *Science, 146,* 951–958.

Stacy, D., Doleys, D.M., & Malcolm, R. (1979). Effects of social skills training in a community-based program. *American Journal of Mental Deficiency, 84,* 152–158.

Tharp, R.G., & Wetzel, R.J. (1969). *Behavior modification in the natural environment.* New York: Academic Press.

Ullman, L.P., & Krasner, L. (1975). *A psychological approach to abnormal behavior.* Englewood Cliffs, NJ: Prentice-Hall.

Watson, L.S. (1967). Application of operant conditioning techniques to institutionalized severely and profoundly retarded children. *Mental Retardation Abstracts, 4,* 1–18.

Whitman, T.L., & Schibak, J.W. (1981). Behavior modification research in the mentally retarded: Treatment and research perspectives. In J.L. Matson & J.R. McCartney (Eds.), *Handbook of behavior modification with the mentally retarded* (pp. 1–28). New York: Plenum.

Whitman, T. L., Schibak, J. W., & Reid, D. H. (1982). *Behavior modification with the severely and profoundly retarded: Research and applications.* New York: Academic Press.

Wolpe, J. (1982). *The practice of behavior therapy* (3rd ed.). New York: Pergamon.

Yule, W., & Carr, J. (1980). *Behavior modification for the mentally handicapped.* Baltimore: University Park Press.

SUPPLEMENTARY RESOURCES

Allyon, T., & Azrin, P. (1968). *The token economy: A multirational system for therapy and rehabilitation.* Englewood Cliffs, NJ: Prentice-Hall.

Baker, B.L., Brightman, A.J., Heifetz, L., & Murphy, D.M. (1976). *Early self-help skills.* Champaign, IL: Research Press.

Baker, B.L., Brightman, A.J., & Hinshaw, S.P. (1980). *Toward independent living.* Champaign, IL: Research Press.

Brown, B.J., & Christie, M. (1981). *Social learning practice in residential child care.* London: Pergamon.

McCarthy, T.J. (Ed.). (1980). *Managing group homes: A training manual.* Nashville: TMAC (P.O. Box 140496).

Sulzer-Azaroff, B., & Mayer, R.G. (1977). *Applying behavior analysis procedures with children and youth.* New York: Holt, Rinehart & Winston.

Chapter 23

Microcomputer Applications in Community Residences

John W. Jacobson, Jason R. Dura, and James A. Mulick

Microcomputers represent a new and still evolving technology that can be used to improve many aspects of community residence management and resident training. The integration of a microcomputer management and training system in a community residence requires managers to be able to recognize the capabilities, limitations, and range of possible applications that exist within this technology. This chapter presents an overview of the functions and uses of microcomputers and orients readers toward managerial and clinical issues involved in using these devices to improve oversight and promote program success.

Microcomputers have been available for a little over a decade. Already these machines have affected both business practices and educational programs as students of all ages prepare to work in an increasingly automated society. What are these devices, and how can they be used in community residences for persons with developmental disabilities?

The short answer is that microcomputers are complex electronic tools that can manipulate any information that can be represented in a binary code, including numbers, letters of the alphabet, graphic images, and instructions to the computer itself or devices attached to it. Microcomputers can be used in community residences to manage a variety of types of records or information critical to a residence's operation. Furthermore, microcomputers can make information management less difficult and more convenient than traditional methods. The computers are increasingly easy to learn to use. Prices are dropping for the basic machines, for the devices they can be used to control and for the commercial programs that make them do useful work. The information or data they ma-

nipulate can be accessed from a variety of sources, such as other electronic machines located nearby or anywhere that telephone lines extend, certain kinds of cameras, typewriterlike keyboards, and electronic drawing pads. Once the computer processes the information through the action of a programmed set of controlling instructions, it can send out new information to control other machines connected to it by cables or telephone lines. These other machines might do such things as create documents or pictures on paper or on televisionlike screens, place orders and pay bills at commercial businesses, request information searches from a giant computerized library, or simply store information—such as resident records and case summaries—conveniently for later use.

The rest of this chapter is spent providing the long answer to the previous question. The focus is on how microcomputers can assist community residence managers and staff. Managerial activities are addressed, including selecting the most appropriate equipment, choosing software that is consonant with programmatic requirements, oversight considerations in assuring the proper use of the equipment, and the integration of the microcomputer within the existing structure and operation of the community residence. The microcomputer applications covered include service documentation and clinical information gathering, and the promotion of resident development and autonomy through the use of computer-assisted instruction and recreation.

First, a simplified orientation to the functions of the various major components that comprise a complete basic microcomputer system is provided. Next, the general types of software that can make the system useful in a community residence are reviewed, with special emphasis on applications that can be utilized to automate various managerial tasks. Some special-interest applications are discussed that are relevant to managers and to the use of microcomputers by residents. Clinical applications are given only minor emphasis in this chapter, because few demonstrations have yet been reported in this area. However, one case example of a community residence is included as an illustration. Lastly, some practical aspects of introducing microcomputers to staff and the community residence environment are presented.

MICROCOMPUTER HARDWARE

A complete microcomputer system consists of a group of components that permit information handling: a console housing the microprocessor or central processing unit (CPU) and memory chips, a keyboard and other input devices, a disk drive or other storage device, a monitor, and a printer. Each performs a function that is discrete and indispensable to the utility of the device. These components are the *hardware*. Because the components are tangible or "hard" and present specific capabilities and limitations, they determine what the computer can do. In contrast, programs, which are the instructions that the computer follows in manipulating information, are called the *software*, because they can be modified.

The central processing unit is usually attached to a keyboard much like a typewriter, including special keys that are used to write or edit programs. The keyboard is the principal means of instructing the computer. The CPU

housing or console also contains the memory for the computer. There are two types of memory: ROM, or "read only memory," where information such as programming languages is stored, and RAM, or "random access memory," where information may be entered or stored. Information can be accessed from ROM, whereas a user can both put in and access information from RAM. The amount of memory space in the computer is expressed in "K" (i.e., 64K, 128K, 256K, 512K) or thousands (actually 1,024s) or characters (or bytes). The amount of memory determines how much information can be entered into the system before it must be saved in a storage device, what type of software can be used, and the speed with which operations can be performed. In general, computers with more memory can perform operations faster.

If information is placed into a computer and then power to the CPU is turned off, all information will be deleted from the RAM. In order to prevent loss of the information that has been entered, the data must be stored permanently using a storage device such as a tape or disk drive. Tape recorders, similar to portable cassette audio recorders, are one means of storage. However, computer cassettes are slow, albeit inexpensive. A better, and not very expensive, alternative is the disk drive, which uses electromagnetically sensitive floppy disks. Disks can retain a considerable amount of information—for example, several hundred pages of text—and with proper care they can provide a reasonably safe means of storing information. The greatest storage capability is provided by a hard disk drive, which uses a different kind of storage medium and may provide from 5 to 40 megabytes (million characters) of storage in commonly available capacities. Many of the more expensive business-oriented microcomputers come with a multimegabyte hard disk and a floppy disk drive. The disk drive is used to load programs onto the hard disk or into the computer's temporary RAM memory. For most beginning community residence staff users, a hard disk is not a necessity, and over the long term, may not be required.

The monitor is the video screen and is used to view the information stored in the computer and to document that a keypress has been received. There are several types of monitors: the most prominent are monochrome, color (separated), and RGB. The monochrone monitor provides a single color and gray/black tones, or a black and white image. Green and amber monochrome tones are also popular. Color monitors reproduce a signal like that used by color televisions. Many monochrome and color monitors contain small speakers and, with an external tuner, can double as a television receiver. RGB monitors also produce a color image, but with increased resolution permitting display of smaller characters on the screen. With a color monitor, small characters tend to blur and can induce eye strain. Depending upon the computer selected, there may be constraints regarding the choice of monitor. Hybrid monitors include those that will accept a monochrome or color signal, and those that accept a monochrome, color, or RGB signal.

The printer serves to transfer a copy of the material in the microcomputer onto paper. Printers vary in the mechanism used to form characters (dot matrix, ink jet, daisy wheel, or laser). Ink jet and laser printers produce high-quality printed copy and graphics at high speed, and at high cost. Daisy wheel printers produce typewriter-quality text at high speed and provide text features like boldface and double-striking, but have limited graphic applications. Dot matrix printers are sometimes slower than the other types, but give the benefit of ready graphics capability and can produce "near-letter-quality" print, multiple faces, boldface, and condensed (reduced) print, at lower cost. The speed and print quality of higher-priced dot matrix printers typically approach those of the daisy wheel printer. A printer may require an interface device (translator) that goes between the computer and the printer.

In order to link the microcomputer to a mainframe computer information service or to exchange information with another microcomputer, a *modem* is needed. A modem is essentially a telephone for the computer. Generally, a regular telephone line is sufficient to transmit data. Most modems come with the necessary software to communicate with different types of mainframe computers. In a multisite agency, the microcomputer can usefully serve as a means of transmitting administrative, individualized program plans or intervention plan data that would otherwise have to be physically, and repeatedly, carried from site to site. This can be accomplished either by direct links between microcomputers via the telephone lines or by connections to mainframe computers providing other information services and temporary storage of messages and data (see Glossenbrenner, 1983).

There are many ways to expand the capability of a microcomputer. For most brands, it is possible to purchase expansion modules that increase the usable RAM. Some software requires 256K or more to operate. Input options abound. For example, graphics tablets, which resemble writing slates, are useful in graphics work. Joysticks are useful for moving material around the screen to change text or graphics. The mouse (a small device moved about by one hand on the work surface) is a useful device to control the user's position on the screen and, with the right software, to input information or make revisions. Some computer brands offer multiple types of input devices with the initial package; others must be expanded by owners.

Selection of your computer hardware should be based on the software applications you expect to use immediately, and perhaps on what you find out about the availability of hardware attachments and modifications needed to use the system with your residents. There is no substitute for informed shopping in an industry that is undergoing such rapid change. It is likely that as educators and rehabilitation specialists become more familiar with microcomputers and experienced in their use, an ever greater variety of adaptive devices and better educational and recreational software will become available.

GENERAL APPLICATION SOFTWARE

Word Processing

Software, the programs that make general purpose microcomputers accomplish specific tasks, is available to automate many routine tasks. Word processing may be the most familiar of these applications. This kind of program provides the capability to generate text and format tables; to combine text from separate sources; to move, delete, reformat, or underline text; and to use different print styles. Word processing programs also permit the user to send commands to the printer; to set page or line length and spacing; and to order multiple original copies. The benefits of word processing over typing are the ability to make changes at any point, to produce text more rapidly, to generate form letters for mass mailings, to prepare customized forms, and to store text compactly on magnetic media rather than paper. Word processing programs enable residence staff to easily update records, complete reports, and carry on correspondence with agencies and families of residents.

Data Base

Data-base programs provide a framework for the entry and manipulation of information when the same categories of data are used for each entry. A data base developed for an individualized program plan, for example, might contain fields for: 1) resident's name, 2) date, 3) goal, 4) objective, 5) means of measurement, 6) trial number, 7) behavior count, 8) staff name, and 9) anecdotal comment. The mechanics of a data base require that you define the field (specify the maximum number of characters that might be used on a line), label that line, and then continue this process until all needed lines are exhausted. Then a keyword is assigned to the screen layout (labels and lines). A blank format can be retrieved at any time using that keyword. By inputting the keyword and a resident's name, all of the information about the resident's individualized program plan can be reviewed, and a ''hard'' (paper) copy can be generated by the printer. If word processing and data-base programs are integrated (part of the same software program) or are compatible (can exchange data back and forth), it becomes possible to combine data-base information with text or to generate multiple, individually addressed original letters. Software is now becoming available to integrate graphic images with text from a word processor or data base, although these tend to be more expensive products. Other common uses of data-base programs

include files for names, addresses, and phone numbers that can be used to print address labels, and inventory management such as might be useful in keeping track of supplies and medical appointments or personal property of individual residents.

Brown (1982) described a centralized computer system used by teachers to generate individualized education plans (IEPs). The system consisted of over 7,000 measurable objectives in all major curriculum areas, allowed teachers to substitute various training and criterion variables for each objective, could be updated with new objectives as teachers wrote them, and produced final IEPs on a letter-quality printer. The system could be accessed by telephone with a terminal or a microcomputer equipped with a modem. The teachers using the system were able to complete the paperwork connected with writing new IEPs in half the usual time, and most teachers were pleased with the flexibility it provided. This is an example of a specialized data-base and report-generating application program. Similar software systems are beginning to be placed on the market for use with large-capacity microcomputers, and can easily be adapted for habilitation goals and objectives for residents of all ability levels.

Spread Sheet Programs

Spread sheet programs were developed primarily as a business accounting tool, but have manifold uses. Like the data base, fields must be defined (in this case in terms of rows and columns), and then numerical data can be inserted within the format. The output looks like a table, with numbers lined up in rows and columns with labels. Equations can be written that use the data in the table to construct new rows or columns or to perform simple calculations and statistics. Some applications where spreadsheets can be useful include agency accounting, documentation of staff work schedules, wage or salary computation, and reviewing of trends in program services and resident activities. Spread sheets permit the user to project trends and assist in decision making by calculating the effects of one decision over another on costs, income, and services, or other important data. Many spread sheet programs can feed data to graphics programs so that graphs can be created without reentering the data.

Outlining Programs

Outlining programs are similar to word processing programs in that they manipulate text. However, they are in the form of an outline with many levels and permit the user to establish a framework and then to modify it. For example, should the user decide that the second main section should be the fifth main section of the document, the header for the second section can simply be shifted to the fifth position and any related material (at a subordinate level in the outline) will automatically follow. Outliners are useful in the early stages of production of a talk or report, in setting up meeting agendas, or as a shell for repeated use in writing professional reports or form letters.

SOFTWARE OF SPECIAL INTEREST

Clinical Management

A number of microcomputer applications have been reported in large residential facilities for persons with developmental disabilities. Many of these applications could be implemented in smaller community residences. For example, in one instance (Romanczyk, 1984) an integrated microcomputer system was used for clerical work, goal planning, and progress assessment, and graphing functions in a nonresidential treatment program. Other authors (Brown, 1982; Crawford, 1980; Nolley & Nolley, 1984; Smith & Wells, 1983) have described the use or benefits of computer- and microcomputer-assisted treatment planning systems. Benefits in terms of savings of staff time on paper work or in clarity of records are generally reported (Smith & Wells, 1983). One study that measured staff activity, however, found that use of the microcomputer decreased staff contact with clientele (Byrnes & Johnson, 1981). Other users of an automated treatment planning system describe benefits of higher-quality reports and records at lower cost, increased staff interaction with residents, and decreased paperwork (Gardner, Swanson, Sutton, & Breuer, in press). Similar benefits have been described by users of the ASPECT (Automated System for Program

Evaluation and Client Tracking) software package developed by Goodwill Industries of America (1986). Another automated record-keeping system introduced recently is the Habilitation Documentation System (Rasmussen, 1986).

An example of a recently developed "expert system" is the Behavior Intervention Plan (BIP), a comprehensive microcomputer-based individualized program planning system, including automated behavioral assessments and an "expert system" that provides assistance in goal and intervention strategy selection (Gardner & Breuer, 1985; Gardner & Breuer, in press; Gardner, Breuer, Souza, & Scabbia, 1985; Gardner, Souza, Scabbia, & Breuer, in press; Gardner, Swanson, Sutton, & Breuer, in press). Expert systems like the BIP are reference guides to decision making that serve as a repository of critical information useful in selecting a strategy in a work or problem situation. Applications integrated with the BIP have been developed to accommodate comprehensive adaptive behavior assessment, generic individualized program plan construction, psychological report preparation, functional analyses of behaviors, progress tracking, case management notes, compliance review, and individualized educational plan construction. (Gardner & Breuer, 1985; Gardner, Swanson, Sutton, & Breuer, in press).

The Behavior Intervention Plan aids in the development of therapeutic interventions for disabled persons with severe behavior problems, using input of individualized data on physical health status, adaptive development, communication skills, socialization, preferences, and reinforcement history. Target behavior elements include the essentials of a functional analysis, including topology, structure, frequency, antecedent and situational relationships, and temporal relations to other behaviors. Data on the effectiveness of up to 50 past techniques are retained in the system and are considered in the construction of intervention recommendations. Although requiring entry of extensive data for full utility, the BIP provides a detailed analysis of the behavior, with suggested data collection strategies, contributing causal factors, and a range of potentially beneficial intervention strategies. External validation studies and studies of the comparative effectiveness of BIP-based interventions are not available at this writing (Gardner & Breuer, in press), and must be considered an essential step in demonstrating the usefulness of any expert system. Meanwhile, the BIP deserves closer study as a harbinger of other systems that will doubtless appear in the near future.

Resident-Oriented Applications

Resident use of microcomputers within community program settings has seldom been reported; however, there is an emerging literature in special education that is relevant. Most of the reported educational applications are tailored to children and adolescents with comparatively mild intellectual impairments or with physical disabilities. Unfortunately, few of the educational software packages have been documented as being of benefit in training efforts, and most cannot be adapted to learner ability level or to special learner characteristics (see Hannaford & Taber, 1982). Hammer (1986) has recently reported on applications relevant to persons with more severe disabilities, and has observed that pertinent applications are being developed for teaching, assessment, recreation, and prosthetic uses. The latter applications lie in such areas as communication, cognitive functions, environmental control, and vocational activities. Katz, Johnson, and Dalby (1981) described an experimental computer-assisted instruction (CAI) program in which moderately and mildly mentally retarded adults who were to be transferred from a residential institution to a group home were successfully taught conceptual discriminations among nutritional food groups. Using slides and a computer-controlled presentation format, Katz et al. (1981) showed the practical value of automated teaching in preparing people with little prior experience in menu selection to recognize foods belonging to the four major food groups.

A range of adaptations useful for prosthetic purposes or improvement of educational uses is now available (see McWilliams, 1984). These include mechanisms to slow down display speed, speech synthesizers, adaptive input switches, add-ons to make display screens touch-sensitive, computer-controlled active stimulation devices, and adaptive keyboards. Many obvious applications, such as those for instructional use, have been hindered by inadequately tested software and the absence, until recently, of inexpensive and suitable hardware adaptations. Of special interest to readers contemplating use of microcomputers as prosthetic or environmental control devices are reviews by Goldenberg (1984), Huguenin, Weidenman, and Mulick (1983), Mulick, Scott, Gaines, and Campbell (1983), and Wilson and Fox (1984).

While habilitation is a primary goal for most community residences, the goal of increasing recreational opportunities is also important. Home computers probably would not exist had they not been promoted in terms of their recreational value, with business and educational applications receiving attention later as they were devised. Microcomputers still should be considered for their recreational value. Persons with mental retardation will probably participate in recreational activities at rates comparable to their nonretarded peers, especially activities centered in the home, if they are available (Matthews, 1979). Commercially available software may be used with little or no modification by the majority of persons with mental retardation. Hardware and software adaptations of these programs may expand their usefulness to persons with moderate to severe mental retardation (Chaffin, Maxwell, & Thompson, 1982; Condry & Keith, 1983). A useful guide to hardware and software adaptations for persons with handicaps is provided by McWilliams (1984). Video games probably can be used with no modification by some individuals with severe mental retardation if sufficient attention is given to training and generalization of the skills required to enjoy the game, as was shown by Sedlak, Doyle, and Schloss (1982). Recreational applications of computers should be high on the list of priorities in any community residence.

Vignette

One recently reported microcomputer application (Andresen, Davis, & LaPaglia, 1985; J. LaPaglia, personal communication, January 1986) employed the Aimstar software package (Hasselbring & Hamlett, 1983) to assist clinical management of group home program activities. Aimstar was de-

Table 1. Components of a group home microcomputer system

1. *Individualized Service Plan:* States long- and short-term goals for each resident
2. *Program Data Book:* Contains program descriptions, data files, graphs, and monthly summaries compiled by the professionals and supervisors (and used by auditors)
3. *Raw Data Book:* Contains data recording sheets and task analyses of training tasks
4. *Community-Based Raw Data File:* Contains laminated index cards on which data are recorded during in-vivo community-based training
5. *Daily Schedule and Summary Sheet:* Contains a list of all the training programs to be conducted on a given day, showing time, name, setting, and outcome summary, and permitting the recording of focal behaviors in terms of frequency, intensity, duration, and time of day
6. *Graph Bulletin Board:* Is prominently displayed in the home and shows progress graphs for each resident's goals (updated weekly and reviewed by training staff)
7. *Supervisor's Reliability Management Book:* Contains information from the Raw Data Book and Program Data Book; used in supervisory reliability checks

Sources: Adapted from Andresen et al. (1985) and LaPaglia (personel communication, January, 1986).

signed to manage individualized education plan records, to graph data, and to analyze data. The computer was used to support consistency and thoroughness in intervention documentation and maintenance of uniform treatment records. Although evaluative data are not yet available, preliminary information suggests that this application has been useful.

This application employed an Apple II series microcomputer, with disk drive, monitor, and printer. This equipment was selected because of compatibility with existing and potentially useful educational software applications. The elements of this system are shown in Table 1.

In this application, intervention data reflecting ongoing resident training efforts are first entered in a standard format data book (providing for coding of prompt level, responses [correct/error], and time required to perform response). Fifteen to 20 current training objectives are identified for each resident. Raw data are summarized and recorded daily for computer entry (task analysis steps completed correctly, response errors, time required, frequency data). These records are similar to those maintained by many community residences. However, in this application, at the end of each day data from the summary sheets are entered into the Aimstar program. Data graphs are printed weekly. Aimstar-generated current program descriptions, data files, and graphs are entered into the program books monthly, as are monthly data summaries.

Direct care staff collect raw data, fill out daily schedules as training is conducted, enter data using Aimstar daily or weekly, and participate in weekly review meetings. Case coordinators develop the raw data sheets and task training specifications, provide monthly updates and revisions to the program books, print out revised plans, update graphs, and summarize data for each goal. They also update the summary data graph, update the reliability data, meet weekly with the trainers, and meet monthly with senior professional staff. Professionals meet monthly with case coordinators and the house manager to review all data, review reliability data, and designate the schedule for reliability checks.

Noteworthy aspects of this system are use of the microcomputer and of off-the-shelf software exclusively for clinical documentation, and the specification of staff responsibility for maintenance of the data. The software also permits maintenance of records on interventions that have been discontinued, thus providing a history of training for each resident. Word processing software is used to develop anecdotal notes and to record rationales for alteration or discontinuation of interventions. Preliminary findings on the advantages of this application, in addition to citing uniform format and consistent content of resident records, have mentioned the enhanced ability to determine instances in which training techniques are ineffective and require modification and the ability to effectively document programmatic activities for review by quality assurance specialists.

MANAGEMENT AND THE MICROCOMPUTER

A range of microcomputer management applications has been described by Jacobson (1985) with regard to publicly operated institutional programs. Many of these managerial applications are relevant to community residential programs. Pertinent management uses for which general application software is suitable include: 1) staff scheduling (spread sheet), 2) documentation of participation in training (data base), 3) documentation of personnel evaluations (outlining), 4) resource or consultant directory (data base), 5) inventory (data base), 6) expenditures (data base and spread sheet), 7) standards compliance information (spread sheet), and 8) individual instructional training for staff working variable schedules (word processing). In addition, the collection and reorganization of objective information is a defining characteristic of many program evaluations (see Jacobson & Regula, this volume). Such analysis can be expedited by microcomputer.

Acquiring a Microcomputer

Considerable time and study should be invested in deciding which microcomputer and which components are needed for an organization. A critical analysis should answer such questions as, Where will the computer be located? Who will be the primary users? Would a portable unit, possibly one compatible with a stationary unit, be appropriate? Will the computer be in constant use or used only at certain times of the day? Will there be such reliance upon the computer that breakdowns cannot be tolerated? Such questions may dictate the form of the system and where it is located. The steps in selecting the most appropriate system and software are shown in Table 2.

Also important are the uses to which the computer is put. If needs are primarily traditional business applications, a very powerful computer may not be needed. However, if the computer may become either the primary means of maintaining fiscal accountability, recording program data, or generating comprehensive proposals and reports, greater capacity will be required to handle the more sophisticated software. Most applications can be developed in BASIC language (all microcomputers will support some form of BASIC). However, for some purposes BASIC is very inefficient, and alternatives like PASCAL and COBOL may be required. If the computer will be used by a multisite agency operation, a high-level microcomputer that can accept input and provide output to several keyboards and screens at the same time may be more appropriate.

Impact on Staff Time Usage

Few objective data are available to determine how staff use of microcomputers affects completion of other assigned duties or contact with residents. Intuitively, one would expect that immediately following acquisition of a microcomputer, extra staff time would be devoted to learning how to use this resource. However, in the long term how the microcomputer is used determines the amount of staff time devoted to it. In general, entry and retrieval of information using the microcomputer should not entail more staff time than handwritten or typed recording of comparable information. However, if an ap-

Table 2. Guidelines for selecting and purchasing a microcomputer

1. Learn as much about microcomputers as possible before entering a store.
2. Carefully assess needs with respect to initial hardware components
3. Consider incremental implementation of uses for the new system, and schedule software purchases correspondingly.
4. Identify sources of expertise within the agency and associates, and draw upon these sources in making choices.
5. Construct an implementation plan that considers supports and routines for use of the computer (as well as a detailed description of its primary functions within the agency) and document its value in regard to management's direction.
6. Specify the hardware and software requirements in functional terms before seeking price quotes from stores.
7. Comparison shop and insist on demonstration of the unique strengths and weaknesses of both the hardware and software.
8. Consider the store's track record in providing technical assistance, demonstration, and maintenance services to customers.
9. Consider the manufacturer's track record on reliability, likelihood of remaining competitive in either the home or business computer market, and the importance of the particular model to be purchased to the manufacturer.
10. Make the selection based primarily on current uses, but with a sensitivity to long-term needs that agency expansion could require.

plication requires data not previously collected, one should anticipate some additional time demands on staff.

As a rule of thumb, the first applications should be those that blend in with the managerial and programmatic processes in the residence or that are not critical to its performance. Thus, if difficulties are encountered with the system, the impact on the overall residence program would be minor. For example, if a residence has a history of problems with the content and quality of individualized program plans, one would not address this problem as the first application, despite the benefits to be gained from uniformity of format and content. Nonetheless, it is reasonable to institute an automated recording component for an already well-documented program component as the first application, especially if off-the-shelf software may be used.

Costs for Purchase and Maintenance

The costs for purchase, maintenance, and improvement of a microcomputer constitute management expenses for programs receiving public funding and are therefore reimbursable. Purchase prices for a typical fully configured microcomputer system range from about $1,300 to $6,000 plus software. Discounts may be available for certain models because of membership in consortia or sole-source agreements made with manufacturers by state agencies. Long-term utility will be enhanced if an agency purchases a system compatible with those used by other local providers or by the lead mental retardation agency. Maintenance of the system encompasses costs for repair of malfunctioning equipment, staff training, and expansion. Depending on geographic location and local dealers, maintenance can be a minor or a serious barrier to microcomputer usage (repairs may take 6 to 12 weeks). In addition, most models have not been on the market long enough to assess their durability or preventive maintenance needs. These considerations make it attractive to lease a computer system—particularly the higher-priced systems—if daily use is planned.

Staff training represents an investment in the microcomputer. Staff expertise reduces the dependency upon the general software market for relevant applications. Many state agencies and community colleges offer staff development programs that include orientation to and use of microcomputers. Programmed learning manuals are also available for most major microcomputer systems. Management personnel should receive training in use of the computer, not only so they can more effectively manage its use but also because training will assist them in identifying capabilities to meet program needs. It should be noted, however, that microcomputers are potentially useful in staff training when used with any of the authoring applications (i.e., those providing built-in assistance in program writing) becoming available or with centralized computer-based instructional services (Bennett, 1982).

Protecting the Physical Integrity of the Computer

The microcomputer is a potentially fragile device. It is also a potentially attractive object of theft, in part because of its cost and general appeal. In a community program, security can be achieved by locating the microcomputer in a limited access area and by physically attaching the CPU and other components to the work surface. Sufficient space should be provided, and components placed so that they may be used readily in combination. Storage for disks, printer paper, manuals, and printer ribbons should be arranged so that these items are within reach. Lighting, heat, ambient noise, and other environmental features should be conducive to working with the computer.

Protecting the Data

Several steps can be taken to promote the reliability and validity of data entered into the computer. The first is staff training. The second is use of uniform data entry formats. The forms on which staff record data should be similar in format to the data base or spread sheet layouts in which they are entered (Andresen et al., 1985). The third step is continuing review of printouts from the data system. The fourth step is completion of spot checks to ensure agreement between handwritten data sheets and information in the computer. The fifth step (used by Gardner, Souza, Scabbia, & Breuer, in press) is an internal review of data entries within the software. Finally, users typically should maintain two copies of each file, on separate disks and in separate locations. If both files are kept current, and one file is lost, damaged, or altered, the time spent in developing this information is not wasted.

Some software will permit the entry of passwords that prevent direct access to data. In large agencies, this may be necessary to assure confidentiality and proper use of electronic records. Another aid to identifying potential sources of bad data, and to controlling access, is the use of a sign-in log for the computer and/or identification of a staff member by name or number of each data entry session.

Establishing Staff Responsibilities

There are several benefits to stipulating that the staff who collect data be responsible for entering that data, rather than making this a permanent responsibility of other staff. This strategy familiarizes more staff with the microcomputer and its use, and diminishes entry errors due to misread handwriting. Each staff person will probably find it necessary to enter daily or weekly data for only a few minutes at a time. Data entry responsibilities (i.e., types and content of data) should also be compatible with the role of each staff person in the program.

The integration of a microcomputer within a community residence requires active and involved oversight by management. Staff resistance to microcomputer usage, possibly perceived in terms of increased clerical load, is to be expected. Because computers can be used as a potent resource in evaluation efforts, staff may have concerns about their ability to learn to use the computer within these contexts. Issues of computer phobia need to be addressed during introduction of a microcomputer system (Davidson & Walley, 1984). Several reports have suggested that: 1) the openness of a group to innovation will affect the adequacy of implementation (Mankin, Bikson, & Gutek, 1984); 2) inclusion in a microcomputer network can promote usage (Anderson & Jay, 1984); 3) acceptance may decrease over time (depending upon the application type, the data entry burden, and utility for staff—Counte, Kjerulff, Salloway, & Campbell, 1984); 4) implementa-

tion must be sensitive to management goals and the interdependencies of diverse program elements (Buchanan & Boddy, 1984); 5) implementation must be consonant with the nature of control or social systems within the organizational unit (Kling & Iacono, 1984); and 6) applications should be oriented toward increasing staff opportunities for self-determination in the work environment (Blackler & Brown, 1985).

Advantages of microcomputer use, such as immediate feedback, improved readability of records, reduced storage of paper records, better data on individual resident progress, and the opportunity to acquire a marketable skill as part of one's regular work (Brown, 1982) should be emphasized during introduction of the system. At the same time, resistance to usage should be investigated to determine whether the resistance is based on: 1) antipathy toward innovation, further education, or technology in general, 2) perceptions of duties as clerical or nonuseful, 3) prior experience with a poorly constructed or a mainframe system, or 4) differences of opinion about which applications are needed (Jacobson, 1985).

SUMMARY

The acquisition and use of a microcomputer by a community residence requires an awareness of computer capabilities, a sensitivity to possible disruptive effects on ongoing activities, consideration and planning for short- and long-term applications, and allowance for needed supports such as staff development. Currently, something of a pioneering spirit is still needed by those who would automate community residence management and habilitation activities, but we believe it is worth the effort by all involved.

Software is now available for most microcomputers to support business applications, including those that entail construction of individualized program plans and the analysis of trends. A limited amount of software, for selected microcomputer brands, is available for educational or prosthetic applications, and most of the existing software is oriented to persons with mild mental or mild to severe physical handicaps. However, in the near future it is likely that some of the existing software will be submitted to more rigorous assessment regarding its utility, and that both educational and prosthetic applications will become increasingly accessible to the group home microcomputer user. Some practical applications to expedite resident development and autonomy are already available, and should be considered in the selection of a microcomputer for everyday resident use in community residences.

REFERENCES

Anderson, J.G., & Jay, S.J. (1984). Physician utilization of computers: A network analysis of the diffusion process. *Journal of Organizational Behavior Management, 6*(3–4), 21–35.

Andresen, C.A., Davis, M., & LaPaglia, J. (1985, October). *Computerized client tracking for small intermediate care and group homes.* Symposium presented at the 32nd Annual Conference of AAMD Region X, Stowe, VT.

Bennett, R.E. (1982). Applications of microcomputer technology to special education. *Exceptional Children, 49,* 106–113.

Blackler, F., & Brown, C. (1985). Evaluation and the impact of information technologies on people in organizations. *Human Relations, 38,* 213–231.

Brown, D.A. (1982, November). *Goal selection and program monitoring using batch and microcomputer procedures.* Paper presented at the 9th Annual Conference of the Association for the Severely Handicapped, Denver.

Brown, N.P. (1982). CAMEO: Computer-assisted management of educational objectives. *Exceptional Children, 49,* 151–153.

Buchanan, D.A., & Boddy, D. (1984). Skills, motivation, and interdependencies: The effective use of new computing technology. *Journal of Organizational Behavior Management, 6*(3–4), 99–108.

Budoff, M., Thormann, J., & Gras, A. (1984). *Microcomputers in special education.* Cambridge, MA: Brookline Books.

Byrnes, E., & Johnson, J. (1981). Change technology and the implementation of automation in mental health care settings. *Behavior Research Methods and Instrumentation, 13,* 571–580.

Chaffin, J.E., Maxwell, B., & Thompson, B. (1982). ARC–ED curriculum: The application of video game formats to educational software. *Exceptional Children, 49,* 173–178.

Condry, J., & Keith, D. (1983). Educational and recreational uses of computer technology. *Youth & Society, 15,* 87–112.

Counte, M.A., Kjerulff, K.H., Salloway, J.C., & Campbell, B. (1984). Implementing computerization in hospitals: A case study of the behavioral and attitudinal impacts of a medical information system. *Journal of Organizational Behavior Management, 6*(3–4), 109–122.

Crawford, J.L. (1980). Computer support and the clinical process: An automated behavioral rehabilitation system for mentally retarded persons. *Mental Retardation, 18,* 119–124.

Davidson, R.S., & Walley, P.B. (1984). Computer fear and addiction. *Journal of Organizational Behavior Management, 6*(3–4), 37–51.

Gardner, J.M., & Breuer, A. (1985). Reliability and validity of a microcomputer assessment system for developmentally disabled persons. *Education and Training of the Mentally Retarded, 20,* 209–213.

Gardner, J.M., & Breuer, A. (in press). Micropsych: Applications in a residential facility for developmentally disabled persons. *Professional Psychology: Research and Practice.*

Gardner, J.M., Breuer, A., Souza, A., & Scabbia, A. (1985). *Using microcomputers to generate non-punitive multi-modal intervention strategies.* (Brief Report). Costa Mesa, CA: Fairview State Hospital.

Gardner, J.M., Souza, A., Scabbia, A., & Breuer, A. (in press). Using microcomputers to help staff reduce violent behavior. *Computers in Human Services.*

Gardner, J.M., Swanson, C., Sutton, T., & Breuer, A. (in press). Microcomputer assessment of persons with developmental disabilities: A cost benefit analysis. *Mental Retardation.*

Glossenbrenner, A. (1983). *The complete handbook of personal computer communications.* New York: St. Martin's Press.

Goldenberg, E.P. (1984). Computers in the special education classroom: What do we need, and why don't we have any? In J.A. Mulick & B.L. Mallory (Eds.), *Transitions in mental retardation: Vol. 1* (pp. 107–127). Norwood, NJ: Ablex.

Goodwill Industries of America. (1986). *ASPECT: Automated system for program evaluation and client tracking.* Bethesda, MD: Author.

Hagen, D. (1984). *Microcomputer resource book for special education.* Reston, VA: Reston.

Hammer, D. (1986, May). *Microtechnologies for persons with moderate to profound mental retardation.* Paper presented at the 109th Annual Conference of the American Association on Mental Deficiency, Denver.

Hannaford, A.E., & Taber, F.M. (1982). Microcomputer software for the handicapped: Development and evaluation. *Exceptional Children, 49,* 137–142.

Hasselbring, T.S., & Hamlett, C.L. (1983). *Aimstar.* Portland, OR: ASIEP Education Co.

Huguenin, N.H., Weidenman, L.E., & Mulick, J.A. (1983). Programmed instruction. In J.L. Matson & J.A. Mulick (Eds.), *Handbook of mental retardation* (pp. 443–453). New York: Pergamon.

Jacobson, J.W. (1985). *Microcomputer applications in public residential facilities: 1984,* (Project Report). Albany, NY: New York State Office of Mental Retardation and Developmental Disabilities.

Katz, L., Johnson, K.P., & Dalby, J.T. (1981). Teaching nutrition to the developmentally handicapped using computer-assisted instruction. *British Journal of Mental Subnormality, 27,* 23–25.

Kling, R., & Iacono, S. (1984). Computing as an occasion for social control. *Journal of Social Issues, 40*(3), 77–96.

Mankin, D., Bikson, T.K., & Gutek, B.A. (1984). Factors in successful implementation of computer-based office information systems: A review of the literature with suggestions for OBM research. *Journal of Organizational Behavior Management, 6*(3–4), 1–20.

Matthews, P.R. (1979). The frequency with which the mentally retarded participate in recreation activities. *Research Quarterly, 50,* 71–79.

McWilliams, P.A. (1984). *Personal computers and the disabled.* New York: Doubleday.

Mulick, J.A., Scott, F.D., Gaines, R.F., & Campbell, B.M. (1983). Devices and instrumentation for skill development and behavior change. In J.L. Matson & F. Andrasik (Eds.), *Treatment issues and innovations in mental retardation* (pp. 515–580). New York: Plenum.

Nave, G., Browning, P., & Carter, J. (1983). *Computer technology for the handicapped in special education and rehabilitation: A resource guide.* Eugene, OR: Rehabilitation Research and Training Center in Mental Retardation, University of Oregon.

Nolley, D., & Nolley, B. (1984). Microcomputer data analysis at the clinical mental retardation site. *Mental Retardation, 22,* 85–90.

Rasmussen, P. (1986). *The habilitation documentation system.* Morgantown, NC: Habilitation Software.

Romanczyk, R.G. (1984). A case study of micro-computer utilization and staff efficiency: A five-year analysis. *Journal of Organizational Behavior Management, 6,* 141–154.

Sedlak, R.A., Doyle, M., & Schloss, P. (1982). Video games: A training and generalization demonstration with severely retarded adolescents. *Education and Training of the Mentally Retarded, 17,* 332–336.

Smith, D.W., & Wells, M.E. (1983). Use of a microcomputer to assist staff in documenting resident progress. *Mental Retardation, 21,* 111–115.

Wilson, M.S., & Fox, B.J. (1984). Software development in language instruction and enhancement. In J.A. Mulick & B.L. Mallory (Eds.), *Transitions in mental retardation: Vol. 1* (pp. 128–150). Norwood, NJ: Ablex.

Williams, P.A. (1983). *The personal computer book.* Los Angeles: Prelude Press.

SUPPLEMENTARY RESOURCES

Budoff, M., Thormann, J., & Gras, A. (1984). *Microcomputers in special education.* Cambridge, MA: Brookline Books.

Goldenberg, E.P. (1984). Computers in the special education classroom: What do we need, and why don't we have any? In J.A. Mulick & B.L. Mallory (Eds.), *Transitions in mental retardation: Vol. 1* (pp. 107–127). Norwood, NJ: Ablex.

Hagen, D. (1984). *Microcomputer resource book for special education.* Reston, VA: Reston.

Huguenin, N.H., Weidenman, L.E., & Mulick, J.A. (1983). Programmed instruction. In J.L. Matson & J.A. Mulick (Eds.), *Handbook of mental retardation* (pp. 443–453). New York: Pergamon.

Mulick, J.A., Scott, F.D., Gaines, R.F., & Campbell, B.M. (1983). Devices and instrumentation for skill development and behavior change. In J.L. Matson & F. Andrasik (Eds.), *Treatment issues and innovations in mental retardation* (pp. 515–580). New York: Plenum.

Nave, G., Browning, P., & Carter, J. (1983). *Computer technology for the handicapped in special education and rehabilitation: A resource guide.* Eugene, OR: Rehabilitation Research and Training Center in Mental Retardation, University of Oregon.

Wilson, M.S., & Fox, B.J. (1984). Software development in language instruction and enhancement. In J.A. Mulick & B.L. Mallory (Eds.), *Transitions in mental retardation: Vol. 1* (pp. 128–150). Norwood, NJ: Ablex.

Williams, P.A. (1983). *The personal computer book.* Los Angeles: Prelude Press.

Note: Readers are referred, in addition, to software reviews presented in Pergamon Press journals, particularly those in *Research in Developmental Disabilities.*

Section V

SAFETY AND DESIGN CONSIDERATIONS

Chapter 24

Fire Safety Practices

Norman E. Groner

Fire safety in housing for handicapped or dependent persons has always been a difficult problem. However, with the growth in the number of community residences for persons with mental retardation and other developmental disabilities in the United States, the concern over fire prevention, fire safety, and safe and effective evacuation has gained prominence as a major issue. Concern has escalated with reports of deaths and injuries as a result of fires in such facilities, coupled with awareness of the need to better assess the "self-preservation" capabilities of many mentally impaired and physically disabled individuals. This chapter describes the *Life Safety Code*. It also explores the key elements of fire safety planning designed to protect residences and improve the abilities of operators to design, implement, and manage favorable evacuation techniques and procedures.

Fire safety in group homes for persons with handicaps has recently attracted much attention—sometimes to the consternation of residence operators. The sudden concern about fire prevention stems both from an increased awareness that residents in group homes and similar facilities have often been exposed to an excessive risk from fire, and from the recent availability of regulatory means to deal with the problem. It is important for group home operators to understand the impetus behind the current regulations so that they can better deal with fire protection authorities.

REGULATORY BACKGROUND OF FIRE SAFETY

An expanded awareness that disabled persons have assumed too high a risk from fire results directly from an unacceptably high rate of fire casualties in what are generally called "board and care facilities." The National Fire Protection Association's (NFPA) *Life Safety Code* (NFPA, 1985), portions of which have been extensively adopted by local jurisdictions, defines a *residential board and care occupancy* as "a building or part thereof that is used for lodging and boarding of four or more residents . . . to provide personal care services." Examples include group homes for developmentally disabled persons, as well as halfway houses, retirement homes for elderly persons, and institutional settings for physically or mentally handicapped persons where health care services are not routinely provided. The general term *board and care facility* is frequently used in this chapter, because much of the materials discussed were developed with all types of personal and supervisory care facilities in mind. Board and care facilities, including group homes, have proliferated rapidly in recent years as a result of the combined forces of deinstitutionalization and the increased interest in providing services in community-based, "least-restrictive" settings (see Lakin, Hill, & Bruininks, this volume). Until recently, the disparity between the demand for affordable facilities and the limited number of board and care homes forced large numbers of disabled persons to be placed in facilities where inappropriate, and often insufficient, fire safety standards were enforced. A sudden increase in fire deaths was the inevitable result. During an 18-month period in 1979 and 1981, 120 elderly and mentally impaired persons died in fires in board and care facilities (Holton, 1981).

The U.S. Congress quickly expressed its concern for fire safety in board and care facilities by holding hearings in the late 1970s (Holton, 1981; Select Committee on Aging, 1979), followed by an attempt to pressure the then U.S. Department of Health, Education & Welfare (HEW) to address the issue. Unfortunately, the situation was not amenable to rapid or inexpensive solutions.

Regarding group homes, HEW was already grappling with the fire safety problem. Department officials endeavored to reconcile the need to provide affordable, community-based housing for developmentally disabled individuals with a justifiable concern for their fire safety. For intermediate care facilities for the mentally retarded (ICFs/MR), the department began to allow conformance to the *Life Safety Code* standards for lodging houses, a relatively lenient requirement compared to fire safety standards for health care facilities. However, this was permitted only where the residents were certified as "ambulatory" and "self-preserving" in the event of a fire.

(The *Life Safety Code* is a model code concerned exclusively with preventing fire casualties. Separate chapters in the code specify requirements for most types of "occupancies." For example, among the provisions for various types of occupancies are separate chapters for new and existing health care facilities, new and existing apartment buildings, one- and two-family dwellings, new and existing hotels and dormitories, and lodging or rooming houses. Each of these chapters has at least occasionally been applied to residential care facilities. The *Life Safety Code* is written by a committee of volunteers who represent various relevant constituencies and areas of expertise. The committee must consider all changes in code provisions that are submitted by concerned persons.)

Unfortunately, like many stopgap measures at protecting people in board and care homes, the certification approach created problems in its own right. Recent audits conducted by the Health Care Financing Administration (HCFA) have decertified facilities because their residents did not meet HCFA's newly developed criteria for "ambulatory" and "self-preserving," demonstrating that subjective judgments of risk are an inadequate substitute for relatively objective standards, because they have inherently low reliability and are strongly influenced by professional roles.

Adequate regulatory responses to the fire problem in board and care facilities were slow in coming, principally because of the uniqueness of the facilities themselves. Regulatory authorities usually respond to the lack of standards by simply adopting model codes with little or no modification. However, board and care facilities presented special problems because the authorities were unable to make valid generalizations about their fire safety characteristics. There is great variability in both the types of buildings in which board and care facilities are located and the types of residents that reside in them. The buildings range from large institutional facilities to small single-family houses and apartment units. The residents range from persons who could take no action on behalf of their own safety to persons who, with some training, would be more likely to take quick and effective action than most able adults.

When regulatory authorities applied existing regulations (e.g., for health care facilities or lodging houses) to the wide range of facilities, they often imposed unnecessarily strict requirements on some facilities, while residents in other facilities were inadequately protected. In many situations, local authorities preferred to misclassify board and care facilities as hotels or lodging houses, or ignored some facilities altogether, rather than close them down by imposing expensive standards originally intended for health care facilities.

Again in the late 1970s, HEW recognized that substantial progress on the board and care fire safety problem would be possible only after suitable model standards were incorporated into the *Life Safety Code*. Some jurisdictions, principally states, did write their own standards with varying degrees of success. However, most coped as well as they could by applying building codes or other portions of the *Life Safety Code* until a standard was incorporated into the National Fire Protection Association's 1985 edition of the Life Safety Code.

HEW enlisted the assistance of the National Bureau of Standards' Center for Fire Research to develop a flexible fire safety standard for group homes that might be included in the code. This work eventually produced the *Fire Safety Evaluation System for Board and Care Homes,* which is the basis for the board and care home requirements in the 1985 edition of the *Life Safety Code* (Nelson et al., 1983). With the availability of an effective model standard for governing safety in boarding homes, an important obstacle to effective regulation was finally surmounted.

As stated earlier, the diversity among types of facilities and their residents was previously the primary obstacle to adapting other standards to board and care homes. Chapter 21 of the *Life Safety Code,* the chapter that delineates requirements for board and care facilities, deals with this diversity in a unique way: as a facility's capability to evacuate its residents improves, less stringent fire safety features are required for the building. Depending on its size and "evacuation capability," a facility is required to conform to requirements ranging in stringency from standards for lodging houses to health care facilities. Facilities are categorized as falling into one of three levels of evacuation capability: "prompt," "slow," and "impractical." Thus, board and care home operators can often qualify for more lenient fire safety standards depending on the extent that they can demonstrate their facilities' evacuation capability.

When the *Life Safety Code* requires additional hardware features as evacuation capability decreases, the more stringent hardware requirements reflect an increasing emphasis on refuge. For facilities demonstrating a "prompt" level of evacuation capability, requirements emphasize alarm systems and the

prevention of the rapid exposure of escape routes to fire and smoke. When facilities can only demonstrate a "slow" capability, requirements increasingly emphasize hardware and building features that limit the spread of fire and smoke, especially to sleeping areas. At the "impractical" level, requirements resemble those for health care facilities and provide refuge within sleeping areas in the event that at least some residents cannot be evacuated within a reasonable time period. As emphasized later in this chapter, these levels of evacuation, in addition to being hardware requirements, are intended to adapt buildings to strategies for emergency planning that will vary according to the abilities of staff and residents to effect an evacuation.

The remainder of this chapter discusses the elements of a fire safety plan designed both to improve the abilities of group home operators to protect residents and, if relevant, to achieve a more favorable evacuation capability judgment from regulatory officials. The elements of a good training program are also outlined, without which even the best thought-out plan is useless.

LITERATURE ON FIRE SAFETY IN BOARD AND CARE HOMES

This author has examined some local efforts at developing fire safety materials for group homes. These materials vary widely in quality and coverage, and are not generally available outside the jurisdiction for which they were developed. (See Rome Fire Department, 1981, for one of the better examples.)

Fortunately, two helpful fire safety manuals, both funded by the U.S. Department of Health and Human Services, have been published recently and are easily obtained. This author wrote the earlier of the two (Groner, 1982) for the National Bureau of Standards. The latter was prepared by two consultants for the National Fire Protection Association (Blye & Yess, 1985). The manuals overlap considerably in content, but their styles and emphases differ substantially.

A Matter of Time: A Comprehensive Guide to Fire Emergency Planning for Board and Care Homes (Groner, 1982) provides detailed information and procedures that can help operators tailor their plans to specific facilities, ranging from large facilities with a few hundred elderly residents to small-group homes where only a few developmentally disabled individuals live. *Fire Safety in Board and Care Homes: A Self-Study Guide for Owners and Operators* (Blye & Yess, 1985), the NFPA manual, differs in that it offers blanket advice for all facilities. Whereas the former manual provides comprehensive discussions of topics related to fire emergency planning, the latter manual is less detailed in most areas, but includes a section on prevention, a topic omitted from *A Matter of Time*. The manual by Groner is written in the style of a college text, whereas the NFPA manual is written and illustrated as a self-study guide, with questions that readers can use as a self-test of the material. As such, *Fire Safety in Board and Care Homes* might be best used as briefing material for staff, while *A Matter of Time* might be more applicable where operators must solve planning problems whose solutions are not readily apparent. (For information on ordering these manuals, see the Note at the end of this chapter.)

At least one package of hands-on training materials is available for facilities serving retarded adults (Coady & MacMillan, 1983). The package *In Case of Fire,* was developed at the Massachusetts Firefighting Academy in an effort to make available materials that are both simply explained and directed toward adults. *In Case of Fire* is distributed by the National Fire Protection Association and includes a slide/tape presentation that teaches basic fire prevention and evacuation skills, a trainer's guide, and student booklets (see Note for ordering information).

INTEGRATING FIRE SAFETY PLANNING AND REGULATORY COMPLIANCE

Traditionally, there has been no explicit connection between fire emergency planning and compliance with fire and building codes. However, as stated earlier, Chapter 21 of the *Life Safety Code* takes a unique approach by basing fire protection building and hardware requirements on the evacuation capability of staff and residents taken as a group. Thus, many group home operators will be able to substantially improve their standing on new and tougher code requirements by improving the fire response capabilities of their residents. This allows operators the possibility of continuing to meet important programmatic goals of maintaining a noninstitutional ambience and of saving money. Where applicable, operators should take full advantage of this unusual feature among fire codes, by demonstrating their improved ability to protect residents from fire. But an added responsibility accompanies this new flexibility. If operators are not honest about documenting improved evacuation capability, regulatory authorities are certain to return to their traditional use of building features as the only acceptable means of determining code compliance. Even operators who do not need to conform to *Life Safety Code* standards will find it informative and helpful to assess their facilities using Chapter 21 of the code and the associated appendices.

Chapter 21 of the *Life Safety Code* does not require regulatory authorities to use any specific means to determine evacuation capability, but it suggests some approaches that regulatory authorities may choose to employ. One of these, the Evacuation Difficulty Index, explained in Appendix F of the code, is particularly important to small facilities (Groner, Levin, & Nelson, 1981; Nelson et al., 1983). (The Health Care Financing Administration currently requires surveyors to use Appendix F when classifying the evacuation capability of small ICFs/MR for the purpose of Medicaid reimbursement.)

Appendix F is included in the *Life Safety Code* as a means to measure how much time could be needed to evacuate residents in the event of fire. An "E-score" is computed, which represents a ratio of the potential assistance needs of residents during a fire emergency divided by the availability of staff members to meet those assistance needs. The higher the E-score, the longer it is likely to take the facility to evacuate its residents. As part of the calculation, the Evacuation Difficulty Index includes a procedure for rating the potential assistance needs of residents. All group homes can profit by using Appendix F as a planning tool, even where regulatory authorities do not require its use. In fact, the two planning manuals discussed earlier (Blye & Yess, 1985; Groner, 1982) use checklists of potential resident problems which were adapted from Appendix F.

Just as important as computing potential evacuation time is that of estimating the time that the building provides by limiting the growth and spread of fire and by alerting residents as early as possible. Appendix G of the *Life Safety Code* estimates the amount of available time for various combinations of fire protection and building features, a method called the Fire Safety Evaluation System for Board and Care Facilities. Regulatory authorities have the option of using this feature of the code to measure whether buildings that do not meet the exact provisions in Chapter 21 are still able to provide a level of protection equivalent to Chapter 21 requirements. If a building provides equivalent protection as determined in Appendix G, then most regulatory authorities will accept the building as complying with code requirements. Operators can also use Appendix G to help them discover and compensate for building problems that could occur during a fire emergency.

PREVENTION

A good fire emergency plan has two essential components: strategies for preventing fires from starting in the first place, and strategies for taking necessary actions in the event that a fire starts anyway (which remains a possibility regardless of preventive measures). These latter strategies are discussed in the next section.

Studies have demonstrated that fires start in group homes for mostly the same reasons that they start in family dwellings (Janicki & Jacobsen, 1985). Chief among the hazards that start fires is the improper use of smoking materials. Every facility that has smokers, whether visitors, staff, or residents, needs a smoking

policy. In most cases, the policy should limit smoking to a specific room or area that is equipped with safe ashtrays and preferably furniture that resists ignition. Upholstered furniture can be purchased that does not easily ignite: the gold label with the letters "UFAC" signifies that the manufacturer is complying with certain voluntary standards. Moreover, if the building is not sprinklered, fire-rated barriers should separate the smoking area from the primary routes of escape. Caution should be used when disposing of ashes from ashtrays. Also, residents and staff should be carefully instructed to avoid resting cigarettes on the arms of chairs, smoking in bed, and other hazardous uses of smoking materials.

Improper use of space heaters is another common and deadly source of fire ignitions. In particular, space heaters should be kept away from combustible materials. For example, many fires have been started by people who try to dry cloths on space heaters or place the heaters next to their beds.

Cooking fires occur frequently, but tend to be less deadly than fires that start late at night. Electrical hazards include frayed wires and overloaded circuits. Local fire departments are usually very helpful in identifying these and other hazards during routine inspections of a home. However, this service should be requested so that the fire service representative does not restrict the inspection to building code violations.

Based on this author's review of board and care home fires, it seems that intentionally set fires are more common in these facilities than in other types of residences. These fires can be especially deadly because they are often set in particularly dangerous locations, such as hallways or bedrooms, and usually spread very quickly. It is impossible to offer advice applicable in all such situations, except to say that it is important to try to identify potential problems and to avoid undue risks. For example, staff references should be carefully checked prior to employment, and client records should be examined prior to admission. Finally, there is a chance that neighbors could set fires at group homes. Good outside lighting, removal of combustible materials from outside the home, installation of fences, and increased vigilance are all helpful where there are poor relationships with neighbors.

EMERGENCY PLANNING TO INCREASE THE MARGIN OF SAFETY

While prevention is critically important, there is always the chance that a fire will start. A fire emergency plan, plus an accompanying training program, is essential for any community residence. (For a more detailed discussion of the content of this section, see Groner, 1982.)

The basic goal of all fire emergency plans is to increase the margin of safety. *Margin of safety* is not simply a slogan; it is a concrete criterion against which all the details of an emergency plan should be evaluated. The *margin of safety* can be defined as the difference between the amount of time that it takes to accomplish the emergency plan and the amount of time available to accomplish the plan. The time available ends when fire, or more typically, smoke creates untenable conditions. The time needed ends when all residents and staff are located where fire and smoke cannot reach them. In other words, the margin of safety is used up when people are still present at any location where fire or smoke becomes an immediate threat to life. In the absence of fire protection features, untenable conditions can be reached within a few minutes, even in areas relatively remote from a fire. The margin of safety can and should be increased by incorporating features that both decrease the time needed to evacuate and increase the time available.

In small-group homes, the staff and residents will usually be safe only when they have moved to somewhere outside and away from the building. However, in some instances (e.g., where a group home is located in a large apartment building), temporary refuge can be found in a well-protected area inside a building. For guidance about where to locate safe areas in large facilities and apartment buildings, consult the fire safety manual by Groner (1982) or familiarize yourself with the definition of "point of safety" in Chapter 21 of the *Life Safety Code* (Lathrop, 1985). Alternatively, a competent fire protection engineer or fire service representative can be consulted.

Increasing the Time Available by Improving the Building

Most fire safety improvements in the building and its fire protection hardware serve to increase the available time. Enclosing staircases and other vertical openings can prevent fire from following its natural path upward, where it represents an immediate and extreme threat to upstairs sleeping areas. Sprinkler systems will usually extinguish fires before they pose a serious threat to life. Walls and doors can be upgraded to resist the spread of fire and smoke. Less flammable furniture and wall coverings can slow the growth of fire and prevent some fires from starting in the first place.

Building changes that slow the growth and spread of fire and smoke are not the only ways to provide more time. Improved alarm systems increase available time by giving the residents and staff an earlier start. Additional smoke detectors enhance the chances of discovering a fire sooner, while interconnecting smoke detectors and installation of manual alarm pull-boxes help notify residents and staff more quickly.

A building should be evaluated to determine where and how it may fail to provide enough time for evacuation. Local fire departments can be an excellent source of information about the preceding safety components and other ways to increase the time available through modifying the building and its features. (Fire safety experts often disagree about the relative merits of different approaches. They may demonstrate biases regarding certain approaches of fire safety and the abilities of group home residents. In this situation, group home operators may want to educate fire service representatives about the abilities of residents or seek advice from an engineer with specific training in fire protection.) Both of the already-mentioned fire safety manuals (i.e., Byle & Yess, 1985; Groner, 1982) provide helpful information on fire protection hardware and building features. For a more comprehensive treatment, consult the National Fire Protection Association's *Fire Protection Handbook* (NFPA, 1986).

Appendix G of the *Life Safety Code,* the Fire Safety Evaluation System for Board and Care Facilities, can be used as a diagnostic tool. An examination of ratings on the evaluation system can assist in the evaluation of the relative usefulness of various ways to upgrade the building. However, these evaluations are best performed by someone trained in the use of the evaluation system. If an inspection for compliance with the *Life Safety Code* has been conducted, then Appendix G may have been used. Where Appendix G is not used, the regulatory authority having jurisdiction may be willing to complete the evaluation system and discuss its findings.

Planning to Decrease the Needed Time

Equally as vital as increasing available time are the actions that residents and staff take to decrease the time needed to get to an area of safety. The starting point for a fire emergency plan is to choose the best protection strategy for each resident.

Choosing the Primary Strategy

Finding the best strategy for a resident is more complex than simply choosing the shortest or quickest route out of the building. It also involves deciding how to alert the resident, anticipating problems that may be encountered, and assisting the resident to overcome those problems. The primary strategy is chosen by considering two criteria, speed and reliability. Speed is simply whatever approach will best protect the resident in the least amount of time. Both the capability of the resident and the availability of staff members to help should be considered.

Reliability is as important as speed, but more difficult to determine. Reliability means the probability that the strategy will be effective regardless of where a fire starts and how fast it grows. For example, an evacuation route that is exposed to common living areas such as the kitchen and living room or den is much more likely to be blocked, because fires often start in such locations. For this reason, the route that people habitually use to enter and leave the building is often not the best to use during a fire emergency. Rather, a preferred route may be through a back door or even out the window (but only if there is a low risk of personal injury).

No single primary strategy works best for all residents in all group homes: interactions between residents, staff, and the building need to be considered. For example, one resident may

be depended on to safely leave through a bedroom window, while another resident may be physically or mentally incapable of reliably performing this same procedure. Thus, either a different approach needs to be used for the second resident, or staff members should be prepared to help the second resident leave through the window. Different strategies can result from physical, sensory, or cognitive limitations of residents or from their locations within the building. In many situations, especially in small-group homes, the life safety strategies for all the residents will be very similar. However, a careful review of the abilities and reliabilities of all the residents is necessary.

Backup Strategies Given the unpredictability of fires, it is rare that a primary strategy alone provides adequate protection. Thus, a backup strategy is needed that can be used in case the primary strategy is unavailable during an emergency. A limited number of combinations of primary and backup strategies will be used for most residents. These are described in the following paragraphs.

First Strategic Option: Use a Direct Exit from Bedrooms In those rare situations where bedrooms have a door leading directly to the outside of the building, relatively capable residents can be taught the simplest and most effective of all strategies: open the door and go outside to a meeting place. Where this approach is feasible, careful consideration must be paid to whether the door is kept locked at night, and whether the residents can unlock the door without difficulty. When possible, this primary strategy is usually sufficient by itself.

Second Strategic Option: Backup with an Alternative Route As most facilities do not have bedrooms with direct access to the exterior of the building, residents will usually have to travel through the building to reach an exit. In this situation, there are two advisable backup strategies: the resident can either use an alternative escape route or wait inside his or her bedroom until rescued. The use of an alternative route is usually the preferable approach, provided that the primary and backup routes are sufficiently separated so that the probability that a fire will block both the primary and backup routes is low. A typical example is where one route leads out the front door and the other route leads out through the bedroom window. Alternatively, the routes are not sufficiently separated when the resident must travel down the same unprotected corridor or stairs to reach both routes. As with choosing the primary route, the residents' physical, mental, and sensory disabilities should be considered. To use the alternative route approach, the resident should have the ability to decide when the backup route should be used instead of the primary route, or provisions should be made to ensure that staff would be quickly available to lead the resident to safety.

Third Strategic Option: Backup by Waiting in the Bedroom When the two best routes are insufficiently separated or when a resident is unable to use the backup route, the best backup strategy is often to have the resident wait inside the bedroom behind a closed door until he or she can be rescued. To make this approach dependable, residents must have the ability to decide when they must leave the door closed (e.g., the door is hot or smoke can be seen around the door) and how to signal for help (e.g., wave from the window, put a sheet outside the window).

Fourth Strategic Option: Evacuate Only with Help A fourth approach is to have the resident not attempt an unassisted evacuation, but rather for him or her to wait inside the bedroom behind a closed door until it is clear that an evacuation is feasible. This strategy is used in health care settings. It is important to note that this approach is only advisable in buildings that satisfy the stringent fire safety requirements imposed on hospitals and other health care facilities. Buildings that meet these requirements are designed to provide safe refuge inside of bedrooms behind closed doors in the event that an evacuation cannot be completed. Accordingly, this approach infrequently will be available to operators of small-group homes: it should only be used where the disabilities of residents preclude independent action and where staffing patterns might prevent a timely evacuation.

Building Design
Affects Choice of Strategies

The four strategic choices just outlined are ordered in an important way: each successive choice more strongly emphasizes refuge because residents will remain in the building longer than the previous choice. Primarily for this reason, an earlier option is safer than latter options when both are feasible. However, due to limitations in the availability of staff and in resident capabilities, these latter options must often be chosen. By limiting the spread of flames and smoke, the building's layout and fire protection features largely determine how much time will be available during a fire. Remaining in the building for longer time periods is advisable only to the extent that the building has the fire protection features needed to provide the additional time.

This same logic underlies the *Life Safety Code* requirements where more stringent building requirements are needed to accomplish more time-consuming protection strategies. For example, buildings that satisfy the requirements for an "evacuation impractical" level of evacuation capability are intended to provide good refuge capability, and the last choice of strategy can be used with considerable confidence. Conversely, having residents wait in their rooms for assistance is ill-advised in buildings that only meet the fire safety requirements for a "prompt" evacuation capability level.

Resident Capabilities
Affect Choice of Strategies

A resident's performance in emergency evacuations is the result of his or her interactions with the building. For example, escaping out a ground floor window may be infeasible for many physically impaired residents, which in turn makes escaping out the window a poor choice as a backup strategy. Therefore, the plan needs to ensure that staff assistance will be available to the extent that residents cannot dependably accomplish a strategy on their own. Moreover, simple changes can greatly affect the usefulness of such an approach. A box can be placed under the window, a window latch can be replaced, or other measures can be taken to ensure that alternative routes of escape are feasible as backup strategies. Also, residents may be moved to rooms from which they can escape more safely. (Such changes may not only reduce the time needed to get everyone to safety, but may also result in more favorable ratings on *Life Safety Code* measures of evacuation capability.) Finally, dramatic improvements in residents' abilities can be accomplished through training, as discussed later in this chapter.

Anticipating Resident Problems during an Emergency Evacuation

Real fire emergencies do not closely resemble any routine events, so it is difficult to predict how residents will react. Nonetheless, staff should anticipate problems that residents may experience during an actual fire. The *Life Safety Code*'s Appendix F, the Evacuation Difficulty Index (Groner, 1982; Nelson et al., 1983), is a measurement instrument specifically designed for such problems, using technology adapted from organizational psychology and with assistance from experts.

Ratings on the Evacuation Difficulty Index are not based on what is most likely to happen during an emergency, but rather on what could go wrong. All good emergency planning takes this same perspective: if there is a reasonable chance that something may go wrong, you assume that it will go wrong.

The index assesses each resident on seven "risk factors" that were determined by a panel of experts as potential problems during an emergency: risk of resistance, impaired mobility, impaired consciousness, need for extra help, response to instructions, waking response to alarm, and response to fire drills. The Evacuation Difficulty Index divides each risk factor into categories with numeric scores that reflect the amount of staff assistance that may be needed to overcome the problem. A specific definition and behavioral examples are supplied for each category. (When using the index, ratings should be based on the definitions and examples provided in the instructions. Worksheets for deriving the index are used only for evaluations, because labels used on the worksheet are too ambiguous in themselves to provide meaningful results.)

While the Evacuation Difficulty Index is too lengthy to reproduce here, an example from it will illustrate its construction and logic. The risk factor called "risk of resistance" is defined as follows:

A reasonable possibility that, during a fire emergency evacuation, the resident may resist leaving the home . . . [and that] staff [may be] required to use some physical force. . . . Resistance may be active (for example, the resident may have struck a staff member or attempted to run away) or passive (for example, the resident may have "gone limp" or hid from staff members.) Mere complaining or arguing is not considered resistance. (Nelson et al., 1983, p. 97)

The index includes three categories for "risk of resistance": "minimal risk," "risk of mild resistance," and "risk of strong resistance." Each category is supplied with specific examples of behavior. For instance, risk of mild resistance is accompanied by the following examples:

1. The resident has mildly resisted instructions from staff. Further, the resistance was brief or easily overcome by one staff member, and occurred in a situation similar enough to a fire emergency to predict that the behavior could recur during a fire emergency.
2. The resident has hidden from the staff in a situation similar enough to a fire emergency to predict that the behavior could recur during a real fire emergency. However, once found, the resident offered no further resistance. (Nelson et al., 1983, p. 97)

These examples are particularly useful in predicting problems that may be encountered during a fire emergency, and can be used as a checklist for the periodic assessment of each resident. In fact, such checklists, adapted from the Evacuation Difficulty Index, are found in both the Blye and Yess (1985) and Groner (1982) fire safety planning manuals.

Summary of Planning Steps

To summarize the theoretical material on fire emergency planning, the following steps can be used to develop a fire emergency plan:

Step 1. A *preliminary* selection of primary and secondary strategies should be made for each resident. The layout of the building; the cognitive, sensory, and physical limitations of the residents; and the availability of staff (especially late at night) should be considered.

Step 2. For each resident, a list should be made of his or her potential problems and needs for assistance in accomplishing the primary and backup strategies. The Evacuation Difficulty

Index or the checklists in the manuals can be used for guidance. Methods for compensating for potential problems should be developed.

Step 3.   The building should be evaluated to determine whether it is likely to provide enough time to accomplish the primary and backup strategies. For guidance, a fire protection engineer or representative from the fire department or regulatory authority should be consulted.

Step 4.   After considering the information obtained from steps 2 and 3, the initial selection of primary and backup strategies (step 1) should be reviewed and changed if a larger margin of safety can be provided.

Step 5.   A good training program should be developed so that both residents and staff are prepared in the event of fire.

Step 6.   If any doubt remains about whether the margin of safety is inadequate even after training, the building should be modified to provide more time.

TRAINING

Once an emergency plan has been developed, it must be implemented. A coordinated response to a fire emergency entails putting into practice a collection of skills that can be reliably learned only by practice. The stress that accompanies real emergencies interferes with the extra cognitive load required to translate the plan into a series of actions. Therefore, the actions themselves should be practiced until they can be performed with little mental effort. To the degree feasible, this principle of "overlearning" should be applied to training for staff as well as residents.

Using Fire Drills to Implement the Fire Emergency Plan

Practicing a fire emergency plan implies the use of fire drills. Unfortunately, fire drills are often poorly conducted, resulting in discord among management, staff, and residents. The problem seems to result from two commonly held but mistaken beliefs. First, fire drills are thought to have little to do with surviving an actual fire. Second, fire drills are valid and acceptable to regulatory authorities only when they are a sur-

prise to residents. These two beliefs should be corrected. First, when residents (to the extent possible) and staff understand the rationale behind the strategies, they will believe that learning the skills can really save lives in the event of a fire. Second, announced fire drills are useful training devices and can often be counted toward satisfying regulatory fire drill quotas. For example, the *Life Safety Code* (NFPA, 1985; section 31-7.3) specifically states that announced fire drills are an acceptable way to meet the quota that drills be conducted at least six times a year, two times per year on each shift.

Although legal requirements are a legitimate reason to run drills, the greatest value of fire drills lies in their use as a means to learn, practice, and evaluate a facility's fire emergency plan and training program. The specific purpose for running a drill should determine whether the drill is announced ahead of time. Surprise fire drills are best reserved for evaluating a facility's success in implementing its emergency procedures. Announced drills are more useful when residents and staff are still learning the procedures. In general, facilities should rely mostly on announced drills until the procedures have become well-learned.

In addition to announced and surprise fire exit drills, group homes should conduct "walkthrough drills," in which staff practice important skills with residents on a one-on-one basis. Once individual residents have learned basic skills, they can participate meaningfully during announced and surprise fire drills.

Content of Fire Drill Training

Three fundamental actions should be accomplished during a fire emergency. They are as follows:

1.   Complete the primary strategy as quickly as possible.
2.   Decide whether the primary strategy is unsafe; if it is, then complete the backup strategy.
3.   Stay at a designated safe location.

To the greatest degree possible, residents should perform these actions without assistance, and staff should be trained to ensure that the actions are carried out quickly and efficiently during an emergency. As an essential part of their training, staff should learn to anticipate problems with individual residents, as discussed earlier. (The three basic actions are the same skills that residents are evaluated on in the "response to fire drills" risk factor in the Evacuation Difficulty Index (see Appendix F in the *Life Safety Code,* NFPA, 1985).

In small-group homes, residents should be trained to respond quickly to a variety of fire stimuli, including the sound of the fire alarm, verbal warnings that there is a fire, and perhaps the smell of smoke or the sighting of flames or smoke. Further, the response must generalize to any time of the day, and especially at night. Appropriate rewards will help to ensure quick responses at inconvenient times.

In the event that their primary evacuation route is blocked, most residents should learn how to implement a backup strategy—to either remain inside a bedroom or use an alternative route of escape. This action, however, requires that residents make a decision and generalize the stimuli for that decision to a real fire. For these reasons, this is often the most difficult skill to teach. Various approaches have been attempted. For example, Haney and Jones (1982) used a heating pad and hair dryer to simulate the heat from a fire that can be felt when feeling the knob and edges of a door. Mentally retarded persons who felt heat were taught to leave the door closed and to signal for help from the window of their bedrooms. As a general guideline, the more that the training stimuli resemble actual fire stimuli, the more likely the training is to generalize to a real emergency.

Staying at some designated safe location is important, because people will often want to return to a burning building to retrieve a valued possession or to look for someone else still in the home. For example, in one instance told to the author, a group home resident evacuated in response to a fire alarm, but then rushed back into the home to save a valued picture when she found out that the fire was real. Therefore, it is important to establish a "safe area" meeting place, and to train residents to remain there even without the presence of staff members.

"Buddy systems" where residents are assigned the task of helping other specific residents are generally not recommended. However, particularly capable residents may still help during an emergency, provided that they are not assigned to help any specific person and that they know not to expose themselves to additional personal risk.

As a general guideline, the same battery of training techniques that are routinely used to train residents in everyday skills should be used to teach fire safety skills. Good use can be made of behavioral techniques such as modeling, rehearsal, shaping, withdrawal of reinforcers, and self-reinforcement (Haney & Jones, 1982).

Other Fire Safety Skills That Residents Should Learn

Learning to Stay Low During a fire emergency, residents trained in the skills just described are likely to avoid serious contact with smoke and flames in a code-conforming building. However, if the strategy fails or is not performed correctly, residents may still be able to avoid injury by staying below the level where smoke concentrates. Because smoke is hot, it first concentrates at the ceiling of a room and then moves towards the floor as it builds up. Therefore, persons can often move through a smoky environment in relative safety if they stay close to the floor. Training residents and staff to crawl or crouch near the floor will increase their chances for survival. However, crawling during an evacuation can cause many residents to travel much more slowly. Therefore, residents should be taught to crawl only in response to the presence of smoke.

Learning to Investigate and Report Fires Fires are often first noticed when someone hears a strange noise, smells smoke, or sees a flickering light. The natural tendency is to investigate, an action that can lead to great danger if not performed with considerable caution. The danger results when someone opens a door to a room where a serious fire has developed. The sudden rush of intense heat can force the person to retreat rapidly, leaving the door open. An open door will provide more oxygen and will remove a barrier, thus helping the fire to spread rapidly to other areas.

When investigating a fire, staff should learn to feel doors for heat and to look for smoke coming from around the doors. If there is reason to believe that a fire is on the other side, then the door should be left closed and the alarm sounded. Even when heat or smoke are not apparent, doors should be opened just a crack so that they can be slammed shut if there is a fire on the other side.

Because the actions taken while investigating a possible fire can make a great deal of difference in the final outcome, only particularly capable and reliable residents should be taught to investigate. Other residents should learn to immediately alert a staff member at the first sign that anything may be amiss. This is particularly important, because there have been instances where a resident has discovered a fire, and used his or her training to evacuate the home, but failed to alert anyone else in the home or to activate the fire alarm.

Staff and capable residents should learn how to report fires to the fire department. In the excitement of a fire, many people hang up before relaying all the information that the fire department needs to respond. The appropriate phone number and instructions should be posted at the telephones. Local fire departments or emergency dispatchers should be asked to list the information needed to respond to a fire. However, it is important that both staff and residents understand that the first priority is to evacuate the home; only then should the fire be reported. A telephone inside the building should only be used if it is obvious that the caller is not in immediate danger from the fire.

Learning to Use Fire Extinguishers
Staff members should be trained to use fire extinguishers. The training program should include the following features: actual practice putting out fires with the type of extinguishers used in the facilities; learning what types of extinguishers should be used on what types of fires; knowing how to check and maintain fire extinguishers; and knowing exactly where to find the extinguishers. Once again, staff should know that their first priorities are to start the evacuation and report the fire. Staff should learn never to attempt to put out a fire unless they are certain that they will succeed. Failing

to extinguish a fire may endanger the individual, and will waste time that could otherwise be used to get everyone to safety. The NFPA manual (Blye & Yess, 1985) includes a good discussion on fire extinguisher training. Most fire departments offer good advice and will help train staff in the hands-on use of extinguishers.

Stop, Drop, and Roll Extinguishing clothing fires is an easily learned skill that has often saved lives. This involves having the person "drop" to the floor and "roll" to smother the fire. The "stop" part is also critical, because the natural response to a clothing fire is to run, which only fans the fire, causing it to burn more rapidly.

CONCLUSION: THERE'S NOTHING SPECIAL ABOUT FIRE SAFETY PLANNING

Fire safety should be routinized into everyday programs. The same techniques and scheduling that are used to train residents in other skills can and should be used in fire safety training. When someone is observed performing an unsafe act that could create a fire hazard (e.g., propping open a fire door or leaving a lighted cigarette on the edge of a table), the problem should be corrected just as though it were a problem that significantly interfered with day-to-day living. By integrating fire safety practices into the everyday management of a group home, a program will be established that remains effective over the life of the group home and the lifetimes of many of its residents.

NOTE

The National Bureau of Standards manual (Groner, 1982) can be ordered from two sources. A photocopy of the original report is available from the National Clearinghouse for Rehabilitation Materials at Oklahoma State University, 115 Old U.S.D.A. Building, Oklahoma State University, Stillwater, OK 74078. A new typeset edition has been published by Project Share, and can be ordered by writing them at P.O. Box 2309, Rockville, MD 20852, or telephoning them at (301) 231-9539.

All materials published by the National Fire Protection Association can be ordered by calling their toll-free customer service number at (800) 344-3555. These materials include the NFPA manual (Blye & Yess, 1985); *In Case of Fire,* a slide/tape package for training mentally retarded adults (Coady & MacMillan, 1983), and the *Fire Protection Handbook.* The 1985 edition of the *Life Safety Code* (NFPA, 1985) and the *Life Safety Code Handbook* (Lathrop,

1985) are also available from NFPA. Both include the Evacuation Difficulty Index (Appendix F) and the Fire Safety Evaluation System for Board and Care Facilities (Appendix G). The author suggests that readers order the *Life Safety Code Handbook* instead of the *Life Safety Code,* owing to the former's excellent annotations and improved organization.

REFERENCES

Blye, P.E., & Yess, J.P. (1985). *Fire safety in board and care homes: A self-study guide for owners and operators.* Quincy, MA: National Fire Protection Association.

Coady, D., & MacMillan, R. (1983). *In case of fire: A fire safety program for mentally retarded adults.* Sudbury: MA: Massachusetts Firefighting Academy.

Groner, N.E. (1982). *A matter of time: A comprehensive guide to fire emergency planning for board and care homes.* Washington, DC: National Bureau of Standards.

Groner, N.E., Levin, B.M., & Nelson, H.E. (1981). Measuring evacuation difficulty in board and care homes. *Fire Journal, 75*(3), 52–58.

Haney, J.I., & Jones, R.T. (1982). Programming maintenance as a major component of a community-centered preventive effort: Escape from fire. *Behavior Therapy, 13,* 47–62.

Holton, D. (1981). Boarding homes—the new "residential fire problem? *Fire Journal, 75*(2), 53–56.

Janicki, M.P., & Jacobson, J.W. (1985). Fire safety, self-preservation, and community residences for mentally re-

tarded in New York State. *Fire Journal, 79*(4), 38–41, 82–86.

Lathrop, J.K. (Ed.). (1985). *Life safety code handbook, 3rd ed.* Quincy, MA: National Fire Protection Association.

National Fire Protection Association. (1985). *Life safety code.* Quincy, MA: National Fire Protection Association.

National Fire Protection Association. (1986). *Fire protection handbook.* Quincy, MA: National Fire Protection Association.

Nelson, H.E., Levin, B.M., Shibe, A.J., Groner, N.E., Paulsen, R.L., Alvord, D.M., & Thorne, S.D. (1983). *A fire safety evaluation system for board and care homes.* Washington, DC: National Bureau of Standards.

Rome Fire Department (1981). *Fire safety manual for personal care homes.* Rome, GA: Bureau of Fire Prevention, Rome Fire Department.

Select Committee on Aging. (1979). *Fire in boarding homes: The tip of the iceberg* (Comm. Pub. No. 96-187). Washington, DC: U.S. Government Printing Office.

SUPPLEMENTAL RESOURCE

Cantor, D. (Ed.).(1980). *Fires and human behavior.* New York: John Wiley & Sons.

Chapter 25

Design Features and Architectural Considerations

Julia Williams Robinson

The architecture of a community residence is discussed in terms of the process and criteria for design. Beginning with a broad overview of the literature relating architecture to the behavior of developmentally disabled persons, the chapter goes on to delineate key issues in the design of community residences. These are: the design process, the relation between housing and program, and appropriate design responses in the context of: 1) individual resident needs, 2) group needs, 3) staff and administrative needs, 4) safety considerations, and 5) designing for handicaps. Principles for design are presented as well as specific design suggestions.

The architecture of the dwelling we inhabit not only enables us to live functionally in a particular way (Altman & Chemers, 1980; Rapoport, 1969), but is also a symbolic representation of ourselves (Cooper, 1974). A community residence for developmentally disabled persons similarly performs at both the functional and symbolic levels: it needs to support the daily activities that occur within it, and it symbolizes integration within the community. For the individual resident, a private dwelling, in contrast to an institutional setting, presents opportunities for developing autonomy, identity, dignity, and a relation to both a community of residents and to the community at large.

Autonomy is promoted in housing design by allowing the resident to control the environment. Insofar as residents are given the opportunity to engage in the normal activities of life (determined by dwelling design, location, and accessibility), are able to choose among different levels of privacy and physical comfort (determined by variation in degrees of privacy in room arrangement and in control of light, temperature, and ventilation), and are provided chances to learn new things (through a challenging, nonoverprotective environment), autonomy will be supported by the housing setting.

Identity, similarly, means that the setting must allow for individual expression, by providing for spontaneity (in the accessibility of activities), by allowing modification of places (materials that are easily manipulated,

This chapter is based on research from two projects. *Architectural Planning of Residences for Mentally Retarded People* was supported by grants from the following University of Minnesota Units: the Center for Urban and Regional Affairs, the Graduate School, the School of Architecture and Landscape Architecture, and the Department of Psychology. Participants on this project included the author, Travis Thompson, Paul Emmons, Myles Graff, and Evelyn Franklin. *Housing Form: Empirical Description* was supported by the National Endowment for the Arts and by the University of Minnesota School of Architecture and Institute of Technology. In addition to the author, participants on the project include Travis Thompson, Myles Graff, Julio Bermudez, Michelle Johannes, and Jan Greenberg. With the exception of the graphs, the chapter illustrations are by Richard Laffin.

room designs that allow multiple furniture arrangements), by creating real choices (selection of furniture, options for room color, ease of decorating rooms), by encouraging an understanding of personal growth and history (places for old things, ways to store photographs and other personal items), and by making places for the person to do things by himself or herself (private territory, adequate room to keep and use equipment, a place to entertain and to experience being alone).

Dignity is provided when a person lives in a dwelling that looks and functions like the dwellings of other citizens, incorporating beauty, convenience, and comfort, and when the dwelling is part of the larger community, affording opportunities for individual growth and change.

The sense of community among residents results from cooperation among residents (as well as between residents and staff) and from the development of a group history. When each person in a community has an identifiable role to play in maintaining the group and is seen as valuable by all, true cooperation is possible. Each group member should be both dependent upon the group and depended upon by the group. The environment can support this by providing each person and the group with a range of places for activities (locations for individual hobbies, places for quiet group activities, spaces that allow boisterous, interactive endeavors, and spaces that are informal and formal), by facilitating group governance and decision making (providing space for organized and casual meetings and discussion), and by making possible individual contributions to the group (minimizing barriers to housework, food preparation, and other daily activities, presenting opportunities for the broad range of talents of residents). The sense of group history can be enhanced by the provision of places where shared needs are met (a dining area for the ritual of eating, places where the group gathers informally), and where shared memories are manifest (places to put group photographs, trophies, etc.).

The resident's integration within the outside community may be enhanced by the location of the residence (proximity to activities and to transportation), and by the dwelling's appearance (its fit with its neighbors, its physical condition, and the status of the life-style it conveys).

The challenge of designing a community residence for developmentally disabled persons entails taking advantage of the opportunities presented by housing to support the broad goals of autonomy, identity, dignity, and a sense of community, while meeting the practical requirements of a given situation, such as resident limitations, staffing necessities, and building regulations.

ROLE OF ARCHITECTURE

Buildings both communicate and perpetuate the culture of a society by limiting or supporting overt behavior (it is difficult, for example, to sleep in a kitchen), and by symbolizing the behavior expected to occur (a kitchen stands for preparing food). A building's design, as a behavior setting (Barker, 1968), affects the nature and character of the activities associated with it. We can all identify certain types of buildings as stores, churches, or schools, for instance, and we have ideas about the type of behavior and kinds of people likely to be found there. Similarly, different types of housing are associated with different kinds of behavior and people.

The architecture of any building, including housing, consists of a complex set of elements. The physical elements of architecture create a cumulative effect, communicating coherent meaning by a positive redundancy of cues (Norberg-Schulz, 1965; Rapoport, 1982). The "storeness," "schoolness," or "houseness" of a building is expressed by such things as geometry, size, setting, materials, windows, doors, furnishings, room size, mechanical systems, and lighting. Within each feature are successive layers of variety. The floor, for example, may be any combination of materials such as wood, carpet, vinyl, terrazzo, or brick. Each variation of materials may be associated with different uses. For example, vinyl tile may be associated with schools and wood may be associated with residential use, depending on the context of other associated features (area rugs, floor drains).

Although the character of the building is communicated through the redundancy of the features, dissonance may also play a role. A single nonconforming cue or element may make a setting noncoherent, so that a room that looks like a living room because of its configuration, finish materials, and furniture, will no longer "read" clearly if it also contains an exit sign or metal fire door. It is therefore not enough to design a setting in a piecemeal fashion: the relation between architectural features is as important as the individual characteristics themselves.

Goffman (1961) described how specific social and physical characteristics of institutions tend to create particular patterns of behavior that are maladaptive in an ordinary community setting. The philosophy of normalization underlying the development of community-based residences similarly includes an awareness of the potential role played by the physical setting of a facility (Gunzburg, 1973; Nirje, 1969; Wolfensberger, 1972). Consequently, the concern to create appropriate housing for developmentally disabled persons has led to research on the physical characteristics of housing.

Although there is evidence that housing plays a role in the support of normal behavior (Architecture, Research, Construction, Inc., 1985; Bercovici, 1983; Thompson & Carey, 1981), the specifics of the relationship between architectural features and behavior are still largely speculative. The ability to detect the effects of any particular environment or environmental element depends, in part, on the use of reliable instruments that describe the physical setting (Craik, 1971; Wener, 1982).

Three approaches have been used to develop environmental descriptions in the study of normalization and persons with developmental disabilities: globally characterizing the setting (Rotegard, Hill, & Bruininks, 1982; Wolfensberger & Glenn, 1975; Wolfensberger & Thomas, 1983); identifying selected physical features based on their observed relationship with behavior (Gunzburg, 1973; MacEachron, 1983; Raynes, Pratt, & Roses, 1979; Rivlin, Bogert, & Cirillo, 1981); and using an inclusive description of setting combined with observed relationships between behavior and setting (Robinson, Thompson, Emmons, Graff, & Franklin, 1984). The environmental description

instruments that have been tested most are PASS (Program Analysis of Service Systems) (Wolfensberger & Glenn, 1975) and PASSING (Program Analysis of Service Systems Implementation of Normalization Goals) (Wolfensberger & Thomas, 1983). These instruments are useful to assess the overall character of a setting (e.g., its institutionality), but lack the specificity necessary to determine the impact of individual environmental characteristics on behavior (e.g., the difference it would make if the living room were smaller). While not oriented to the principles of normalization, Moos and Lemke's (1979) Multiphasic Environmental Assessment Procedures (MEAP), provides a specific description of settings for the elderly. The work of Robinson et al. (1984) and Robinson (1986) is directed to the creation of a descriptive tool for normalization that could complement more general instruments by providing specific descriptions of environmental elements. This would allow for the development of more definitive research on the role of housing design in supporting behavior.

Although in some cases the assessment techniques, and the specificity of the population or the settings studies, limit the applicability of the research findings, there is a sizable body of research on housing for persons with developmental disabilities (Architecture, Research, Construction, Inc., 1985; Bercovici, 1983; Butterfield, 1984; Environment Design Group, 1976; Hendrickson, Akkerman, Speggen, & Thompson, 1985; Holahan, 1979; Knight, Weitzer, & Zimring, 1978; Landesman-Dwyer, Stein, & Sackett, 1976; Mazis & Canter, 1979; Richer, 1979; Rivlin & Wolfe, 1979; Sime & Sime, 1979; Thompson & Carey, 1981). These investigations form the basis for further study to relate behavior in designed settings to the character of the environments.

BUILDING DESIGN PROCESS

The relationship between a community residence's program and the architecture of the facility is usually not explicitly considered. However, the role of the physical setting in facilitating or impeding daily activities is obvious when we find the places where we work or live either delightful on the one hand or inconvenient and uncomfortable on the other. The design process plays a critical role in making a community residence of high quality.

Designing a community residence typically follows a three-phase architectural process: program design and site selection, building design or modification, and construction. A fourth phase may also be added: evaluation and adjustment.

The architectural program is usually a written document describing what the community residence building is to be like and articulating cost constraints and criteria for site selection and design. Starting with broad principles, moving on to desired activities, and finally to the spaces necessary to house the activities, the program defines the character of the facility. In order to allow an appropriate fit between the buildings and a resident program, the following issues are generally included in the program: 1) philosophy, 2) characteristics of the residents to be served, 3) type of staffing and anticipated schedule, 4) programmatic activities (both formal and informal), and 5) identification of individual resident needs and desires. In addition, the requirements of codes and zoning regulations must be considered. The architectural program should be well developed before a new building is designed or an existing building is modified.

The site selection process involves the architect and agency in identifying key selection criteria. Location must be considered in terms of transportation needs, accessibility of key services, character of the neighborhood, and zoning regulations. For new construction, the suitability of the site for the building must be determined, and requires a surveyed plot plan and possibly soil borings. The site must have soil that will support a structure and allow proper drainage. The topography must allow for appropriate building orientation and access by vehicles. To determine this, the services of a landscape architect and/or engineer may be required.

In chosing a building to be remodeled, it is important to consider both the building's type and condition, as modification costs to meet practical needs and codes may be prohibitive if major changes are necessary. (For a more complete discussion of choosing a building for remodeling see Architecture, Research, Construction, Inc., 1985.) If a zoning variance is needed, community acceptance of a project is usually a prerequisite (see Freedman & Freedman, Chapter 4, this volume, for a discussion of zoning and community residences.)

In creating a building design, or a modification of a building, the architect works with the agency to ensure that the plan is implemented at the required cost. Design aspects that need to be considered include physical access (parking, service, sewer, gas, and water), code requirements (for fire, health, emergency, handicaps, energy), structural and mechanical concerns, organization of rooms, and the character of the building's exterior and interior spaces. The more experienced the architect, the more options can be considered. An experienced architect will be able to identify alternative solutions to particular design problems because of working knowledge of building materials and a thorough understanding of the numerous intricate relationships between building parts.

The design process generally progresses from schematic design (where a number of options are explored), to design development (where a single design is completed), to the construction drawing phase (where documents describing the construction techniques and specifying the materials are made). During the design phase, engineers, landscape architects, and/or interior designers commonly enter into consultant or cooperative roles with the architect and agency. Usually, at the end of the design phase, the construction documents are put up for bid to a number of reliable contractors, and the best bid is selected. Because bids may include substitutions of materials and involve subcontractor relationships, the best bid is not always the lowest in cost. Sometimes architects work with one reliable contractor from the beginning, alleviating the need for the bidding procedure between contractors. In times of low inflation, the contractors' bids should be close to the costs estimated by the architect. When bids are higher than expected, minor redesign may be required.

In the fortunate circumstance where the bid is lower than anticipated, improvements to the design may be made.

Generally, the actual construction process is supervised by the architect, who acts as the agency's representative on the site. Inevitably, changes in the original plans will be required as unforeseen circumstances arise, but changes are carefully monitored by the architect, who consults with the agency when revisions are necessary.

Once the building is constructed and the residents and staff move in, the fine tuning begins. There is likely to be continued contact with the architect as questions arise, which may be formalized in a consultant relationship.

After a facility has been occupied for a year or more, it may be desirable to have the designer or another architect do an evaluation, termed a postoccupancy study. A postoccupancy study compares the original architectural scheme to the actual performance of the building. It is an opportunity for the architect and the agency to communicate with the actual users. If the building is not being used as intended, it may be that the reasons for a particular design were not communicated to the users. Or, the design may be used in innovative and unintended ways that can educate the designer and client. Sometimes, with slight modifications, the building can perform better for the users. This kind of fine-tuning can be very beneficial to all involved.

The importance of choosing a good architect cannot be overestimated. As with the selection of any professional, it is wise for an agency to interview more than one potential architect. While experience with housing may play an important role, an architect who is sensitive to the issues of normalization may be equally important. If an architect has designed community residences before, a visit to these homes is recommended to see whether they convey an understanding of issues of importance to the agency.

THE RELATION BETWEEN HOUSING AND PROGRAM

The character of a residential program is represented to the outside world through the facility that houses it. For example, large isolated campuses of institutions have come to symbolize negative things that traditionally occurred there, despite the many improvements that may have occurred in particular facilities. But the relationship between a facility and its program is not simply limited to appearance. The organization and character of the spaces have a practical effect and create an ambience that is more or less supportive of the activities that are intended to occur there. Particular building forms are either more or less supportive of specific types of programmatic goals.

This point can be illustrated by observing the larger community to discover how different forms of housing are generally used and perceived. Recent work (Robinson, 1986) has indicated that when slides of interiors and exteriors of a variety of housing types (including hospitals, nursing homes, dormitories, apartment buildings, group homes, rooming houses, and single-family detached dwellings) are assessed as institutionlike or homelike by students, the types have tended to fall along a continuum between the two qualities (see Figure 1). When the mean scores for each building type are graphed (Figure 2), three broad categories of setting emerge: the medical facility (hospitals and nursing homes), the single-family detached homes, and what was termed the ambiguous setting. Within the middle group, walk-up apartments were assessed closest to the single-family dwelling, and dormitories were assessed closer to the medical settings. For the individual ratings, one group home (G3) and one walk-up apartment (W1) were rated more homelike than one of the single-family detached units (Figure 1). This suggests that while the most homelike settings are likely to be single family residences, other housing forms also may be perceived as homelike.

The American dream of owning a single-family dwelling on its own plot of land (Rapoport, 1969) is a powerful one. However, for most single people, this is not a practical reality. Only 17% of unmarried people who do not live in group quarters (dormitories, boarding houses, group homes, etc.) own single unit detached housing (U.S. Department of Com-

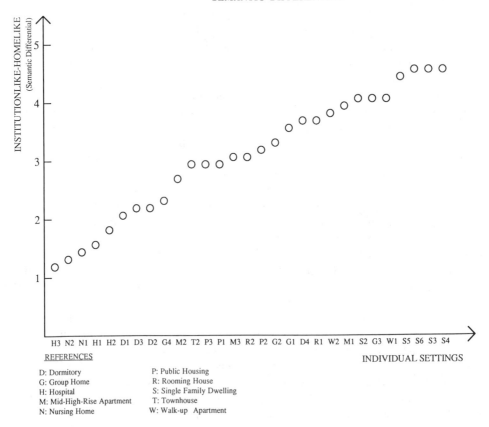

Figure 1. Ratings of individual housing settings.

merce, 1984), whereas 65% live in buildings with two or more housing units, largely as renters. Of this same unmarried group, 59% live by themselves, 26% share a unit with one other person, and the remaining 15% share a unit with two or more people (only 1% share a unit with five or more individuals). Within the context of the normalization principle, housing opportunities in a given society should conform to the cultural expectations of its citizens. Thus, the ideal form of long-term housing for unmarried, developmentally disabled persons in the United States is an apartment or single-family house. When, because of the level or character of a disability, this is not a viable option, the alternative that is most typical of situations where adults share a single residence is a room of one's own. As with a typical adult popula-

tion, for short-term occupancy, such as for vacations or for a term of study, group living situations such as dormitories, hotels, and rooming houses are appropriate settings. However, these are unlikely to be the dwelling of choice for nondisabled adults who are financially free to make a choice.

The design of a community residence, whatever its overall form as a housing type, must respond to five concerns common to all such facilities: 1) private space for the resident; 2) shared space; 3) staff and administrative space; 4) building regulations and fire safety; and 5) accommodation of handicaps. The remainder of the chapter discusses the relation between these concerns and specific design features that create the character and support the uses of a community residence.

MEANS FOR BUILDING TYPE
SEMANTIC DIFFERENTIAL

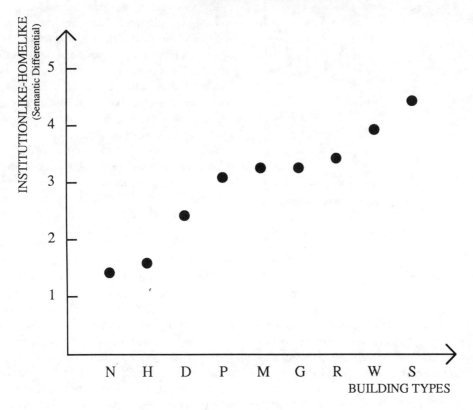

REFERENCES

D: Dormitory
G: Group Home
H: Hospital
M: Mid-High-Rise Apartment
N: Nursing Home

P: Public Housing
R: Rooming House
S: Single Family Dwelling
W: Walk-up Apartment

Figure 2. Ratings of housing types.

RESIDENT PRIVATE SPACE

One's own room is the territory over which an inhabitant has ultimate control. In American society, this need is most often served by the bedroom (Altman & Chemers, 1980). A private room enables the developmentally disabled person to make choices and to mark territory. It was noted earlier that unmarried adults most often have a housing unit all to themselves. While this may not be practical in all communi-ty residences, wherever possible the resident should be provided with a private room. As with the nondisabled adult, this space should not simply be a place to sleep, but should be a place of retreat, a place for hobbies, a place to indulge personal preferences for colors, materials, and furniture style (Figure 3). It is important that each person within a dwelling have a unique territory, identifiable as different from others in order to discover who he or she is. If a room for each resident is not possible, the next

Figure 3. Bedrooms express individual identity.

best option is to provide a large enough shared space so that each person can have a clearly defined area within the room that can serve some of these same functions.

Ideally, individuals' rooms should be large enough to have a bed and dresser, a comfortable chair, a work surface (table or desk), and plenty of storage for clothes, radios, records, collections, sports equipment, or other personal objects. As for the nondisabled adult, the bedroom may be a place to entertain as well, which should be reflected in the size and furnishings.

If at all possible, residents should be encouraged to select wall coverings, curtains, rugs, bedcovers, and items of furniture. For example, a resident might prefer a sofabed to an ordinary one, so that the room may be easily transformed from a sleeping room. Whatever the preferences of the inhabitants, they will learn about themselves through the necessity to create a territory of their own. If residents are truly incapable of making choices about their rooms and furniture, the uniqueness of spaces can be maintained by having different people help them to select their furniture and arrangement. An available family member, or if this is not possible, several different staff people, may assist residents, thereby assuring that no two rooms will be alike. When more than one person occupies a room, agreement on decorating will have to be reached. Nonetheless, if two people differ strongly about a preference, it may well be more important that both roommates be allowed to express themselves, even

though some of the aesthetic unity of the room is sacrificed.

In most houses and apartments, each bedroom has a different character. They vary in size, window placement, window style, exterior orientation, proportions, and architectural details. Even with no furniture, each room would be identifiable. These differences among rooms increase the likelihood of different furniture arrangements, thus making each person's room more likely to be special.

The design of bedroom storage can assist the resident in several ways. If a large closet is provided, dressing activities may be separated from others, facilitating the use of the room for a range of nonsleeping-dressing activities, hobbies, and entertaining. In addition to good closet space, adequate shelf space will make it easier to keep the room organized and neat.

In addition to the bedroom, the other private area is the bathroom. In short-term dwellings like dormitories, the bathroom may be a communal facility with stall toilets and showers, and rows of sinks. In private residences, the bathrooms are typically designed to be used by one person at a time. This smallness requires that the bathroom be a private place. It generally holds only one toilet, one sink, and one shower or bath, although when a married couple share a bathroom, sometimes two sinks are included to allow simultaneous use of the space.

For people who do not need assistance in hygiene-related activities, the traditionally designed bathroom will help them to learn modesty and the rules of privacy, which are a part of our culture. Even when disabled persons need assistance, the character of the intimacy of the space should not be eliminated altogether. The concern for efficiency, which may require a larger area than usual or special kinds of fixtures, should be balanced with a concern for materials that express the concern for comfort. This attitude is expressed in typical bathrooms by carpeted floors, pictures hung on the walls, the use of colorful towels, and the existence of a vanity and mirror. Regardless of their functional utility, such furnishings should be included for the symbolic role they play in creating a homey character. Equipment such as paper towel dispensers or air hand dryers are out of place in private bathrooms. If they are necessary, they should be placed inconspicuously. Ways to symbolically differentiate the home bathroom from that found in the hospital setting are very important in maintaining the feeling that this is primarily a dwelling, not a workplace.

While it is common for adults who share an apartment or house to share one bathroom, the fewer the people who share, the less the likelihood of conflicts about different standards of cleanliness or about territorial claims. Furthermore, the typical medicine cabinet and vanity will not hold a great deal of shaving equipment, shampoo, curling irons, and other items that accompany bathing. The convenience of having all of these materials always in the room is one thing that makes the room feel like it belongs to the resident. If residents must always bring their items with them, they are likely to feel more like visitors than inhabitants. Adequate storage is therefore important. Another factor that affects sharing of bathrooms is timing. At hours of peak use, such as the morning rush, the more people who share the bathroom, the greater the lag time for getting ready to go. In most families, conflicts seem to arise when more than four people share one bathroom, and for most situations, the fewer sharing the bathroom, the better.

The bathroom needs to be located within the private part of the house so that the travel space between it and any bedroom will be short and discrete. It is also typical in larger houses to have a half bath in the public part of the house so that the private bathroom territory will not have to be seen by visitors. If a resident is sick, or if one occupant retires early, this will assure that privacy is maintained.

SHARED SPACES

Group territory presents opportunities for residents to learn social skills. For a space truly to be shared, however, each resident must have reason to use it and have a sense of investment in it. Territory that is intended to be shared, but whose use is dominated by only some residents, will come to be seen as belonging only to those

people who use it. While this is not necessarily bad (people who use a space tend to be more responsible toward it), the space may be regarded as alien territory by those who don't use it. Planners should be aware of this potential problem as they design a residence. For this reason, part of the discussion of group space that follows is directed toward ways to encourage the use and personalization of space.

Decisions about which shared spaces are appropriate to have depend on the programmatic requirements, and are made relative to decisions about other spaces. For instance, if bedrooms are small, more shared area is needed than if bedrooms can easily house personal activities and hobbies.

Location of shared spaces will depend upon the types of activities they are to contain, and upon whether the spaces are essentially public or private. In most housing there is a clear separation between public and private areas (Goffman, 1961). This separation is created by having a change in level, by a corridor that narrows or turns a corner or has a closing door, or by some other spacial device that inhibits movement and impedes sight lines into the private part of the dwelling. The distinction between private and public spaces is critical to keep in mind when designing and locating shared spaces. For instance, in some houses the kitchen is directly accessible from the bedroom areas without being visible from the living room. This could mean, for example, that at night if one person is entertaining in the living room, someone else could come down and get a midnight snack without being seen.

The distinction between private and public territories can best be understood by imagining which activities residents might want to be able to engage in in their pajamas while other people are dressed. When someone is sick, he or she will want to be able to use the bathroom, for example, without the knowledge of people in the living room. Or on a Saturday morning, some people may want to relax over the paper in their pajamas, while others are up and about.

Shared spaces offer different opportunities depending on the activities that occur within them, their architectural character, and their location within the residence.

Living Rooms

The most obvious group space is the living room, which serves all the residents, and also represents them to visitors. Therefore, the living room's symbolic role may be as important as its functional role. In many private homes, the living room or parlor serves purely symbolic purposes. It is used only when guests come, while other spaces, such as the kitchen table, recreation room, or den perform as gathering places for the family. In group homes, however, it is assumed that the living room will play a dual role, and will represent itself as an active place.

The dual role played by the living room may be a source of conflict, for a presentation space may need to be neat, while a gathering space will promote a variety of activities. In planning a residence, therefore, it is important to consider which activities are likely to take place in the living room, and which will probably take place elsewhere. The living room design cannot and should not determine what occurs there, but it is not necessary for it to be all things to all people. For example, the kitchen or dining room may be the place that is designed for community meetings, or the bedroom may be the designated place for television watching. This does not mean that the living room could not also accommodate these activities, but that its design would be primarily responsive to other intended uses. Some factors one may want to consider are whether or not the living room will be a place for large gatherings, whether it will serve noisy and/or quiet activities, and how its use will relate to other rooms in the dwelling. These questions will affect the placement of the living room within the home, as well as its size, the design of doors, windows, heating and lighting, and the furnishing of the space.

In most private residences, the living room is adjacent to the entry. As the most public room, it serves as a filter to the house and opens onto other spaces, allowing living room activities to merge easily with others. While the living room normally seats no more than 5 or 6 people, if a larger group is expected, chairs may be easily obtained from the dining room. Or when the dining room, which may seat no more than 10

people, is too small for a large sit-down meal, a dinner may be served buffet style, with both spaces serving to hold the larger group. In this way, both the living room and dining room spaces have their own identity, and remain intimate in scale, without inhibiting the versatility needed for special occasions.

When nondisabled persons share a dwelling the living room belongs equally to all. Its furnishings are negotiated by all, and all residents are likely to have some of their own furniture in the room. If people move out, they take their furniture with them, and if new people move in, they expect to be able to add theirs to what is already there. In this way, people invest in the space and make their own mark. When a furnished place is rented, the individuals simply add their own items to what is there. For developmentally disabled persons as well, the personal investment made in a space by participating in its furnishing can have an important relation to the way the place is used and maintained. Carelessness toward one's own possessions is much less easily tolerated than carelessness toward objects of unknown ownership.

Because the use of the living room space will probably vary greatly among community residences, it is difficult to discuss furniture in detail, but several principles may be helpful to consider in designing a living room to make it noninstitutional in character. In institutions, living room space is more symbolic than useful, reflecting the values of the institution rather than of the individual residents. In such facilities, this room is therefore characterized by order. The chairs are placed at the perimeter of the room. There is little or no clutter, and there are few horizontal surfaces to leave things on. The furniture is likely to be either chairs, sofas, end tables, or card tables. All of the furniture tends to be the same, with the same colors or the same upholstery pattern. The lighting is predominantly overhead lighting. The walls are typically sparsely decorated with reproductions of famous paintings. No knick knacks or personal mementos are found in the room. Symbolically, these characteristics are those of a space that is not inhabited by any particular person, but that is seen as the territory of staff or of administration.

Figure 4. Living room furniture is arranged to facilitate conversation.

In private dwellings, to encourage activity, living room seating is arranged for easy conversation, with sofa and chairs placed no more than 10 feet apart, facing each other or at right angles (Figure 4). Magazines or books on a coffee table or bookshelf encourage people to come in and read. A piano, stereo, or desk implies the possibility of still other activities. Several kinds of chairs, not necessarily matching, provide for people with different seating preferences. Furniture may also show the history of the inhabitants: the chair bought at an estate sale, or grandmother's old clock. Floor lamps or table lamps light tasks, and highlight certain places in a room rather than give uniform light throughout. Wall decorations and the choice of curtains are special to this room, and reflect the tastes of the inhabitants. Wall surfaces are likely to be covered with a variety of items—hangings, photographs, plants, as well as art. Shelves and other horizontal surfaces (end tables, mantelpieces, desks) hold not only books but art objects and mementos belonging to residents.

Kitchens

Perhaps the most active space in any dwelling is the kitchen, often referred to as the heart of the house. Food preparation and meal cleanup occur here at least twice a day, and often eating happens here as well, making this place a natural generator of activity and a draw for social interaction. If one person does most of the cooking, that person tends to claim this territo-

ry, possibly inhibiting its use by others. If, however, everyone in a group uses and makes decisions about this area, it can easily become shared territory.

The four functions that are most commonly found in the kitchen are food preparation, meal cleanup, eating, and storage. Other activities that may also occur here include telephoning, desk activities, laundry, and ironing. Careful consideration of the activities for which the kitchen will be used allows the space to be effectively designed to minimize interference between activities and to create a lively focus for daily life.

A natural place for snacking, the kitchen is also often a place where intimate conversation occurs easily. Having a kitchen near to, but separated from, the living room permits two different sets of people to socialize at the same time while remaining in the public part of the house. The kitchen, then, needs to be large enough to house all the activities that may occur within it, or it should be associated with the dining area or other space in such a way that it can handle the overflow activity.

In a program that stresses learning daily living skills, the kitchen is a natural focus of education. Its layout can assist the learning process, especially if the arrangement of appliances and storage is related to the natural sequence of events. Having the spatial sequence reinforce the time sequence not only assists the learning process but minimizes the pain of doing chores. For example, meal cleanup will be aided if there are places to store cleared dishes close to the dining table. Next to this would be located a place to scrape and rinse dishes, a place to wash dishes, a place to dry dishes, and a cupboard for storing clean dishes.

Although food preparation and meal cleanup are usually separated in time, there may be occasional conflicts when, for example, dessert is being prepared while main course dishes are being cleared. Depending on the number of residents, and the desired size of the kitchen, it may be useful to have one sink for preparation and one for cleanup. Generally, speaking, it is possible to simply segregate the preparation-related functions from those of cleanup. The food preparation sequence can be seen as food storage (refrigerator and can shelves), washing, chopping and can-opening, cooking, draining, serving, and cleaning up of cooking utensils. Except food washing and draining and cleanup, these activities do not have to occur in direct contact with the sink, and in the small kitchen, may be seen as more related to refrigerator, stove, and chopping area (counter or table). When one person is using the kitchen, the traditional approach to kitchen design, which seeks to minimize the triangle between refrigerator, stove and sink, is desirable. When several people are using the kitchen, this old rule of thumb may not be so directly applicable.

A key part of any kitchen is the kitchen table. The table is what creates the social character of the kitchen. This allows for companionship when tasks are being done. The function of the table can certainly be substituted by the use of eating counters with high stools, but kitchens that do not have a place to sit will not be able to maximize the social potential of the kitchen space.

The relation between the kitchen and other rooms should be taken into account. Clearly the kitchen needs to be adjacent to the main eating area, and should also be close to the living room to allow easy serving of snacks and drinks. In addition, the kitchen should be closely related to the outdoor living area so that the latter area will be a handy place to eat and entertain. Lastly, the kitchen should be accessible to a vehicle area, to facilitate carrying in of groceries.

Eating Areas

Whether or not a formal dining room is provided, the eating area is important. The meal traditionally symbolizes the coming together of a community. Thus, the eating area and its furnishings ought to be designed to hold at least all the members of the community as well as a guest or two. The advantages of having a separate dining room are twofold: eating is allowed to be a formal activity, separate from the bustle of preparation and cleanup, and the dining room may provide additional space to be used throughout the day. A number of activities benefit from being related to a table surface. Meetings that take place in upright seating may have a more formal character. Certain types of

games, sewing, studying, and paying bills are activities commonly done in the dining room. The usefulness of having a dining room must be evaluated in the context of the other types of spaces in the home.

The character of the eating area is vital, too. This is not a place where notions of efficiency should dominate. A warm open feeling may be created by having a single wood table where all residents can gather. Incandescent light will emphasize the intimacy of eating, especially if it is not general lighting but is focused on the table or located in free-standing lamps or wall fixtures. The addition of a dimming feature on the light switch makes it possible to create a variety of moods at night. The use of large windows to admit plenty of natural daylight also makes this room pleasant to be in and practical for many purposes. Aside from the dining table, the eating area is often furnished with cupboards or buffets for storage of dishes and decorative items. Wall surfaces are rarely left blank, but are used for hanging art. Plants placed in the dining room provide a link to the natural world, especially valuable in places that have a long winter.

In most places, there are times in the year when outdoor eating is a great pleasure. Patios, decks, and screened porches offer opportunities for outdoor living. As stated earlier, the more direct the link between the kitchen and outdoor area, the more likely that eating outdoors will occur, since to eat out-of-doors may require the transporting not only of eating utensils and food but also of tables and chairs. Sturdy, weatherproof furniture that can be kept out-of-doors during the good weather months will promote outdoor life. Providing a place for outdoor cooking or barbecuing will also encourage use of the outdoors, and will provide opportunities for learning new cooking skills, which can be applied in other outdoor settings as well.

Circulation Space

One type of shared space that is often overlooked for the opportunities it provides is circulation space: entry, corridor, and vertical movement. The process of coming in and going between places is one of transition. The places between allow one to survey an activity before entering, provide opportunities for chance meetings between people, and allow movement patterns to be controlled.

The entry experience provides the introduction to a residence. Between the street and the front door is a series of barriers, depending on the type of building and the context. This area is the point where the private and the public realms meet. When a building entrance is right off the street, there may be a level change, or a stoop, or a vestibule separating an internal entrance door from the first door. In an area with front yards, there may be a path that changes direction or levels, and there may be a porch or platform to define the doorway area (see Jenkins, Chapter 26, this volume).

Other Areas

A number of possible activities exist in a dwelling, which may need their own space or may be located in other areas. Some of these are laundry, workshop for crafts or home repairs, television watching, large games such as Ping-Pong or pool, and sewing. When bedrooms are large, hobby space for activities like sewing, which may be hard to put away in the middle of a project, may be accommodated in the private bedroom area. But if this is not possible, other space where projects may be left partially complete may be important to provide if such activities are to be encouraged.

A workshop, on the other hand, would be difficult to have in one's bedroom. Most houses have a space for a workshop in the basement, although this may not be an ideal location if it is far removed from staff supervision. The opportunity for learning home-maintenance skills, however, is significantly augmented by easy access to tools in an area sufficiently large for working.

Another space often found in the basement is the laundry area. This is not the most convenient place for a laundry area. Since most dirty laundry is created in the bedroom (clothing, sheets), the laundry area is most conveniently located in close proximity to the bedroom area. Doing laundry involves intermittent attention, so it is good to have it located near a place where one can accomplish something else at the same time. This could be the bedroom, the kitchen, the living room, a den, or recreation room.

Television watching can take place almost anywhere in a dwelling, but it is wise to plan ahead for it. If individuals will be able to own their sets, the sound barriers between bedrooms need to be sufficient to maintain acoustical privacy. Many people object to having television in the living room, because it interferes with other activities that normally take place there. But if there is to be a shared TV, a place will be needed for it. As this activity not only creates noise but also cannot be engaged in when there is noise nearby, it may be best placed in an isolated location. This area is frequently the den, which may be in either the private or the public part of the house. If the den is placed in the private realm, its use will be limited to residents and close friends. If in the public realm, it can be used as a place to entertain visitors. It is also possible to limit television watching to special occasions, in which case renting or borrowing a television is a possibility, or else a permanent storage place may be provided.

Many single-family houses have a recreation room or game room where boisterous activity takes place. At some distance from the normally quieter living room, this room does not contain precious objects, is easy to clean, and is a place for casual entertainment. Sometimes this room opens directly to the outdoors. The recreation room is where playing pool or other table games like Ping-Pong can occur without bothering others. Here, too, loud music is also possible.

A last kind of necessary, shared space is storage space. Every kind of hobby or activity that requires the use of equipment requires storage area. While, ideally, there will be sufficient space within the bedroom area for most types of personal equipment, some, such as bicycles, may need a separate place to be kept, and storage that is easily accessible will greatly increase the likelihood of people using the equipment. In addition, space for communal equipment used in normal house maintenance must be provided. Convenience will encourage responsible use. Provision of a garage with plenty of extra space for ladders, lawn mowers, hoses, snow shovels, and gardening equipment will reduce the amount of in-house storage required. Chemicals associated with gardening and barbecuing should be placed in a locked area for protection. Within the house, provision of areas on every level of the house where cleaning equipment may be kept will reduce the amount of carrying, and also the chances for accidents related to housework. Here too, a locked place for storing chemicals is advocated.

STAFF AND ADMINISTRATIVE SPACES

While a community residence should not be primarily a workplace, it must be a pleasant and comfortable place for staff to work. The type of space to be provided will vary greatly with the nature of the program. Where the residence is to be the primary dwelling place of staff, a different kind of space will be required than when staff are only working on a shift basis. Then, too, with live-in staff, the staff area will be different if staff need to be directly adjacent to resident areas. Also, depending on the housing type, the staff area will be more or less difficult to provide. The following brief discussion deals with two of the most common types of staffing circumstances, the apartment residence and the single-house facility.

The simplest situation is the apartment-type community residence. In this type of building, the natural way to solve the administrative and staff space problem is to set aside one or two units for this purpose, depending upon the size of the units. This allows the staff to have a natural and inconspicuous territory of their own.

In a single-house community residence in which staff work in shifts, staff space will not be used for permanent dwelling, and does not have to be large. In addition to being a place to sleep, it may serve as a space to retreat to when tensions are high and as a place to do paperwork. Ideally it should be located away from the entrance to the house, so that the entrance is clearly residential and not an administrative zone. A place in the basement is practical, and will not detract from the residents' territory. Alternatively, a location near the kitchen or alongside the residents' bedrooms may be appropriate.

BUILDING REGULATIONS, SAFETY, AND HOUSING DESIGN

One of the most demanding aspects of designing community residences is that of meeting the concerns of the state for safety of residents without creating an inhospitable environment. By their very nature, building codes are designed to protect people from risk, whereas the ordinary dwelling unit has as its primary motivation the concern for comfort. These two concerns do not necessarily have to be incompatible, but historically, they have been so. In the concern to build environments that are safe for persons with developmental disabilities, care must be exercised not to create the institutional setting that is implied by most building codes, which assume that developmentally disabled persons are uniformly incapable of self-preservation.

Most discussions of risk focus on the relationship between risk taking and independence and autonomy (for example, see Wolfensberger, 1977). Every learning activity involves a certain amount of risk, and if the risk is not taken, autonomy cannot be attained. On the other hand, the state and others have a reasonable concern that persons with disabilities not be subjected to undue risks. In housing design, this is a difficult issue, for the capabilities of individuals who are housed in community residences vary, and no blanket rules can be applied.

The principles of safety discussed here are primarily related to fire. Fire safety regulations are governed by three general rules (see also Groner, this volume). First, the materials used should not be combustible. Second, the design of the facility should inhibit the spread of fire. Third, in case of fire, exiting should be quick and safe. To adhere strictly to these principles, a building would be made of noncombustible materials such as masonry, it would be subdivided into discrete areas with fire separation between them, fire extinguishing equipment and alarm systems would be provided, exits would be designed to limit corridor lengths, and fire stairs, as well as certain types and sizes of doors, would be included. But even fire regulations do not require that all of these criteria be met for every situation, as this would be unduly restrictive. In each circumstance, one or more of the options may be sufficient to create a safe setting.

The link between safety, resident behavior, and design makes balancing all of the factors complex. The first preference is to create fire safety through behavior, without having to effect substantial alterations to a typical residential setting. However, this will not always be possible. The first limiting factor, therefore, is the nature of the residents' abilities. If all residents are able to exit quickly, fire considerations should not have to compromise the residential character.

Apartment buildings are generally designed for fire safety. The corridor on each floor of the building is a discrete space, separated by a fire door from fire stairs that are located so that residents will not be trapped by smoke or fire. The materials of halls and stairs are noncombustible, and alarms and fire extinguishing equipment are provided in the corridors. However, within the dwelling unit, the design is comfort-based. Materials are selected for aesthetic reasons, and the space is organized for privacy over safety.

Because each unit in an apartment is discrete, supervision from outside is inhibited; the concern for safe living practices is balanced by a concern to assure independent living. Where residents can significantly provide for their own welfare, and where only minimal supervision is needed, design features can assist with this. In the design of housing for developmentally disabled persons in Saint Paul, Minnesota (see the vignette later in this chapter), the concern that appliances accidentally left on not lead to fire was met by a design that allowed for a master control of each apartment at its entrance. The resident leaving for the day could turn off the current to all of the appliance outlets (including the stove but excluding the refrigerator). Discretely placed and unobtrusive fire alarms provide security while not substantially interfering with resident independence and control of the unit.

Most free-standing houses are designed with the assumption that exiting will be the main source of fire safety, and that exiting through existing doors will not be a problem. Because houses are generally small, they are conceived of as being one discrete space. But large houses that have large open spaces may be fire hazards, especially with traditional open staircases, which may act as a chimney for fire to spread between floors. Similarly, the openness between rooms that promotes easy transition between activities may allow fires to spread quickly. In balancing between the inherent design of the spaces of a house and the concern for fire safety, keep in mind that trade-offs are possible. There are likely to be several ways to solve any one problem: one is to change the design of the spaces themselves, another is to assure that the exiting will be so easy that the room design will not be a problem, and the third is to add equipment such as sprinklers, which inhibit the spread of the fire.

When a building is one story, exiting is possible at many points, so a typical house design may be employed without requiring unusual equipment or substantial change in design, beyond the addition of extra doors. With two-story buildings, fire safety may be achieved in a variety of ways. The problem of openness between rooms may be addressed by placement of exits, or by retaining the openness between some rooms while maintaining separation between others. The use of sprinklers is also an option, but should be avoided unless other considerations outweigh the negative visual impact.

The vertical circulation space presents a special challenge. The staircase is often the focal point of the house, especially as it is usually located by the front door. The residential symbolism of such a space gives great character to a house, and it is undesirable to destroy it (Figure 5). The problem is how to keep the symbolic character without having it be a fire hazard. While adding sprinklers would inhibit the spread of fire in this area, they would detract from the residential character. In some circumstances, the main staircase may be kept intact, while fire stairs are added. This, however, may create negative symbolism on the exterior. It may also be possible to create a discrete space within the circulation itself. This is sometimes done by placing doors at both the base and top

Figure 5. Open stair lends character to a residence and should be kept intact, if possible.

of the stairs. Depending on the configuration of the stairway and its placement within the house, this may be handled in a number of ways. When the front door and the staircase are closely related, it may be best to include the front door and the entry within the isolated vertical circulation area, thus creating the separation between these spaces and the other downstairs rooms. At the head of the stairs, the placement of the separation door should respond to the design of the hall. If the stair is at one end of the hall, a door may be easy to place without disturbing the appearance of the stair itself. If the stair divides the hall in two, the best solution may be to have two different doors. If the hall is a roomlike area, the best door placement may be dictated by the concern to maintain the integrity of the room shape. These same methods may be used to subdivide other areas of the dwelling so that natural separations between areas are reinforced, rather than adding new and incompatible divisions between areas.

When creating separations between areas within a residence, the choice of materials becomes very important. As pointed out previously, within a house or an apartment it is unusual, and aesthetically undesirable, to have fire doors. Even in apartment buildings, where fire doors sometimes are used in the public corridor, they will be disguised with paint, or will be placed in a low-visibility location and will not be found within the dwelling unit itself.

Doors used within houses for public rooms, or in corridors, are frequently made of glass, so that approaching people can be seen easily, or so that the activity inside one area is visible from without. Alternatively, residential doors are made of wood and are left open unless the situation warrants closing them. Depending on the attitudes of the local inspection officials, it may be possible to create fire separations using typical residential doors so long as door closers activated by smoke, or automatic door closers, are used. If the inclusion of automatic door closers will permit the use of more residential styles of doors, this trade-off should be taken advantage of.

Whenever possible, entrance doors should also be of a typical residential form. Standard fire doors not only symbolize nonresidential uses, but they are heavy and hard to open and close. Such doors make going in and out difficult, and may inhibit the easy and informal use of outdoor areas.

RESPONDING TO HANDICAPS

Many developmentally disabled persons have physical handicaps, which may span a variety of impairments, including mobility impairments, sensory disabilities, and balance and seizure disorders. Since a number of excellent resources exist on designing living spaces for handicapped persons (see Supplementary Resources), this section offers only a brief introduction to this area of concern.

Because our society is oriented toward specialization, there is a tendency to group persons with certain types of handicap together. This approach to serving disabled persons is not always beneficial. When people with similar problems are grouped together, the tendency is for the problem to become magnified, and for the disability, rather than the strengths of individuals, to be emphasized. For instance, if a blind person is housed with people who are not blind, the blind person may be able to provide nonvisual assistance to others, while reciprocally being helped with tasks that require sight. As another example, whereas a normal-width corridor may serve a household in which there is one wheelchair-bound person, when there are two such persons, the corridor will need to be unusually wide in order for them to pass each other. Overall, allowing space for one handicapped person in every residence may be a better solution than providing single residences that house only persons with particular physical disabilities. Adapting an environment to a specific handicapped person's needs may be more useful than trying to make a setting work for a generalized grouping of handicapping conditions, since the generalization process creates a situation in which no one person's needs are really met well.

A person who uses a mobility prosthesis, whether a cane, walker, wheelchair, or some other device, will need more room to maneuver than will others. Areas like entries, bathrooms, and bedrooms, where complicated activities like putting on overcoats or getting in and out of the shower take place, will need to be more generous in size than usual. In the bathroom, the addition of grab bars will assist the use of these facilities.

For most mobility-impaired persons, vertical movement is difficult. The addition of ramps and elevators to supplement stairs will be useful. While the wheelchair cannot surmount even one step, the person with a balance disorder may find it impossible to use a ramp; therefore, there is likely to be no one solution that suits everyone's needs. By providing several alternatives, everyone will be free to select the approach that best serves him or her.

Vignette

In 1983, a group of six developmentally disabled persons decided they wanted to live together. Working with a social worker, the group decided that new construction would be the best solution, and they selected architects to draw up plans for two apartment group homes.

From the beginning, the architects met with the prospective residents, to discuss their desires and to explain the proposed designs. Group members decided that the best type of dwelling would be one in which each resident had a self-contained unit, but where group spaces were also provided.

A number of special features were incorporated into the design proposal so that it would meet the divergent needs of codes, of fitting into the neighborhood, of creating a place to support group interaction, and of fostering independence and competence of residents (see perspective and plans in Figures 6 and 7). As the figures show, the entry and corridor design allow for the six units (B–H) to be independent, and for the group spaces to be centrally placed, while the architectural details are like those of a house. The roof is

Perspective

RAMSEY COMMONS

Community Development Corporation
Hokanson·Lunning Associates, Inc.

Figure 6. Perspective of a proposed community residence.

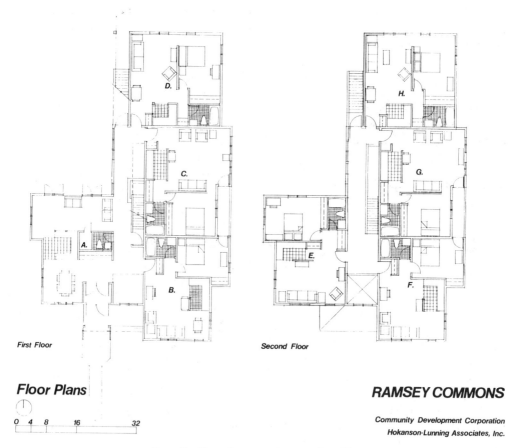

Floor Plans

0 4 8 16 32

First Floor

Second Floor

RAMSEY COMMONS

Community Development Corporation
Hokanson-Lunning Associates, Inc.

Figure 7. Plans of a proposed community residence.

pitched, and windows are of varying sizes. An open stair with wooden balusters connects the two main levels. Fire codes are met through the provision of a fire stair. The shared area is placed so that access to the backyard and to a deck is convenient and natural. The space allows for shared meals and gathering activities. A laundry room is also shared by the group.

Each unit is designed to maximize the number of windows and to provide for good natural ventilation. Although every unit has a living area, a kitchen-eating area, a bedroom and a bathroom, variety in unit arrangement generates character differences among the units.

A particular innovation was designed especially for this proposal, which has application to other situations as well. The group members decided that a useful piece of furniture to have would be a special organizer right by the door, which would store all the things that they would need to take with them when they went out; coat, backpack, pocketbook, keys, and so forth. And along with this, they wanted a way to make sure that they had not left any appliances on that might cause a fire. The special storage arrangement, designed by the

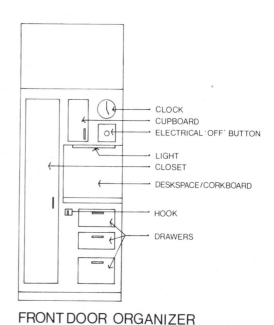

CLOCK
CUPBOARD
ELECTRICAL 'OFF' BUTTON

LIGHT
CLOSET

DESKSPACE / CORKBOARD

HOOK

DRAWERS

FRONT DOOR ORGANIZER

Figure 8. Front door organizer.

architects (see Figure 8), not only provides a place to keep things but also has a special electrical switch that turns off all the electrical outlets in the unit (with the exception of the refrigerator and kitchen clock).

CONCLUSIONS

While the design of a community residence for developmentally disabled persons entails solving many complex practical problems, its main purpose must never be forgotten. A home is a dwelling place and must serve as the physical and psychological base for its residents individually and collectively. Sensitive design in combination with a strong program can support the development of autonomy, identity, and dignity of the residents, by providing a place with maximum opportunity to control the environment and to express individuality and group spirit. Both the process of design and the building itself can engage residents in a sense of responsibility for themselves, for their group, and for their dwelling. The creation of a practical, beautiful, and meaningful place in which to live is the primary goal and desired outcome for community residence design.

REFERENCES

Altman, I., & Chemers, M. (1980). *Culture and environment.* Monterey, CA: Brooks/Cole.

Architecture, Research, Construction, Inc. (1985). *Community group homes.* New York: VanNostrand Reinhold.

Barker, R.C. (1968). *Ecological psychology.* Palo Alto, CA: Stanford University Press.

Bednar, M.J. (1977). *Barrier-free environments.* Stroudsburg, PA: Dowden, Hutchinson & Ross.

Bercovici, S.M. (1983). *Barriers to normalization: The restrictive management of retarded persons.* Baltimore: University Park Press.

Butterfield, D. (1984). *Design guidelines for exterior spaces of group homes.* Urbana, IL: Housing Research and Development Program, University of Illinois at Urbana-Champaign.

Canter, D., & Canter, S. (Eds.). (1979). *Designing for therapeutic environments: A review of research.* New York: John Wiley & Sons.

Cooper, C. (1974). The house as symbol of the self. In J. Lang, C. Burnette, & W. Moleski (Eds.), *Designing for human behavior* (pp. 130–146). Stroudsburg, PA: Dowden, Hutchinson & Ross.

Craik, K. (1971). The assessment of places. In P. McReynolds (Ed.), *Advances in psychological assessment: Vol. 2.* Palo Alto, CA: Science & Behavior Books.

Environment Design Group. (1976). *Design standards: Intermediate care facilities.* Boston: Massachusetts Department of Mental Health.

Goffman, E. (1961). *Asylums.* Chicago: Aldine.

Gunzburg, H.C. (1973). The physical environment of the mentally handicapped: 39 steps toward normalizing living practices in living units for the mentally retarded, *British Journal of Mental Subnormality, 10,* 91–99.

Hendrikson, K.C., Akkerman, P.S., Speggen, L., & Thompson, T. (1985). Dining arrangements and behavior of severely mentally retarded adults. *Applied Research in Mental Retardation, 6,* 379–388.

Holahan, C.J. (1979). Environmental psychology in psychiatric hospital settings. In D. Canter & S. Canter (Eds.), *Designing for therapeutic environments: A review of research* (pp. 213–231). New York: John Wiley & Sons.

Knight, R.C., Weitzer, W.H., & Zimring, C.M. (1978). *Opportunity for control of the build environment: The ELEMMR Project.* Amherst, MA: Environmental Institute, University of Massachusetts.

Landesman-Dwyer, S., Stein, J., & Sackett, G.P. (1976). *Group homes for the mentally retarded: An ecological and behavioral study.* Olympia, WA: Washington State Department of Social and Health Services.

MacEachron, A. (1983). Institutional reform and adaptive functioning of mentally retarded persons: A field experiment. *American Journal of Mental Deficiency, 88,* 2–12.

Mazis, S., & Canter, D. (1979). Physical conditions and management practices for mentally retarded children. In D. Canter & S. Canter (Eds.), *Designing for therapeutic environments: A review of research* (pp. 119–157). New York: John Wiley & Sons.

Moos, R., & Lemke, S. (1979). *Multiphasic environmental assessment procedures (MEAP): Preliminary manual.* Palo Alto, CA: Social Ecology Laboratory, Stanford University.

Nirje, B. (1969). The normalization principle. In R.B. Kugel & W. Wolfensberger (Eds.), *Changing patterns in residential services for the mentally retarded* (pp. 231–240). Washington, DC: President's Committee on Mental Retardation.

Norberg-Schulz, C. (1965). *Intentions in architecture.* Cambridge, MA: MIT Press.

Rapoport, A. (1969). *House form and culture.* Englewood Cliffs, NJ: Prentice-Hall.

Rapoport, A. (1982). *The meaning of the built environment.* Beverly Hills, CA: Sage Publications.

Raynes, N., Pratt, M., & Roses, S. (1979). *Organizational structure and the care of the mentally retarded.* London: Croom-Helm.

Richer, J. (1979). Physical environments for autistic children—four case studies. In C. Canter & S. Canter (Eds.), *Designing for therapeutic environments: A review of research* (pp. 63–86). New York: John Wiley & Sons.

Rivlin, L.G., Bogert, V., & Cirillo, R. (1981). *Uncoupling institutional indicators.* Paper presented at the Environment Design Research Association Conference, Ames, IA.

Rivlin, L., & Wolfe, M. (1979). Understanding and evaluating therapeutic environments for children. In D. Canter & S. Canter (Eds.), *Designing for therapeutic environments: A review of research* (pp. 29–61). New York: John Wiley & Sons.

Robinson, J.W. (1986). *Housing—exploring the ordinary: Home and institution in Minneapolis.* Unpublished manuscript.

Robinson, J.W., Thompson, T., Emmons, P., Graff, M., & Franklin, E. (1984). *Towards an architectural definition of normalization: Housing for severely and profoundly mentally retarded adults*. Minneapolis: University of Minnesota, Center for Urban and Regional Affairs, School of Architecture and Landscape Architecture.

Rotegard, L.L., Hill, B.K., & Bruininks, R.H. (1982). *Environmental characteristics of residential facilities for mentally retarded people in the United States*. Minneapolis: University of Minnesota, Department of Psychoeducational Studies.

Sime, J.D., & Sime, D.A. (1979). A therapeutic environment for forensic patients. In D. Canter & S. Canter (Eds.), *Designing for therapeutic environments: A review of research* (pp. 175–198). New York: John Wiley & Sons.

Thompson, T., & Carey, A. (1981). Structured normalization: Intellectual and adaptive behavior change in residential setting. *Mental Retardation 18*, 193–197.

U.S. Department of Commerce. (1984). *Structural characteristics of the housing inventory. 1980 Census of Housing: Vol. 3* (Subjects Reports, Chapter 4.) Washington, DC: U.S. Department of Commerce.

Wener, R.E. (1982). Standardization of testing in environmental evaluation. In P. Bart, A. Chen, & F. Francescato, (Eds.), *Knowledge for design* (pp. 77–84). Washington, DC: Environmental Design Research Association.

Wolfensberger, W. (1972). *The principle of normalization in human services*. Toronto: National Institute on Mental Retardation.

Wolfensberger, W. (1977). The normalization principle, and some major implications to architectural-environmental design. In M.J. Bednar (Ed.), *Barrier-free environments* (pp. 135–169). Stroudsburg, PA: Dowden, Hutchinson & Ross.

Wolfensberger, W., & Glenn, L. (1975). *Program analysis of service systems (PASS): A method for the quantitative evaluation of human services (3rd ed.). Handbook and field manual*. Toronto: National Institute on Mental Retardation.

Wolfensberger, W., & Thomas, S. (1983). *PASSING: Program Analysis of Service Systems' Implementation of Normalization Goals. Normalization criteria and ratings manual* (2nd ed.). Toronto: Canadian National Institute on Mental Retardation.

SUPPLEMENTARY RESOURCES

A number of helpful resources are listed here, on designing a community residence. Three that address this task based on environment-behavior research are *Community Group Homes* (Architecture, Research, Construction, Inc., 1985), which presents practical advice on the entire process of design; *Design Guidelines for Exterior Spaces of Group Homes* (Butterfield, 1984), which describes factors in the design of the site; and *Towards an Architectural Definition of Normalization* (Robinson et al., 1984), which details the difference in design between the traditional institution and the private dwelling.

For a broader set of resources on the design of housing, the following may be consulted. For discussions of cultural norms and perceived status: *House Form and Culture* (Rapoport, 1969), "The House as Symbol of the Self" (Cooper, 1974), *Housing Messages* (Becker, 1977), *Culture and Environment* (Altman & Chemers, 1980). Practical aspects of the design of housing such as unit layouts and design to allow for furniture are covered in *Low-Rise Housing for Older People: Behavioral Criteria for Design* (Zeisel, Epp, & Demos, 1978) and *Designing for Aging* (Howell, 1980). Qualitative considerations in design are presented in *Pattern Language* (Alexander et al., 1977).

Resources on design for handicaps, which discuss attitudes as well as practical advice, include *Designing for the Disabled* (Goldsmith, 1976), *Barrier-free Environments* (Bednar, 1977), and *Design for Independent Living: The Environment and Physically Disabled People* (Lifchez & Winslow, 1979). For additional practical advice, the following material may be helpful: *Accessible Housing* (North Carolina Department of Insurance, 1980), *Handbook for Design: Specially Adapted Housing* (Veterans Administration, 1977), and *Housing Interiors for the Disabled and Elderly* (Raschko, 1982). The following is a bibliography of the works just cited.

Alexander, C., Ishikawa, S., Silverstein, M., et al. (1977). *A pattern language*. New York: Oxford University Press.

Altman, I., & Chemers, M. (1980). *Culture and environment*. Monterey, CA: Brooks/Cole.

Architecture, Research, Construction, Inc. (1985). *Community group homes*. New York: VanNostrand Reinhold.

Becker, F.D. (1977). *Housing messages*. Stroudsburg, PA: Dowden, Hutchinson & Ross.

Bednar, M.J. (1977). *Barrier-free environments*. Stroudsburg, PA: Dowden, Hutchinson & Ross.

Butterfield, D. (1984). *Design guidelines for exterior spaces of group homes*. Urbana, IL: Housing Research and Development Program, University of Illinois at Urbana-Champaign.

Cooper, C. (1974). The house as symbol of the self. In J. Lang, C. Burnette, & W. Moleski (Eds.), *Designing for human behavior* (pp. 130–146). Stroudsburg, PA: Dowden, Hutchinson & Ross.

Goldsmith, S. (1976). *Designing for the disabled*. London: RIBA (Royal Institute of British Architects) Publications.

Howell, S. (1980). *Designing for aging*. Cambridge, MA: MIT Press.

Lifchez, R., & Winslow, B. (1979). *Design for independent living: The environment and physically disabled people*. Berkeley, CA: University of California Press.

North Carolina Department of Insurance. (1980). *Accessible housing*. Raleigh: Special Office for the Handicapped, North Carolina Department of Insurance.

Rapoport, A. (1969). *House form and culture*. Englewood Cliffs, NJ: Prentice-Hall.

Raschko, B.B. (1982). *Housing interiors for the disabled and elderly*. New York: VanNostrand Reinhold.

Robinson, J.W., Thompson, T., Emmons, P., Graff, M., & Franklin, E. (1984). *Towards an architectural definition of normalization: Housing for severely and profoundly mentally retarded adults*. Minneapolis: University of Minnesota, Center for Urban and Regional Affairs, School of Architecture and Landscape Architecture.

Veterans Administration. (1977). *Handbook for design: Specially adapted housing*. Washington, DC: Architectural and Transportation Barriers Compliance Board.

Zeisel, J., Epp, G., & Demos, S. (1978). *Low-rise housing for older people: Behavioral criteria for design*. Washington, DC: U.S. Government Printing Office.

Chapter 26

Design Features and Exterior Spaces

Dorothy Butterfield Jenkins

This chapter discusses how the design of the exterior spaces of community residences can create an environment that is supportive to residents and acceptable to neighbors. Design strategies that help the home to fit within the existing neighborhood context and create a positive image are explored. Suggestions are offered for ways to structure the spaces so that they challenge residents to expand their social and manual skills, while respecting the needs of the neighbors. Finally, two vignettes illustrate designs that incorporate many of the recommended suggestions.

Little attention is typically given to the aesthetic or therapeutic design of the outdoor features of community residences. Yet, the exterior aspects of such homes can function to support the home's goals for community integration in two major ways. First, the design can help make a home more acceptable to neighbors, and second, it can have a positive influence on residents' behaviors and opportunities. This chapter explores how exterior design features can make a home more acceptable by creating an image that fits the neighborhood, supports appropriate resident behaviors, and is sensitive to the rights and needs of neighbors. The chapter also discusses how these components can support residents' needs for an environment that enhances their ability to achieve environmental control, adequate privacy, socialization opportunities, new skills, and personal growth. Specific examples show how design can support or defeat these goals, and vignettes of two group homes are used to further illustrate these principles.

When designing the exterior spaces of a community residence, the potential always exists for conflict, since residents' needs and desired behaviors may require an environment whose design does not match neighborhood standards. The question is, Whose values should prevail? One point of view favors the neighbors and suggests that as little as possible should be done to attract attention to the residents' potential ''differentness'' (Wolfensberger, 1972). An alternative point of view holds that the environment should support residents' needs even if it ignores the neighborhood norms. This latter view developed because of research that noted that the most normal-looking settings do not neces-

Figures 1 through 7 were drawn by Van Cox, associate professor, School of Landscape Architecture, Louisiana State University. Figures 8 through 12, accompanying the two vignettes, were designed by Anne Roane as a project toward a bachelor's degree in landscape architecture at Louisiana State University.

Support for writing this chapter was provided by Louisiana State University. The research on which this chapter is based was supported by the National Endowment for the Arts, the University of Illinois, Illinois Department of Mental Health and Developmental Disabilities, and Louisiana State University.

sarily result in the most normal behaviors or the greatest skill development and personal growth for residents (Knight, Weitzer, & Zimring, 1978; Landesman-Dwyer, 1981). The solution to this dilemma is not clear-cut. Often a balance can be reached that is acceptable to both neighbors and residents. An effective designer can suggest creative ways to provide supportive environments that are also palatable to neighbors (see the Appendix for guidelines on choosing a landscape architect). Yet, achieving a balance can also be difficult, and each situation is different. In this writer's view, the goal should be to achieve a design that provides the most supportive setting to residents, while ensuring neighborhood tolerance.

ACCEPTABILITY TO NEIGHBORS

In order to be acceptable to neighbors, community residences need to look as though they fit within the neighborhood, the residents' behavior needs to be appropriate in the outdoor space, the house needs to look as homey as possible, and the design of the yard must be sensitive to the rights and needs of neighbors.

Image and Neighborhood Context

In most residential neighborhoods the facade and design of the outdoor spaces of a home give clues about the socioeconomic status and values of the residents. Research conducted at multi-family housing sites suggests that neighbors find each other more acceptable when they perceive their values and attitudes to be similar (Francescato, Weidemann, Anderson, & Chenoweth, 1978). Therefore, community residences should look similar to other homes in the neighborhood and should be more acceptable than those that do not. Furthermore, since some persons with mental retardation often look and behave differently from other persons, designing an exterior home environment that is congruent with others in the neighborhood may contribute to the perception that residents and neighbors share like values, and that the home "belongs" in the neighborhood even though the residents themselves may appear different. Thus, careful design of the outdoor features may help residents to become better integrated into the neighborhood.

Neighborhood norms must be respected if the residents and their home are to look like they belong. Flagrant violations that call attention to the home should be avoided. For example, a naturalistic yard planted in wild flowers is not typical in middle class neighborhoods and would be considered unusual. While a non-retarded neighbor may develop one and merely be considered eccentric, the same yard at a community residence could be problematic and might cause adverse concern among neighbors toward the home and its occupants. Likewise, if the home is located in a run-down neighborhood, the house, at a minimum, should conform to the better examples in the neighborhood, and the grounds should be as neat and well maintained as possible to assure a positive comparison with other homes in the neighborhood.

In addition, new homes being built in established neighborhoods and older homes being chosen for adaptation should be as compatible with the existing housing stock in terms of style and building materials as possible. For instance, if most homes in the neighborhood are brick, ranch-style homes, the residence should be made of brick in a single story, elongated design. Similarly, if most of the homes are Victorian, the community residence should be too. In an eclectic neighborhood there is more room for deviation but the principle is the same; the style and materials of the home should reasonably blend with the general tone of the neighborhood.

Size compatibility is also important. If the home needs to be much larger than the surrounding residences, it can be placed on the lot so the narrow side faces the street and the bulk space the depth of the lot (see Figure 1). This technique helps to hide the home's larger size and gives an appearance of modest proportions. Trees and shrubs can be planted near the front corners of the home to further hide its unusual length from pedestrians.

When placing a new home in an existing neighborhood, it is especially important to respect the existing setback line, or distance from the street right of way. Even though most zoning ordinances only require a minimum, but not a maximum, setback, new community residences should be placed approximately the

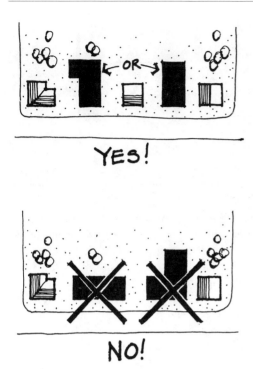

Figure 1. The size of larger homes should be minimized on the lot. (Drawn by Van Cox. Reprinted, by permission, from Butterfield, 1984.)

same distance from the right of way as the existing housing stock. Homes placed much farther back destroy the visual rhythm of the block, appear to be isolated, and call attention to themselves in a negative manner.

Appropriate Behaviors

Besides expecting an image that conforms to the neighborhood, most neighbors also have definite ideas about what behaviors are appropriate for the exterior spaces. The appropriateness depends not only upon the specific composition of the neighborhood but also upon a generally accepted convention for use of the outdoor spaces. This convention consists of a hierarchy of space from public to private (see Figure 2).

The areas closest to the street are the most public, while those closest to the home are the most private. The street, grass right of way, and front sidewalk are public territory. Nonresidents may drive down the street, or walk on the sidewalk or along the grass strip near the street, but usually do not stop or linger there without suspicion. The front yard is semipublic, and an outsider may walk past and look at but not enter into this space without permission. The home's entry or porch are semiprivate, and visitors are allowed into this space only with the resident's permission or for the time required to seek entry into the home. The backyard may be either private or semiprivate and outsiders, once again, are only allowed to view or enter this area with the resident's permission. This hierarchy implies a range of design features and uses that are acceptable within each specific area.

The best outdoor designs respect this hierarchy and are more likely to be acceptable to neighbors than those that do not. For example, the front yard in a typical, suburban, residential neighborhood is for show. Since it is the space where residents frame their home and create the impression of themselves they want to display to the world, it is especially important that this

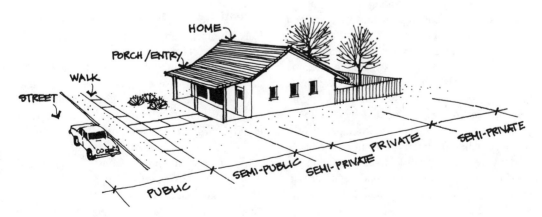

Figure 2. The home's outdoor spaces should reflect a hierarchy from public to private. (Drawn by Van Cox. Reprinted, by permission, from Butterfield, 1984.)

area be reasonably maintained. Although it may be acceptable for children to play in this space, adults are not usually seen in these spaces unless they are performing maintenance chores either on the home or in the yard. In older city neighborhoods and in some ethnic communities, the front yard is still used for social gatherings, but in most suburban neighborhoods those functions now occur more frequently in the backyard.

Neighbors are likely to look askance at inappropriate behavior in the front yard of a home. One report of research at group homes in the Midwest noted several examples of inappropriate "front yard behavior" (Butterfield, 1984). At a home located on a busy street in a metropolitan suburb, one of the residents, a young woman in her 20s, sat down on the grass right of way in front of the home and waved at passing vehicles. At another home, the residents used the area directly in front of the home for relaxing, lounging, courting, and listening to music. At this same home, residents played basketball in their front yard, which consisted of a paved area serving both as a parking lot and basketball court. All these behaviors are typically incongruous with accepted use for a front yard. While the policy of encouraging neighborhood youngsters to play ball with the residents is helpful and can result in some positive interaction, playing basketball is still an unacceptable front yard activity for a typical residence.

There are various ways to handle behaviors inappropriate for a space. One way is to accommodate the behavior elsewhere on-site. For example, the basketball court could be displaced to a side or backyard where this activity would be more acceptable. Another way to handle behaviors inappropriate for a space is to alter the design of the space along the public to private hierarchy. For instance, the courting/lounging behavior can be accommodated by creating a semiprivate space (such as a front porch or a screened galleria) directly in front of the home (see Figure 3). Such alternatives respect neighbors' expectations that residents' behavior will match the appropriate hierarchy of the space in which it occurs.

Design can support and encourage desirable behavior as well as displace or discourage inap-

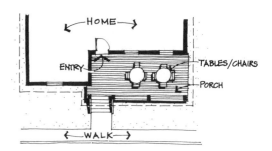

Figure 3. A porch can be added to provide a semiprivate space. (Drawn by Van Cox. Reprinted, by permission, from Butterfield, 1984).

propriate behavior. Of course, the home's program and staff must encourage residents to participate in desirable behavior; otherwise, residents may be likely to sit inside the house watching television, for instance, and ignore the opportunities the exterior design offers.

Residents can participate in the maintenance of the home and its yard space. Residents can mow the lawn, rake leaves, trim shrubs, and plant flowers. Residents of one home this writer is familiar with built a sturdy wooden planter and filled it with blooming annuals. The residents take care of the flowers themselves and are proud of their results, which add beauty to the neighborhood and create a "well cared for" impression of the home. Through such activities residents can learn basic skills and have the opportunity to exchange "hellos" with their neighbors while working in the yard. Furthermore, neighbors have the opportunity to see residents engaged in "normal" activities such as they themselves perform, thus emphasizing a similarity between neighbors and residents.

Sensitivity for the Rights of Neighbors

Careful placement and choice of design elements can contribute to the perception that group home residents are considerate of their neighbors. The use of the surrounding neighbors' yards needs to be considered in the exterior design, so that activities in contiguous spaces do not conflict. Quiet areas need to border quiet areas, private areas should be respected, and active areas should not flow onto the neighbors' yard spaces. Disregard for such commonsense design can result in poor relationships with neighbors. For example, neighbors of one group home complained because the residents' activity area bordered their garden. Plants were being unintentionally damaged by stray balls and trampled when residents went to retrieve them. Meanwhile, the group home residents' garden was located on the opposite side of the yard, near an abandoned structure. If the two activity areas had been switched, the adjacent usage would have been much more compatible. In addition, residents and neighbors would have had the opportunity to exchange hellos while working in their respective gardens.

Should a situation occur where conflicting areas cannot easily be switched (such as a hard court basketball area bordering a patio), then some form of barrier or privacy fence should be erected to minimize conflict. Unfortunately, such a feature will also limit opportunities for neighbor interaction. Sometimes conflicts occur because of when, and not how, the spaces are used. For example, the neighbors with the patio may only be bothered by residents using the basketball court while they are entertaining company. In this situation a fence may not need to be erected, and the two groups could negotiate a compromise that works for both.

Besides designing spaces for compatible usage, yard elements that may be offensive should be placed away from the neighbors' lot line or placed contiguous to a similar use in the neighbor's yard. At one home for instance, the garbage dumpster was placed at the end of the group home's driveway adjacent to the neighbor's patio. While the dumpster's location makes sense if one only considers the design layout of the group home, its placement was extremely inconsiderate and offensive to the neighbors, and surely negatively affected their impression of the group home and its residents.

Besides avoiding offensive design and incompatible placement, sensitivity to neighbors implies that design features will accommodate a homey environment. For example, staff at a community residence should choose a few, regular-sized garbage cans and screen them from view, instead of using an institutional-size dumpster. Furthermore, handicapped parking spaces should be reserved by policy rather than by markings on the ground or a sign on a metal standard. The amount of parking space designed for the home also should be consistent with that available for the other homes in the neighborhood. If more staff parking is abso-

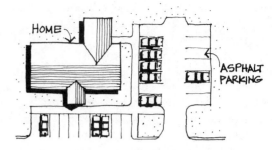

Figure 4. Homes should not "float" on asphalt. (Drawn by Van Cox.)

lutely necessary, it should be as inconspicuous as possible. Shrubbery and fencing should be used to screen the area from view, and the access driveway should be as narrow as feasible.

In general, the provision of adequate parking should not result in the impression that the residence is surrounded by asphalt (see Figure 4). Such an insensitive design is an effrontery to neighbors. If extra parking must be available for occasional use, a polymer grid can be laid on a granular base below a sod carpet, which will be stable enough to support a car so it will not ruin the lawn by forming deep ruts. One alternative design solution is the use of grass impregnated concrete, which is not as aesthetically pleasing as pure sod, but is less offensive than concrete or asphalt. Or a more decorative hard surface such as brick or pavers could be located in an appropriate yard space for use as a patio or game area when not needed for parking (see Figure 5).

While design alone cannot be expected to make community residences acceptable to their neighbors, it can avoid some potential conflicts,

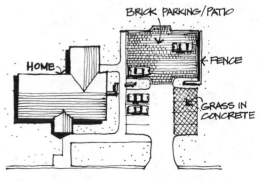

Figure 5. Decorative surfaces can be used in place of asphalt. (Drawn by Van Cox.)

encourage acceptable resident behavior, and help homes at least to look as though they belong in a neighborhood.

ABILITY TO MEET RESIDENTS' NEEDS

Design of the exterior can also help create an environment that is physically supportive and homey in appearance. The space can be arranged so that residents develop a sense of control over both the environment and their privacy. It can provide a setting in which residents can learn skills, socialize with neighbors, and live comfortably.

Physical Needs

One of the most obvious ways in which the exterior environment can meet residents' needs is through physical support. This is especially important, since some of the residents may have multiple disabilities. Some residents must use a cane, walker, wheelchair, or gurney, and may require special design adaptations such as a handrail or ramp. When such aids are needed, it is important that they be unobtrusive and blend in with the home's building materials. Care should be taken that the material and design of environmental supports not look institutional. When a handrail is needed, for example, the use of a metal tubular rail (see Figure 6) gives the dwelling an institutional look and detracts from a homey appearance. A better solution would be to construct the rail of wood in a style more

compatible with the home, so that it more resembles an additional, planned amenity rather than a standardized institutional support.

Similar care should be taken when designing ramps. Nothing is quite so unasthetic as a makeshift ramp that dissects a yard in two. It is better to construct a ramp that hugs the house and becomes an integral part of its design, as though the ramp were planned as a creative design solution for a change in grade (see Figure 7). Several good resources are available that give specifications for designing ramps that meet the needs of residents who use wheelchairs (see Supplementary Resources). A ramp should reflect the home's materials, style, and color, and thus blend in with the existing architecture.

Some residents may have conditions such as arthritis and poor muscle control. Design details such as the style and height of a door handle may make the difference between access or no access to the home's features. While it is best to keep the design details as normal and homey as possible, sometimes decisions must favor extra environmental support at the expense of creating a "homey" appearance. However, in most cases the trade-off is not so obvious, and a creative solution can be developed that satisfies both goals.

Moreover, residents who may not be physically disabled when they first move into a home may, over time, need additional support, owing to the effects of aging. Their potential

NO!   YES!

Figure 6. Avoid institutional details. (Drawn by Van Cox. Reprinted, by permission, from Butterfield, 1984.)

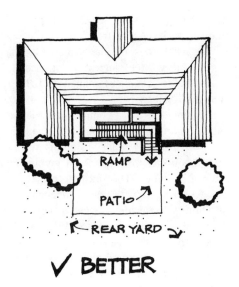

✓ BETTER

Figure 7. Ramps should be planned as part of the design. (Drawn by Van Cox. Reprinted, by permission, from Butterfield, 1984.)

needs for physical support must also be considered. In some cases this may be as simple as providing seating with arm rests for ease of getting out of a chair (Koncelick, 1976), or careful attention to changes in grade so they are obvious to ailing eyes.

Another consideration is that some residents may be taking medications whose side effects increase their sensitivity to the sun (for example, thorazine). Such residents need shade if the exterior spaces are to be at all useful. The long-term solution is planting trees for shade; however, other more immediate options include structures that would support canvas awnings for heavy shade, or vine-covered arbors for more dappled light.

Thoughtful design, then, can mitigate a variety of impairments. Environments can also be designed so that they match the competence level of their residents (Lawton, 1980). The environment should not be overly supportive so that residents lose acquired skills, nor should it be so challenging that residents give up trying to negotiate it. A delicate balance must be reached for each resident to meet his or her potential. Some excellent references are available (see Supplementary Resources) that can help managers learn more about special design features.

Design Features
That Enhance the Home

Besides meeting the residents' needs for physical support, exterior design features can make the residence more of a home. For most homes the front door and entry are the home's focal point. Several design strategies can be used to emphasize the importance of the home's entry. Design features and landscaping that create a visual edge should be directed to the front door. The largest plants can be used at the sides of a home and smaller ones placed toward the door so the eye is carried to the door. Planting beds can also be designed to emphasize the door. Another strategy is to accent the entry by using colorful or unusually shaped plants on either side of the door. The door can also be painted a color that contrasts with the rest of the home, or a small rug or doormat can be added for further definition. Of course, care must be taken so that the techniques used do not destroy the fit of the home within the neighborhood context.

A design feature that is particularly important is the placement of the pedestrian walkway to the door. A strong visual connection is created when the sidewalk leads directly from the street to the front door, indicating to the pedestrian or visitor where to enter the home. Although some suburban homes have a sidewalk leading from a side driveway, this solution is less effective visually, and less convenient for pedestrians and visitors who may have to jockey between cars to reach their destination. The addition of a second walk directly from the street to the door will also avoid the unsightly development of a footpath by those not parking in the driveway. If none of the other homes in the neighborhood has a direct walk, it may be advisable to play down this feature out of respect for neighborhood norms. Moreover, the walk from the driveway can be composed of stepping stones or pavers set in the lawn, making the physical link less obvious.

In addition to creating a focal point of the entry, the facade and yards of community residences should be as neat, or neater, than those of the surrounding homes, thus helping to assure a positive comparison. Neatness is especially important if the residence has been an object of neighborhood opposition. For example, one midwestern group home was an older home previously inhabited by members of a cult who painted all the upstairs rooms black and did not tend the vegetation around the house. Under such circumstances it was particularly important to immediately trim trees and shrubs and clear out the underbrush to create an impression of tidiness so that the new residents were not associated with the old ones.

The choice of planting materials can contribute to, or detract from, an impression of neatness. Plants that tend to collect trash and leaves and are difficult to maintain should not be included in planting plans. The cotoneaster, for example, would be a poor choice for a community residence, since its spindly, spreading arms gather leaves and stray bits of trash.

Sense of Environmental Control

A major potential benefit of a carefully designed exterior is the enhancement of the individual resident's feeling of control over his or her environment. Control adds to a person's sense of competence and self-esteem. A resident can be given a small section of the yard over which he or she has direct physical control. Even a plot as small as 2 square feet can provide the resident with a space he or she "owns" and controls. The resident could be helped to choose the plants within the area and taught how to care for them.

Another strategy for increasing a resident's control over the environment is to allow the resident to help personalize the space with personal decorations or outdoor furniture. A homemade wreath for the front door or handmade pot for a plant gives character to the home while conveying to the resident a satisfying sense of ownership. Allowing the resident the opportunity to add a favorite lawn chair, rather than having the manager purchase six identical models that defy personal identification, is another way to enhance a resident's sense of control.

A sense of environmental control can be further aided by allowing residents to participate in choosing landscaping materials. Once the basic conceptual design for the yard spaces is developed, there are usually a variety of building materials and plants that would be appropriate choices. The residents, rather than the manager, could make the final decisions. In addition to control, the process of selecting plants is a learning experience, and residents could learn about the properties of plants and materials, their durability, the interplay of aesthetic qualities, identification of plants, and the requirements for their care.

Developing a sense of control over one's environment extends beyond physical manifestations, however. It includes the ability to regulate the amount of one's personal involvement in exterior activities. The ability to preview activities occurring in these spaces enhances a resident's ability to decide whether or not to participate. By being able to first observe activities, the resident can see who is outside, how they are dressed, and what type of behavior seems appropriate. This allows the resident a chance to size up the situation before deciding whether or not to participate.

The addition of a porch or partially screened galleria is a design feature that supports the ability to preview. Lawn furniture and potted plants provide comfort and a further invitation to the outside. The resident could choose to sweep the porch, water the plants, or straighten the furniture in order to place himself or herself in a position to preview yard activities before choosing to join in.

Another design strategy that may allow residents to preview is that of careful selection of size and placement of windows. Windows should be large enough for residents to easily view the outdoors but not so large that the resident is readily viewed by persons outside, as if he or she were on stage. Ranch-style homes built in the 1950s have ideal windows for previewing. The opening is about 4½ feet from the ground and allows the resident to look out without becoming enframed by the window.

PRIVACY

Privacy means being able to control others' access to oneself (Altman, 1975). When a group of unrelated adults share a residence as a family, satisfying a residents' needs for privacy may be difficult. In situations where residents share bedrooms, finding a place to be alone may be nearly impossible. Residents who sometimes have behavior problems have special needs for private space. The demands for privacy place intense pressure upon interior spaces. Some of this pressure can be alleviated by creative use of portions of the exterior space. Secluded areas, for example, can be developed as part of the design. A narrow side yard is ideal for this use. It is often bounded on one side by the house and can be enclosed with privacy fencing on the other sides. A far corner of the backyard may also be made into a secluded place by using a combination of berms, planting materials, or structures. A wealth of creative options is available for screening an area for privacy. Chain-link fencing can be covered quickly by planting at its base morning glories or more permanent vines such as honeysuckle or, in warm climates, bougainvillea. Wooden lattices makes a beautiful semipermeable screen, as do some larger shrubs and evergreens.

For residents of a community home privacy also means the ability to control visitors' and other outsiders' access to more private areas of the home such as the bedrooms and bathrooms. Privacy furthermore means the right to have group social functions without interruption. The design of connections between the inside and outside of the home is vital to controlling unwanted access. For example, locating visitor parking near the bedroom wing, with a sidewalk directly from the parking lot to this private entry destroys any control by residents of access to these private areas. Likewise, placing the center of the group social area or patio adjacent to the back door, with a sidewalk leading from the door to staff, or worse yet, visitor parking, means that people using the parking area will be directed to the back door through the middle of any group social activities occurring at the time.

The best designs provide spaces with a variety of degrees of privacy from very secluded—for an individual's use—to very open—for large social gatherings where the whole household and guests are able to congregate. A diversity of spaces allows residents to choose the desired amount of access to themselves.

DEVELOPMENT OF SKILLS AND PERSONAL GROWTH

The use of the exterior spaces as a classroom for developing basic living skills has also been overlooked in many community residences.

Many residents move into homes after living in institutions, nursing homes, or much larger community homes where they had only limited opportunities to learn the basic skills necessary to maintain a home. For instance, residents can learn how to care for plants (i.e., when to water and fertilize them); they can mow the lawn, edge sidewalks, and rake lawns; they can be taught simple carpentry skills such as how to pound in a nail, saw a board, or use a screw driver. And, of course, there are always pragmatic jobs like washing the exterior of windows, painting the house, and washing yard equipment or furniture. Each exercise can provide residents the opportunity to develop a range of necessary life skills and to improve their competence.

Only a few design features are needed to support such activities. A corner of the garage or a storage shed can be used to store tools and equipment. Water can be made available either by placing an outdoor faucet near the work area or by use of a hose. The work area should also have a hard surface work pad (asphalt or concrete), which can easily be hosed down for cleaning. However, the most important aspect for developing the outdoors as a classroom is a program to teach residents these skills.

Beyond basic homemaking skills, the outdoor areas can support residents' personal growth. Residents can become involved, for example, in hobbies and caring for pets, with the specific design features tailored to the type of hobby or pet. A hobby such as growing a garden gives the resident an opportunity not only to learn gardening skills but, as indicated earlier, also provides an opportunity for neighbors and visitors to engage in casual social conversation. In a study of outdoor spaces of group homes, almost all social interaction occurring outdoors between residents and their neighbors took place either while residents were performing maintenance chores or tending their gardens (Butterfield, 1984). By laying out the garden next to a neighbor's garden or along a visually permeable fence, a situation is created where a neighbor can say ''hello'' while remaining on home turf, and can see residents performing ''normal'' yard activities. Furthermore, the encounter can be comfortably ended by either party without embarrassment.

A pet, such as a well-trained dog, allows similar opportunities and expands the social encounters beyond the yard spaces as residents take the dog for walks. It allows the resident an opportunity to go beyond personal needs and develop awareness of the needs of another living thing. Learning to care for an animal involves valuable skills and can help a resident develop sensitivity. It also teaches responsibility, since a pet cannot take care of its own basic needs.

DESIGNS FOR TWO GROUP HOMES

The final section of this chapter includes vignettes of and illustrations for the designs of two group homes. The designer analyzed the exterior spaces, working closely with the administration, staff, and residents of the homes to ensure that the designs were as sensitive as possible to residents' individual needs. Both homes were already sited and built before the project began. The entire design process was quite lengthy and incorporated many opportunities to discover the needs of the home's residents, neighbors, and staff.

Vignette: Home #1

The first home was chosen at the request of a service agency who operated several similar homes and felt this particular home most needed a designer's skill. The home was located in a multifamily housing area where most of the neighbors rent, rather than own, their homes. The home was designed originally as a duplex and fit in well with the rest of the neighborhood. The lot was located on a quiet deadend street located off another deadend street.

The home was anchored in a concrete front yard, which also served as staff parking (see Figure 8). The only landscaping consisted of a 4-foot by 20-foot strip of dirt along the front of the building, a grass backyard, and one willow tree in the far southeastern corner of the lot. An unsightly, unscreened garbage area was located adjacent to the neighbors' yard at the side entry to the backyard. The rear yard was enclosed by a cyclone fence offering no privacy. Two 7-foot-wide sidewalks wrapped around the sides of the home and culminated in two individual patios joined with an undifferentiated boundary. The backyard lacked definition, was very open, and, as stated, was devoid of shrubs and flowers. The patios were unscreened with views directly into the neighbors'

yards. The view toward the rear lot line was of undeveloped woods.

The residents of this home were six women ages 22 to 29, two of whom were nonverbal. Residents reported knowing only one neighbor, an 18-year-old boy, whom they met "around." During an interview the designer conducted with three of the residents to gain information about specific resident needs, none reported ever gardening, although all said they would like to learn how to grow flowers and vegetables. One of the residents reported she knew how to run a lawnmower. However, outdoor maintenance chores were being performed at the time by a maintenance crew.

The designer used an extensive process to develop the designs for the homes, which included a survey of relevant literature, analysis of the site, and interviews with the administration, staff, neighbors, and residents (see Figure 9). Since the first home's landscaping was so sparse and residents had trouble visualizing design possibilities from pictures or verbal descriptions, the designer arranged for them to visit an arboretum. This technique was most successful for learning about the specific preferences of the residents. It also allowed the designer to observe what aspects of the environment appealed to each resident. For example, one of the residents enjoyed birdwatching, another digging in the garden, and another just sitting in a secluded nook.

The information gleaned from the various sources was used to develop a program for each of the homes, which served as the basis for the design. In addition, the design had to work within a sparse budget. While a larger budget would have enhanced the aesthetic possibilities, the designer felt obligated to work within a realistic framework.

As the plan and sketches show, modifications incorporated many of the principles previously discussed (see Figure 10). Raised planting beds, trees, and flowers were used to direct pedestrian circulation to the front door and to create a visual focal point. Ambiguity about which entry should be used was cleared up by placing a lattice screen across the staff entry, still allowing physical access but creating a visual barrier. Unfortunately, no space was available for the needed parking other than that existing in front of the home. Although tearing out the concrete and replacing it with a grasscrete would have been preferable, this measure was not feasible.

The front planting beds not only allowed color, texture, and form to be added but also provided an opportunity for residents to learn plant care skills and to be available for casual social interchanges with neighbors. The unsightly service area was screened with a wooden fence and structure for garbage to eliminate this irritation to neighbors.

Private areas for residents were created in the side yards with wooden fences and appropriate

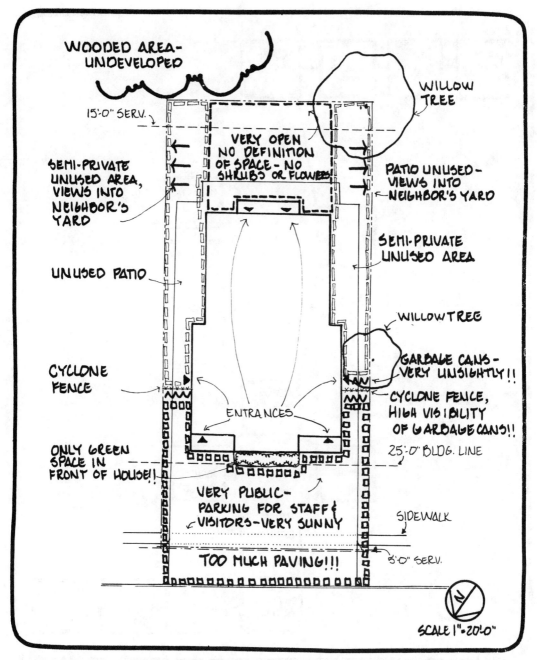

Figure 8. Site analysis for home #1. (Drawn by Anne Roane.)

screening. Since there were two private areas, the one on the side away from the front entry was used as a retreat for staff or for residents who needed a timeout for behavior problems, while the other enabled residents to meet their privacy needs. A lattice screen enclosed a hard surface area with access to water and electricity for messy hobbies such as woodworking, potting, or painting. A small vegetable or cut-flower garden bordered the hobby area and was placed adjacent to the neighbors. The backyard retained the patio, but a border of trees and flowering shrubs was added to attract birds; and finally, an open area for lawn games and socializing was created adjacent to the patio so that the space could be used in a flexible manner according to the activities planned for it.

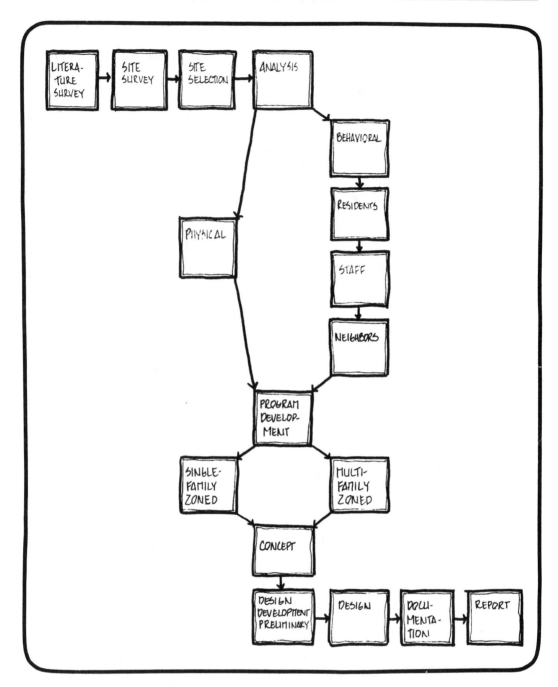

Figure 9. Design process for home #1. (Drawn by Anne Roane.)

A view from the recreation room at the rear of the home allowed residents to preview yard activities.

A list of appropriate plant materials for each of the areas accompanied the design plan so that the residents themselves could participate more fully in decision making. Another trip to an arboretum or nursery helped residents make more informed decisions and functioned as a learning aid. The planting beds needed also to be edged and mulched in order to be neat; this allowed residents to participate in maintenance. Staff were encouraged to revise outdoor policies so that each resident could be responsible for some aspect of the environment to reinforce feelings of proprietorship.

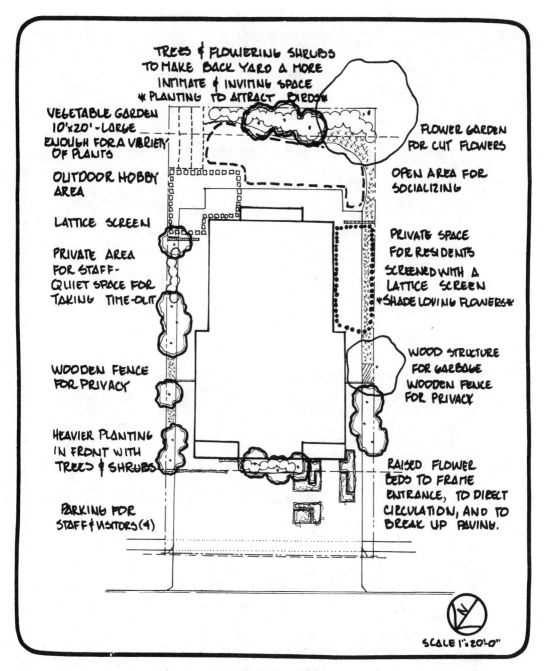

TREES & FLOWERING SHRUBS TO MAKE BACK YARD A MORE INTIMATE & INVITING SPACE * PLANTING TO ATTRACT BIRDS*

VEGETABLE GARDEN 10'x20' - LARGE ENOUGH FOR A VARIETY OF PLANTS

FLOWER GARDEN FOR CUT FLOWERS

OUTDOOR HOBBY AREA

OPEN AREA FOR SOCIALIZING

LATTICE SCREEN

PRIVATE AREA FOR STAFF - QUIET SPACE FOR TAKING TIME-OUT

PRIVATE SPACE FOR RESIDENTS SCREENED WITH A LATTICE SCREEN *SHADE LOVING FLOWERS*

WOODEN FENCE FOR PRIVACY

WOOD STRUCTURE FOR GARBAGE WOODEN FENCE FOR PRIVACY

HEAVIER PLANTING IN FRONT WITH TREES & SHRUBS

RAISED FLOWER BEDS TO FRAME ENTRANCE, TO DIRECT CIRCULATION, AND TO BREAK UP PAVING.

PARKING FOR STAFF & VISITORS (4)

SCALE 1": 20'-0"

Figure 10. Design for home #1. (Drawn by Anne Roane. Reprinted, by permission, from Butterfield, 1984.)

Vignette: Home #2

The second home chosen was newly built and designed for a mixture of ambulatory and nonambulatory residents. It was centrally located in a new, upper-middle class neighborhood consisting of primarily owner-occupied, single-family residences. The basic structures of sidewalks and driveways were in place, but there was little landscaping, giving the home an unfinished look.

Six severely and profoundly disabled young men ages 22 to 29 lived in the home. Of these, five were either nonambulatory or nonverbal, and two were both. The home, specially designed to house severely disabled persons, was built to provide a barrier-free environment. However, few oppor-

tunities were included in the design for the residents to experience the outdoor environment.

The home itself was similar in size and style to the others in the neighborhood, although it was constructed of wood rather than the predominant brick. There were neighbors to the east, a vacant lot to the west, and a large, open-space neighborhood park with a small lake to the south (see

Figure 11). The home had a covered 4-foot gallery that could be screened lightly with plantings to function as a semiprivate area for the residents. There already was a sidewalk leading from the front door to the street, and a long drive with an awkward bend leading to staff parking in the back. The driveway divided the east side yard into long narrow strips. The bend created a problem be-

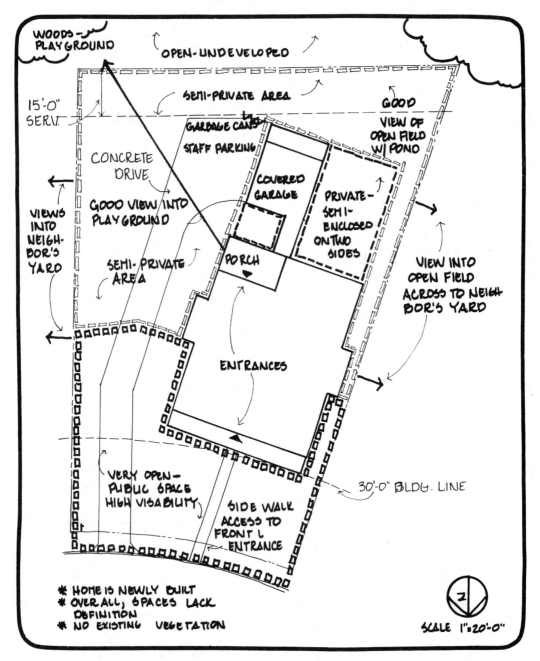

Figure 11. Site analysis for home #2. (Drawn by Anne Roane.)

cause cars tended to misjudge the change of direction and ran off the paving, creating ruts and an unsightly muddy area.

In the back of the house was a large concrete pad and a covered garage for staff parking. There was also a small covered back porch near the rear entry on the east side of the house. The yards were completely undifferentiated.

Because of the residents' limited communication abilities, the development of the design program for this home relied heavily upon staff input and the available literature. The goal of the design was to provide more opportunities for limited or passive recreation. The new design suggested additional plantings for the front of the home to emphasize the entry and define the gallery (see Fig-

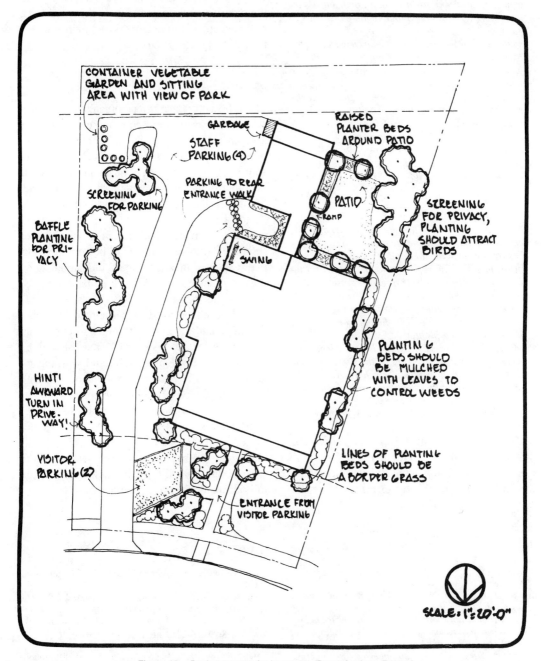

Figure 12. Design process for home #2. (Drawn by Anne Roane.)

ure 12). A tentative grass parking area with underlying structural support for visitors was suggested if the available street parking proved insufficient. A group of shrubs was planted as a warning to drivers that the driveway was switching directions. An additional grouping of shrubs served as a baffle for sound and as a screen to increase privacy from neighbors.

Since residents in wheeled vehicles were unable to negotiate a soft surface, additional hard surfaces were added to the plan to enable residents to use more of the yard space. A paved area in the southeast corner extended the driveway for this purpose. It was located adjacent to the neighbors and was the area of the lot closest to the playing fields and equipment in the park. It was also a perfect location for container gardening. Since the residents had limited physical ability, containers allowed them to grow a few plants with little physical effort. Once again, an opportunity was created where residents could learn skills while they could be observed participating in normal behavior. The location would also encourage children who are in the park to come over and speak with the residents.

A more private patio bordered by raised planter beds was planned for the southwest corner adjacent to the rear of the house and garage. It had a beautiful view of the lake and trees and would be a pleasant place for residents to be alone or with friends. Shrubs and small trees were used to give privacy from the adjacent lot, and residents who were able participated in the design by selecting from a list plant materials that are attractive to birds. The raised planter beds would serve as informal seating for visitors and allow residents who were more able to take care of the flowers. Some of the flowers that residents selected were suitable for cutting so that they could enjoy a touch of their garden indoors. A canvas or fiberglass canopy was added to provide shade for extended usage.

The designs presented form an underlying structure for the development of exterior spaces. Unfortunately, the homes' locations and buildings were already in place before the designer was called upon to develop a plan for the exterior spaces. The range of design solutions was therefore necessarily limited. The most effective treatment of the exterior spaces can only occur if these spaces are considered when the major decisions such as location, style, and design of the home are being made. However, even if the homes are already built, the exterior environment can be designed to be more acceptable to neighbors and more supportive of residents' needs.

SUMMARY

The following general recommendations reflect strategies that can be used to increase a home's acceptability to neighbors and enhance support of residents. The exterior spaces should be designed to appear at least as neat and attractive as the other homes in the neighborhood. The function and use of each space should be clear, and should be constructed within a hierarchy from public to private. The design of the spaces should encourage residents to behave in a normal, expected manner, and should capitalize on opportunities for resident participation in the maintenance and care of yard spaces. Residents should be encouraged to participate in design decisions and given opportunities to control an area or aspect of the yard. Areas should be planned for developing skills and working on hobbies. The environment should be safe and negotiable for physically handicapped residents and should incorporate the necessary special design features. Finally, the spaces should be designed with the neighbors in mind. The hope, ultimately, is that such careful attention to the exterior spaces will bring increased satisfaction to both residents and neighbors.

REFERENCES

Altman, I. (1975). *The environment and social behavior.* Monterey, CA: Brooks/Cole.

Butterfield, D. (1983). Neighbors' perception of outdoor spaces surrounding group homes for the developmentally disabled adult. In *Proceedings of the Environmental Design Research Association, 1983.* Lincoln, NE: Environmental Design Research Association.

Butterfield, D. (1984). *Design guidelines for exterior spaces of group homes.* Urbana, IL: Housing Research

and Development Program, University of Illinois at Urbana.

Francescato, G., Weidemann, S., Anderson, J., & Chenoweth, R. (1978). *Residents' satisfaction in HUD-assisted housing: Design and management factors.* Washington, DC: U.S. Department of Housing and Urban Development.

Knight, R., Weitzer, W., & Zimring, C. (1978). *Opportunity for control of the build environment: The ELEMR*

Project. Amherst, MA: Environmental Institute, University of Massachusetts.

Koncelik, A. (1976). *Designing the open nursing home.* Community Development Series No. 27. Stroudsburg, PA: Dowden, Hutchinson & Ross.

Landesman-Dwyer, S. (1981). Living in the community.

American Journal of Mental Deficiency, 86, 223–234.

Lawton, M. (1980). *Environment and aging.* Monterey, CA: Brooks/Cole.

Wolfensberger, W. (1972). *Normalization.* Toronto: National Institute for Mental Retardation.

SUPPLEMENTARY RESOURCES

American Society of Landscape Architects. (1977). *Barrier free site design.* Washington, DC: U.S. Government Printing Office.

Bednar, M. (1977). *Barrier-free environments.* Stroudsburg, PA: Dowden, Hutchinson and Ross.

Booth, N. (1983). *Basic elements of landscape architectural design.* New York: Elsevier/North Holland.

Brockman, C. (1968). *A guide to field identification: Trees of North America.* New York: Golden Press.

Jones, M. (1978). *Accessibility standards.* Chicago: Capital Development Board.

Odenwald, N., & Turner, J. (1980). *Plants for the south.*

Baton Rouge, LA: Claitor's Publishing Division.

Perry, F. (Ed.). (1974). *Simon and Schuster's complete guide to plants and flowers.* New York: Simon & Schuster.

Robinette, G. (1983). *Barrier-free exterior design: Anyone can go anywhere.* New York: Van Nostrand Reinhold.

Simonds, J. (1983). *Landscape architecture.* New York: McGraw-Hill.

Symonds, G. (1963). *The shrub identification book.* New York: William Morrow.

Symonds, G. (1985). *The tree identification book.* New York: William Morrow.

APPENDIX

How to Choose a Landscape Architect

A landscape architect may be located through several sources. The first and most obvious is the yellow pages in the telephone book under "Landscaping." Most design firms who have a landscape architect will note so in their advertisement. Another good information source is the local university, which, if it does not have a school of landscape architecture, can refer you to the one nearest by. Most schools, too, are glad to recommend some of their alumni. A third source is the American Society of Landscape Architects (ASLA), the professional organization for landscape architects. Information may be obtained by writing the ASLA at: 1733 Connecticut Ave., NW, Washington, DC 20009.

Whomever you select to be your landscape architect should have the appropriate credentials. Most landscape architects are members of the American Society of Landscape Architects. Landscape architects (as opposed to landscape designers) will either have a bachelors (B.L.A.) or a masters degree (M.L.A.) in landscape architecture from a school accredited by the ASLA. If your state requires a license to practice, then the landscape architect you choose should be licensed.

You will also want to be sure that the individual you hire will be sensitive to the needs of the individuals who will use the community home. A few carefully chosen questions will help you evaluate this characteristic. Ask if the designer has ever worked on a project for a client with special needs. Ask also if the designer is willing both to review the literature about those needs and to incorporate such information in the design. Finally, ask what process is used to be sure the clients' needs are met. The landscape architect should be hired only if you are satisfied with the answers and convinced that he or she will give clients' needs first priority. Such a person will design an environment that not only meets the needs of your client but is also functionally and aesthetically pleasing.

Epilog

Agenda for Service, Policy, and Research

Matthew P. Janicki, Marty Wyngaarden Krauss,
and Marsha Mailick Seltzer

The evolution of a broad range of community residential programs serving individuals with developmental disabilities represents one of the most significant advances in the history of publicly supported services for this population. In the short span of 20 years we have observed a profound shift in the attitudes expressed by local, state, and federal governments with respect to the public sector's role in the care of and provision of services to persons with lifelong cognitive and functional disabilities. It is now considered a legitimate state activity to provide community-based residential and related services for persons with developmental disabilities. These services are intended not just to sustain residents, but rather to stretch their abilities to achieve as independent and dignified a life as possible. Notwithstanding the "growing pains" experienced by providers of community residential programs, the fact that a variety of types of residential programs are available in every state (see Lakin, Hill, & Bruininks, Chapter 3, this volume) attests to the integration of these programs into the service delivery system.

However, community residential programs do not operate without serious constraints. Perhaps the most commonly stated limitation is their precarious fiscal basis. It is almost a truism to note that community residences are underfunded and that the expectations for high-quality care and services often exceed the ca-

pacities of the available staff. Neighborhoods in which programs are located are not always congenial hosts to the residents who live in community residences. Localities may try to restrict the development of new programs through the passage or application of discriminatory zoning laws (see Freedman & Freedman, Chapter 4, this volume). An additional operational limitation is that residents typically have less access to the full range of community activities and resources than do nonhandicapped citizens. Of particular concern, operators of community residences may be more compelled to respond to regulatory requirements rather than to build in programmatic features that lead to high quality.

All large systems of human services face management, programmatic, and clinical constraints and challenges. A major challenge for the future of community residences, however, is to bring to today's problems the same degree of energy, commitment, and innovation that characterized the initial stage of program development 20 years ago. The ability to meet the challenges of the next 20 years will rest, in large part, on the creative adaptation of traditional management strategies to ensure that programs operate optimally as viewed from three perspectives: business, human services, and clinical services.

The business perspective requires that programs remain within their budgets, utilize the best-qualified staff, provide the required range of services, and operate in as efficient and safe a manner as possible. Good business acumen was rarely considered a prerequisite for operating a human services program in the early days of community residential program development. It is now generally considered a minimum qualification of operators.

The human services perspective requires that the residents are treated with respect and dignity and are provided an environment that capitalizes on their strengths and works to minimize the impact of their weaknesses. It is in this domain that community residences have had the most success, owing to the influence of dominant ideologies such as normalization, the least restrictive alternative, and the right to habilitation.

The clinical perspective requires staff to develop an active treatment program for each resident, which provides a blueprint for professional service delivery. In this domain lies both the greatest need for improvement and the greatest potential for future success.

Observers of the community residence movement have witnessed a series of changes during the past two decades in the characteristics, goals, and organizational concerns of such programs (see Turnbull, Chapter 2, this volume). Twenty years ago, the community residence movement operated at the local grass roots level, staff were considered pioneers in a new social reform movement, and residential programs were organized in diverse and usually poorly monitored ways. Today the situation is vastly different. A highly differentiated community-based service system has developed and matured. This system intersects with other national systems such as federal housing (see Allard, Chapter 6, this volume), wage (see Fritz, Chapter 21, this volume), legal (see Freedman & Freedman, Chapter 4, this volume), and health care (see Rowitz, Chapter 16, this volume).

There has been a remarkable change during this period in the primary challenges facing community residences. Whereas 20 years ago, the goal was to demonstrate that it was possible for developmentally disabled persons to live in such programs, community residential living is no longer considered novel or atypical. Today,

the most important challenge facing community residential programs is to ensure the stability, security, and quality of the service system.

There has been a shift as well in the way community residences have defined quality of life for residents. Twenty years ago, a high-quality program was often conceived of simply as the antithesis of a public institution ward. Today, the human services field defines a high-quality program as one that provides for comfort and safety, promotes residents' personal growth and independence, and lends residents a high degree of satisfaction (see Landesman, Chapter 8, this volume). We have thus moved from an ideological definition of *quality* to one with more practical components.

The individuals now served in community residences are a much more diverse group than they were two decades ago. At that time, residences were targeted for mildly handicapped and employable young adults. In contrast, it is now the norm for the community residence system to serve mildly, moderately, severely or profoundly, and multiply handicapped persons who range in age from children to the elderly.

Operators of community residences have expanded the types of residents they are willing to accept, in part because the technology for providing residential services to persons formerly considered "hard to serve" has improved substantially. No longer are community residences intended to be just ordinary homes in the community; now many are expected to have a rehabilitative intent even in their recreational programming (see Hawkins, Chapter 17, this volume) or communication milieu (see Kenefick, Chapter 15, this volume). Similarly, whereas it was once assumed that mere exposure to the community would promote more typical behaviors, as Manfredini and Smith (Chapter 10, this volume) pointed out, active treatment is now generally viewed as the foundation on which services are based. In today's interventionist context, anyone, no matter how severely disabled, can be effectively served in a small community setting.

There has also been a major shift in the characteristics of staff who work in community residences and in the structure of staffing patterns. Twenty years ago, most staff were young, educated, and frequently willing to work for low pay because of their idealism and dedication to social and political reforms that would improve the conditions and treatment of persons considered "disenfranchised" by society. Today's community residence staff are not typically bolstered by a social and political reform activist spirit. In addition, as Lakin (Chapter 18, this volume) explained, the demographic structure of our society has changed; there are fewer persons in their early to mid-20s who traditionally formed the core of direct service workers. In response, community residences are searching for other ways to motivate and retain staff—career ladders, higher salaries, and educational benefits (see Levy, Levy, Freeman, Feiman, & Samowitz, Chapter 19, this volume). However, the challenge of ensuring competent staff remains a particularly vexing one for community residences, owing to limitations in the resources needed to implement such benefits and programs.

The agencies that sponsor community residences have also undergone profound changes in the last 20 years. Initially, it was common for an agency to sponsor a single residence or a single type of program. Today, it is more typical for agencies to operate multiple residences as well as nonresidential programs such as work or day activity centers. Whereas individual programs have remained geographically diverse, they are now administratively linked. The benefits of multiple-program agencies include efficiency of operation, the possibility of specialization of function (e.g., by type of individual served), and the possibility for a large enough financial base to support professional staff (e.g., physical therapists, social workers) operating across programs.

Further, the infrastructure of the community residence movement has become more complex and sophisticated. Now many protections are built into the system—accreditation standards, state regulations, human rights committees, licensure requirements—most of which were absent 20 years ago. As Gelman (Chapter 5, this volume) noted, the agency's board of directors is increasingly required to take an active role in the development, monitoring, and coordination of the agency's programs and to attend to lia-

bility issues of greater complexity. Better methods to monitor service delivery and ensure accountability have taken the place of trusting in the good intentions of operators and staff.

It is difficult to calculate the net effect of these changes on the residents and on the viability of the community residence service delivery system as a whole. While acknowledging the unpredictability of the future, we conclude this volume with an agenda for service delivery, policy development, and research culled from a review of each of the contributing chapters in this book.

Agenda for Service Delivery

1. Develop strategies for resolving conflict between individual needs and regulatory requirements. Community residences are unlikely to experience a decrease in the amount of regulatory, administrative, and fiscal oversight that currently exists. Indeed, the pressures for increased monitoring, for increased standards development and conformity, and for increased fiscal accountability grow unabated. There is an unquestioned need to ensure that programs provide what they are contracted to provide, that they spend resources according to carefully developed and negotiated plans, and that they protect the rights of residents and staff. Further, regulations have been widely implemented regarding a myriad of diverse objectives, including limiting the risk of fires in community residences (see Groner, Chapter 24, this volume), paying staff according to strict wage and hour requirements (see Fritz, Chapter 21, this volume), and conducting evaluations of the services provided to residents (see Jacobson & Regula, Chapter 7, this volume) among others. However, the number of "masters" to which programs are accountable requires a degree of management sophistication that may soon compete with equally needed attention to clinical and programmatic goals of community residences. Without a conscious effort to acknowledge clinical and programmatic initiatives as the highest priority for community residences, there is a risk that management or administrative concerns will dominate the tone and context in which programs operate. For example, a satisfying and active retirement may be an individual need of an aging developmentally disabled person, but the regulatory requirements of providing a set number of hours of active treatment each day might preclude an agency's ability to respond adequately to the elderly person's needs.

It is extremely important for community residence operators to periodically take stock of the extent to which new program decisions are made on the basis of residents' needs as reflected in programmatic goals and on the need to ensure a high quality of life or on the basis of the accountability requirements of the numerous oversight agencies. This recommendation also applies to the need to keep the physical environment of the residence homelike as well as responsive to regulatory requirements (see Robinson, Chapter 25, this volume, and Jenkins, Chapter 26, this volume).

2. Increase the extent to which community residences have an outcome orientation. Historically as well as currently, community residences have paid greater attention to process issues than to outcome issues. There are at least two reasons for the pervasiveness of the process orientation. First, many community residences are guided by the normalization principle, which involves putting into place environments and conditions that approximate typical homes. Evaluation of the quality of the residence is often made on the basis of whether such environmental and programmatic conditions have been implemented, rather than on the effect of such elements. Second, the extent of regulatory oversight characteristic of community residences forces operators to assume a process orientation in their efforts to comply with the specifications of the regulations.

It will be increasingly important to emphasize the extent to which community residence operators are guided by the impact of program elements on residents rather than on assessments of whether the program elements exist. As Blunden (Chapter 9, this volume) pointed out, a high-quality program should be defined as one in which residents develop new functional abilities consistent with their developmental stage and feel a sense of satisfaction with their life-style. This recommendation does not diminish the importance of attention to pro-

cess issues but, rather, implies an additional focus on outcome.

3. Develop community residence staff expertise in case management and service coordination. A third pressure on the service delivery system likely to persist in the future is the increased emphasis on the residence as a "learning center" or "skill building environment" as well as being simply a home for its occupants. As already noted, a dominant theme in the initial development of community residences was the emphasis on substituting the virtues and rewards of a natural home setting for the sterility and impersonal nature of institutional programs. Today, however, community residences are expected to be the hub of an individual's multispoked service wheel.

Serious thought needs to be given to the appropriate role of the community residence within the total arena of an individual's service needs. Although in many states a formal case management system is operated by the state's administering agency for mental retardation/developmental disabilities, community residential staff often act as informal service coordinators. The extent to which community residence staff are qualified or competent to function as a clearinghouse of information and service coordination may be limited by the lack of technical information available to them about eligibility for services, entitlements, resources, and alternative options. Whether it is desirable to shift formal case management responsibility from the state agency to the residence is a question for debate. However, given the informal responsibilities for case management and service coordination assumed by residential staff, a training program should be instituted to increase staff members' ability to carry out this function.

4. Develop a partnership between the community residence and the resident's family. With the dramatic reduction of institutional placement, it will be increasingly common for developmentally disabled individuals to enter community residences directly from their family homes. Concern over the effects of relocation on a developmentally disabled person calls for careful planning (see Heller, Chapter 12, this volume). Whereas in the past, many individuals became estranged from their families as a result of the long years of institutionalization, in the future it will increasingly be the norm for continuous family relationships to be maintained. As Baker and Blacher (Chapter 14, this volume) suggested, currently there may be a sense of discomfort, tension, or mistrust between community residential staff and family members. Given the shift in placement patterns, development of a more positive approach to working with families must be given priority by community residences. Ideally, both staff and family members should function as components of a resident's support network. While in individual instances there may be strained relationships between staff and family, the dominant orientation should now shift to one of partnership and continued collaboration.

Agenda for Policy Development

1. Establish a legal basis for the community residential system. A critical step in the development of public policies for the community residential system is the establishment in federal and state law of the legitimacy of this system and of all the features necessary to its support. Neither at the federal nor the state level do community residences enjoy an unambiguous legal basis. Many American states have yet to translate prevalent practice into codified statute. Legislation is needed that clearly defines the basis and rights associated with community living for disabled citizens in order to ensure that such residences are "here to stay." Systems in many jurisdictions are vulnerable to the vagaries of "the budget" or other political influences that potentially jeopardize the stability of care that is critical to the public's confidence in community residential systems. Public policy makers, when confronted with budgetary pressures, may yield to a simple solution, such as economies of scale rather than to compelling arguments regarding quality of care.

The public policy agenda should include the passage of enabling legislation that legitimizes government's commitment to community services, diminishes support to institutions, enhances public agency policies and practices to promote equal treatment for all disabled citizens, acknowledges the importance of the fam-

ily, and ensures that the frames of reference for "alternative" is not the institution, but the individual's own home.

2. Establish minimum standards for community residences. There is no national policy regarding the development, operation, and management of community residential programs. This is a result of many historical forces, including the traditional dominance of state government in the creation and funding of programs for persons with mental retardation, the absence of a single federal agency responsible for service delivery to this population, and the general political support for the concepts of decentralization and local decision making. Even within the individual state, policies governing community residential services may vary widely from one jurisdiction to another.

The only residential program that has the capacity to impose uniformity within and across states is the federally supported Intermediate Care Facilities for the Mentally Retarded (ICF/MR) program. Its mandated staffing, programmatic, and design standards ensure consistency within the program, and its reimbursement mechanisms enable operators to develop fiscal plans with greater confidence in their accuracy. The operating characteristics of ICFs/MR are not without their critics; however, the issues of programmatic consistency and relative fiscal soundness represent powerful considerations for the future development of other types of community residential programs. The reported variability in programmatic quality and fiscal stability of residential programs across the country may come under increasing scrutiny within policy-making circles. Professional and public opinions regarding the assets and liabilities of such diversity and variability need to be ascertained in order that policy deliberations incorporate "best practice" principles.

3. Rationalize the distribution of residential services. Another policy issue that already confronts the service delivery system is the lack of enough "slots" or "places" within existing residential programs to serve the number of developmentally disabled persons who need out-of-home residential care. Most states have extensive waiting lists for residential services, especially among the adult and elderly groups of developmentally disabled persons. The criteria used for selecting among those on waiting lists for available openings have yet to be seriously analyzed. Policies governing the distribution of residential places also need to be considered. For example, a policy could be adopted at the state or substate level whereby new "slots" would be allocated to those with the "greatest need." Assuming a rational definition of "greatest need" were developed, the policy would effectively implement a system of vertical equity whereby public resources were expended on those who were ranked as more in need of those resources than others. An alternative policy could be adopted whereby the service system would be expanded to enable all those in need to obtain a residential setting. This policy would ensure horizontal equity in the distribution of public resources such that no preset criteria were utilized to differentiate among similarly situated citizens. While these examples represent improbable extremes, it is likely that at the local, state, or federal level, pressures to control the utilization and distribution of publicly supported residential programs will continue.

4. Develop a state-level initiative to attract, train, motivate, and retain community residence staff. A number of chapters in this book have described the staffing constraints characteristic of the community residence system today (in this volume, see Burchard & Thousand, Chapter 20; Levy et al., Chapter 19; and Lakin, Chapter 18). While staffing problems are endemic in most human service sectors, community residences currently are faced with chronic staffing shortages, high staff turnover, and a consequent less-than-optimal level of staff competency to carry out their mandated functions.

Lakin and other authors in Section IV of this volume have pointed out the high costs of staff turnover and the implications of a shrinking labor pool for this service sector. As Burchard and Thousand (Chapter 20, this volume) described, the obvious association among the capability of staff, the quality of the program, and the growth, change, and satisfaction among the residents calls for a well-developed and properly funded response to this problem.

Individual community residence programs are not capable of rectifying this situation, as they do not control a sufficient level of needed resources. Rather, a state-level response is needed, whose components should include: 1) the development of a career ladder so that upward mobility is a possibility and an incentive; 2) reasonably standardized training models that permit transferability of skills across employers and throughout (and outside of) the state; 3) increases in salary linked to greater competence and job longevity; and 4) both preservice and in-service training components.

The expense of a state-level initiative, however, obviously can be quite high. In many instances, state agencies possess the coordinative and technical capacities, but do not have the fiscal resources to mount major support and training efforts. A federal initiative is needed to provide support for the technical development of training methods, evaluation of "best practices" for the provision of training materials, and financial resources to underwrite the state's development activities. Such a federal initiative would have the added effect of developing core training modules and models that would aid in the standardization of skills and in the mobility of skilled workers who move from state to state.

5. Increase the access to quality health care for residents. Some developmentally disabled individuals, particularly those with certain syndromes, severe impairments, or multiple handicaps, receive their health care from specialists located at major medical centers with special units or expertise in the area of developmental disabilities. However, most residents of community residences have less specialized health care needs and may best be served through the generic health care system. Barriers exist that impede the receipt of quality health care by residents; in some instances, hindrances to available health care cause certain residents (e.g., those who are elderly and are becoming more impaired) to have to move to a more restrictive setting. These barriers, detailed by Rowitz (Chapter 16, this volume) call for a policy-level response.

Obviously, mechanisms to overcome these impediments are extremely complex. The provision of quality health care must be an integral ingredient of the community care system. Models using health maintenance organizations (HMOs), preferred provider organizations (PPOs), or other agreement-based health service linkages may be one solution. Another possibility is to draw upon the network of University Affiliated Programs for Persons with Developmental Disabilities (UAPs), established under the Developmental Disabilities Act, to serve as linking agents between local hospitals, medical centers, physicians, and community residences. Local health providers could use the area's UAP as a source for technical assistance and as a referral source in the case of a resident who needs specialist services. Any or all of these means of establishing responsive health care services, and, more important, of ensuring that the health care providers understand the health care needs of persons with developmental disabilities, will have the effect of increasing health care accessibility at the grass roots level.

Agenda for Research

1. Develop closer linkages between community residences and university programs. Although much research has been conducted *about* community residences, little has been carried out *within* these facilities. Because of staff shortages and the pressing day-to-day needs of residents, research has received a low priority in community residences. Further, some have considered it inappropriate to conduct research in what is essentially a home. However, the need for program evaluation (see Jacobson & Regula, Chapter 7, this volume) makes research a necessity in community residences.

The potential for pursuing both broad and specific research questions in community residences exists because of the detailed data kept for regulatory purposes about residents. Individual service plans routinely are based on current assessments and on longitudinal data regarding the extent to which the resident has achieved specified objectives. As Seltzer and Apolito (Chapter 22, this volume) noted, the current record-keeping requirements have resulted in a wealth of individualized data that could be utilized for research studies conducted in community residences. Further, the in-creased utilization of computers for record keeping has the effect of facilitating data analysis for research (see Jacobson, Dura, & Mulick, Chapter 23, this volume).

Although research may not be a priority activity for direct care staff or administrators, it may well be the key to the survival of the community residence movement. The more that is known about the viability of community care and about how to best deliver it, the more firmly entrenched community care becomes as the basis for services in practice, in public policy, and most important, in the allocations of monies. Consequently, while staff may feel that research efforts detract from their primary activities, they may be able to productively collaborate with others, such as university faculty, for whom research is a priority. Such a relationship, exemplified by Felce's (Chapter 11, this volume) and Burchard and Thousand's work (Chapter 20, this volume), has produced valuable knowledge about the optimal ways to develop programs and services for persons with developmental disabilities who live in community residences. A fair exchange of university research expertise for access to the community residence site and residents, guided by human subjects review and monitoring, would be productive in establishing research *within* the residence environment.

2. Conduct studies of differential outcomes for residents. No single type of residential program (i.e., foster family care, group home, ICF/MR, semi-independent living program, etc.) is equally effective for all types of developmentally disabled persons. While few would disagree with this assertion, there is, nonetheless, little to guide program administrators regarding the differential effectiveness of residential programs for different types of persons. More rigorous research is needed to increase our understanding of the relationship between specific program characteristics (including staff, treatment, and facility characteristics) and different types of relevant outcomes for the program's occupants. Further, a program model that is effective for some residents (i.e., mildly impaired residents) may be less effective for other types of residents (i.e., residents with severe behavior problems).

Despite the considerable volume of research that is available concerning the impacts of residential programs on their occupants, few principles or generalizable guidelines are available that can be offered to program administrators regarding the appropriate placement of particular types of residents into specific types of programs in order to achieve specific types of outcomes. Furthermore, although the literature commonly refers to a "continuum of service models," little is known about how the models fit together or when an individual should move from one model to another (see Close & Halpern, Chapter 13, this volume). Until these knowledge areas are further developed, the research community will have skirted a particularly valuable role that it must assume in order to maintain a high-quality system of residential services.

3. Conduct studies on family relationships. It is also important that studies be conducted examining the preferences and goals of the families of persons served in community-based residential programs. As discussed in several chapters in this text (see Baker & Blacher, Chapter 14, in particular), the relationship between community residential programs and the residents' families is an underexplored area in need of more reliable information. The need to expand and strengthen the informal support networks of persons with developmental disabilities is frequently articulated. However, the adult services system can be justly criticized for, at worst, ignoring, and

at best, undervaluing, the powerful contribution that family members may make to their disabled relative. Research should be focused on identifying ways in which programs can effectively tap this important support network. Similarly, research should focus on ways in which programs can be responsive to the needs and preferences of family members. The insight and knowledge that family members have, based on years of living with or knowing a developmentally disabled person, should represent a respected source of information for program staff and administrators.

CONCLUSIONS

The diversity of concepts and approaches represented by the chapters in this text shows that much has happened over the past 20 years to cement the acceptance and use of community residential options for developmentally disabled persons. What began as a few isolated "alternative" programs has now expanded to encompass a system of services that are here to stay. However, as we have noted, the nation's community residential programs are still bound by constraints and subject to challenges that need creative and constructive responses and solutions. Thus, the task that remains is to create a fully supported, flexible, and responsive system of residential program models and accompanying services that allows persons with developmental disabilities to live in dignity and as independently as possible.

Index